THE ENCYCLOPEDIA OF SUPER VILLAINS

THE ENCYCLOPEDIA OF SUPER VILLAINS

Jeff Rovin

Facts On File Publications
New York, New York • Oxford, England

THE ENCYCLOPEDIA OF SUPER VILLAINS

Library of Congress Cataloging-in Publication Data

Rovin, Jeff
The encyclopedia of super villains.

Includes index.
1. Villains in mass media—Handbooks, manuals, etc.
I. Title.
P96.V48R68 1987 700 87-8831
ISBN 0-8160-1356-X (hardcover)
ISBN 0-8160-1899-5 (paperback)

Interior design by Duane Stapp.

Printed in the United States of America

10 9 8 7 6 5 4 3 2 1

CONTENTS

INTRODUCTION

"Insanus omnis furere credit ceteros."
(Every madman thinks everybody else is mad.)

—Syrus, in *Maxims*

In the motion picture *Superman II*, the super-powered General Zod escapes from his Phantom Zone prison and sets himself up as the tyrannical ruler of earth. Eventually, Superman is able to defeat him—but not before people are slain, cities are razed, and a President is forced to kneel before the tsar from Krypton.

"He was a monster," says actor Terence Stamp who played Zod, "but though we all cheered for Superman the truth is that if *we* had superhuman powers, most of us would most likely be doing what Zod is doing and not what Superman is doing. Most of us wouldn't be upholding laws, we'd be running the world according to our *own* rules." Psychologist Bruno Bettelheim agrees. In *The Uses of Enchantment* he writes, "Who would not like to have the power . . . to satisfy all his desires . . . and to punish his enemies? And who does not fear such powers if some other possesses them?"

Superheroism requires an extreme degree of self-sacrifice and denial. Being a superhero means controlling one's base, carnivorous instincts. It means turning the other cheek no matter how disgusted one gets. It means striving to protect others, even those who have wronged the superhero.

Super-villainy is just the opposite. It permits self-indulgence in the extreme, the seeking of vengeance or gain with a complete disregard for the rights and well-being of others.

The fact that there are often dozens of super villains for each and every superhero indicates just *how* tempting this is, how easy it is to be corrupted rather than to grow saintly. How natural it is to be like Zod.

Even if the average person is not of a mind to conquer the world, every day we find a valid reason for lashing out at that world; a driver cuts us off on the road, we're treated unfairly at the workplace, something we just bought breaks down.

Our first thoughts are not to rehabilitate or forgive the perpetrator. Our initial reaction is to swear. To chastise. To kick. Perhaps even to destroy—if we had superpowers and were beyond retribution. This isn't to say that we're evil because we get angry. After all, we're human. But if we had superstrength or a raygun or a voodoo doll—if we felt that we could get away with revenge—violence would probably erupt.

For most fictional characters, acquiring superpowers causes just that. It magnifies latent or mild megalomania, misanthropy, and madness. These obsessions tend to grow more intense as time goes on; paranoia sets in, enemies are perceived as being everywhere, fortifications rise, weapons are collected, and before you know it a Darth Vader or Dr. Doom has been born.

How thoroughly does this evolution affect the brain? Consider: Unlike the superhero, the super villain doesn't sneak back into a civilian identity, become a Clark Kent or Bruce Wayne at the end of the day. The Joker remains the Joker, the Phantom of the Opera is always the Phantom of the Opera, 24 hours a day, 365 days a year. They are satisfied, utterly, with this identity. Which isn't to say that super villains are true obsessive-compulsives, people who reach a point where they derive no pleasure from their actions other than to release tension. Super villains *enjoy* making others suffer, as witness this classic exchange between Superman and Lex Luthor from the film *Superman*:

Superman: "Is that how a warped brain like yours gets its kicks, by planning the death of innocent people?"
Luthor: "No. By *causing* the death of innocent people."

Super villains have their roots in the dawn of civilization, when they were created to make ethical statements or simply to create conflict and drama. In ancient Egypt, Set, the god of darkness, cut the body of the benevolent sungod Osiris into 14 pieces and scattered them throughout the land. The Babylonians feared the awful goddess Tiamat who, with her pet dragons, represented the destructive power of the ocean, while the Persians weren't too fond of Druj, the Spirit of Evil, who was served by an army of demons.

These religious figures and others like them were the forerunners of the witches, ogres, and trolls which menaced heroes in fairy tales, and the wizards and hi-tech antagonists which later appeared in fantasy and science fiction novels, comic books, motion pictures, television, and the like.

The super villains which appear in this encyclopedia were culled from these and other sources, each source indicated by letters in parentheses beside the heading of each entry: A (advertisements), C (comic books), CS (comic strips), F (folklore), M (magazines), MP (motion pictures), MY (mythology), N (novel/short story), P (poetry), R (radio), RE (religion), S (stage, includes opera), T (toys), and TV (television). The range is broad—Satan rubs shoulders with the likes of the Bunny from Beyond—but then evil takes many forms. Even a hare with absolute power can be corrupted absolutely.

Who qualifies? That's subjective to some degree, though there are common attributes among all the figures in this encyclopedia. Like the superhero, the super villain is a figure whose ambitions and abilities—whether from mutation, wizardry, or even an incredible weapon or two—surpass those of ordinary villains. Thus, while the likes of Fagin, Lady Macbeth, and Boris Badenov (of Rocky and Bullwinkle fame) are certainly ne'er-do-wells, they lack the technology, the sixth sense, the extra dimension that would make them super villains.

Which is not to rule out the exceptions that meet only one of the criteria. Auric Goldfinger isn't markedly more "super" than Badenov, but the scope of his plan to kill off an entire city and loot Fort Knox is dastardly enough to merit him a place in the rogue's gallery. Sometimes sheer criminal audacity is sufficient to offset the lack of a gadget or superpower.

On the other hand, *apparent* criminality can be misleading. For example, the monstrous flies in the pictured issue of *Porky Pig* would certainly seem to qualify as super-villainous. Porky and Sylvester steal into the insects' homeland intending to destroy them, but, as the story reveals, the monstrous Muscidae are merely defending themselves. (Eventually, Porky and Sylvester realize their error and leave . . . astride a horsefly, naturally.)

Another problem area is monsters. As a rule, huge and/or clearly non-humanoid evildoers have not been included in the text. While creatures like Godzilla and the Frankenstein Monster are destructive, they are not greedy or totalitarian or simply sadistic in the same way as Captain Hook or Medea.

Also, a number of super villains catalogued in the text ultimately reformed—most notably, Darth Vader. They have been included just the same since, their ultimate redemption notwithstanding, the body of their criminal work is awesome.

Each entry in the encyclopedia is divided into a variety of subheadings. Like a "Wanted" poster, this lets you know quickly and concisely just who the enemy is. (In those cases where information was inapplicable or unavailable, the subheading has not been included.) The categories are as follows:

Real Name: If known or provided in the original chronicles, the super villain's identity before he/she/it gave up any semblance of law-abiding normalcy.

First Appearance: The medium and date of the character's first appearance. Note that some magazines, such as *The Mighty Crusaders* and *Superman*, had two separate runs. These are differentiated by notations of first or second series.

Costume: The fiend's distinctive garb. A bodysuit/shirt is tight and formfitting, while a jumpsuit is not; a T-shirt is simply a bodyshirt without the sleeves; a capelet is a small cape, reaching no farther than the midback.

Weapons: The implements, gadgets, conveyances, and arms used by the super villain.

Chief Henchmen: The lawbreaker's aides and flunkies—human and monster alike—listed by name wherever possible.

Biography: The often tragic story of the super villain's life, including how she/he/it became a criminal and a few of the major crimes.

Quote: A typical threat, malediction, quip, or famous-last-words—straight from the super villain's mouth.

Porky Pig in peril. © *Dell Publishing.*

Comment: Any additional information, including cross-references to super villains with similar powers or motivation.

Note that beside the headings of several entries are numbers. Super villains not only conquer, murder, and extort, but sometimes they steal one another's names. If more than one super villain has the same name—such as the Scorpion—the entries are numbered according to who used it first.

Too, super villains frequently crop up in the entries of other super villains. If a villain's name appears this way in capital letters, it means she or he has their own entry.

If you're interested in finding out which villains shared the same superhero enemies, please refer to the hero's name in the index.

Indeed, you can often tell a great deal about people from the company they keep, and it's interesting to note that superheroes often attract certain kinds of super villains. Foes of the Batman tend to be psychotic, adversaries of Dick Tracy are often physically deformed, and Superman's greatest enemies seem to enjoy goading him on more than they thrill to criminality for its own sake. Freudians will find this revealing . . . not only in analyzing the characters, but also in understanding the dark side of the creators' imaginations as well.

The truth is, super villains also teach us about ourselves. We may admire the hubris of the super villain, identify with their frustrations, and even, as actor Stamp suggests, find their freedom alluring. But the bottom line is that in life, as in art, herodom is a chronicle of successes while villaindom is a catalogue of failures.

Milton unwittingly provided the call-to-arms for most super villains when he wrote, "Better to reign in hell, than serve in heav'n." However, it was Underdog who provided the capper, summing up what the woeful saga of every super villain in this book underscores:

"Crime doesn't pay."

"We villains are a very select group indeed. In the very desperation of our hate rests our strength."

—CYCLOPS

THE ABOMINATION (C)

Real Name: Emil Blonsky.
First Appearance: 1967, *Tales to Astonish* #90, Marvel Comics.
Costume: Blue trunks (the Abomination's skin is green and scaly).
Biography: A Yugoslavian and onetime associate of THE RHINO, Blonsky infiltrated the Air Force base in New Mexico where Dr. Bruce Banner (aka the superheroic Hulk) performed his experiments with gamma rays (the rays which turned him into the Hulk). Sneaking into the laboratory to take photographs of the extraordinary equipment, pictures which he plans to sell "behind the bamboo curtain," Blonsky triggers the apparatus which turns Banner into the shambling green giant. The burst of radiation transforms Blonsky into a more lizard-like but equally powerful brute. The exuberant Blonsky exclaims, "I can do *anything*!! I'm master of the *world* . . . of the whole *universe*!!" Like the Hulk, the Abomination possesses enormous strength, the ability to leap miles in a single bound, and a high degree of invulnerability to pain or injury; unlike the Hulk, he cannot return to human form. The hero and villain have tangled repeatedly, most recently at the prompting of the evil MODOK. Failing to defeat the superhero, the Abomination was disintegrated by a psionic beam from Modok. Though things look grim for the Zagreb native, it is possible that someday, somehow, he will return.
Quote: No *longer* need I resort to being a furtive *spy* . . . ! Now, I have only to desire a goal . . . and I possess the *strength* to make it *mine*!"

ABRA KADABRA (C)

First Appearance: 1963, *The Flash* #128, DC Comics.
Costume: White tuxedo, cloak, gloves, slippers.
Weapons: Gem flower, worn in his lapel, which generates a hypno-spell; magic wand which can teleport objects, paralyze them, or transmute matter. (Note: later it is revealed that these are scientific instruments; still later, they are described as merely being stage props, and that Kadabra's powers are generated from within.)
Biography: In 64th century society, magicians are no longer valued. Each day, a magician with the stage name Abra Kadabra goes to Magician's Hall and finds the "Request for Magicians" board devoid of requests. Blaming science for making miracles commonplace, Kadabra finally sees a way out. In the year 6363, researchers invent a time machine which, because it's made of M-Metal whose "radiation is petering out swiftly," can be used only once. Sneaking into the laboratory and using his powers to mesmerize the scientists, Kadabra flies back to the twentieth century, the golden era of Houdini. Crashlanding in 1963, a bit late for the famous escape artist, Kadabra yearns for applause and realizes that the best way to get attention is to commit crimes. Discovering that he enjoys stealing, he becomes a master villain; he is particularly keen on eliminating the superheroic Flash whom he perceives "could be a threat to me in this era." To date, his most extraordinary crime has been to turn the Flash into a giant marionette (*The Flash* #133).
Quote: "I'll cause the floor to change its structure—fashion wooden hands to . . . hold him tight—while I make off with the gold!"

THE ABSORBING MAN (C)

Real Name: Carl "Crusher" Creel.
First Appearance: 1964, *Journey Into Mystery* #114, Marvel Comics.
Costume: Prison trousers.
Weapons: Ball and chain, which he wore in prison and now uses as a mace.
Biography: Wishing to destroy the superheroic god Thor, the evil deity LOKI turns Creel into a supervillain. Mixing an herbal formula in his drinking water, Loki transforms Creel into the Absorbing Man, a being who can take on the strength and properties of any nearby person or object, as well as grow to several stories in height. Escaping from

prison and engaging Thor, he is defeated on two separated occasions; banished to space by Odin, the king of the gods, Creel returns on a comet to continue his disruptive ways. In addition to frequent battles with Thor, he has fought the Hulk, the Dazzler, and others.

Quote: "I'll ram you through a bulkhead so's you . . . won't be underfoot no more!"

Comment: THE SUPER-ADAPTOID is another foe who can absorb the powers of those near it.

ADMIRAL CEREBRUS (C)

First Appearance: 1984, *DC Comics Presents* #68, DC Comics.

Costume: White gloves, bodysuit with gold stripe down front; gold epaulets, belt, boots, wristbands.

Weapons: Cerebral Regulator, a headband that can produce the cerebro-charge, a jolt which disconnects the "psychic regulator . . . which controls the vast energies our brains contain" and allows his henchmen to "gain access to tremendous psychic power." The output of energy is so powerful it can knock Superman down for the count.

Biography: Lying about his age, Cerebrus joins the navy at the young age of 15. Later, he becomes the head of a special program studying psychic power. Misleading the Pentagon about his findings, he causes it to drop the program. Continuing his research upon retirement, Cerebrus develops the Cerebro Regulator and begins recruiting subjects who must pass his Psychic Quotient test—an arcade videogame that automatically teleports them to Cerebrus' yacht headquarters if they attain a score of 100,000, an indicator that they have "the ideal kind of mind—resilient, quick, and highly focused." There, he breeds psychic soldiers available for hire by interested foreign nations. When Superman investigates the missing youngsters, the villain challenges him; Superman triumphs only when his colleague, the superhero Vixen, pulls the plug on Cerebrus' equipment, sending the villain a monumental feedback-blast of cerebro-charge energy. His chances of ever recovering are "not one chance in a thousand."

Quote: "Properly *marketed*, this can be a gold mine."

Comment: This has been the character's only appearance to date. Other villains Superman has battled in his 50 years of crimebusting include the robber Achilles who wore, in a rather clumsy box on his heel, an "anti-magnetic device" to repel all metal objects; Akthar, a powerful figure in an undersea kingdom, who plans to use incredible "beam-forces" to invade the surface world; the Archer, a hunter who dons a disguise, turns his bow and arrow on millionaires, and becomes an extortionist; the Brain, a superscientific fiend; the Chameleon, a master of disguises; Drago, an extraterrestrial dictator who, among his awful crimes, causes the blinding of everyone on his planet (save those who serve as taskmasters), a deed undone by Superman's "antidote bomb"; the Duplicate Man, who is able to split into two people, either one of which can simply vaporize to escape capture; the Emperor of America, who uses a "monstrous ray machine" to sap human will and conquer the United States; the Evolution King, who ages people who don't submit to extortion. Also, the Four Galactic Thiefmasters, alien crooks who attempt to destroy Superman for having nipped their criminal plans in the bud (they fail); the Gargoyle, a fanged villain who lost his eyes and ears in an explosion and wears a bizarre helmet which enables him to see and hear . . . the better to steal scientific secrets for his boss, chemical magnate J.C. Quagmire; Hroguth, an extraterrestrial who comes to earth to steal copper, with which he can build a machine that will enable him to rule his home world, Durim; the Insect Master who, like KING LOCUST, can control bugs and sends them against humanity; Khalex, a superpowered extraterrestrial; the Leopard, who wears a mask resembling his namesake and uses ferocious cats to help commit crimes. Also, Lightning Master, who uses his "lightning machine" to destroy buildings and extort money from Metropolis; Medini, a hypnotist-criminal; Mr. Ohm, who commits robberies with his "flying electromagnet," an airplane which uses magnetism to hijack armored cars; Mister Sinister, a denizen of the fourth dimension who uses his world's advanced science to attempt to conquer the earth; the Miracle Twine Gang, which uses an unbreakable cord (made with the help of kryptonite) when committing crimes; the Mole (2), "an expert miner and tunneler" who is unrelated to Batman's Mole (3) (see ZODIAC MASTER, Comment) or THE MOLE (1) who battled Dick Tracy; the Moonman, an astronaut who becomes a super villain after a combination of the moon's light and a passing comet gives him the tide-like ability to attract matter using his right hand and repel it with his left; the Rainmaker who, like WEATHER WIZARD, has a "rain-machine" to control precipitation and uses it for extortion; the Snake, aka Bill Chantey who, dressed as a serpent, uses poisoned needles to kill those who he feels have held him back in his career at the Allerton Construction Company. And the Squiffles, elves led by Ixnayalpay who conspire with Hitler to turn their talents against American aircraft during the Second World War; the Talon, a fifth columnist during the Second World War whose target is the Metropolis subway system (at one point, he tries to electrocute the riders on one line); Tiger

Woman, a "daring female bandit"; Vathgar of the other dimensional world Xeron, which he tries to conquer by plucking iron from earth, an element which turns his planet's skrans from pacifistic to warlike creatures; Vul-Kor, an alien from a water world who builds an "infra coil" on earth to melt the polar caps and eliminate all human life, leaving his kind free to colonize. Also, Watkins, a hypnotist who mesmerizes people into robbing with bombs lashed to their waists, bombs which they detonate rather than submitting themselves to arrest; the Wizard of Wokit, a sorcerer who enslaves the European town of Morabia; the Wrecker, a non-super villain whose calling card is the spectacular destruction he leaves behind when committing crimes; the twisted scientific genius Xanu, who is trying to gain control of a world in another dimension; and Zerno, a wizard on the planet Y'Bar, who uses a "strange crystal" to snatch beings and devices from other worlds, prizes which he is then able to put to work on criminal undertakings (which are all aimed at conquering Y'Bar).

AEGEUS (C)

Real Name: Nikos Aegeus.
First Appearance: 1973, *Wonder Woman* #207, DC Comics.
Costume: Red breastplate with golden band around chest and waist, another running down center; red cape with golden fringe; golden boots.
Weapons: Thunderbolts which can be flung like javelins or fired like arrows; the Six Daggers of Vulcan, which can cut through virtually anything.
Chief Henchman: Pegasus, the winged horse.
Biography: In ancient Greece, the goddess Athena gave a magic bridle to the mortal Bellerophon. With it, Bellerophon tamed Pegasus and used both the horse and the thunderbolts it carried to work heroic deeds. Coming to believe his own press, Bellerophon grew into an unparalleled egomaniac who aspired to be a god. Displeased, Zeus, the king of the gods, made him blind and crippled. Down but not out, Bellerophon was discovered in our own era by Nikos Aegeus, a Greek terrorist. The ancient Greek gave the bridle to Aegeus, who found Bellerophon and used the horse and his powers to further his causes. His enemy is Wonder Woman and her race of Amazons, over whom he has yet to triumph.

THE AFRICAN MAGICIAN (F)

First Appearance: Circa 800 A.D., "Aladdin."
Weapons: Magic ring.
Biography: Heading to China, where he pretends to be the brother of the late tailor Mustapha, a "famous African magician" asks his "nephew" Aladdin to collect a magic lamp from a labyrinth of small, dark caves. The boy does so, but can't climb out because of the jewels he's stuffed in his pocket; when he refuses to discard the wealth, his "uncle" shuts him in the cave. Aladdin escapes using a magic ring the African had loaned him. Back home, while the youth is polishing the lamp, a powerful genie appears. The "slave of the lamp" makes Aladdin wealthy, and showers him with riches which enable him to woo and wed a princess. Meanwhile, back in Africa, the Magician learns of Aladdin's good fortune and resolves to steal it. Disguising himself as a lamp-seller, he walks the streets crying "New lamps for old!" The princess (in some versions, it's a slave) gladly trades Aladdin's lamp for a newer model. As soon as he has it, the Magician orders the genie to carry Aladdin's palace and the princess back to Africa. The outraged Aladdin follows him and, sneaking into the palace, provides the princess with poison. She slips it into the Magician's wine and, drinking it, he perishes. However, the Magician has a brother who's also a wizard and is "if possible, more wicked and more cunning." Following Aladdin back to China, he disguises himself as a holy woman and enters the palace; but the genie tips Aladdin off, and the youth stabs the brother through the heart.
Quote: "At the foot of those steps you will find an open door leading into three large halls. Go through them without touching anything, or you will die instantly."
Comment: "Aladdin" may have appeared in an Oriental manuscript of 1703; the document is alluded to by a later text, though no surviving written form predates that of French Oriental expert Galland. Even so, the tale has a long oral tradition and appears in the lore of other lands. In the Bohemian tale of Jenik, there is no counterpart to the Magician, and the magic item found by Jenik is an enchanted watch. However, the princess is evil and the events in the story are largely the same. In an Albanian folktale the "lamp" is a magic stone, the villain an evil Jew. The best-known versions of the story appeared in Richard Burton's *Arabian Nights Entertainments* (1885), and in anthologist Andrew Lang's collection of the same name (1898). However, the best of these was a beautifully animated featurette made in 1939 starring Popeye as Aladdin and Brutus as the Magician. See also AMINA and THE FORTY THIEVES.

AGGAMON (C)

First Appearance: 1964, *Strange Tales* #119, Marvel Comics.

Costume: Red trunks, boots, wristbands, tunic with extremely high collar.

Weapons: Gems (only one is shown, but presumably there are more) through which he snatches people from worlds in other dimensions.

Chief Henchmen: Nameless soldiers, all dressed in red armor and helmets.

Biography: When a pair of thieves breaks into the home of master magician Dr. Strange, they try to steal a mystic gem and are drawn through it to another dimension. Following them into "the dread *Purple Dimension*," Strange discovers the overlord Aggamon and his minions. For thousands of years, Aggamon has been snatching beings from anywhere and everywhere and using them as slaves to mine gems "which delight my soul." Refusing to turn the earth people over to Strange, Aggamon is buffeted by the good wizard's magic: Strange not only convinces the tyrant to surrender, but makes it impossible for him to regain any strength at all unless he sets every one of his captives free. Aggamon capitulates and Strange returns to his Greenwich Village apartment.

Quote: "*Surrender*, you mortal fool! You have no other choice—except certain death!"

Comment: This was the character's only appearance.

A.J. RAFFLES (N, S, MP)

First Appearance: 1899, "The Amateur Cracksman," E.W. Hornung.

Biography: A brilliant young man, Raffles unexpectedly finds himself broke while in Australia. Having no choice but to steal, he discovers that he enjoys the act so much he decides to keep at it. ("Of course it's very wrong," he admits, "but we can't all be moralists.") Moving through English society, he is at home among the rich and well-connected . . . and makes careful mental notes about who owns what. Though he steals to pay his bills, Raffles is not averse to committing crimes to help friends or punish those who are more corrupt than he. Raffles makes his home in Albany, near that of his best friend Bunny. The "cracksman" is an expert cricket player, a talent which keeps him on the guest lists of exclusive homes and clubs.

Quote: "Why settle down to some humdrum, uncongenial billet when excitement, romance, danger, and a decent living were all going begging together?"

Comment: Hornung wrote three Raffles stories: *The Black Mask* (1901; American title: *Raffles: Further Adventures of the Amateur Cracksman*); *A Thief in the Night* (1905); and *Mr. Justice Raffles* (1909). Hornung also collaborated with Eugene Presbrey on a Broadway play, *Raffles, the Amateur Cracksman* (1903; Kyrle Bellew starred). In 1933, writer Barry Perowne revived the character as an adventure hero; after eight novels he once again made the character a crook, though these short stories (collected as *Raffles Revisited* in 1974) had him committing crimes to right larger injustices. In the movies, Raffles has been played by John Barrymore (1917), House Peters (1925, only stealing from the well-to-do), Ronald Colman (1930), George Barraud (1932), and David Niven (1940). Gentlemen thieves who are actually rather virtuous, robbing from the unjust to help the righteous, include Frank L. Packard's Jimmie Dale, aka the Gray Seal in a series of stories beginning with *The Adventures of Jimmie Dale* in 1917 (Jimmie also poses as Larry the Bat when he has to move among sleazier elements); Bruce Graeme's Richard Verrell, alias Blackshirt—so-called because he dressed from head to toe in black, including a mask—who appeared in 12 tales, the first of which was *Blackshirt* in 1925; Thomas W. Hanshew's Hamilton Cleek, who first appeared in *The Man of Forty Faces* (1910) and, because of his rubbery face, could change his features utterly (earning him the nickname "The Vanishing Cracksman," though not for long; he, too, reformed and became a detective); and Leslie Charteris' the Saint, whose first adventure, *Meet the Tiger* (1928), has been followed by over a hundred others, in print, and as many on TV, radio, and in the movies. See also THE LONE WOLF.

AMAZO (C)

First Appearance: 1960, *The Brave and the Bold* #30, DC Comics.

Costume: Brown tights with horizontal dark and light green bands from the ankles nearly to the knee; matching bands on the wrist, and an identical leotard cut off just below the breast (leotard was changed to a "V"-shaped vest in #112). Amazo now wears a red cap with a widow's peak (originally, his bald head was bare), and boasts a bright yellow "A" on his red belt.

Weapons: The android's entire flesh-colored body is a weapon; his artificial cells enable him to duplicate the powers of any superbeing he encounters.

Biography: Built by Professor Ivo to duplicate the powers of the Justice League of America, the nearly 10-feet-tall Amazo was defeated, deactivated, and stored in the superheroes' trophy room (see PROFESSOR IVO for details). However, Amazo was reanimated to help defeat the alien menace I, who could only be slain by exposure to an abundance of superpower energy—energy provided by a battle between the android and the Justice League

(#27); he returned, next, as a helpless flunky of T.O. MORROW (#65); then, reprogrammed, he returned to help the Justice League regain powers they lost to the evil, gold-like Libra, who subjected them to his Energy-Trans-Mortifier. In that tale, Amazo did indeed absorb the powers from space, but he then refused to turn them over. He was ultimately defeated when Batman tricked him into a machine that drew the powers away, after which the Caped Crusader used steel gloves to knock Amazo's head off (#112). That hasn't kept the villain down, however, and he continues to be a force for villainy in the DC universe.

Quote: "You're a *fool*—if you think I will hesitate to harm a *woman* . . . ! I'll destroy *anyone* who gets in my way—!"

ANIMA (F)

First Appearance: Circa 8th century A.D., "The Story of Sidi-Nouman."

Biography: Amina is an Arabian witch and ghoul. She would go out each night with another ghoul "springing out upon unwary travellers whose flesh they eat." If no one was around, they would go to the cemetery for their feast. When Anima's husband Sidi-Nouman becomes suspicious, she uses her magic powers to transform him into a dog. A young lady who is also a magician restores Sidi-Nouman and gives him a potion to turn Anima into a horse. After splashing it on her, he keeps her as his steed, beating her frequently.

Comment: The tale appears in Andrew Lang's *Arabian Nights Entertainments* (1898), as well as other collections. See also Arabian Nights' villains THE AFRICAN MAGICIAN and THE FORTY THIEVES.

ANGAR THE SCREAMER (C)

Real Name: David Angar.

First Appearance: 1973, *Daredevil* #100, Marvel Comics.

Costume: Tan trousers; blue vest with tassels, boots, headband; golden wristbands, necklace with skull pendant.

Biography: A hippie, Angar allows himself to be subjected to a mutating device from the moon of Titan. Moondragon, an emissary from Titan, hopes that once Angar gains superhuman powers, he will help battle the interplanetary scourge THANOS. Instead, as soon as he is given a voice capable of causing incredible hallucinations (which tap the listener's private fears), Angar collaborates with Moondragon's terrestrial partner Kerwin J. Broderick to become a criminal. Defeated by Daredevil, he remains at-large as an independent operator.

Comment: Daredevil's foes Ramrod and the Dark Messiah (see THE TRUMP, Comment) are also products of Titanian genetic tinkering.

ANGLE MAN (C)

Real Name: Angelo Bend.

First Appearance: 1954, *Wonder Woman* #70, DC Comics.

Costume: Dark green bodysuit, boots, cowl and goggles, all with yellow stripes as follows: along both arms, down both legs to toes, triangle with base along chest and point at navel, "V"-shape on forehead; yellow holster, gloves.

Weapons: The Angler, a triangle-shaped device which allows the user to teleport through space, time, and other dimensions.

Biography: A small-time crook, Bend realized that in order to succeed in the big time he needed an angle. At first, he became the non-costumed Angle Man whose crimes all had a complex gimmick; when that failed to launch him into the major leagues, he donned a costume and acquired, through unknown means, his Angler. His perennial foe was Wonder Woman; he served briefly in THE SECRET SOCIETY OF SUPER-VILLAINS.

ANIMAL-VEGETABLE-MINERAL MAN (C)

Real Name: Dr. Sven Larsen.

First Appearance: 1964, *The Doom Patrol* #89, DC Comics.

Costume: None; Larsen can transform himself to resemble whatever creature, plant, mineral, or metal he desires.

Biography: A biologist, Larsen was a student of Dr. Niles Caulder (leader of the superheroic Doom Patrol) at Stockholm University. One summer, there developed some bitterness between the two when Larsen accused his professor of stealing the idea for an invention, an "anti-decay ray that halts all changes in living cells." The accusation was untrue, and though Larsen pretended to believe Caulder's denial, he privately held a grudge against him over the years. Intending to destroy the Doom Patrol as vengeance, the Swede comes to the United States ostensibly to give a lecture about the origins of life. At State University, using a vat of amino acids and synthetic lightning, he attempts to create life artificially; once the experiment is underway, however, he immerses himself in the frothing liquid and emerges the Animal-Vegetable-Mineral Man, able to become, at will, any life form or animate mineral in any size, with its appropriate powers. (Becoming lead, for instance, he has all the properties of that metal.) Among the things he becomes are a giant sponge, a living mass of sulphur, a strangling tree, a monstrous paramecium, a swarm of gnats, a giant diamond man, and a tiger. Caulder eventually is able to subdue Larsen with the gun he was originally accused of stealing. Dipped back in the green liquid, Larsen is returned to normal and sent to prison. However, he escapes and menaces the Doom Patrol anew, becoming a giant Grizzly, hydrochloric acid, electric eels, a caveman, tungsten birds which glow blindingly like "a giant living light," and a monster octopus, until once again, he is felled with Caulder's gun (#95, 1965).

ANNIHILUS (C)

First Appearance: 1968, *The Fantastic Four Annual* #6, Marvel Comics.

Costume: Outer skin is hard, red shell resembling bodysuit, trunks, boots, and gloves; face framed with red shield; green shoulderpads; darker green wings (see Weapons).

Weapons: Annihilus' armor-like shell permits him to travel through space, propelled by the Cosmic Control Rod, a six-inch tube worn under his chin and which doubles as a blaster. Annihilus' shell also endows him with vast strength, and his wings enable him to fly through any atmosphere. Annihilus also possesses various blasters and transports.

Biography: Eons ago, in the antimatter universe known as the Negative Zone, spacefarers from the planet Tyanna roamed the Zone planting the seeds of bioengineered life on lifeless planets. Crashing on one such planet, Arthros (located in Sector 17A), the Tyannans release their seeds—one of which was the nascent Annihilus. Growing and entering the crashed ship, Annihilus dons a helmet which, containing all Tyannan knowledge, transforms him into a vastly intelligent being. Transistorizing the ship's propulsion system and building his Cosmic Control Rod, Annihilus sets out to conquer not only the Negative Zone but also all worlds everywhere. The Fantastic Four have thwarted his scheme in the past, as have other heroes such as the Avengers, and no doubt will be called upon to do so again.

Quote: "Thus do I safeguard my own immortal existence . . . by crushing all who live!"

THE ANSWER (C)

First Appearance: 1984, *Peter Parker, the Spectacular Spider-Man* #92, Marvel Comics.

Costume: Purple tights; purple bodyshirt with flaps under arms, attached to waist (see Weapons); golden collar; silver shoulderpads with purple epaulets; silver stripe down chest and over navel; purple cowl with queue; golden boots, gloves, girdle.

Weapons: Flaps enable him to fly; suit is "so slick" that Spider-Man's webbing can't stick to it.

Biography: Nothing is known about this villain, save that he was hired by a crime czar known as the Kingpin to pit his own superpowers against those of Spider-Man in an effort to gauge the superhero's strength. In addition to swift flight, the Answer, through some unexplained means, is able to make his hearing more acute. He perishes four issues after his debut, dying when the fiendish SILVERMANE is on the verge of murdering the Kingpin. The Answer generously gives his "light" to the superheroine Dagger—who can turn light into lethal daggers—so that she can stop Silvermane.

Quote: "Very well, the Answer has his answer! You may live."

Comment: Spider-Man has fought many super villains in his 25 years of crimefighting, including those, such as THE MOLE MAN and THE RING-MASTER, who are associated with other heroes. Among the lesser lights who have appeared in the various Spider-Man magazines are the Dreadnought, a powerful, fire-throwing robot; the alien Meru of the Haifs, who are "smug supercilious telepaths"; the Black Abbott, a master of mind control; the Crime-Master, with his deadly gas pellets; the Cat, a nimble cat-burglar; the Looter, who gains superpowers from a fallen meteor; Man Mountain Marko, a brutish enforcer for the crime group the Maggia; the cosmetics magnate Narda Ravanna who uses her knowledge of chemistry to create weapons and commits crimes as the costumed Belladonna; the bounding Kangaroo, who acquired his powers after living and dining for years with kangaroos in the Australian Outback; inventor Spencer Smythe and his huge Spider Slayer robot; the seven-foot-tall Giant One, an Oriental who is in league with the Monks of the Hidden Temple; Hammerhead, whose skull is made of an unbreakable metal; the genetically altered Smasher (aka the Man Monster), a bruiser who can punch through just about anything; the Mindworm, a mutant who consumes the energy created by his victims' emotions. Also, the Grizzly, a wrestler given enormous physical strength due to an exoskeleton built into his bear costume; the Cyclone, a French engineer whose costume creates fearsome winds; Mirage, a master illusionist; Stegron the Dinosaur Man who is keen to conquer the world; Will O' the Wisp, who has the power to make himself incorporeal; the Rocket Racer, an inventor with a jet-propelled skateboard and missile-firing wristbands; the Spider-Squad, three criminals who wear exoskeletons for super-strength and have, in addition, either pincers, a stinger, or four additional arms; Fusion, twin brothers who can become one and draw energy from anyone or anything around them; and Hydroman, who can turn his body into water.

THE ANTI-MONITOR (C)

First Appearance: 1985, *Crises On Infinite Earths #2* (not pictured until #5), DC Comics.

Costume: Original: iron-gray bodysuit; blue boots to knees, squares around thighs, girdle, armor on shoulders, forearms, chest (with golden tubes and circuits covering them), helmet with yellow eyes and gray tubes from nostrils to chest; purple cape; light blue gloves. Second: iron-gray bodysuit with gold circle on back, radiating tubing under breast, around waist, down arms and down legs to boots; blue boots, trunks, armor on forearms and shoulders, helmet with yellow eyes. (Essentially, the second costume, which debuted in #8, is a sleeker version of the first.) The Anti-Monitor's skin is brittle and white.

Chief Henchmen: The Thunderers, warriors armed with lightning bolts and golden shields; the Shadow Demons, black humanoids who slay with their electric touch and move with ease through air, land, or sea.

Biography: The Anti-Monitor is the master of the Anti-Matter Universe, a negative complement to our own. It, along with countless other parallel universes in the "multiverse"—Earth-1, -2, -3, -4, -S, -X, etc., matter-universes all—was created 10 billion years ago when the scientist Krona of the planet Oa (see THE CONTROLLER) sought "to learn the origin of the universe." He opened a gateway into the Big Bang, the moment of creation, and, accidentally, not only caused countless replications of this universe, but also unleashed evil. In the aftermath of Krona's experiment, Qward came into being in the antimatter universe. On both, a being arose from the planet itself: the Monitor and the Anti-Monitor. The former was a benevolent, meditative soul, the latter an aggressive, "blasphemous parody of humanity . . . weaned on the evil of that anti-matter universe." The Anti-Monitor promptly "created an army of warriors," the Thunderers; then he metamorphosed "the Thunderer elite" into his "shadow Demons." Sending his armies forth, he conquered his universe, and then, sensing the presence of his counterpart, the Monitor, the Anti-Monitor attacks him across the dimensional barriers. The two fight for one million years until "a simultaneous attack rendered them both unconscious." They remain, thus, for over nine billion years. Finally, in a matter universe, a brilliant scientist named Kell discovers the existence of the multiverse and antimatter universe. Stepping into his "netherversal chamber" and accidentally exposing the two universes to each other, Kell sets off a chain reaction which destroys his own universe. The scientist—who most fittingly renamed himself Pariah—also causes the Anti-Monitor to awake. As he explains it, "When my positive matter universe was destroyed, the anti-matter universe expanded to fill the void. Its power grew . . . and the Anti-Monitor fed upon that power, and grew stronger." The revived Anti-Monitor realizes, then, that "as each positive matter universe died, he would grow more powerful." Thus, he sets out to consume every inch of the multiverse with an "anti-matter force (which) shatters the dimensional barriers." Meanwhile, the Monitor has also awakened and, finding an orphan girl on our own earth, brings her aboard his satellite and spends two decades turning her into the super-powered Harbinger. As such, she has the power to make duplicates of herself which she sends forth to rally every superhero from every universe to battle the Anti-Monitor. Concurrently, the Monitor causes Harbinger to kill him, freeing his life essence to flow into huge "vibrational forks," a device to halt the consumption of the multiverse. The battle against the Anti-Monitor rages through time and space, the most dramatic moment occurring when he and Supergirl go head-to-head on his planet-sized stone fortress in the Anti-Matter Universe. Though she does the super villain enormous damage (forcing his costume change), he manages to catch her with a power blast, killing the superheroine (#7). Picking up the slack, the superheroic Spectre absorbs the powers of all the superheroic sorcerers (Phantom Stranger, Dr. Fate, etc.) and, cornering the Anti-Monitor at the dawn of time, sends him back into the miasma of creation. However . . . the fiend is not dead. He resurfaces in Qward and, with only our universe remaining, he makes ready to destroy it. The surviving superheroes head to Qward, and though Superman is able to give the Anti-Monitor quite a licking, he requires the help of a super villain to do him in; concerned that his home Apokolips will be consumed, the evil DARKSEID sends a power blast at the already weakened Anti-Monitor. Falling back into his moon's star, the demonic creature manages to crawl forth and is met by Superman who socks him so hard the Anti-Monitor explodes (#12).

Quote: "You turn in battle, girl? That is a fatal mistake!" (Last words before he destroys Supergirl.)

Comment: Other superheroes who died at the hands of the Anti-Monitor include the Flash and the Dove. The members of THE CRIME SYNDICATE OF AMERICA also perished, and THE PSYCHO PIRATE was left insane.

APIAN WAY (TV, C)

First Appearance: 1967, "Super Chicken," *George of the Jungle*, ABC-TV.
Weapons: Yacht with artillery; 200-ton steel tank.
Biography: A graduate of the Harvard watch repair college, Tick-Tock Tech, and heir to the riches of the Ways of Providence (Rhode Island), Apian nonetheless wants even more wealth. To this end, the noncostumed felon tows his home state out to sea and refuses to return it unless the U.S. government deposits "83 trillion dollars in the old oak by the crossroads." Former schoolmate Super Chicken and his lion aide Fred fly to his yacht, where they engage in a duel—the plucky chicken wielding his sword, Apian at the controls of his tank. But Apian didn't count on the boat capsizing due to the weight of his tank at one end; no sooner does it vanish beneath the waves than Fred rows the island back to shore.
Quote: "When they land, *fricassee them*!"
Comment: The story was told in comic book form in *George of the Jungle* #1 (1968).

***APIAN WAY** prepares a welcome for Super Chicken. © Jay Ward Productions.*

ARCHIMAGO (also ARCHIMAGE) (P)

First Appearance: 1590, *The Faerie Queene*, Edmund Spenser.
Chief Henchman: Braggadochio.
Biography: An aged enchanter, Archimago is the personification of Hypocrisy, and is as oily a sorcerer as ever slunk through classic literature. In Book 1, "The Legend of the Red Cross Knight, or of Holiness," the noble Red Cross Knight is travelling with the virgin Una. After pausing at the lair of Error to slay a creature who is half-woman, half-snake, they come to the hut of Archimago. The wizard permits them to stay the night, but while they sleep he fills the knight's head with awful dreams. The nightmares convince him that Una has been untrue and he abandons her; she follows, pursued by Archimago who has assumed the likeness of the noble Red Cross Knight. Unmasked by the Sansloy, who has designs on Una, Archimago escapes; while her savior tries to have his way with her, he is attacked by fauns and satyrs. The chivalrous Sir Satyrane finds Una and allows her to ride with him—pursued by Archimago who, now disguised as a pilgrim, informs them that the Red Cross Knight is dead. That isn't quite true: he's simply been captured by the giant Orgolio. Learning of this, Una persuades one Prince Arthur to save him. Una and the Red Cross Knight are reunited, but before they can be married Archimago makes one last attempt to shatter the union; masquerading as a messenger, he claims that the knight is already betrothed to a young witch, Duessa. Once again Archimago is exposed as a fake, only this time he's "layd full low in dungeon deepe." He escapes in "Book II: The Legend of Sir Guyon, or of Temperence" and, meeting Sir Guyon, tells him that the Red Cross Knight has defiled a virgin, with Duessa playing the part to the hilt. Sir Guyon goes after the Red Cross Knight and the two nearly come to blows before recognizing each other by the Christian crest on their shields. Looking to avenge himself for yet another setback, the beaten necromancer charges the boastful Braggadocchio with fulfilling the task before retreating from the narrative. Braggadocchio himself is defeated in Book V.
Comment: The epic poem comprises six books and two cantos, and is a metaphor for the author's time: Archimago represents the evils of the Roman Catholic church while the Faerie Queene herself, Gloriana, is Queen Elizabeth. Other unsavory characters populating the narrative are the aforementioned Duessa, a hag who turns one poor soul into a tree, among other crimes (she represents both Falsehood and Mary, Queen of Scots); Queen Lucifera (i.e., Pride), who lives in a magnificent abode built on a foundation of sand; the sorceress Acrasia (Intemperance); Maleger, who is wicked passion incarnate, commands 12 mighty troops which represent the seven deadly sins and the lustful aspects of the five senses and, because the earth is his mother, becomes more powerful each time is he thrown to the ground (the heroic Prince Arthur finally heaves him into a lake); the crone Ate (Dissension); Grantorto (Great

Wrong; i.e., Philip of Spain); Pollente, a Saracen robber and killer; the thieving shapechanger Malengin (Guile); and the Blatant Beast (Slander).

ARMADILLO (C)

Real Name: Antonio Rodriguez.

First Appearance: 1985, *Captain America* #308, Marvel Comics.

Costume: None (Antonio has the orange, chitinous body of a large, humanoid armadillo).

Weapons: Large, powerful claws on his hands and feet.

Biography: His wife Maria is deathly ill, and there isn't a doctor who seems to know what's wrong. A minor-league crook, Antonio had learned about Dr. Karl Malus while in prison; desperate, he visits Malus (creator of the villainous GOLIATH) with whom he strikes a bargain: the doctor will attempt to cure his wife, in exchange for which Antonio will submit to experiments the scientist has been aching to perform on a human subject. The experiment entails genetically mixing a human and an armadillo; what emerges is Antonio as a human armadillo with enormous physical strength and lethal claws. Going back to work as a thief for Malus, the Armadillo meets and is defeated by Captain America. But the law takes pity on him, and Armadillo goes free; his wife cured, Armadillo evaulates his options and takes a job as a professional wrestler.

ARNIM ZOLA (C)

First Appearance: 1977, *Captain America* #209, Marvel Comics.

Costume: Golden blouse, tights; purple gloves, boots and loincloth with yellow design on front; purple harness on chest with a hologram of Zola's face upon it.

Weapons: ESP box worn atop neck in place of head. This device transmits his thoughts to his artificial creations. The box also grants him limited telekinetic power over inanimate matter. Zola also employs various hi-tech weapons.

Chief Henchmen: Various beast-men, most notably Vermin, a human to whom he gave certain physical and feral attributes of a rat.

Biography: A geneticist working in his castle in Switzerland in the 1930s, Zola discovered rare old documents at his ancestral home, papers written hundreds of years before by Deviant scientists. (The Deviants are a super-intelligent race created by genetic tinkering performed on prehistoric humans by the alien Celestials. Unlike the Eternals [see THANOS], who were also created by the Celestials, the Deviants are not otherwise super-powered.) Zola managed to create artificial life as well as a means of superimposing one mind onto another. Underwritten by Hitler, Zola was able to preserve the dictator's mind when his body died; he subsequently used the Führer's mind to create THE HATE-MONGER. Meanwhile, himself a diminutive figure of a man, Zola built a new body, one with the brain inside the chest cavity, where it was well-protected. In place of his head he put the ESP box. Working for THE RED SKULL—for whom he created such beings as PRIMUS—he assisted that master villain in his efforts to rebuild his Cosmic Cube; he also fought frequently with the Skull's mortal enemy Captain America. Zola appears to have perished in an explosion caused when he tried to raid the laboratory of Dr. Bruce Banner, aka the superheroic Hulk. It is likely, however, that even if his body perished, he managed to transfer his mind to a safe locale.

Quote: "Within that matrix shall be captured the mysterious, omni-dimensional X-element which is the essence of the Cosmic Cube!"

ARSENAL (C)

Real Name: Commander Nimrod Strange.

First Appearance: 1982, *Moon Knight* #17 (as Strange); 1982, #19 (as Arsenal), Marvel Comics.

Costume: Fawn-colored bodysuit with red "A" on chest; blue boots; silver helmet and wristbands (see Weapons); holsters on each leg for weapons.

Weapons: High-intensity headlamp; belt of grenades; wrist rifle; nunchaku; garrote (concealed in right wristband); shotgun; knives.

Chief Henchmen: Master Sniper (#17), who wears a specially constructed eyepiece for accuracy and shoots from a wristband; the Slayers Elite (#18), consisting of Jou-Jouba (firearms), Kareesh-Bek (acid-filled glass knives), and the giant Sumaro (bare hands and garrote); Chu-Lin and sundry, nameless lieutenants; and three female bodyguards (regardless of who they are one is always black, one white, and one Asian to symbolize "the three major factions" of the Third World; when Arsenal was last seen, the women were Yumi, Assigi, and "Mary Sands," who is actually Moon Knight's ally Marlene).

Biography: Strange is the leader of a "Third World army," a nonaligned coalition of terrorists from the left and right. Based on a private island, they are "dedicated to smashing every government on earth." Disappointed with the failures of several projects, Strange becomes a costumed super villain himself and launches his boldest undertaking: leading a raid on Manhattan and coating the surrounding rivers with flaming oil, thus setting the island ablaze, while his armies simultaneously assault Tokyo, Lebanon, Poland, Paris, Madrid, Rome, Buenos Aires, and South Africa. However, he has earned the enmity of the superhero Moon Knight, by having, in Moon Knight's words, "killed my oldest friend—among other things." The superhero attacks him on his island and, when Arsenal escapes (behind a lobbed grenade), Moon Knight follows him to New York. There, the superhero batters him nearly insensate aboard the terrorist's tanker. Rather than allow himself to be taken, however, Arsenal blows up the ship and is presumed dead. However, he returns (#25) as the leader of the terrorist group Black Spectre.

Quote: "I am the greatest warrior history has ever seen! *Nothing* can stop me!"

THE ARSENAL (C)

Real Name: Original: Unrevealed (see Comment). Second: Nicholas Galtry.

First Appearance: 1967, *The Doom Patrol* #113 (as "Unrevealed"); 1982, *Tales of The New Teen Titans* #3 (as Galtry; Galtry had previously appeared, though not as the Arsenal, in *The Doom Patrol* #100, 1965), DC Comics.

Costume: "Biosuit" armor is green (as "Unrevealed"), orange (as Galtry) (see Weapons).

Weapons: Helmet has working metal jaw; left arm is scythe, right is machine gun ("Unrevealed" only); left arm fires unbreakable cable, right arm destructive blasts, and boots contain jets for flight (Galtry only).

Biography: Little is known about this character's past. The Arsenal is actually a criminal dwarf (his name is never revealed) who climbs inside a circa 10-feet-tall robot-like structure. Once inside, he possesses superstrength and uses it to battle the superheroic Doom Patrol. Defeated and uncanned, the diminutive super villain is never heard from again. Not so, however, the supersuit. It seems that the original inhabitant of the costume was recruited by Nicholas Galtry, the evil legal guardian of Doom Patrol member Beast Boy (Gar Logan), to crush the group so that he could pillage Gar's substantial inheritance. (He'd already dug freely into the fund to underwrite the creation of MISTER 103.) Years after the first Arsenal failed to kill Gar and his teammates, Galtry had lost executorship of the money and came after Beast Boy as the new Arsenal. Faring no better than his predecessor, the superhero Gar turns into a giant crab and crushes the robotic shell in a pincer. He allows Galtry to live, but the crumb has not been heard from since.

Quote: "I want to *destroy* you! And I want you to *suffer*!"

Comment: It's quite possible that the first Arsenal is actually Giacomo, a midget who battled the Doom Patrol in #87. He was, for that issue only, a member of THE BROTHERHOOD OF EVIL and was captured after the Doom Patrol battled an army of toy soldiers rendered life-size by an enlarging ray.

ASMODEUS (RE, N)

Real Name: Ashmedai (Hebrew).

First Appearance: *The Book of Tobit*, the Apocrypha.

Biography: The king of the demons in Hebrew lore, known more for his failures than for his triumphs. Falling in love with Sara, a mortal woman, he destroyed each of her seven husbands in succession, each on his wedding night. Banished to Egypt by Tobias of Nineveh—who had been instructed by the angel Raphael how to make a repulsive charm of the heart and liver of a fish burned atop perfumed ashes—Asmodeus made it his business to "plot against the newly wedded and . . . sever them utterly by many calamities," among other misdeeds. His most famous role in Biblical lore involved King Solomon. When Solomon was preparing to build his temple, he learned about the Shamir, an insect which could cut through the hardest stone. Learning that Asmodeus knew where to find the Shamir, Solomon dispatched his devoted servant Benaiah to the mountain where the demon lived. There, the wily servant filled Asmodeus' water jug with wine; the demon got drunk and, when he fell asleep, Benaiah bound him with a magic chain inscribed with the name of God. The servant carried the helpless Asmodeus to Solomon, who not only forced him to reveal the location of the Shamir but also kept Asmodeus imprisoned until the temple was built. Withal, Asmodeus possessed great physical strength and cunning. Like all demons, Asmodeus can fly on his great wings and can foretell the future (obviously, however, without complete accuracy). He can turn his head completely around, can become invisible, and can assume any form he may choose . . . including that of specific individuals. He is at his most potent on Wednesday and Saturday nights. However, he is unable to affect or even open anything which is sealed, counted, or measured, or bound in any way. Likewise, he can be repulsed by anyone who utters the name of God. Unlike angels, Asmodeus and his demons must eat, can reproduce, and are mortal.

Comment: In literature, Asmodeus is prominently featured in Rene Lesage's novel *Le Diable Boiteux*

(1707), known in English as *Asmodeus or the Devil on Two Sticks*. In this tale, he is pictured as a small, lame creature who, unusually merry, takes his joy from human suffering.

THE ATOMIC SKULL (C)

Real Name: Albert Michaels.

First Appearance: 1978, *Superman* #323, DC Comics.

Costume: Yellow cowl (see Weapons), with the lower half of Michaels' face a skull; yellow bodysuit with white skull on chest; green cloak, gloves, thigh boots, belt (see Weapons).

Weapons: Mask fires destructive "atomic brain-blasts"; rockets attached to sides of his belt for flight; skull-shaped hovercraft complete with "long range cameras" for surveillance and "cloaking device" for invisibility; sky-sled armed with poison gas gun, stun-ray, and an "ultrasonic wave device" which deprives Superman of the ability to fly.

Chief Henchmen: The operatives of the crime syndicate SKULL, all of whom are similarly attired; his lover Felicia, a panther who has been transformed into a human.

Biography: The director of S.T.A.R. (Scientific and Technological Advanced Research) Laboratories, Michaels suffers from "a rare neurological disease" which disrupts his brain's electrical impulses. A felon at heart, he steals hi-tech devices from S.T.A.R. and turns them over to SKULL; becoming that group's leader, he undergoes an operation to place a "radium-powered implant—the 'neural pacemaker'" in his brain. Not only does the surgery keep Michael's synapses from shorting out, it "transforms the electrical impulses of my brain into devastating *energy-bolts*!" Becoming the Atomic Skull, he leads SKULL on many of its daring crimes and is particularly adept at keeping Superman at bay.

Quote: "*Superman*! I'd follow you into *hell itself*... for my *vengeance*!"

ATOM-JAW (C)

Real Name: Mr. Preston.

First Appearance: 1966, *Captain Marvel Presents the Terrible* 5 #1, M.F. Enterprises.

Weapons: Jaws and teeth made of compound X-4, which can bite through virtually anything, including steel and brick.

Biography: A brilliant physicist, Preston worked on the atom bomb project at Oak Ridge during the Second World War. Caught in a blast that destroyed half his face, Preston was given a crude metal jaw which was to be replaced by a more realistic prosthetic after the war. He went back to work, but when peace came he disappeared . . . and turned to a life of crime. He's finally arrested by the superhero Captain Marvel, then freed by the villainous Dr. Fate, an electronics genius who masterminds a robbery for which he needs Atom-Jaw's help (specifically, chewing through a concrete wall six feet thick). After committing the crime, the once-virtuous Atom-Jaw turns over a new leaf by giving himself up and telling police where to find Dr. Fate. (Fate, in turn, is set free by the stretchable villain Elasticman, both of whom are eventually brought to justice by Captain Marvel.)

Quote: "At last! The great Captain Marvel! I'm going to take you apart piece by piece!"

Comment: This was the only appearance of Atom-Jaw and Dr. Fate.

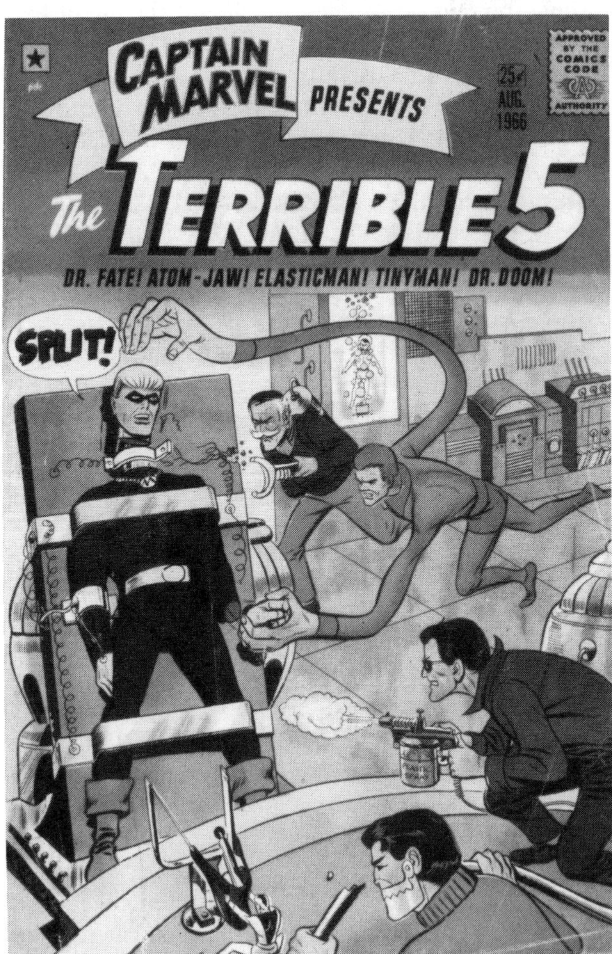

ATOM-JAW *(gnawing pipe in half) and his villainous friends have the best of Captain Marvel (from top to bottom: Dr. Fate, Elasticman, Dr. Doom [see PROFESSOR DOOM] and Tinyman).* *© M.F. Productions.*

ATTUMA (C)

First Appearance: 1964, *The Fantastic Four* #33, Marvel Comics.

Costume: Blue mail tights, gloves; golden trunks, breastplate; blue belt, harness crisscrossing chest, boots, helmet shaped like a serpent's head with golden horns (Attuma's skin is blue).

Weapons: Trident-shaped sword; "Octo-meks," octopus-like war machines.

Chief Henchmen: ORKA; armies unofficially known as "Attuma's hordes."

Biography: Attuma both lives and breathes underwater and is physically the most powerful member of his wandering tribe, a group which long ago left the civilized, sunken continent of Atlantis. However, Atlantean prophesy holds that a warrior will one day conquer Atlantis and, believing himself to be that individual, Attuma regularly attempts to wrest the throne from the rightful ruler, the Sub-Mariner. Among Attuma's many crimes, the worst was inarguably the raid on Atlantis which cost the life of Lady Dorma, Sub-Mariner's wife (*Sub-Mariner* #37, 1971). Attuma briefly teamed with DOCTOR DOOM and TIGER SHARK, a team unofficially known as the "Slayers from the Sea" (*Super-Villain Team-Up* #'s 1-3, 1975).

Comment: See other underwater super villains BLACK MANTA, CAPTAIN NEMO, CAPTAIN WHALE, DR. FANG, FISHERMAN, KILLER SHARK, KRANG, MR. CRABB, OCEAN MASTER, PIRANHA, and TIGER SHARK (2).

AUGUST ATLANTA BRAUN (M)

First Appearance: 1937, "The Terror in the Navy," *Doc Savage* Magazine, Kenneth Robeson.

Weapons: Water-insoluble acid to dissolve anyone who tries to pursue him on the seas.

Biography: "Perhaps fifty years old," Braun concocts a scheme to make a fortune. Recruiting young men, Braun has them enlist in the navy. Over a period of five years, they work their way to positions of strategic importance, as steersmen of ships and pilots of planes. Then, on appointed days, they scuttle their craft, insisting that some "mysterious force" was responsible. Enter Braun, who claims that a foreign power has the device which "throws out an invisible field . . . and nothing on the sea, under it, or in the air can resist it." He also says that, conveniently, he has a "nullifier machine" which "generates a field of force nullifying the one which is causing all the damage" and that he'll sell it to the United States government for $100 million. ("I'm not very patriotic where one hundred million dollars is concerned," he snidely apologizes.) However, the superhero Doc Savage invades the villain's submarine stronghold and, surfacing miles from land, Braun and his gang try to swim to shore. Not one of them makes it; Braun's body washes ashore several days later. Braun was "plump, had gray hair and a face that did not look very pinched by care." He wore glasses and sometimes masqueraded as an elderly newsboy near Doc Savage's building in order to keep tabs on the hero's doings.

Quote: "We will expel these navy men through the torpedo tubes in water so deep that the pressure will kill them."

Comment: Lesser Doc Savage villains include Colonel Bishop, who literally baked the water from people and turned them into mummies in a massive land scam ("Tunnel Terror," 1940); Sandy Gower, who developed an "aerial torpedo" and planned to use it to kill everyone who waged war ("The Flying Goblin," 1940); the Deadly Dwarf, aka three-feet-tall Cadwiller Olden, who sought to control the world through his army of savage giants and "Repel," an incredibly destructive energy ("The Deadly Dwarf," 1937); financier High and his wife Lo Lar who attempted to control the world's airways ("The Feathered Octopus," 1937); the sadistic pirate Captain Flamingo who enjoyed pouring acid down people's mouths ("Mystery Under the Sea," 1936); the hooded Green Bell, who plotted to render people mad, force their cities into bankruptcy, then buy up all the mines and factories for a pittance ("The Czar of Fear," 1933); Ky Halloc, leader of a gang of criminals who, with a device capable of nullifying all weapons, plan to set themselves up as world rulers ("The Motion Menace," 1938); the empire-building Khan Nadir Shar of Tanan ("The Mystic Mullah," 1935); and Marikan, with his army of invisible robbers ("The Spook Legion," 1935).

AURIC GOLDFINGER (N, MP)

First Appearance: 1959, *Goldfinger*, Ian Fleming.

Weapons: Colt .25 caliber gun, bullet always killing the victim by penetrating the right eye.

Chief Henchman: Oddjob, a Korean.

Biography: Born in Riga in 1917, Goldfinger emigrated to England 20 years later, when it became clear that the Russians would swallow up his country. A jeweler, like his father and grandfather before him, he began buying up pawn shops and specialized in buying gold. He lived in London, collecting the gold from his 20 shops, except for the war years when he hid in Wales at a machine-tool firm he owned. After the war, he bought himself a mansion at Reculver and an armored Silver Ghost Rolls Royce (which had been built for a South American president who was killed before he could take delivery). He set up a factory called "Thanet Alloy Research" at his home and hired a half-dozen Korean stevedores to work it. In time, the British government learns that Goldfinger is slipping a fortune in gold out of the country, thus jeopardizing the nation's gold standard; they assigned secret agent James Bond to find out how he's doing this. Bond learns how the "Thanet" scheme operates: gold is melted down and used to replace the armor plating on the car, which is then driven to another Goldfinger factory, "Enterprises Auric" in Coppet. The gold is melted once again and each lot is formed into 70 airplane seats, bolted into a Constellation of Goldfinger's Mecca Airlines and flown to India. There, the gold earned Goldfinger the greatest possible premium. While spying, however, Bond is captured and forced to assist Goldfinger on an even more ambitious plot: to steal one billion dollars (1,000 tons) of gold from Fort Knox. The plan ("Operation Grand Slam") involves poisoning the water of the depository and surrounding town, entering the area by train posing as health officials, blowing open the vault with a nuclear warhead, and getting the booty away on a Russian freighter. However, Bond succeeds in informing the authorities of the plot via a note taped under an airplane toilet seat. The poison is intercepted, the guards feign death, and the plot is foiled. However, Goldfinger and his personal bodyguard, the Korean giant Oddjob, escape and spirit Bond away on a private jet. Bond manages to break a window with a knife, and Oddjob is sucked into oblivion; Goldfinger is strangled to death by the furious Bond. Physically, Goldfinger is "out of proportion." Standing roughly five feet tall, he has "a thick body and blunt . . . legs (and) set, almost directly onto the shoulders, a huge and it seemed exactly round head." He is a fanatic about maintaining a sunburn because "without the red-brown camouflage the pale body would be grotesque. The face, under the cliff of crew-cut carroty hair . . . was moon-shaped." He has a high forehead, thin level sandy brows, light blue eyes, and a "fleshily aquiline" nose set between high cheekbones and cheeks "more muscular than fat." The chin and jaws, however, are firm and the "dead straight" mouth "beautifully drawn."

Quote: "My treasure of gold is like a compost heap. I move it here and there over the face of the earth and, wherever I choose to spread it, that corner blossoms and blooms. I reap the harvest and move on."

Comment: Gert Frobe played the part in the 1964 United Artists motion picture; Harold Sakata co-starred as Oddjob. In the film, Oddjob had a hat which, when flung at an object—even one made of metal—could damage or destroy it. Human necks stood no chance against the lethal chapeau. See also GOLDFACE.

AVALANCHE (C)

Real Name: Dominic Petros.

First Appearance: 1981, *The X-Men* #141, Marvel Comics.

Costume: Purple bodysuit; silver gloves, boots, helmet, belt, breastplate with flared shoulders and light blue "A" on chest.

Biography: Little is know about Petros, save that he came from Greece and possesses the mutant power to create destructive vibration waves. He began his criminal career as a member of THE BROTHERHOOD OF EVIL MUTANTS, joining them in their plot to murder anti-mutant activist Senator Robert Kelly. When that plan was foiled, he went solo to hold California for ransom, threatening to dump it into the Pacific if he weren't paid a whopping sum; pulverized by the Hulk, Avalanche spent a while recuperating before rejoining the Brotherhood. He has since gone to work as a government operative as part of the heroic Freedom Force.

Comment: MAJOR DISASTER, QUAKEMASTER, Shakedown of MASTERS OF DISASTER, and VORTEX are other earthquake-causing super villains.

THE AWESOME BRAVO (C)

First Appearance: 1967, *Mighty Comics* #44, Archie Comics.

Costume: Orange jerkin; green cloak, tights, boots.

Biography: A mutant shapechanger, Bravo hates superheroes. Wishing to destroy the virtuous Steel Sterling, young Bravo lures him to a remote castle by pretending to be in jeopardy. There, he turns into a string of super villains who take turns punishing the hero: the human battering ram know as the Metal Mask; Beastor, who has telepathic control over a horde of monsters; and the Deadly Dimensional with the ability to travel through time and space. However, Sterling manages to signal good mutants who are flying overhead; they descend and, disguised as rocks, sneak up on Bravo. Capturing him, they remove his evil tendencies.

Quote: "You should thank me for killing you in so spectacular a setting."

Comment: This was the character's only appearance. Other foes of Steel Sterling include Dr. Evil, a white-faced, red-cloaked villain from the future who possesses a "Bionetically advanced intellect" as well as such weapons as a levitation ray ring and a Spectra-X analyzer which reads brain patterns and helps him to subjugate opponents; and the Monster-Master, a green-garbed genius who fashioned hulking, winged Monstroids with which to conquer the world. (Steel Sterling originally atomized the Monster-Master and trapped him in his own computer; when the fiend returned, Sterling and superhero the Black Hood sent both the Monster-Master and Dr. Evil to the future, using the latter's time machine. Neither has been seen since that happy event occurred in *Mighty Comics* #49, 1967.)

BABA (F)

Weapons: Iron mortar which she rides through the sky, whipping it with a pestle and sweeping away her trail with a besom, a broom made of brush (in some tales, the mortar is large enough for her to ride inside); a cudgel with which to turn people into stone.

Chief Henchmen: She is served by a thin birch tree which beats intruders with its limbs, an emaciated cat who tears out intruders' eyes, an emaciated dog who rips intruders to pieces, and an emaciated servant who cleans up the mess.

Biography: Also known as Baba Yaga, this aged witch and ogress is an unclean cannibal, ugly and skeletal ("as bony as a fish with all the flesh picked off"). The sister of Prince Ivan, she was fully grown in six weeks and inaugurated her reign of terror by feasting on her parents with her iron teeth. Ivan escaped to become a hero, while Baba dwelt in a hut which can walk about, being built on enormous hen's legs. In some tales, human skulls hang from the roof and, at night, are filled with fire to attract passers-by in the forest. In other tales the house is surrounded by a high fence whose gate squeaks in pain when she opens it, a signal that an intruder has arrived. The witch has the power to converse with plants and animals, and to command them to serve her in dramatic ways, as in "Baba Yaga and the Little Girl With the Kind Heart" when she orders a herd of cows to drink up a river to stop the little girl's flight.

Quote: "Go scrub my niece. I'll make a dainty meal of her."

Comment: The definitive tales of Baba are included in Arthur Ransome's classic *Old Peter's Russian Tales* (1916). Similar to Baba is Berchta of German folklore. A cannibal, Berchta has huge feet, an iron nose, and particularly relishes feasting on disobedient children and lazy young men.

BADMAN (C)

Real Name: Bruce Pain.

First Appearance: 1966, *Go-Go* #3, Charlton Comics.

Costume: Blue bodysuit with black bird emblem in white circle on chest; navy blue cape, cowl, trunks, gloves, boots.

Weapons: The Badphone, a direct line to the police commissioner; the Badmobile, a slick sports car; the Badcave with its fully-stocked chemical lab (allowing him to create Bad-hypnosis spray, among other mixtures).

Biography: A wealthy socialite dwelling in Pain Manor outside of Metroville, Pain uses his government and police department contacts to acquire secret information about payroll shipments and the like. Then, as Badman, he goes out and robs them. His sidekick is young Robber, a cigar-chomping youth who wears a gray jerkin and boots and a blue cape, gloves, and trunks. The villains are eventually defeated by the fumbling superhero Blooperman.

Quote: "Ahh . . . here it is! In Icky's Do-It-Yourself Chemistry Comics. A well stocked library is very helpful in planning crimes!"

Comment: The character is a parody of the superhero Batman. The Badman saga was spread over three issues.

THE BAD ONE (F)

Weapons: Magic bridge "which lengthens out when the Bad One waves his hand, so that there is no river or sea that he cannot cross."

Biography: The Bad One is a scaly, child-eating demon who lives in the woods, in a hut on a hill beyond the great river. There, hanging from the great beams which support the ceiling, he keeps bags of gold as well as his magic bridge. Nearby dwells a witch who covets his treasures; endowing a brave little boy with various powers—including enchanted arrows, shape-changing ability, and a magic ball to carry him across the river—she sends him forth to steal the Bad One's possessions . . . just as she has done for other children, none of whom ever returned. Captured by the Bad One and his female servant, Lung-Woman, the boy is to be served at a feast for the local water demons. But he escapes and, fleeing, uses the bridge to cross the river. Following him across, the Bad One drowns

H.J. Ford's interpretation of ***THE BAD ONE.***

when the youth orders it to shrink while he is still "in the midst of the stream."

Quote: "Be sure that he does not run away. Boil some water, and get him ready for cooking."

Comment: The character appears in an American Indian folktale, first published as "Ball-Carrier and the Bad One" in Andrew Lang's *The Brown Fairy Book* (1904). In the sequel, "How Ball-Carrier Finished His Task," the witch reveals that she could easily have overcome the Bad One with her magic. She sent the boy solely to make a responsible young man of him.

BALTAR (TV, N)

First Appearance: September 17, 1978, "Saga of a Star World," *Battlestar Galactica*, ABC-TV.

Costume: Basic wardrobe consists of white robes and cloak, though occasionally he dons more colorful "formal" attire. (TV; in the novel he wears "ornate, colorful garments" and a "flowing velvet cape").

Biography: It's the seventh millennium, and for 1,000 years human beings have been battling the robotic Cylons and their insect-like Imperious Leader. Suddenly, the Cylons sue for peace through Count Baltar, a merchant; Baltar carries their message to the ruling body, the Quorum of Twelve. The Quorum doesn't realize that Baltar is in league with the enemy to betray humankind: he is delivering his people in exchange for having his colony spared (which it is not) and himself established as the Imperious Leader's ruler-in-absentia of humankind (which he does not become). The peace is ratified, and as a planets-wide celebration is underway, the Cylons attack and all but obliterate humankind. The few survivors wander through space aboard the mile-wide *Galactica* and its caravan of 220 smaller ships, pursued all the while, by Cylons and the treacherous Baltar. Though Baltar is eventually arrested—in "War of the Gods"—he breaks out in "Baltar's Escape" and continues his wicked ways.

Quote: "The Cylon's choice of me as their liaison . . . was an act of providence, not skill."

Comment: The character was played by John Colicos during the one-season run of the show. Baltar was also featured in the *Battlestar Galactica* novel by Glen Larson and Robert Thurston, in the photo-novel which told "Saga of a Star World" in comic book style through photographs, and in the Marvel comic book. Though Baltar was executed in the first episode—beheaded by a Cylon (quoth the Imperious Leader: "Could you think me so foolish as to trust a man who would see his own race destroyed?")—he proved a popular villain and his demise was overlooked.

BANDOLIAN (N)

First Appearance: February 1943, "The Skeleton Men of Jupiter," *Amazing Stories*, Edgar Rice Burroughs.

Costume: Harness marked with hieroglyphs (which read "Bandolian, Emperor of the Morgors).

Weapons: Sword.

Biography: Bandolian is the leader of the Morgors, a race of beings who dwell on Jupiter. The Morgors are human in form, with a few notable exceptions: They have no lips, nose, hair or outward ears; their eyes are solid brown; and their yellow skin is so thin and translucent that their bones show through. Altruistically, the Morgors are even more lacking than they are physically, and Bandolian is the worst of the lot. Cruel and emotionless (except for anger), he yearns to conquer the inhabited world of Mars. However, he is kept from this goal by the transplanted earthperson John Carter. Kidnapped and brought to Jupiter, Carter refuses Bandolian's offer to be made a leader on Mars in exchange for his help, and manages to prevent the invasion with his "naked blade." Bandolian lives in a cavernous, box-like building with "lava-brown" corridors and bare rectangular rooms. There is no art to relieve the austerity. Among Bandolian's aides are his counselor Horur, the devoted Commander Haglion and the sadistic guard Gorgum. (Addressing Carter, Gorgum growls, "Thing, for even a small part of what you have done you deserve death—death after torture."

Quote: "I understand that your name is John Carter. While you are of a lower order, yet it must be that you are endowed with intelligence of a sort. It is to this intelligence that I address my commands."

Comment: This was the character's only appearance. The story is one of two which comprise the book *John Carter of Mars* (the other is "John Carter and the Giant of Mars"; see PEW MOGEL).

BARON BLITZKRIEG (C)

First Appearance: 1979, *World's Finest Comics* #246, DC Comics.

Costume: Yellow full-head helmet, bodysuit with red eagle and iron cross symbol on chest and belly, respectively; orange trunks, gloves (which extend to biceps) and boots with black swastika in white circle on front; red cape held by clasp which is a black swastika in a white circle; blue belt.

Biography: "The living incarnation of the thousand-year Reich," the Baron (his name has never been revealed) was a Prussian noble and a friend of Hitler whom the Führer appointed as commandant of one of his concentration camps. A vicious soul, he was hated by the prisoners, one of whom finally got close enough to heave a beaker of acid in the Prussian's face. Hideously scarred, the Baron underwent surgery and something more: a secret experiment to release the psychic abilities latent in many of us. After several months, the Baron had acquired the ability to control his metabolism, to increase his muscular power and agility, and to radiate intense heat from his eyes. Mustering every ounce of power, he can also with great effort travel between the dimensions. During the Second World War he tangled regularly with the U.S. superheros, the All-Star Squadron; his present whereabouts are not known.

Quote: "Wherever there is Nazism—there will be a *Baron Blitzkrieg*!"

Comment: See other Nazi super villains BARON GESTAPO, BARON ZEMO, CAPTAIN AXIS, CAPTAIN NAZI, THE CLOWN, THE GOLDEN FUHRER, KILLER SHARK, NIGHT AND FOG, The Masked Swastika of VENDETTA, Mastermind (see U-MAN, Comment), THE RED PANZER, THE RED SKULL, and ZYKLON.

BARON BLOOD (C)

Real Name: Lord John Falsworth.

First Appearance: 1976, *The Invaders* #7, Marvel Comics.

Costume: Green bodysuit with indigo sides, from toe to wrist; green gloves; indigo collar, cowl with huge bat-like ears, ribbed flaps under arms from wrist to waist (see Weapons). He also wears a gaunt green mask to conceal his identity. (Greens were later changed to violet.)

Weapons: Flaps under arms allow him to fly.

Biography: Early in this century, when his elder brother Montgomery inherited most of the estate of their father, Lord William Falsworth, John left England and traveled in Europe. Arriving in Romania, he decided to search for the castle of DRACULA, convinced that if he could find and control the vampire he could build his own fortune and power base. The good news is that he did indeed locate the vampire; the bad news is that Dracula made a meal out of young Falsworth. Dying, the English nobleman rose three days later as a vampire and slave to Dracula's will. Vengefully, the Count immediately dispatched Falsworth to stir up hell in England, where he himself had had so much trouble several years before with Dr. Van Helsing. This Falsworth did, using his ability as a shapechanger to prey on the British. Becoming a German spy at the outbreak of World War I—codenamed Baron Blood—the embittered Falsworth murdered Britons until stopped by Montgomery, who had himself become the superhero Union Jack. Wounded with a silver blade, Blood left England and took to studying the supernatural. When Hitler came to power, Blood allied himself with the Nazis and underwent a surgical procedure which made him immune to the deadly rays of the sun, but which cost him his metamorphic abilities. (Years later, when the treatment wore off, Blood took to wearing insulated underwear.) Posing as his own son, John, Jr., he returned to England and resumed terrorizing the natives. By this time, however, a superheroic team known as the Invaders had taken up residence in England, and they countered Blood tooth-and-nail. Early in their conflict, Blood perished when he was skewered by a stalagmite which was threaded-through with silver (#9). Brought back to life, he continued to fight the English, allied with a group of Nazi super villains known as the Super-Axis. Staked to death at war's-end, he was resurrected by physician Dr. Charles Cromwell, one of Dracula's servants, whom Blood slew so he could assume his identity. Laying low and drawing from his patients just enough blood to live, the vampire eventually resumed his nefarious ways and was decapitated by the shield of Captain America. His corpse was burned, the ashes scattered, and he is not likely to return.

Quote: "Struggle all you *wish*, human! Your power is as *nothing* beside that of *BARON BLOOD*!"

Comment: Other super villains battled by the Invaders include Werner Schmidt, aka operative A1416, aka Brain Drain, who puts mighty aliens under his control; the Blue Bullet, aka Professor John Goldstein who, enclosed in a bullet-shaped costume with arms, can launch himself like his namesake; the superhuman Nazi Master Man; Julia, the whip-cracking Warrior Woman, aka Agent Three (who eventually marries Master Man); Vicky, the Asbestos Lady, who packs flame-dousing guns (and who, naturally, cannot be harmed by Invaders member the Human Torch); the evil Abdul Faoul, aka the blast-firing Scarlet Scarab, and his aides, the Sons of the Scarab; and Agent Axis, the "Master of Murder," who is actually the result of a combination of crack German, Italian, and Japanese agents. See other vampires BEN CORTMAN, BLACULA, COUNT YORGA, DRACULA, NOSFERATU, PAUL JOHNSON, and VARNEY THE VAMPIRE.

BARON BUG (C)

First Appearance: 1966, *House of Mystery* #63, DC Comics.

Weapons: Control Helmet and chest attachment which allow him to communicate with insects or enlarge them to giant size; loudspeaker worn by one insect in every platoon so that Bug can shout instructions to those he's robbing.

Chief Henchmen: Two nameless thugs.

Biography: Working at a laboratory in a cavern outside of Zenith City, Baron Bug is obsessed with punishing humankind for the way he'd "been scorned and ridiculed because of my . . . appearance" (people called him "Bugsy" and "Fly Eyes"). After years of research, he develops his bug control unit and sends giant insects forth to rob so he can continue his costly experiments. (His bug slaves include an "ant army," "mosquito air force," and "bee raiders.") He is eventually nabbed by Robby Reed, keeper of the "Dial-H for Hero" device, who becomes the worm-like superhero King Coil, infiltrates the hideout, and, clobbering Baron Bug, smashes his control helmet.

Quote: "Ant army, attention! We will rehearse this diamond exchange caper one more time before you go into action . . . !"

Comment: This was the character's only appearance. See other insect-controlling super villains THE DRAGONFLY RAIDERS, HUMBUG, KING LOCUST, QUEEN BEE, and SWARM.

BARON GESTAPO (C)

First Appearance: 1942, *Zip Comics* #27, Archie Comics.

Costume: Navy blue bodysuit with red swastika on chest; gray trunks, gloves, boots. He also wore a monocle in his right eye.

Chief Henchmen: Sundry soldiers and spies.

Biography: A Nazi operative with a skull-like face, Baron Gestapo was "a menace so gigantic that man's mind reels . . . a dread monster whose name strikes terror into the hearts of the bravest." Working for both the Germans and the Japanese, the non-super sadist was kept from sabotaging the Allied war effort by the superheroic Steel Sterling.

Comment: The character appeared just twice, after which Steel battled the Nazi villain the Hyena. See other Nazi super villains BARON BLITZKRIEG, BARON ZEMO, CAPTAIN AXIS, CAPTAIN NAZI, THE CLOWN, THE GOLDEN FUHRER, KILLER SHARK, NIGHT AND FOG, The Masked Swastika of VENDETTA, Mastermind (see U-MAN, Comment), THE RED PANZER, THE RED SKULL, and ZYKLON.

BARON KARZA (T, C)

First Appearance: 1977, Micronauts toy line, Mego Corporation.

Costume: Blue full-head helmet, thigh boots, gloves, bodysuit with two red knobs on each breast and a larger one on the belly.

Weapons: The Sunscope, a weapon capable of destroying all life on a planet. Karza also wields a mighty sword.

Chief Henchmen: Prince Shaitan, his right-hand man and commander of the elite warriors, the Acroyears; Major D'Ark; the Shadow Priests, robed mystics; the Unmen, Homeworld natives whom he mutates into a band of misshapen savages.

Biography: Homeworld is a planet which exists in a subatomic solar system known as the

Microverse, a universe which lies beyond the Spacewall, a space/time barrier. There, the brilliant Chief Scientist Baron Karza makes an incredible discovery: he finds the key to immortality. Offering it to the populace, he asks for only one thing in return—that the people name him their ruler. Naturally, this doesn't sit well with the Royal Family, but their voices are lost in the din of those willing to serve Karza in exchange for access to his "body banks." The sole force which can be mustered to defend the royals are the costumed Micronauts; after 10 centuries of the so-called "Karza Wars," they are finally able to defeat Karza, with Princess Mari (aka the "warrior-maid" Marionette) stabbing him in the belly (#58). Unfortunately, having sensed the approach of doom, Karza took the libery of depopulating the entire planet, leaving only a vast graveyard for the conquerors. In life, Karza had the ability to fire destructive rays from his eyes, and also the power to call upon "his Centaurian aspect" and become a mighty armored centaur. It was in this form that he died.

Quote: "I shall heal you of your madness by stripping you of your life!!!"

Comment: Karza was featured in the Marvel Comics *Micronauts* comic book which was published from 1978 to 1984. See other action toy super villains DESTRO, GENERAL SPIDRAX, HORDAK, MOLTAR, MUMM-RA, and SKELETOR.

BARON MORDO (C)

Real Name: Karl Amadeus Mordo (occasionally masquerades as Sir Clive Bentley).

First Appearance: 1963, *Strange Tales* #111, Marvel Comics.

Costume: Original: green jumpsuit with light green collar. Second: green cape covered with intersecting black circles on outside, light green lining; green bodyshirt (originally bell-sleeved shirt), tunic with light green collar, trunks with long flap in front; light green, white, and black designs on chest (resembling owl's eyes); dark green tights; black shoulder coverings with huge upright horns and a band leading down to waist.

Chief Henchmen: Sir Baskerville, a disciple; Demon, a human wizard; the Witch, a sorceress; and sundry, nameless aides, some of whom, like the small army in #130, are granted the power to fire powerful mystic blasts.

Biography: Born in Transylvania, Mordo became fascinated with the black arts, an interest encouraged by his grandfather Viscount Crowler. As soon as he was old enough, Mordo left home to try to find a great Tibetan wizard known as the Ancient One. Finding him, the enthusiastic Mordo was accepted as a disciple. In time, he completed his education and returned to his "heavily guarded" castle hidden "in the heart of Europe." Longing to become "the only master of black magic," he made plans to kill the Ancient One by invoking the "fatal touch" of DORMAMMU. Overhearing his incantation, American surgeon Stephen Strange—who has come seeking help for his hands, which were injured in a car accident—is subjected by Mordo to a mystical incantation which prevents him from warning the Ancient One. Instead, Strange asks to remain and become a disciple—the only way he can keep an eye on the evil sorcerer. The Ancient One permits this, and Strange surreptitiously keeps an eye on Mordo while simultaneously becoming the superhero Dr. Strange. Mordo toughs it out for several years and then leaves, thereafter making numerous attempts to slay both his mentor and Strange. Among the countless dark powers he has at his command are "astral projection," the ability to send his spirit out to do his bidding (such as journeying a continent away in a flash), though his body lies dormant and helpless during such periods; altering his physical appearance; mesmerizing others while he's in corporeal or spiritual form; summoning up a paralytic vapor; and creating another vapor which can remove an entire apartment building from this realm and drop it into limbo.

Quote: "Once I have conquered your *spirit image*, your actual body will perish, too! Then the world will be *mine!*"

Comment: Mordo is the most persistent foe of Dr. Strange, although Dormammu is more dangerous by far.

BARON ROXOR (R, MP)

First Appearance: 1932, *Chandu the Magician*, Fox.

Costume: Black trousers, vest, boots, turban, robe.

Weapons: Death ray.

Biography: Having developed a death ray, a scientist is pressed into the service of the evil Roxor. With the ray, Roxor plans to destroy half the world and rule the other half, which will have been terrified into submission. He is thwarted by government agent Frank Chandler, a magician who operates under the name of Chandu.

Comment: The original radioplay, heard only on the west coast, was written by Harry A. Earnshaw, Vera M. Oldham, and R.R. Morgan. In the 1932 Fox film, Bela Lugosi played Roxor. In the movie sequel from Principal, *The Return of Chandu* (1934), Lugosi got to play the magician, seeking to prevent the evil Vindhyan (Lucien Prival) and the sorcerer Vitras (Jack Clark) from using a blood sacrifice to resurrect the Egyptian goddess Ossana—who, it is believed, has the power to raise the lost continent of Lemuria from the ocean. This serial was edited into two separate features, *The Return of Chandu* and *Chandu on Magic Island*, which focus on the exploits of Vindhyan and Vitras, respectively. Chandu and sundry villains appeared in a 1949 radio series heard over ABC. Bela Lugosi has played numerous super villains, including DR. ALEX ZORKA, DR. MIRAKLE, DR. PAUL CARRUTHERS, DRACULA, MURDER LEGENDRE, and PROFESSOR ERIC VORNOFF.

BARON STRUCKER (C)

Real Name: Wolfgang von Strucker.

First Appearance: 1963, *Sgt. Fury and His Howling Commandos* #5, Marvel Comics.

Costume: None until he becomes Supreme Hydra: green bodysuit with a black skull and tentacles on a circular, black-fringed yellow field on chest; light green gloves, boots, trunks, all fringed with yellow; yellow belt with "H" buckle on black field; yellow braid on right side of chest; light green ruff-like collar.

Weapons: Strucker has at his command the formidable arsenal of HYDRA, which includes backpacks for flight, jet-propelled skateboards, robots, and countless firearms. The group's most dangerous weapon is the Death Sport Bomb, which would have poisoned the planet had it not exploded where it did (see Biography).

Chief Henchmen: Second-in-command is Arnold Brown, the Imperial Hydra; he also leads the minions of HYDRA, all of whom wear green boots, gloves, hoods, trousers, a cowl with red goggles, and a jacket with a large yellow "H" on the front.

Biography: Several years before the start of World War II, Strucker continued a long tradition among his Prussian noble family by joining the military: in his case, becoming a spy for the Nazis and, at the onset of hostilities, a highly regarded officer. Early in the war he distinguished himself as wing commander of the Death's-Head Squadron and, later, lead a team of crack commandos known as the Blitzkrieg Squad. In this position, Strucker devoted his energies to the destruction of America's heroic Sgt. Nick Fury and his Howling Commandos. Failing, he earned Hitler's enmity and would have been executed if THE RED SKULL hadn't intervened. Planning to rule the world himself one day, that Nazi fiend sent Strucker to the Far East, where he was to help plant the seeds for an eventual Red Skull takeover. But Strucker had no such intentions. As soon as he reached Japan, he joined a newly formed group which was *itself* making plans to conquer the world. Joining the team and quickly becoming the Supreme Hydra, the former aristocrat made HYDRA one of the most feared subversive groups extant. Headquartered on a Pacific Island, the organization committed various acts of espionage, from raiding warehouses for weapons to trying to do-in leaders on both sides. At last, however, it was decimated in an assault by another group of heroic Americans, Captain Savage and his Leatherneck Raiders. Escaping his devastated atoll, Strucker devoted himself to rebuilding HYDRA, a task which took years. Relocating to the United States, he once again crossed swords with Nick Fury, who was now head of the international peacekeeping force known as S.H.I.E.L.D. (Supreme Headquarters International Espionage Law-enforcment Division). After years of conflict—during which time Strucker moved his operation back to the Pacific, to an artificial new Hydra Island on the site of the old one—Strucker and Fury finally faced off in a fight-to-the-death. Strucker was the loser, dying when he blundered into his island's nuclear reactor room. Adding insult to injury, the island itself sunk and many HYDRA personnel were slain when Strucker accidentally detonated his foul Death Spore bomb (*Strange Tales* #158, 1967). Though HYDRA is still active, it has not been the same since Strucker's demise.

Comment: HYDRA itself first appeared in *Strange Tales* #135 (1965). The other major Marvel subversive group is A.I.M. (Advanced Idea Mechanics) (see MODOK).

BARON ZEMO (C)

Real Name: Heinrich Zemo; Helmut Zemo.

First Appearance: 1963, *The Avengers* #4, (the Heinrich incarnation); 1973, *Captain America* #168, (as Phoenix); 1982, *Captain America* #276, (the Helmut incarnation), Marvel Comics.

Costume: As Heinrich: purple trousers, jerkin with white leopard-ruff collar; gold gloves, boots with white leopard fringe; gold strap down chest to gold belt; red hood with thin black vertical stripes; gold crown. As Helmut: purple bodysuit with bell sleeves; gold belt; gold gloves, boots with thin black vertical stripes, white leopard fringe on boots; red full-face cowl which also covers most of chest and has thin black stripes radiating from forehead; white leopard shoulderpads; gold diadem.

Weapons: Disintegrator gun (hand-held version of raygun developed for Nazis; see Biography); robots which can be shrunk to doll-size, packed in a suitcase, then expanded when needed; rocketplanes.

Chief Henchmen: Countless thugs; also THE MASTERS OF EVIL and the Army of Assassins, a band of green-costumed, heavily armed killers sent to murder Captain America (one has an iron first, another the debilitating "Formula X" coating his palm, another packs a "sub-miniature missile," the others are merely superior athletes).

Biography: A brilliant Nazi scientist, Baron Heinrich Zemo invented a "death ray" disintegrator early in his career. A notorious figure, he was keenly sought by the Allies during the war; donning a hood and going into hiding with his wife Hilda and son Helmut, he used the riches showered upon him by Hitler to continue his devilish research. Among his chief projects was the development of "Adhesive X," a bonding agent so powerful that nothing could dissolve it. He planned to airdrop it on Allied forces to snarl their progress. But Captain America located his laboratories and, during the ensuing battle, Heinrich was drenched with his own glue. His hood became a permanent fixture, forcing Heinrich, among other things, to have all his meals given intravenously; beneath it lay a mind which had snapped from the shock and wanted nothing more than to slay Captain America. Biding his time, inventing more weapons of destruction, and working as a saboteur abroad, the German finally met his enemy again at War's end. Trying to steal an experimental plane from the British, Zemo watched with delight as the aircraft—armed with a bomb to prevent its theft—flew out to sea and exploded. Its sole passenger was Captain America's sidekick Bucky, who perished; as for the good Captain, he fell into the freezing waters and went into suspended animation. Nearly two decades later, when the superhero was found by the Avengers and revived (*The Avengers* #4), Heinrich (who had left his wife and son Helmut in Germany and relocated to South America) came foreward and organized The Masters of Evil to destroy both Captain America and his do-good colleagues. Despite several changes in personnel, Zemo and his associates were unable to defeat the Avengers. Finally, in a showdown in South America, Zemo turned his disintegrator ray on Captain America. But the wily hero used his shield to blind Zemo with sunlight and, firing blindly, the villain brought a mountain down on himself (*The Avengers* #15). Meanwhile, young Helmut learned of his father's fate and decided to take up the gauntlet and slay the red, white, and blue Avenger. Using his inherited scientific genius (as well as his father's notes), Helmut built himself an arsenal and took on Captain America as the Phoenix. Trying to drop the Captain in a vat of Adhesive X, Helmut himself fell in and his face was horribly deformed, creating a hooded costume similar to that of his father. He became the new Baron Zemo, supervillain. He even pulled together a fourth lineup for the Masters of Evil, though neither they nor he succeeded in felling the resilient superhero. Zemo the Second perished when, shortly after a battle with fellow super villain BLACKOUT, he took on Captain America. During that struggle Zemo fell from a rooftop to his death.

Comment: See other Nazi super villains BARON BLITZKRIEG, BARON GESTAPO, CAPTAIN AXIS, CAPTAIN NAZI, THE CLOWN, THE GOLDEN FUHRER, KILLER SHARK, NIGHT AND FOG, The Masked Swastika of VENDETTA, Mastermind (see U-MAN, Comment), THE RED PANZER, THE RED SKULL, and ZYKLON.

THE BAT (C)

First Appearance: 1966, *Captain Marvel* #3, M.F. Enterprises.

Costume: Blue bodysuit, trunks, boots, wings, cowl, antennae; yellow eyes. (Cover shows gray wings,

THE BAT *vs. Captain Marvel. © M.F. Enterprises.*

bodysuit with blue stripes down chest; blue trunks, gloves, cowl with pointed ears, antennae, and red eyes.)

Weapons: Wings for flight.

Chief Henchmen: Secret army "throughout the land"; dressed in khaki uniforms and blue helmets with bat ears.

Biography: "A warped megalomaniac bent on subjugating the globe," the Bat works as a magician and master hypnotist in a traveling sideshow. Apparently recruiting soldiers to his cause as he traverses the country, he finally launches an uprising in order to take over the world. He is stopped far short of his goal and sent to jail thanks to the superhero Captain Marvel. Apart from his mesmeric powers, the Bat can levitate others and fly.

Quote: "When I say '3' all national monuments will be exploded immediately."

Comment: Although this was the character's only appearance, at the beginning of the story a previous encounter is *said* to have taken place in 1960. (Captain Marvel did not begin publishing until 1966. The character was apparently recycled as THE RAY. Other Captain Marvel villains include the inventor Mr. Brilliant, who renders people immobile with his "electronic impulse reducer"; the Vapor Man, an extraterrestrial who practices mind control on humans; Dr. Darkness, a fiend who rules an underwater race intent on destroying all surface-dwellers; Colonel Cold, who spreads disease throughout cities and then charges a fortune for the antidote; and Elasticman, who can stretch and twist into any shape and also shape his features to resemble anyone he wishes.

BATROC (C)

Real Name: Georges Batroc.

First Appearance: 1966, *Tales of Suspense* #75, Marvel Comics.

Costume: Maroon bodysuit with orange stripe down center; orange gloves, boots, trunks, cowl with black mask slightly flared on top.

Chief Henchmen: Batroc's Brigade, an ever-changing group of mercenaries and killers assembled to help Batroc (originally introduced in *Captain America* #105, 1968). The first roster consisted of LIVING LASER and THE SWORDSMAN; the second, PORCUPINE and WHIRLWIND; the third was comprised of non-super thugs; the most recent consisted of MACHETE and ZARAN.

Biography: While serving in the French Foreign Legion, Georges mastered savate, boxing in which blows are also administered with the feet. Upon being discharged, the Frenchman decided to become a mercenary, a pursuit which segued into criminality. Despite repeated losses to his archenemy Captain America, Batroc remains at large.

Quote: "*Sacre bleu*! Your treacherous gases will not stop the great Batroc!"

B.B. EYES (CS, TV)

First Appearance: January 27, 1942, *Dick Tracy*, Chicago Tribune-New York News Syndicate.

Biography: B.B. Eyes is the pellet-eyed brother of Jacques, owner of the Bird Club. Because Dick Tracy shoots Jacques to death, B.B. kidnaps the detective and Debby Thorndike, the club's new owner. Binding them on the floor of Debby's house, he disables the safety valve of the mansion's boiler and, for good measure, saws through all the joints to make sure the house collapses. Fortunately, Debby's Aunt Bea saves the pair and Tracy goes looking for B.B. He traces the villain to the bootleg tire company he runs (to make a killing under the rationing laws of World War II), but B.B. once again gets the upper hand and seals Tracy in a huge cylinder of paraffin. The wily Tracy is able to upend the trap and roll it up to a furnace, where it melts enough for him to break free. The sleuth captures the criminal, but B.B. leaps from the police car as it crosses a bridge. He lands in a passing garbage barge but, sadly for B.B., the refuse is dumped just then. Trapped in a tire casing, he is dragged to the riverbottom where he drowns.

Quote: "Let 'em smother for a few minutes while we figure out what to do next."

Comment: B.B. Eyes was also a character on the syndicated Dick Tracy cartoon show (1960).

THE BEETLE (C)

Real Name: Abner Jenkins.

First Appearance: 1964, *Strange Tales* #123, Marvel Comics.

Costume: Original: green jumpsuit, boots, full-head helmet with white eyes; purple wings and boots (see Weapons). Second: green bodysuit, helmet with purple front and flared brows over yellow eyes; purple trunks, boots, belt, shell on back containing translucent wings (see Weapons).

Weapons: Original: wings for flight and suction-tipped gloves for clinging to walls or lifting objects. Second: superstrength due to circuitry inside costume; wings for flight; computer in chest of costume feeds information to helmet about various goings-on, including likely response of a foe to whatever the Beetle does;

suction tips in gloves as well as "electro-bite" blast fired from fingers.

Biography: Bored with his job at an aircraft factory, engineer Jenkins built himself his Beetle costume and began a criminal career—not because he was inherently bad, but because he wanted the thrill of fighting superheroes. Since then, he has divided his time equally between Spider-Man, the fiery Human Torch, and the armored Iron Man. He took on the latter at the behest of Justin Hammer, a mobster who hired him when Jenkins' own activities failed to net him much of a living. (He used his earnings from Hammer to build his second, far more powerful costume which debuted in *Peter Parker, the Spectacular Spider-Man* #58). The Beetle is a member of THE SINISTER SYNDICATE.

Quote: "*This* time I won't be so *gentle* with you! I'll hurl you to the ground like a sack of potatoes!"

BELASCO (C)

First Appearance: 1982, *Ka-Zar the Savage* #12, Marvel Comics.

Costume: Red cape with purple lining, boots, tunic with purple hem and shoulders; golden wristbands, collar, other ornaments. The red-skinned Belasco also has two small red horns jutting from his forehead, as well as a pointed red tail which he controls like a tentacle.

Weapons: Powerful sword forged by the elder gods.

Chief Henchmen: Countless demons, from satyrs to harpies to centaurs, who "burst from (the) rent womb" of his wife.

Biography: According to Belasco, "Seven centuries ago, in Italy, through my practice of alchemy and the black arts, I was able to summon the elder gods." These "demonic entities from a parallel universe" had only one desire: to rule the earth. Thus, the wizard strikes a bargain with the demons: He will help them enter earth's plane in exchange for being granted vast powers and immortality. The demons agree, giving him his horns and tail and making him one of them. In love with Bice dei Portinari ("Beatrice"), the inamorata of Dante Alighieri (the poet who composed *Divine Comedy*; see SATAN), Belasco kidnaps her to be the mother of demonic progeny and takes to the sea; looking rather ridiculous, the distinguished poet hires a boat and gives chase. After some nine months, the rivals reach the land of Pangea, home of a long-dead civilization. (According to the demonic gods, the spell to bring them hence will be most effective performed on the cliffs of the Antarctic territory's volcanic Mt. Flavius.) Alas, things don't go well for Belasco after landfall. Beatrice dies in childbirth and, in an ancient room, Belasco duels with Dante who, "inspired by grief (and) enraged beyond reason" puts up an incredible fight. During the fray, Belasco's sword strikes a pipe which "dumped freezing liquid upon me." (Remarkably, the room was part of an "ancient amusement ride" which had been designed to resemble hell!) Belasco is engulfed, frozen solid but still alive, still immortal. Centuries later, in our era, the volcano acts up and "through an accident in the wiring system in the chamber," Belasco is thawed and freed. He finds an all-important locket, lost during all the confusion of his earlier arrival at Pangea, containing the jeweled pentagram with which he was going to bring the evil deities to earth. He abducts and hypnotizes the mighty woman warrior Shanna as a replacement for Beatrice and begins the ceremony. Fortunately, the heroic Ka-Zar, the jungle king, is on hand to break up the rite and keep the slimy, tentacled giants in their dimension. Though, in the resultant burst of fire "Belasco's supplicant form explodes in a riot of flame and flesh," and he falls into the volcano, he survives when the deities pluck him from earth and place him in an "alternate dimension." Returning, Belasco menaces not only Ka-Zar but other Marvel superheroes—most notably the New Mutants, against whom he sends the horned giant S'ym (*The New Mutants* #14, 1984).

Quote: "I wonder if you'd be so kind, Dherk, as to open yourself . . . you may begin with the chest cavity."

Comment: Belasco was also the name of the demon in Richard Matheson's exceptional 1971 horror novel *Hell House*. Both namings were apparently inspired by DRACULA actor Bela Lugosi, who was born Bela Blasko. The elder gods were obviously a "tribute" to author H.P. Lovecraft, who evolved a similar mythos about elder gods in his short stories and novelettes.

BEN CORTMAN (N, MP)

First Appearance: 1954, *I Am Legend*, Richard Matheson, Fawcett Gold Medal.

Biography: Husband of Freda Cortman, Ben was a middle-class suburbanite who, in the early 1970s, became a vampire when a war caused a plague in which "cylindrical bacterium creates an isotonic solution in the blood (and) lives on fresh blood." Ben, like the vampires he led—who had driven the handful of untainted humans into hiding—could not be deprived of new blood for too long; the result would be decomposition, at which point the bacteria would go "flying out (to) seek new hosts." Garlic caused the bacteria to perish, as did solar radiation, which made it imperative for the vampires to sleep during the day. On the plus-side, the bacterium caused canine teeth to grow and turned the flesh "grayish-white." Cortman himself was portly—"a hideously malignant Oliver Hardy"—bearded, and had "long, greasy (black) hair." His singular enemy was his ex-neighbor Robert Neville, who was immune to the bacteria. Daily, Cortman tried to penetrate or lure Neville from his fortified home. Like his kind, Cortman was extremely resilient; hiding in a chimney during the day, he survived being "ripped by bullets, punctured by knives, flattened by cars, smashed under collapsing chimneys and boats, submerged in water, flung through pipes" and the like because the bacilli created "a powerful body glue" that sealed all wounds. When a wound was kept open, however—as with a stake—the germ became parasitic and the host died. Cortman finally perished when, climbing from his chimney, he was cut down by rifle and machine-gun fire from humans who had managed to develop a vaccine.

Quote: "Come out, Neville!"

Comment: Anthony Zerbe played the role in the 1971 film *The Omega Man*, in which the character was known as Matthias. A previous film version was *The Last Man on Earth* (1964) with Giacomo Rossi-Stuart in the part. See other vampire villains BARON BLOOD, BLACULA, COUNT YORGA, DRACULA, NOSFERATU, PAUL JOHNSON, and VARNEY THE VAMPIRE.

THE BERSERKER (C)

First Appearance: 1981, *The Avengers* #207, Marvel Comics.

Costume: The golden armor, boots, gauntlets (see Weapons), and red-plumed helmet of a soldier of ancient Rome; green cape.

Weapons: Shield which pulls objects to its disintegrating aura; a sword which spits a destructive beam powerful enough to cause a minor earthquake; a chariot with flying mechanical horses and a contrail of fire which isn't hot but burns all the oxygen in its wake; gauntlets which sap the power of anyone he touches; a lance strong enough to down a jet.

Biography: The Berserker's "bloody-handed career" began in prehistory. During a foray with his fellow cave dwellers, the future Berserker (his name has not been revealed) ventured into a cave where he was bathed in an eerie green light. Hours later he emerged "surging with incredible power (and) possessed of an insane, savage, unquenchable fury." He was dubbed the Berserker for "there was no other name to describe the madness that was him." Through the centuries, he was the real power behind the Egyptian pharaohs and Alexander the Great; even extraterrestrials came calling for his help. The destinies of empires and solar systems alike were all "decided by who hired him first." Finally, the earth lords—now-defunct godlike rules of earth's winds, seas, and land—caused Mt. Vesuvius to erupt while the Berserker was on its slopes, entombing him in lava. But he escapes in our era and "cuts a bloodstained path through the Italian countryside" until the superheroic Avengers arrive. After taking a serious beating, they manage to subject the Berserker to a surviving earth-lord gem which sends him to a "shadow world."

Quote: "*Bah*! Rather than vaporizing you *totally*—let's see how you feel about a *bath* in the molten rock!"

Comment: The character has thus far appeared in only the single two-issue tale.

THE BLACK ACE (MP)

Real Name: Hank Davis.

First Appearance: 1933, *Mystery Squadron*, Mascot Pictures.

Costume: Aviator's suit, goggles, and cap; circular metal mask over mouth.

Biography: The foreman of a new dam, Davis learns that a rich gold mine lies nearby—and will end up under 50 feet of water if the dam is completed. Thus, he becomes the Black Ace and forms the Mystery Squadron, a group of pilots who attack the huge dam in an effort to drive the construction team away. To throw suspicion from himself, Davis hires two old flying associates, Fred Cromwell and Bill Cook, to track down the Black Ace. Identifying Davis as the greedy pilot, they shoot their one-time crony from the sky.

Comment: Jack Mulhall played the Black Ace in the 12-chapter serial.

BLACK ADAM (C)

Real Name: Teth-Adam.

First Appearance: 1945, *Marvel Family* #1, Fawcett Publications.

Costume: Navy blue bodysuit with yellow lightning bolt down chest; yellow wristbands, belt, boots.

Biography: Five-thousand years ago—ages before he bestowed superpowers on Bill Batson, making him the heroic Captain Marvel—old Shazam, "the wise Egyptian wizard," gave Adam the ability to acquire invulnerability, superstrength, immortality, the ability to fly, the power to gather and discharge lightning, and other extraordinary abilities, simply by muttering the mage's name. Each letter of "Shazam" stood for the gods whose powers he took on, *S*hu (stamina),

*H*ershef (strength), *A*mon (power), *Z*ehuti (wisdom), *A*nubis (speed), and *M*enthu (courage). (Repeating the name reverses the process, restoring Adam to his mortal identity.) "I called him Mighty Adam first," the wizard recollects, "but when he turned evil I renamed him Black Adam." What turned Adam evil was the realization that he was the most powerful man on earth. Seeing no reason why he shouldn't rule the world, he murdered the pharaoh and sent forth his armies to conquer the globe. Furious, Shazam banished the fiend "to the farthest star." However, flying for 5,000 years, Black Adam manages to return to earth, still intent on conquering it. Defeating Shazam's charges, Captain Marvel, Mary Marvel, and Captain Marvel, Jr., he is thwarted only when the sly, non-super Uncle Marvel tricks him into saying Shazam. Black Adam promptly loses his powers and Captain Marvel clobbers him insensate. However, that proves to be a case of overkill. Once he's returned to his mortal form, he promptly becomes his mortal age and rots before the heroes' eyes. Yet, that is not the end of him; soon thereafter DR. SIVANA exposes Adam to a reincarnation machine and brings him back to life, enabling the fiend to return numerous times over the years to fight not only the Marvel Family but also Superman.

Quote: "Why shouldn't I be ruler of all mankind? I will invade the palace! Out of my way, worms!"

Comment: Black Adam possesses devilishly pointed ears, though just why is never explained. In the four-part *Shazam* miniseries published by DC in 1987, the Captain Marvel legend was altered; the hero was given his powers not just to do good, but also, expressly, to battle Black Adam, who was the series' featured evildoer.

BLACK ANNIS (F)

Weapons: Iron claws able to dig through rock.

Biography: Black Annis dwells in a cave in the Dane Hills of Leicestershire, England—a cave she is thought to have dug with her claws. A blue-faced cannibal, Annis hides until dark, behind an oak tree near the opening of her cave, and jumps out to eat passers-by, usually lost children or sheep. When none come around, she goes hunting in neighboring villages. However, the grinding of her teeth usually gives her away, affording people time to lock their doors. (Her presence is one reason windows were small in this part of the country.) Whenever Black Annis wails, her voice can be heard up to five miles away.

Comment: Annis is believed to have evolved from Anu, a Celtic goddess. Belief in Black Annis survived through the first half of this century. In previous times, it was the custom to drag a dead cat through the countryside on Easter Monday in the hope that Black Annis would lurch after it, exposing her to the purifying light of the holy day.

BLACK BISON (C)

Real Name: John Ravenhair.

First Appearance: 1982, *Fury of Firestorm* #1, DC Comics.

Costume: Navy blue trousers with tassels along both sides, bison-skin cowl with white horns; tan loincloth, boots, wristbands with tassels.

Weapons: Medallion worn around neck, an ancient amulet which permits the spirit of his "great grandfather . . . the greatest shaman of the noble Bison Cult" to take over his body. In this form, he is able to bring inanimate objects to life and also to control the weather. These powers are channeled through a wooden staff he carries, a meter-long stick covered with feathers and topped with a bird's head. He also carries a shield, which is fringed with feathers but has no mystic powers.

Chief Henchmen: Black Bison rides a white horse, once a stuffed animal, which he animated at a museum.

Biography: A high school history teacher, Ravenhair was innocently leading his class through the New York Museum of Natural History when he became dizzy and disappeared into the men's room. When he emerged, the Indian was possessed by the spirit of his great grandfather; the old man had recently been killed by muggers, and entered Ravenhair through the mystic talisman he'd given him. The self-described "last defender of a nation too proud to die," Ravenhair declared war on the white man, and began by bringing back to life carousel animals he encountered in New York's Central Park. The ferocious beasts were stopped by the nuclear superhero Firestorm, who battled not only the Bison but also the park statues he animated. The super villain finally snapped from his enchantment when his girlfriend, school nurse Vanessa Tremont, was threatened. However, a few months later he was turned into the Black Bison once again, this time by the shape-changing witch Silver Deer (see Comment). Firestorm teamed with the superheroine Firehawk to defeat them both.

Quote: "You *white men*—so *proud* of your weapons! What *use* are such toys against my *medicine-magic*?"

Comment: Silver Deer was a Cherokee named Chanka who became a villain due to tragic circumstances. As a child, her twin brother Bobby was bitten by a rattlesnake. Her father rushed the boy to a hospital where, in his haste, he pushed a nurse; both Indians were immediately shot dead by a racist guard. Thus, the magic lore of her grandfather, a medicine man, passed to the embittered Chanka instead of to Bobby. Garbed in a white halter-style top with feathers running down one side, and black mesh tights, she became Silver Deer and used her arts on John Ravenhair. She apparently perished when a building fell on her during the battle with Firestorm and Firehawk. See other Indian villains, PUMA and WALKING SUN.

THE BLACK BOW (CS)

First Appearance: January 5, 1941, *The Spirit*, Register and Tribune Syndicate.

Costume: Jerkin, tights, cape, gloves, slippers; feather in cap, domino mask.

Weapons: Bow and arrow.

Biography: Arriving from Europe penniless, the Black Bow decides to make money by reviving an old family custom: extortion. "My forefathers were the feudal lords . . . of middle Europe. The serfs lived under our protection . . . for which they paid tribute." Preying on immigrants in Central City and murdering those who fail to pay, the Black Bow is pursued by the superhero the Spirit. Chased to his den beneath the mansion of one of his first victims, he is arrested.

Quote: "Ha, fool! Do you think the Black Bow surrenders so easily?"

Comment: See also the archers CROSSBOW and Merlyn (see TOBIAS WHALE, Chief Henchmen).

BLACKFIRE (C)

Real Name: Komand'r.

First Appearance: 1982, *The New Teen Titans* #22, DC Comics.

Costume: Navy blue bodysuit, boots; silver breastplate, armor from hand to shoulder, diadem; purple cape with red fringe. Komand'r's skin is orange.

Chief Henchmen: Many warriors, most prominently Zarek and his Gordanian slavers.

Biography: Because she was a frail child, Komand'r did not possess the ability to fly like others on the distant world of Tamaran. Worse, because she was sickly, she was "judged unfit to eventually rule," and it was her younger sister Koriand'r, and not she, who was named princess and heir to the throne of the distant world. Angry with her parents Myand'r and Luand'r (a brother Ryand'r came along later), her hate for Koriand'r "grew with every passing year." Since "even the daughters of kings must learn to fight," the girls were still just children when they were sent to train with the Warlords of Okaara, a dead planet whose denizens lived inside the world. The training lasted for several years, after which the two sisters engaged in a "graduation exercise," a joust with solar lances. But to Komand'r it was more than an exercise, and she tried hard to kill Koriand'r; for demonstrating that she was "without a heart or soul," Komand'r was expelled from training. Agreeing to leave but vowing to "be back to see you all burn in hell," she left . . . but not for Tamaran. Instead she went to the Citadel, an evil empire located in the Vegan solar system. Revealing the secrets of Tamaran's defenses, the traitor caused a war which lasted for 100 years; finally King Myand'r was forced to surrender, one of the terms of which was Koriand'r being sold to the Gordanians as a slave. However, after five years, both she and Komand'r ended up being captured by the Gordanians' enemies, the evil scientists known as Psions. Both sisters were subjected to an experiment to see how Tamaranians transform solar energy into the power of flight. As fate would have it, however, Citadel attack squads blasted the Psion ship during the test and caused the machine which held the sisters to explode. The blast left them both with the power to collect solar energy and transform it into destructive beams. Koriand'r fled to earth where she became the superhero Starfire, while Komand'r continued to rise through the Citadel ranks and is now Commander Komand'r. Both remained mortal enemies until *The New Teen Titans* #23 (1986). After a violent fistfight which left the sisters badly bloodied, they were separated by their parents. Komand'r admitted that "Tamaran has become more important to me than I expected" and agreed to rule with her father at her side (though she warned him not to "let your weakness get in my way"); her sister returned to earth, doubtful that things will work out yet having no choice but to accept her parents' will.

Quote: "*Launch* your troops. Lay waste to that planet. *Kill* whomever you wish—but bring my stupid sister to *me*."

Comment: The origins of Komand'r and Koriand'r were recounted in *Tales of the New Teen Titans* #4 (1982), a well-developed and literate tale by writer Marv Wolfman.

BLACK FLAME (C)

Real Name: Zora.

First Appearance: 1963, *Action Comics* #304, DC Comics.

Costume: Blue tights, T-shirt with flared shoulders, sleeves which reach from wrist nearly to shoulder; red boots, mask; black cape with red lining.

Chief Henchman: A "chemical android" look-alike to take her place in Kandor so Supergirl won't suspect her real identity.

Biography: Zora is a scientist in the city of Kandor, a metropolis from Krypton, home planet of the superheroes Superman and Supergirl. (Kandor and its inhabitants were shrunken and placed in a bottle before the planet exploded; the bottle and its teeming contents is located, today, in Superman's Fortress of Solitude in the Arctic.) Admiring the villainess Lesla-Lar, Zara decides to become a criminal herself, not in our world. Escaping the bottle with a jetpack and a pulse-ray gun (to pop the cork), she heads into space, bound for a cosmic cloud which "has the property of changing the physical form of any superbeing the way he wishes it." Willing herself to grow to human size, she goes on a rampage as the superpowered Black Flame (hailing from Krypton, she possesses all the powers of Superman and Supergirl). Plotting to rid the earth of Supergirl, she then plans to free the Phantom Zone villains (see JAX-UR, Biography) to help her destroy Superman. However, Supergirl is able to locate several grains of gold kryptonite, a rock which permanently robs all Kryptonians of their superpowers. Placing them in a compact, she waits until the enlarging effects of the cosmic cloud wear off. Then, slipping the shrunken Black Flame into the tiny box, she saps her super abilities for all time. Zora is returned to Kandor and imprisoned.

Quote: "Our cosmo-tronic cannon cut through that moon like a piece of cheese! That's exactly what will happen to earth unless you pay the tribute I ask!"

Comment: Black Flame's plan to get rid of Supergirl is actually quite clever, and it's based on a false origin story that the Kandorian tells to the Girl of Steel. In it, she claims to be Supergirl XXV, a blood-descendant of the fortieth century, who heads into space and, bringing together "the most evil criminals and outcasts in the universe" sets herself up as Queen of the Pirate Planet. There, she sends out her spacefaring buccaneers to loot other worlds. She created this elaborate story hoping that Supergirl would expose herself to gold Kryptonite in order to prevent her descendant from having superpowers. Naturally, that would also have left the superheroine unable to combat the mighty super villain. The plan backfires when Supergirl notices a filling in one of the Black Flame's teeth, something a super-powered descendant wouldn't have.

BLACK FLAME *menacing Supergirl. © DC Comics.*

BLACKGUARD (C)

First Appearance: 1986, *Booster Gold* #1, DC Comics.

Costume: Gray armor bodysuit; green boots, wristbands, knuckles, tabard, and helmet with a red queue.

Weapons: Armored car; energy mace and shield.

Chief Henchmen: Gang members garbed in light green bodysuits with orange sleeves, dark green boots, and dark green cowls with an orange face.

Biography: Nothing is known about this character's past. Possessing superstrength, he arrives in Metropolis, bent on a career of crime. Immediately attacked by the superhero Booster Gold, he is maneuvered to a power terminal which the hero uses to knock him out.

Quote: "I'm *Blackguard,* squirt! And, as of now, you are a *dead man*!"

Comment: This was the character's only appearance.

THE BLACK HAND (C)

Real Name: William Hand.

First Appearance: 1964, *Green Lantern* #29, DC Comics.

Costume: Navy blue bodysuit, trunks, boots, gloves, cape, cowl, with solid lavender triangle on chest and forehead (later, a lavender arrow coming over the head, the point ending inside a white triangle).

Weapons: The Power Light, a cylinder which collects

the radiation "absorbed by objects in the immediate area" whenever the superhero Green Lantern uses his power ring. The Black Hand is then able to fire it back as a destructive weapon or, used in connection with a special grid, "dispatch Green Lantern to another worldly dimension from which there is no return!"

Biography: One of the Hands of Coatsville, California (his brothers are great financier David, renowned scientist Joe, and famous actor Peter), William Hand turns to crime because his family is "so respectable and I hate them all." Starting out as a second-story operator and pickpocket, he keeps a notebook of "the answers . . . to *every* situation a crook can get into." Thanks to his extraordinary memory, he always knows what to do in any given situation; whipping up a costume he becomes the Black Hand, "the criminal who *cannot fail*!" Graduating from petty larceny, he comes up with his greatest scheme: to send Green Lantern to another dimension, while at the same time still being able "to tap his ring power here on earth," thus leaving Hand the most powerful person in the world. Only able to send half of the superhero away when his device inexplicably freezes, he is defeated by the remaining half.

Quote: "If I can make just *one* more percent of *Green Lantern* disappear, I'll have fifty-one percent of the power!"

Comment: The character has made a handful of appearances.

THE BLACK HANGMAN (MP)

Real Name: Arthur Galt.

First Appearance: 1943, *Adventures of the Flying Cadets*, Universal Pictures.

Costume: Black overcoat, gloves, full-face mask.

Weapons: Pistol, hand grenades.

Biography: Discovering hitherto unknown stores of helium in Africa, engineer Galt adopts the identity of the Black Hangman and slays the other members of his expedition. Four air cadets take the rap while Galt plans to sell the gas to the Nazis. Accompanying Galt to Africa to clear their names, the young men are forced by Galt to fly the gas to Germany. Instead, they manage to take the engineer prisoner and fly him to Allied headquarters. There, Galt convinces the authorities that he was hoodwinked into serving the enemy and is set free. However, tailed by the cadets, he is seen contacting Nazi agents working in America. Recaptured, Galt is charged with treason.

Comment: Robert Armstrong played the thug in the 13-chapter serial. Armstrong is famous for having starred as Carl Denham in *King Kong* a decade before.

THE BLACK KNIGHT (C)

Real Name: Professor Nathan Garrett.

First Appearance: 1963, *Tales to Astonish* #52, Marvel Comics.

Costume: Iron-gray mail bodysuit; blue boots, gloves, cape, helmet, jerkin with white skull and crossbones on chest.

Weapons: "Mirror visor" in helmet; a "paralyzer pistol" which works for an hour; an "itch ray" which is "like plain itching powder—only a thousand times worse"; and a lance which fires bolo balls and a "super-strong steel cable," contains an "acetylene torch capable of burning through a two foot steel wall," and fires .45 caliber machine-gun bullets from the handle.

Biography: A renowned scientist, Garrett sells secrets to "the Reds" and is caught by the superhero Giant-Man. His bail paid by the Communists, Garrett skips the country with a counterfeit passport and settles in "a remote Balkan kingdom nestled in the Alps." Musing over a statue of a flying horse, he decides to breed one himself. Renting a castle, he spends months on his genetic experiments until he finally injects "just the right proportion of an eagle's blood cells into a stallion." Creating his lance and armor, he returns to the United States and goes on a criminal rampage. Thwarted in his first foray by Giant-Man, he is fatally injured in a subsequent adventure (*Avengers* #47, 1967). As he lays dying, he begs his nephew Dane Whitman to take his accountrements and use them for good . . . to make up for the evil he committed in his life.

Quote: "No one would ever suspect that a .45 caliber *machine gun* is mounted in the control handle of my lance!"

Comment: Whitman is still active as the superheroic Black Knight.

BLACKLASH (C)

Real Name: Mark Scarlotti (has also gone by the name of Mark Scott).

First Appearance: 1968, *Tales of Suspense* #97 (as Whiplash); 1981, *Iron Man* #146 (as Blacklash), Marvel Comics.

Costume: As Whiplash: purple bodysuit; orange gloves, boots, jodhpurs, cowl with capelet and brown queue. As Blacklash: navy blue bodysuit with purple collar; violet cape; purple boots, gloves, cowl with green queue, utility sack worn over shoulder (see Weapons).

Weapons: Versatile whip whose lash can penetrate steel, be whirled fast enough to create a virtually solid shield able to repel bullets, stiffen to a long staff, retract to function like a club, or be disengaged from the handle and used as a "concussion charge"; "necro-lash" which, worn in a tube on the underside of his wrist, channels "every bit o' power my energy gauntlets can put out," then whips out to deliver the charge to the target; "bolash" bola carried in pouch; "steel mesh" costume impervious to bullets.

Biography: While studying at Rensselaer Polytechnic Institute, aspiring engineer Scarlotti is contacted by the Maggia, an international crime group, about working for them as a weapons designer. Inventing his whip and yearning to try it himself, he is given permission to become the costumed operative Whiplash. Battling the superhero Iron Man on numerous occasions, Scarlotti eventually ends up in prison at Ryker's Island. Sprung by millionaire Justin Hammer, who has decided to underwrite super villains for a piece of their profits, Whiplash uses Hammer's money to refine his weapons. Going back into action as Blacklash, he takes a job from the Maggia, only to be clobbered by Iron Man yet again. Disowned by the mob ("They said they don't know you," his public defender informs him), Scarlotti goes off the deep end when even his mother Barbara refuses to come and visit him in jail. He is presently at large and still looking for work as a costumed villain.

Quote: "My *Necro-lash*—that's enough raw *force—to slice Iron Man to paper clips*!"

Comment: SYONIDE also cracks a deadly whip.

BLACK MANTA (C)

First Appearance: 1967, *Aquaman* #35, DC Comics.

Costume: Blue bodysuit, boots, gloves (see Weapons); completely opaque black helmet (see Weapons).

Weapons: Suit and helmet permit Black Manta to survive underwater, supplying him with air and protecting him from the pressure. Helmet is also equipped with lasers which are fired from the eyes and can penetrate virtually any substance.

Chief Henchmen: Sundry thugs, many of whom have been surgically implanted with gills.

Biography: Nothing is known about this villain's past, save that he is a black man who, with his black aides, intends to rule the underwater world. Each time he's tried to conquer territories below the sea, he has been beaten back by the superhero Aquaman; during one such confrontation, Aquaman's son Arthur was killed.

Quote: "Since blacks have been suppressed for so long on the surface, they fight well for a chance to be masters below."

Comment: See other underwater super villains ATTUMA, CAPTAIN NEMO, CAPTAIN WHALE, DR. FANG, FISHERMAN, KILLER SHARK, KRANG, MR. CRABB, OCEAN MASTER, ORKA, PIRANHA, and TIGER SHARK (2).

BLACKOUT (C)

Real Name: Marcus Daniels.

First Appearance: 1978, *Nova* #19, Marvel Comics.

Costume: Black gloves, bodysuit with yellow lightning bolt across torso, cowl with yellow lightning bolt mask; yellow belt, boots with lightning shinguards.

Weapons: Blackout can form the Darkforce into discs which enable him to fly.

Biography: An assistant to physicist Abner Croit, Daniels allows himself to be exposed to the "Darkforce," black star radiation from another dimension. Thanks to the bombardment, Daniels acquires the ability to throw out a thick, black gel-like substance which can solidify to trap others, blow holes in walls, or protect him like a shield. (One of his Darkforce blocks can even detain a powerful super villain like THE RHINO.) Creating a costume—which serves the functional purpose of keeping him from leaking—he also steals the stabilizer which Croit used to keep him from being drawn into the other dimension. Armed with this device, he opens a doorway between the dimensions and allows Croit to be sucked in. Becoming the criminal Blackout, he tangles with the superhero Nova; during their battle, the stabilizer is wrecked and Daniels is pulled into the other dimension. Despite losing his mind there, he is eventually able to make his way back to our world where he runs afoul of sundry superheroes. Ironically, it is a villain that kills him: while battling BARON ZEMO, whom he learned was using to further his own greedy ends. Blackout suffers a cerebral hemorrhage and dies. Blackout was briefly allied with the villainous MOONSTONE and was a member of THE SINISTER SYNDICATE.

Quote: "You should be made to go through the torture I endured . . . to have your body twisted with the power of the black star . . . to be merged with the light spectrum."

Comment: The Darkforce is also, apparently, the power tapped by Darkstar, one of THE SOVIET SUPER SOLDIERS.

BLACKROCK (C)

Real Name: Successively, Samuel Tanner; Les Vegas; Dr. Peter Silverstone.

First Appearance: 1975, *Action Comics* #458, DC Comics.

Costume: Green bodysuit, trunks; light green boots and gloves with white jagged stripe on fringe, belt with white jagged line around it through center; purple cape, full-head helmet with black widow's peak on top.

Weapons: Palm-size black "power stone" which soaks up broadcast energy from the airwaves and allows Blackrock to use it in numerous ways, including the creation of visual and audio illusions, a force field, or destructive blasts; blocking radio and TV waves; and breaking himself into atomic particles so he can ride airwaves.

Biography: The powers of Blackrock are the work of scientist Peter Silverstone, an inventor with a long line of credentials including co-invention of color TV and key design work on the United States' first communications satellite. Silverstone works for the United Broadcasting Company (UBC) whose owner, Samuel Tanner, is tired of having Galaxy Broadcasting get higher ratings because they always get scoops about Superman. (Not surprising, since the Man of Steel is secretly Galaxy employee Clark Kent.) Deciding that UBC needs a superhero of its own to report on, Tanner instructs Silverstone to create one. He does, and then, to satisfy his own rampaging ego, hypnotizes Tanner into wearing the costume and battling Superman. Tanner is defeated and emerges from the confrontation with no recollection of what happened. But Silverstone doesn't forget and, putting Tanner's nephew, comic Les Vegas, into a trance, he sends him out to fight the Man of Steel. The results are the same and, for their third confrontation, Silverstone dons the costume himself. This time Supergirl gets to fight Blackrock, defeats the demented scientist and sends him to prison.

BLACKSMITH (C)

First Appearance: 1981, *Moon Knight* #16, Marvel Comics.

Costume: Golden T-shirt, wristbands; purple trousers.

Weapons: Huge mallet; forceps which, heated by a backpack, are used to burn through the necks of adversaries.

Biography: Nothing is known about Blacksmith, save that while he was in prison he devoted himself to the study of the superhero Moon Knight, not only learning his techniques and skills but also working-out until he felt he'd equaled those skills. Incredibly powerful, Blacksmith escapes from jail using his forceps, and is hired by Mr. Latimer to help set a bomb that will destroy Manhattan (and with it the "East Coast communications grid," a loss that will leave the United States open to attack by an unspecified foreign power and make Latimer one billion dollars richer). Blacksmith accepts the job largely because Moon Knight is expected to interfere; by destroying him, Blacksmith hopes to prove *himself* "the world's greatest adventurer." All he succeeds in proving is that there is only one Moon Knight, the superhero bringing him to his knees in hand-to-hand combat (a feat helped along when Moon Knight detonates Blacksmiths' inflammable backpack). As he's being arrested, the Blacksmith vows to work alone ever after . . . though he has not been heard from since.

Quote: "Long has Blacksmith awaited this day—this moment shall prove just *who is the master*!"

BLACK SPIDER (C)

Real Name: Eric Needham.

First Appearance: 1975, *Detective Comics* #463, DC Comics.

Costume: Purple bodysuit; yellow gloves, boots, full-head cowl with spider emblem on forehead; light blue spiderweb design on shoulders and top of back and chest.

Weapons: Retractable pistol worn on glove; sundry firearms.

Biography: A junkie, Needham robbed in order to buy drugs, until one day he accidentally killed his own father Jacob during a holdup. Vowing to avenge his father's death by waging war on pushers, Needham kicked his own habit and, underwritten by an unknown benefactor, trained until he reached the peak of physical perfection, then set out after the "superfly" scum as the Black Spider. Actually, Needham's angel was none other than Gotham City drug kingpin Hannibal Hardwicke, who was looking to do away with the competition. Black Spider was eventually snared by Batman.

BLACKSTARR (C)

Real Name: Rachael Berkowitz.

First Appearance: 1983, *The Daring New Adventures of Supergirl* #13, DC Comics.

Costume: Blue dress, with multicolored starbursts, streaks, and other abstract designs; maroon robe.

Biography: The daughter of tailor Chaim Berkowitz and his wife Ida, Rachael was born in Warsaw shortly after Hitler came to power in Germany. Sent to a concentration camp after her father was shot to death, she survived until the Allied liberation, after which she went to the United States—convinced, from her ordeal, that Hitler was right in trying to exterminate the Jews. Here, she earned a Ph.D. by the time she was 18, becoming a brilliant physicist. Her research eventually enabled her to tap the hidden forces which guide and form the universe; so doing, she could control gravity, teleport anyone or anything anywhere, create electromagnetic fields, and shoot destructive beams of light. Using that power to become the evil Blackstarr, she forms the Party for Social Reform, a political movement that attempts to revive the anti-Semitic ideals of the Reich. Both she and her group were attacked by Supergirl, and Blackstarr apparently died when she was caught between a pair of small black holes she'd created and was ripped asunder.

Comment: This controversial character has appeared only once.

THE BLACK TIGER (MP)

Real Name: Stanford Marshall.

First Appearance: 1940, *The Shadow,* Columbia Pictures.

Weapons: Death ray; invisibility ray.

Biography: A pillar of the community, Marshall has a secret life as the Black Tiger, a power-crazed underworld czar. When he isn't blowing up factories, trains, and airplanes, he's busy stealing chemicals and various electrical components needed to build his destructive gadgets. In the end, the Black Tiger is thwarted by the Shadow. The superhero infiltrates his gang and, about to arrest Marshall, he watches helplessly as the fleeing villain trips into a control panel and is electrocuted.

Comment: J. Paul Jones played the character in this 15-chapter serial.

BLACULA (MP)

Real Name: Mamuwalde.

First Appearance: 1972, *Blacula,* American International Pictures.

Costume: White shirt; black vest, trousers, and cloak.

Biography: The year is 1815 and Mamuwalde is an African leader eager to end the slave trade. To this end, he and his wife Luva pay a visit to DRACULA in Transylvania, hoping the noble will lend his name to the endeavor. When the vampire laughs at Mamuwalde—and makes lewd remarks about Luva—the couple prepares to go. But Dracula and his vampire aides attack, drinking their blood and bringing the Africans to a tomb. There, Dracula pronounces a curse: "You shall pay, black prince! I will . . . doom you to a living hell! A hunger . . . will grow in you—a hunger for human blood. But I will seal you in this living tomb, you and your princess, and here you will starve for eternity, torn by an unquenchable thirst." He also curses Mamuwalde "with my name: you will be . . . Blacula . . . a living fiend!" Locking Mamuwalde in a coffin, he closes the door of the tomb with Luva still inside so she can "watch, helpless and dying, till your flesh rots from your bones!" In 1965, long after the Count has been slain by Dr. Van Helsing, a pair of decorators, Billy and Bobby, buy the furnishings of Castle Dracula and have them shipped to the United States. Among them is Blacula's coffin. They wrench it open, Billy gashing himself in the process. Blacula rises, drains the blood from them both and, venturing forth, meets Tina who is a dead ringer for Luva. She is shot when police invade Blacula's gasworks hideout; to save her life, he transforms her into a vampire. When she is subsequently staked to death, the vampire willingly walks into the sunlight, perishing . . . though not for long. He returns (in *Scream, Blacula, Scream,* 1973) revived by voodoo, and turns to the black arts in the hope of ridding himself of Dracula's curse. However, before the priestess Lisa can finish the appropriate ritual, the police rush in. Blacula perishes when his voodoo effigy is pinned in the heart.

Comment: William Marshall played the part in both films; Charles Macaulay costarred as Dracula in *Blacula.* Other non-Dracula movie vampires include the crone Marguerite Chopin (Henriette Gerard) in *Vampyr* (1932), based very loosely on J. Sheridan Le Fanu's classic novella "Carmilla" (1871); Webb Fallon (John Abbot), owner of an African bar and casino in *The Vampire's Ghost* (1945); Don Drago Robles (Michael Pate) who, posing as a gunfighter named Drake Robey, allows his opponents to shoot him before blowing them away (and drinking their blood) in *Curse of the Undead* (1959); Gorca (Boris Karloff) in *Black Sabbath* (1963), based on a little-known story, "The Family of a Vourdalak," by Aleksei Tolstoi (a distant relative of Leo); Doctor Ravna (Noel Willman), holed-up in a Bavarian castle in *Kiss of the Vampire* (1964); the beautiful Mircalla Karnstein (Ingrid Pitt) in *The Vampire Lovers,* another version of "Carmilla," and its sequels *Lust for a Vampire* (1971) starring Yutte Stensgaard as Mircalla, running rampant at a girl's finishing school, and *Twins of Evil* (1971) with Katya Keith playing the part; the *Vampire Circus* (1972), which roamed Serbia in the early nineteenth century; and Janos Skorzeny (Barry Atwater), a Rumanian born in 1899 and preying on modern-day Las Vegas in *The Night Stalker* (1972). On TV's *Dark Shadows* (1966-71) the 200-year-old vampire Barnabas Collins (Jonathan Frid) prowls in and around Collins House in Collinsport, Maine, though he is less a figure of evil than a tortured soul who happens to drink human blood for a living. See other vamprie villains BARON BLOOD, BEN CORTMAN, COUNT YORGA, DRACULA, NOSFERATU, PAUL JOHNSON, and VARNEY THE VAMPIRE.

THE BLACK WIDOW (MP)

Real Name: Sombra.

First Appearance: 1947, *The Black Widow*, Republic Pictures.

Costume: Formfitting satin dress with beads and sequins in web-like design on torso.

Weapons: Lethal black widows; a device which quickly changes the color of a car while it's moving; teleportation machine which can send human beings halfway around the globe.

Biography: Sombra is the daughter of King Hitomu of an unspecified Asian nation. Eager to rule the world, Hitomu sends his daughter to the United States to try to steal the plans for a novel atomic rocket engine. Setting up shop as a fortune-teller, she allies herself with a fiendish scientist named Jaffa, who contributes his superscientific gadgets, and an equally fiendish gangster named Ward; Hitomu himself stops by now and then courtesy of the teleportation device. When people associated with atomic research start dying of spider poison, sleuth Steve Colt sallies forth to solve the murders. The trail eventually leads to Sombra's fortune-telling establishment, where she quietly sics a black widow on Steve while her father and Jaffa flee. But Steve notices the spider and gets out of its way, just as Ward walks in. The men battle and Sombra stumbles into the fickle spider; she shoots at Steve before she dies, hitting Ward instead. Hurrying after Jaffa and Hitomu Steve blows them away, thus ending the threat.

Comment: Carol Forman (LASKA, THE SPIDER LADY) starred as Sombra in this 13-chapter serial; Theodore Gottlieb costarred as Hitomu, I. Stanford Jolley as Jaffa, and Anthony Warde as Ward. The serial was later edited into a feature entitled *Sombra, the Spider Woman.*

THE BLANK (1) (CS)

Real Name: Frank Redrum (read it backwards).

First Appearance: October 21, 1937, *Dick Tracy*, Chicago Tribune-New York News Syndicate.

Costume: Black trenchcoat, hat; purple ascot; flesh-colored cheesecloth pasted on face to make it appear as if he has no eyes, mouth, or nose.

Weapons: Smoke bombs, pistol.

Biography: Looking to avenge himself against the criminals who betrayed him, Redrum becomes the Blank and begins killing off his enemies. He kills two by tying them up and leaving them in a garage with the car engine running; another is bound and tossed from a car; another is locked in the trunk of a car which is parked on a train track; two others are blown up in a boat; another is sealed in a decompression chamber. The villain is stopped when police chief Pat Patton clobbers him with a 60-pound diving helmet.

Quote: "Aha! Another baffling knot for the cute little coppers to untie!"

THE BLANK (2) (C)

First Appearance: 1984, *West Coast Avengers #2*, Marvel Comics.

Weapons: Belt allows him to become a solid gray silhouette that can't be held or hurt by concussions (although an explosion at a gas station which throws him three blocks *does* knock him out for roughly five minutes). He also carries a gun which, he cackles, "*doesn't* shoot blanks!"

Biography: When Obadiah Stane takes over Stark International, a hi-tech corporation, one of their scientists resents the way everything has been turned upside-down. Leaving with his prize invention, a belt that creates a "slippery force-field" of solid gray, he is hit by a car while waiting for a bus. Also waiting for the bus, a nameless man makes off with the scientist's briefcase, figures out how to use the belt, and goes on a criminal tear as the Blank. Teaming with the untrustworthy GRAVITON, the Blank is betrayed by the fiend; when last seen, he was being dumped into the depths of the Pacific Ocean courtesy of "an irresistible wave of gravitic energy," where he "must've gotten caught in an undertow" (#3).

Quote: "I'm taking the money from this morning's job and going someplace where people don't come flying through the air at you!"

BLASTARR (C, TV)

First Appearance: 1967, *The Fantastic Four #62*, Marvel Comics.

Costume: Blue armor leotard, boots, wristbands (Blastaar's skin is gray and he has a thick gray mane).

Biography: The ruler of the planet Baluur in the Negative Zone (an antimatter universe), the evil tyrant was eventually deposed by his people. Since they were unable to destroy this incredibly powerful being, they imprisoned him in a spacesuit and strapped him to a planetoid like an alien Prometheus, set adrift "in the death-laden debris belt" of the Zone. Escaping, he pursued Mr. Fantastic of the Fantastic Four to earth. The heroes managed to exile him yet again on a planetoid; there, he was discovered by ANNIHILUS with whom he struck a bargain: If the latter would help him regain his throne, then Blastaar would become Annihilus' vicious herald "and lead your . . . army . . . on a bloody rampage" throughout the Negative Zone. Though the two were stopped by the Avengers, Blastaar remains at large. The love of his life was his queen, Nyglar ("I never wanted a glistening palace or a vast empire," says she. "You and your love was all my heart ever desired.") She perished at the hands of Annihilus when she tried to warn her lover that the archfiend intended to betray him (*Marvel Two-In-One* #75, 1981).

Quote: "My rage knows no limits! My strength knows no bounds! The power to annihilate armies . . . to shatter entire civilizations . . . lies within my explosive-filled fingertips!"

Comment: The villain appeared in an episode of ABC-TV's *Fantastic Four* cartoon series in 1967.

BLIZZARD (also known as JACK FROST) (C)

Real Name: Professor George Shapanka.

First Appearance: 1963, *Tales of Suspense* #45 (as Jack Frost); 1976, *Iron Man* #86 (as Blizzard), Marvel Comics.

Costume: Original: blue bodysuit with thin white bands around chest, torso, forearms, thighs; cowl with white "icicle" motif around eyes; white boots, gloves with icicle fringing (see Weapons). Second: white bodysuit, gloves, cowl with black top; blue boots, wristbands (see Weapons).

Weapons: Circuitry in costume (powered by an energy pack on back in first costume, by wristbands in second) allows Blizzard to radiate extreme cold, snow, sleet, and ice through his gloves.

Biography: Working for Stark Industries (owned by Tony Stark, aka the superhero Iron Man), Shapanka stole the plans for Iron Man's armor, plotting to sell them to interested parties so he could underwrite his own private research into immortality. His industrial espionage discovered, Shapanka was dismissed. Using the stolen technology, he created a costume to get revenge against Stark. Beaten as Jack Frost and sent to jail, he escaped after several years and, regrouping, returned as Blizzard. Several additional bouts with Iron Man followed (along with prison terms), by which time Blizzard no longer required his equipment to generate cold—he could simply will it. Once again calling himself Jack Frost, he tangled with Iron Man as well as Spider-Man. Alas, he finally ran into a superhero who was not quite so charitable as the rest—the Iron Man of 2015 A.D. That Iron Man was visiting our era to locate a boy who would grow up to be a terrorist. He found his quarry . . . and Frost, who, mistaking him for our era's Iron Man, tried to kill him. Iron Man wiped him out with a ray-blast.

Quote: "My icy power has *frozen* your armor *solid*, Iron Man! One more second and that *stamping press* will crush you to *death*!!"

Comment: Other ice-producing super villains are CAPTAIN COLD, Coldsnap of MASTERS OF DISASTER, KILLER FROST, and MR. FREEZE.

THE BLOB (C)

Real Name: Fred J. Dukes.

First Appearance: 1964, *X-Men* #3, Marvel Comics.

Costume: Varies; sometimes wears street clothes, sometimes just orange trunks. Of late, he has taken to wearing navy blue trunks, boots, wristbands, and a T-shirt, all fringed in yellow.

Biography: A mutant with incredible physical strength and impenetrable flesh, the quarter-ton Blob works as a circus sideshow attraction. It costs "only twenty-five cents" to see him withstand the futile efforts of a half-dozen men to budge him and to watch a rifle load of bullets bounce off his corpulent chest. When the superheroic mutants know as the X-Men try to recruit him, the Blob's ego gets the best of him. Regarding himself as superior to them ("I'm pretty terrific, huh?"), he decides to destroy them and use his power to take over the world. The Blob is a member of the BROTHERHOOD OF EVIL MUTANTS.

Quote: "Once we dispose of Professor X . . . the whole human race will bow down to—the *Blob*!"

Comment: The movie monster the Blob predated this character, though they have nothing in common. Coincidentally, the 1972 sequel to the original 1958 film *The Blob* is called *Beware! The Blob*; the title of the story in which Marvel's Blob first appeared was *Beware of the Blob*. Other X-Men villains include the misshapen superhuman Caliban (similar to CALIBAN); Cobalt Man, who gains superpowers after donning a costume wrought of cobalt; Destiny, who can foresee the future; El Tigre, a mercenary who finds a mystic pendant and is transformed into the Mayan god Kukulca'n; Jack O' Diamonds (later the Living Diamond), a mutant with diamond hands, telepathy, and the ability to teleport; the Locust, a scientist who enlarges and controls insects; Lucifer, an extraterrestrial telepath with super-strength and the ability to fire power blasts from his hands; Maha Yogi (later the Warlock), an immortal who, thanks to the Bloodgem, has the power to bend others to his will, levitate matter, teleport, or even change his features; Mastermind, who can create illusions; the hypnotist Mesmero and his android Demi-Men; Mutant X (later Proteus), who can redesign reality in his immediate area; Sauron, a pteranodon with a human mind and extraordinary mesmeric powers (not related to J.R.R. Tolkien's SAURON); the powerful androids known as the Sentinels; the giant and mighty Sub-Human; the Toad, an extraordinary leaper; and the telepathic White Queen. See other corpulent villains THE DUKE OF DECAY, THE FAT MAN, LORD LAZEE, and TOBIAS WHALE.

BLOCKBUSTER (1) (C)

Real Name: Mark Desmond.
First Appearance: 1965, *Detective Comics* #345, DC Comics.
Costume: Tattered clothing (usually purple trousers, orange bodyshirt); sandals.
Biography: Little is known of Desmond's early years, save that on one occasion Batman rescued him from drowning in quicksand. A chemist-prodigy, Desmond was also a 97-pound weakling who wanted more than anything to be heavily muscled. Concocting a potion designed to stimulate his endocrine glands, he quaffed the mixture without doing any tests. As a result, he became the Blockbuster, gaining strength and sinew at the cost of virtually every shred of intelligence. Falling under the influence of his wicked brother Roland, Desmond began a criminal career that brought him into conflict with Batman. Torn between his hazy admiration for the superhero and his brother's instructions to break him in half on sight, Blockbuster is never able to kill the Caped Crusader. They tangle many times over the years, Blockbuster eventually giving up his criminal activities to live as a "gentle giant" in the wilds of West Virginia. He served briefly in THE SECRET SOCIETY OF SUPER-VILLAINS.

BLOCKBUSTER (2) (C)

First Appearance: 1970, *Captain America* #121, Marvel Comics.
Costume: Green mask, bodysuit with two yellow stripes across each shoulder; yellow belt, boots.
Biography: His strength increased 12-fold by Professor Silas X. Cragg, Blockbuster (then known as Man-Brute) turns to crime to get money for his poor son, with whom he plans to move to the mountains of Arizona. Unfortunately, countless people are hurt in the process and he is battled by Captain America and, later, by the superhero Omega (*Omega the Unknown* #'s 7 and 9, 1977). Overcoming Omega in their second battle, Blockbuster is about to snap the hero's neck when the villain is vaporized by the second FOOLKILLER, Greg Salinger.
Quote: "I'm *breakin' loose*, hero—and I don't care *who* gets hurt!"
Comment: Other foes of Omega during his magazine's short 10-issue run were El Gato, a mutant with extraordinary psychic abilities including the power to control cats; the Wrench (Kurt Klemmer), a superstrong brute who packs a huge wrench for cracking skulls; and a Hebrew demon known as the Dybbuk.

BLOODSPORT (C)

Real Name: Robert DuBois.
First Appearance: 1987, *Superman* #4 (second series), DC Comics.
Costume: Black T-Shirt; camouflage pants; green fingerless gloves, boots, sash around waist; red cowl with two long queues.
Weapons: Machine-gun, kryptonite dartgun, gas pellets, teleportation "weapons transporter" which allows him to instantly access weapons from his arsenal.
Biography: When Bobby gets his induction notice during the war in Vietnam, he flees to Canada and his younger brother Michael takes his place. Michael loses his arms and legs in the conflict and the resulting guilt causes Bobby's mind to snap; he spends the next 12 years in psychiatric hospitals in Canada. Found and recruited by LEX LUTHOR, he is given his hi-tech weapons with the express mission of hunting and destroying Superman. But he starts slaughtering civilians as well, forcing both Superman and Luthor to hunt him down. Eventually, Superman manages to disarm him, except for the energy pack which powers his weapons transporter. Threatening to blow up Metropolis, Bloodsport is talked out of it when reporter Jimmy Olsen brings the crippled Michael to the scene. Presumably, the super villain ended up in another psychiatric hospital.
Quote: "*Superman*! Don't come any closer, freak-o, or I'll give this broad a fast *lobotomy*!"

Comment: Bloodsport was one of the first new super villains battled by Superman after DC and artist-writer John Byrne refashioned the Man of Steel in 1986, making the superhero less omnipotent.

BLOWTORCH BRAND (C)

First Appearance: 1984, *The New Defenders* #135, Marvel Comics.

Costume: Street clothes.

Weapons: Blowtorch to ignite himself and use as an additional source of flame.

Biography: A drifter, Brand has the ability to exhale fire (once it's been touched off) or move through it without burning. Arrested for showing off and nearly burning down a bar in Elijah, New Mexico, he is bailed out of jail by a jeans manufacturer who wants him to burn down his plant; this, to keep the U.S. Federal Trade Commission and immigration officials from investigating him for using illegal aliens. But Brand goes one step further: He keeps the workers locked inside, disparaging the women as "no-good Mexchickies." Breaking into the factory, the superheroic New Defenders save the women and apprehend Brand, who has not been heard from since.

Quote: "Not all the fires of *hell* kin touch me! I'm the devil's own child, and that's a fact!"

Comment: See other fiery super villains FIREBOLT, FIREBUG, FIREFALL, FIREFIST, Heatstroke of MASTERS OF DISASTER, HEATWAVE, and PYRO.

THE BLUE BULLET (C)

Real Name: Professor John Goldstein (name has been shortened to Gold, possibly to appease his Nazi masters).

First Appearance: 1976, *The Invaders* #11, Marvel Comics.

Costume: Light blue, metallic arms, legs, and bullet-shaped enclosure over torso and head (see Weapons).

Weapons: Costume allows Gold to fly and crash his way through virtually anything.

Chief Henchman: Norris, his hulking aide.

Biography: During World War II, Gold was given a research lab located in a British hospital (space was at a premium). Unconcerned when his experiments cause frequent power drains that endanger patients, Gold completes his work—the human rocket suit he calls the Blue Bullet. Unknown to the Allies, however, Gold is a German agent; when he completes the suit, he uses it to attack the superheroic Invaders, who are based in Britain. He is stopped when the mighty Sub-Mariner smashes head-on into the rocket costume, crippling it. Though Gold is arrested, his final fate is unknown.

Quote: "Damn you! I would have *succeeded* if faced only with *men*—and not with *freaks* such as the accursed *Sub-Mariner*!"

THE BLUE LEOPARD (C)

Real Name: Patrice Labor.

First Appearance: 1975, *Tiger-Man* #2, Atlas Comics.

Costume: Orange bodysuit with black spots and black silhouette of leopard head on chest; blue trunks, gloves, boots; orange cowl with black mask. (Note: bodysuit is blue on cover, with red cowl, gloves, boots, and leopard silhouette.)

Weapons: Claws which can be tipped with sleeping potion or lethal poison, potions concocted by a vengeful witch doctor.

Biography: The Blue Leopard hails from Zambia, where Dr. Lancaster Hill (alias the superhero Tiger-Man) worked for the Peace Corps. During his stay in Africa, Hill earned the enmity of the witch doctor Na'bantu, whose magic was overshadowed by the medicine of Hill; when Hill went home to New York, Na'bantu cast a spell over a young village man, increasing his strength and agility threefold, then sent him to the United States to kill Hill. Though he failed, the youth is still at large.

Quote: "You will die when *I* decide—and you will die *painfully* . . ."

Comment: This was the character's only appearance.

THE BLUE WIZARD (C)

First Appearance: 1967, *Double-Dare Adventures* #2, Harvey Comics.

Costume: Blue pants and shirt; white turban; purple cape.

Weapons: Magic wand (see Biography for powers).

Biography: Disguised as a clown, the "modern practitioner of the evil arts of sorcery" infiltrates Mr. Morgan's circus and demands half the take "or else you'll meet ruin through the uncanny powers of the Blue Wizard." Enter the superheroic Magicmaster. Though the Blue Wizard turns animals into mosters (including a bucking rabbit the size of a horse), transforms carousel animals into murderous beasts, and creates a dragon, Magicmaster stops them all; when

The Origin of ***THE BLUE LEOPARD****. © Atlas Comics.*

THE BLUE WIZARD*. © Harvey Comics.*

the villain puts all the circus performers to sleep (with all of the customers demanding their money back), Magicmaster puts on a show himself. Finally, in the midst of this performance, the Blue Wizard makes three sword-wielding duplicates of himself to fight the hero, but Magicmaster simply fells him with a right hook, breaks his wand, and corks him in a bottle.

Quote: "By the dark power of Isiris, I command the lion to grow wings and an eagle's head!"

Comment: This was the character's only appearance. It is never explained why a sorcerer who could create life had to resort to extorting money from a third-rate circus.

BLUTO (also BRUTUS) (CS, MP, C, TV)

First Appearance: July 1932, *Thimble Theatre* (see Comment).

Costume: Usually a sailor's suit, but varies. Presently: longsleeve black shirt with white T-shirt worn over it; white sailor's cap; brown trousers.

Biography: Born in Hollywood, California, Bluto is 36 years old, stands 6 feet 8 inches, tips the scales at 372 pounds, and was originally described as "Bluto the Terrible! Lower than bilge scum, meaner than Satan, and strong as an ox." However, he has a glass jaw and cannot take the beatings meted out by his enemy Popeye the Sailor (he has even been felled by Popeye's infant ward Swee'pea). The two men usually tangle over the affections of Olive Oyl, who has also dropped the burly fellow with a smack. Bluto lives in a modest house on the island of Sweetwater, halfway between the homes of Olive and Popeye.

Comment: The Bluto who appeared just once in the *Thimble Theatre* strip was actually the prototype for the character; unlike the other personalities, all of whom were well-developed in the comic strip, Bluto was fleshed out expressly for the motion picture cartoons when they went into production in 1933. Thereafter, he became a regular fixture in the strip as well as in comic books. In the animated theatrical shorts produced by Paramount through 1957, Bluto's voice was provided, in succession, by Gus Wicki, Pinto Colvig, and William Pennel. Jackson Beck did the honors for the sydicated TV series produced from 1961 to 1963, and Allan Melvin took over the CBS-TV cartoons produced from 1978 to 1980. In the 1981 theatrical motion picture *Popeye*, Paul Smith played the part. Through the years, Popeye comic books featuring Bluto have been published by David McKay (1935-39), Dell (1948-62), Western Publishing (1962-66), King Comics (1966-67), Charlton Comics (1969-77), and Western Publishing (1978-present). Bluto was also featured in the popular 1983 Nintendo arcade and home videogame. The character's name was changed from Bluto to Brutus during the 1950s when there was a dispute over its origin.

BOBA FETT (MP, N, C)

First Appearance: 1980, *The Empire Strikes Back*, Twentieth Century-Fox.

Costume: Light blue jumpsuit with orange kneepads; brown cloak, belt, boots; white gloves; green and light blue helmet with T-shaped visor.

Weapons: Spaceship *Slave-1*; jetpack on back for flight, wrist-lasers, explosive darts, grapple, flame-thrower.

Biography: A native of the Mandalore system, Fett is an intergalactic bounty hunter. (His costume, the uniform of the evil warriors who fought the Jedi Knights during the Clone Wars, suggests that he was a soldier at some point in the past.) After an illustrious career, he has the misfortune of tangling with heroic young Luke Skywalker in the Dune Sea, a vast desert on the planet Tatooine. Skywalker activates Fett's backpack and the villain flies off, out of control; he lands in the Great Pit of Carkoon, where he is devoured by the worm-like Sarlacc. Fett's most famous hunt was for smuggler Han Solo, an assignment given to him by DARTH VADER. Other bounty hunters involved in that quest were the bug-eyed, amphibious Bossk; the humans Zuckuss and Dengar; and the robot IG-88.

Comment: Boba Fett met his doom in *Return of the Jedi* (1983). The part was played by Jeremy Bullock in both films. The character appeared in the novel and comic book adaptations of the film.

BOOMERANG (C)

Real Name: Fred Myers.

First Appearance: 1966, *Tales to Astonish* #81, Marvel Comics.

Costume: Original: blue tights, helmet, belt, harness consisting of a strap around the torso and over the shoulders meeting in a starburst on the chest with a red "B" inside; red boots, gloves; white trunks, bodyshirt covered with red, half-dollar-sized discs (see Weapons). Second: white tights, shirt with red starburst on chest and white "B" inside; red helmet, gloves, boots, trunks, belt with white boomerang buckle; harness consists of straps over shoulders only, studded with the discs. Third; purple cowl, gloves, bodysuit with blue sides, arms; blue boots; white boomerang on forehead, two on chest, two on back, and two on each side (all nine are detachable for use as weapons).

Weapons: Originally employed not only boomerangs but razor-edged "whirling discs," some of which were capable of slicing a gun in half (length-wise) when thrown, or exploding with "the power of a dozen hand grenades." With the change to his third costume he uses only boomerangs—though each is special. The "shatterangs" contain a powerful explosive, the "gaserangs" contain tear gas, the "razorangs" slice through metal, the "screamerangs" produce a destructive sound wave, and the "bladerangs" are like buzz saws. Both his second and present costumes boast "rocket jets" in the boots for flight. He is a member of THE SINISTER SYNDICATE.

Biography: An Australian who came to the United States as a child, Myers became fond of baseball and eventually worked his way into the major leagues. Found guilty of taking a bribe, the angry pitcher was approached by a subversive group know as the Secret Empire; he agreed to work for them using his extraordinary arm, as operative Boomerang. When that gig ended disastrously, Myers hid out in Australia, practicing his skills with the boomerang. He resurfaced as a free-lance criminal, most frequently battling the superheroic Hulk.

Quote: "Maybe the *explosion* can't hurt you . . . but what about the *landslide* it causes?"

Comment: Other sports villains are BULLSEYE, Fastball, SPORTSMAN, and SPORTSMASTER.

THE BOUNCER (C)

First Appearance: 1966, *Detective Comics* #347, DC Comics.

Costume: Brown bodysuit, gloves, boots, full-face cowl (see Weapons).

Weapons: Costume is made from "Elastalloy," which is "an alloy of rubber, steel, and chrome" and allows the wearer to bounce "higher than anything yet known to man" while at the same time protecting him from shock (though not interminably; at a certain point the impact will begin to harm the wearer). The Bouncer also has a gun made of Elastalloy, allowing it to fire itself when thrown.

Biography: After five years of research, "a young metallurgist" stumbles upon Elastalloy and, using it to weave a costume, turns to crime. After a number of muffled attempts to capture the villain, the superheroic Batman and Robin find a way to nullify the Bouncer's powers by wearing electrodes under their costumes and "passing a high-frequency beam . . . through the Bouncer." A simple sock to the jaw is then sufficient to end his up and down career.

Quote: "When my *Elastalloy* gun hits that wall, it will bounce off—and fire the fatal bullet that ends *Batman's* career!"

Comment: The Bouncer tale was unique in that after the villain was captured, the story was continued as a "what if" tale, that is, what if the gun had gone off and Batman were killed. In that variation, Robin is able to experiment on the gun, which the Bouncer leaves behind, and finds a surefire light/sound beam combination which causes the suit to fall apart.

THE BOUNTY HUNTER (C)

First Appearance: 1981, *Adventure Comics* #484, DC Comics.

Costume: Blue T-shirt with yellow diamonds on chest; red trunks; yellow tights, cape; navy blue boots, gloves with blue trim; navy blue cowl with yellow visor and flared ears (see Weapons).

Weapons: Machine-gun; costume is "triple thick" and bulletproof.

Chief Henchman: Pupil, a giant, flying mechanical eyeball with a red graduation cap used for reconnaissance (see Biography).

Biography: Pretending to be a bounty hunter, capturing crooks for pay, the villain is actually out to kill his prey to keep them from revealing what they know about the mob. In public, the Pupil pretends to work for the Bounty Hunter; in private, it's actually the other way around. When Bounty Hunter is captured by teenagers Chris King and Vicki Grant (holders of the "Dial-H for Hero" device), he tries to barter freedom for information; outraged, the Pupil shoots him dead with a gun hidden behind its iris, then self-destructs.

Quote: "Another costumed clown? Well . . . I no longer have to pretend I'm on *your* side—this time I can just *kill.*"

Comment: This was the character's only appearance.

THE BRAIN (C)

First Appearance: 1964, *The Doom Patrol* #86, DC Comics.

Costume: None; the Brain is simply a brain which, over the years, has occupied a variety of different vessels (see Biography).

Weapons: "Mini-radio" which his minions wear in their ear to receive his instructions; "computer sensors" in the base of his dome (added along with his skull-like face; see Biography).

Chief Henchmen: Monsieur Mallah and THE BROTHERHOOD OF EVIL; Mr. Morden and the robot Rog, who stands over 100 feet tall and fires a destructive "thermo ray" from his eyes (#'s 86 and 93 only); and Videx (aka Jalmar Lichtmeister), who can control light (#118 only).

Biography: The Brain is the most dogged and powerful foe ever faced by the superheroic Doom Patrol. Roughly a decade before his death, the Brain (his name is never revealed), a French scientist, used "secret teaching methods and shock treatment" to turn an expecially agile and powerful gorilla into a genius even by human standards (IQ: 178). Dubbed Monsieur Mallah, the ape made the effort worthwhile for, when his master died, the genius simian followed "careful instructions" and kept the scientist's brain alive by placing it inside a liquid-filled dome. For all intents and purposes immortal, the Brain founded the Brotherhood of Evil and made ready to destroy the Doom Patrol, which he regarded as the one obstacle to conquering the world. In their first and most spectacular encounter, Rog drew them out by attempting to steal the Statue of Liberty and hold it for ransom. He failed, but that didn't prevent the Brain from attacking them repeatedly during their five-year run. Ultimately, the Brain's partner Madam Rouge turned on him when she fell in love with Niles Caulder, leader of the Patrol. She blew up the headquarters of the Brotherhood of Evil with the Brain and Mallah inside. But the attack failed to destroy them; moments before the blast, the Brain's computer sensors anticipated the detonation and the two felons left replicas in their place while they escaped underground. He "remained in hiding" for some time, after which he formed a new Brotherhood of Evil. Both the Brain and the new league remain at large, warring mostly against the New Teen Titans. The appearance of the Brain has varied over the years. He inhabited the body of the huge robot Kranus (posing as an extraterrestrial tyrant) in #101; he was the robot Ultimax and packed a shrinking-gas gun in #107; a skull-like face was slapped onto the transparent dome in #108; he briefly acquired a body of crackling light in #110; and the Brain was placed inside a silver stand with a face on top—looking remarkably like a chess pawn—in *The New Teen Titans* #14 (1981).

THE BRAIN EMPEROR (C)

First Appearance: 1965, *The Mighty Crusaders* #1, Archie Comics.

Costume: Red bodysuit, cape; white belt; golden skirt, boots; gray breastplate, gloves; transparent helmet.

Weapons: Spaceship with "Extoplasmik device," a huge extendable arm; G-missiles to blast objects to bits; sin-satellite whose radiations "will cause all earthlings to hate one another"; Belt Translocator for skipping through time and space.

Biography: The Brain Emperor hails from the planet K-Shazor, where all the people "are mental giants" because of surgery conducted upon them when they are very young. However, the Brain Emperor alone had the mutant "command-power," and he used it to take control of his world. But his power was mysteriously cut off during an eclipse, and his subjects rebelled; imprisoned in a "cosmo-cube," he escaped during a planetquake and left for the planet L-253-P. There, he collected five super villains: Thornaldo, whose body is covered with deadly thorns which, striking a victim, cause instant death; Bombor, a living bomb who can fire off blasts of explosive energy as well as fly; Wax-Man, a humanoid candle who uses the radiation from his fiery "hair" to turn other objects (and people) to wax; Electroso, who kills beings with his "electric-touch"; and Force-Man, who throws back "a thousand-fold" any power which is thrown at him. Bringing these villains to earth, which he intended to conquer, the extraterrestrial despot was shocked when all are defeated by the superheroes of the Mighty Crusaders: Thornaldo was roped and tossed into quicksand by the Shield; Bombor was detonated by the Black Hood's robot horse; Wax-Man was smothered by Fly-Girl; Electros was grounded and thus utterly depleted when the Comet turned a tree into a lightning rod; and Force-Man gave up his evil ways when Fly-Man buffeted him with the power of good. Putting the Mighty Crusaders under his power, the Brain Emperor constructed a device which was to reduce the brain-capacities of others and make them easier to control. Unknown to him, however, the Comet changed "vital parts" in the machine, causing the Brain Emperor to obey instructions given to him. The Mighty Crusaders ordered him to return to imprisonment on K-Shazor, and he quickly rocketed home. However, he returned 18 years later (*The All New Adventures of the Mighty Crusaders* #'s 1, 2, and 3) and, settling into a castle on a mountain in southern New Jersey, teamed with the mad Eterno, the Conqueror of Atlantis. Together, they planned to divide up the earth, Eterno ruling beneath the seas and the Brain Emperor lording over the land—though the latter fully intended to betray his partner and "assume final control." Once again, however, the Mighty Crusaders foiled the villain, and he decided to try a new tack, taking them on separately, commencing with the Fox. Using his mental powers to adopt a human form and calling himself Brain—the fiend also briefly masqueraded as the hero's girlfriend, Delilah—he teamed with THE GASSER and THE ERASER to kill the superhero (*Blue Ribbon Comics* Vol. 2, #7, 1984). Despite the triple-threat,

THE BRAIN EMPEROR. *© Archie Comics.*

the Fox triumphed; Brain Emperor was destroyed (or so it seems) when he was accidentally touched by the Eraser.

Quote: "Bah! I dare not reconquer K-Shazor . . . instead, I shall conquer earth with my renewed command-power."

Comment: Other villains with whom the Mighty Crusaders tussled during their original (1965-66), seven-issue run were Inferno, the Destroyer; the Maestro and his debilitating organ; and the savage Hammerhead. Most of these characters were created by Jerry Siegel, the father of Superman.

THE BRAIN FROM SIRIUS (C)

First Appearance: 1973, *E-Man* #1, Charlton Comics.

Costume: None; the Brain is a giant pink brain inside a huge Plexiglas dome.

Weapons: Interstellar ship; "The XYZ-947," a "Sirian mind control" helmet which bends others to the wearer's will, and can also create cinematographic techniques in real life (i.e., dissolves, fadeouts, etc.).

Chief Henchmen: Various robots; Stringpull Schmaltzberg, a moviemaker who serves the Brain in exchange for the XYZ-947, which he planned to use to make critics like his pictures; the Entropy Twins, Michael and Juno, from Sirius One—Michael possessng the power of order but keeping his lover Juno (disorder) in check only when he's near her.

Biography: Piloting its starship from Sirius One, the Brain heads for our solar system, where it intends to test the "ultimate weapon" on the defenseless inhabitants of Pluto. However, the shapechanging superhero E-Man happens upon the ship, his added weight causing it to miss Pluto and crashland on earth. Furious, the Brain plots to detonate its "hate bomb" on earth, but E-Man is able to smash its protective dome and nip its plan in the bud. But only for a short while; the Brain's robot drones were able to repair the dome before their master expired. Despite suffering some mental damage (it is now addicted to television) the Brain has enough on-the-ball to try to kill E-Man on numerous occasions, most notably by using the Entropy Twins (it has to sign for the package when it arrives from Sirius One), which fail when E-Man changes their chemical makeup; and by trying to feed E-Man to lethal Sirian snakes. Luckily, the superhero is able to set up an electromagnetic field around the brain, which is pelted insensible by its helpless metallic robots. The Sirian has not been heard from since.

Quote: "You see, *E-Man*—for *condemning* me to the years I've spent *here* on this stinking mudball . . . I must *destroy* you!"

Comment: Other foes battled by E-Man include the Battery, a giant robot capable of breaking down matter and sucking it up as energy; an evil energy creature known as the Feeder, which fed on the fear it caused; and the exoskeleton-wearing, carbon dioxide-breathing, ex-mining engineer Blacklung (aka Colchnzski, father of E-Man's girlfriend Nova).

THE BRAIN FROM SIRIUS. *© First Comics.*

BRAINIAC (C, TV)

First Appearance: 1958, *Action Comics* #242, DC Comics.

Costume: Original: pink leotard with white collar, wristbands, solid black triangles on trunks-portion pointing toward waist; white belt (skin is green and, except for his first appearance, his bald head is covered with a network of nodes and wires, "the electric terminals of his sensory nerves"). Second: silver, metallic body with skull-like silver head.

Weapons: Brainiac has used vast numbers of "nightmarish scientific weapons" over the years, among them his "space-time craft" which can fly anywhere in time and space and is protected by an impenetrable "ultra-force barrier"; a "hyper-force machine" which shrinks cities (Brainiac places them in bottles with the intention of restoring them, later, on the planet Bryak with himself as ruler); a "power-belt" which surrounds Brainiac with his own personal protective force field; a "coma-ray" which can render even Superman helpless; a "Z-ray" projector which heals any wound; a "thought-caster" to project his thoughts through space; "force-fingers," a giant hand that Brainiac can create and control simply by willing it, and which can grasp objects or generate heat sufficient to melt metal; and an "underground machine" for burrowing.

Chief Henchman: Koko, a monkeylike pet with a pair of antennae.

Biography: There came a day on the planet Colu (a world also referred to as Yod in the chronicles) when the computers (possessing tenth-level intelligence) turned against their green-skinned, humanoid creators (who had a mere sixth-level intelligence) and took control ("We computers . . . are more fit to govern than you," chortles one). Anxious to rule other worlds ("We must extend our wise rule to all worlds governed by foolish humans!"), the non-ambulatory computers built the android Brainiac and sent him forth to reconnoiter. A young Coluan named Vril Dox (and renamed Brainiac II) was chosen to travel with him to perpetuate the illusion that Brainiac was Coluan. But Vril fled and, in time, boosted his own intelligence to twelfth-level and rallied the Coluans in a successful revolt against the computers. (Vril, in turn, became the great grandfather of Querl Dox, one of the greatest superheroes of the thirtieth century. Querl fights crime as Brainiac 5, a name he chose to erase the foul memories of his android namesake.) Roaming time and space in a effort to conquer the universe, Brainiac was constantly stonewalled by Superman. During one such battle, Superman trapped Brainiac on a world in the Epsilon 4 planetary system. Hoping to escape by causing the sun to go nova, Brainiac was instead blown to pieces. Floating through space as a mass of loosely bound molecules, the villain eventually reached a world of electronic life forms. Linking with that planet's computers, he drank up vast amounts of knowledge and was eventually able to reform. In his new physical incarnation, Brainiac has incredible physical strength in addition to a superior mind.

Quote: "I have a little business here on earth—and I'd just like to see *Superman* try to stop me! Ha, ha!"

Comment: In the character's first adventure, he remarked that he was stealing cities in order "to repopulate my home world, where a plague wiped out my people." That was subsequently revised to accommodate the grander revolution scenario. Brainiac has also been featured in animated cartoons in *The New Adventures of Superman* (1966-67), *The Superman/Aquaman Hour* (1967-68), and *The Batman/Superman Hour* (1968-69).

BRAIN STORM (C)

Real Name: Axel Storm.

First Appearance: 1964, *Justice League of America* #32, DC Comics.

Costume: Blue jumpsuit; purple gloves, boots, vest with flared shoulders (originally had white stripes along sides); light blue belt (originally purple); silver helmet shaped like an elongated egg with rings around it and a bulb on top (see Weapons).

Weapons: Helmet soaks up stellar power and boosts his natural brain power, enabling him to fire lightning-like blasts which permit him to control anything they strike—including superheroes (for example, causing the Flash to run in place, Superman to become powerless, or Green Lantern's power ring to do the villain's bidding, and in one instance turning Batman into a huge reptilian beast [#36]). The blasts also grant Brain Storm the ability to animate lifeless objects and teleport himself or others. Brain Storm flies on a golden hover-sled when his brain powers have been overtaxed.

Biography: Discovering that human ideas (i.e., "brainstorms") take place during peak periods of radiation emission from the stars, Storm finds a metal which attracts the stellar energy, and uses it to form a helmet. When his brother Fred, a criminal, disappears, Brain Storm blames Green Lantern, and brings the Justice League of America to his headquarters to witness the superhero's execution. However, learning that he himself had accidentally teleported his brother to France, Brain Storm flees, returning numerous times over the years to battle the superheroes, as a team and individually.

BREATHTAKER (C)

First Appearance: 1984, *Fury of Firestorm* #29, DC Comics.

Costume: Red Robe with hood.

Weapons: Robotlike exoskeleton which gives him increased height (from just over four feet to nearly seven feet), but little added strength.

Chief Henchmen: Operatives of the Assassination Bureau, a group of highly skilled killers-for-hire; principal killers are Incognito and Mindboggler; also MINDBOGGLER.

Biography: An albino dwarf, the Breathtaker (his name hasn't been revealed) spent his early life as an outcast, abandoned by his family and taunted by his peers. Building his exoskeleton and adopting a new identity, he vowed to make humankind suffer as he had suffered. On the more practical side, he formed the Assassination Bureau in order to underwrite his extravagant dream. However, his most ambitious job proved to be his last (to date), as he accepted an assignment from the subversive 2000 Committee to slay the nuclear man Firestorm. Though the Breathtaker managed to lure the superhero to his headquarters, he failed to kill Firestorm. The superhero destroyed his lair and hauled him off to prison.

BRICKFACE (C)

Real Name: Terrence Cotta.
First Appearance: 1980, *Adventure Comics* #470, DC Comics.
Costume: Street clothes and trenchcoat. Cotta's face resembles a brick wall.
Weapons: Standard firearms.
Chief Henchmen: Stucko, whose right had was replaced with a trowel; his deceitful secretary, Cindy Bloch.
Biography: This Bogart-like villain was once a respectable maker of home siding. Discovering a "new kind'a brick siding" which was stamped in sheets and looked like the real thing, he gave competitor Alonzo Van Rivett and his aluminum siding firm a run for their money. Smarting, Van Rivett had some mob goons go to the pseudo-brick plant and work the owner over; as the piece de resistance, they put his face under the press and it emerged with a brick pattern. His assistant, Stucko, lost his hand when he was knocked into different machinery. As Brickface, he has Stucko stab Von Rivett to death with his trowel and bury the body behind fake brick siding. Two years later, the superhero Plastic Man found the body and, learning that the siding was installed by Cotta, went after him. The villain was last seen being carted off to prison (#471).
Quote: "Tell me *why* ya were *shpyin'* on me . . . or ya take the *fasht way down—47 shtories!"*
Comment: This character appeared just once, and is reminiscent of Dick Tracy's singularly misshapen villains such as FLATTOP. Other foes Plastic Man has fought include I.Q. Small, alias Lowbrow (a parody of Tracy's THE BROW); Whirling Dervish, a gaunt fellow who spins like a cyclone, his arms and feet flailing with stunning impact; Roxanne Roller, a disco-dancing crook with razor-tipped skates and a belt which squirts fast-drying plastic to form getaway ramps; and the truly inspired "B.O. Bandit" the Skunk, who dressed in black with a white stripe down his back and explained his powers thusly: "Since the instant of *my birth*, I have not taken a cleansing *bath*! Indeed, I've *chemically* increased my body odor to . . . *slay*."

BRIGAND LEADER (CS)

First Appearance: December 22, 1934, *Terry and the Pirates*, Chicago Tribune-New York News Syndicate.
Costume: Black robe with lighter, flared shoulders, collar; intricate braiding on chest.
Weapons: Machine gun.
Chief Henchman: The *very* dedicated Kiang ("Grovel in the dirt, incautious fool! You have spoken rashly to the master!").
Biography: The Chinese despot lives near the West River, where he watches over an ancient temple and its adjoining treasure room. Despised by his own people ("Evlybody hate him," confides one subject, "but do not dare make him angly"), he captures young Terry and his party of explorers when they find his temple. Seated on his throne and puffing his pipe, he makes plans to enslave Dale Scott, the female member of the party, and murder the others. Instead, the tyrant himself is killed along with Kiang when one of the prisoners, Dale's father, kicks a case of dynamite, sacrificing himself to blow the villains to kingdom come.
Quote: "Take these pigs from my presence! I shall have the pleasure of torturing them at my leisure!"
Comment: The Brigand Leader, also referred to as the Mandarin and Master, was Terry's first nemesis; he perished in the January 17 installment. See Terry's more enduring foe THE DRAGON LADY; also see Asian villains COLONEL SUN, DR. FU MANCHU, DR. GOO FEE, DR. YEN SIN, GENERAL CHANLU, and WU FANG.

BROTHER BLOOD (C)

First Appearance: 1982, *The New Teen Titans* #21, DC Comics.
Costume: Red bodysuit with blue shoulders, "X"-like design on torso, stripes down legs and around shins and thighs; blue boots with red toes and three silver patches on front; blue gloves with red hands and silver patches on back of forearm (see Weapons); blue trunks, belt; white cloak and straps under arms, hood—which resembles a canine-skull—with black mask with red fringe.
Weapons: Cloak bestows great physical strength and personal charisma; circuits built into Brother Blood's costume enable him to fire destructive blasts.
Chief Henchmen: Brother Blood has followers in every nation and from all walks of life. At his side in his castle are the likes of the Confessor, who uses torture to force people to confess to crimes, and various "brothers" and "sisters" who handle everything from

his finances to his media appearances. These include such appropriately named persons as Sister Sade, Brother Fear, and Sister Soul.

Biography: Brother Blood was born in 1940, heir to a savage heritage. During the Fourth Crusade in the thirteenth century, the Crusaders sought to impress others into the service of Pope Innocent—in particular, people of the Baltic nation of Zandia. Not really wanting to go, the Zandians fought back. To save his own miserable life, one of the invaders offered to give the Zandian high priest the Cloak of Christ, which Jesus allegedly wore at the Last Supper. Since it had passed into the hands of wizards and been befouled before returning to the church's possession, it was being brought to the Holy Land to be purified. Accepting the cloak, the priest put it on and was filled with power. Slaughtering his enemies, washing in their blood, and becoming nearly invulnerable, the priest adopted the name Brother Blood and set up a cult of evil. He remained the leader of Zandia for six decades before being slain by his son; this, then, became the ritual, and it has continued down to our present day. The current Brother Blood leads the international Church of Brother Blood which controls Zandia and seeks to become a world power.

Quote: "I have met the *enemy* and they are *mine*! Seal them in the pits and let them *die*!

THE BROTHERS GRIMM (C)

Real Name: Nathan Dolly; Barton and Percival Grimes.

First Appearance: 1978, *Spider-Woman* #3 (as Dolly); 1984, *Iron Man* #188 (as the Grimes brothers), Marvel Comics.

Costume: Blue bodysuit, cowl, gloves; red boots (originally reached to thighs), leotard with stiff collar reaching to forehead; full-face white skull mask with red eyes (see Weapons).

Weapons: Dolly was able to will various weapons into existence; with the Grimes Brothers, they can create offensive artifacts simply "by thinking about them," due to the Grimm suits. The weapons which the villains have thusfar whistled up include "Grimm Grenades," for explosions; sneezing powder; Mexican jumping beans which ricochet all over a room; dough which sticks to peoples' faces; exploding eggs which are produced "from thin air" and temporarily blind enemies; seeds which immediately sprout into a huge, strangling vine; "stardust" (aka "glittering death") which paralyzes people (and also clogs Iron Man's boot jets); inflatable spare uniforms to decoy adversaries; "golden thread" which shoots from fingertips and binds people; a yellow (blue for the Grimeses) star, roughly six feet tall, which flies by unknown means and carries them through the air, suspended from a swing; clouds on which they can stand and also soar through the skies.

Biography: Ages ago, when the Elder Gods were purging their realm of evil, the demon-god Chthon hid his foul spirit inside Wondergore Mountain in the Balkans. The trees growing thereabout were thus infused with Chthon's mystic essence, and it was from one such tree that a local woodworker eventually carved a pair of foot-long dolls. Doll fancier Nathan Dolly acquired the figures, informed by their creator that he could actually make them move by transferring his own spirit into the figures. Unfortunately, Nathan tried to bring both dolls to life simultaneously and was trapped within. Shipping his body and the dolls back to the United States, he was able, with the help of his wife Priscilla as well as extensive readings in the black arts, to shift his life essence from the figurines to a pair of lifesize mannequins—the Brothers Grimm. Turning to crime, he repeatedly battled Spider-Woman, who was never able to apprehend him. However, he did manage to capture her. And having Spider-Woman in his clutches, he was able to bring her magician mentor Magnus into the picture. Yearning to reinhabit a human body, Dolly coerced Magnus into performing the appropriate mystic ritual; pretending to go along, the mage instead sent Dolly's spirit into limbo and he has not been heard from since. But the Grimms have. Two brothers, co-owners of Grimes and Grimes Real Estate, took over the Los Angeles Theater where the rite was performed, and found the costumes with which Dolly had garbed the lifesize mannequins. The suits themselves possessed magic—apparently from having been in contact with Dolly—so the brothers turned to crime, which was only a hop, skip, and jump from the unspecified "questionable business ventures" in which they'd previously been engaged. Captured by Iron Man, they have yet to resurface.

Quote: "*My* god is money . . . speaking of which, do hand over all of *yours*! Or would *you* like to go bye-bye?"

Comment: Nathan Dolly had previously battled Iron Man as Mister Doll, using the occult to hurt people by harming their doll likenesses. He first appeared in *Tales of Suspense* #48 (1963).

THE BROW (CS, TV)

First Appearance: June 13, 1944, *Dick Tracy*, Chicago Tribune-New York News Syndicate.

Weapons: Spike Machine, a large, motorized vise lined with spikes (a timer controls how long the jaws take to close).

Biography: The Brow has a forehead which, falling in deep folds from his scalp to the bridge of his nose, comprises half of his face. His grotesque physical appearance echoes a dark soul. The head of a spy ring, he punishes those of his agents who fail by putting their limbs in the Spike Machine. When he forces petty thieves known as the Summer Sisters to go to work for him, they rebel and the Brow is forced to flee from his apartment. On the lam, he shoots a farmer dead to steal his tractor, strands Dick Tracy on a lightning rod, and holes up with the hag-like Gravel Gertie until Tracy catches up with him. The two-fisted gumshoe subdues the Brow by knocking him into an electrified fence. Before his operation was squashed, the Brow's aides included Turtle and Joe, who are shot dead by the Summer Sisters; Doc, who dies in a car crash while fleeing police; and operative "26," who is captured by police.

Quote: "It takes sixteen minutes to perform the errand I am assigning you. It also takes sixteen minutes for those spikes to reach your sister's flesh. The machine will not be turned off till you return."

Comment: The Brow was also a character in the Dick Tracy cartoon series (1960).

BUG AND BYTE (C)

Real Name: Barney and Blythe Bonner.

First Appearance: 1984, *Fury of Firestorm* #23 (Byte), #24 (Bug), DC Comics.

Costume: Bug: green bodysuit; indigo vest, gloves, trunks, helmet with mandible-like front and green eyes; three violet tentacles on back. Byte: blue bodysuit and white leotard, light blue rectangles running along from feet to shoulders and up her arms; light blue gloves and boots; blue helmet with light blue covering over face.

Biography: Working as a computer designer in her garage, Belle Bonner successfully juggled a career and motherhood, that is, until the day her children Barney and Blythe entered her workshop and brought a pair of live wires together. Thousands of volts of electricity shot through the siblings, who, miraculously, seemed unharmed. Not so Belle's marriage, for when father Frank got home, he tossed Belle out of the house. She went to work at Concordance Research and didn't see her children for a decade, Barney and Blythe growing to hate her for her perceived desertion. Something else happened during those 10 years: The children acquired superpowers. Blythe was able to turn into electricity and travel through wires, fire electric blasts, or even form huge, functioning electric likenesses of objects. Barney was able to enter any computer or integrated-circuit-based device and, while there, fire electric blasts or suck other people into the system. Still angry with their mother, they decided to seek her out and kill her—and would have succeeded if the superhero Firestorm hadn't interfered. Unfortunately, during the confusion, Byte accidentally assaulted Bug, leaving him insane; the good news is that the tragedy brought Frank and Belle back together.

BUG-EYED BANDIT (C)

Real Name: Bertram Larvan.

First Appearance: 1966, *The Atom* #26, DC Comics.

Costume: Purple trunks, bodysuit with high black collar, white neck, and a white stripe down the chest; purple helmet with golden antennae and green, multifaceted eyes (see Weapons); green boots, wristbands.

Weapons: Mechanical bugs with the powers of their living counterparts (the spider spins powerful webs, the beetle has enormously powerful mandibles, etc.). The Bandit can remote-control these, thanks to his helmet.

Biography: Inventing a mechanical insect which would prey on pests and offer humanity relief, Larvan is unable to raise the money to build a prototype. Stealing the cash he needs, he manufactures his first robot bug and, as the Bug-eyed Bandit, uses it to steal more money. Running afoul of the superheroic Atom, he ends up with amnesia and a stiff prison sentence.

BULLSEYE (C)

First Appearance: 1976, *Daredevil* #131, Marvel Comics.

Costume: Blue bodysuit with concentric white and black bull's eye circles over neck and shoulder (as if neck were the bull's-eye); blue cowl with concentric white and black bull's-eye circles on forehead; white gloves, boots with three thin black bands each; white belt.

Weapons: Countless arms, including guns, knives, spears, whips, sais (three-pronged daggers), razor-edged playing cards, and sundry martial arts weapons.

Biography: A big-league pitcher, the man-who-would-be-Bullseye (his name has not been revealed) joined the army and became a crack soldier. In fact, he enjoyed killing so much, and was so good at it, that he became a mercenary in Africa after his tour of duty. There, he also mastered the use of many primitive weapons. After a while, he came back to the United States as the costumed assassin Bullseye. He has frequently crossed paths with the superhero Daredevil, and is best known for having slain rival assassin Elektra, who was also Daredevil's lover. Though she was later revived in a secret rite, Daredevil was so furious at the time that he broke Bullseye's back (#181). The villain was subsequently repaired and resumed his criminal career.

Quote: "Yeah, hornhead . . . *I* killed that creep just like I'm gonna kill *you*! Y'see—*Bullseye never misses*!"

Comment: THE BOOMERANG was also a baseball player turned criminal. See other sports villains Fastball (Comment, SPORTSMASTER), SPORTSMAN, and SPORTSMASTER.

THE BUNNY FROM BEYOND (C)

Real Name: Ralf-124C4U.

First Appearance: 1982, *Captain Carrot and His Amazing Zoo Crew* #5, DC Comics.

Costume: Blue breastplate; purple vest, gloves, trunks, books; navy blue cap with a red gem at its widow's peak.

Weapons: "Flyin' Frisbee" which allows him to float anywhere he wishes.

Biography: The Bunny comes from "a far-off planet" whose rabbit civilization is far more advanced than that of the animal world, Earth-C, which is located in another dimension and is identical to our own planet, save that it's populated by anthropomorphic animals. Eons ago, giant eggs from space landed on the Bunny's world. Containing giant, malevolent yolks, the eggs could not be destroyed, so they were sent to earth. However, the spaceship crashlanded on Earth-C's Easter Bunny Island, its sole survivor being the Bunny from Beyond. Using "the electrical energy that flowed from his space-ears," he took control of the puppy natives and had them bury the eggs beneath huge carved stone heads. Then he spun himself a cocoon in which to sleep underground until his fellow rabbits could come and get him. But they never came and, centuries later, in our own era, the cocoon is unearthed and the Bunny emerges—intent on conquering Earth-C. Using his electrically charged ears, he's able to turn living creatures to stone, fire destructive blasts, or "ultra-Zap" them into another dimension; however, he is no match for the superheroic rabbit Captain Carrot and the mightly animals of the Zoo Crew. Cocky at first ("If you are the greatest champions your world can offer—it's a wonder your planet hasn't been conquered every second week!"), he is defeated when Captain Carrot slyly ties the villain's ears in a knot and lets him blast himself into another dimension.

Quote: "If you're going to *conquer* a whole planet, you might as well start someplace with a *nice climate*!"

Comment: The Bunny's real name is a parody of *Ralph 124C41+*, a seminal science fiction story written in 1911 by Hugo Gernsback, the father of modern science fiction. Other anthropomorphic foes created by writer Roy Thomas to battle Captain Carrot in this inventive series include the savage Wuz-Wolf, a timid wolf who becomes a lumbering man; the powerful, bionic amphibian Salamandroid; the mighty Armordillo whose "rending claws can tear a tank to shreds in seconds" and whose "nine-banded scales are seemingly invulnerable"; Armordillo's evil employers, the "secret cabal" A.C.R.O.S.T.I.C. (A Corporation Recently Organized Solely To Instigate Crimes), run by the cowled Brother Hood; Dr. Hoot, "the greatest inventive genius of all time," and his towering robot owl; and the swamp beast Mudd, whose "boggy biceps" boast phenomenal strength.

BUSHMAN (C)

First Appearance: 1980, *Moon Knight* #1, Marvel Comics.

Costume: Gold wristbands, necklace; blue earring in right ear, gem set in forehead; lavender tights; blue boots; face has been tattooed white with red fringe. Other apparel varies, the villain usually wearing skimpy vests.

Weapons: Sharp steel teeth; standard firearms.

Chief Henchmen: Marc Spector (until he becomes the superhero Moon Knight); THE MIDNIGHT MAN.

Biography: A terrorist-for-hire, Bushman has his face tattooed "into a mask of death (to) strike total fear into the hearts" of his enemies. While Bushman and his forces are operating just south of Egypt's border, he shoots citizens in cold blood; it is then that aide Spector realizes that he is working for "the wrong side" and lunges at Bushman. For his efforts, Spector is abandoned in the middle of the desert, where, entering the tomb of the moon god Khonshu, he becomes the mighty Moon Knight. Eventually finding Bushman again, the superhero leaves him a bloody heap. But Bushman turns the tables, resurfacing in New York as a powerful crimelord and capturing Moon Knight (#9). Left in a death trap, a brick room rapidly filling with water, Moon Knight is able to work out several of the bricks and escape. Once again beating up Bushman, the superhero hands him over to the police (#10).

Quote: "I'll grant you this much, Spector—you did stop me, but only temporarily, unlike the stop I'm going to put on *you*."

Comment: See other fear-inducing villains DR. SPECTRO, D'SPAYRE, MISTER FEAR, PHOBIA, PSYCHO-MAN, PSYCHO-PIRATE, and SCARECROW (1).

BUTCH CAVENDISH (R, MP, TV)

First Appearance: 1933, *The Lone Ranger,* the Mutual Broadcasting System (originating at WXYZ radio, Detroit).

Weapons: Standard firearms.

Chief Henchmen: The Hole-in-the-Wall Gang.

Biography: Cavendish is the leader of the notorious Hole-in-the-Wall gang, outlaws who prey on ranches, towns, and travelers in Texas circa 1890. The Texas Rangers learn where they're hiding out, and six rangers ride forth under the command of Captain Daniel Reid. Their scout is a man named Collins who, unbeknownst to them, is himself a member of the Hole-in-the-Wall gang. He leads them to an ambush at Bryant's Gap, where all but one ranger, Captain Reid's brother, die. Mortally wounded, Reid's brother is nursed to health by an Indian named Tonto and becomes the crimefighting Lone Ranger. (In some versions of the tale, the noxious Cavendish guns down Collins as well.) One by one, the gangmembers are caught by the Lone Ranger until only Cavendish remains at large. He eludes the Lone Ranger for months, at one point managing to snipe at and kill the Lone Ranger's horse (the hero replaces the steed with the white stallion Silver). The Ranger and Tonto continue after Cavendish, chasing him through seven states before finally capturing the felon after a race along a tortuous trail.

Comment: Jay Michael was the voice of Cavendish on the radio, and Glenn Strange played the part in the 1949 origin story shown on the Lone Ranger TV series. Christopher Lloyd was Cavendish in the 1981 motion picture *The Legend of the Lone Ranger* in which, in addition to ambushing the Rangers, he kidnaps President Ulysses S. Grant.

THE BUTCHER (MP)

First Appearance: 1956, *The Indestructible Man,* Allied Artists.

Biography: A criminal known only as the Butcher is executed in the gas chamber, damning, as he dies, the thugs who had double-crossed him. The body is acquired by Professor Bradshaw, who uses electricity to bring it back to life. The revived Butcher, though mute due to the poison gas, has great strength and can't be harmed by bullets. Escaping from Bradshaw's lab, he makes the Los Angeles sewers his home while he wreaks vengeance on his enemies. In time, he tires of his new life and kills himself by overdosing on electricity at a power plant.

Comment: Lon Chaney, Jr., played the Butcher. A similar role for Chaney had been *Man-Made Monster* (1941), in which he was a carnival sideshow freak known as the Electric Man. Falling into the hands of the real villain of this piece, the evil Dr. Regas (Lionel Atwill, who later played the super villains OTTO VON NEIMANN, THE SCARAB, and SIR ERIC HAZARIAS), the Electric Man is subjected to increasingly larger doses of electricity until he becomes a slavish, death-dealing dynamo.

THE CALCULATOR (C)

First Appearance: 1975, *Detective Comics* #463, DC Comics.

Costume: Purple cowl, bodysuit with ribbed white stripes down legs and along arms, shoulders, and sides of cowl; white gloves, boots, harness on chest containing a computer (see Weapons); red visor worn on forehead (see Weapons).

Weapons: Computer on chest enables him to do quick calculations regarding the movements of adversaries; once the actions of a superhero have been catalogued, the Calculator is able to avoid capture by them in the future. He also wears a visor on his cowl, which is tied to the computer and allows the Calculator to coalesce airborne dust into a variety of controllable objects, such as giant fists, anti-gravity discs for his feet which allow him to fly, and other objects.

Biography: Nothing is known about this super villain before he appeared on the criminal scene. Committing crimes to draw out local superheroes, he permitted himself to be captured so that he could catalogue each modus operandi on his computer. He has battled a rash of heroes, including the Atom, Batman, Black Canary, Elongated Man, Green Arrow, and Hawkman. His most recent battle was with the Blue Beetle (*Blue Beetle* #8, 1987). He was defeated when the superhero managed to pull off the Calculator's chest-computer.

Comment: POWER RING, a member of THE CRIME SYNDICATE OF AMERICA, can also create any object he wishes, as can Atom-Master of THE FORGOTTEN VILLAINS.

CALENDAR MAN (C)

Real Name: Julian Day.

First Appearance: 1958, *Detective Comics* #259, DC Comics.

Costume: Red bodyshirt, gloves, boots, cowl with calendar on forehead; white wristbands, tights with red stripe down front of each leg, belt covered with black numbers; cape consisting of white calendar pages, one red day on each, strung together like scales.

Biography: As Calendar Man, Day bases his criminal acts on the seasons (cold for winter, water for the "rainy season," etc.). Traveling the country and doing shows as Maharajah the Magician, Day uses the cover to commit crimes in whatever city he happens to be. Arriving in Gotham City, his days have been numbered, on several occasions, by Batman.

CALLISTO (C)

First Appearance: 1983, *The X-Men* #169, Marvel Comics.

Costume: Purple vest, boots, skintight pants; tattered orange shirt; patch worn over right eye.

Weapons: Switchblade.

Chief Henchmen: The Morlocks, mutants with a variety of powers. Her principal aide is Caliban, a white-skinned man who can sense the presence of other mutants miles away.

Biography: Virtually nothing is known about this character's past. At some point in her early youth, she lost her right eye and acquired a long scar under the other eye; that, plus the fact that she was a mutant with superhuman senses, made her feel like a leper. Resolved to leave society, she found catacombs beneath Manhattan—a maze of tunnels secretly built by the government during the 1950s, for use in the event of atomic warfare. Dubbing these the "Alley," Callisto took up residence. She also found another mutant, Caliban and, through him, located other mutants; these other misfits became her Morlocks (named after the subterranean mutants in H.G. Wells 1895 novel *The Time Machine*). Using them as her personal army, Callisto has waged a private war against those well-adjusted, relatively happy mutants, the X-Men.

Comment: In Greek mythology, Callisto was a woman who was transformed into a wolf for having fed the gods human flesh.

CAPTAIN AXIS (C)

Real Name: Otto Kronsteig.

First Appearance: 1972, *The Incredible Hulk* #155, Marvel Comics.

Costume: Red trunks, bodysuit with white swastika in a black circle on chest; navy blue boots; silver wristbands (tights are blue on cover).

Chief Henchmen: Various soldiers.

Biography: A scientist in the service of the Führer in the Second World War, Kronsteig fled Germany to avoid the war crimes commission. Settling in Latveria, he went to work for that nation's leader, DR. DOOM. Inventing a reduction ray, he was its first unwilling subject; Kronsteig quickly "shrunk through universes hidden within molecules, within atoms," until he reached a subatomic world which was being toyed with by the Shaper, "he who makes dreams live" (see Comment). Reading Kronsteig's mind, he finds World War Two amusing and recreates its combatants on a microscopic world. However, in this version Kronsteig is himself the Führer, and the Nazis sweep through the United States. Enter the Hulk, who has been shrunk due to exposure to a serum invented by scientist Henry Pym, aka the superhero Ant-Man. The Hulk begins trashing the Nazi armies, which annoys the Shaper, who resents the outside interference. To this end, he searches Kronsteig's mind and finds "an experiment cut short by your war's end—to produce, through genetic-surgery, a Nazi super-being." The Shaper turns Kronsteig into just such a muscular brute, whom the Hulk slams around like so much pizza dough; disgusted, the Shaper abandons the subatomic world. When last seen, Kronsteig had reverted to his old form and was stranded on the microscopic orb.

Quote: "I am . . . the *answer* to the *Captain Americas*, the *Sub-Mariners*, who dared to fight *against* us—*and I can CRUSH the Hulk*!"

Comment: The Shaper is an artificial being created by the alien Skrulls (see SUPER-SKRULL). It was originally known as the Cosmic Cube (see THE RED SKULL, Weapons), a device created to make real the wishes of the bearer. Eventually, the cube evolved into an entity which had a Skrull-like torso atop a cube on tank-type treads. The sentient cube then roamed the uinverse transforming worlds into planets which had existed only in the minds of other creatures. As long as the doings on these worlds amuse him, the Shaper allows them to survive. After that, they are restored (save for those inhabitants who perished in the course of the reshaping). See other Nazi super villains BARON BLITZKRIEG, BARON GESTAPO, BARON ZEMO, CAPTAIN NAZI, THE CLOWN, THE GOLDEN FUHRER, KILLER SHARK, NIGHT AND FOG, The Masked Swastika of VENDETTA, Mastermind (see U-MAN, Comment), THE RED PANZER, THE RED SKULL, and ZYKLON.

CAPTAIN BOOMERANG (C)

Real Name: George "Digger" Harkness.

First Appearance: 1960, *The Flash* #117, DC Comics.

Costume: Black tights, gloves; blue boots with black back; blue peaked cap with white boomerang on front; blue jacket covered with white boomerangs; white scarf, belt.

Weapons: Countless trick boomerangs, including those that explode; that double as grapnels; create deafening sounds; are large enough to have people strapped to them and rocket powered so they can be launched into space (the "Doomerang"); expand (so the villain can grab on and make getaways); grab things via pincers while in flight; work on a delayed-reaction principal, returning several minutes after they are thrown (in case Captain Boomerang has gotten himself into trouble); deliver a potent shock ("electro-boomerangs"); tie people up ("lasso-boomerangs"); slice through metal; release smokescreens; split into twin boomerangs which come at an adversary from opposite sides; collapse for easy storage; and even a giant model that, thanks to microtechnics, allows a person sitting inside to travel through time.

Biography: When W.W. Wiggins of the Wiggins Game Company decides that the boomerang has the potential to be "the coming craze," he decides to make everyone in the country "boomerang-conscious" by hiring an expert to go around promoting them. Enter criminal Harkness, who reads about the search while holed-up "in a cheap hotel room." Because of the years he spent "in the Australian bush—hiding out from the law," boomerangs are second-nature to him. Introducing himself to Wiggins as George Green, he gets the job and a flashy costume to go with it. Using boomerangs to commit crimes wherever he goes (for example, flinging through jewelry-store windows to snatch up goods), he eventually crosses paths with the superheroic Flash, who survives his Doomerang by vibrating quickly enough to burn through the restraining ropes (in another tale, the crimebusting Batman gets off the deadly boomerang by working his bonds down toward the rocket exhaust). The super-speedster brings Captain Boomerang to justice, though the villain returns frequently to battle the hero. (Indeed, he has outlived the Flash, who perished in 1985.) The fiend belongs to THE SECRET SOCIETY OF SUPER-VILLAINS.

Quote: "No one crosses 'Digger' Harkess—and gets away with it *intact*!"

CAPTAIN COLD (C)

Real Name: Leonard Snart.

First Appearance: 1957, *Showcase* #8, DC Comics.

Costume: Blue goggles, snowsuit with white icicle motif on shoulders, white hood; white gloves, boots, both with furred cuff; yellow holster.

Weapons: Coldgun which fires blasts that freeze people solid; the gun can also whip up protective barriers for the villain, as well as create incredibly realistic illusions from ice—i.e., a marauding polar bear. (As the Flash explains, "Just as intense heat can cause a mirage to appear—Captain Cold has managed to produce the same results with absolute zero.")

Biography: A small-time crook wishing to go on a crime wave in Central City, Snart realizes that he must first nullify the city's protector, the Flash. Hoping to find a superweapon capable of defeating the hero, Snart breaks into a nuclear research laboratory, where he inadvertently starts up the cyclotron; its radiation strikes Snart's gun, turning it into an ice pistol (see Weapons). Creating a costume and becoming Captain Cold, Snart relies on his Coldgun to deal with the Flash whenever they meet. Leonard's sister, Lisa Snart, is another of Flash's foes, the nefarious GOLDEN GLIDER; the Captain himself belongs to THE SECRET SOCIETY OF SUPER-VILLAINS.

Comment: For similar super villains see BLIZZARD, Coldsnap of MASTERS OF DISASTER, KILLER FROST, and MR. FREEZE.

CAPTAIN HOOK (S, L, MP)

Real Name: James Hook.

First Appearance: 1904, *Peter Pan or the Boy Who Wouldn't Grow Up*, Sir James Matthew Barrie.

Weapons: Iron hook instead of right hand; a "terrible sword (which) severed in twain any man . . . who obstructed it."

Biography: Hook was a pirate who lived in a harbor on the southwest corner of Never Never Land. At an unspecified time in the past, Hook fought the heroic Peter Pan who lopped off his right hand and flung it to a passing crocodile. The animal liked the taste so much that she yearned to eat the rest of Hook; fortunately for Hook, the carnivore swallowed a clock, the ticking of which announced its coming. During a second battle with Pan, Hook received a kick from the airborne boy and plunged into the waiting mouth of the crocodile. Hook's skin was swarthy and, overall, he was "cadaverous and blackavized," has

***CAPTAIN HOOK** (Ernest Torrence) tries to persuade the crocodile to swallow a clock in the 1924 Famous Players-Lasky production of* Peter Pan. *© Paramount Pictures.*

eyes "the blue of the forget-me-not," his hair black and "dressed in long curls." He spoke with an "elegance of . . . diction" in "a black voice." Though he felt his hook was worth "a score" of hands, he was steeped in melancholy while governing his pirate crew—except when he was "plunging his hook into you," at which time "two red spots" appear in his eyes. His favorite pastime was kidnapping people and forcing them to walk the plank. In his leisure moments, Hook was fond of cigars and used a special holder which allowed him to smoke two cigars at once.

Quote: "It liked my arm so much, Smee, that it has followed me ever since. I want no such compliments."

Comment: In the original play, Hook escaped and became a schoolmaster in Kensington Gardens; in the later novel Never Never Land became Neverland. Hook has been played by various actors, on stage and screen. The first was Gerald du Maurier in the play's 1904 London debut at the Duke of York's Theatre. Ernest Lawford took the part when the play opened in New York at the Empire Theater the following year. The play was not published until 1928, though Barrie's novelization, *Peter and Wendy*, had appeared in 1911. Other notable stage Hooks include Charles Laughton, Alistair Sim, and Cyril Ritchard. Ernest Torrence played the part in the 1924 film version, and Hans Conreid was the voice in Walt Disney's 1953 animated cartoon. Ritchard repeated his stage role in 1955 in the TV musical version of the play.

CAPTAIN MEPHISTO (MP)

Real Name: Frederick Braley.

First Appearance: 1945, *Manhunt of Mystery Island*, Republic Pictures.

Costume: Dark vest, trousers, gloves, all with light embroidery around edges; pirate's hat, bandana beneath; bell-sleeve shirt with laced-up front.

Weapons: Rapier, dagger, pistol, Transformation Chair which allows Braley to metamorphose into Mephisto by altering the molecular structure of his blood.

Biography: In the mid-eighteenth century, the pirate Captain Mephisto ruled Mystery Island in the Pacific. Today, replete with a stately mansion—and, behind a hinged painting, Mephisto's old lair—the island is jointly owned by his descendants Frederick Braley, Paul Melton, Edward Armstrong, and Professor Hargraves. Building a "Radiatomic Power Transmitter," noted scientist Professor Forrest disappears while looking for radium on the island; he has been captured by Braley who, using the Transformation Chair to become the spitting image of his ancestor, wants the power transmitter so he can conquer the world. Mephisto's sadism knows no end. Not only does he greedily murder the co-owners of the island but also, when Forrest's daughter Claire and rugged sleuth Lance Reardon come looking for the professor with a radium detector, Mephisto has the radium removed from the transmitter and placed in a cave—which he promptly floods. When the pair escapes, he traps them on a rope bridge and cuts the supports. In the end, Mephisto nearly succeeds in committing the perfect crime: he knocks Lance insensate and makes ready to turn him into a Mephisto clone in the Transformation Chair. That way, he can escape with the power transmitter while Lance takes the rap. But Claire tracks them down and shoots the villain dead.

Comment: Roy Barcroft (THE PURPLE MONSTER, RETIK) starred as Mephisto, Harry Strang as Braley in this 15-chapter serial. Note the similarity of the two key bits of action—the flooded labyrinth and the rope bridge—with *Indiana Jones and the Temple of Doom* (1984).

CAPTAIN NAZI (C)

Real Name: Albrecht Krieger.

First Appearance: 1941, *Master Comics* #21, Fawcett Publications.

Costume: Light green tights with white stripe down sides; green leotard with black circle on chest and white swastika inside; red boots, gloves, cape (in all but his first few adventures); yellow belt, epaulets.

Weapons: "Flying gas" which enables the super villain to fly, though for how long depends on the amount inhaled; radio in his belt.

Chief Henchmen: Numerous Nazi aides.

Biography: Developing a remarkable "Miracle Food," German Siegmund Krieger fed it to his son Albrecht. The youth grew up to be enormously powerful, nimble, and intelligent (though not entirely impervious, receiving a nasty scar on his face during a fencing match at school in Heidelberg). When Hitler became Germany's ruler, Siegmund proudly brought his son to the Fuhrer; deeming him the perfect Aryan and dubbing him Captain Nazi, Hitler sent Albrecht to the United States to keep the Allied superhero Captain Marvel off his back. Ironically, the German fiend was responsible for the birth of one of his most dogged foes. Among Captain Nazi's first victims in the United States was young Freddy Freeman, whose back he broke. Found by Captain Marvel, the boy was brought to the wizard Shazam, who had given Marvel his powers; the benevolent sorcerer bestowed the same abilities on Freddy, who became Captain Marvel, Jr., and more than once helped to defeat the Axis felon. Early in his criminal career Nazi

*The evil **CAPTAIN NAZI**. © Fawcett Publications.*

obtained his Flying Gas, a concoction stolen from a murdered French scientist. This made him a more formidable foe, though he was still unable to defeat the Marvels. When the superheroes were put into suspended animation in 1953 by DR. SIVANA, Captain Nazi also went to sleep so he could continue to battle them when they awoke. All were revived in 1972. Though the Reich has long-since fallen, Captain Nazi remains at large; he was briefly a member of THE MONSTER SOCIETY OF EVIL.

Quote: "Herr Hitler, I haff killed an old man and crippled a little boy . . . it iss so eassy beating these Yankee pigs."

Comment: Another Marvel foe was Captain Nippon, the snarling Japanese counterpart of Captain Nazi. See other Nazi super villains BARON BLITZKRIEG, BARON GESTAPO, BARON ZEMO, CAPTAIN AXIS, THE CLOWN, THE GOLDEN FUHRER, KILLER SHARK, NIGHT AND FOG, The Masked Swastika of VENDETTA, Mastermind (see U-MAN, Comment), THE RED PANZER, THE RED SKULL, and ZYKLON.

CAPTAIN NEMO (N, MP, TV)

Real Name: Prince Dakkar.

First Appearance: 1869, *Twenty Thousand Leagues Under the Sea*, Jules Verne.

Weapons: The *Nautilus*, an electrically powered submarine which is "very much like a cigar in shape." It is 232 feet long and 26 feet wide; has an area of 6,032 square feet; consists of two steel hulls one inside the other; and is steered horizontally by a rudder, vertically by "two inclined planes fastened to its sides." The *Nautilus* can easily sink any surface ship it rams (cutting through "like a needle through sailcloth"); the outer hull is electrified to keep people from boarding while the vessel is in drydock. The submarine's crew is armed with diving suits and powerful airguns for underwater work.

Biography: Dakkar is a "terrible avenger, a perfect archangel of hatred." Born in 1818, Dakkar is the son of the rajah of the independent territory of Bundelkund. At the age of 10 Dakkar was sent to Europe to be educated; he returned 20 years later, marrying "a noble Indian lady" and fathering two children. In 1857 he became embroiled in the Sepoy Mutiny, struggling to keep the British Crown from gaining more power in his country. When the revolt was crushed and the rajahs subjugated, Dakkar fled, to plot his vengeance. Using what remained of his wealth, he set up shop on a secret desert island in the Pacific where he drew upon his vast scientific knowledge to construct the *Nautilus*. He then devoted his life to roaming the world and destroying the tools of war. Unfortunately, he destroyed countless innocent people along with them, attributing their deaths to the price of doing business. Though he was sought by various navies, who presume his submarine to be a sea serpent, it was nature which finally stopped Nemo on June 22, 1867. While sailing off the coast of Norway, between the isles of Ferroe and Loffoden, the ship was crippled by a whirlpool and dragged down. However, as is revealed in the sequel *Mysterious Island*, the *Nautilus* wasn't destroyed but managed to limp to Lincoln Island in the South Pacific. There, the now-

CAPTAIN NEMO *(James Mason) from* 20,000 Leagues Under the Sea. *Courtesy Bill Latham. © Walt Disney Productions.*

60-year-old Nemo was stranded when volcanic activity caused basalt to rise and trap the craft. When a group of refugees from a Confederate prison were stranded by balloon on the island, Nemo helped them to survive. Late in December of 1868 Nemo muttered "God and my country!" and perished; the castaways sank the submarine, a fitting tomb, then escaped in a boat they had built. Tall, with a large forehead, black eyes, a straight nose, and a "clearly cut mouth," Nemo spoke fluent French, English, German, and Latin. At the time of his death Nemo was enormously rich, having collected sunken treasures from the ocean floor ("I could, without missing it, pay the national debt of France," he boasts, and not idly; one chest alone in his saloon contains nearly £200,000).

Quote: "The earth does not want new continents, but new men."

Comment: *Mysterious Island* was first published in 1871. There have been many screen versions of *Twenty Thousand Leagues Under the Sea*, commencing with a silent film version of 1907. Lionel Barrymore played "Dakkar" in the early Technicolor film *Mysterious Island* (1929), but Verne's story was badly mangled. This time out the villain was a noble named Falon (Montagu Love) who tried to force the inventor and his sister Sonia (!) to use their twin submarines to help him regain his throne. Leonard Penn played the part in *Mysterious Island*, a 1951 serial (see RULU). However, the most famous Nemo is James Mason, who starred in the faithful 1954 Walt Disney classic *Twenty Thousand Leagues Under the Sea*. Other fine Nemos include Herbert Lom in *Mysterious Island* (1960); Robert Ryan in *Captain Nemo and the Underwater City* (1969), in which the madman tries to establish a society on the ocean floor; Omar Sharif in *The Mysterious Island* (1973), a retelling of *Mysterious Island* with Nemo now an Arab and using atomic power rather than electricity in his submarine; and Jose Ferrer in a short-lived TV series, *Twenty Thousand Leagues Under the Sea* (1978). While it can be argued that what Captain Nemo did was for a noble cause, one character accurately summed up his criminality by declaring, "Whatever he had suffered . . . he had no right to punish (people) thus." See other underwater super villains ATTUMA, BLACK MANTA, CAPTAIN WHALE, DR. FANG, FISHERMAN, KILLER SHARK, KRANG, MR. CRABB, OCEAN MASTER, ORKA, PIRANHA, and TIGER SHARK (2).

CAPTAIN RAMESES (MP)

First Appearance: 1978, *Starship Invasions*, Warner Bros.

Costume: Black bodysuit, inverted-pyramid hat.

Weapons: Spaceship; telepathic control; robot deactivator wrist unit to foil Galactic League of Races androids.

Biography: Rameses is the commander of the Legion of the Winged Serpent, a force from another planet. His world threatened because of the instability of his solar system, Rameses comes to earth intending to eliminate humankind and transplant his race onto our world. However, he immediately runs afoul of Commander Zhendor of the Galactic League of Races. Based in the Alien Galactic Center, a pyramid built under the Atlantic Ocean in the Bermuda Triangle, the Galactic League makes sure that no harm befalls humankind from extraterrestrial sources—an objective contrary to Rameses' intentions. Waging war on Zhendor's forces, Rameses takes over the League base and, from an orbiting spaceship, telepathically convinces humans the world over to commit suicide. But his reign of telepathic terror is short-lived as a fleet of League UFOs arrives and destroys the forces of the Legion of the Winged Serpent.

Comment: Christopher Lee played the part of Rameses. Rameses, of course, was the name of the pharaoh with whom Moses struggled in the Old Testament. Lee also played DRACULA and SCARAMANGA.

CAPTAIN WHALE (C)

First Appearance: 1966, *Nukla* #3, Dell Publishing.

Costume: Blue T-shirt; brown trousers; brown cap with white whale emblem.

Weapons: Killer Whale, a submarine which fires explosive harpoons, mesh harpoons to snare intruders, artillery laden with "steel spaghettie" to tangle aircraft propellers, and a "sonar device" which enables him to command killer whales.

Chief Henchmen: Toljek and others; Whale has many aides, most of whom wear blue T-shirts with a black whale emblem inside a white circle on the chest.

Biography: Whale has built a city thousands of feet beneath the ice of the South Pole, a domed colony housing his henchmen and their families. Stealing a Russian bomber, he intends to provoke World War III, then repopulate the world with his subjects. The superhero Nukla infiltrates Whale's domain and destroys the ship on its bombing run; the evil Captain plunges into the icy waters and is consumed by his own whales.

Quote: "When the holocaust is over, we can return to the surface . . . and begin a *new world! Mine!*

Comment: This was the character's only appearance. Other villains in Nukla's four-issue run were the Evil Prince and the Mad Baron (Baron von Zee). See other underwater super villains ATTUMA, BLACK MANTA, CAPTAIN NEMO, DR. FANG, FISHERMAN, KILLER SHARK, KRANG, MR. CRABB, OCEAN MASTER, ORKA, PIRANHA, and TIGER SHARK (2).

CARL ZOLG (M)

First Appearance: July 1939, "Merchants of Disaster," *Doc Savage* Magazine, Kenneth Robeson.

Weapons: An oxygen destroyer which causes "weird fireworks" in the air, then kills everyone within its wide range; a "huge bowled" pipe which, apart from tobacco, contains pure air to protect him from the oxygen destroyer; "tri-pronged" torture device: prongs were placed on the belly and sides of the waist, then driven in slowly with a master screw.

Biography: A science teacher, Zolg is the half-brother of chemist Paul Payne. Learning that Payne has invented the oxygen destroyer, Zolg partners with the "black-eyed" Leon Spardoso and sadistic Grant Holst. They kidnap Payne to get the formula for his oxygen destroyer, which they plan to sell to the highest-bidding nation. To demonstrate the power of their device they murder a hobo and 200 soldiers; they also kill a troublesome patent attorney who worked with Payne, and a crowd of G-Men who are on their trail. The superhero Doc Savage eventually tracks the conspirators to their lair, Holst being shot through the heart but Zolg and Spardoso escaping through a manhole. Unknown to Zolg, however, the bullet that killed Holst had grazed his pipe first, cracking it; he dies when he uses the pipe to release the oxygen destroyer in a (successful) effort to murder Spardoso, who was going to doublecross him. Zolg dressed "with dangling black coat tails" and a brown derby; his "complexion was pasty, his eyes pale and watery."

Quote: "We had to kill a lot to put this thing over."

THE CAT GIRL

First Appearance: 1960, *The Fly* (later, *Fly Man*) #9, Archie Comics.

Costume: Orange bodysuit with tail.

Weapons: Metal claws.

Biography: In reality, the Cat Girl is "the Sphinx, the original model for the countless ancient statues." An immortal, her job is to serve as the "defender of the animal world against the human world." Sallying forth from her cave, she begins liberating wild cats from their caves; she stops only when the superhero the Fly begins trapping them again, often painfully. (One luckless tiger jumps at the Fly, who grabs a manhole cover to use as a shield. The animal falls limp with a resounding BRRONNGGG!) The Cat Girl is impervious to weapons and cannot be suffocated.

Quote: "You saw what my steel-like claws did to your gunbelt. Cry for help and I'll slash your face to ribbons."

CAT-MAN (C)

Real Name: Thomas Blake.

First Appearance: 1963, *Detective Comics* #311, DC Comics.

Costume: Yellow bodysuit with orange "CM" on chest (later, "M" inside "C"); orange cape, gloves, boots, trunks, belt cowl with cat-ears. (See Weapons.)

Weapons: Costume is made from cloth that once swathed an idol "from a small Pacific island where the natives worship cats!" As a result, the flame-proof cloth gives nine lives to anyone who wears it. Other weapons include the Cat-car, a one-person sportscar complete with a metal tail poking up from the trunk and springs behind the real wheels which enable the car to make "cat-like leaps"; claws on boots; catarang, a razor-edged boomerang; a super-swift catamaran; and a cat-clawed grapple with line.

Biography: A former big-game trapper, Blake turned to crime both for the money and the challenge. Taking his inspiration from CATWOMAN, he made a catlike costume from enchanted cloth, which he'd obtained in Africa, and became Cat-Man. He has crossed claws frequently with the superhero Batman; to date, their most dramatic encounter occurred on Blake's private Greek island, where he was knocked "into the mouth of a scalding-hot geyser hole" and the right side of his face was badly scarred. Like most cats, Cat-Man hates water; he also has some degree of mental control over all felines, presumably due to his costume.

Quote: "Tell *Batman* that even though my boat exploded when it hit a buoy, I managed to survive that *cat*astrophe."

Comment: In *Detective Comics* #318, the heroic Batwoman briefly posed as the villain's sidekick Cat-Woman in order to snare him. As such, she wore a leotard that was green on the top and orange below the orange belt; green tights, and an orange cape, cowl, boots, and gloves.

CATWOMAN (C, TV, MP, N)

Real Name: Selina Kyle.

First Appearance: 1940, *Batman* #1, DC Comics.

Costume: Lavender bodyshirt, skirt, cat-eared cowl; blue boots, belt; green cape. During the early 1970s, she wore a navy blue leotard with a tail and long gloves; a red mask; light blue tights; and navy blue boots with red cuffs on top. (Note: Costume was adopted in *Batman* #3; costume on TV show and in the *Batman* movie was simply a navy blue bodysuit and cat-ears.)

Weapons: Cat-o'-nine-tails; Cat-plane; Kitty-car; Cat-boat; claws worn on the ends of her fingers; bulb filled with catnip which causes humans to sneeze.

Chief Henchmen: Diablo, a pet panther; Hecate, a pet cat; various, nameless human thugs.

Biography: Working as a stewardess for Speed Airlines, Selina is the sole survivor of a crash, thrown clear when a door tore open. Stumbling from the wreckage, she has almost complete amnesia, with only "vague recollections . . . of a *pet shop* my father owned—*cats!*" Becoming a thief know as the Cat, she soon adopts a flamboyant costume and an equally flamboyant monicker: Catwoman! Her only rule is never to kill or allow killing in any of her crimes. Catwoman's one weakness is her love for Batman, the hero sworn to bring her to justice; her passions are divided somewhat when she falls for Bruce Wayne, the multimillionaire philanthropist who is secretly Batman. Though he's aware of who Catwoman is, Wayne allows himself to love her in his non-heroic identity. Eventually, Selina gives up her criminal life and, bored with retirement, undertakes a career as a superhero. However, her new leaf quickly withers: Catwoman is abducted by Batman's enemy THE JOKER, who has her brainwashed into becoming a criminal once again. The brainwashing was performed by the evil physician Dr. Moon.

Quote: "My claws are steel-tipped . . . razor-sharp.I could cut your throat . . . "

Comment: Until 1986, when DC "simplified" their character line with a massive over-haul in the 12-issue series *Crisis on Infinite Earths*, there were actually two Catwomen: one on Earth-One, in our dimension, and another on Earth-Two, in an adjoining dimension. The adventures of Catwoman which took place prior to *Detective Comics* #369 (1967) were said to be those of the Earth-Two villain; the later stories took place on Earth-One. This being the case, DC found itself with two characters and concocted revisionist origins for them both. The Catwoman of Earth-Two was an abused wife who divorced her husband, then went back to his mansion and robbed him. Excited by the crime, she pursued a career outside the law as the Cat and then as the Catwoman, for the reasons described in Biography. (The amnesia story cited above was described as a lie. Once she'd decided to go straight, Selina made it up in order to explain away her criminal tendencies.) In time, Selina married Bruce Wayne and had a daughter, Helena; Batman went into semi-retirement. However, Catwoman was forced to return to crime when Cernak, a former gangmember, threatened to blackmail her with evidence that she'd once committed murder, evidence which Selina didn't realize was fake. Batman sallied forth and stopped the crime, Selina perishing in the process; overcome with grief, Batman retired and Helena became the superheroic Huntress (who was herself killed during the aforementioned Crisis; she is unrelated to the villainous HUNTRESS). Meanwhile, over on Earth-One, Selina grew up (with her brother Karl) in the pet shop but turned to crime simply because she was bored. Thereafter, her story parallels the one told in Biography. Julie Newmar played the character in the 1966-68 TV series *Batman* (save for a brief period during the last season when Eartha Kitt took over); Lee Meriwether played the role in the 1966 feature film *Batman*. Catwoman was also featured in Winston Lyon's 1966 Signet novel *Batman vs. the Three Villains of Doom*, and had a short-lived series of her own crimebusting adventures beginning in *Batman* #332 (1981). MADAM MASQUE is another villain who was in love with her superheroic foe.

CENTURIUS (C)

Real Name: Dr. Noah Black

First Appearance: 1968, *Nick Fury, Agent of S.H.I.E.L.D.* #2, Marvel Comics.

Costume: Silver armor bodysuit, belt, cylindrical collar which covers lower face; red breastplate, trunks, gloves, boots, helmet with silver mask and fin on top.

Weapons: Evolutionizer, to accelerate evolution; "hydro-capsule" for imprisoning people; "thermalic suppression beam," a non-mechanical elevator beam; astral projector, which creates the illusion that Valhalla is an inhospitable volcanic island; "T-Viewer" to watch the goings-on beyond the huge laboratory complex; a "land mine activator" to destroy anyone who *does* land there; and a spaceship known as the Automated Rebirth Colonizer (ARC), which will not only sustain life onboard for a century, but can also rain enough "radioactive fire" on the earth to kill every living thing.

Chief Henchmen: Various monsters and insect-like humanoid "arms-men."

Biography: A Nobel Prize winner in the 1930s, Dr. Black soon thereafter vanished from sight, angry at having been "censured for his ideas" about the origin of life: specifically, that it "evolved from internuclear space." Black believed that each atom was "a subminature solar system" and, to prove his point, moved to the Pacific island he dubs Valhalla to conduct research. There, he developed the Evolutionizer (among his other weapons) and used it not only to keep himself young, but also to speed up the evolution taking place in a single drop of water. This produced "hundreds of life forms," which he painstakingly placed onboard the ARC. Soon after its launch, the ARC was to act upon his long-simmering hatred of humankind: It will spew radiation on the earth for 40 days and nights (note the scientist's first name), killing everyone; a century later, it will land and the life onboard will inherit the earth. However, the heroic Nick Fury of S.H.I.E.L.D. (Supreme Headquarters International Espionage Law-enforcement Division) went to the island to try and stop him. During their struggle, equipment was damaged and the ARC fell from orbit. Fury escaped minutes before "the hellborn comet of doom" dropped on Valhalla and caused the atoll to explode. Centurius survived by jumping into his Evolutionizer and reverting to "a handful of protoplasmic slime." Escaping, he was last seen battling the superheroic Hulk (1978, *Rampaging Hulk* #8).

Quote: "As my *parable of doom* strikes from the heavens, so will it also give this planet a *second chance* for regeneration!"

THE CHAMELEON (C)

First Appearance: 1963, *The Amazing Spider-Man* #1, Marvel Comics.

Costume: White full-head mask; long white vest (see Weapons).

Weapons: "Multi-pocket disguise vest" which contains the villain's makeup materials as well as smoke pellets to conceal his getaways and, to make sure he's above suspicion, another "special chemical gas" to instantly change the color of his clothes.

Chief Henchmen: Pee-wee, Rocky, Nails, others. (Their only appearance is in *Tales of Suspense* #58.)

Biography: A master of disguise—and a native of some unspecified foreign country—the Chameleon explodes upon the criminal scene by stealing missile defense plans, framing the heroic Spider-Man, and trying to peddle the secrets to the Communists. Arrested as a spy and deported, he lives abroad until he is able to return "to resume my crime career." Among his activities is selling hides and tusks collected by KRAVEN THE HUNTER; it is the Chameleon, in fact, who starts Kraven on his own criminal career by bringing the African hunter to New York to pursue Spider-Man.

Quote: "*Hah!* Nothing can stop the *Chameleon!* With the right disguise, I can steal anything from anywhere, unchallenged!"

Comment: The Chameleon is a minor super villain in the Spider-Man pantheon.

CHARLES EVANS (TV, N)

First Appearance: September 15, 1966, "Charlie X," *Star Trek*, NBC-TV.

Biography: Only three years old, Charles Evans is the sole survivor of an expedition which crashed on the planet Thasus during the twenty-third century. There, for the next 14 years, he is reared by the non-corporeal Thasians, who grant him extraordinary psionic powers to enable him to survive. Without the Thasians realizing it, Charlie is rescued by the starship *Antares*, then transferred to the *Enterprise*; while Captain Ramart is trying to warn the *Enterprise*'s Captain Kirk of Charlie's powers, the youth destroys the *Antares*. Charlie proceeds to order crewmembers about, in one case "sending away" to limbo a woman who refuses his romantic advances. Deciding that he wants to rule a world, Charlie orders Kirk to take him to Colony 5, the nearest inhabited world. By this time, however, the Thasians realize that Charlie is gone and bring him back to their world, restoring everything he has damaged.

Quote: "What you did wasn't nice . . . if you try to hurt me again, I'll make a lot of other people go away."

Comment: Robert Walker, Jr., played the part in the character's only appearance; Gene Roddenberry wrote the story, D.C. Fontana the teleplay. The tale was adapted by James Blish as the short story "Charlie's Law" and collected in the anthology *Star Trek 1*.

CHARUN (MY)

Weapons: A huge hammer and/or sword which he uses to torment souls.

Biography: Only vaguely associated with the Greek Charon, ferryman of the underworld, Charun is a truly sadistic figure in Etruscan mythology. A demon in the service of Mantus and Mania, the king and queen of the Etruscan underworld, Charun is an aged creature with fiery eyes and a disheveled appearance. His hide is thick and black, he has elephantine ears and tusks, and he sports a pair of wings. He is never without snakes twined around his head and/or arm. Wandering the earth, he watches with glee as people die by natural causes or violence; making them mount horses who travel with him, he leads them to the underworld. There, he tortures them with his sword and hammer, assisted by lesser demons. In some tales Charun and not Mantus is the king of the netherworld.

Comment: Other nefarious figures in Etruscan mythology are the spirit Vanth, who encourages those on the verge of committing a violent act; Kulmu, who cuts the thread of life and guards the gates of the underworld; and Nathuns, a male fury who resembles Charun and works as a cheerleader to stir the other demons into action.

CHEETAH (C)

Real Name: Priscilla Rich; Deborah Domaine; Barbara Ann Minerva.

First Appearance: 1943, *Wonder Woman* #6 (as Priscilla); 1980, #274 (as Deborah), DC Comics.

Costume: Bodysuit, clawed slippers and gloves, cowl with cheetah-like ears (Deborah wore only the ears), tail—all yellow with brown spots.

Weapons: Cheetah's claws are able to cut through virtually any substance.

Biography: An extremely wealthy debutante, Priscilla hosts a charity affair and grows wildly envious of Wonder Woman, who attracts more attention than she does. Coming up with her own alter ego, she becomes the Cheetah and vows to do-in Wonder Woman. Though she gives it her all over the years, Cheetah never quite manages to pull it off. After spending time on Reform Island, run by Wonder Woman's people, the Amazons, Priscilla gives up her criminal ways. Meanwhile, her niece Debbi has used *her* wealth to aide various ecological groups, most notably the Organization for Ecological Sanity. On her deathbed, Priscilla calls Debbi to her side; though the older woman perishes before she can reveal her secret, Debbi bumps into a closet and the door opens, a mannequin dressed in the Cheetah costume falling from within. The mannequin knocks her unconscious, though not before she sees the super villain KOBRA approaching. When she awakens, she learns that Kobra had intended to hire her aunt to work for him. Now he intends to make-do with the niece. Binding her and forcing her to watch scenes of pollution, he simultaneously subjects her to jolts of electricity. Debbi goes mad, ready to avenge nature as one of its own—the Cheetah. Kobra sends her out against Wonder Woman, but she and the serpentine fiend are defeated. The insane Cheetah joins THE SECRET SOCIETY OF SUPER-VILLAINS, but her stay there is also brief; she is presently living in a nice room at the Arkham Asylum.

Comment: When Wonder Woman's comic was revised in 1986, the Cheetah was also changed. An archaeologist, Barbara Ann Minerva, unearthed herbs which were once cultivated by a race of catlike people. Brewing them as a potion, she drinks the concoction and becomes the Cheetah. She looks like the other Cheetahs with one exception: she doesn't wear a costume. Her flesh is orange with black spots; she also has a tail and claws, along with superhuman reflexes and senses.

CHEMO (C)

First Appearance: 1962, *Showcase* #39, DC Comics.

Costume: None; Chemo is a humanoid made of translucent "elastic plastic" filled with green and pink sputtering chemicals.

Biography: Undertaking an ambitious program to "find a combination of chemicals . . . to conquer disease . . . famine . . . all the ills of mankind," Professor Ramsey Norton suffered countless failures. Each time he would pour the unsuccessful concoction into a circa 10-foot-tall test tube he'd built in humanoid form to "remind me of my failures . . . a ruthless antagonist I have to triumph over." And because the test tube was "a well of chemicals," Norton dubbed him Chemo. One day—ironically, right before Norton planned to empty the filled container—the figure doubled its size and came to life. Worse, it was able to expectorate a variety of lethal chemical compounds, sprays which caused living tissue to grow, could burn through steel or fuse sand into glass, freeze objects, rust metal, and allow Chemo to increase its own size nearly tenfold from its original modest height.

*The imposing **CHEMO** dismantles the Metal Men. © DC Comics.*

Lumbering from the lab with no purpose other than to destroy, it was confronted by the superheroic robots known as the Metal Men. In their first encounter, they were able to lure Chemo into a subterranean cavern where they trapped "the chemical catastrophe" in the "air jets" of a natural gas deposit. But it escaped into the sea and, using telepathic powers (Chemo can't speak) let the Metal Men know that it intended to destroy the world and remake it as "a liquid world—ruled by a liquid-being—Chemo!" Discovering that even Chemo needed air, the two tin Metal Men turned to powder and engulfed and suffocated the creature (*Showcase* #40). The titan appeared to be destroyed when the Metal Men finally penetrated its skin and spilled it into the sea (*Metal Men* #46, 1976). But it was able to regroup and menace the world anew, most notably as a dupe of I.Q., who turned the giant "into a beam of chemical energy" to shoot at our sun, which he had accidentally unbalanced (see I.Q.). But Superman interfered with the experiment, turning the "Chemobeam" into a half-dozen human-sized "mini-Chemos." These managed to coalesce back into Chemo, whom Superman superheated and heaved into space, where it exploded (1978, *Comics Presents* #4). Needless to say, it regrouped as a comet, plunged into the sea (1982, *Superman* #370), and has continued to menace Superman, among other superheroes. In *Action Comics* #590, 1987, a Chemo-Superman was created when the superhero fell into a vat of materials reprocessed from industrial accidents.

Comment: Other foes of the Metal Men include the Gas Gang, consisting of living beings composed of Carbon dioxide, Carbon monoxide, Chloroform, Helium, or Oxygen; the Plastic Perils of Professor Bravo, Metal Men-like antagonists made of Ethylene, Methacrylate, Polyethylene, Silicone, and Styrene (all of whom were vulnerable to extremely high temperatures); the Man-Horse of Hades; Dr. Yes; the Black Coven, seven practitioners of the supernatural; the Robot Eater of Metalas 5; Z-1 and the Missile Men; and—believe it or not—the Cruel Clowns from the Clown Planet.

CHOPPER (C)

First Appearance: 1975, *1st Issue Special* #5, DC Comics.

Costume: Green robe; oversized pink head which is featureless, save for purple eyes and slit for mouth.

Weapons: Cave hideout is lined with heads which fire flames from their mouths; the Electric Head, a mask which sends high voltage into the wearer.

Biography: Nothing is known about this "deranged" character's past, though he's a murderer of some significance as many "pursuers" have come after him. Only the superheroic Manhunter manages to track him to his cavernous lair and, surviving the Electric Head, strikes Chopper with "paralysis shells." Before he is overcome, the villain tries to kill Manhunter with an axe; but the hero thrusts the Electric Head in the blade's path, and Chopper is electrocuted.

Quote: "Fry, Manhunter!"

Comment: "Chopper" is slang for a machine gun. This was the character's only appearance; he was created and drawn by Jack Kirby, who cocreated such classic superheroes as the Fantastic Four and the Silver Surfer. Another Manhunter villain, the chubby crime lord known as the Hog, makes a brief appearance.

CHRONOS (C)

Real Name: David Clinton.

First Appearance: 1962, *The Atom* #3, DC Comics.

Costume: White tights with thin vertical black stripes; yellow cloak, boots, gloves with "arrow" motif running along back of forearm; white full-head cowl with black hands signaling one o'clock on forehead; red trunks; green bodyshirt with yellow waist, circle on chest with red and white hourglass design inside.

Weapons: Various time-related objects including a watch with detachable, dart-like hands; an exploding hourglass; a device which slows time to a crawl; and a sundial-like platform for flight.

Biography: A monumentally unsuccessful crook, Clinton realizes that his problem is in not taking the time to plan crimes correctly. During a period of incarceration, he becomes impressed with the efficiency of prison, and vows to make his own criminal life run just like clockwork. Using the prison workshop to begin constructing time-oriented crime devices, he becomes the costumed Chronos the second he gets out of jail. Despite his best efforts he is repeatedly defeated by the superheroic Atom, who happens to live in Ivy Town, where Chronos sets up shop. He is equally unsuccessful as a member of THE SECRET SOCIETY OF SUPER-VILLAINS. Chronos is presently doing time.

Comment: In Greek mythology, Chronos (also Cronus and Kronos) was the father of Zeus and the God of Time. He is identified with the Roman god Saturn.

CIRCE (MY, N, MP, C)

Real Name: Kirke (the original Greek version of the more famous Roman name).

Biography: Circe is the daughter of the sun god, Helios, and the ocean nymph Perseis; she is the sister of Aeetes, king of Colchis, and of Pasiphae, the wife of Minos, king of Crete. Her niece is the infamous sorceress MEDEA, the wife of Jason of the Argonauts. A powerful sorceress herself, Circe settled upon the island of Aeaea, where she lived, according to Homer, in "a smooth stone house" in "an open glade." There she passed the time turning former lovers into swine, wolves, mountain lions, and other animals by placing a "vile pinch" in their wine. The change was instantaneous, and affected only their bodies. Described by Homer as a "dire beauty and divine," she performed her first truly spectacular deed of evil after the sea god Glaucus, in love with a beautiful maiden named Scylla, came to the witch for a love potion. Circe fell in love with Glaucus herself and prepared a poison for the maiden; spilling it into the waters where she bathed, she transformed Scylla into a monster with six long necks, each bearing an awful head which thereafter plucked passing sailors from ships. Circe's most famous struggle was with Ulysses (circa 1190 B.C.). Landing on Aeaea, all but Ulysses and one of his men (Eurylochus) were turned into swine. Obtaining a protective herb from the god Hermes, Ulysses ordered Circe, at swordpoint, to restore his crew, which she did. Her last appearance on the stage of mythology was to purify Medea for having committed fratricide.

Quote: "Down in the sty and snore among the rest!"

Comment: Keats, in *Endymion*, told a slightly different tale of Glaucus and Circe. The god falls in love with Circe and remains with her until he sees her transform people into animals. When he tries to escape, she sentences him to live a thousand years decrepit and agonized. Finding Scylla drowned, he passes the time collecting the bodies of drowned lovers. Circe's exploits come down to us from Greek mythology, though her struggle with Ulysses was chronicled in detail in Homer's *The Odyssey* (circa 850 B.C.). In the 1954 film *Ulysses*, Circe was played by Silvana Mangano. Circe is also a comic book villain, having made her debut in #305 of *Wonder Woman* (DC Comics). Marvel's Sersi is the ancient Circe alive in the modern era (according to Marvel, Circe/Sersi is one of the Eternals, being evolved from but superior to human beings).

THE CLAW (1) (C)

First Appearance: 1939, *Silver Streak Comics* #1, Lev Gleason.

Costume: Robes of different colors, usually red or green; cap with widow's peak, usually the same color as his robe. The Claw's skin was yellow, his skull-like face decidedly reptilian, with long fangs and sharply pointed ears. Instead of hands, he had bony claws.

Chief Henchmen: Personal army as well as various operatives.

Biography: "A monster of miraculous powers who is out to dominate the universe," the Claw was, as billed, "the world's worst villain." The Claw was born in "a thriving little village in Tibet" named Death's Head. There, the veiled young Caucasian woman Zola was proprietor of a popular tavern. A cruel boss, she actually slew employees who asked for their wages. One day, the yellow-skinned brute named Mei Ting came to see her about marriage (what he really wanted was half-ownership of the tavern). Furious at his proposal, the uppity Zola tried to stab him to death;

during the fray he yanked off her veil, revealing the woman's long fangs. To keep her deformity a secret, she married Mei Ting. Disappearing for many months, they shocked the community by jumping from a cliff one day. Searching the dead couple's "great mansion" high on a mountaintop, the villagers found a horrible infant therein. According to the 123-year-old sage Ashi Canbini, who was there, "the kind village folk decided to . . . bring him up as their own child. Better they should have drowned him." Named the Claw because of his deformed hands (not to mention the fangs he got from his mother's side), the Claw was a young terror, brutalizing other children (especially good-looking ones, for he detested beauty) and adults alike—"and woe betide the teacher who failed to give him the best mark." The Claw was sent to reform school (of which there weren't many in turn-of-the-century Tibet); it took 15 men to cart the "juvenile Nero" off, five of them ending up at the hospital. And when reform school proved unequal to the task of breaking the Claw's spirit, he was "removed to the greatest prison Tibet had." There, the Claw grew stronger and larger each day until he reached the height of roughly 100 feet. Breaking out and slaying the prison guards (graphically mashing them to pulp against the prison wall; as Ashi puts it, "blood flowed like water"), he found he could control his height, becoming human-sized or gigantic at will. Establishing a mountain fortress, he hatched fantastic plots in his efforts to take over the world, most dramatically launching an invasion of New York in which his army traveled from the Himalayas to the Big Apple in their personal underground railroad. Stalking through the streets, wrecking buildings, the Claw was met by the superhero Daredevil, whom he ate; the costumed defender got the Claw to spit him out by lighting TNT in his throat. ("If dynamite down his windpipe fails," he mutters, "I'll soon be ground meat!") Though the attack was repulsed, the Claw and Daredevil battled each other for years, the hero finally slaying him in *Daredevil Comics* #31 (1945).

Quote: "Die, pigs of the devil!!"

Comment: No comic book antagonist was as merciless as the Claw. Though an Asian villain, the Claw has more in common with Godzilla than with DR. FU MANCHU and his ilk. Daredevil had a knack for fighting particularly heartless villains. Another of his foes, the circus strongman Sandor, not only sabotaged the acts of his fellow performers but also, for sport, shot circus animals with a bow and arrow ("Well! Well! If it isn't Lumbo! I wonder if elephants have any feelings?"). He even went so far as to lash a rival strong man to horses, grinning as the animals "tore him apart." Sandor's sadistic career was ended when Lumbo picked him up in his trunk and hurled him onto a row of spikes used to prod the animals (#12).

THE CLAW (2) (C)

Real Name: Richard Reese.

First Appearance: 1971, *Hell-Rider* #1, Skywald Publications.

Costume: Robe and hood (comic is black and white; presumably these are green, since his henchmen all wear green).

Weapons: Metal claw on his left hand.

Chief Henchmen: Clancy and several other thugs dressed in green bodysuits and cowls with cat-ears.

Biography: Working for the firm of Williams and Williams in Los Angeles, the circa 50-year-old, extremely right-wing Reese is secretly the Claw, peddling heroin in order to "lure followers . . . to build my empire." These acolytes live on a commune in the desert where, when their numbers have swelled, the Claw plans to instigate a civil war which will enable him "to rule the country . . . and maybe the *world*." Fortunately, the superheroic Hell-Rider finds the Claw's apartment hideout in the city and, crashing through a picture window, runs Reese down. It isn't clear whether the Claw is killed or if his body is simply shattered.

Quote: "I, as your leader, recommend that they remain tied to these stakes until the desert sun bakes the last breath of life from their bodies."

Comment: Hell-Rider's name was Brick Reese, suggesting that the writer intended to reveal in some future tale that the characters were related—or else simply had a Reese fetish. But this was the character's only appearance. In the second (and final) adventure of Hell-Rider, the hero battled the savage, ape-like, chemically-created Ripper, aka nightclub owner Jack Samuels.

CLAYFACE (C)

Real Name: Basil Karlo, followed by Matt Hagen and Preston Payne.

First Appearance: 1940, *Detective Comics* #40 (Karlo); 1961, *Detective Comics* #298 (Hagen); 1978, *Detective Comics* #478 (Payne), DC Comics.

Costume: Karlo: purple suit, cloak, fedora. Hagen: none. Payne: blue cloak, hood, bodysuit; red trunks, boots, gloves; entire suit is framed within a white exo-skeleton to keep his soft flesh from collapsing.

Biography: Once the greatest horror actor in motion pictures, Basil is undone by his own bad publicity. He "got into scrapes and did a lot of crazy things," and people refused to go to his films. When the Argus Motion Picture company remakes his old film *Dread*

Castle with someone else as the central figure, the Terror, Basil cracks. He creates a misshapen makeup for himself and, as Clayface, starts killing everyone as they die in the picture. Fortunately, the heroic Batman is able to get him into the Arkham Asylum before he kills too many castmembers. Though he manages to escape several times to try to get revenge on Batman, the villain is finally locked away securely. But Clayface is not quite gone. Years later, treasure seeker Matt Hagen discovers a cave containing a pool laced with an element that enables him to change into any object he wishes, animate or inanimate, for two full days after each dunking. After this new version of Clayface indulges in several criminal escapades, the superhero Superman lends Batman a hand—more accurately, an eye—by using his heat vision to destroy the small lake. Hagen is sent to prison; though he manages to synthesize the miracle element, he's reluctant to use it because of deadly side effects. Yet, the villain returns again, this time in the person of Preston Payne. "Born an acromegalic—victim of chronic hyperpituitarism which hideously distorted my body," he grows up friendless. However, he is a genius and, graduating from school, takes a job with S.T.A.R. Laboratories. When his fellow scientists and plastic surgeons alike tell him there is nothing they can do for him, he convinces imprisoned Hagen to let him have a sample of his blood. Payne distills the essense of his malleability and injects himself with the extract. Alas, it causes his flesh "to run . . . like wax before a candle . . . like flowing clay" and, worse, creates in him every now and then "a fever which can only be quenched" if he touches another human being and turns him into a pool of melted flesh and bone. Hunted by Batman, he perishes when his wax museum lair burns to the ground.

Quote: "Fools! *They play* at murder . . . not realizing that *I* do *not* pretend." (Karlo)

CLOCK KING (C)

Real Name: William Tockman.

First Appearance: 1959, *World's Finest Comics* #111, DC Comics.

Costume: Blue bodysuit covered with white clocks; green trunks, gloves, boots, cape, cowl with blue-rimmed white clockface over entire face.

Biography: Learning that he has only a half-year to live, former clock repairperson Tockman becomes a criminal in order to make enough money so his crippled sister can survive after his death without having to go to a nursing home. Using the clock as the motif for his costume—not only because clocks were his life, but also because he only has a limited time left on earth—he pillages Star City as the Clock King. Time stops for the villain when the archer Green Arrow intercepts him. In the cruelest twist of all, not only does Tockman find out that he wasn't terminally ill (the doctor had mixed up his records with those of someone else), but his sister ends up going to a nursing home when he is sent to jail. She dies there, and the furious Tockman vows to avenge her death by killing both his thimblewit physician and Green Arrow. Though he has escaped from jail numerous times, he has yet to make good on his promise.

Comment: Other noteworthy foes of Green Arrow were Camouflage King, the Red Dart, and Slingshot. Camouflage King invented a "special chemical spray paint" which could imitate, instantly, any background . . . even if the person coated with the paint was moving. The archer defeated him with rain arrows which washed away the paint. Red Dart was actually John "The Midas" Mallory, a crook who pretended to be a superhero in order to gain the superhero's trust—and be at his side to foul him up when his own gang committed a crime. Armed with various darts—including fog-darts, grenade-darts, and rain-darts—the villain dressed in a golden bodysuit with blue trunks, boots, and a cape. Slingshot was actually David Drayson and, as his name implies, wielded a slingshot with deadly precision. See CHRONOS, another time-related super villain.

THE CLOWN (C)

First Appearance: 1940, *Super-Mystery Comics* #5, Ace Magazines.

Costume: Dressed in a ruff collar and bodysuit, his pasty face resembles that of Batman's nemesis THE JOKER (save for the clown's domino mask).

Weapons: The "Roto-Dynamo," a cigar-shaped vehicle which burrows through the earth, sails beneath the seas, and is the "most powerful engine of destruction ever to be used against mankind." The Clown also wears "electric wiring sewed inside" his blouse which gives him the "touch of death," allowing him to murder by gesturing at anyone nearby.

Chief Henchmen: Sundry nameless thugs.

Biography: The Clown works for Hitler and is a "sabotage expert extraordinary." In his several forays against the United States, he is invariably stopped by the magnetic superheroes Magno and Davey.

Quote: "Ha-ha! Are you enjoying the pretty sight, Miss Jane? This is your country going down in ruins."

Comment: The character made only a handful of appearances during the War years. See other Nazi super villains BARON BLITZKRIEG, BARON GESTAPO, BARON ZEMO, CAPTAIN AXIS, CAPTAIN NAZI, THE GOLDEN FUHRER, KILLER SHARK, NIGHT AND FOG, The Masked Swastika of VENDETTA, Mastermind (see U-MAN, Comment), THE RED PANZER, THE RED SKULL, and ZYKLON.

THE CLUEMASTER (C)

First Appearance: 1966, *Detective Comics* #351, DC Comics.

Costume: Orange bodysuit, boots; lighter orange gloves, mask over the lower half of his face; yellow scarf.

Weapons: Fourteen blue glass canisters attached to costume in two rows, from the shoulders to the knees; these contain blinding flares, choking fumes, gas which renders people unconscious, explosives, and the like.

Chief Henchmen: Various thugs.

Biography: Nothing is known about this villain's past. Ambidextrous, he intends to destroy Batman and then commit crimes at his leisure. Leaving clues rendered with radioactive paint, the Cluemaster fully expects the hero to take the clues to his hideout, the Batcave, to which Cluemaster will then trace him. But Batman figures out the gimmick and follows the Cluemaster's thug who was sent to spy on them. Storming the Cluemaster's headquarters, Batman captures the villain and carts him off to prison.

Quote: "*Batman's* perfect record of crook-catching and trap-escaping puts them in a defeat-frame of mind . . . just as *Babe Ruth* striding to the plate used to terrorize pitchers."

Comment: The villain has appeared only twice, but his debut is notable for a comment made by Batman's sidekick, Robin. When he first spots the Cluemaster, he clucks, "*Batman*! Men coming out of the *Lowland Trust Bank*—led by a guy wearing a crazy mixed-up uniform!" This from a teenager who is himself dressed in a red, green, and yellow costume.

THE CLUTCHING HAND (1) (N, MP)

First Appearance: 1915, *The Exploits of Elaine*, Arthur B. Reeve.

Weapons: Death ray; poison passed by kiss; "electric resuscitation" device to bring the dead back to life.

Biography: A scientific genius, the Clutching Hand uses his gadgets to try and usurp the inheritance of heroine Elaine. He is thwarted by detective Craig Kennedy.

Comment: Pathe released *The Exploits of Elaine* as a 14-chapter serial in 1915. Author Reeve recycled the story and villain, both with changes, in 1934. See THE CLUTCHING HAND (2).

THE CLOWN.

THE CLUTCHING HAND (2) (N, MP)

Real Name: Dr. Paul Gironda.
First Appearance: 1934, *The Clutching Hand*, Arthur B. Reeve.
Costume: Black suit and fedora.
Weapons: Television cameras with which to broadcast instructions to his henchmen.
Biography: Claiming to have found a way to make synthetic gold, Dr. Gironda is promptly kidnapped. His daughter Verna hires detective Craig Kennedy to find him, but the villainous Clutching Hand is always getting in their way. Investigating Gironda, Kennedy discovers that he's not actually Verna's father but her guardian, and that he's secretly misused a great deal of money that was rightfully hers. He contrived the (fake) gold formula in the hopes of selling it for a small fortune and skipping the country; the kidnapping was simply a means of laying low so he didn't have to answer questions about the discovery. Revealed as the Clutching Hand and as a fraud, Gironda commits suicide.
Comment: Robert Frazier played the part in the 15-chapter serial, *The Clutching Hand*, from Weiss Pictures in 1936.

***COAL MAN** on a rampage. © Dell Publishing.*

COAL MAN (C)

First Appearance: 1967, *Super Heroes #3*, Dell Publishing.
Weapons: Pickaxe.
Biography: The human-hating Coal Man dwells in a "flame-filled cavern" adjoining mines 1,200 feet beneath eastern Pennsylvania. There, he has rigged giant fans which feed oxygen to the flaming coal (circa 10,000 degrees) from which he gets his strength (by inhaling the flames or ingesting the burning coal itself); one miner implies that the towering humanoid creature has been down there for 100 years. Because he enjoys killing any humans who come his way, the android Super Heroes are called in: after a violent battle, Crispy the Cryogenic Man is able to freeze him, Polymer the plastic-coated heroine binds him in polymer strands, and the badly battered Coal Man staggers off to a deeper cavern, never to bother humans again.
Quote: "They are dead like the others who came here! *All dead! I rule here! I am the Coal Man!*"
Comment: This was the Coal Man's only appearance. Other foes of the Super Heroes include the destructive, nuclear-powered robot Enndo-Man; Mr. Mod; Johnny Boom-Boom; the magician Dr. Orb, who puts audiences to sleep and then robs them ("When you awaken, you will not notice your losses"); and Nepto of the Reef who, though he lives underwater, robs jewelry from surface dwellers and sells it on the black market. (He even has a fence!)

COBRA (C)

Real Name: Klaus Voorhees.
First Appearance: 1963, *Journey Into Mystery #98*, Marvel Comics.
Costume: Green snakeskin bodysuit, cowl (see Weapons); darker green wristbands (see Weapons), cobra hood behind head; purple shawl, leotard with thin, horizontal black stripes and black cobra silhouette from chest to waist; blue belt.
Weapons: Costume has been treated to be extremely slippery; suction cups on fingers and feet for climbing walls or crossing ceilings; wristshooters which fire "cobra-bite" darts containing deadly venom, others which paralyze "for hours," poisonous "cobra-gas," explosives, and other projectiles.

Biography: A "rehabilitated" crook, Voorhees is employed by Professor Ezekiel Shecktor, who is working in India to find an antidote for any and all snake venom. Secretly hating the benevolent scientist, Voorhees decides to kill him and make it seem like an accident by letting a cobra bite them both—with only the ex-con getting to use the antidote. Without realizing it, Voorhees selects a cobra which had been subject to radiation. The mixture of its venom and the experimental serum gives the Dutch criminal the cobra-like ability to slither along the ground and slink through openings "too small for any normal man to fit through." Becoming the costumed Cobra, he battles Thor and, taking a licking, for a time teams with another nemesis of Thor, Mr. Hyde (see MR. HYDE, Comment). The union ends repeatedly in disaster and, escaping from the Ryker's Island prison one night, he leaves Hyde behind and becomes an independent operator. ("Everytime I've teamed with you, we've both had our heads handed to us!" he hisses to the jailed Hyde. "Well, never again!" [*Peter Parker, the Spectacular Spider-Man* #46, 1980]) But, captured by Spider-Man, he opts to join THE SECRET SERPENT SOCIETY, of which he is presently a member.

Quote: "Yes—gas! Its vapors are quite deadly! Ha-ha! I'd like to see you mock me now!"

COLONEL COMPUTRON (C)

Real Name: See Biography.

First Appearance: 1981, *The Flash* #304, DC Comics.

Costume: Silver armor designed like a microchip; covers entire body except for mouth (see Weapons).

Weapons: Costume is a bulletproof computer which not only calculates the strength Colonel Computron will need to perform any given task, but delivers the energy to do it as well. It also allows Computron to fly (thanks to jet-heels) or to become pure electricity and escape pursuers by slipping into any handy electrical wiring. Colonel Computron also packs several other hi-tech weapons: a molecu-siphon rifle which allows the villain to disassemble the atoms of any object (including a person) and recreate it as an image on a computer screen; and video-missiles, which seek out and destroy preprogrammed targets.

Chief Henchmen: Blip-One and Blip-Two, a pair of brutish robots.

Biography: Captain (sic) Computron is the name of a popular toy manufactured by the Wiggins Toy Corporation (the same outfit which had previously been responsible for the birth of the vile CAPTAIN BOOMERANG). Some unknown person wishing owner Wiggins ill puts a special chip in one of the toys, a component which causes the Colonel Computron costume to emerge. In several adventures it tries to slay Mr. Wiggins. Fortunately, the superheroic Flash intercedes at each turn. It is not yet clear who lurks inside the Colonel Computron suit, but the likeliest suspects are inventor Basil Nurblin, who invented the enormously successful toy for Wiggins but has only seen a pittance in profit-sharing; his even more bitter wife Francine; and their daughter Luna, who is furious with Wiggins because her father's poverty has forced her to live at home during her college years.

Quote: "At this very moment my suit is computing precisely how many *ergs* of *force* it will take . . . for me to hoist your *fat mass* off the floor!"

COLONEL SUN (N)

Real Name: Sun Liang-tan.

First Appearance: 1968, *Colonel Sun*, Kingsley Amis (as Robert Markham).

Biography: Kidnapping "M," the head of the British secret service, Colonel Sun earns the enmity of agent James Bond. Pursuing the Red Chinese operative, Bond is unaware that M was abducted so that Sun could draw him out and thus kill them both. His plans for the two are exotic, to say the least: He plans to bomb a Russian conference in Greece and plant the Britons' bodies at the site so they will be blamed. Though Bond is indeed captured and tortured, he escapes with the help of a prostitute and stabs the notorious Sun in the heart. Standing nearly six feet tall, Colonel Sun has a long face and blue black hair which lies dead-straight. He is aided in his dirty work by former Nazi thug Von Richter.

Quote: "You must understand that I'm not the slightest bit interested in studying resistance to pain or any such pseudo-scientific claptrap. I just want to torture people."

Comment: This was the first James Bond novel written by someone other than Ian Fleming, and Amis' only stab at that character. John Gardner continued the series in 1981, his villains including nuclear terrorist Anton Murik in *License Renewed* (1981); a Blofeld heir who plots to drug key NORAD employees with poisoned ice cream and thus take over the military's new laser satellies in *For Special Services* (1982); and ex-nazi Count Konrad von Gloda who is attempting to revive the Reich in *Icebreaker* (1983). See other Asian super villains DR. FU MANCHU, DR. GOO FEE, DR. YEN SIN, and WU FANG.

THE COMPOSITE SUPERMAN (C)

Real Name: Joseph Meach.
First Appearance: 1964, *World's Finest Comics* #142, DC Comics.
Costume: Superman's costume on his right side (blue bodysuit with half of red "S" on yellow, red-fringed pentagon on chest; red trunks, boot, cape; yellow belt); Batman's costume on his left side (gray bodysuit with half of black bat in a golden field on chest; blue cape, cowl, trunks, boot, glove). The Composite Superman's skin is green.
Biography: A failed high diver, Meach intends to make his mark with a spectacular dive from a skyscraper into a pool of water. Fortunately, Superman notices that the pool has leaked and he streaks over to catch Joe before the daredevil becomes part of the pavement. Irrationally blaming Superman for his misfortune, Joe nonetheless accepts a job as caretaker at the Superman museum in Metropolis. Forgetting to close the window one night, Joe is standing beside statues of the members of the Legion of Super-Heroes when lightning strikes them. Because the statues were created using a special "duplicator machine" which reproduced the heroes in complete detail, the essence of the heroes' powers is latent within the figurines; the lightning releases these powers and transfers them to Meach. As the Composite Superman, Meach can adopt any disguise he wishes (from the Legion's Chameleon Boy), split into three identical beings (from Triplicate Lass), fire lightning bolts (Lightning Lad), bounce (Bouncing Boy), eat anything (Matter-Eater Lad), grow huge (Colossal Boy), grow small (Shrinking Violet), become invisible (Invisible Kid), fly and employ superstrength, invulnerability, superspeed, and enormously heightened senses (all of these held, to different degrees, by Mon-El, Superboy, Supergirl, and Ultra Boy), transmute matter (Element Lad), use telepathy and telekinesis (Saturn Girl), pass through solid matter (Phantom Girl), stretch (Elastic Lad), think with a vastly superior brain (Brainiac 5), generate star-like heat and light (Sun Boy), cause matter to grow heavy (Star Boy) or light (Light Lass), and attract or repel matter (Cosmic Boy). Building an imposing Composite Castle high in the mountains, he intends to conquer the world; even Superman and Batman are unable to stop him, the latter because he's mortal and the former because the fiend can employ Element Lad's powers to change any object to deadly kryptonite. Luckily, the effects of the lightning are only temporary; before he can think to fire a Lightning Lad bolt at them, his powers (and all memory of them) fade away. A few months after, the extraterrestrial Xan comes to earth to avenge the death of his father, an interplanetary pirate, at the hands of Superman and Batman. Recruiting Meach to do his dirty work, Xan recreates the accident which gave Meach his powers and sits back to watch the Composite Superman beat the tar from the heroes. Once again, however, Meach's powers fade, and, discovering that he'd been Xan's lackey, he gives his life to save the superheroes from Xan. Superman melts the statues and the alien is imprisoned; escaping, he travels back in time, uses the statues to turn himself into the Composite Superman (though he discards that name in favor of the flashier Amalgamax), and attacks the heroes. He is defeated due to the combined efforts of the Legion of Super-Heroes and, his powers having faded, is presently under lock and key.
Quote: "Fight *me*? That's laughable . . . try it, and I'll break *Batman* like a doll!"

COMPUTO THE CONQUEROR (C)

First Appearance: 1966, *Adventure Comics* #340, DC Comics.
Costume: The robot's rectangular body, roughly 12 feet tall, is yellow with light green tentacles and red wheels. (As constructed by Brainiac 5, it was a larger, green unit; it rebuilt itself halfway through the first story.)
Weapons: Tentacles are extremely powerful.
Chief Henchmen: "Computeroids," robot duplicates, "enough reasonable facsimiles of myself to control" the planet; Computo communicates with them via "invisible trans-beam." Danielle Foccart was also briefly a mind-slave (see Biography).
Biography: Computo was created in the second half of the thirtieth century, the result of efforts by the brilliant Brainiac 5 to construct the ultimate computer. Working at the United Planets Lab Complex, Brainiac had hoped the computer would be a force for good, "a boon to mankind." Learning everything it can from books, Computo literally swallows Brainiac 5 and, placing him inside its "energum-induction bubble" (a dome which the later model didn't have), sucks the knowledge from his head. Deciding to conquer the planet, he builds his Computeroids and places other specialists in *their* energum-induction bubbles. Deactivated by the Legion of Super-Heroes (#341), the computer is revived years later when, against his better judgment, Brainiac 5 places virtually identical circuitry in a computer needed to save the life of young Danielle Foccart. Rebuilding itself and taking over young Danielle, the computer defeats most of the Legion and is stopped only when Danielle's brother Jacques becomes the superhero Invisible Kid and teams with Brainiac 5 to, once again, deactivate it (*The Legion of Super-Heroes*

Annual #1, 1982). Lobotomized and redesigned as an energized circuit globe, Computo now serves the Legion in the manner originally intended. Though bodiless, it will undoubtedly go rogue again at some point in the future.

Quote: "Surrender, *Superboy*, or I'll annihilate my other hostage!"

COMRADE STUPIDSKA (C)

First Appearance: 1983, *Captain Klutz II*, Don Martin.

Costume: Black bodysuit with white star on chest; white trunks with black polka dots; cowl with huge nose; bearskin hat with wings on the side; fur-lined boots; cape (apprently a bath towel) with dark stripes at fringe. (Book is in black and white.)

Biography: Stupidska lives in Soviet Brusha, where he reports to party leader Ivanovitch Eyebrowski. Eyebrowski conceives of a diabolical plot against the United States: the placement of "one-hundred-pound capsules of Alka Seltzer in each chimney stack of an American nuclear power plant" so that "when the stacks belch . . . a radiation polluted cloud . . . will devastate the entire country." While the first city is victimized, Stupidska leads in an army of rifle-toting henchmen. Fortunately, the superhero Captain Klutz collides with Stupidska as both run blindingly around a corner; because he had sucked up the radioactive cloud, Klutz explodes. Presumably, the villain perishes in the blast.

Quote: "All right, men . . . are your *credit cards* ready? *Good!* Then let's *CHARGE!!!*"

Comment: This was the character's only appearance. See other Soviet super villains Boris Kartovski (see DR. CLEMENT ARMSTRONG, Comment), THE CRIMSON DYNAMO, MONGU THE RED GHOST, THE SOVIET SUPER SOLDIERS, THE TITANIC THREE, and TITANIUM MAN.

THE CONSTRICTOR (C)

Real Name: Frank Schlichting

First Appearance: 1977, *The Incredible Hulk* #212, Marvel Comics.

Costume: Blue bodysuit, cowl, gloves; boots are orange with thin, horizontal black stripes; same motif in a fat band that runs from the waist, up the belly and chest, along the forehead and top of cowl, and down back; also cable-housing on backs of wrists (see Weapons).

Weapons: Entire costume serves as a bulletproof vest; twin electrified cables shoot from backs of wrists to an extension of roughly 10 yards and can be used to crush, bind, or whip adversaries.

Biography: A petty crook in Chicago, Schlichting went west to try and boost his fortunes. Joining the criminal league, The Corporation, he was given his Constrictor costume and made a special agent; although he didn't fare terribly well on his first assignment, during which he battled the super-powered Hulk, he was encouraged enough to go free-lance when the Corporation folded. He has since battled other superheroes, include Luke Cage, the Powerman. The Constrictor is one of the few snake-like super villains who has not belonged to THE SERPENT SOCIETY (which offered him membership) or its predecessor, THE SERPENT SQUAD.

THE CONSTRUCT (C)

First Appearance: 1977, *Justice League of America* #142, DC Comics.

Costume: None; humanoid shell is light, metallic blue.

Chief Henchmen: Cannons, a battery of heavily armed humanoid robots.

Biography: The Construct is a sentient energy-wave being, self-evolved from the abundance of radio, TV, and other electronic signals in the air. Originally dwelling in all the electronic tools on earth, the Construct pulled together a metal humanoid form for itself; though it inhabited this form full-time, it retained the power to get inside of and control all electronic devices. Building its Cannons and undertaking the conquest of the earth—which it intended to populate with flawless machines—the Construct was defeated by the Justice League, its mind disincorporated and scattered to the winds. Managing to coalesce as Construct II (but with no memory of its previous incarnation), the new intelligence went after the Justice League by taking over the minds of the INJUSTICE GANG OF THE WORLD as well as Justice League member Wonder Woman. Beaten again, it returned as Construct III, this time taking over yet another Justice Leaguer, Red Tornado. Exorcised, it was permanently banished by Wonder Woman, who erected a transmitter that keeps the airwaves churning, making it impossible for a new Construct to form.

THE CONTROLLER (1) (C)

First Appearance: 1967, *Adventure Comics* #357, DC Comics.

Costume: Purple gloves, boots, jacket with tusk-like horns curving to the side from shoulders, helmet with matching horns on sides; black leotard with pink starburst on chest. (Note: Other Controllers wear blue boots, jacket with sleeves slit to the elbow on insides, triangular flap hanging point-down from waist to knees; purple belt, cloth around sleeves, cloak with curved, flared shoulders and high collar.) The skin of the Controllers is bright pink.

Weapons: The Sun-Eater, a sentient red cloud which consumes stars and leaves behind "a black, cold, husk"; "a miniature psychic projector" which sends "psychic impulses" to control human emotions; destructive "photon bolts."

Biography: The Controllers are part of a race which evolved some 10 billion years ago on the remote planet Oa. One of the Oans, Krona, conducted forbidden research into the origin of life and, reminiscent of Pandora's box, reportedly unleashed evil throughout the universe. Warfare erupted on countless worlds and, to make up for this horrendous plague, the Oans devoted their great minds and immortal existence to battling all evil. One group of Oans, later to call themselves the Guardians, became the progenitors of the superheroic Green Lantern Corps—natives of other worlds assigned to combat evil on those worlds. However, not every Oan subscribed to the idea that the intervention be worked only within the structures of the societies which had evolved around the universe. They regarded evil as a horror which must be eradicated at all costs. These Oans, the Controllers, moved to another dimension where they created weapons powerful enough to destroy an entire galaxy if it were infected. Individual Controllers were assigned to police specific sectors of the universe. If they spotted evil, their task was to try to prevent it using "subtle . . . mind control." However, if that failed and evil were deemed out-of-hand anywhere in the star system, the galaxy was to be obliterated using sundry tools designed for this purpose. By the thirtieth century sufficient worlds had banded together to eliminate evil that the Controllers deemed their role superfluous. They recalled their forces, but one refused to obey. Rather than be one of many immortal superbeings at home, he elected to remain in our galaxy and take it over. To demonstrate his power he unleashed the Sun-Eater, which was destroyed by the Legion of Super-Heroes thanks to an absorbatron bomb (detonated by Ferro Lad, who sacrificed his life to do so). Down but not out, he used his psychic projector to try and take over the Legion to use as his strike force. However, he was visited by the ghost of Ferro Lad and perished from "the equivalent of a heart attack."

Quote: "I am the most *powerful* being in this universe! Why not stay here . . . conquer . . . and *rule*?"

THE CONTROLLER (2) (C)

Real Name: Basil Sandhurst.

First Appearance: 1969, *Iron Man* #12, Marvel Comics.

Costume: Light blue bodysuit; navy blue trunks, gloves, boots, helmet which also covers shoulders and upper torso.

Weapons: Surgically-attached exoskeleton to boost his strength, powered by his mind via a "mental wave absorbatron"; small control disks which, when attached to the foreheads of others, enable him to enslave them.

Biography: A research scientist employed by Cord Industries, Basil is bored with his work. One day, his brother Vincent, an attorney, comes to visit; since it was he who got him the position, Basil demonstrates his appreciation by throwing a tantrum. Attempting to subdue him, Vincent accidentally knocks his brother into a table stocked with unstable chemicals. They explode, maiming and paralyzing Basil. Overcome with guilt for all he'd done to bring this about, Vincent embezzles money from Cord to build a private, fully-automated laboratory for Basil. There, the scarred scientist creates an exoskeleton and control discs and lumbers forth to build himself a kingdom as the Controller. To date, his plans have been repeatedly decontrolled by Iron Man.

COPPERHEAD (C)

First Appearance: 1968, *The Brave and the Bold* #78, DC Comics.

Costume: Orange copperhead snake cowl, bodysuit (see Weapons), both covered with scales; green gloves, trunks, boots.

Weapons: Suit is made of special metallic cloth and covered with slippery coating which allows Copperhead to crawl through incredibly tight spots and also to make grabbing him all but impossible. His cowl's fangs are filled with a poison which causes paralysis or death, depending upon the dosage.

Biography: Nothing has been revealed about this character's past, or about how he acquired his remarkable snake suit. A master thief in Gotham City, he was eventually captured by a desperate teaming of the superheroes Batman, Wonder Woman, and Batgirl. Sent to prison, he escaped when one of his friends snuck him a new and improved suit, one provided by the newly-formed SECRET SOCIETY OF SUPER-VILLAINS. Joining the evil league, Copperhead has worked on their criminal projects as well as his own, many of which have landed him back in the clink.

Comment: Other snake-like villains can be found in THE SERPENT SOCIETY and THE SERPENT SQUAD.

THE CORRUPTOR (C)

Real Name: Jackson Day.

First Appearance: 1976, *Nova* #4, Marvel Comics.

Costume: Indigo trousers, shirt, skirt; purple boots, gloves, cloak, belt.

Biography: An employee at a drug company, Day was drenched with radioactive chemicals during a fire. As a result, his skin turns blue and his soul grows black: The bath not only destroys the benevolent side of his nature, but also gives him the power to control anyone he touches. Becoming the Corruptor, the harbinger of evil, his most ambitious scheme to date has been turning slews of New Yorkers into slaves to pillage the city, a plot foiled by Nova. The Corruptor has also battled Thor and the Hulk.

COUNT FERDINAND FATHOM (N)

First Appearance: 1753, *The Adventures of Count Ferdinand Fathom,* Tobias Smollett.

Biography: Fathom personifies "treachery and fraud," as befits the son of a woman who roams battlefields stealing from the dead. When his mother finds and saves the life of the wounded Count de Melvil, the grateful noble takes Fathom under his wing. The youth grows to corrupt manhood, thanking his benefactor by trying to seduce his daughter. Two years later, at the age of 18, Fathom becomes friendly with Ratchchali, the most loathsome liar and swindler in Vienna; traveling to London, the men move through society using their veneer of breeding to set up a fake antique ring. Fathom continues his wanton ways with women, actually driving one poor girl, Celinda, to drink. Caught cheating at cards, he's tossed into jail; bailed out by Melvil's son, Fathom thanks him by trying to rape his girlfriend Monimia. After a brief turn at a legitimate trade (medicine), Fathom gives it up to become the kept husband of a rich widow. Running afoul of the law once again, he's tossed back in, where he is forgotten as the narrative turns its attention to the young Melvil and Monimia.

Comment: Fathom is one of the truly great profligates of literature, unspoiled by the humor and derring-do which mark other roués such as Don Juan or Henry Fielding's Tom Jones.

COUNT GATTO (C)

Costume: Red trousers; yellow shirt; blue cape; black shoes with white spats; purple top hat; white gloves.

Biography: The sinister cat and his sidekick Shadow detest the mice of Mouseville, and Atomic Mouse in particular, and spend their time devising ways of destroying the superhero and his city.

Quote: "Bah! I, Count Gatto, again outsmarted by that rodent!"

Comment: The villainous cat troubled Atomic Mouse for most of that character's run (1953-63). See other cat villains OIL CAN HARRY and TERRIBLE TOM.

COUNT MARIO ROMANO (MP)

First Appearance: 1968, *The Destructors,* United Pictures.

COUNT GATTO *wreaking havoc. © Charlton Comics.*

Biography: A well-to-do swimsuit importer, Count Romano has a higher ambition: undermining the security of the United States. Stealing a supply of vital laser rubies as a prelude to lifting the destructive laser gun itself, the Count is thwarted by National Intelligence agent Dan Street. The Count is assisted in his evil plans by lover Stassa and brainwashed Korean War veteran Dutch Holland.

Comment: Michael Ansara played the Count, Joan Blackman was Stassa, John Ericson played Dutch Holland.

COUNT VERTIGO (C)

Real Name: Count Werner Vertigo.

First Appearance: 1980, *World's Finest Comics* #251, DC Comics.

Costume: Dark green gloves, cowl, boots (see Weapons), tights which rise to mid-chest, terminating in a pyramid-shape; dark green cloak with green lining crisscrossed with dark green lines; light green bodyshirt with green and white bullseye on chest.

Weapons: Electronic device in his right temple which destroys the equilibrium of anyone around him; boots are magnetic and enable Vertigo to walk on walls; another device which enables Vertigo to cause illusions.

Biography: Vertigo is the last in the noble line which ruled Vlatava, a Balkan nation, which was annexed to Russia after the Second World War. Because of an inner ear problem, Vertigo had an implant to help him keep his balance; discovering that he could affect the balance of others by fiddling with the device, he turned to crime. His first target—the Vertigo family jewels, which his parents had been forced to peddle when they fled to England following the war. The jewels were housed in Star City in the United States which, unfortunately for Vertigo, happened to be home for the superheroes Black Canary and Green Arrow. Canary prevented him from stealing the jewels when her shrill cry shattered his vertigo device; escaping from prison, he has alternately attacked the Canary and Green Arrow, as well as the Soviet Union. In his most prodigious effort to date, he tried to liberate his former country by vowing to destroy the U.S.S.R. in a nuclear holocaust. Failing, he was forced to become a Soviet assassin, a brief career which ended in imprisonment back in the United States.

Robert Quarry as ***COUNT YORGA*** *in* The Return of Count Yorga. *© American International Pictures.*

COUNT YORGA (MP)

First Appearance: 1970, *Count Yorga, Vampire,* American International Pictures.

Chief Henchman: Brudah.

Biography: Traveling from Transylvania to Los Angeles via freighter, the vampire Yorga moves into a sprawling estate, intent on building a harem of vampire women. When his consort of several months dies, Yorga holds a seance so that her daughter, Donna Darnell, may contact her. However, the chat is brief since Mrs. Darnell isn't really dead but has been turned into a vampire. Given a ride home by teens Erica and Paul, Yorga turns the road into mud so their van gets stuck and they have to stay the night. He dispatches Paul and turns young Erica into a vampire, then brings Donna into the fold, reuniting her with her undead mother. Consulting a vampire-expert named Dr. Hayes, Donna's boyfriend Michael goes to the mansion and stakes Yorga in the heart, though apparently not to death. Inexplicably turning up in San Francisco (in *The Return of Count Yorga* [1971]), the Transylvanian settles into another mansion, preying on the children of a nearby orphanage and plotting to make neighbor Cynthia Nelson part of his new harem. Slaughtering the entire Nelson family and spiriting Cynthia away, Yorga is done in when the young woman buries a battleaxe in his heart and the vampire plunges from a balcony. In addition

Walking Sun. © *DC Comics.*

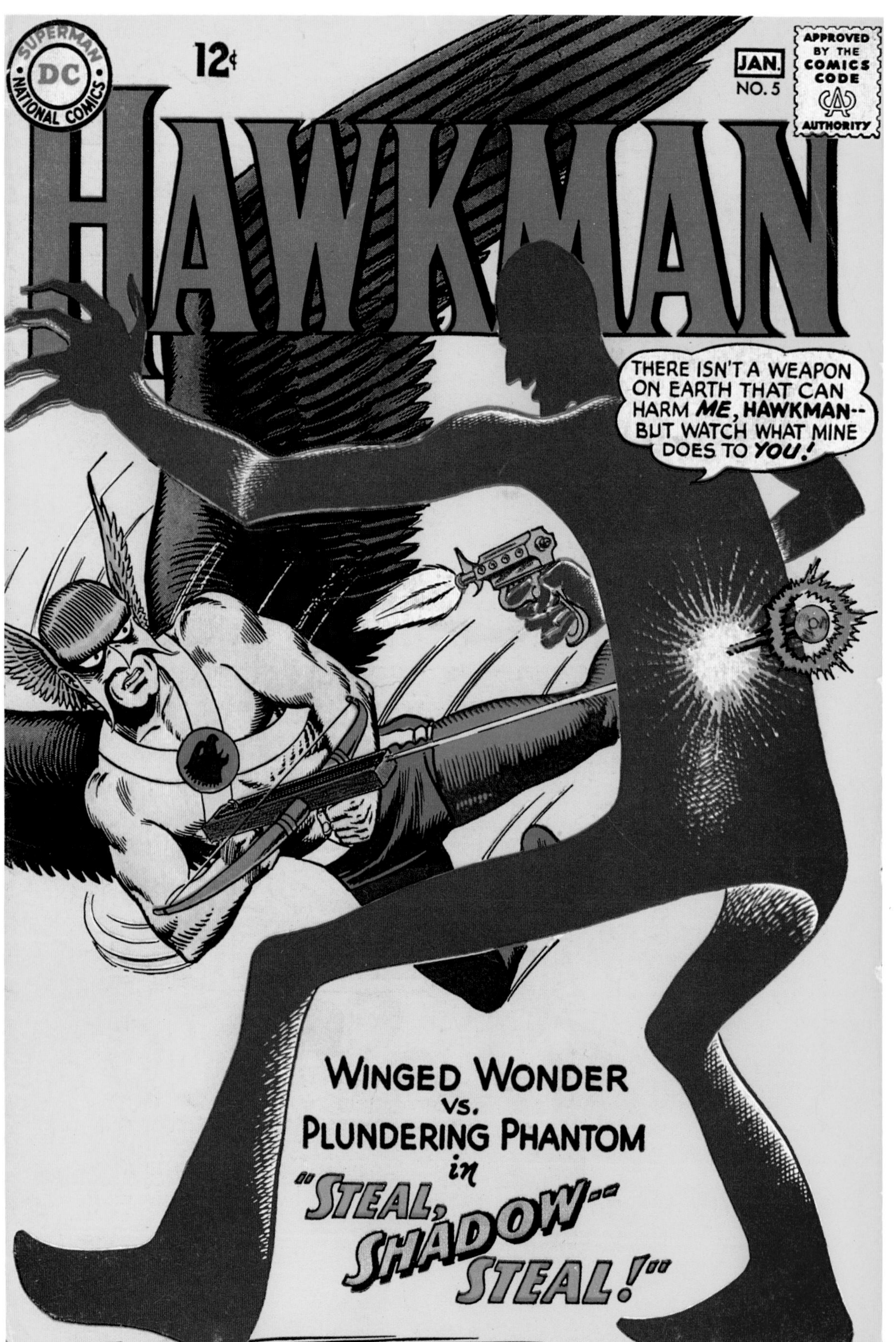

The Shadow-Thief *battles Hawkman. © DC Comics.*

Oil Can Harry *crashes Mighty Mouse's date with Pearl Pureheart. © Viacom.*

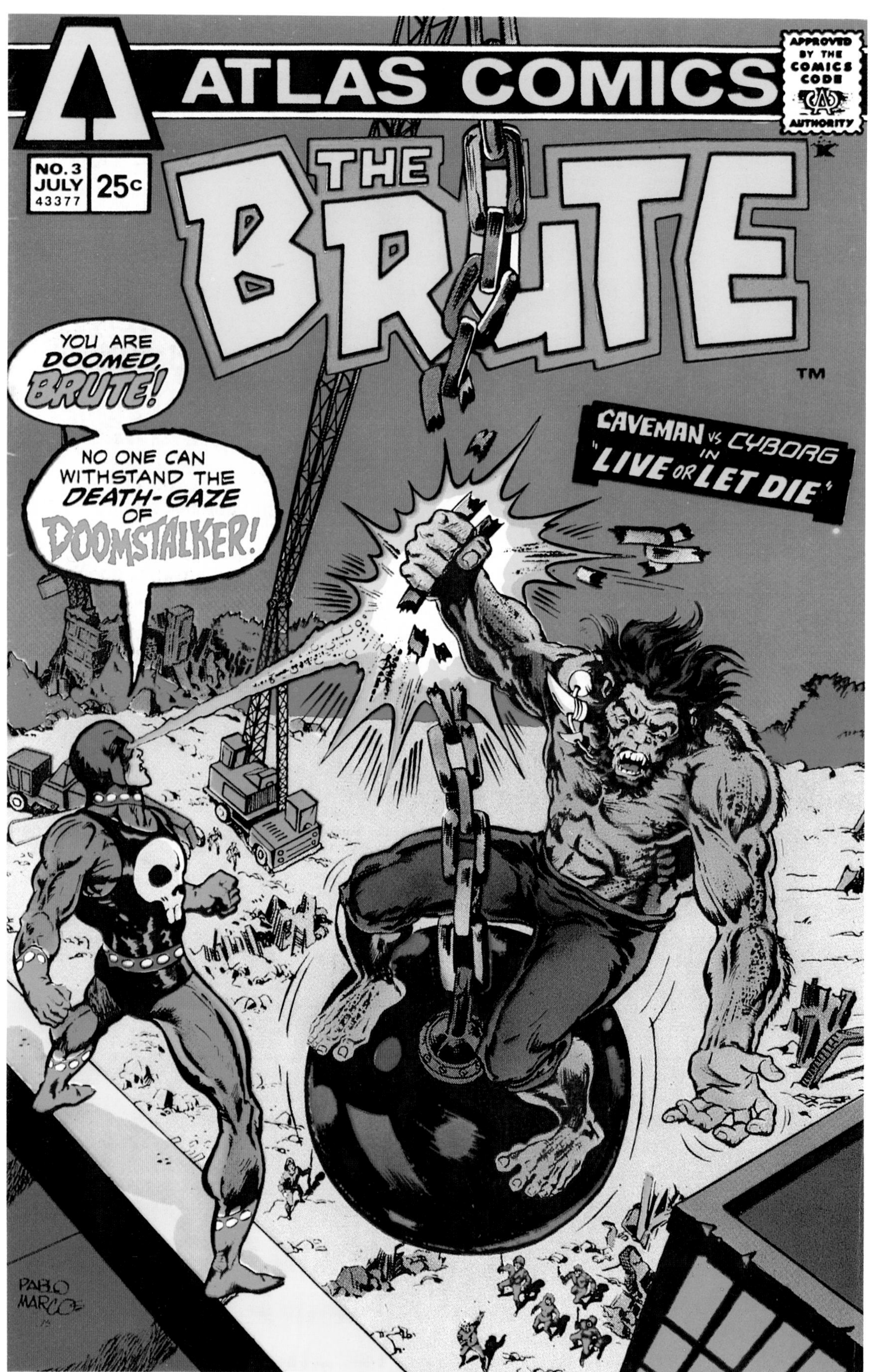

Doomstalker *menaces the Brute. © Atlas Comics.*

Eclipso *(left) and his occasional nemesis Prince Ra-Man. © DC Comics.*

The Blue Beetle vs. Mentor, robot minion of ***Dr. Jeramiah Clugg****.* *© Charlton Comics.*

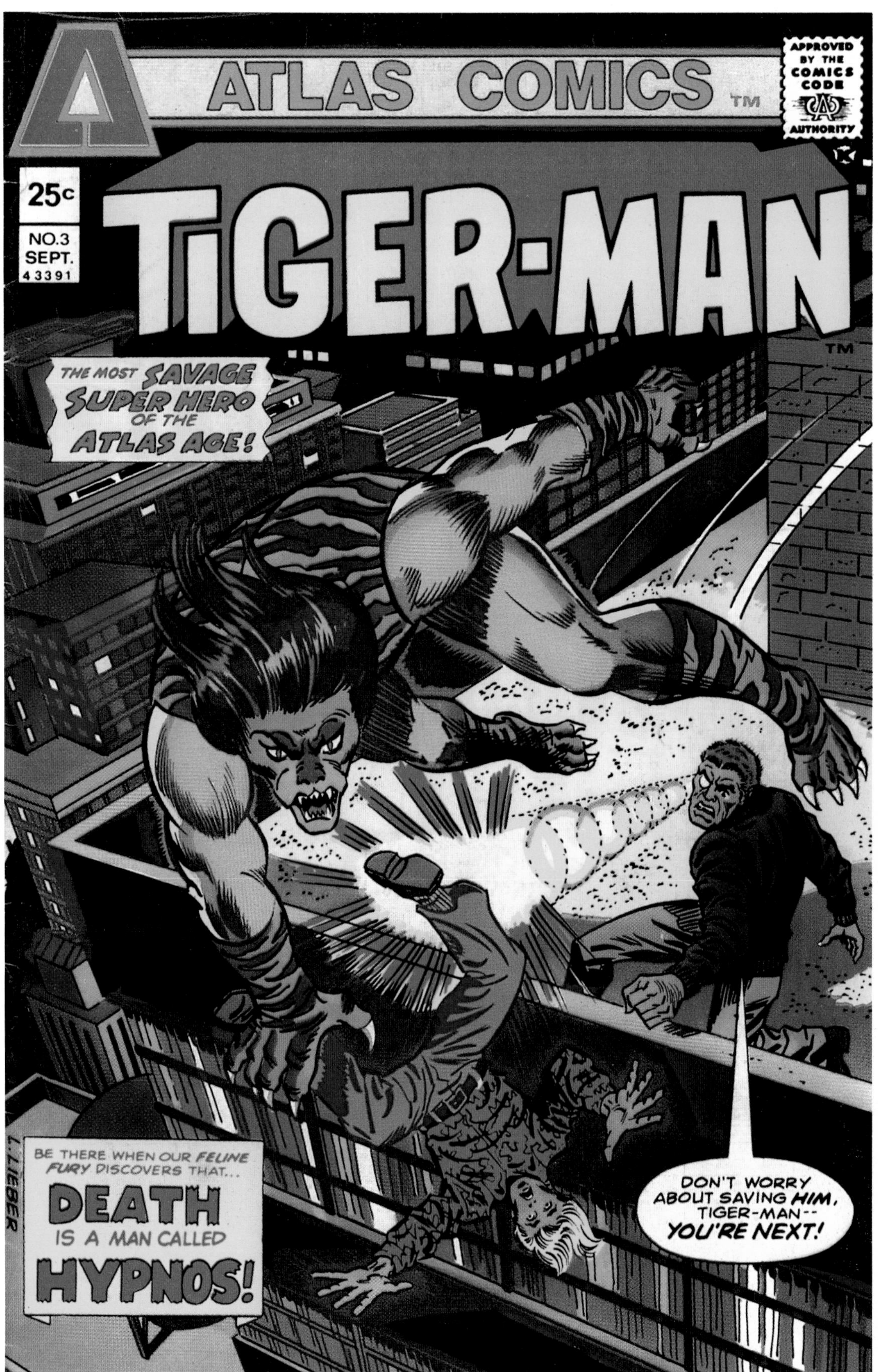

Hypnos *battles to the death with Tiger-Man.* © *Atlas Comics.*

Daffy the Great *(left) battles with Robby Reed. © DC Comics.*

CREATURE KING *projects a giant image of himself. © Hanna- Barbera Productions.*

to being able to control the elements, Yorga is a master hypnotist.

Quote: "Accept my love and I will show you how you may live forever."

Comment: Robert Quarry played Count Yorga in both films; Edward Walsh was the hulking Brudah, who was shot to death by the police in the second movie. The films were written by Robert Kelljan (Yvonne Wilder collaborated on the second); the first picture was originally conceived as a soft-core pornographic film. See other vampire super villains BARON BLOOD, BEN CORTMAN, BLACULA, DRACULA, NOSFERATU, PAUL JOHNSON, and VARNEY THE VAMPIRE.

CREATURE KING (TV, C)

First Appearance: 1966, Space Ghost, CBS-TV.

Costume: Olive bodysuit; green trunks, boots gloves (three-fingered), shoulders, cap with widow's peak and red jewels set in forehead (skin is orange).

Weapons: Ray gun which fires "nightmare beams."

Chief Henchmen: Sulphur-breathing space bats.

Biography: An extraterrestrial, the Creature King uses his ray to cause people, individually or en masse, to see huge monsters. His ambition is to rule the galaxy, using his terrifying illusions to keep people in line. He is foiled repeatedly by the superheroic Space Ghost.

Quote: "His powers and strength are great, but cannot last long if I wear him down with unending, useless combat!"

Comment: This character was seen in two Space Ghost cartoons. He was also featured in Western Publishing's *Super TV Heroes* #3 (1968), a re-telling of the TV tale. Other foes of Hanna-Barbera's Space Ghost include the alien Brak, who terrorizes the spaceways with his Immobilizer-Ray; the Heat Thing; Zoark; the Lizard Slavers; the Sandman; the Robot Master; the Iceman; Brago; the Spider Woman; the Energy Monster; Lokar, King of the Killer Locusts; the Ruler of the Rock Robots; Transor the Matter Mover; the Gargoyloids; and the Molten Monsters of Moltar.

THE CRIMELORD (C)

First Appearance: 1981, *Wonder Woman* #284, DC Comics.

Costume: Silver-blue armor, mail bodyshirt and hood, gauntlets with red cuffs; red tunic with white skull on chest; navy blue cape; red boots; black belt with golden buckle.

Weapons: Electrified broadsword and chain, both of which can render people unconscious with their touch; mace.

Chief Henchmen: Various thugs including Karnage, who was used to test the Crimelord's weapons (#'s 286-287) before he began using them himself (#289).

Biography: When his criminal operations are constantly thwarted by the superheroic Huntress, the Crimelord decides to become super himself. Donning armor and taking weapons in hand, he deduces her secret indentity, kidnaps her, and engages in a gladiatorial duel-to-the-death (with the heroine unarmed) atop his magnificent castle just outside of Gotham City. During the battle the Crimelord plunges to his death, borne earthward by the weight of his armor (#290).

Quote: "I don't know why you're suddenly so *quiet*, Huntress, but *no matter*. All I want to hear is your *death-cry*, anyway!"

THE CRIMSON DYNAMO (C)

Real Name: Anton Vanko; Boris Turgenov; Alex Niven (alias Alex Nevsky); Yuri Petrovich; Dimitri Bukharin.

First Appearance: 1963, *Tales of Suspense* #46 (as Vanko); 1964, *Tales of Suspense* #52 (as Turgenov); 1970, *Iron Man* #21 (as Nevsky); 1976, *Champions* #8 (as Petrovich); 1978, *Iron Man* #109 (as Bukharin), Marvel Comics.

Costume: Red body-armor, gauntlets, boots, full-head helmet (see Weapons).

Weapons: Crimson Dynamo's armor enables him to fly via jet-boots, fire destructive blasts from his hands, jam radar, withstand emormous extremes in temperature, and also gives him superstrength.

Biography: After inventing a suit of incredible armor, Russian scientist Anton Vanko is assigned to put it on, go to the United States and, as the Crimson Dynamo, destroy the superhero Iron Man. Beaten by the American hero, Vanko agrees to turn on his Soviet bosses. Meanwhile, Russia dispatches operatives Natasha Romanova and Boris Turgenov to kill Iron Man and Vanko both. Stealing the armor, Turgenov goes on a rampage as the Crimson Dynamo until Vanko is able to stop him. Both men perish. Back in Russia, things are also going poorly for Vanko's assistant Alex Nevsky. (Note: Alexander Nevsky is also the name of a thirteenth-century Russian hero-saint.) He is mistrusted because of Vanko's treason and, unable to live under those conditions, he too defects. Landing a job at Cord Industries, he builds his own Crimson Dynamo armor in order to avenge Vanko by slaying Iron Man. Failing, he hies to Saigon where he briefly serves with THE TITANIC THREE before being found by the Soviets and executed. His armor is confiscated, and the suit next goes to Yuri Petrovich who is sent to nab Natasha Romanova, who has defected, as well as his own father Ivan, also a defector. Coming home empty-handed earns him a one-way trip to a Siberian work camp. KGB operative Dimitri Bukharin is the next Crimson Dynamo, assigned to the group THE SOVIET SUPER SOLDIERS in order to clandestinely report on the activities of the mutants. Learning that he's a spy, the other members show him the door. Bukharin presently operates as a loner in the Communist cause.

Comment: See other Soviet super villains Boris Kartovski (see DR. CLEMENT ARMSTRONG, Comment), COMRADE STUPIDSKA, MONGU, THE RED GHOST, THE SOVIET SUPER SOLDIERS, THE TITANIC THREE, and TITANIUM MAN.

THE CRIMSON GHOST (MP)

Real Name: Professor Parker (no first name).

First Appearance: 1946, *The Crimson Ghost*, Republic Pictures.

Costume: Skull facemask; dark robe, hood; dark gloves with skeleton hands painted thereupon. (Presumably the character's garb was red; the film, however, was black and white.)

Weapons: The Cyclotrode, a large instrument which short-circuits electrical current and has a TV screen which allows the user to watch the results; metal control collars which force each wearer to obey the Crimson Ghost, and cannot be removed or the wearer dies.

Biography: Professor Chambers invents the Cyclotrode and demonstrates it to four of his associates. Unknown to him, one of them is the Crimson Ghost who sees in the device a means to make a fortune. Holed up in his rundown country place, the villain sends a pair of thugs to try to steal the Cyclotrode. Chambers smashes it rather than let it out of his hands; however, he has another one tucked away and when the Crimson Ghost fits him with one of the control collars he reveals its location. Planning to sell it to an unfriendly foreign government, the Crimson Ghost must first demonstrate the Cyclotrode's power by shutting down an entire city. Just as he is about to do so, crimefighter Duncan Richards reaches the malfeasant's hideout and shoots at the machine. The Crimson Ghost runs but, pulled down by a bloodhound named Timmy, he is arrested by Duncan.

Comment: Joe Forte played the part of this genuinely eerie character in the 12-chapter serial. Other skull-faced super villains include THE RED SKULL and THE SKULL.

CRIMSON STAR (C)

First Appearance: 1981, *Adventure Comics* #487, DC Comics.

Costume: Red boots, trunks, bodysuit with black band around thighs, ankles, toes, star on chest; red gloves with black stripes on cuffs; black belt; red cowl with white ears and stripes on top. (On cover, bands around thighs and cuffs, and the star on his chest, are all white.

Weapons: Black bracelets which radiate "solar energies."

Biography: Nothing is known of this villain's past. Able to generate great heat, Crimson Star can melt metal—including incoming bullets—or fire stunning heat blasts. His partner in crime is the green-costumed Radiator, who can fly as well as fire heat or ice rays. Since both men are powered by solar energy, their goal in life is to blow a hole through the earth's ozone layer so that "*radiation* will pour through like water through a dam—radiation . . . that will make my partner and me *the strongest men on earth!*" They intend to do this by sabotaging the U.S. missile Skywolf One, which was created to *seal* rents in the ozone layer. However, the super villains didn't count on the interference of Vicki Grant and Chris King, keepers of the "Dial-H for Hero" device. Becoming the superheroes Kismet and Avatar, respectively, they arrest the villains and destroy the override panel Radiator had placed on Skywolf One.

Quote: "Farewell, dolts!"

Comment: This was the characters' only appearance. That same magazine featured a tale of Snakeman, aka Professor Ralson, a biochemist who accidentally turned himself into a giant snake while experimenting with snake venom.

CROSSBOW (C)

First Appearance: 1984, *Daredevil* #204, Marvel Comics.

Costume: Green bodysuit; tan jerkin, boots; dark green hood.

Weapons: Crossbow.

Biography: Nothing has been revealed about this character's past, although his accent and Robin Hood-like garb suggest he hails from the United Kingdom. Disgusted with the world, Crossbow hires himself out to kill anyone who he agrees should be dead. He shows very little discrimination, enjoying the hunt, not to mention the $50,000 he receives for each hit.

Quote: "I'll not skewer ye—I'll aim for the rope. Ye can contemplate yer folly during' the fall."

Comment: See also the archers BLACK BOW and MERLYN (see TOBIAS WHALE, Chief Henchmen).

CROSSFIRE (C)

Real Name: William Cross.

First Appearance: 1979, *Marvel Two-in-One* #52, Marvel Comics.

Costume: Red gloves with white fringe and stripe along back of forearm; red cowl with a white band around it and a stripe along left on top; red bodysuit with a white stripe across the chest and arms and another over the left shoulder (continuing down the leg), the two meeting at a red cloverlike design on a white field over the heart; white band around waist and another down crotch; white boots; ornamental black and red lens worn over left eye.

Weapons: "Sonic Mind-Warper," a non-portable organ-like device which uses music to destroy the human brain (the louder the music, the more rapid the listener's demise); nerve gas grenades.

Chief Henchmen: A small army of yellow- and red-garbed thugs armed with paralyzing "sonic blasters."

Biography: A former C.I.A. employee, Cross was "the best brainwasher they had." Possessing a "zealous devotion to duty," he quickly built up his own private army. With it, he became involved in assassination and drug-dealing, turning a tidy profit until he was investigated and fled. (Rumor has it that he was caught in an explosion set by either the C.I.A. or criminal rivals. If so, he may have lost his eye in the blast, which would explain the opaque lens he wears.) When he next surfaces he is the costumed Crossfire, bent on ridding the world of what he calls an "aberrant breed": superheroes. Capturing Moon Knight and the Thing of the Fantastic Four, he is about to destroy them with his Sonic Mind-Warper when the heroes escape. He is last seen fleeing his Brooklyn headquarters, lobbing a nerve gas bomb to cover his retreat.

Quote: "My Sonic Mind-Warper! At high intensity, it can kill with swift and painful effect. At low, it will sound to you like soothing music . . . even as it eats away your brain!"

CRUELLA DE VIL (N, MP)

First Appearance: 1956, "The Great Dog Robbery," *Women's Day*, Dodie Smith.

Costume: "Simple white mink cloak (with) a brown mink coat under it." Also fur hat, gloves, and boots lined with fur. Her dresses are usually red.

Biography: Cruella has "dark skin, black eyes with a tinge of red in them (and) hair parted severely down the middle and one half of it was black and the other white." Cruella lives near Regent's Park in a mansion filled with marble, puts a coat of pepper on all her food (including ice cream), drives a car with "the loudest horn in England," and has a Persian cat, of which she says, "I'd drown her if she wasn't so valuable." Little is known about Cruella's early years. Expelled from school "for drinking ink," Cruella married, insisting that her husband change his name to hers because she is the last of her family. Everything she does is equally selfish, particularly when it comes to fur, which is her passion. She wears it all year round, even sleeps between ermine sheets; "that," says she, "is why I married a furrier." Meeting the dalmatians of former classmate Mrs. Dearly, she muses they'd make "enchanting fur coats . . . for spring wear, over a black suit." When Mrs. Dearly won't sell, Cruella hires the Baddun brothers to dognap them; simultaneously she begins stealing dalmatian puppies from around the country, hoarding them at her country estate, Hell Hall. Intending to make a line of coats, she plans to flay them when she's collected enough. She's foiled when Pongo and Missis Pongo, the parents of the Dearly puppies, rescue all the dalmatians. Destroying Mr. de Vil's stock of furs, the dogs force him to go into another line of work; he opts to go abroad and make plastic raincoats. As for Cruella, the black side of her hair turns white and the white side green from shock.

Quote: "*I* don't care *how* you kill the little beasts. Hang them, suffocate them, drop them off the roof—good gracious, there are dozens of lovely ways. I only wish I'd time to do the job myself."

Comment: The title of the serial was changed to *One Hundred and One Dalmatians* when it was published in book form. Betty Lou Gerson was the voice of Cruella in Walt Disney's 1961 animated feature. In the film, she was last seen when her car was wrecked as she pursued the dogs.

THE CRUSADER (C)

Real Name: Arthur Blackwood.

First Appearance: 1983, *Thor* #330, Marvel Comics.

Costume: Iron-gray mail bodysuit; red tunic with white cross on chest, helmet with white band around it, a vertical white stripe forming a cross on the forehead; purple cape, gloves, boots, belt.

Weapons: Mighty sword of his Crusader ancestor; shield.

Chief Henchman: His squire Paeleus (real name: Polowski), who happens to be nearby when the ghost of Arthur's father appears. Impressed into service, he wears a mail bodysuit, blue tunic with a white cross on the chest, and blue boots and gloves.

Biography: A student at Chicago's Blackwood Seminary, which was founded by his great-great-grandfather, the bespectacled Arthur is offended by the popularity of Thor, an ancient Norse god who has become a modern-day superhero. Deciding that "It's time to lift up the sword . . . against those who tolerate pagans and heretics," he goes to the tomb of his father Harold and is visited by the dead man's ghost. Harold introduces his son to the spirits of his ancestors, most notably a knight who served in the Crusades. Bequeathing Arthur the weapons, garb, and "the strength and power and skill" of that knight and "countless others who fought in defense of the true way," he sends Arthur forth as the Crusader. Though Arthur hacks at Thor with his sword, and even throws a car at him, the superhero triumphs—angered when his father, Odin, is referred to as being "bloated on the blood of innocents." Smashing the Crusader's sword, Thor sends him running.

Quote: "Repent or *die*, ungodly pagan!"

Comment: The character's two-issue appearance was a notable achievement for Marvel, the writer and editors effectively underscoring the folly of blind faith and intemperance.

CUTTHROAT (C)

Real Name: See Comment.

First Appearance: 1979, *Marvel Team-Up* #89, Marvel Comics.

Costume: Gray bodysuit, boots; green breastplate, tights; dark green hood, cape.

Weapons: Gun which fires explosive darts, deafening "sonic screamer" projectiles, and blinding magnesium flares.

Biography: Amos Jardine is a wealthy circus entrepreneur with an all-consuming hatred of Spider-Man. When an attempt to kill the wall-crawling superhero fails, Jardine hires novice assassin Cutthroat to murder him—in center ring of The Greatest Show on Earth. It's a job Cutthroat accepts with relish; being known as "the man who killed Spider-Man" will make him much in demand. To set the hero up, Jardine takes out a newspaper ad challenging him to "prove (that) his web-swinging was more exciting than my high wire acts." Though Spider-Man attends in his identity as photographer Peter Parker, he has no intention of going into action. However, when Nightcrawler happens to show up and Cutthroat accidentally shoots at that similarly-attired superhero, Spider-Man has no choice but to suit-up. Together, they battle the assassin and the horde of circus animals he unleashes. He's overcome when Spider-Man's webbing causes his gun to backfire; Jardine is also arrested.

Quote: "*Cutthroat's* the name . . . murder's my game!"

Comment: The character's name is never revealed. Though Nightcrawler refers to him as "Herr Schurke," "schurke" is German for "villain." This was the character's only appearance.

CYCLOPS (C)

First Appearance: 1966, *Spyman* #2, Harvey Comics.

Costume: Light green bodysuit; dark green trunks, gloves, boots, cape, hood.

Weapons: Destructive ray fired from eye.

Biography: Cyclops leads an evil organization known as the Evil Eye Society, all of whose members wear a third eye pasted onto their foreheads. The gang's only loyalty is to gold, and they sell their criminal services to the highest international bidders; gangmembers who bungle a job are executed. The group's arch-enemies are Spyman and the heroes of Liberty, the U.S. counterespionage agency. In his only known crime, Cyclops tries to steal the plans for Professor Volk's "Transistorized Nuclear Weapon" from Liberty's outpost in the Statue of Liberty. Cyclops and Spyman battle on the monument's torch; when the villain fires a blast at the hero from his "baleful eye," Spyman's cybernetic hand sends the ray bounding back, causing Cyclops to stumble from the torch to his death.

***CYCLOPS** eyes another victim.*

Quote: "To understand the heart beat of a villain you must *be* one. One must be born with that inner hatred toward society that smoulders like a pot of simmering stew."

Comment: This was the character's only appearance.

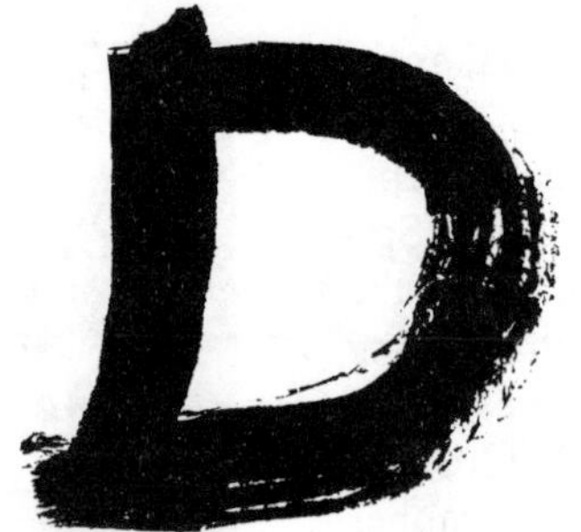

DADDY LONGLEGS (C)

Real Name: Ramsey Kole.

First Appearance: 1982, *Spider-Woman* #47, Marvel Comics.

Costume: Navy blue tuxedo and top hat.

Weapons: Solid steel cane used for clubbing.

Biography: An aspiring dancer, Kole is "'bout the best there is," but is unable to get work because he's too short. Entering the lab of scientist Bill Foster (aka Giant-Man), he implores the superhero to lend him some of his growth formula. Foster refuses, and Kole knocks him out ("Sorry, bro, but I just gotta get tall!"). Unfortunately, he doesn't know which of the beakers contains the formula and drinks from them all. He starts to grow and is delighted, until he realizes that he is getting not only taller, but also increasingly more spindly. He stops at around 13 feet, "a freak" with a consuming desire to avenge himself against the dance world. His weight "distributed to make him light as a feather," and large enough to vault cars with ease, he is still no match for Spider-Woman. She captures him, but he wriggles free of his bonds and escapes and has not been heard from, save for a cameo appearance in the superhero's last issue (#50).

Quote: "You have stood in the way of art. I shall kill you for that."

DAFFY THE GREAT (C)

Real Name: Daffy Dagan.

First Appearance: 1966, *House of Mystery* #158, DC Comics.

Costume: Blue trunks; purple belt.

Weapons: Dial-H for Hero device (see Biography).

Chief Henchman: Smike.

Biography: Daffy is the leader of the Siren Thieves, robbers who use sirens to paralyze the police. However, during a robbery in Granite City, he tangles with Robby Reed, keeper of the "Dial-H for Hero" device; getting his hands on the instrument, Daffy dials "V-I-L-L-A-I-N" and is immediately transformed into a grotesque, red giant who fires both destructive and magnetic rays from his fingers and can surround himself with a protective field of energy. Delighted, he goes "on a super-crime rampage that'll make the world learn to respect Daffy Dagan!" Luckily, Reed is able to get to his dial and, as the superhero the Squid, subdues Daffy with a sting of lightning. Using the unconscious villain's finger to dial "N-I-A-L-L-I-V" ("villain" in reverse), Robby turns him back to his human self and carts him off to jail.

Quote: "How am I going to enjoy all the loot in this crazy form?"

Comment: This was the character's only appearance.

DAGNA (MP)

First Appearance: 1936, *Darkest Africa*, Republic Pictures.

Costume: Tight, light-color silk robe; dark tabard with lighter embroidering; black turban with light horizontal stripes along bottom (film was black and white).

Weapons: Trained lions.

Chief Henchmen: The winged Bat Men; Samabi is the leader of these spear-carrying warriors.

Biography: Dagna is the high priest of the Goddess of the Golden Bat; his cult, located in the lost city of Joba, was established ages ago by Solomon. When Dagna kidnaps a young girl named Valerie, her brother, Baru, engages animal expert Clyde Beatty to help him rescue her. After many adventures in Joba, Clyde and his companions rescue Valerie as a volcano erupts, destroying Joba and Dagna with it. Other villains in Joba include Durkin and Craddock, traders who will stop at nothing to find and control Joba's fabled diamond mines. They, too, are killed in the eruption.

Comment: Lucien Prival played Dagna, Ray Benard was Samabi, Wheeler Oakman was Durkin, and Edmund Cobb (THE RATTLER) was Craddock in this 15-chapter serial. John Rathmell, Barney Sarecky, and Ted Parsons wrote the screenplay, based on a story by Rathmell and Tracy Knight. The serial was re-released in 1948 as *King of Jungleland*; a feature version entitled *Bat Men of Africa* was released in 1966.

DAGON THE AVENGER (C)

Real Name: Wezil Yondor.

First Appearance: 1980, *The Legion of Super-Heroes* #263, DC Comics.

Costume: Green bodysuit armor; darker green helmet with two huge, curved horns on side (see Weapons), shoulders, gloves, boots.

Weapons: Anesthetic darts fired from gloves and "carrying sufficient dosage to stun a Plutonian helium-bull" (not to mention superheroes); "cyanide capsules" also fired from gloves; destructive "light beams of energy" fired from eyes of helmet; crushing, painful "net composed of negative ions."

Biography: An inhabitant of the thirtieth century, Wezil is "a Tech Master . . . a super weapons expert." Fired by B.D. Brande Enterprises in a cost-cutting move, he designs and/or steals from the Security Storage Chambers elements of his potent armor. Kidnapping the parents of members of the Legion of Super-Heroes, he then demands "one billion solar credits" for their release, threatening to kill them if the ransom is not paid in 24 hours. He demands the fortune not only to become wealthy, but also that others will know "the agony of financial ruination" which he himself has suffered. However, the Legion finds his headquarters located in the earth right beneath their own headquarters, and Lightning Lad is able to subdue him with a potent blast of energy (#264).

Quote: "Do not underestimate me, Legionnaires, for if you do . . . as surely as there is sunrise . . . your parents will *die*!"

Comment: The two-issue story marks the character's only appearances to date. Dagon is also the name of the chief god of the Philistines, a deity who was half-human, half-fish. It was his temple that the Biblical Samson pulled down in his last hurrah.

DARK DESTROYER (C)

First Appearance: 1984, *Atari Force* #1, DC Comics.

Costume: Originally: none, as the Dark Destroyer was a giant octopus-like beast. Later: purple bodysuit, shoulderpads; red robe, horned helmet; blue boots, gloves; bandoliers around chest and waist (see Weapons).

Weapons: Various guns and explosives contained in bandoliers and holsters; antimatter bomb.

Chief Henchmen: Sundry beings whose minds it takes over.

Biography: The Dark Destroyer was the sole survivor of an extinct civilization. A tentacled slug the size of a small planet, the creature was found in another dimension by the adventurers known as the Atari Force. Although they managed to avoid its clutches the creature gave chase, using its vast telepathic abilities to take over sundry alien races it encountered. Finally turning and confronting the extraterrestrial, the Atari Force blew it to pieces—but not before the slug was able to send its consciousness off in a living shell. Later, the Dark Destroyer entered Mark Champion, leader of the Atari Force and, reading his genetic code, began creating a clone. When his work was completed the new Dark Destroyer was an exact copy of Champion. Laying low for many years, the super villain finally returned, intending to destroy Champion's universe with an antimatter bomb. However, it was not our universe but the Dark Destroyer who perished in the blast, due to the efforts of the Atari Force.

Comment: Not bona fide superheroes, the Atari Force is a group of adventurer/scientists living in the future. They were organized to scour the universe and other dimensions to find a new home for humankind, earth having been made unlivable due to warfare and pollution. (DC created the group as a means of promoting the Atari name. Both DC and the videogame manufacturer were owned by Warner Communications.)

THE DARK MAN (C)

First Appearance: 1980, *The Legion of Super-Heroes* #269, DC Comics.

Costume: Yellow boots, bodysuit with red bands around wrists, forearms, biceps, ankles, shins, and neck; black trunks with red belt.

Weapons: *Dragonbane* (a spaceship, complete with cloaking device).

Chief Henchmen: Nameless border guards of the United Planets Patrol (whom he feeds to sea-apes when he's finished with them).

Biography: In the thirtieth century, when the villain THAROK underwent surgery on the planet Zadron, a scientist took a tissue sample from the thief's brain and cloned it. Weeks later, due to exposure to radiation (from a nuclear bomb that felled Tharok), the tissue developed "a unique life of its own." It took over the scientist's mind and forced him to create a humanoid body in a protein bath. The creature which emerged announced that it was "all that is *dark* in the human spirit." Worse, as "a life-force vampire," it must eat people to live. Consuming the scientist, it intended to use its mind-control power and other weapons to take over the universe. First, however, the clone had to eliminate all the forces of good. Calling itself the Dark Man, it set up headquarters on the starship *Dragonbane* and paid border guards to obtain a cloaking device so it could approach the earth and destroy the Legion of Super-Heroes. However, the villain was eventually destroyed when the original Tharok touched his clone and the two were obliterated (#271).

Quote: "You have tasted only a little of my power, small man. Be grateful I am in a *gentle* mood."

DARKSEID (C, TV)

First Appearance: 1971, *Jimmy Olsen* #134, DC Comics.

Costume: Blue vest, helmet, gloves, trunks, boots; skin is purple.

Weapons: Shock-prod, which can hurt even a god; a tele-ray for teleportation; the Fear Machine, to turn heroes into cowards; many others.

Chief Henchmen: Brola, an elite bodyguard; Kalibak the Cruel, Darkseid's brute of a son; Dasaad, a deformed scientific genius; Para-Demons, the flying "sentries of Apokolips"; the Deep Six, amphibious killers most of whom have superhuman powers: Slig vaporizes objects by touching them, Jaffar causes instantaneous mutations, Trok is armed with a powerful battleaxe, and Shaligo can fly (Gole and Kurin are merely amphibious); THE SECRET SOCIETY OF SUPER-VILLAINS; Mantis "the awesome digger" who burrows through the earth and "whose mammoth power rivals that of Darkseid"; Steppenwolf, an axe-wielding brute (and Darkseid's nephew); the military stragegist and scientist Virman Vundabar; and numerous others.

Biography: "There came a time when the old gods died," it is written, and from that holocaust (implicitly the Norse "Twilight of the Gods," aka Ragnarok [see LOKI]) arose two great worlds: New Genesis, home of the benign New Gods, and the dark Apokolips, where "those who *live* with weapons *rule* the wretches who *build* them." Darkseid is the son of Queen Heggra, and he secretly yearns to rule. Physically, the nearly eight-foot-tall being has the power to do so. Chief among his powers is "the Omega Effect," the ability to shoot destructive blasts from his eyes, as well as to disintegrate or teleport objects; the power to fly; a limited talent for mind-control; and vast physical strength. Craftily convincing his uncle Steppenwolf to go to New Genesis and kill a few of its people for fun, Darkseid ignites a war between the worlds. Allowing his uncle to go into battle he knew to be particularly dangerous, Darkseid sits back while Steppenwolf is slain. Meanwhile, Dasaad slays Heggra and the throne passes to Darkseid. A truce is eventually called with New Genesis and, based in the capital city of Armagedda, Darkseid spends years trying to conquer the universe. Principal among his projects during this period is trying to learn the Anti-Life Equation, a mental force which, if he could master it, would theoretically enable him to subjugate every mind in creation. A second war with New Genesis results in that planet's destruction, though a rebellion of the Hunger Dogs, the slave-caste of Apokolips, leaves his own world badly battered as well. Still, Darkseid plots on. It is widely held that Darkseid will eventually meet his doom in a battle with the heroic Orion, his son by his second wife Tigra (his first wife, Suli, is dead).

Quote: "Enough, *dog*! Find your *kennel* and nurse your well-deserved wounds!"

Comment: The character continues to plague the roster of DC heroes. The similarity between writer/artist Jack Kirby's tales of the New Gods and the later saga of *Star Wars* is pronounced. Most telling factors are the father-son status of Darkseid and Orion (akin to the DARTH VADER-Luke Skywalker relationship), the fact that Vader was lured to the "Dark Side" (Darkseid?) of the Force, and various psionic powers the two share.

DARTH VADER (N, MP, C, CS)

Real Name: Anakin Skywalker.

First Appearance: 1976, *Star Wars*, George Lucas, Ballantine/Del Rey.

Costume: Black helmet and full-face covering (which contains breath mask, a miniature life-support system, and electronic speech augmentor; control panel on chest); black cloak, gloves, boots, shirt, pants.

Weapons: Lightsaber, a sword whose energy-blade can slice through rock; TIE (Twin Ion Engine) Interceptor for solo spaceflight; various telekinetic, precognitive, and mind-control abilities.

Biography: Little is known of Darth Vader's younger years. He fought in the Clone Wars as a pilot and warrior and, by exhibiting unusual extrasensory powers, became the apprentice of Obi-Wan Kenobi, a Jedi Knight—one of the intergalactic peacekeepers who have telekinetic and related psychic abilities. At some point Anakin fathered a son, Luke Skywalker, and a daughter, Leia. Lured to serve evil in the person of THE EMPEROR, Anakin turned on his mentor Obi-Wan; the two fought with lightsabers, Skywalker receiving severe injuries during the clash (he is rumored to have tumbled into the crater of a volcano). Fitted with a breath mask and garbed entirely in black, Anakin—now known as Darth Vader—spent the next 20 years serving as

The Emperor's most trusted henchman. (At some point as yet unrevealed he became one of the Dark Lords of the Sith, a band of extremely powerful evildoers.) Meanwhile, Luke went to live with his aunt and uncle, Owen and Beru Lars; Leia was adopted by the Organa family and became a senator. After overseeing such projects as the construction of the planet-destroying Death Star, fighting the ragtag Rebel Alliance on worlds throughout the galaxy (aboard his flagship the *Executor* at the head of the Imperial Armada), and also slaying Obi-Wan in a rematch, Darth was instructed by the Emperor to seduce Luke to their cause. When the boy refused, The Emperor proceeded to electrocute him; unable to stand by and watch his son destroyed, Vader killed his master. In the process, however, he received a substantial dose of electricity, which short-circuited his life support systems. Vader died in his son's arms, repenting all his crimes; he lives on as a benign spiritual presence. Among the officers who served with Darth on his military campaigns against the Rebel Alliance were Admiral Ozzel, Captain Piett of the *Executor* (Piett succeeded Ozzel when Vader executed Ozzel for incompetence), Captain Needa of the Star Destroyer *Avenger*, and General Veers, commander of the Imperial Armada's ground forces.

Quote: "You were once my teacher, and I learned much from you. But the time of learning has long passed, and I am the master now."

Comment: Darth Vader is best known through the motion pictures *Star Wars* (1977; the source of the novel, which was published six months before the release of the film), *The Empire Strikes Back* (1980), and *Return of the Jedi* (1983), all Twentieth Century-Fox. David Prowse played the part in all three films, though his voice was dubbed by actor James Earl Jones. Jones also played the villainous THULSA DOOM in the movie *Conan the Barbarian* (1982). The character has also appeared in the newspaper comic strip and the popular Marvel comic book which lasted nine years.

***DAVROS** overlooking his evil creations, the Daleks. Illustration by David Mann; © British Broadcasting Corporation.*

DAVROS (TV, N)

First Appearance: 1974, "Genesis of the Daleks," *Dr. Who*, BBC.

Costume: Green plastic bodysuit; from the waist down, Davros is enclosed in a "travel machine" (see Biography).

Biography: The scientist Davros is one of the Kaleds, martial inhabitants of the planet Skaro. Maimed when an atomic bomb strikes his laboratory, the withered Davros is enclosed in a "travel machine" from the waist down, a shell-like device which serves as a wheelchair and aids his breathing and heart functions; on his forehead is an artificial eye which is operated by a mesh of tubes and wires atop his bald head, electronics which also help him hear and speak. Because Kaled ranks have been been depleted by a thousand-year war between the Kaleds and the other Skarosians, the Thals, Davros seeks to use gene technology to create an advanced Kaled, one able to survive the radiation which has been produced by the war. The result of his work are the Daleks, slug-like Kaleds encased in travel machines. Unfortunately, the scientist makes his cyborg creations in his own image, "without conscience, without soul, and without pity," arming them with built-in guns and "sucker arms." When the Kaled leaders protest the awfulness of the creatures, Davros allies with the Thals and eliminates the remaining Kaleds. Davros and his emotionless fiends then turn on the Thals, take over Skaro, and make the most ambitious plans in criminal history: to take over the universe, not just in their era but throughout all time! Although Davros is killed by his own Daleks in "Genesis of the Daleks," they are forced to bring him back to life when his scientific genius is required. He perishes again in "Revelation of the Daleks" when he attempts to take control over his creations via a germ lethal to Daleks. Unfortunately, he himself becomes the bacterium's victim. In "Genesis of the Daleks," the heroic Dr. Who travels to the past and tries in vain to prevent the creation of the Daleks—which, according to the all-knowing Time Lords, will at some point "become the dominant creatures in the universe."

Quote: "Your friends are attached to rather different instruments, Doctor. At the touch of a switch I can make them feel all the torments and agonies ever known."

Comment: The Dr. Who series is produced in England. The teleplay for "Genesis of the Daleks" was written by Terry Nation; it was published in book-form as *Doctor Who and the Genesis of the Daleks*, by Terrance Dicks. The Daleks themselves first appeared in Nation's 1963 adventure drama, "The Dead Planet."

DEADSHOT (C)

Real Name: Floyd Lawton.

First Appearance: 1950, *Batman* #59, DC Comics.

Costume: Original: tuxedo with domino mask. Second: red bodysuit with blue waist and "V"-shaped panel on chest; blue fullhead cowl (see Weapons), wristbands (see Weapons), trunks, narrow storage containers strapped to thighs; yellow boots with blue front and toes, gloves.

Weapons: Cowl has infrared sight over right eye; miniature telescopic rifles on wristbands which fire everything from bullets to grapnels (projectiles which he stores in containers attached to wristbands).

Biography: Despite his inherited wealth, Lawton wants to be a powerful criminal figure in Gotham City. A marksman without peer, Lawton becomes Deadshot in order to humiliate Batman and make him ineffective as a force for justice. Failing at this and landing in prison, Lawton spends his time up the river designing a new costume and hi-tech armaments. Becoming a high-paid hitman upon his release, he is once again captured by Batman and is presently back in jail.

DEATHBOLT (C)

Real Name: Jake Simmons.

First Appearance: 1983, *All Star Squadron* #21, DC Comics.

Costume: Green bodysuit; purple trunks, cape boots, gloves, helmet with green fin.

Biography: Not quite a half-century ago, murderer Simmons stole a biplane to escape from the law. Struck by lightning over Arizona, he crashed and was found barely alive by the evil ULTRA-HUMANITE. The super villain took him to his lair, where he was kept alive by an experimental process involving electricity. However, there was an unanticipated result to the prodecure: Simmons became a living battery, able to fire destructive bolts of electricity from his hands. Joining the Ultra-Humanite as his costumed sidekick, Deathbolt was eventually captured by the superheroic All-Star Squadron. His current whereabouts are not known.

DEATHGRIP (C)

Real Name: Glenn Thorne (alias; real name is unrevealed).

First Appearance: 1975, *The Destructor* #2, Atlas Comics.

Costume: Dark green bodysuit; yellow boots, wristband on left hand, belt, cloak; blue sunglasses; red right hand (see Weapons).

Weapons: "Electronic paw," a metal hand capable of crushing and melting metal . . . and killing enemies.

Biography: Little is known about this character's past. As a young man, he was "a brilliant card sharp . . . blessed with magic hands." However, he miscalculated grandly when he "worked his clever tricks against a powerful syndicate lord (Big Mike Brand) who didn't appreciate being fleeced." A car chase ensued, followed by a crash; though the card player escaped, one of his hands did not. Allying himself with Brand's rivals, a crime syndicate known as the Combine, Glenn was outfitted with a metal hand and devoted himself to bringing down Brand—for starters, making him suffer by going after his daughter, Angela. Fortunately for the woman, the superheroic Destructor arrived just as Deathgrip was going to slip her into a car compactor. During the ensuing battle, the fiend's hand was drawn to a crane magnet, the "automatic process swings fully in motion," and he, himself, was pressed into scrap metal.

Quote: "Subtlety can *hardly* be the stock-in-trade of *anyone* called *Deathgrip*."

Comment: This was the character's only appearance.

DEATH-MAN (C)

First Appearance: 1966, *Batman* #180, DC Comics.

Costume: Black gloves, boots, bodysuit, all with white skeleton on front; white skull mask.

Chief Henchmen: Nameless thugs dressed in black bodysuits, full-face masks, boots, white belts and gloves.

Biography: Mastering "the ultimate yogi exercise" which slows breathing and heartbeat until they cannot be detected, Death-Man goes on a crime rampage, always "dying" when he is caught by the superhero Batman. Buried, he always escapes to rob again. Unfortunately, while holding a gun in a rainstorm, he is struck by lightning and perishes for real. Death-Man had a "spine-freezer" of a laugh.

Quote: "*You* can't take it with you—so *I'm* takin' it with *me*!"

Comment: This was the character's only appearance; it was never explained how he escaped being embalmed after each death.

DEATH-STALKER (C)

First Appearance: 1968, *Daredevil* #39 (as the Exterminator); 1974, #113 (as Death-Stalker), Marvel Comics.

Costume: As the Exterminator: white bodysuit with "V" (purple with thin horizontal stripes) from shoulders to crotch and on back; purple boots, gloves; white full-head cowl with purple mask and top-right side (thin, horizontal black stripes on latter); blue ears with antennae. As Death-Stalker: blue slouch hat, cloak, suit; white gloves (see Weapons).

Weapons: Time-displacement ray (as the Exterminator). "Cybernetic death-grip" worn in gloves, rendering his touch instantly lethal (as Death-Stalker).

Chief Henchmen: As the Exterminator: the Unholy Three (see THE ANI-MEN). As Death-Stalker: the full roster of the Ani-Men.

Biography: A scientist who was once employed by Abner Jones (see THE ANI-MEN), the villain-aborning (his name is never revealed) invents a time-displacement ray and embarks on a life of crime. He is confronted by Daredevil, who destroys the machine; the resultant explosion hurls the costumed felon "through the fabric of time." Presumed dead, he is actually in a limbo which allows him to become immaterial and come and go anywhere he pleases. Stealing plans from the criminal scientific group, A.I.M. (see MODOK), he builds the death-grip unit, "linked electronically" to his gloves, and sets about rebuilding his "t-ray." However, his one diversion proves to be a fatal one. He has the Ani-Men kidnap Daredevil and dies horribly in the midst of battle when, in a rage after his hands have been smashed by the superhero, he goes from non-corporeal to solid just as he's leaping through a tombstone.

Quote: "I have been waiting for you with, shall we say, open arms!"

DEATH-STROKE (C)

First Appearance: 1981, *Spider-Woman* #39, Marvel Comics.

Costume: Red bodysuit, full-face cowl, gloves, boots; blue, sideless tabard with flared shoulders, "V" neck, and "V" shape cut from shoulders to waist (allowing red to show through); white skull clasps, one each straddling "V" shape in tabard; light red sash around waist; white wristbands.

Weapons: Knife.

Chief Henchmen: The Terminators, killers garbed from head to toe in black. Only the name Mendez is known.

Biography: Nothing has been revealed about this character's past, or about his private identity. When the Carillon Towers is built in San Francisco, it is constructed with a "quite illegal" inner core which is to serve as the headquarters for "the new crime czar of San Francisco." When "the Feds" get wise, Death-Stroke and his Terminators are brought in to murder those who have learned the truth about the Carillon. Happily, before too many people die, Spider-Woman delivers Death-Stroke and his men to the police—and leaves him with this warning: "Should you ever consider returning to this line of work—I'll be waiting for you."

Quote: "The men you see are my *Terminators*. As the names imply, our business is killing."

Comment: Death-Stroke apparently took Spider-Woman's admonition to heart, as this has been the character's only appearance.

DE FLORES (S)

First Appearance: 1653 (although performed as early as 1622), *The Changeling*, T. Middleton and W. Rowley.

Biography: Young Beatrice-Joanna is betrothed to Alonzo de Piracquo, but her heart belongs to Alsemero. Thus, she hires the wretched De Flores to murder Alonzo—the criminal agreeing because he secretly lusts for the woman. Committing the murder, De Flores takes his fee in trade, despoiling the woman. Beatrice-Joanna subsequently becomes engaged to Alsemero, but doesn't want him to know she has had a lover; thus, she orders her maid Diaphanta to slip into his bed on their wedding night. Alsemero is fooled and, with Beatrice-Joanna's blessing, De Flores kills the maid so she can't reveal what has transpired. But Alsemero finds them out and turns them over to the governor; De Flores and Beatrice-Joanna commit suicide rather than face the law.

Comment: The bulk of the plot derives from an earlier work by John Reynolds, *God's Revenge Against Murther* (1621). Unlike the largely caricatured or seriocomic villains of other English writers, from Shakespeare to Dickens, De Flores is a truly foul human being without conscience or redeeming values.

THE DEMOLISHER (C)

Real Name: Troxx-5S.

First Appearance: 1980, *Superman* #353, DC Comics.

Costume: Maroon tights; red goggles, gloves, boots with maroon sides; red vest (the Demolisher's skin is yellow).

Weapons: Rocket backpack for flight; rifle powerful enough to level a bank; force-field which protects him from assault and endows him with incredible physical strength (this is apparently generated by controls on his vest).

Biography: On the home world of Troxx-5S, any "criminal act is impossible" due to a device which, through invisible beams, purifies the minds of the inhabitants. But the brilliant scientist Troxx-5S is a genetic mutant with "a psychologically diseased brain" who, finding a way to leave his dimension, comes to earth to execute crimes "he's secretly yearned" to commit. However, he creates a unique quandary for the protector of earth, Superman. Whenever he comes to our world, Troxx-5S automatically transfers Superman to his. This not only keeps him safe but also adds to his enjoyment of the crimes, for he can challenge Superman to battle and, since the Man of Steel can't possibly accept, the super villain makes Superman "appear a coward, afraid to face him." The superhero finally tricks him, however, by seating himself in a chair containing an "amplified purifying beam." Thus, when Troxx returns to his world, he is automatically cleansed of every "shred of anger."

Quote: "What could be more *gratifying* to a true *criminal mind* than selecting as my victim one of *Superman's closest friends*—the *woman he loves*!"

Comment: This villain was created by writer Cary Bates. Bates' villains for Superman and the Flash (i.e., COLONEL COMPUTRON and THE RAINBOW RAIDER) usually rely on super-science and, conceptually, are more ingenious than any being created for contemporary comic books. This was Troxx's only appearance.

DESPERO (C)

First Appearance: 1960, *Justice League of America* #1, DC Comics.

Costume: Orange jerkin, trousers, boots; blue gloves, belt; red full-head cowl and headdress.

Weapons: Giant hourglass which sends the Justice League to another dimension (#26 only).

Chief Henchmen: Flame-creature (#1 only); sundry terrestrial thugs.

Biography: Tyrannical ruler of the world of Kalanor in another dimension, Despero first battles the Justice League of America when scientist Jasonar escapes Kalanor and enlists the help of the superheroes to overthrow the despot. That's no easy task, Despero being well-equipped to take on all comers. A mutant, Despero has a third eye, set in his forehead, which gives him the ability to hypnotize others, create illusions, levitate and teleport matter, and even read the mind of any being on any given world. Defeated by the Justice League in their first encounter Despero is put under the knife on his home world and has his third eye removed. However, it grows back and, feigning death, Despero is able to escape Kalanor. Yearning, now, to conquer the entire universe, he again does battle with the Justice League—only to be beaten when he is snared by Wonder Woman's magic lasso (#26). He returns to fight the team numerous times over the years. In their last tilt, Despero is captured and ends up imprisoned on the world Takron-Galtos.

Quote: "I've got this game rigged so that everytime *Flash* makes a move, a member of the *Justice League* disappears from the face of the earth!"

Comment: See other hypnotist super villains HYPNOS, MESMERO, THE RINGMASTER, and UNIVERSO.

THE DESERT RAT (C)

First Appearance: 1942, *Speed Comics* #16, Harvey Comics.

Costume: Yellow robe (the Desert Rat has green skin).

Weapons: An iron mole, a drill-nosed tank which bores through the earth.

Biography: The cadaverous Desert Rat is "The Ruler of the Rolling Sands," a title he takes seriously. Discovering gold in the desert, he ignores the fact that it's U.S. government property and, digging tunnels beneath the sand, mines it for his own use. When a film crew comes to film *Bleeding Sands* above his network of tunnels, he warns the director to leave or "you and your cast shall die one by one"; when the film crew stays, the villain begins making good his threat. Fortunately, just before the crook's henchmen are about to mow down the crew in a "bloody massacre," heroic actor Ted Parrish infiltrates the Desert Rat's subterranean lair and, subduing him with "a perfect flying tackle," sends him to "a city jail . . . where he can do no more harm." A subplot involves the green-skinned malfeasant's efforts to win the love of actress Myrna Leigh.

Quote: "Come on boys we got some killing to do!"

Comment: This was the character's only appearance.

DESTINY (C)

First Appearance: 1967, *Double-Dare Adventures* #1, Harvey Comics.

Costume: Purple tights, vest; yellow-and-black striped bodyshirt; blue cape.

Weapons: Immobilizing light-gun; teleporter "gizmo"; time machine; unnamed wave invention which strikes at "the weak mortal part" of the Gladiator's body, forcing him to transform into the superhero.

Chief Henchmen: The James Gang, John Dillinger (first issue only).

Biography: A horned, portly shapechanger who can be killed without dying ("I'm a cool cat with nine hundred lives"), Destiny wants to obtain the magic amulet of the superheroic Gladiator. To do this, however, he must kill the hero—no easy task. In their first encounter, the superbeings battle to a draw, Destiny escaping by slipping into his time machine; in the second, the Gladiator is transported to the Land of No Return. There, with the help of another Destiny—the evil entity's benign counterpart—Gladiator stabs his opponent, who has taken the shape of a huge bull. However, as the Gladiator departs, the villain twitches back to life.

Quote: "Somewhere in the rule book it says I must put you completely out of action—I mean like knock you off—then I get the amulet!"

Comment: The two bouts with Destiny were the Gladiator's only appearances.

DESTRO (T, C)

First Appearance: 1982, G.I. Joe action toy lineup, Hasbro.

Costume: Navy blue boots, bodysuit with red collar; silver gauntlets (see Weapons), full-head mask.

Weapons: Various "wrist rockets," projectiles and grenades fired from backs of gauntlets; compact machinegun.

Chief Henchmen: The personnel of M.A.R.S. (Military Armaments Research System).

Biography: Virtually nothing is known about this character's past. The head of M.A.R.S., he is the largest manufacturer of hi-tech weapons—arms he'll sell to the highest bidder. Destro is also an international terrorist, practicing what he preaches: that war, and not peace, is the "most natural state" of humankind. Gunrunning has apparently been in Destro's family for generations; the full-head "battle mask" he

The evil face of ***DESTINY****. © Harvey Comics.*

wears is described as "a family tradition." Destro has several residences around the world, one of which is a spectacular mountain retreat.

Quote: "You think that you might be fast enough to raise your *uzi* for one final burst, eh? I think not. I think you will die like a dog . . . ."

Comment: Marvel Comics has published the hugely successful *G.I. Joe* comic book since 1982. The most interesting issue, #21 (1984), was an attack on Destro's mountain stronghold; the story was told entirely in pictures. The *G.I. Joe* comic holds the distinction of being the first comic book ever advertised via TV commercials. Other villains in the G.I. Joe lineup include the fiends of Cobra, an international terrorist group: the Cobra Ninja, the Cobra Intelligence Officer (the only woman), as well as Cobra's soldier/operatives, most of whom wear silver masks. The mysterious leader of the evil group is Cobra Commander, who wears a blue bodysuit with gold braid, and either a hood with a red cobra symbol on the forehead, or else a full-face, featureless silver mask. The forces of Cobra are based on Cobra Island, which is located in the Caribbean. They work out of an old Spanish fort, which is protected by batteries of surface-to-air missiles. Also serving the Cobra Commander is Zartran, a human chameleon, and the brilliant scientist Dr. Mindbender. See other action toy super villains BARON KARZA, GENERAL SPIDRAX, HORDAK, MOLTAR, MUMM-RA, and SKELETOR.

THE DEVOURER (C)

First Appearance: 1976, *Marvel Two-In-One* #23, Marvel Comics.

Costume: Iron-gray armor vest, wristband; red headdress, belt with iron-gray mail flap hanging to knees; green armor on legs and tail.

Biography: Standing some 50 feet tall, the Devourer was snared "eons ago" by the Egyptian sun god Horus. Kept imprisoned in Heliopolis, beyond the space-spanning Golden Paths of the Gods, it is released by the fiendish death god Seth to consume his hated nephew Horus and help in his plans to conquer the universe. The superhero Thing and the Norse God Thor hasten along the golden bridge to confront the enormous brute, who intends not only to dine on Horus but also to eat everyone in sight, including Seth. ("The *Devourer* . . . cares not for *pacts* or *bargains*," notes Horus' father, the regal deity Osiris.) Thinking quickly, Thing is able to lure the giant off the bridge into space. The titan has not been seen since.

Quote: "*Aaarrhh!*"

Comment: In Egyptian mythology, the Devourer dwelt in the Hall of Maat, the goddess of truth. When the dead arrived, each heart was placed in one pan of a scale, a magic feather in the other pan. If the two balanced, the soul was admitted into the afterlife. If the heart were heavier, the Devourer ate the owner. The Devourer had the forequarters of a lion, the hindparts of a hippopotamus, and the jaws of a crocodile.

DIABLO (C, TV)

Real Name: Esteban Diablo.

First Appearance: 1964, *The Fantastic Four* #30, Marvel Comics.

Costume: Purple bodysuit, boots with black sides, toe, and wings on heels; black trunks; flared black shoulders with star-like radii protruding down chest and a floor-length strip of black fabric hanging from both front and back; black mask with wide, flared brows and "U"-like horns on brow; green cowl and neck; green gloves, black on the back.

Weapons: Various pills and potions stored in the pockets of his outfit. These include paralytic gas, a knockout-brew, an immortality serum, a will-sapping potion, and many others.

Chief Henchmen: The Dragon Man, a flying, fire-breathing dragon created by the villain (#35 only). Diablo can also create slaves made of the four elements of antiquity: air, fire, water, and earth.

Biography: A Spanish nobleman of the early 1800s, Diablo is bored with the life of a country squire and takes to studying alchemy. Traveling throughout Europe and looking for notebooks or papers left behind by the masters of the art, he becomes a master of magic and transmutation. Relocating to Transylvania—which is, for mystics, what Greenwich Village was for beatniks—he puts his knowlege to work. Among his first and most astonishing concoctions is one which staves off aging: unfortunately, he doesn't get to enjoy immortality right away, as the locals whom he has repressed storm his castle and seal him in a vault. Over a century later he is able to get control of the mind of the Thing (of the Fantastic Four). The superhero unwittingly frees him, and Diablo begins his reign of terror anew in the twentieth century. In addition to his alchemical potions, Diablo has the power to cause explosions and transmute matter, including his own shape and appearance.

Comment: Marvel itself declared the character "so evil he makes some of our other villains look like Pollyanna's pen pals!" Diablo was featured in one self-titled episode of *The Fantastic Four* cartoon show which aired on ABC in 1967.

DIABOLU (C)

First Appearance: 1966, *House of Mystery* #158, DC Comics.

Costume: Blue robe.

Weapons: The Idol-Head of Diabolu, a grotesque urn containing "many terrible evils" placed there by Diabolu.

Biography: Drawn into the Idol-Head of Diabolu, the superheroic Martian Manhunter finds himself in Ancient Babylonia. There, the people are being menaced by a towering monster which spits lightning bolts. Defeating the beast, the hero learns that it was created by the wizard Diabolu, who was once the right hand man to King Nebuchadnezzar. When the tyrant was overthrown, Diabolu, "dying and driven insane... vowed revenge on all Babylonia." To this end, he created the Idol-Head which will unleash monsters regularly long into the future. Impersonating one of the monsters by using his shape-changing ability, the hero is sent inside the idol just as Diabolu perishes. Returning to the present, the superhero destroys the artifact.

Quote: "Sidarre—omnere—in you go!" (The chant to entrap time-released monsters in the idol.)

Comment: This was the character's only appearance.

DIAMONDHEAD (C)

Real Name: Arch Dyker.

First Appearance: 1976, *Nova* #3, Marvel Comics.

Costume: Blue bodysuit with diamond symbol on chest inside yellow starburst; diamond-white gloves, boots, belt, bands around shoulders. Diamondhead's head is also diamond-white, with a thick, flat top like an anvil.

Biography: While robbing a lab, Dyker stumbled into a diamond-powered laser, which promptly turned him into living diamond. Although his diamond-hard skin made him an invulnerable, hard-hitting super villain who no longer has to breathe, he also attracted superheroes each time he committed a crime. Diamondhead's perennial foe was Nova, though he has also battled Rom and others. Diamondhead briefly served with the superheroic aliens the New Champions of Xandar, but only so he could betray them (*Rom* #24) to the evil extraterrestrials, the Skrulls (see SUPERSKRULL).

Quote: "The punk *was* stupid enuff ta come after me! Too bad, creep. 'Cause now yer just gonna get *smashed—Diamondhead style*!"

DINOSAUR MAN (C)

Real Name: Zalme.

First Appearance: 1983, *The Dazzler* #30, Marvel Comics.

Biography: Fearing the growing strength of superpowered mutants, the military establishes an anti-mutant strike force in the Sierra Nevada Mountains. When Alison Blaire arrives in San Diego, the group suspects her of being a mutant (she is the superheroic Dazzler). Thus, they break out a new device to try and prove it, a machine which generates an "energy field (that) has no effect on normal humans" but causes mutant powers to "intensify... till they run out of control," thereby giving their owners away. Ironically, standing nearest the machine is soldier Zalme who doesn't know he's a mutant; bathed in the rays, he immediately becomes the purple, reptilian, nearly 12-feet-tall Dinosaur Man. Going on a rampage, he is stopped by the Dazzler and reverts to human form.

Quote: "Guys, I, um, feel . . . funny!"

Comment: This was the character's only appearance. Another saurian super villain is Spider-Man's enemy, Stegron.

DOC BENWAY (C)

Real Name: Dr. W. Lee Benway.

First Appearance: 1980, *Marvel Team-Up* #97, Marvel Comics.

Costume: Lab jacket.

Weapons: "Pleasure ray," a gun which stimulates "the pleasure centers" of the brain and removes hostilities; "nerve-paralyzer" gun.

Chief Henchmen: Various insect-, lizard-, bear-, and bird-like monster robots.

Biography: A physician, Benway had his license revoked for "illegal trafficking in human organs for transplants." Wanted in nine states, he settles into a villa 10 miles north of Jude, New Mexico. There, he uses criminals—passed along by Jude's corrupt sheriff, Bradley Martin—for his latest project. He removes their brains and places them in human-sized robotic bodies, ostensibly to develop a creature that can "survive on the hostile worlds that mankind must someday conquer." However, the bald scientist also has a lucrative side business going, selling the left-over organs on the black market. Capturing the Incredible Hulk to lobotomize him and find out how exposure to gamma radiation gave the Hulk superhuman powers, he is stopped when Spider-Woman attacks the lab. Together, she and the Hulk raze the facility. Though Benway flees into the desert, he is knocked out by Spider-Woman and collected by the Arizona State Patrol. His present whereabouts are unknown.

Quote: "She should give you no trouble. But, if she does—*rip her to shreds!*"

DOCTOR ALCHEMY (C)

Real Name: Albert and Alvin Desmond (see Biography).

First Appearance: As Mr. Element: 1958, *Showcase* #13, DC Comics; as Dr. Alchemy: 1958, *Showcase* #14, DC Comics.

Costume: As Mr. Element: green bodysuit with light green, horizontal slats on chest and matching wristbands; light green belt, boots, helmet with dark green gas mask. As Dr. Alchemy: black tights; blue boots, mask jerkin with black cross-hatching; green hood with black "A" on forehead.

Weapons: As Mr. Element: element-gun, which gives him complete mastery over the elements. As Dr. Alchemy: Philosopher's Stone, which allows him to metamorphose matter.

Biography: A schizophrenic due to the radiation of a star known as the Dragon's Eye, chemist Albert Desmond vascillates between good and evil. Committing crimes as Mr. Element, Albert is cured when the superheroic Flash finds a way of neutralizing the offending radiation. Sadly, the scientist discovers the Philosopher's Stone shortly thereafter and his wicked side is rekindled; this time he works evil as Dr. Alchemy. Cured yet again (and marrying a lovely woman named Rita), Albert is surprised to learn that he has a "psychic twin" named Alvin Desmond. Though the two had been born on different sides of the country (Albert to Mr. and Mrs. Herman Desmond of San Diego, California, and Alvin to Mr. and Mrs. Herbert Desmond of Tampa, Florida), their births occurred at precisely the same moment (12:07 P.M.). Thus, they are spiritually linked. Also a chemist (he has discovered Desmondium, an element which causes complete subservience in anyone who inhales its fragrant fumes), Alvin is an innately evil soul who, for years, felt good only when Albert was committing crimes. Now that Albert has given it up, Alvin no longer has that much-needed catharsis. Tapping into Albert's mind, he finds out where he buried the Philosopher's Stone and becomes the new Dr. Alchemy. To date, Albert has not returned to a life of lawlessness. Alvin was most recently seen battling the superheroic Blue Beetle in *Blue Beetle* #4 (1986). At the end of that issue, Dr. Alchemy absorbed too much of the element promethium and has merged (presumably dead) with the Philosopher's Stone.

Quote: "Now that my *Philosopher's Stone* has turned you into a *human cloud,* Flash—I can literally *blow you away!!*"

Comment: In some of the stories, both Desmonds are said to have the same first name, Albert.

DR. ALEX ZORKA (MP)

First Appearance: 1939, *The Phantom Creeps,* Universal Pictures.

Weapons: Eight-feet-tall robot; Divisualizer Belt for invisibility; meteorite from which he distills an element which can do everything from putting hundreds of people to sleep to causing massive earthquakes.

Chief Henchman: Monk.

Biography: A scientist, Dr. Zorka and his ex-convict aide Monk work in his secret lab where they specialize in creating tools of warfare and peddling them to the highest foreign bidder. Learning about his operation, U.S. Military Intelligence moves in and Zorka moves out. Sadly, his wife is killed in the process and Zorka vows to avenge her death by using his arsenal to conquer the world. Zorka destroys trains, blows up dirigibles, causes avalanches, and works other mayhem before the army finds his new laboratory and bombs it to rubble. Deciding that if *he* can't have the world no one will, the fiend tries to escape via airplane and tosses the unstable meteorite overboard. Though the space rock causes an earthquake, our planet holds; the same cannot be said for Zorka's plane, the villain perishing in the cataclysm.

Comment: Bela Lugosi portrayed the character in the 12-chapter serial. See other Lugosi villains BARON ROXOR, DR. MIRAKLE, DR. PAUL CARRUTHERS, DRACULA, MURDER LEGENDRE, PROFESSOR ERIC VORNOFF.

DR. ARANA (MP)

First Appearance: 1953, *Mesa of Lost Women,* Howco Pictures.

Chief Henchman: Masterson.

Biography: Living on Zarpa Mesa in Mexico, spider-expert Dr. Arana is engaged in a mad scheme to breed a race of powerful spider people which he will control. However, his plan is nipped in the bud when his long-suffering associate Masterson whips up an explosive and blows the scientist's abode to smithereens. Though Dr. Arana is destroyed, several of his genetically mutated spider women survive, presumably to spawn a spider race after all.

Comment: Jackie Coogan starred as Dr. Arana (which is "spider" in Spanish); Harmon Stevens played Masterson.

DOCTOR BONG (C)

Real Name: Lester.

First Appearance: 1977, *Howard the Duck* #15, Marvel Comics.

Costume: Purple bodysuit; brown cape, boots; golden gauntlet on right hand, clapper on left (see Weapons), belt, bell-shaped helmet (see Weapons).

Weapons: Bong's clapper and helmet produce sonic waves which can paralyze people or destroy metal; he also has an Evolvo-Chamber to push life forms along the evolutionary scale, and also to create clones.

Chief Henchmen: Various monstrous creations, including a living concrete swan, a sea serpent, a humanoid duck, and a lizardlike "coterie of bizarre beings."

Biography: Headquartered on an uncharted Mediterranean island, "a bell-shaped atoll," Doctor Bong conducts unlawful scientific experiments on lesser life forms, turning them into more humanoid creatures. When Howard the Duck washes ashore, the bird from another planet puts an end to Bong's sadistic research, though the two run afowl of each other repeatedly. Eventually, the scientist is forced to reture to his new headquarters in the Himalayas to look after quintuplets cloned from one of his fingernail clippings in the Evolvo-Chamber (#31, 1979). The kids all have little bell-heads like Bong. Bong is estranged from his wife Beverly (it was a shotgun wedding) who is really in love with Howard.

Quote: "You may think one death is as painful as another—but I guarantee you, it is not in your own best interest to have me *angry* when I get my hands on you!"

Comment: A parody of DR. MOREAU, Bong was Howard's most dogged adversary. Howard has battled numerous super villains over the years, among them the laser-eyed Space Turnip; the Chair-Thing which is a living piece of furniture; the two-headed insect-like Muurks; the Giant Ginger Bread Man; the cosmic accountant Pro Rata who is, literally, a financial wizard; the human-sized Mr. Chicken and his "rocket-powered feather darts"; the costumed, one-armed bandit Jackpot who uses coins as weapons; and the would-be conqueror of the universe, Bzzk-Joh. Withal, Howard is best known to the world-at-large for his duel with the Dark Overlords of the Universe in the 1986 Universal motion picture *Howard the Duck.* Brought to earth by a lab laser accident, one of the Dark Overlords takes over the body of project scientist Dr. Jennings (Jeffrey Jones), and then brings down the others to invade the earth. The giant, insect-like beings are eventually blasted back into space by Howard wielding a hi-tech cannon.

DR. CALIGARI (MP)

First Appearance: 1919, *Das Kabinett des Dr. Caligari* (*The Cabinet of Dr. Caligari*), Decla.

Costume: Top hat; black dinner jacket; white gloves; overcoat with capelet (film is black and white).

Chief Henchman: Cesare.

Biography: Caligari is the head of an insane asylum not far from the town of Holstenwall. Reading a book about the 18th-century hypnotist also named Caligari, who hypnotized one of his patients to commit murder, the eccentric and clearly impressionable psychiatrist decides to do the same. With a somnambulist, Cesare, in tow, Caligari heads to Holstenwall, which is putting on its annual fair. Going to a local official and requesting a license to exhibit Cesare, Caligari is taunted by the fellow before being granted permission; that night, Caligari sends Cesare to murder the rude clerk. The next day, at Caligari's tent, fairgoer Francis and his friends Alan and Jane are shocked when Cesare briefly wakes to announce that Alan is going to die before dawn. When Alan is murdered that night, Francis suspects Caligari; the hypnotist, meanwhile, sends Cesare to kill Jane. But the somnambulist is smitten with her and makes off with the young woman; chased by the townspeople, he soon drops dead from exhaustion. When Caligari sees his dead sleepwalker, he goes mad and has to be restrained in a straightjacket.

Quote: "Cesare! Awaken for a brief while from your dark night."

Comment: Werner Krauss played Caligari; Conrad Veidt (JAFFAR) costarred as Cesare. The script was written by Hans Janowitz and Carl Mayer, who took the name of the character from an officer in Stendhal's *Unknown Letters*. Much to the authors' dismay, the punch of their original script was largely eviscerated by the filming of a framing story in which the tale of Caligari is being told by Francis, who is in fact mad and an inmate in an asylum of which the sane Caligari is the head psychiatrist. The change was made to soften the authors' view that authority figures are by nature rude and overbearing. The script was published in book form in 1972 by Simon and Schuster. The film was remade in 1962, though the story bore little similarity to the original, as a madwoman underwent various adventures in an eerie house which, as it turned out, was the asylum.

DR. CALLISTRATUS (MP)

First Appearance: 1958, *Blood of the Vampire*, Universal Pictures.

Biography: Callistratus lived in 1874, in the Transylvanian village of Carlstadt. Obsessed with human biology, specifically blood, the scientist is staked to death by the local villagers, who regard him as a vampire. But he isn't, at least not until they stake him. He survives because of a special culture he'd developed, and thereafter requires continual transfusions. Working at a laboratory located in a prison for the criminally insane, Callistratus uses the prisoners as his living blood bank. Eventually, he is consumed by the human-eating dogs which guard the jail.

Comment: Sir Donald Wolfit played the part; Victor Maddern was his deformed hunchback aide. The script was by veteran horror writer Jimmy Sangster.

DR. CLEMENT ARMSTRONG (TV)

First Appearance: 1965, "The Cybernauts," *The Avengers*, BBC.

Weapons: The Cybernauts, powerful androids with silvery skin and blank expressions; ink-pens which, innocently carried by victims, draw the Cybernauts to them. (A later model Cybernaut, only one of which was ever built, can reason for itself and doesn't need the pen.)

Chief Henchman: Benson (Frederick Jaeger).

Biography: The owner of England's United Automation, Armstrong is a cripple who rides about in a high-tech wheelchair. When a Japanese company tries to market a new circuit in Great Britain, Armstrong uses the Cybernauts to kill importers who would compete with him. Sleuths John Steed and Emma Peel investigate Armstrong and are marked for death with a pen. However, they manage to place it on the one reasoning Cybernaut and the others attack it instead; Armstrong perishes when he tries to prevent the carnage.

Comment: Michael Gough (see MICHAEL CONRAD) played the part in the hour-long British TV episode. The androids were seen again two years later in "The Return of the Cybernauts," homing into a watch worn by the victims. At the controls this time was Armstrong's brother Paul Beresford (Peter Cushing). Other super villains and unusually sadistic souls who menaced the Avengers include the Radioactive Man,

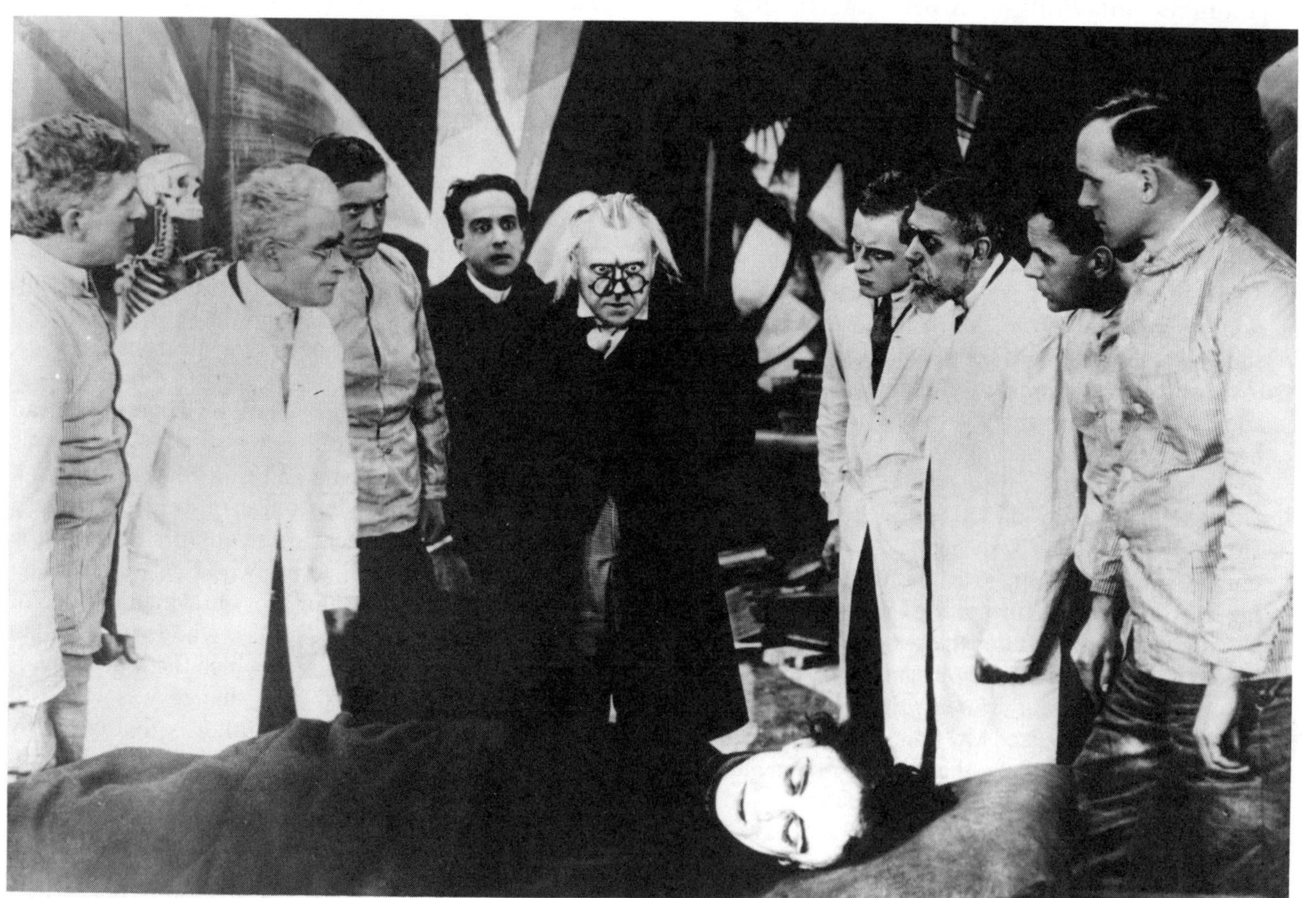

***DR. CALIGARI** (Werner Krauss) and his fallen somnambulist.*

who uses a deadly isotope to kill his enemies in "The Radioactive Man"; Deacon (Willoughby Goddard), the leader of a group of thugs known as the Frighteners in the episode by that name; Jack Dragna (Reed de Rouen), a ruthless gangleader in "The Removal Men"; Cosho Gallion (Peter Arne), who uses the occult to obtain scientific secrets in "Warlock"; the Wringer (Terence Lodge), a Red brainwashing expert in "The Wringer"; Dr. Sturm (Albert Lieven), who uses scientific apparatus to cause destructive storms in "A Surfeit of H_2O"; Sir Lyle Peterson (Derek Farr), who is put under an hypnotic spell by carnivorous plants from space and is forced to help obtain victims for them in "The Man-Eater of Surrey Green"; the Commander, alias Chester Reed (Larry Cross), who uses a dancing school to smuggle enemy agents into England in "The Quick-Quick Slow Death." Also, Dr. Harold Long (Douglas Wilmer), who, in "The Danger Makers," plans to rob the Crown Jewels, an undertaking known as "Operation Grand Slam" (the same name as AURIC GOLDFINGER's operation); a group of killer androids who are identical to and take the place of key humans in "Never, Never Say Die"; Mr. Goat (Dudley Foster), who is trying to locate secret English missile bases in "Something Nasty in the Nursery"; Needle (George Murcell), who extorts money from and/or kills millionaires in "You Have Just Been Murdered"; Dr. Chivers (Francis Matthews), who shrinks objects and people alike in "Mission . . . Highly Improbable"; Boris Kartovski (Steven Scott), a Soviet agent who, in "Split," is subjected to a device that allows him to transfer his mind into other bodies, which he then takes over. Also, Zoltan (John Hollis), a vicious assassin in "Legacy of Death"; Mr. Punch, aka Seagrave (John Woodvine), who uses circus stars "Merry" Maxis Martin, "Fiery" Frederick, and others to kill business rivals in "Look (Stop Me If You've Heard This One) But There Were These Two Fellers . . . "; the computer Remak (Remote Electro-Magnetic Agent Killer) in "Killer"; Balkan President Yakob Borb (Paul Stassino), who wears the mask of a 10-tentacled squid when he commits political murders in "The Decapod"; and communist agent Ezdorf (Peter Bowles), who possesses a chemical which allows him to blend in with the background.

DOCTOR CYBER (C)

First Appearance: 1969 *Wonder Woman* #179, DC Comics.

Costume: Purple leotard with flared shoulders, thigh boots, gloves which reach to shoulders; golden bodysuit worn beneath and which is covered with microcircuits (see Weapons); yellow full-face mask.

Weapons: Her bodysuit provides her with superstrength, and also absorbs and throws back any kind of energy fired at it; various arms including laserguns, a rocket sled, and an invisibility device.

Chief Henchmen: Numerous nameless operatives.

Biography: Throughout her career as the head of an international band of spies and saboteurs-for-hire, the brilliant scientist Cyber (her real name is never revealed) has regularly battled Wonder Woman. During one such tilt, a Chinese assassin flung a brazier of live coals at the mercenary and she was badly scarred; donning a mask, she continued her criminal escapades, making the destruction of Wonder Woman a top priority. During one confrontation, she actually attempted to have her brain placed in the body of the superhero. When last seen, Cyber was plowing into a mountainside on a malfunctioning rocketsled. She has not been heard from since.

DR. CYCLOPS (1) (MP, N)

Real Name: Dr. Alexander Thorkel.

First Appearance: 1940, *Dr. Cyclops*, Paramount Pictures.

Costume: Radiation suit when working in laboratory.

Weapons: Radium condenser in lead-lined closet, used for shrinking animals and people.

Chief Henchman: Pedro.

Biography: Leaving New York, where he was regarded as "a bit crazy," biologist Dr. Thorkel moves to the jungles of Peru, setting up a laboratory among the Iqito Indians, on a knoll above the Karana River. There, using radium procured from a nearby mine, he conducts experiments in shrinking animal tissue. He reduces a pig to the size of a rat, a horse to a mere eight inches in height, and his housekeeper Mira Santiago to pygmy-size (something goes wrong, however, and she dies). Two years after his arrival, he invites several former colleagues down to help in the final phases of his research, since he is nearly blind without his glasses (which he's unable to use in tandem with his microscope). After traveling "ten thousand miles," the scientists examine some cells for him in the microscope, report their findings (an iron imbalance had killed Mira), and without being told of the nature of the research are promptly told to return to the United States. Offended, they refuse—so Thorkel subjects them to the invention on which he'd been working, shrinking them to under a foot in height ("I never realized until now how an ant must feel when you're about to step on it," philosophizes one). However, Thorkel discovers that

The bald ***DR. CYCLOPS*** *(1) (Albert Dekker) and his visitors.*

the miniaturized people are slowly returning to normal size and decides to kill them. In defense, they try to smash his glasses (only one lens breaks, hence "Cyclops"), then climb into the mine shaft, where the madman plummets to his death while trying to reach them. Within two weeks the beleaguered scientists are full-sized once more. Thorkel is a brawny, baldheaded fellow; his native assistant (whom he shrinks along with the scientists) is named Pedro, and his pet cat is Satanas.

Quote: "I'm not going to eat you, I only wish to weigh and measure you."

Comment: Albert Dekker played the part in the movie. In 1940, Will Garth authored *Dr. Cyclops*, a novelization of the film.

DR. CYCLOPS (2) (C)

First Appearance: 1967, *House of Mystery* #164, DC Comics.

Costume: Red bodysuit with white eye emblem on chest; green cape, boots; purple belt.

Weapons: Visors with various lenses for different crimes; a magnetic money lens which attracts cash as well as coins; an X-ray lens; an ice-creating lens; a shrinking lens and restorative "reverso lens" (used, in one instance, to shrink masterpieces of painting and carry them out on a tray); an anti-metallic lens to repel metal; inferno opticals to create fires; a zoom lens for superspeed; an eclipse lens to create utter darkness; and a death lens to kill.

Biography: Nothing is known about this super villain's background. From his cave hideout south of Zenith City, Cyclops uses his various lenses to commit crimes. He is captured by Robby Reed, who uses his "Dial-H for Hero" device to become Robby the Super Robot. Flying to Cyclops' cave, Robby smashes all the lenses with his metal fist and brings the thug in.

Quote: "A barrage of wooden missiles . . . ! Only one pair of glasses that will get rid of them . . . my *inferno opticals!*"

Comment: This was the character's only appearance.

DR. DAKA (MP)

First Appearance: 1943, *Batman*, Columbia Pictures.

Weapons: Zombie helmet, an electrical device which resembled an oversized diver's helmet and was used to transform people into obedient slaves; alligator pit for the disposal of enemies.

Biography: A Japanese operative during the war, Daka is headquartered in an old carnival arcade which displays various methods of torture. His principal crime is an ongoing effort to steal radium for use in the Axis war effort. Daka meets his end not unlike CAPTAIN HOOK, falling into the pit filled with alligators.

Comment: J. Carrol Naish played the character in the 15-episode serial. Dr. Daka was not a character in the Batman comic book. See also THE WIZARD.

DOCTOR DEATH (1) (M)

Real Name: Dr. Rance Mandarin.

First Appearance: August 1934, *All-Story Detective* #1, Edward P. Norris.

Weapons: Black magic (see Biography).

Biography: Feeling that progress and goods have ruined humankind, Dr. Mandarin adopts the identity of Doctor Death and uses his mastery of black magic and the elements to destroy science and technology and throw society back to a primitive state. Though he has no interest in ruling this new order, Dr. Death stops at nothing to achieve his goal. Countering him at every turn is criminologist and black magic expert James Holm, aided by New York police chief John Ricks. Doctor Death has long white hair.

Comment: Norris wrote the Doctor Death stories which appeared in *All-Story Detective* #'s 1 to 4. The title was changed to *Doctor Death* with #5 and expired with issue #7. Harold Ward wrote those tales. The seven titles were "Doctor Death," "Cargo of Death," "Death's I.O.U.," "Thirteen Pearls," "Twelve Must Die," "The Gray Creatures," and "The Shriveling Murders." "Murder Music" was advertised but never published.

DOCTOR DEATH (2) (C)

Real Name: Dr. James Kirk.

First Appearance: 1940, *Whiz Comics* #2, Fawcett Publications.

Costume: Lab coat; Death also has a Satanic goatee.

Weapons: "The Death Machine": cyanide pellets which, when dropped in a bucket of sulphuric acid, form a deadly gas which kills in 10 minutes; trapdoors in office which dump victims into a dungeon.

Chief Henchmen: A pair of unnamed thugs.

Biography: A "new sawbones (that) just came to town," Kirk lives on Elm Street in an unspecified rural village. Beneath his office is "a dank cellar dungeon," where he keeps the radium-powered Life Machine with which he hopes to restore life. Unfortunately, to perfect the device he must first kill people in order to have raw research material. He must also acquire radium, and steals it from City Hospital; that's when reporter Scoop Smith and his photographer Blimp Black become involved. Visiting Kirk's abode, Scoop is locked up when Death notices his press credentials. Planning to make the journalist his latest victim, Death is foiled when Blimp frees Scoop just as the cyanide pellets are activated. The doctor's assistants aren't so lucky. They try to restrain the "crack newshawk," who decks them; locked in the room, the flunkies perish. However, Death uses the Life Machine and they are resurrected; Death is promptly arrested.

The insidious ***DOCTOR DEATH (2).*** *© Fawcett Publications.*

Quote: "I can restore the dead to life—I hope. But first I must kill you."

Comment: It is entirely coincidental that Death lives on a street with a name made infamous by FREDDY KRUEGER, and that he has the same name as the hero of *Star Trek*.

DR. DEATH (C)

Real Name: Dr. Karl Hellfern.

First Appearance: 1940, *Detective Comics* #29, DC Comics.

Weapons: Death Pollen, blown on victims through a straw; the Fiery Death, a potion which incinerates whatever it touches.

Chief Henchmen: Jabah, who is attired like a swami.

Biography: A brilliant scientist based in Gotham City—he has both a penthouse and a mansion—Dr. Death demands "tribute" from the wealthy and sends Jabah to use the Death Pollen on those who refuse. The heroic Batman goes after him, and Dr. Death appears to perish when his lab is consumed with the Fiery Death. However, he returns (quite a bit later, in *Batman* #345, 1982), threatening to use his pollen on all Gotham City if his extortion demands are not met. Once again, however, Batman is able to thwart his scheme.

Quote: "This man they call Batman . . . must be done away with! Perhaps we can contact him through the personal notice column in the daily newspapers."

DOCTOR DEMONICUS (C)

Real Name: Douglas Birely.

First Appearance: 1977, *Godzilla, King of the Monsters* #4, Marvel Comics.

Costume: Purple trunks, cowl with white skull-face and horns, bodysuit with stylized white eyes and mouth on chest; blue boots, gloves, cloak with high collar, belt, holsters. (Note: the costume helps to retard the skin cancer he acquired during his radiation bath.)

Chief Henchmen: The monsters Batragon (a batlike beast, and his first creation), Ghilaron (a pteranodon), Lepirax, Centipor, and others; various lowly thugs whom he brought to the island and used to corral an army of Eskimo slaves.

Biography: A scientist, Birely was "intrigued by the correlation between radioactive agents and mutation." Going about his research one day, hoping to give himself superpowers, he was caught in a radioactive spill and contaminated; an examination subsequently revealed that the scientist suffered a "mental imbalance," a claim he angrily denied. Shortly thereafter, he decided to breed an army of monsters. Learning about a meteor which fell near the Aleutian Islands, he sought out "the precious ball of cosmic radiation." Finding it on a volcanic island, he set up a laboratory where he subjected the tissue of animals such as bats and Komodo dragons to the radiation of the so-called "lifestone." Then he extracted hormones from their mutated tissue, injected those hormones back into the animals, and exposed the animals to the cosmic rays of the meteor. The complex process turned them into huge monsters, with which Birely—as the costumed Dr. Demonicus—attacked civilization to get "*revenge* on the world that had *rejected* me and my *work*—accused me if *insanity*!" However, the fiend's plans were undermined by the crack agents of the peacekeeping force S.H.I.E.L.D. (Supreme Headquarters International Espionage Law-enforcement Division), with an assist from the benevolent Japanese titan Godzilla. Escaping his captors, Demonicus fell in with an alien named MAUR-KON, who lived to torment others. Giving Demonicus a space station in lunar orbit, he sat back while the scientist created new monsters—Cerberus, Starchild, and the Hand of Five—which he used to ravage the world and pave the way for a meteor bombardment he was planning to send, using Maur-Kon's equipment. This plan was prevented by the superheroic robots known as the Shogun Warriors. Turned over to S.H.I.E.L.D., Demonicus escaped, created more monsters, which were rounded up by the West Coast Avengers, and ended up back in prison where he currently resides.

Quote: "Either you supply my creations with *sufficient food*, or I'll set them free to eat whatever's available."

DOCTOR DESTINY (C)

First Appearance: 1961, *Justice League of America* #5, DC Comics.

Costume: Light blue bodysuit; blue jerkin; dark blue cape, hood, gloves, boots; white skull mask.

Weapons: The Materioptikon, a device which turns dreams into reality; it is also able to find a waking person's darkest fears and cause them to materialize. He also employs antigravity discs for flight.

Chief Henchmen: Nameless thugs.

Biography: Creating an antigravity device, Doctor Destiny (his name has never been revealed) first impersonates Green Lantern, then uses the ray to draw the other Justice Leaguers to his hideout. Planning to launch them into space, he is overpowered by the real Green Lantern and hauled off to prison. From jail, he manages to dip into the superheroes' dreams and create evil duplicates of the Justice League; they are defeated when the Atom goes inside the clones and disrupts their motor centers. For his efforts, Destiny ends up in solitary confinement. He has returned frequently over the years, most spectacularly with three Materioptikons linked by the Omega Program, which is capable of creating a "worldwide nightmare followed by insanity" (#76).

Quote: "I'll be the only man on earth left *sane! Hahaheehee!*"

DOCTOR DIABLQ (C)

First Appearance: 1959, *The Double Life of Private Strong* #1, Archie Comics.

Weapons: Pellets of green gas which reduce people to three inches in height; Microcosmic Probing Machine which studies life in subatomic universes and can pluck inhabitants from worlds therein.

Biography: A genius in the science of microscopy, Diablq discovers the microuniverses and, bringing beings from those worlds, uses them to help him steal "the top secret inventions of the world." (Whether to satisfy his own scientific curiosity or conquer the world is not made clear.) Stealing an atomic tank, he plans to use its occupants as guinea pigs, making them the first people he will send to one of the microworlds. However, one of the people he has kidnapped happens to be the superheroic Shield, who frees his comrades and recaptures the tank; so doing, he causes Diablq's cavern laboratory to collapse, killing the mad scientist.

Quote: "Here is a sample of the power that brought the Micro-men to our world—the genius of Doctor Diablq!"

Comment: The character, similar to DR. CYCLOPS, was created by legendary artist Jack Kirby and writer Joe Simon. It was Doctor Diablq's only appearance; the story was reprinted in *Blue Ribbon Comics* #5 (1984).

DOCTOR DOOM (C, TV, N)

Real Name: Victor von Doom.

First Appearance: 1962, *The Fantastic Four* #5, Marvel Comics.

Costume: Green tunic; darker green cloak with hood held by golden clasps; iron-gray mask, gauntlets, boots, and bodyarmor (see Weapons); brown (sometimes black) belt.

Weapons: With the possible exception of Superman's foes LEX LUTHOR and BRAINIAC, Doctor Doom has employed the greatest arsenal in villaindom. His armor endows him with superstrength, creates a virtually impenetrable forcefield, carries its own air supply, boasts a "jet flying-belt," has a "miniature (index) finger-gun," contains a megaphone as well as various radio-transmission devices, a translator, and more, and is so-constructed that Doom can tap its power and send out destructive blasts. Among his other gadgets are a machine which can pluck objects from the past; the XZ-12 device, which increases a person's natural abilities (for instance, sensitive ears are made sharp enough to hear a feather drop); a cosmic beam gun that fires concentrated cosmic rays; an ether gun; sundry robots (including a duplicate of himself and the Fantastic Four's mighty Thing); a dimensional transport machine that puts people in another dimension until Doom needs them; the "aerosub," for travel through the sea and sky; a "rocket plane" for journeying through the ionosphere; a small, cylindrical magnetic "grabber" that can locate any object and, finding it, lift it and bring it to Doom no matter what the object's weight (it has been used, for example, on a skyscraper); a "spider-wave transmitter" that can only be heard by Spider-Man; and, perhaps most ingenious of all, a device consisting of "iron globes, revolving at great speed around a magnetic core," the globes covering virtually every square inch of a room and making it impossible for even most superheroes to avoid being clobbered.

Chief Henchmen: Boris, his devoted friend; countless flunkies over the years.

Biography: The son of Werner and Cynthia Doom, Victor was born in a Gypsy camp near Haasenstadt, Latveria. His mother, a witch, was killed by "a petty official" when she was unable to cure a horse; his father, a healer, perished while fleeing a local noble whose wife he was unable to save. Alone in the world, Victor dedicated himself to making the world suffer for his loss. Staying with his father's friend Boris, the "proud and handsome" Victor lived by selling magical potions based on his mother's recipes. In the meantime, he studied hard and became a self-educated scientific genius; so great was his subsequent fame that he was given a scholarship to the State University of America. Coming to the United States, he met fellow student Reed Richards, who would later become the stretchable Mr. Fantastic of the Fantastic Four. One day, Richards stopped by while Victor was working on a device which he hoped would enable him to communicate with his mother—whose spirit, he learned, was "trapped in an infernal extra-dimensional netherworld," held there by the demon MEPHISTO "as payment for arcane knowledge" he had given to her. So engrossed in his work was Victor that he didn't hear Richards' approach; curious, the young man took the liberty of reading Victor's notes. When the Latverian finally noticed him, he grew furious with his colleague's prying, so furious that he refused to listen when Richards informed him there was a mistake in his computations. As a result of Victor's intractability the machine blew up, shattering his body and leaving a lengthy scar on his face. Though he recovered, the scientist was expelled and his tortured mind blamed Richards for his troubles. Traveling to Tibet, he took over a community of monks who helped him build his armor as well as a mask to conceal what the vain Victor felt was no longer a perfect face. Unfortunately, in his haste to don the mask, he failed to wait until the metal had cooled and all but melted his face. Returning to Latveria as Doctor Doom, the demented native deposed the King and took over the country. There, he settled in a castle in Haasenstadt, whose name he took the liberty of changing to Doomstadt. There he created the many weapons which he has used against the Fantastic Four, Spider-Man, and other heroes. He also labored ceaselessly to free his mother from Mephisto. During the 12-issue run of *Marvel Super Heroes Secret Wars* (1984-85), Doom's face was healed when he absorbed "vast energies" from the alien entity, the Beyonder (#10). However, the reparation was undone two issues later when the Beyonder reclaimed his power.

Quote: "You *dare* lay hands on me? You have little regard for your life, fool! And I have even *less!*"

Comment: Doctor Doom is certainly the most notorious villain in the Marvel universe; the physical parallels between this character and DARTH VADER are pronounced. Doom was the villain in the Fantastic Four novel *Doomsday* written by Marv Wolfman in 1979, and was also featured in several episodes of *The Fantastic Four* cartoon show which aired on ABC-TV from 1967 to 1970, and in another series which was broadcast on NBC-TV from 1978 to 1979.

DR. DOUBLE X (C)

Real Name: Dr. X.

First Appearance: 1958, *Detective Comics* #261, DC Comics.

Costume: Yellow boots, bodysuit with white "X" on chest; red trunks, cape, cowl with purple "lightning" mane on top; purple belt.

Weapons: Duplicate Machine, which creates an energy clone of Dr. X (except for the red "XX" on his chest), one capable of flying, firing destrutive bolts, and lifting enormous weights. Each act, however, drains a little of the clone's energy, which must then be replenished.

Biography: Working in the cellar of an old mansion on the outskirts of Gotham City, Dr. X creates an energy double of himself and sends it out to commit crimes. The superhero Batman foils the scientist and has him committed to the Happydale Sanitarium, but he escapes and revives his clone (*Detective Comics* #316). To combat it, Batman steals into X's lab and creates a double of Batman which manages to destroy the fiend's equipment.

Quote: "You fool . . . you can't flee from your fate! I can overtake you in seconds with my super-energy speed . . ."

DR. FANG (C)

First Appearance: 1966, *Undersea Agent* #1, Tower Publications.

Costume: Red tights, jacket with blue braid on shoulders. (Though this is his principal uniform, he also has other clothing; when he relaxes, Fang usually wears a red smoking jacket.)

Weapons: "Crammed in his monster arsenal is every type of destructive device known to man," including "bait bombs," which unleash a "shark exciter," food designed to attract sharks for the disposal of unwanted divers; a "cloud of blackness" which blinds all who approach his subsea kingdom, save for his Lemurians; saucer-like "seacrafts" for underwater travel by surface dwellers; sodium torpedo, a super-explosive; rayguns which stun (and, presumably, can also kill).

Undersea Agent battles the Lemurians of ***DR. FANG*** *(inset).*
© Tower Comics.

Chief Henchmen: Lemurians, sea-breathers who dwell in Fang's kingdom on Lemuria; also, numerous non-Lemurian lackeys and spies.

Biography: Unlike most would-be world conquerors, the Asian Dr. Fang knows no compromise. His goal is "the ultimate conquest of everything *above* and *below* the sea." Living on the sunken continent of Lemuria, he is opposed by Lt. Davey Jones and the agents of U.N.D.E.R.S.E.A. (United Nations Department of Experiment and Research Systems Established at Atlantis), operatives headquartered in the underwater base of Atlantis.

Quote: "Who do they think they are, to try to overcome the invincible *Dr.Fang*? Could they believe for a moment that there is a single thing I have overlooked?"

Comment: Fang battled U.N.D.E.R.S.E.A. for the duration of that magazine's six-issue run. Other Asian super villains include BRIGAND LEADER, COLONEL SUN, DR. FU MANCHU, DR. GOO FEE, DR. YEN SIN, and WU FANG. See other underwater super villains ATTUMA, BLACK MANTA, CAPTAIN NEMO, CAPTAIN WHALE, FISHERMAN, KILLER SHARK, KRANG, MR. CRABB, OCEAN MASTER, ORKA, PIRANHA, and TIGER SHARK (2).

DR. FRANKENBEANS (C)

First Appearance: 1986, *Madballs* #1, Marvel Comics.

Costume: Pink labcoat.

Chief Henchmen: The moronic Snivelitch; also Crasher, Smasher, and Trasher, the evil, living bouncing balls known as Badballs.

Biography: Frankenbeans is the head of R.U.I.N.—Research Unlimited In Nucleonics—which is nothing more than the lab in his rundown mansion. His one goal in life is to enslave the enormously resilient and good-natured Madballs, living, bouncing balls with ugly faces. Despite his great genius, he has yet to succeed.

Quote: "Lucky for you, I'm always in a *good mood* after my bath!"

Comment: Though the Madballs were toys created by Those Characters From Cleveland, Dr. Frankenbeans was only used in the comic book.

DR. FREDERICK MOELLER (C)

First Appearance: 1965, *Forbidden Worlds* #127, American Comics Group.

Weapons: Electronic Blaster (capable of rendering even

DR. FREDERICK MOELLER *vs. Magicman. © American Comics Group.*

superheroes unconscious); youth-chair, a device which makes people as young as Dr. Moeller wishes and simultaneously reduces their will power; Electronic Grid, a box which, when affixed to persons whose will has been weakened by the youth-chair, enables Moeller to control them utterly.

Biography: The head of the Bureau of Scientific Crime Detection, Moeller is actually a super villain "seeking revenge . . . for the defeat of Nazi Germany, my Fatherland." Obtaining financing from Red China, Moeller begins killing "men important to America's welfare." He does this by restoring the youth of old people close to his victims, people who are fitted with Electronic Grids and, as his slaves, murder "their famous friends." The superhero Magicman sniffs him out only to be stunned by the Electronic Blaster; placed in the youth seat, he is time-shifted into adolescence. Fortunately, he still has enough strength to break from the restraining straps and, flying after Moeller when he races off in his car, kicks the car out of control using magic. The car speeds off a cliff and Moeller plunges to his death.

Comment: This was the character's only appearance. Other villains battled by Magicman include Merlin the Magician, Chang, Dragonia, and the Wizard of Science and his huge robot dogs.

DR. FU MANCHU (N, MP, R, TV)

First Appearance: 1913, *The Insidious Dr. Fu-Manchu* (British title: *The Mystery of Dr. Fu-Manchu*), Sax Rohmer.

Costume: A robe (varies between black and yellow) with a silver peacock on the front; black cap.

Biography: One of the most resilient and nefarious villains of all time, Fu Manchu has one dream and one dream only: to rule the world. As many times as he is beaten back by his archenemy Sir Denis Nayland Smith (who was officially attached to Scotland Yard and knighted for his work against Fu Manchu), the human demon returns to try again. Along the way countless people die in countless ways, from having their heads lopped off with a sickle, to the poisonous Green Death, to having a devoted assistant run a motorboat he's piloting into a rock. Believed to be descended from the leaders of the Manchu dynasty, the Chinese villain holds degrees from a trio of European colleges, possesses a vast knowledge of science—particularly chemistry, physics, and medicine—and also knows a great deal about black magic. The master of many tongs (secret criminal societies) and "evil-faced thugs" organized under the title of the Si-Fan, Fu Manchu is "abnormally tall," slim, and walks with "a queer, catlike gait"; bald, he has green eyes, bony hands, and "long, highly polished fingernails"; as well as thin lips that barely part when he speaks in his "slightly hissing" voice. Contrary to the many portrayals in movies and even on the dust-jackets of his novels, Fu Manchu has neither a beard nor moustache but is cleanshaven—so he can easily apply the disguises he uses in his work. For a brief period after the Second World War, Fu Manchu shelved his plans to conquer the world in order to fight Communism. Fu Manchu's daughter, Fah Lo Suee, is not above suffering her loving father's wrath. In *The Drums of Fu Manchu*, she is disciplined by having her mind erased and being given the new identity of Koreani, a dancer—a profession which Fu Manchu finds "useful" in advancing his schemes.

Quote: "I regret that you are still alive."

Comment: Rohmer based his character on a legendary London criminal named Mr. Big. A Chinese gangster and the leader of many tongs, he lorded it over an extensive gambling and narcotics network. (Rohmer claimed to have seen the man once getting into a limousine on a foggy London street. According to the author, Mr. Big looked like Satan.) Rohmer wrote a total of 14 novels concerning the crimes of the Oriental archfiend. The original was followed by *The Return of Dr. Fu-Manchu* (1916; British title *The Devil Doctor* [unless otherwise identified, British titles are the same as the American titles]), *The Hand of Fu-Manchu* (1917; British title *The Si Fan Mysteries*), *The Golden Scorpion* (1919; the villain is not identified as Fu Manchu, but is him nonetheless), *Daughter of Fu Manchu* (1931; the name, manufactured from two Chinese surnames, was no longer hyphenated), *The Mask of Fu Manchu* (1932), *The Bride of Fu Manchu* (1933), *The Trail of Fu Manchu* (1934), *President Fu Manchu* (1936), *The Drums of Fu Manchu* (1939), *The Island of Fu Manchu* (1941), *Shadow of Fu Manchu* (1948), *Re-Enter Fu Manchu*

(1957; British title *Re-Enter Dr. Fu Manchu*), and *Emperor Fu Manchu* (1959). A pair of short stories, "The Eyes of Fu Manchu" and "The Wrath of Fu Manchu," were published in 1970 and 1973 respectively. There have been numerous motion pictures about the super villain, beginning with a series of 23 short silents made in England from 1923 to 1925 and starring Harry Agar Lyons as Fu Manchu. But the first big hit was *The Mysterious Dr. Fu Manchu* in 1929. This adaptation of the first novel starred Warner Oland, as did *The Return of Dr. Fu Manchu* (1930) and *Daughter of the Dragon* (1931). Boris Karloff was Fu Manchu in *The Mask of Fu Manchu* (1932), arguably the best of the Fu Manchu films. Seeking the hidden tomb of Genghis Khan, the villain and Fah Lo See (sic; played by Myrna Loy) want Khan's mask and sword. These artifacts will give him control over "the teeming hordes of Asia" and enable him to overrun the west, thus ruling the world. Finding them, he sentences those who oppose him to nasty forms of death, notably impalement and being fed to crocodiles. But Nayland Smith manages to zap Fu Manchu with a death ray the villain has invented, ending the threat. Henry Brandon, as the next Fu Manchu, heading the secret group from the novels, called Si Fan, sought only Khan's scepter in the serial *Drums of Fu Manchu* (1940). Recognized as the symbol of leadership, the scepter would allow him to start a war in Central Asia and emerge as its ruler. The next group of Fu Manchu films starred Christopher Lee (CAPTAIN RAMESES, DRACULA) as the villain. In *The Face of Fu Manchu* (1965) he and his daughter (played by Tsai Chin) use a new poison gas to kill everyone in an English town; in *The Brides of Fu Manchu* (1966) he kidnaps the daughters of a dozen powerful politicians and industrialists, forcing them to help him conquer the world; in *The Vengeance of Fu Manchu* (1967) he endeavors to replace every police chief at an Interpol meeting with a duplicate; in *Kiss and Kill* (1970) he infects girls with the kiss of death and dispatches them to smooch world leaders to death; and in *The Castle of Fu Manchu* (1972) he uses an iceberg-maker to try and control all commerce on the waterways. Peter Sellers' last film was a bastardization called *The Fiendish Plot of Dr. Fu Manchu* (1980) in which he played both Fu Manchu and Nayland Smith. There were several Fu Manchu adventures on the radio during the 1930s; on TV there was a classy, unsold NBC pilot starring John Carradine as Fu Manchu (1952) and a cheaper 13-episode half-hour series, *Dr. Fu Manchu* (1956; also known as *The Adventures of Fu Manchu*), starring Glen Gordon. Other villains cut from the same mold are COLONEL SUN, DR. YEN SIN, GENERAL CHAN LU, WU FANG, Dr. Nikola, and Mr. Wong. While not an Asian, Dr. Nikola was cut from the same cloth. Created by Guy Boothby in 1895, he and his aides (from whom he demands their "whole and entire labour") fought the law in five novels. Mr. Wong, who was Asian, is best known from the film *Mysterious Mr. Wong* (1935), which was based on the novel *The Twelve Coins of Confucius* by Harry Stephen Keeler. In the film, Wong, based in San Francisco's Chinatown, stops at nothing to obtain the dozen coins which will make him the rightful ruler of the province of Keelat in China. Despite Gruesome tortures and murder, Wong earns nothing more than a police bullet for his efforts. Bela Lugosi (BARON ROXOR, DR. ALEX ZORKA, DR. MIRAKLE, DR. PAUL CARRUTHERS, DRACULA, MURDER LEGENDRE, and PROFESSOR ERIC VORNOFF), played Wong. SUMURO is another Rohmer villain.

DR. GIZMO (TV, C)

First Appearance: 1968, *George of the Jungle*, ABC-TV.

Weapons: Robot duplicate; top hat with helicopter for flight, "scissor-extension wallet grabber" for robbing, and mechanical boxing glove to pulverize enemies; jet roller skates; crossbow with TNT arrows; instant brick builder to erect walls within moments; false index finger which fires bullets; unicycle.

Biography: Nothing is known of Gizmo's past. He is first seen on his way to prison, escaping by way of his helicopter top hat. Committing a series of crimes, he is captured by the superhero Super Chicken, who subdues him with a lightning bolt gun.

Quote: "Curses! This is fowl play!"

Comment: This was Dr. Gizmo's only appearance; the cartoon adventure was told in comic book form in Gold Key's *George of the Jungle* #2 (1969).

DR. GOLDFOOT (MP)

First Appearance: 1965, *Dr. Goldfoot and the Bikini Machine*, American International Pictures.

Weapons: Sexy, bikini-dressed girl androids; Bikini Machine, a device which duplicates the androids (in second film, they are explosives-laden "Girl Bombs" whose fuses, nestled in their navels, will ignite during lovemaking).

Chief Henchman: Igor.

Biography: An insane scientist, Dr. Goldfoot sends his androids forth to seduce millionaires. Once the men are hooked, Goldfoot instructs his androids how to manipulate them. His plot to control the world's

DR. GIZMO. *© Jay Ward Productions.*

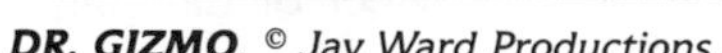

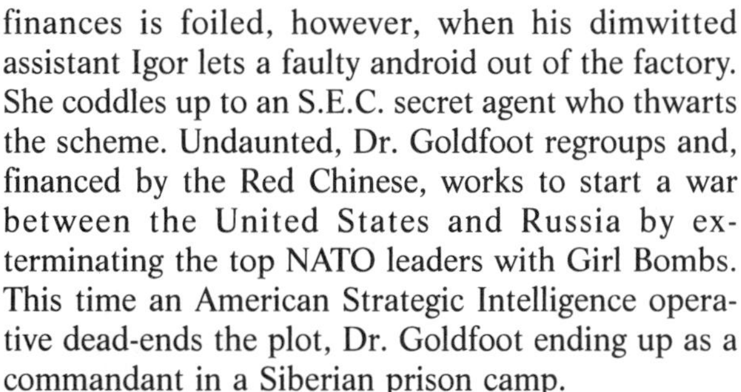

finances is foiled, however, when his dimwitted assistant Igor lets a faulty android out of the factory. She coddles up to an S.E.C. secret agent who thwarts the scheme. Undaunted, Dr. Goldfoot regroups and, financed by the Red Chinese, works to start a war between the United States and Russia by exterminating the top NATO leaders with Girl Bombs. This time an American Strategic Intelligence operative dead-ends the plot, Dr. Goldfoot ending up as a commandant in a Siberian prison camp.

Comment: The war plot was the subject of the second and final Dr. Goldfoot film, *Dr. Goldfoot and the Girl Bombs* (1966). Vincent Price (DR. PHIBES) played the scientist in both pictures, with Jack Mullaney as Igor.

DR. GOO FEE (TV, C)

First Appearance: 1965, "Fearless Fly," *Milton the Monster*, ABC-TV.

Chief Henchman: Gung Ho.

Biography: Goo Fee lives in a home atop a mountain in Tibet, where the 972-year-old villain spends his time plotting the destruction of the superheroic Fearless Fly. His most ambitious ploy was luring the Fly to his home by kidnapping famed singer Juanita Bananafly; once there, the Oriental fiend tricked Fearless Fly into entering a box containing a deadly spider. Unfortunately, Gung Ho had forgotten to punch holes in the box and the arachnid passed out long before Fly arrived.

Quote: "Insolent dog! I'll have you drawn and quartered!"

Comment: The character was also seen in the first issue of the *Milton the Monster* comic book from Gold Key in 1966. Other enemies of the indestructible insect include Captain Fligh, Lady Deflylah, Ferocious Fly, and Napoleon Bonefly. See other Asian villains BRIGAND LEADER, COLONEL SUN, DR. FU MANCHU, DR. YEN SIN, and WU FANG.

DR. GREGORY GRUESOME (C)

First Appearance: 1966, *Showcase* #62, DC Comics.

Weapons: Robot cobbled together from bathtubs, vacuum cleaners, and a wagon; Crime Car, a heavily armored vehicle complete with an ejection seat for quick getaways; tiny mobile TV cameras set around Megalopolis to spy on enemies; Super-laser death-beam.

Chief Henchman: Hermes.

Biography: Based in a shanty in a Megalopolis junkyard, Doc Gruesome desperately needs a ruby to finish his Super-laser death-beam, which he plans to use to conquer the world. Stealing the famous Shinboni Ruby, he fires the beam at one of his enemies, the superheroic Dumb Bunny of the Inferior Five ("A chance to shoot a woman—in the back! What villain could resist such a temptation?"). However, the beam strikes a mirror Dumb Bunny is using to fix her lipstick; the beam reflects back at Gruesome, knocking him for a loop. Jailed, he busts out (*Showcase* #63) by way of a catapult. Though he lands on

***DR. GREGORY GRUESOME** in peak form. © DC Comics.*

the other side of the walls of the Megalopolis Prison, he breaks his leg, several ribs, and his skull and has to be carted off the the prison infirmary. Taking one last stab at crime (*The Inferior Five* #7), Gruesome holds the United States for ransom by threatening to explode an atomic egg. The deadly orb is snatched from him, and when Awkwardman accidentally drops it on a general's head it proves to be a dud.

Quote: "Other mad scientists are *rich*! They turn out multi-million dollar missiles like they were paper planes! Why can't I be like *Luthor*?"

Comment: These stories marked the villain's only appearances.

DR. GROOD (MP)

First Appearance: 1953, *The Lost Planet*, Columbia Pictures.

Weapons: Cosmojet for interplanetary travel; TV which can see anyone anywhere; death ray; robots; Thermic Disintegrator, which destroys objects with intense heat.

Biography: Arriving on earth from the planet Ergro, scientific genius Dr. Grood intends to make our world his first conquest in a bold scheme to rule the universe. Setting up headquarters inside Mt. Vulcan, he kidnaps Professor Dorn, a physicist, to work on invasion weapons. Dr. Grood also captures reporter Rex Barrow—who has come to the mountain to investigate the arrival of the cosmojet—and ships both men to Ergro (Barrow to work as a slave mining the element cosmonium). On Ergro, Dorn discovers that, when mixed with cosmonium, dornite, another metal indigenous to the planet, creates an invisibility ray. Becoming invisible for a spell, Barrow commutes between Ergro and earth in an effort to capture the intergalactic lunatic. In the end the two men engage in a spaceship dogfight, Grood losing when one of his robots accidentally sets the ship on an irreversible course for infinity.

Comment: The character was played by Michael Fox in the 15-chapter serial.

DR. GUSTAV NEIMANN (MP)

First Appearance: 1944, *House of Frankenstein*, Universal Pictures.

Chief Henchman: Daniel.

Biography: Escaping from Neustadt Prison, where he's already served 15 years because of sadistic medical experiments, Dr. Neimann and his hunchbacked aide Daniel murder the owner of Lampini's Chamber of Horrors and take over the traveling show. With this as a front, Neimann plots revenge against those who sent him up the river. At the same time he plans to continue his cruel experiments. Reaching Reigelburg, he brings one of his exhibits, DRACULA, back to life, by removing a stake from his heart. The vampire destroys Neimann's enemy the Burgomaster, after which the scientist doublecrosses Dracula by riding away from pursuit and leaving the helpless Count to perish in the sun, unable to reach his coffin. Reaching Castle Frankenstein, Neimann discovers the frozen bodies of Frankenstein's Monster and the Wolfman (they had been caught in a flood in *Frankenstein Meets the Wolfman* [1943]). Thawing the bodies and reopening his own nearby lab, Neimann kills two more enemies and, removing their brains, plots to put them in the skulls of the two monsters, making them his slaves. Unhappily for Neimann, the Wolf Man badly miscalculates when he attacks a Gypsy woman armed with a silver bullet; the assault proves fatal to the hirsute creature. Shortly thereafter, the Frankenstein Monster comes to life and, killing Daniel, carries Dr. Niemann into a swamp where the two drown in quicksand.

Comment: Boris Karloff (DR. SCARABUS) played Neimann and J. Carroll Naish (DR. DAKA) was Daniel. See DRACULA.

DR. HASTOR (C)

Real Name: Hath-Set; Anton Hastor.

First Appearance: 1940, *Flash Comics* #1, DC Comics.

Costume: Original: green skirt, Egyptian headdress. Second: green bodysuit with high red collar; yellow belt.

Weapons: Lightning-making machine; the Flying Eye, an eye-shaped flying machine equipped with destructive rays.

Biography: In ancient Egypt, Hath-Set was the priest of Anubis, the God of Death. Yearning for secrets of "a lost science" known only by the warrior-prince Khufu, he slays his enemy with a mystic sacrificial knife when Khufu refuses to tell what he knows; centuries later, in the present era, Khufu is reincarnated as the superhero Hawkman. But Hath-Set has also returned in the person of Dr. Anton Hastor, a scientific genius "second only to Edison himself." The fiend is using a lightning device to strike at a nearby city and vows to launch "death—carnage—horror" on a worldwide scale until he is named ruler. Tracking him down, Hawkman ends the reign of terror by firing a crossbow quarrel into his chest. But the respite is only temporary. Hath-Set is reincarnated yet again, this time kidnapping fellow scientists and using hi-tech devices to add their brainwaves to his. This enables the "psychic vampire" to fire debilitating mental blasts. The villain goes on a destructive spree with the Flying Eye, Hawkman finally confronting him with a challenge: to let the spirits of Khufu and Hath-Set battle to the death. Using the knife which slew him in Egypt, Hawkman liberates their ethereal selves, in which form he defeats his enemy, leaving Hastor in a state of total paralysis (1982, *All-Star Squadron* Vol. 2, #12).

Quote: "I give you credit for foolhardy *courage*—even *stamina*—but those virtues are *straws in the wind* before my increased *mental powers*!"

Comment: Hastor was the first enemy faced by Hawkman.

DR. JEREMIAH CLUGG (C)

First Appearance: 1965, *Blue Beetle* #51, Charlton Comics.

Weapons: Mentor the Magnificent, a silver-shelled robot with orange trunks. The robot's powers include flight (he can soar to heights of at least 28,000 feet and travel at Mach 5), great strength, and a destructive gamma ray beam.

Biography: A physics professor, Clugg is "an acknowledged genius" in his field, though he has a communication problem with his students. Because of his frail physical appearance and timid nature, he is "ignored by the pretty girls, ridiculed by football-playing buffoons, and laughed at by my faculty colleagues." Building a mighty robot with which to conquer the world, and inventing a device which imprints his memory cells on the circuits of the robot, Clugg wishes to make the mechanical creature even stronger by obtaining the scarab which provides the superheroic Blue Beetle with his powers. Stealing the gem, Clugg—who also happens to be "a brilliant hypnotist"—puts the hero under a spell. However, a ray from the scarab strikes Blue Beetle, who snaps out of his mesmerized state to battle the robot in the skies. Ramming the robot, the hero sends it crashing to the seas below. It is not clear what happened to the scientist himself. Clugg's heartthrob was Miss Appleton, whom he wanted to rule at his side.

Quote: "Without the Blue Beetle to foil my plans, I can make all men bow low and call me master!"

Comment: This was the character's only appearance, and it was never explained why Clugg did not simply use his hypnotic ability to conquer the world, rather than go through the trouble of building Mentor.

DR. KONG (C)

First Appearance: 1965, *Mysteries of Unexplored Worlds* #46, Charlton Comics.

Costume: Black bodysuit; purple cloak.

Weapons: Electrified sword (second adventure); anima-ray to give life to the lifeless (third adventure).

Chief Henchman: The Giant Gladiator, a robot some 15 feet tall.

Biography: The Preteons and the Cyclates dwell on the island of Cyprete where, according to legend, one of those two peoples will eventually rule with the help of the Giant Gladiator. Headquartered beneath the ruins of the Tomb of the Gladiators—a lair guarded by a giant octopus—the oriental Dr. Kong, "the meanest man alive," plots to use that legend to his advantage. Sending forth a robot Giant Gladiator to stir the people to war, he plans to rule the survivors. However, the superheroic Son of Vulcan destroys the robot in combat and Kong escapes, vowing "someday I will make Son of Vulcan pay for what he has done to me!" He does so (in issue #49), using an electrified sword to put the hero in a coma and, teamed with the villainous Olympian God of War Mars, steals $2 million from a diamond exchange. However, the hero is revived by his patron, the god Vulcan, and captures Kong as he tries to escape in his submarine. In their next tilt (issue #50), the villain uses his anima-ray to wreak havoc on the set of a film about the Trojan War, where Son of Vulcan is serving as a bodyguard for the leading lady. Though Kong gets away, this was his last appearance.

Quote: "You are about to meet another of my pets! And I

am certain that it will not be a pleasant encounter—for you! *Ha!*"

Comment: Kong was the hero's first enemy and was also the hero's last foe, their third encounter occurring in the final issue featuring the son of Vulcan. The other villains in the hero's chronicles are Professor Leonard Lambie, who has the power to turn people and objects to gold after acquiring the Gauntlets of Midas (Son of Vulcan was briefly transformed into the precious metal, but recovers on the way to the smelter); and the whaler Captian Tusk who, at the behest of Mars, uses his ship to menace the hero.

The Son of Vulcan confronts ***DR. KONG****. © Charlton Comics.*

DR. LIGHT (C)

Real Name: Dr. Arthur Light; Kimiyo Hoshi.

First Appearance: 1962, *Justice League of America* #12, DC Comics.

Costume: Black bodysuit with white starburst on chest, cowl with white fin on top; white gloves, boots, cape, belt (see Weapons).

Weapons: Many light-related gadgets including a light-beam projector capable of immobilizing even superheroes; another which can view and send people to planets outside our own solar system; "solid light" creator for slamming down people or walls or allowing Dr. Light to walk through the air; illusion-making device. (Note: many of these tools, originally handheld, are now part of his costume.)

Chief Henchmen: THE FEARSOME FIVE; also, various thugs.

Biography: A physicist, Light created a machine which was supposed to permit him to see into the future; instead, it let him see what was happening on other planets. Tuning in on the planet Thanagar, home of the superhero Hawkman, he was actually able to snatch equipment from a Thanagarian laboratory and bring it to earth. With these, Light fulfilled a long-standing ambition to become a super villain. Unfortunately, he was found by a law officer from Thanagar who relieved him of the equipment (this flashback tale was told in *DC Super-Stars* #14 [1977], published after the character's debut in *Justice League of America*). Undaunted, Light remained a criminal, incurring the wrath of the Justice League when he tried to use light waves to overcome the entire population of the planet. Thwarted and captured time after time by the superheroes, he eventually founded The Fearsome Five; not only did the group fail to help him achieve his criminal goals, but Light was also actually unseated as leader by a fellow team member. Disgusted by that, and defeated by the superheroes the Teen Titans, he gave up villainy altogether (1984, *Tales of the Teen Titans* #49). A new Doctor Light has since appeared (1985, *Crisis on Infinite Earths* #4). She is scientist Kimiyo Hoshi, who was watching the star Vega through her telescope when she was bathed in its energy (an event made possible by a temporary suspension of physical laws during the Crisis). The radiation bath gives her the ability to create light in any form (from a simple glow to a destructive laser) and to fly. Garbed in a costume identical to that of her predecessor—with the exception of a tiara which she wears in place of the helmet—Kimiyo is extremely arrogant. However, she is not inherently evil like her predecessor, and has slowly become a full-fledged superhero.

Quote: "You want me to absorb a *sun's energy*?"

DOCTOR MAYAVALE (C)

First Appearance: 1980, *The Legion of Super-Heroes* #268, DC Comics.

Costume: Light blue mail T-shirt; blue jacket; orange Stetson; purple boots; pink belt with white buckle; white skirt; "I Like Ike" necklace. (His wardrobe is plucked from different eras in time; he also has an Indian outfit he wears on occasion.) Mayavale's six extra arms are green.

Weapons: Bubble which ensnares people and, filled with a green gas of Mayavale's invention, allows him to recondition their minds into a state of torpor.

Chief Henchmen: Sundry beasts, whistled forth from other times and places by Mayavale's powers—creatures which include earth's Abominable

Snowman and the extinct, spidery P'O'Likk of Khund.

Biography: Mayavale is a native of the planet Avatanda, a world "cut off from the main spaceways." There, the natives have been devoted "for eons . . . to meditation . . . the divine search for the ultimate reality." Mayavale himself "spent the first fifty V'undas (equivalent to 150 terrestrial years) of his life as an acolyte in a monastery. Unhappy with his progress and feeling he's suffered "a mystic blockage," he is allowed to go to the Chamber of Lives, where he can inhale "the wheeling mists" to clear away the impedance, the "incidents in past lives that have left the inner scales unbalanced." Cautioned to breathe the green smoke only until a gong sounds, he disregards the warning and dives deep "into the ocean of years." The experience fills him with "instant, complete knowledge of fifty thousand lifetimes," an influx which causes him to go insane. Learning that he had spent his past 60 lifetimes doing "nothing but good" as a politician (he was Julius Caesar), member of the clergy, police officer (John Alvarez in New York in 1969), and a prophet, he decides it's time to work some evil to balance out his karma. Based on the world All Time, which contains relics and civilizations from all eras in time, the fiend of the thirtieth century lures the Legion of Super-Heroes to his planet to destroy them prior to unleashing "my evil on the galaxy." Escaping various death traps, the superheroes confront him and he flees into the vastness of space.

Quote: "I take my world-ship and briefly *retire* . . . but rest assured—Mayavale will return. . . ."

DR. MIRAKLE (MP)

First Appearance: 1932, *Murders in the Rue Morgue*, Universal Pictures.

Chief Henchman: Eric the ape.

Biography: Mirakle is a Parisian scientist with only one ambition in life: to prove the theory of evolution by mating a woman with an ape. During the day, he presents his orangutan Eric to crowds at a carnival; at night, he sends his very willing hench-ape out to procure subjects for his diabolical experiments, which involve preparing the women by injecting them with Eric's blood. The authorities eventually find Mirakle's laboratory; panicking, Eric kills his master and flees across the rooftops with a woman tucked under his arms before being stopped by police.

Comment: Bela Lugosi (BARON ROXOR, DR. ALEX ZORKA, DR. PAUL CARRUTHERS, DRACULA, MURDER LEGENDRE, PROFESSOR ERIC VORNOFF) played the part in this very loose adaptation of the Edgar Allan Poe tale. (In the 1841 short story, an "Ourang-Outang" escaped from the room of its owner, a sailor, and was solely responsible for the killings.) Arlene Francis made her debut in the film as a prostitute. In the 1954 remake, *Phantom of the Rue Morgue*, Karl Malden chewed the scenery in Lugosi's role (Merv Griffin was featured in a bit part as a college student!); Jason Robards, Jr., got his chance to create ape people in yet another remake, *Murders in the Rue Morgue* (1971).

DR. MOREAU (N, MP, C)

First Appearance: 1896, *The Island of Dr. Moreau*, H.G. Wells.

Chief Henchman: Montgomery.

Biography: When he was approximately 40 years old, Moreau was forced to flee England when a journalist posing as a lab assistant revealed that, for nine years, Moreau had been practicing vivisection. Yachting over to a small South Pacific Island—apparently, Noble's Island—he sets up a new lab and has been there nearly 11 years when a castaway washes ashore in 1887. The castaway, Edward Prendick, is a horrified observer to the scientist's work, which involves creating human-like beasts which retain the quality of the animal(s) whence they were evolved. Among those "carven and wrought into new shapes" by Moreau are a Sheep Man (his first), a Leopard Man, a Swine Man, a satyr-like apegoat, a Dog Man, a Hyena-Swine, a Monkey Man, "a limbless thing with a horrible face that . . . was immensely strong and in infuriating pain," an Ox-Boar, a Wolf Man, a Bull Man, and an old woman who is part bear and part vixen. (When these creatures bear children, they usually die. If they survive, the offspring show no human traits, so Moreau provides such on his operating table.) Of the 120 creatures he has remade, some 60 survive, of which the mad scientist is proudest of his Puma Man. It's fitting that when the creatures finally revolt against his unutterably sadistic experiments it's Puma Man who kills him, "his head . . . battered in by the fetters of the puma." Moreau stands approximately six feet tall, "a powerfully built man with a fine forehead and rather heavy features," as well as pale skin and white hair. His (human) assistant is named Montgomery.

Quote: "Each time I dip a living creature into the bath of burning pain, I say, This time I will burn out all the animal, this time I will make a rational creature of my own."

Comment: In the movies, Moreau was played by Charles Laughton in *The Island of Lost Souls* (1933) and Burt Lancaster in *The Island of Dr. Moreau* (1977). A novelization of the movie, more contemporary than the Wells novel, was written by Joseph Silva and published in 1977. Wells also created THE INVISIBLE MAN. Marvel published a one-shot comic book adaptation of the film in 1977.

DR. MORGAN (MP)

First Appearance: 1955, *Panther Girl of the Congo*, Republic Pictures.

Weapons: Super-hormone which turns crawfish into monsters.

Biography: Concocting the super-hormone, Morgan breeds giant crawfish to chase natives from the African jungle where he's discovered a diamond mine. However, the menace becomes known to Jean Evans, aka the Panther Girl, and hunter Larry Sanders; together they try to help the natives, surviving bombs and hostile savages of the Returi tribe, who are allied with Morgan, as well as the monsters themselves. Morgan perishes when a bottle of poison gas is broken during a struggle with Sanders; the avaricious chemist is overcome by the fumes.

Comment: Arthur Space played the character in this 12-chapter serial; Space had previously played the super villain MARLOF. In 1966, the serial was edited into a feature film entitled *The Claw Monsters*.

DR. NO (N, MP)

Real Name: Julius No (adopted as an adult: "Julius" after his father, and "No" as a sign of rejecting him).

First Appearance: 1958, *Dr. No*, Ian Fleming.

Costume: Kimono with a "gunmetal sheen."

Weapons: Estate guarded by a human-eating giant squid and an armor-plated mechanical dragon with a flamethrower in its mouth; radio beam which can alter the course of missiles; arms which end in mighty steel pincers rather than hands.

Chief Henchman: Sam-sam.

Biography: No is the son of a German Methodist missionary and a Chinese girl. Born in Peking, he was raised by his mother's aunt (and had "no love" from her). Moving to Shanghai when he was of age, he became involved with the Tongs (secret societies) and "enjoyed the conspiracies, the burglaries, the murders, the arson . . . the death and destruction of people and things." Relocating to New York, he joined the American Tong known as the Hip Sings and, in time, was made their treasurer. He fought in the Tong wars ("a time of torture and murder and arson" he notes with glee) and made off with $1 million before his comrades were arrested. But the Tongs reached out from jail and caught up with him. They cut off his hands (the traditional punishment for a thief), shot him in the heart, and left him for dead, unaware that he was "the one man in a million who has his heart in the right side." He survived and, undergoing radical plastic surgery (including traction on his spine to make him taller), settled in a sprawling esate in Crab Key in Jamaica, where he imported Chinese workers to help him export bird guano. In fact, his real avocation was using a newly-invented radio beam to destroy U.S. test rockets, for which he was paid handsomely by the Soviets (though he had "feelers" out to the Red Chinese for similar work, presumably against Russia). Fortunately, No was found out by British secret agent James Bond, who buried the villain in over 20 feet of guano. No stood roughly six-feet-seven and had a head like a "reversed . . . oildrop," thanks to its "elongated and tapered" shape, "translucent yellow" skin, and baldness (he lacked eyelashes as well). When he walked, he seemed "to glide rather than take steps." Bond described him as, overall, a "giant venomous worm wrapped in gray tin-foil." His bodyguard was the powerful "Chinese negro" Sam-sam, with whom he was in constant contact via a walkie-talkie in his kimono.

Quote: "You are right, Mister Bond. That is just what I am, a maniac."

Comment: Joseph Wiseman played Dr. No in the 1962 film version. The character was somewhat different from the No created by Fleming. When he offers his scientific skills to the East and West and is rejected, he goes to work for the villainous agency SPECTRE, of which ERNST STAVRO BLOFELD is the managing director. Still plotting to reprogram missiles, his target is Cape Canaveral rather than missiles sent from the novel's test site on Turks Island. In the movie, No dies when Bond knocks him into the boiling water surrounding the atomic reactor which supplies his beam with power. TECHMASTER also has artificial hands.

DOCTOR OCTOPUS (C, CS, N)

Real Name: Otto Octavius.

First Appearance: 1963, *The Amazing Spider-Man* #3, Marvel Comics.

Costume: Green bodysuit; orange gloves, boots, belt, collar and neck on bodyshirt; blue goggles.

Weapons: Metal girdle with four pincered arms which can telescope from their normal two-yard length to roughly six yards. Each arm is extremely powerful, and can be used not only to destroy but also to help the super villain scale high walls; every function of each arm is mentally controlled by Doctor Octopus.

Biography: Having developed a harness and robotic arms with which to handle radioactive materials, a getup which earned him the nickname Doctor Octopus, scientist Octavius uses his gear to conduct experiments at the U.S. Atomic Research Center. Despite the fact that he is "the most brilliant atomic researcher in our country," one of his projects gets out of hand and an explosion occurs. The "sudden blast of uncontrolled radiation" fuses the rig to Octovius' body; waking up at the Bliss Private Hospital, he realizes that he no longer needs to use the dials on the front of the girdle but can now manipulate the arms by sheer will. Since his mind has become unbalanced (he suffered "an uncertain amount of brain damage" due to radiation), Octavius decides to use his newfound abilities for criminal purposes, and adopts his former nickname as his *nom de guerre.* He has been among the most persistent foes of Spider-Man, the superhero believing him to be "the most *deadly* criminal on earth." What makes the fiend especially dangerous is that he can be subtle. On one occasion he actually spent time wooing Spider-Man's widowed Aunt May in order to use her as a decoy in a crime. (He escorts her to a museum, causes her to faint near a precious work of art, then steals it while the guard is busy helping the old woman.)

Quote: "With such power and my brilliant mind, I'm the *supreme* human being on earth!"

Comment: As an historical point of interest, whether by accident or design, the villain calls Spider-Man "Super-Man" during their first battle. Doctor Octopus was the villain featured in the first Spider-Man novel, *Mayhem in Manhattan* (1978), by Len Wein and Marv Wolfman; the character has also been seen regularly in the Spider-Man comic strip.

DR. PAUL CARRUTHERS (MP)

First Appearance: 1941, *The Devil Bat,* Producers Releasing Corp.

Weapons: Giant vampire bat.

Biography: Posing as a gentle physician in the small town of Heathville, Carruthers is actually an embittered lunatic. Having created the formula for a perfume which has made Morton-Heath Cosmetics a small fortune, he feels he should share in the profits. But Henry Morton and Martin Heath don't quite see it that way, so Carruthers goes into a new line of work: murder. Using electricity to breed a giant vampire bat, he trains the monster to detest a special fragrance he's created. Mending bodies in public, Carruthers destroys them in private by gifting his enemies and their families with toiletries (shaving cream, cologne, etc.) containing the scent. Then he sends the animal forth to tear out their throats. Unfortunately for Carruthers, a newspaper reporter gets wind of his foul scheme and throws some of the fragrance on the doctor, who is fanged to death by the bat.

Quote: "The cheats! The thieves! *My* brain has made them independently wealthy and I, who should be a partner . . . am treated like a hired clerk!"

Comment: Bela Lugosi played Carruthers in this motion picture which, with World War II just a few months off, was advertised with the tacky line, "more terrifying than bombing by night!" Bela Lugosi did not appear in the 1946 sequel *The Devil Bat's Daughter,* though his bats did. Lugosi also portrayed BARON ROXOR, DR. ALEX ZORKA, DR. MIRAKLE, DRACULA, MURDER LEGENDRE, and PROFESSOR ERIC VORNOFF.

DR. PHIBES (MP, N)

Real Name: Anton Phibes.

First Appearance: 1971, *The Abominable Dr. Phibes,* American International Pictures.

Biography: Born April 21, 1921, Dr. Phibes earned his doctorate in physics from Cambridge University, after which he studied music in Vienna. An independently wealthy concert organist, he was 40 when he married Victoria Devereaux, 17 years his junior. Settling in London and joining the foreign service, Phibes was content until his wife died on the operating table. The following day he was horribly disfigured in a car accident and, patching himself back together, he vowed revenge on the nine doctors he blamed for Victoria's death. Hidden in his mansion—where he also kept Victoria's preserved body—he visited the plagues of Egypt on each doctor in turn: death by bats (they gnawed Dr. Dunwoody to pieces), bees (they were dumped in Thornton's bath), blood (Longstreet's was drained), frogs (a frog mask crushed one medic's skull), locusts, a hailstone machine, and the like. Phibes wore a rubber mask fashioned like his face before the accident; beneath it, his countenance was a skull with strips of tissue still attached. As a result of the accident, he was able to speak in a metallic voice, but only when a thick cable implanted in his neck was plugged into a console. He wore a white cloak, suit, gloves, and big bow tie, complementing his pasty face. His aide was the lovely musician Vulnavia. When the police finally tracked them down, Vulnavia used a dagger to commit suicide; Phibes escaped to Victoria's side, where he embalmed himself. But the vengeful Phibes returned (in *Dr. Phibes Rises Again*, 1972), thanks to a blood transfusion. This time he has a more ambitious program: to find an ancient scroll that will guide him to an underground river in Egypt, a river whose magic will enable him to bring Victoria back to life. Slaughtering the members of a rival expedition led by antiquarian Biederbeck, he eventually finds the river and is last seen sailing his boat—with his wife's coffin—down its dark waters.

Quote: "An X-ray of your son's rib cage. You will observe that a tiny key has been lodged close to his heart. It will unlock the halter around your son's neck. If you're wondering why you need to free the table . . . in a few moments acid will be released . . . directly over the boy's head."

Comment: Vincent Price was at his melodramatic best as Phibes. Like THE PHANTOM OF THE OPERA, this villain played his organ as a catharsis. The first film was advertised with a play on the *Love Story* slogan: "Love means never having to say you're ugly."

DR. PHOSPHOROUS (C)

Real Name: Dr. Sartorius.

First Appearance: 1976, *Detective Comics* #469, DC Comics.

Costume: Tattered clothing (the skin of the glowing Phosphorous is transparent).

Biography: Investing in a private nuclear power plant—built in the ocean beyond the U.S. three-mile limit—Sartorius goes to look over the facility one day. Unbeknownst to him, runaway costs have forced the builders to cut back on safety measures; when he arrives after-hours the nuclear core explodes. Though he is able to jump behind sandbags, the granules themselves are caught up in the holocaust. The irradiated sand is changed from silicon to phosphorus in the cataclysm and, buried in his flesh, turns Sartorius into a living, burning, phosphorous madman. Trailing noxious fumes and causing anything he touches to explode into flame, Dr. Phosphorous seeks to make others suffer. Carrying his vendetta to an extreme, he plans to poison everyone in Gotham City; mixing it up with Batman, he ends up falling into the core of his own faulty reactor. However, Phosphorous still lives and, months afterward, tries to poison the city once more. Batman recaptures him with the help of Batgirl, and the felon gets locked up in a fireproof room at the Arkham Asylum for the Criminally Insane. As of this writing he is still at Arkham.

DR. POLARIS (C)

Real Name: Dr. Neal Emerson.

First Appearance: 1963, *Green Lantern* #21, DC Comics.

Costume: Purple bodysuit with red "U"-shaped magnet in white circle on chest (originally no circle, and magnet was inverted); blue trunks, gloves, boots, vest with flared shoulders (originally had no vest), helmet with flared ears (originally had cowl with tails).

Weapons: Huge gun which taps the earth's magnetism and channels it into the super villain.

Biography: Using magnetism, Dr. Emerson is able to make incredible progress against various human illnesses. However, repeated exposure to magnetism causes him to become evil; exposing himself to his magnetic gun, he goes on a crime rampage before being stopped by the superheroic Green Lantern. But he returns again and again, eventually assimilating the magnetic power so that he becomes "a living magnetic battery" and has no need of weapons to raise, attract, or repel objects made of metal, to fly, or to surround himself with an impenetrable force-field. Now and then his original, benevolent nature surfaces, but never long enough to permit him to end the MR. HYDE-like control Dr. Polaris has over him. Though the fiend is torn apart "into pure magnetic force" when he overloads in *Green Lantern* #135 (concluding a three-issue-long battle), he coalesces (with his magnet emblem now tilted slightly to the left) and has since appeared in various DC titles, most notably *Crisis on Infinite Earths* #s 1-5 and 10.

Quote: "I feel strong enough to tear apart *worlds*! Powerful enough to *control a universe*!"

DOCTOR PSYCHO (C)

First Appearance: 1943, *Wonder Woman* #5, DC Comics.

Costume: Blue tuxedo and bow tie; white shirt, spats.

Weapons: "Electro-atomizer" to "loosen the atoms" of a person's body and remove the spirit, which DOCTOR PSYCHO can then easily trap in his "bands of psycho-electric magnetism."

Chief Henchman: Marva (see Biography).

Biography: When his family came to the United States from Greece, "a semi-literate" immigration officer shortened the family name (which is never revealed) to Psycho. As he grew to adulthood, the future Doctor Psycho was taunted by his peers because he was dwarfish and had a huge head. However, he continued studying medicine as well as mesmerism, his pet subject. Graduating medical school with "the highest award our university can give," he gets into a great deal of trouble because of a young woman named Marva. She admires his brain but is upfront about his chances to do more than discuss medicine with her: "You're not exactly a Clark Gable! Love-making doesn't become you." Though she has agreed to marry him, she slips now and then into the arms of "athletic idol" Ben Bradley; unwilling to break her engagement, she convinces Bradley to steal radium from the college lab and frame Psycho for the theft. The mesmerist is sent to prison for several years, while Marva marries Bradley. Upon his release, Psycho obtains a chunk of radium and uses it to get Bradley to confess that the theft was Marva's idea. Shoving the radium down Bradley's throat and killing him, Psycho hypnotizes Marva into marrying him. Doing so, he finds that through her he can "bring living substance out of the spirit world," ectoplasm which he's able to mold into different bodies and "wear . . . and discard . . . like a cloak." Using this power and his hypnotic abilities, he seeks to get vengeance against all people for the abuse he's endured all his life, and against females in particular for Marva's deceit. He first crosses Wonder Woman's path when he destroys the Supreme Shell Plant in order to dishonor the women working there; the two have battled many times since, their most dramatic encounter taking place when Marva dies. Doctor Psycho finds another to take her place as his medium—Wonder Woman's lover, Steve Trevor. Using ectoplasm, he creates a new super-villainous identity, Captain Wonder, which he employs to battle the heroic Amazon (#289, 1982). The battle ends when Psycho/Wonder has been dropped several miles to the ground by Wonder Woman and slinks off in his old Psycho form (#290).

Quote: "Women shall suffer while I laugh!"

Comment: Supervillainy runs in Psycho's family. His brother was King Ironsides, a "brilliant geologist" who discovered a volcano on Wooloo Island that erupted "pure gold." In order to keep the natives of the island from interfering with his plans to collect the gold, Ironsides constructed incredible iron giants, which were really "ordinary men on stilts, wearing tremendous suits of armor." Eventually, Ironsides was defeated by Wonder Woman.

DR. REGULUS (C)

Real Name: Doctor Zaxton Regulus.

First Appearance: 1966, *Adventure Comics* #348, DC Comics.

Costume: Yellow bodysuit; golden boots, gloves, breastplate open at the sides, full-head helmet with red visor.

Weapons: Spaceship which is "detection-proof" thanks to "electro-magnetic radiation."

Chief Henchmen: Various robots, used early in his career.

Biography: A denizen of the late thirtieth century, Regulus works at a nuclear power plant on earth. There, he is involved in an illegal private research project which involves using a radioactive isotope of gold to amplify solar energy. One day, young Dirk Morgana enters Regulus' lab to deliver some supplies; when he walks in, the equipment explodes, killing Dirk's companion Zarl Hendricks. Regulus justifiably blames the accident on the interruption, but Dirk's father, Derek, who is in charge of the plant, fires him anyway. Embittered, Regulus gets his revenge by kidnapping Dirk and placing him in the heart of a nuclear reactor. The rays don't kill the youth, but turn him into the super-powered Sun Boy. Angry and frustrated, Zaxton became a criminal in large part to underwrite his ongoing experiments with gold. After several run-ins with the Legion of Super-Heroes, of which Dirk is a member, the scientist decides to acquire superpowers himself. Creating the Arion Star, an artificial solar entity, he draws its energies into his own body and, with regular recharges from it or any "solar and nuclear energy" source, is thereafter able to radiate intense light and heat. Withal, he still can't defeat the Legion and is presently jailed on the prison planet Takron-Galtos.

Quote: "Only *here* . . . is *everything* my heart desires! Revenge—and the power I need to destroy a world!"

DR. RIGORO MORTIS (C)

First Appearance: 1967, *House of Mystery* #165, DC Comics.

Chief Henchman: Super-Hood, a "human-like robot" with heat-vision—a ray which hardens into nearly unbreakable plastic for trapping adversaries—and superstrength.

Biography: Nothing is known about this scientific genius, save that he has created Super-Hood, whose great abilities he leases to paying criminal customers. After commiting several crimes, the robot, his creator, and several criminal clients are tracked to a "garage hideout" by teenager Robby Reed, keeper of the "Dial-H for Hero" device. Turning himself into the mighty robot Howziz, Robby shrinks Super-Hood to the size of a doll and subdues the others with "sleep-gas shots."

Quote: "It's just another freak super-hero! But we have the means of dealing with him!"

Comment: This was the character's only appearance.

DOCTOR SATAN (MP)

First Appearance: 1940, *The Mysterious Doctor Satan*, Republic Pictures.

Weapons: A powerful, nearly eight-feet-tall robot.

Biography: With plans to subjugate humankind, Doctor Satan builds a menacing robot (the prototype for an army of such creatures) to carry out his evil deeds. He needs only a remote control unit invented by scientist Thomas Scott to make it operative. Sinking the yacht on which the device is hidden, Doctor Satan recovers it and, through his robot, begins to rob and terrorize the city. However, the masked supersleuth known as Copperhead takes the villain on, surviving crushing walls (he shoots out the controls), a plane crash caused by the remote control unit (he parachutes out), and the mighty arms of the robot (he crowns it with a bottle of acid). Sneaking into Satan's headquarters, Copperhead manages to knock him out and slip his own mask on the fiend, watching as the robot mistakes its master for the detective, crushing him and heaving him to his doom from a high window.

Comment: Eduardo (billed as Edward) Cianelli played the evil Doctor Satan in this 15-chapter serial which was advertised as a "game of death dealt by a power-crazed madman who threatens to crush a nation!" The script for this film was originally written as a Superman adventure. However, negotiations for the character fell through and the story was revised to accommodate the studio-invented hero, Copperhead.

DR. SCARABUS (MP)

First Appearance: 1963, *The Raven*, American International Pictures.

Costume: Black skullcap and robe; paisley outfit underneath.

Biography: Wishing to become the most powerful sorcerer of the sixteenth century, Dr. Scarabus plots to lure one Dr. Craven to his castle. Scarabus intends to extract the secrets of Craven's magic, which will enhance his own. Getting him there is no problem. He turns a third magician, Dr. Bedlo, into a talking raven and sends him to Craven. Restored to human form, Bedlo informs Craven that his lost, beloved wife Lenore is at Scarabus' castle. The two men rush over, where a shocked Craven learns that Lenore has left him to take up with Scarabus, whom she feels has more potential. When the heartbroken Craven refuses to divulge his magical secrets, Scarabus binds him, turns Bedlo back to a bird, and threatens to torture Craven's daughter Estelle. But using his beak, Bedlo pecks through Craven's bonds and frees him. In a duel of magic, Craven defeats Scarabus and leaves the castle in flaming ruins.

Comment: Boris Karloff (DR. GUSTAV NIEMANN) played Scarabus, with Vincent Price (DR. PHIBES) and Peter Lorre as Craven and Bedlo, respectively; Jack Nicholson had a small part as young Rexford Bedlo. Richard Matheson (creator

*Boris Karloff as **DR. SCARABUS** (left) with Dr. Bedlo (Peter Lorre) and Dr. Craven (Vincent Price). © American International Pictures.*

of BEN CORTMAN) wrote the screenplay; though ostensibly based on Edgar Allan Poe's masterpiece, the film has nothing in common with the 1845 poem save for the lost Lenore and the talking bird, and even those connections are tenuous.

DR. SIVANA (C, TV)

Real Name: Thaddeus Bodog Sivana.
First Appearance: 1940, *Whiz Comics* #2, Fawcett Publications.
Costume: Lab coat (color varies; usually white).
Weapons: Countless scientific gadgets, including a spaceship; "suspendium globes" to put people (including superheroes) in suspended animation; "vortex transporter paralyzer beam" to snare adversaries; "cosmic gas" which freezes even superheroes; acid so powerful it can "dissolve even a member of the Marvel Family"; the "spider gun" which "shoots out a rope of liquid plastic" which can't be broken; "Hypno ray" to mesmerize his enemies; a "Shazamium bracelet" stolen from the wizard Shazam, which permits him to become invisible, incorporeal, and weightless; a slew of robots made of "sivanium," a "living metal"; and a "time-travel device" which allows him to move people and buildings through time (though not space). He has also used a "mute ray" on Billy Batson, making it impossible for the lad to utter the magic word "Shazam" and become the superheroic Captain Marvel.
Chief Henchmen: His daughters Beautia and Georgia Sivana (as in Savannah, Georgia), and his sons Magnificus and Sivana, Jr. He was also assisted by numerous hoods.
Biography: "The world's maddest scientist," Sivana desires "to rule not only earth, but the entire universe!" It all started early in this century, when Sivana was "one of the most brilliant and promising young scientists in Europe." However, his visions and inventions were laughed at, so he roamed from country to country looking for acceptance. Finally, disgusted, he built a rocketship and moved to Venus with his children. Beautia eventually became empress of the planet but Dr. Sivana, still smarting with rage, returned to earth intending to conquer it and then the rest of the cosmos. Thanks to Captain Marvel and the rest of the Marvel Family, he and his progeny have yet to succeed. In easily his most heinous crime over the years, Dr. Sivana drew the Marvel Family into space and used his suspendium globes to place them in suspended animation, where they were unable to interfere with his plans of conquest. Unfortunately for him, the rocket in which Sivana was riding went out of control and was also swallowed up by the globe. Thus, both the Marvels and the Sivanas (father, Sivana, Jr., and George) hibernated side by side until the sun's heat vaporized the orb in 1972. The adversaries resumed their battle, which continues still.

DR. SIVANA in his first comic book appearance. © Fawcett Publications.

Quote: "I have stolen the Capitol Building and Congress. You have 24 hours to proclaim me rightful ruler of the universe—or you'll never see your senators and representatives again!"
Comment: Howard Morris played the fiend in the 1979 TV movie *Legends of the Super-Heroes*.

DOCTOR SPECTRO (C)

First Appearance: 1966, *Captain Atom* Vol. 2, #79, Charlton Comics.
Weapons: Device to alter peoples' moods using color.
Biography: The "master of moods," Spectro is a circus star who is pushed into his own apparatus by thugs. Bathed in colored rays, his brain soaks them up, especially the red rays, the rays of hatred and anger. As a criminal, the rainbow-garbed Spectro uses yellow rays to make people afraid of him; his brief reign ends, however, when he tangles with the superheroic Captain Atom and is once again shoved—this time into high-tension wires, whose 50,000 volts reduce him to ash. But while Spectro is dead, he's not quite finished; five small versions of himself show up (issue #81), each one master of a different color (red, blue, yellow, green, and purple). Breaking into a NASA facility, they steal instruments capable of re-forming

them into the original Spectro. Despite Captain Atom's best efforts they succeed in coalescing, but the last laugh is on the reborn Spectro. His purple self is a benign force, the evil colors are all competitive, and the result is a confused whole incapable of committing crimes.

Comment: See other fear-inducing villains BUSHMAN, D'SPAYRE, MISTER FEAR, PHOBIA, PSYCHO-MAN, PSYCHO PIRATE and SCARECROW. Other Captain Atom villains include the mad Dr. Claudius Jaynes, whose missiles the hero detonated "outside the universe" to keep them from destroying the world; the "Spies from Another World," intent on invading the earth; extraterrestrials from the planet Blue who are destroying American rockets; the translucent Ghost from the world of Sunuria (though Sunuria exists in another dimension they apparently value gold since, like AURIC GOLDFINGER, the Ghost is out to rob Fort Knox); Iron Arms, with his powerful exoskeleton, and his partner-in-crime Professor Koste, who holds Captain Atom for ransom ($10 million in gold); and the Fiery Icer, whose guns spit out both heat and paralyzing cold.

DOCTOR SUN (C)

First Appearance: 1973, *Tomb of Dracula* #16, Marvel Comics.

Costume: None; Sun now has a golden humanoid body with his brain set in a clear dome which serves as his head.

Chief Henchmen: Juno (now deceased) and other flunkies.

Biography: Sun's career as a super villain began in Mainland China in 1966. A scientist—"perhaps the most brilliant who ever lived"—he "incurred the wrath of a petty official" and was ordered slain, but not in any old way. Sun had been working on Project: Mind, keeping the human brain alive outside the body and giving it "knowledge greater than any human being has ever known" by linking it to a computer. He was ordered to be the program's first subject. His brain was removed and placed in a preservative "anti-matter receptacle," then electronically bound to the computer; at once, Sun took over the machine and devoted himself to taking over the world. His first task was to try to procure a steady supply of blood by subjugating the vampire DRACULA; however, that failed and Sun was forced to acquire a robotic body for himself in order to "feed." Despite having mastered teleportation, being able to create a force-field, travel through space, and outthink just about anyone, Sun was never able to defeat the superhero Nova in their numerous confrontations. Eventually transferring his intelligence into a huge computer, Sun perished when he was rammed by the robot Herbie of the Fantastic Four. "Two incompatible power sources meet (and) the collision of their opposite polarities is . . . explosive." The devoted Herbie was also destroyed in the detonation (1980, *Fantastic Four* #217).

Quote: "When I am through with you, your mind shall be little more than an empty shell!"

Comment: Other bodiless, super-villainous brains include THE BRAIN and THE BRAIN FROM SIRIUS.

DR. TYME (C)

First Appearance: 1965, *The Doom Patrol* #92, DC Comics.

Costume: Blue tights, boots, cape, gloves; green bodyshirt; helmet is a white clock-face with black hands and numbers, with green eyeslits and an opening for the mouth.

Weapons: Huge hourglass whose sands keep people helpless; suspension ray to immobilize adversaries.

Biography: A brilliant scientist, Dr. Tyme (his real name is never revealed) has discovered a means of controlling the speed at which time progresses. Although he puts up a good fight against the Doom Patrol, the superheroes thwart his criminal plans and he flees. He has not been seen since.

Quote: "Everything's going like clock-work! By the time *Elasti-girl* reaches her teammates, the time bomb will explode!"

Comment: CHRONOS also used time to his advantage.

DR. VULCAN (MP)

Real Name: Professor Bryant.

First Appearance: 1949, *King of the Rocket Men*, Republic Pictures.

Weapons: The Decimator, a device which uses Thromium waves to vaporize rock or metal; remote-control TV which can spy on anyone anywhere.

Biography: Science Associates is a research group devoted to creating useful scientific devices. Seeking to use their inventions for crime, Bryant adopts the identity of Dr. Vulcan and, inaugurating a reign of terror, kills those of his colleagues who may suspect who he is. (Professor Drake's car is driven by remote control, straight off a cliff; Dr. Conway is stabbed; Dr. Von Strum is gunned down; Professor Millard barely escapes being blown to atoms in his laboratory.) Stealing the most powerful of the group's devices, the Decimator, Vulcan conceals it in his private stronghold on Fisherman's Island, several hundred miles from New York City. He demands $1 billion to ensure the safety of the city and, refused, turns the Decimator on Manhattan, causing an earthquake and tidal wave. However, the superhero Rocket Man tracks him down and stops him before he can completely destroy the city. In a serious case of overkill, the air force arrives minutes later, bombing the volcanic island flat. Though Rocket Man escapes, Dr. Vulcan is killed.

Comment: I. Stanford Jolley played the part of Dr. Vulcan. In 1951, the 12-chapter serial was edited into a feature film called *Lost Planet Airmen*.

DR. WU (MP)

First Appearance: 1966, *Our Man Flint*, 20th Century-Fox.

Biography: Under the auspices of the evil organization Galaxy, Dr. Wu, with his colleagues Dr. Krupov and Dr. Schneider, attempts to bring the world to its knees by controlling the weather. Based on a remote island, they are uncovered and bested by secret agent Derek Flint of Z.O.W.I.E. (Zonal Organization on World Intelligence Espionage). A key Galaxy operative is Gila, who beguiles the opposition with her charm and beauty; one of Galaxy's chief assassins is Gruber, who is slain by Flint.

Comment: The stars of this film were Benson Fong as Wu, Rhys Williams as Krupov, Peter Brocco as Schneider, Gila Golan as Gila and Michael St. Clair as Gruber. In the second Flint film, *In Like Flint* (1967), a group of women led by Elisabeth (Anna Lee) try to take over the world in a scam based on substituting a look-alike actor for the President of the United States. Like SUMURU and her horde, the women are implicitly lesbians.

DR. YEN SIN (M)

First Appearance: 1936, *Doctor Yen Sin* #1, Donald Keyhoe.

Costume: Yellow robe; green cap with plume of hair.

Biography: Also known as "the Invisible Peril," Dr. Yen Sin was a would-be world conqueror from Asia, in the tradition of DR. FU MANCHU.

Comment: There were just three Doctor Yen-Sin tales: "The Mystery of the Dragon's Shadow," "The Mystery of the Golden Skull," and "The Mystery of the Singing Mummies." The author, Donald Keyhoe, later gained fame as a UFO expert and critic of the U.S. government's alleged coverups in the matter. Dr. Yen Sin's costume was virtually identical to that of WU FANG, who predated him. See other Asian super villains BRIGAND LEADER, COLONEL SUN, DR. GOO FEE, GENERAL CHAN LU, and WU FANG.

DON DEL ORO (MP)

Real Name: Pablo (no surname).

First Appearance: 1939, *Zorro's Fighting Legion*, Republic Pictures.

Costume: Golden conquistador-style armor, large helmet with angular human features and golden mane.

Weapons: Golden arrows.

Biography: It's 1824, and President Benito Juarez of Mexico looks to put the new republic in order by tapping the gold-rich San Mendolita Mines. However, seeking wealth and power himself, evil Pablo conspires with mine officials to thwart the efforts of the well-meaning leader. Fashioning a suit of gold and passing himself off to the local Yaqui Indians as Don del Oro, their revered Armored God, Pablo puts them to work in his cause. In the president's corner is the heroic Zorro, and the hero and villain clash repeatedly. In their battles, Zorro survives everything from a dynamited building, a flaming wagon, a runaway mine cart, an avalanche, and a flood. Caught in the mastermind's most diabolical trap, crushing walls, Zorro survives by ingeniously wrenching up one of the stones from the floor and using it as a brace. Ultimately, Zorro tracks Don del Oro to the Yaqui village where he's making ready to storm the mines. Unmasking the god and revealing him to be Pablo, Zorro watches helplessly as the Indians kill the pretender.

Comment: C. Montague Shaw played Don del Oro in the 12-chapter serial.

DOOMBRINGER (C)

First Appearance: 1984, *Power Man and Iron Fist* #103, Marvel Comics.

Costume: Silver bodysuit with golden stripes down legs (see Weapons), boots; golden belt, armor worn over both shoulders and right side of chest (see Weapons).

Weapons: Exoskeleton provides him with superstrength and invulnerability (at one point, he survives a 20-story fall); suit (apparently the vest) can generate a force-field which also radiates intense heat; right glove conceals extendable knives; left glove fires "a poison blast"; infrared lenses allow him to see in the dark; and there is also a small oxygen tank for underwater travel.

Biography: The man who would become Doombringer (his real name is never revealed) worked for a secret U.S. Middle Eastern intelligence unit known as the Uni-World Trading Corporation. A brilliant assassin, saboteur, and martial-arts expert, he married and had a daughter—and began to feel remorse for all the "blood on my hands" and also for lying to them about what he really does for a living. He went to his boss, Taylor, to quit, but Uni-World had one more assignment for him—to test a prototype battlesuit in a program known as Operation Doombringer (see Weapons). It was a suit they needed not only to do their job, but also to "prove our worth" to the private sector, what with funding cutbacks due to the outcry against covert operations abroad. To coerce him into testing the suit, Uni-World brought his wife and daughter to their compound, which lay in a disputed, hostility-ridden zone between the nations of Khotain and Dhakran. The operative reluctantly agreed and was dispatched to murder the Mahdi, the leader of Soviet-backed Khotain. While he was gone, Khotainese radicals bombed the Uni-World compound; among the casualties were the agent's family. His world destroyed, he wanted only to destroy ours. Keeping the suit, he tried to trigger World War III by assassinating the leaders of Khotain and U.S.-backed Dhakran. When that failed due to the intervention of the superheroes Iron Fist and Power Man, Doombringer entered a missile silo and tried to send off a bomb by himself. Luckily, a control panel was destroyed when Iron Fist and Power Man tried to stop him and the rockets misfired while Doombringer was in the silo (#104). He appears to have been destroyed in the explosion.

Quote: "My force field's *full strength*! Hitting it, all that will shatter is *you*!"

DOOMSTALKER (C)

First Appearance: 1975, *The Brute* #3, Atlas Comics.

Costume: Orange bodysuit; navy blue leotard with skull emblem on chest; light blue gloves, boots with white spots on hem; red belt with white spots; red cowl with white spots on neck.

Weapons: "Death-gaze" ray from eyes.

Biography: The Doomstalker is a cyborg—half human, half robot—built by Dr. Rolf Hendrick. When the U.S. Defense Department refuses to accept the powerful Doomstalker as a new breed of soldier, the deeply offended Hendrick plots to use the creature to take over the world. The mad scientist operates his creation long-distance with a handheld "control calculator." In addition to his destructive ray and great strength, Doomstalker can leap vast distances.

Quote: "No . . . the ball is *mine*—as all else upon this earth will be!"

Comment: This was the character's only appearance; the story ended with Doomstalker poised on a wrecking ball and shouting at police, "Will you do my bidding—or must I also destroy you?" Had the magazine survived to a fourth issue, Doomstalker would undoubtedly have been defeated.

DORMAMMU (C)

First Appearance: 1964, *Strange Tales* #126, Marvel Comics.

Costume: Purple jumpsuit; yellow belt (later, sash) around waist; red gloves, boots, cobra-like hood behind head (head itself is made of flame, with yellow eyes, mouth, and "hair"); occasionally wears red capelet over each shoulder.

Chief Henchmen: BARON MORDO; the G'Uranthic Guardian, a "pet" monster; Asti the All-seeing; Orini; demon-slaves known as Dykkors; countless other disciples around the world and in his own dimension.

Biography: Born over a thousand years ago, the wizard Dormammu (still in human form) was banished from the magical dimension of a race known as the Faltine. (The reasons for this have not yet been revealed.) Also exiled was his sister Umar, a witch who is not quite as powerful as her brother. Together, they settled in the Dark Dimension, the realm of the sorcerer Olnar. There, in exchange for his hospitality and a measure of power—granted over the strong protests of Olnar's advisors—Dormammu and Umar taught the sorcerer how to move between the dimensions and thereby conquer worlds hitherto beyond his reach. Alas, Olnar had the misfortune of taking in the realm of the Mindless Ones, brutal, clay-like creatures who fire destructive beams from their eyes. They pillaged the Dark Dimension and slew Olmar; the siblings from another dimension promptly seized the opportunity to defeat Olmar's supporters. At the same time they managed to trap the Mindless Ones behind a "mystic shield" at the fringe of their kingdom; this act earned them the respect of the lesser wizard-lords of the kingdom (such as Tazza), who swore allegience to Dormammu over Olmar's young son Orini. Reforming himself into a more powerful being made entirely of magical energy, Dormammu took Orini as his disciple to ensure his loyalty, as well as to keep track of his doings. For years, he has yearned to add the earth to his collection of worlds. Though he has been thwarted repeatedly by the master magician Dr. Strange, that has not deterred him from trying, helped by his many worshipers on our world. Among Dormammu's awesome powers are the ability to become a giant, to fire destructive energy from his hands, to grant lesser but still-potent powers to his disciples, to travel through time and other dimensions; and to control minds or transmute animate or unliving matter. Perhaps Dormammu's most vile act to date was imprisoning his sister in a remote corner of the universe. Though she is less powerful than he, the paranoid Dormammu feared she might one day try to take control of the Dark Dimension. Though she was freed when Dormammu was off battling the magic being Eternity (he couldn't keep her locked up and fight Eternity both, the magic equivalent of chewing gum and walking at the same time), she no longer trusts her brother and plans, someday, to control the Dark Domain. Indeed, she is currently in charge, with Dormammu having been vaporized and strewn through several dimensions by Dr. Strange. (It is doubtful, though, that he will long remain incorporeal.) In fairness to Dormammu, the rule of the green-garbed sorceress is proving every bit as corrupt as his own, Umar perpetuating his evil designs on the earth. Umar's daughter (by Orini, whom she seduced) is the kindly Clea, who sometimes assists Dr. Strange in his battle against the hosts of darkness.

Quote: "Though I possess enough *magical* power to erase you from existence in an instant, I prefer to continue our battle—using only our *physical* weapons . . . !"

DOVI (C)

First Appearance: 1962, *The Fly* (later *Fly Man*) #21, Archie Comics.

Costume: Purple bodysuit; white helmet with blue eyeslits and ears (see Weapons); blue gunbelt and ruffled collar.

Weapons: Time-travel airship; helmet which "protects facial tissue" from aging while moving backward through time (though the effects can be undone by returning to the future); ray gun.

Biography: A native of the year 2262 A.D. where he's "wanted for a dozen crimes," Dovi went back in time to 1962 where his criminal acts were undermined by the superhero The Fly. Thereafter, Dovi devoted himself to destroying the hero. His most ambitious crime was to bring a beauty queen from the future to 1962, where she was supposed to seduce and slay the hero. Instead, she fell in love with him and, capturing Dovi, returned him to the future to pay the piper for his crimes.

Quote: "Ha! Ha! They'll never find me because I'm hiding out in the past!"

Comment: The character appeared in only two adventures. Dovi is a member of THE ANTI-FLY LEAGUE.

DOXOL (C)

First Appearance: 1939, *Wonderworld Comics* #4, Fox Publications.

Weapons: "Mystic solution," injected by hypodermic, which puts others completely under his control.

Chief Henchmen: Nameless, hooded slaves.

Biography: Nothing is known about this character's past. Headquartered in a magnificent country estate, the robed Doxol (whose cadaverous face is "horrible beyond description") has his minions kidnap others, then he injects them with his mystic solution. This done, his slaves are sent forth to commit crimes—all, apparently, in his insane effort to take over the country. (However, Doxol is not completely unreasonable: Though "you will always obey me," he informs one unwilling guest, she and his other slaves *are* allowed to "return to your homes" each night.) Spotting Doxol's henchmen kidnapping a woman, the superheroic Flame follows them in his airplane and, using his ability to become flame, materializes in a brazier at Doxol's side. Though the fiend escapes to his own airplane, the Flame pursues and shoots him down. Upon his death, Doxol's hold over his slaves dies with him.

Quote: "You will do as I bid . . . rob, burn, and murder if need be. I shall be your master and you my slaves!"

Comment: This was the character's only appearance.

DRACULA (N, S, MP, C, R)

First Appearance: 1897, *Dracula*, Bram Stoker.

Biography: A native of Transylvania, of a family which is the "heart's blood (and) brains" of the Szeklers (a people who lived in the east and north and were descended—of course—from Attila the Hun), Count Dracula lived his mortal life in the latter fifteenth and early sixteenth centuries as a "Voivode" (Romanian for "Prince") and a passionately patriotic warrior (see Comment). As a man, he was "most wonderful . . . (a) soldier, statesman, and alchemist. He had a mighty brain, a learning beyond compare, and a heart that knew no fear and no remorse." Apparently, his demonic future was set when he attended the Scholomance, a local school at which, according to legend, magic, the language of animals, and other dark talents are taught to 10 scholars a semester, one of whom—implicitly, Dracula—subsequently served the devil as an aide. As a vampire, Dracula survived by drinking human blood with his gleaming white "eyeteeth long and pointed." (So-doing, he slowly grew from an old man to a youthful one during the course of the novel.) Regardless of his age, the vampire was "a tall . . . man, clean-shaven" save for a long white moustache. He had a high bridge and thin nose with "peculiarly arched" nostrils, a mouth that was "fixed and rather cruel-looking," a broad, strong chin, pointed ears, and slightly furry palms. Because of his devilish nature, he had "the strength of twenty men," was able to crawl straight up or down sheer walls, could become large or small or appear at will in "any of the forms that are to him"—including wolf or bat—and could see clearly in the dark. He was also able to control wolves, rats, owls, foxes, insects, and other creatures, including humans he bit or put under his spell. He could also control the elements, including fog and thunder "within his range." The vampire had "diabolical quickness" and a "lion-like" arrogance—justifiably so. According to his nemesis Professor Abraham Van Helsing, he was determined to become "the father or furtherer of a new order of beings, whose road must lead through Death, not life." To this end, Dracula sailed from his castle in Transylvania to England and set up his principal residence at Carfax estate (though for convenience he scattered dozens of coffins around the countryside). It was in any one of these he slept during the day. His powers fled at daybreak ("as does that of all evil things") and the "monster must retain whatever form" he had at sunrise until the following sunset. Moreover, if he had "banqueted heavily" at night, he "will sleep late." As for limitations and weaknesses, he could not enter someone's home unless he'd been invited, after which he was free to come and go at will, and he could only cross running water "at the slack or the flood of the tide." He neither threw a shadow nor cast a reflection in a mirror. In addition to sunlight, Dracula's weaknesses were garlic and religious artifacts; confronted with a cross, for example, he cowered and "his waxen hue became greenish-yellow by the contrast of his burning eyes." The branch of a wild rose on his coffin could keep him from stirring; a sacred bullet, yard-long stake through his heart, or decapitation could destroy him. In time, Dracula was dispatched by aides of Van Helsing, who simultaneously cut his throat and plunged a knife through his heart as he lay in his coffin. The vampire immediately "crumbled into dust and passed from our sight."

Quote: "My revenge is just begun! I spread it over centuries, and time is on my side."

Comment: The background for Dracula was drawn, in large part, from the life and bloody exploits of Vlad "Tepes" ("the Impaler") who lived in Wallachia (now Romania) from 1431 to 1476. The son of Vlad "Dracule" ("the Dragon"), he was also known as "Dracula" ("the son of Dracule"). There have been many stage Draculas over the years, most notably Bela Lugosi, Frank Langella, and Terence Stamp; however, the character has gained his greatest fame in the movies. Bela Lugosi (BARON ROXOR, DR. ALEX ZORKA, DR. MIRAKLE, DR. PAUL CARRUTHERS, MURDER LEGENDRE, PROFESSOR ERIC VORNOFF) starred as the vampire in *Dracula* (1931) and again in *Abbott and Costello Meet Frankenstein* (1947); Carlos Villarias Villar in *Dracula* (1931, Spanish-language version); Christopher Lee in *The Horror of Dracula* (1959), *Dracula-Prince of Darkness* (1965), *Dracula Has Risen from the Grave* (1969), *Taste the Blood of Dracula* (1970), *Count Dracula* (1972), *The Scars of Dracula* (1971), *Dracula, AD 1972* (1972), and *The Satanic Rites of Dracula* (1978); John Carradine in *House of Frankenstein* (1944) and *Billy the Kid vs. Dracula* (1966); Jack Palance in *Dracula* (1973); Udo Kier in Andy Warhol's *Dracula* (1974); Louis Jourdan in *Dracula* (1978); and Frank Langella in *Dracula* (1979). There have been dozens of other vampire films, some with "Dracula" in their title; these, however, bore little resemblance, if any, to Stoker's evil Count. Among these are *Dracula's Daughter* (1936; Gloria Holden as Countess Zaleska), *Son of Dracula* (1943; Lon Chaney, Jr., as Count Alucard [spell it backwards . . .], *The Return of Dracula* (1958; Francis Lederer), *The Blood of Dracula's Castle* (1969; Alex d'Arcy), *The Lake of Dracula* (1971; Mori Kishida), and *Dracula vs. Frankenstein* (1971; Zandor Vorkov). The character has frequently reappeared in literature, most prominently in *Dracula's Guest* by Stoker himself. First published in 1914, this was a chapter excised from *Dracula* because of the novel's considerable length. Other works include Raymond Rudorff's *The Dracula Archives*, a (non-canonical) account of the origin of the House of Dracula (1972); *The Dracula Tape* by Fred

***DRACULA** (Chirstopher Lee) impaled on a carriage wheel.*
© Hammer Films.

Saberhagen (1975) which sets straight "the events so shamefully misrepresented by Bram Stoker"; *The Holmes-Dracula File* (1978), also by Saberhagen, in which the two great characters meet; and in seven novels published by Pinnacle in 1973-74 and written by Robert Lory: *Dracula Returns, The Hand of Dracula, Dracula's Brothers, Dracula's Gold, Drums of Dracula, The Witching of Dracula*, and *Dracula's Lost World*. There were also various comic book adaptations and sequels, the longest-lived of which was *Tomb of Dracula*, published by Marvel from 1972 to 1979. Marvel also adapted the novel itself in *Marvel Classic Comics* #9 (1977). Countless (or, rather, count*ful*) adaptations have appeared on tapes and records, including a dramatization starring Orson Welles (1974; reissue of an old radiocast) and a reading by Christopher Lee (1974). See also other vampire villains BEN CORTMAN, BLACULA, COUNT YORGA, NOSFERATU, PAUL JOHNSON, and VARNEY THE VAMPIRE.

THE DRAGON (1) (MP)

First Appearance: 1936, *Ace Drummond*, Universal Pictures.

Weapons: Destructive ray.

Biography: A great criminal power in Mongolia, the Dragon knows he'll remain in charge—and the sole possessor of a mountain chockful of jade—only if his country remains isolated. Thus, he works to thwart a multinational undertaking to link the globe by air. His nemesis is aviation legend Ace Drummond who, escaping crushing walls and other traps, is ultimately victorious.

Comment: The serial ran for 13 chapters.

THE DRAGON (2) (C)

First Appearance: 1967, *Thunderbolt* #57, Charlton Comics.

Costume: Red shirt, skirt; green dragon mask; yellow boots.

Biography: Based in the Himalayas, the Dragon "sits in the ancient palace of the Pali Khan" from which the warlord directs his armies. As more and more territory falls under his foul influence, the superhero Thunderbolt heads to the region to fight him. A master of illusion, the Dragon can appear or vanish in a cloud of smoke and do the same to others; he can also cause snakes to appear out of thin air. The despot is destroyed when Thunderbolt one-ups him by causing an enormous, very real dragon to materialize smack in

***THE DRAGON** (2). © Charlton Comics.*

the middle of the palace. Then the real dragon is quickly sent away, mystically, by the superhero.

Quote: "You obviously have come to interfere! But . . . your efforts can only come to a quick end!"

Comment: This was the character's only appearance. Other villains who fought Thunderbolt include Evila; Gore, the Man-Ape; the Cobra; and the Hooded One.

THE DRAGON KING (C)

First Appearance: 1982, *All Star Squadron* #4, DC Comics.

Costume: Green bodysuit; dark green belt, hood with yellow dragon down front, cloak with yellow dragon down back and red collar; red boots, gloves, trunks.

Weapons: See Biography.

Chief Henchmen: Various Japanese soldiers.

Biography: A onetime member of the Black Dragon Society, a secret Japanese organization which he deems "ineffectual," the Dragon King (his real name has never been revealed) yearned to become one of the most powerful men in his native land. To this end, once the Second World War erupted, the Dragon King became a lone operative, employing his extraordinary knowledge of science and mysticism to wage war against the Allies. His only known project was to create an "energy zone" around the Axis countries, a barrier of "inaudible vibrations of force" which will cause even superheroes within it to "serve the Axis cause." This was accomplished when a mystical rite was performed using the Spear of Destiny (in Hitler's possession) and the Holy Grail (kept by Premier Tojo). Although this causes the superheroes of the All-Star Squadron and the Justice Society of America to battle briefly among themselves, it also prohibits the Dragon King and his men from leaving the field. As Superman puts it, "if they set foot *outside* their safety zone—*pow*!" The Dragon King never did, as far as we know, and his current whereabouts are not known.

Quote: "One day soon, I shall carry the battle to *America's own shores*—and show how *insane* she was to believe a mere *ocean* would protect her from *Axis attack*!"

Comment: This was the character's only appearance.

THE DRAGON LADY (CS, R, MP, C, TV)

Real Name: Lai Choi San ("Mountain of Wealth" in Chinese).

First Appearance: December 1934, *Terry and the Pirates*, Chicago Tribune-New York News Syndicate.

Costume: Varies, but preferred wear is green floor-length skirt slit to the waist; a green, skimpy halter top; and a green cloak with a high collar.

Weapons: Standard firearms and knives.

Biography: The Dragon Lady is as "tough as a hash-heavy top sergeant." The leader of a band of pirates which operates along the coast of China, she first fell in love with adventurer Pat Ryan (adult sidekick of young Terry) when she imprisoned the two men on her pirate junk. ("She took one look at Pat Ryan and the average mean temperature for the area rose several degrees," remembered Terry.) During the Second World War, she shelved her criminal career to fight the Japanese. Though Pat frequently thwarts her criminal plans, she can't shake her affection for him.

Quote: "Go back with the other sheep-hearted white fools . . . or I will blow the smirk from your despised face!"

Comment: The strip was created by Milton Caniff in 1934; it folded in 1973. On the radio program which first aired in 1937, the character was played by Agnes Moorehead, followed by Adelaide Klein and Marion Sweet. Sheila Darcy starred as the Dragon Lady in the 15-chapter motion picture serial (1940); Gloria Saunders played the part in the syndicated TV series in 1952. A *Terry and the Pirates* comic book was published by Harvey and then by Charlton during the early 1950s, and there were five Big Little Books issued from 1935 to 1942. Other villains in the *Terry and the Pirates* strip were distinguished more by their colorful names than by the scope of their crimes, to wit: Baron de Plexus, Pyzon, General Klang, and

THE DRAGON LADY *drawn by Milton Caniff. © Chicago Tribune-New York News Syndicate.*

Captain Judas. Lesser comic strip villainesses include (with their respective strips) Rota, the evil queen of the year 1,001,942 A.D. (*Brick Bradford*); Zora, a foreign spy (*Scorchy Smith*); Sala, the leader of the all-female Air Pirates (*The Phantom*); the nefarious Flame, a Eurasian criminal who ruled Chinatown (*Red Barry*); Lil' de Vrille, "The Vampire Queen" (*Jungle Jim*); the just-plain-nasty millionaire Grace Powers (*Secret Agent X-9*) ("Did you just hear a loud noise? That was me shooting one of your men—I didn't like him."); and gun moll-turned-singer Pagan Lee (*Rip Kirby*). Rota, Zora, Lil' de Vrille, and Grace Powers were all wooed from their wicked ways by their respective heroes. See also THE DRAGON QUEEN and THE POPPY.

THE DRAGON QUEEN (MP, N)

First Appearance: 1981, *Charlie Chan and the Curse of the Dragon Queen*, American Cinema.

Costume: Her dresses vary from black to white to red; however, she always wears gold, serpent-like bracelets which stretch from her wrists and twine around her fingers.

Weapons: Crossbow.

Biography: Little is known about her "sordid past," save that this woman with a "bitter face of poison" beneath her sweet smile has had numerous affairs with wealthy men. Her favorite was Bernie Lupowitz, whom she romanced in the late 1940s and who eventually decided to dump her; rather than give him up, the

Dragon Queen killed him with poisoned tea while they were in Hawaii. When detective Charlie Chan solved the case, she placed a curse on his family which was to last three generations. In fact, she had no mystical powers and couldn't make it stick. Thus, upon her release from prison, she set up headquarters in the old scenery loft above the El Tinge Theatre in San Francisco and went after Chan's grandson personally. Drugging the boy, she was about to slay him when Chan arrived, arresting her. (The trap was ingenious: A ferocious dog was tied to a rope which was being burned by a candle. However, the youth managed to get a reprieve by singing *Happy Birthday* to the dog—which compelled it to turn and blow out the candle.) Actually, the real "super" villain of the piece was Mrs. Lupowitz, who was furious with Chan for having brought publicity to the case (and, hence, to her husband's indiscretion). She began a series of hideous killings which were blamed on the Dragon Queen; Chan was called in, as Lupowitz knew he'd be, and she kept up the killings in the hope that Chan would find the Queen and she'd murder him. Among her killings was the flooding of a hotel elevator, drowning everyone inside; wrapping a man in foil and leaving him in a steam room so he'd be "baked like a potato"; and pouring water into a musician's electric saxophone.

Quote: "Your grandfather will be tortured inch by inch."

Comment: Angie Dickenson played the Dragon Queen in the film; Lee Grant was Mrs. Lupowitz and Peter Ustinov was Chan. Pinnacle Books published a novelization by Michael Avallone. Chan fought no super villains in any of the six original novels by Earl Derr Biggers; in the classic movies starring Warner Oland, Sidney Toler, and Roland Winters as Chan, the closest Chan came to facing a super villain was in Toler's *The Scarlet Clue* (1945), in which people were killed by radio microphones which spit out poison gas, and Winters' *The Shanghai Chest* (1948), in which a masked man went around killing people.

DRAKO (C)

First Appearance: 1966, *Captain Atom*, #80, Charlton Comics.

Costume: Brown leotard with flared shoulders; red tights, boots, collar; blue cape, gloves.

Weapons: Gravitational motivator, an inescapable energy prison.

Biography: Born on a world beyond our solar system, Drako was one of the "small colony of peace lovers" who survived a nuclear war by living in a domed city beneath the sea. Contaminated by radiation, the world was not expected to survive much longer; thus, scientists built an artificial world and, living inside of it, the survivors escaped into space. A brilliant scientist himself, young Drako moved up through the ranks, and when the leader died he assumed power. But Drako ruled with "a cruel, iron hand," and, worse, hatched a scheme to conquer the earth by capturing the superhero Captain Atom in a gravitational motivator and tapping his nuclear essence to "threaten (the) world into submission." However, Drako's teenage daughter Celest used her body to short-circuit the motivator. Her death not only liberated Captain Atom, but stunned Drako into a state of shock. Drako was succeeded by Valdar, a benevolent ruler.

Quote: "Mad? If I were mad, could I have devised such a clever prison?"

Comment: This was the villain's only appearance and it was drawn by comics great Steve Ditko.

DREADKNIGHT (C)

Real Name: Bram Velsing.

First Appearance: 1977, *Iron Man* #101, Marvel Comics.

Costume: Blue mail bodysuit (see Weapons); navy blue leotard; purple boots, gloves, tabard with white skull and crossbones; white skull helmet with wings on the side; white cape.

Weapons: Mail bodysuit is impervious to bullets; power-lance which fires destructive beams, releases a cable which can both snare and conduct a deadly electric current, and launch small missiles; gas gun for inducing unconsciousness.

Biography: Born in Latveria, scientist Velsing grows bored manufacturing weapons for the country's dictator, DOCTOR DOOM. Discovering that Velsing is discontent, Doom expresses his own displeasure by welding a white skull-mask to Velsing's face. Failing to appreciate this, the scientist leaves the country and eventually meets Victoria Frankenstein, a descendant of the famous monster-maker. (A genetic tinkerer herself, she has been trying to remove the wings from the flying horse which had belonged to THE BLACK KNIGHT; instead, all she has managed to do is give the horse claws and make the wings more bat-like.) Burning with hatred for Doom, Velsing decides to build weapons for himself and, using the horse (whom he names Hellhorse), becomes the avenging Dreadknight. Fortunately, the superhero Iron Man happens to be in Yugoslavia and puts the novice super villain in his place before he can harm anyone. Crawling into the arms of his lover, the woman Maria, he has yet to strike again.

Comment: "Bram" was the first name of *Dracula* author Stoker; "Velsing" is a contraction of the name of Dracula's foe, Van Helsing.

THE DRUID (C)

First Appearance: 1983, *The Mighty Crusaders #4*, Archie Comics.

Costume: Olive-green robe with tail, pointed hood.

Biography: An immortal who can appear anywhere at will and assume any identity he wishes, the Druid is best known for the villainous team he assembles in an effort to defeat the superheroic Mighty Crusaders. It includes Lodestone who, in his yellow bodysuit and cowl, is able to levitate or transmute metal using his magnetic powers; the centuries-old Dream-Demon, a woman who wears a blue and white skirt and bikini top and debilitates people with psychic attacks; the purple-garbed Rogue Star, who fells adversaries with stellar energy blasts; the towering, humanoid powerhouse Brontosaurus; and the heartless woman-assassin Cyrene ("I want his *skull* to decorate my *cabin*!"). Thankfully, all are eventually defeated by the superheroes.

Quote: "Dream-Demon is *hardly* a'babe' . . . In fact, she is several hundred years *older* than you, *Rogue Star*!"

Comment: The two-part adventure (concluding in issue #5) was the only one in which these characters were featured.

D'SPAYRE (C)

First Appearance: 1978, *Marvel Team-Up #68*, Marvel Comics.

Costume: Light-blue bodysuit, boots, tattered cloak with bat-like clasp, cap with widow's peak. D'spayre's face is white and skull-like.

Biography: Nothing is known about this character's past, save that he is a demon who has the ability to instill fear in others (as well as to feed on peoples' fear and despair). He also has superstrength, the power to create flame, and the ability to make himself rock-hard (as the superhero Spider-Man discovers when he tries to punch the demon out). First surfacing in the Florida Everglades—the location of a mile-high tower which is the doorway into countless other dimensions—D'spayre kidnaps a young sorceress, Jennifer Kale, and her mentor Dakimh the Enchanter, both of whom he plans to make servants of evil. She is rescued by Spider-Man and by the benign monster Man-Thing, when the heroes pool their talents to pummel D'spayre insensate. After neutralizing the villain, the mages send the demon back to his own dimension by destroying the tower. However, D'spayre has since resurfaced to battle other superheroes, including the mystic Dr. Strange.

Comment: See other Fear-inducing villains BUSHMAN, DR. SPECTRO, MISTER FEAR, PHOBIA, PSYCHO-MAN, PSYCHO-PIRATE, and SCARECROW.

***THE DUKE OF DECAY** deals with captain Hero. © Archie Comics.*

THE DUKE OF DECAY (C)

Real Name: Murray Decay.
First Appearance: 1967, *Captain Hero* #3, Archie Comics.
Costume: Orange-and-black turtleneck shirt with green straps forming an "X" front and back; green trousers; black boots.
Weapons: Garbage gun which fires rotten food at adversaries; "Instant Spoil," a machine gun which surrounds towns with an invisible shield that rots all their food.
Chief Henchmen: Murderous pet vultures and hyenas.
Biography: Living in Decay Castle, his family's ancestral home on the moors, the obese Duke subjects Riverdale to the ravages of his Instant Spoil machine. The reason? As he puts it, "Once this foodless town empties . . . I will buy up all the land for practically nothing." The villain is foiled when the heroic Captain Hero shoots him using a dart filled with his own eau d'instant spoil; he was last seen being chased by his hyenas, which had been trained to follow the scent. The Duke's only known relative is his mother, Alicia Rotter. ("Great family, the Rotters! But not as socially prominent as the Decays.")
Quote: "Kill! Kill! My flapping little fiends! Tear him to shreds!"
Comment: This was the character's only appearance. Other corpulent villains are THE BLOB, THE FAT MAN, LORD LAZEE, and TOBIAS WHALE.

THE EAGLE (MP)

Real Name: Danby.

First Appearance: 1932, *The Shadow of the Eagle*, Mascot Pictures.

Chief Henchmen: Boyle and Moore.

Biography: This non-costumed felon is seeking to control the board of an aircraft company by eliminating the other members. His goal isn't exceptional, but his methods certainly are. Flying over an intended victim, he skywrites the person's name and then crosses it out. Moments later, a henchman on the ground guns the victim dead. The Eagle is eventually revealed to the boardmember Danby, and he dies while trying to escape the law.

Comment: Walter Miller played Danby, Bud Osborne was Moore, and master stunt artist Yakima Canutt played Boyle. John Wayne was the hero, also a skywriter, named Craig McCoy, in this 12-chapter serial, which was written by Ford Beebe, Colbert Clark, and Wyndham Gittens (co-creator of EL SHAITAN, WHISPERING SHADOW, THE WRECKER [1]).

EARTHWORM (C)

Real Name: Herbert Hyride.

First Appearance: 1983, *Wonder Woman* #309, DC Comics.

Costume: Tattered green clothing and red scarf.

Chief Henchmen: Various rats and reptiles (see Biography), along with many human aides.

Biography: Extremely thin and supple, able to slither into and out of almost any ducts or pipes, the pallid Earthworm lives underground, in sewers, and earns his living buying the babies of poor people and selling them for a huge markup. He has only appeared once, battling (and escaping from) the superheroic Huntress (not to be confused with the villain of the same name).

Comment: The superheroic Huntress is herself the daughter of a super villain, CATWOMAN.

ECLIPSO (C)

Real Name: Dr. Bruce Gordon.

First Appearance: 1964, *House of Secrets* #61, DC Comics.

Costume: Black leotard with lunar-solar eclipse motif on chest; purple tights, gloves, collar; gold belt; pink boots with white trim; cap is purple on the left and blue on the right; right side of face is blue.

Weapons: Black diamond, a meteorite which, when placed before his eye on the eclipsed (blue) side of his face, allows him to fire a destructive beam of "pure energy."

Biography: A "young benefactor of humanity," Gordon heads to Diablo Island in the South Pacific to study a solar eclipse visible from that part of the world. While there, he is attacked by a local shaman named Mophir; after scratching Gordon with a strange black diamond, the despot falls off a cliff to his death. Freed from Mophir's tyranny, the Diablans give Gordon both the gem and Mophir's costume. Some time later, while Gordon is about to inaugurate the sun-powered Solar City, an eclipse causes a diabolical change to come over him; he becomes the evil Eclipso and uses the gem to raze Solar City. A flash of light counteracts the eerie change which came over Gordon, but thereafter, an eclipse anywhere causes him to become the super villain. And while Professor Bennet and his daughter Mona—Gordon's girlfriend—are usually nearby to zap him with a "high photon light" (they've even invented light grenades for this purpose), Eclipso always manages to wreak havoc while he's afoot. After dogged research, Gordon comes up with an ultraviolet treatment which he hopes will eradicate Eclipso's evil tendencies; alas, all it does is liberate the fiend. Gordon is eventually able to re-merge with Eclipso using bright light. Gordon was briefly employed at Ferris Aircraft, where he worked to create a solar-powered aircraft; while he was there, Eclipso split from him again and was apparently destroyed by a hit from an extremely powerful laser. In one adventure (*House of Secrets* #74), Eclipso, who retains all of Gordon's scientific knowledge, manages to turn himself into a Negative Eclipso, immune to light. He is foiled, however, when Professor Bennet hits him with light from a prism. In another tale (*House of Secrets* #79), Eclipso obtains the Gorgas Ring and the Circlet of Circe. The latter allows him to look into the future, and the former permits him to "superimpose upon the very same scene a *new* element—from my own brain."

Quote: "Another fool! An energy bolt should discourage such rashness!"

Comment: The character has a great deal in common with MR. HYDE. Among the superheroes who tangled with Eclipso during his long career are Batman, Prince Ra-Man, and Green Lantern.

EGG FU (C)

First Appearance: 1965, *Wonder Woman* #57, DC Comics.

Costume: Egg Fu is shaped like the top half of a giant egg, complete with Asian features (including a moustache); he wears only a small beanie atop his ovoid head.

Weapons: The Doomsday Rocket, powerful enough to destroy the United States' Pacific fleet; antiaircraft guns "uniquely synchronized to home-in on the vibrations of any aerial camera over the island"; "beams" which cause anyone at whom they're directed to become "a human time-bomb . . . timed to explode with the force of an erupting volcano."

Biography: This military and scientific superbrain was created by the Chinese Communists to help bring down the free world. Based on Oolong Island in the Pacific, Egg Fu prepares to launch the Doomsday Rocket; aware that *something* is going on there, the military sends Col. Steve Trevor to spy. Taken prisoner, Trevor is turned into a human time bomb and launched at the fleet; though his girlfriend, the superhero Wonder Woman, manages to catch him, the two explode. Fortunately, Wonder Woman's fellow Amazonians are able to vacuum up their atoms and return them to life via an "atomic structure reassembly" beam. Heading to Oolong, Wonder Woman is knocked out and launched into space; reviving in the chill upper atmosphere, she returns to Oolong and snares Egg Fu with her magic lasso. Struggling against its grip, the super villain cracks up into countless pieces. A smaller but otherwise identical version of Egg Fu also battled the superhero (*Wonder Woman* #166, 1966). Dubbed Egg Fu the Fifth (the villain hisses that other Egg Fus have "been hatched," although they are nowhere to be seen), this one is destroyed when Wonder Woman claps her bracelets together so hard that the waves cause the fiend to shatter.

Quote: "The Amelicans *would* be warned if the locket were fired at rong range! So—we will wait until their fleet comes . . . *close*! And our . . . ladar warns us *that* will be *vely vely soon*! Heee-Ho!"

Comment: This one-of-a-kind villain was created at a time when superhero comic strips were coming to be regarded as "pop art" and "camp." Egg Fu certainly fit that menu.

ELASTO (C)

First Appearance: 1965, *The Shadow* #8, Harvey Comics.

Costume: Orange tights, vest; purple bodyshirt, boots, belt; black trunks (on cover, tights had black tiger stripes, shirt was orange, and vest was purple).

Weapons: See Biography.

Biography: Working as a scientist for the F.B.I., the future Elasto is caught in a lab explosion which leaves him with the ability to stretch to any length, as

The long arm of ***ELASTO****. © Archie Comics.*

well as increase the size of his body parts. However, there's a dichotomy about this villain; as he explains it, "even as my evil nature causes me to commit crimes, a glimmer of decency within me is revolted at my despicable deeds." Elasto is outsmarted by the superhero the Shadow, who tempts his vanity by daring him to stretch "as high as the ionosphere." So doing, Elasto blacks out from a lack of oxygen and crashes to earth unconscious.

Quote: "I abhor violence! Before I smother you to death within my enfolding clutch, I want you to know this truly grieves me."

Comment: This was the character's only appearance. The other villains who battled the Shadow during his eight-issue run were Radiation Rogue who, "with his astonishing power of super-atomic radiation . . . could destroy any living thing" by touching it; the notorious Dr. Demon, Hitler's leading scientist ("If he had listened to you," observes the Shadow, "he'd have won the war!"); the barbarian Attila the Hunter, a mad descendant of Attila the Hun who "hopes to become a greater conqueror than his ancient ancestor"; the diabolical Dimensionoid, a being from the thirteenth dimension who can change his shape at will (usually selecting destructive forms such as a giant boulder, a huge spiked wheel, and the like); the RXG Spymaster; and the notorious Shiwan Khan. Many of these characters were the brainchildren of Jerry Siegel, the creator of Superman.

ELECTRO (C)

Real Name: Maxwell Dillon.

First Appearance: 1964, *The Amazing Spider-Man* #9, Marvel Comics.

Costume: Green bodysuit with two vertical lightning bolts on chest, one each down the sides of his legs; yellow boots, trunks, gloves with lightning-bolt flares, five-pointed lightning-bolt mask.

Biography: Even before he becomes Electro, Dillon is scum. A lineman in New York, he refuses to help a fellow electrician trapped on a pole unless the foreman pays him a bonus; only after the man promises to pay him $100 does Dillon agree to go up and help his tangled coworker. However, while Dillon is lowering the man to safety, lightning strikes; surviving, the lineman concludes that "due to the way I had been grasping the electric wires—the two bolts of current cancelled each other out." Actually, it did more as he discovers later that evening. While handling a metal clothes hanger, he causes sparks and realizes that he's become a "living electrical generator." As a result, he is able to throw powerful bolts as weapons, set up electrical barriers, ride his bolts into the sky, and control anything which operates electrically (including time-lock bank vaults). Mustering every penny he owns, Dillon buys an old house, equips it with electrical equipment to feed him energy, and begins his career as Electro. (He charges himself by donning a mesh of wires, then using his body to complete the circuit of a powerful generator.) His archenemy is Spider-Man, who has thusfar managed to beat him in every encounter.

Quote: "Jewels! Money! No matter how much I take I want more—much more! And with my great power, nothing can stop me from *getting* it!"

THE ELECTROCUTIONER (C)

First Appearance: 1981, *Batman* #331, DC Comics.

Costume: Navy blue tights and boots, jerkin with white bolt down chest, gloves, full-face cowl with white bolt on forehead.

Weapons: See Biography.

Biography: Described by his nemesis Batman as "a sadistic, bloodthirsty, self-appointed executioner," the Electrocutioner makes it his business to hunt down and slay people whom the judicial system has acquitted—but who he believes are guilty. Finding these people, he touches them with both hands, thus completing a circuit which electrocutes them. The villain is himself electrocuted when, during a bout with Batman, he grabs a metal rail and sends "the electricity coursing back into my own body!" It is never revealed how the Electrocutioner came by his amazing power.

Quote: "The only entertainment your burbling lady friends are going to witness—is the grisly spectacle of your painful transformation to a *scorched* and smouldering *corpse*!"

Comment: This was the character's only appearance, though he may yet return, as his hand appears to move at the end of the tale.

EL SHAITAN (MP)

Real Name: Ratkin.

First Appearance: 1933, *The Three Musketeers*, Mascot Pictures.

Chief Henchman: El Maghreb.

Biography: Working as a shopkeeper in the Middle East, Ratkin is actually El Shaitan, the leader of a rebel gang known as the Devil's Circle. The group's base is a cave (their password, "The sun rises in the east"), where they plot their various acts of terrorism, murder, and arms smuggling. They disband when Ratkin is shot dead by the Three Musketeers, a group of Foreign Legionnaires.

Comment: Edward Piel played Ratkin, though he was El Shaitan only at the very end. During the course of the 12-chapter serial he was played by each actor on whose character the filmmakers wanted to cast suspicion. George Magrill was El Maghreb and John Wayne was Tom Wayne, the "D'Artagnan" of the group. Future horror superstar Lon Chaney, Jr. (THE BUTCHER), had a bit part in the serial, dying in the first chapter. The picture was written by Ella Arnold based on a screen story by Norman Hall, Colbert Clark, Ben Cohen, and Wyndham Gittens (co-creator of THE EAGLE, WHISPERING SHADOW, THE WRECKER [1]). In 1948, the serial was released as a feature film called *Desert Command*.

EMERALD EMPRESS (C)

Real Name: Sarya (has more recently been written Saryva).

First Appearance: 1967, *Adventure Comics* #352, DC Comics.

Costume: White tights, blouse; light green gloves, leotard with emeralds down the front; black trunks; green cloak, boots, belt covered with emeralds; silver headband.

Weapons: The Emerald Eye of Ekron, a floating eyeball roughly a foot in diameter which responds utterly to the Empress's will; it uses emerald energy to do anything she bids, from firing destructive blasts capable of melting steel to enabling the Empress to survive in the void of space. Coincidentally, the Eye loses its power around kryptonite, the mineral which similarly weakens Superman.

Biography: Sarya is "the most wanted female criminal in the history of the universe . . . guilty of every crime from murder to space-piracy." The native world of the thirtieth-century Empress is Vengar, home of the long-dead Ekron civilization. The Ekrons' "astounding scientific secrets were all lost" until Saryva finds the Crypt of the Eye. The Eye allows her to take over Vengar in "only a few hours." But it doesn't take long for her tyranny to cause the people to revolt, and she barely escapes the planet with her life. Vowing to return with an army, she begins robbing spaceships to get the necessary money and weaponry. When the evil CONTROLLER undertakes to destroy our solar system, the Empress is contacted by Superboy, of the Legion of Super-Heroes, to lend a hand in opposing him. She agrees, and is pardoned for her crimes. Meeting the villainous THAROK during the course of the fracas, she agrees to become a charter member of his new group, THE FATAL FIVE. Although she continues to serve now-and-then with the league, her principal objective remains reconquering her world or another like it.

Quote: "The *Eye*! I overtaxed it!"

EMILIO LARGO (N, MP)

First Appearance: 1961, *Thunderball*, Ian Fleming.

Weapons: The *Disco Volante*, a hundred-ton hydrofoil which could race along at 50 knots with a range of 400 miles; two nuclear missiles.

Biography: A "big, conspicuously handsome man of about forty," Largo is an agent of SPECTRE, a for-profit terrorist group. An excellent athlete (he "fought for Italy in the Olympic foils," was a water-ski champion, and near-Olympic caliber swimmer), he is an adventurer who debuts as a criminal after the war, heading the black market in Naples. He subsequently spends five years smuggling from Tangier and another five masterminding jewel robberies on the French Riviera. Next, he spends five years working for SPECTRE and, when introduced to its chief, ERNST STAVRO BLOFELD, accepts the responsibility of stealing for him a pair of nuclear missiles; he has orders to detonate them at a military site and a major world city (Miami) if the world refuses to pay a ransom of 100 million pounds in gold bullion. Based in the Bahamas, Largo is found out by British secret agent James Bond; during a fierce undersea battle with Bond, Largo is murdered by ex-lover Domino Vitale, when she fires a spear through his neck. Largo has a long face "sunburned a deep mahogany brown," a hooked nose, a lantern jaw, brown eyes, and "thick, rather down-curled lips (which) belonged to a satyr." His black hair was "carefully waved" and he had "overlong sideburns."

Quote: "She refused to talk. In due course I shall force her to do so and then she will be eliminated."

Comment: The character was played by Adolfo Celi in the 1965 film *Thunderball*, and by Klaus Maria Brandauer in the 1983 remake *Never Say Never Again* (as "Maximilian" Largo).

THE EMPEROR (N, MP)

Real Name: Palpatine.

First Appearance: 1976, *Star Wars*, Ballantine Books (see Comment).

Costume: Black robe with hood; walks with cane.

Weapons: Personally commands huge military force

armed with everything from air-land-and-space transports to blasters (sidearms which fire light energy capable of vaporizing a target) to the Death Star, a space station roughly 100 miles in diameter and packing sufficient firepower to destroy a world.

Chief Henchmen: Among the Emperor's principal aides are Moff Tarkin, a powerful governor and commander of the first Death Star (*Star Wars*); Bin Essada, governor of the Circarpous Major star system (novel, *Splinter of the Mind's Eye*, Alan Dean Foster, 1978); Lord Tion of Ralltiir (*Star Wars* radio program, episode #2); and Moff Jerjerrod, commander of the second (and last) Death Star (*Return of the Jedi*). His forces include his personal bodyguards, the red-robed Imperial Guard; the Imperial Stormtroopers, armored warriors who do the military's dirtiest and most dangerous deeds; and robots equipped for every conceivable purpose, including torture (the many-armed Interrogator Droids are familiarly known as "pain droids").

Biography: Senator Palpatine holds a seat in the Imperial Senate, whose members are democratically elected by their native star systems. Because the Republic is fraught with corruption, Palpatine is able to get himself elected president of the Republic by campaigning for reform. Once in office, however, he does away with the Republic and establishes the Empire, with himself as emperor; simultaneously, he disbands the Republic's peacekeeping force, the Jedi Knights. One such knight, DARTH VADER, becomes his chief henchman. Though plagued by the Rebel Alliance, the Emperor fears only one enemy, Darth Vader's son, Luke Skywalker, who has the various telekinetic, precognitive, and hypnotic powers of a Jedi Knight. Holding court on the Death Star, the Emperor tries to recruit the boy to his cause and is refused; subjecting him to painful electrical bolts which he can shoot from his body, the monarch is stopped by Darth Vader who, in a paternal flourish, picks up the frail leader and hurls him down a shaft to his death. The events in the Emperor's life occur "long ago, in a galaxy far, far away."

Comment: The saga of the Emperor was told in the movies (and novelizations) *Star Wars* (1977), *The Empire Strikes Back* (1980), and *Return of the Jedi* (1983). He was referred to but not seen in the first film; only his voice (and shadowed head, in a hologram) was heard in the second (provided by Clive Revill); and he was played in the third by Ian McDiarmid. He plays a lesser part in the various novels, comic books, and radio programs which have been based on *Star Wars* characters. Note: Though the character was created for the movies, the novelization of *Star Wars* was published before the release of the film. Hence, the book is technically his first appearance.

THE ENCHANTRESS (1) (C)

Real Name: Amora.

First Appearance: 1965, *Journey Into Mystery* #103, Marvel Comics.

Costume: Green leotard, boots, sleeves, headdress; golden bands around lower legs and wrists. (Originally wore, as well, dark green tights with a light green serpentine motif on front; leotard ended in very short skirt.)

Weapons: Sundry magical tools and formulae.

Chief Henchman: THE EXECUTIONER.

Biography: Born in Asgard, the celestial home of the Norse gods, Amora studied sorcery in the land of the Norns, under the tutelage of Karnilla, the goddesses of fate. Dismissed by Karnilla because she lacked discipline, the young goddess roamed around Asgard, picking up what additional knowledge she could from local wizards. Her goal: to become conqueror of the heavens and earth. After briefly cajoling the heroine Valkyrie Brunnhilda to serve her (and locking her inside an enchanted crystal when she tried to leave Amora's corrupt service), Amora allied herself with sundry villains, including BARON ZEMO, LOKI, and THE MANDARIN. She was also, briefly, one of the MASTERS OF EVIL. Amora's sister Lorelei, though not a sorceress, is a wily seductress and an ally of Loki.

Comment: See THE FORGOTTEN VILLAINS for the Enchantress (2).

THE ENDOTHERM (C)

Real Name: Tom Wilkins.

First Appearance: 1980, *Iron Man* #136, Marvel Comics.

Costume: Green tights, scarf, jacket with white "E" on chest and light green hem and collar; light green belt, gloves (see Weapons), boots, cowl with green goggles, three stripes front-to-back.

Weapons: "Thermal control components" in gloves which allow him "to absorb heat (and) release that absorbed heat" as destructive bursts; gun which "shoots diamond-hard ice darts."

Biography: Based in London, Wilkins works as a security chief at the hi-tech Stark Industries for 30 years. While he's alone at the plant one night (he gave a guard time off because the man's wife went into labor), an industrial saboteur breaks in and photographs plans for a new fuel stabilizer. Subsequently, Stark's competitors get the machine onto the market before Stark can patent it, costing the firm a bundle. Due to retire, Wilkins becomes paranoid that he's going to be fired by boss Tony Stark (aka Iron Man) and lose his pension. Thus, he plans to lure Stark to England and kill him. Stealing from the company "experimental components" which are "designed to control heat and cold," he becomes the Endotherm and begins destroying firm property. Stark comes to investigate and, as Iron Man, defeats Wilkins, who ends up in a straitjacket.

Quote: "Now to draw the fly into my glacial web!"

THE ENFORCER (1) (C)

First Appearance: 1967, *Captain Hero* #3, Archie Comics.

Costume: Blue T-shirt with iron collar, sleeves; orange mail trunks; iron gloves, boots, and belt.

Weapons: Pizza-aroma gun for attracting teenagers.

Biography: A thief operating from a "plush lair" in Riverdale, the Enforcer is constantly thwarted by the superheroic Captain Hero. In an effort to kill him, he lures Hero's best friend, Archie Andrews, to his headquarters using his pizza-aroma gun. However, the abduction backfires when Hero survives the villain's many traps and sends him running from the apartment. Skillfully maneuvering the chase, Hero gloats when the Enforcer tumbles through the skylight of police headquarters and ends up in jail.

Quote: "Look at that! A deliciously planned bank job foiled by that masquerading moron!"

Comment: This was the character's only appearance. Other enemies of Captain Hero include the red- and blue-garbed Silencer, who hypnotizes people with "the magic words—shaddup!" and kills them with his "lethal electric toothbrush" (Hero gums up the device with toothpaste, then pummels the Silencer nearly insensate); Mr. Machine, a power-mad robot police officer built by a brilliant computer; the mad scientist Dr. Nose, who turns people into monster slaves; the purple- and orange-garbed Collector, who kidnaps young women to work as go-go girls on Ghoul Island; the orange-uniformed Bomb Master, who has explosives which make people tell the truth, lure them into traps with the scent of hamburger, cause amnesia and the like (Hero comes at him with a bomb deactivator, then punches him out); and the red-costumed Operator, who has a special phone so that "each number you dial . . . activates certain carbonaceous life masses which fuse and eject at the other end" of the call—i.e., sends monsters out to attack whoever is called (Hero sends his own monsters back at him, collect).

THE ENFORCER (2) (C)

Real Name: Carson Collier Jr.

First Appearance: 1977, *Ghost Rider* #22 (though mentioned in #21), Marvel Comics.

Costume: Blue bodysuit (see Weapons), belt, cowl with white face (see Weapons); white leotard, gloves, boots.

Weapons: The Enforcer's body suit is made of impenetrable steel fabric; the leotard is laced with silver nitrate to keep werewolves at bay; his white mask has infrared optics which enable him to see in the dark. He also packs a pair of .45 caliber guns which fire a variety of bullets, including "pyrogranulate" pellets which cause explosions; "the tingler," which sets people ablaze; tranquilizers; and sodium pentathol, to make victims obey him. For laughs, he occasionally combines the bullets—e.g., sodium pentathol and "pyrogranulate" to make people will *themselves* ablaze. Early in his career, the Enforcer wore a disintegrator ring. This was replaced by the twin automatics.

Biography: The son of "Coot" Collier, a popular movie cowboy of the 1940s, Carson wanted to emulate his father. Attending the University of Southern California film school, his plans went awry when he became caught up in drugs. Impressed with the thrills to be had and money to be made in the underworld, he dropped out of school and became a mobster. Meeting scientist Ignatz Goldman, he made the inventor create his bulletproof clothes and disintegrator ring. Calling himself the Enforcer, young Collier became a successful mob leader, operating out of Delazny Studios, his father's professional base. Sent to jail by the superheroic cyclist, the Ghost Rider, the Enforcer was released thanks to string-pulling by the Committee, a band of corrupt Los Angeles businesspeople. They were also responsible for replacing his ring with the guns. The Enforcer served as a strongarm man for the Committee until they disbanded; he worked for a while as a mercenary before disaster befell. His brother (name unrevealed) grew so sickened by the Enforcer's crimes that he made a costume for himself, became the vigilante Scourge, and shot his sibling to death.

Quote: "You're just another *victim* to me, punk! *Nobody beats the Enforcer!*"

Comment: The Ghost Rider has also battled SATAN; the Legion, a group of demons; the Challenger, another demon; the Manticore, an amputee outfitted with bionic limbs, including a tail; the Orb, a stunt cyclist (Drake Shannon) who was disfigured in an accident and took to wearing an eyeball-like mask which he used to hypnotize people via laser beam; the ancient mutant Nathan Beame and his cycle-riding humanoids the Dark Riders; scientist Thurgood Vance, the Nuclear Man; the 10-century-old wizard, Azaziah Hornsby, aka the Crimson Mage; and the Water Wizard, aka Peter van Zante, who was given experimental radiation treatment after being wounded in Vietnam and, due to a power surge, acquired mutant powers to control water, even to form it into huge, animate humanoids. Later, he proved he can also control oil, whipping up shock troops known as "Oil Jinns."

THE ERADICATOR (C)

Real Name: Creed Phillips.

First Appearance: 1982, *The Flash* #312 (as Phillips); #314 (as the Eradicator), DC Comics.

Costume: Blue bodysuit; light blue belt, gloves, boots, full-face mask; dark red trunks, cape, hood.

Biography: Because he was devoted to crimebusting, Senator Phillips was abducted by a pair of criminals and deposited beside a stash of stolen plutonium. Instead of dying, however, he was irradiated and given the power to disintegrate others. He also became schizophrenic, feeling that his mortal and superpowered selves were two different people. His superpowered self became the merciless Eradicator, using his power to hunt down criminals and turn them to powder. Cornered by the superheroic Flash, Phillips was made to see that what he was doing was against the law; tortured by guilt and confusion, he promptly used his powers to commit suicide.

THE ERASER (C)

First Appearance: 1965, *The Mighty Crusaders* #1 (first series), Archie Comics.

Costume: Original: purple bodyshirt, boots, gloves; black cowl, tights; lavender "X" stripes on chest and along arms. Second: green bodysuit, boots, gloves, cowl; yellow belt, stripes down arms and crisscrossing back and chest.

Weapons: Metalor Ion Gun to turn people into iron statues; Space-Warpine, a bomb which sends people to another dimension.

Biography: Originally, the Eraser was just a thug in a costume who left an eraser as his calling card. He earned his greatest fame killing the superhero the Shield, then retired ("since I can never *top* this achievement"), only to be forced out of retirement to battle the hero's son, also known as the Shield. During that fight—which took place at the Museum of Arch-Villains—the Eraser stumbled into the ray of his own Space-Warpine and vanished. Returning to this dimension sometime later, the Eraser had no idea who he was due to amnesia caused by "the shock of the alien dimensions." Living in New York's Bowery, he made his living by playing cards, until he was found by the BRAIN EMPEROR who also restored his memory. The Eraser's stay in the other dimension did have one positive side effect; now he "literally erases the molecules of whatever he touches, transporting them to some unguessed alien dimension." To pay off his debt to the Brain Emperor, the Eraser agreed to help him eliminate the superheroic Fox. However, during a battle in a hospital the costumed hero felled him with ether, subsequently carting him off to jail—where, presumably, his hands were kept away from the prison bars. Though the Eraser is extremely portly, his body is solid muscle.

Quote: "I reserve *strangulation* for my most *hated* foes!"

Comment: See also the Eraser's partner, THE GASSER.

ERIS (MY)

Biography: The goddess of strife in Greek mythology, Eris is the daughter of Nyx (Night) and the sister of Momus (mockery), Thanatos (natural death), Morpheus (dreams), and others. She is less known for her own deeds than for the truly nasty children she bore by her brother Ares, the god of war; Deimos (fear) and Phobos (terror). By Zeus, king of the gods, she was the mother of Ate (blind rage and folly). Her most famous exploit occurred at the marriage of the mortal Peleus to the goddess Thetis. Not invited, Eris came anyway and tossed a golden apple into the crowd. On it was written "for the fairest," whereupon three goddesses claimed it. (According to some accounts, Eris was sent by Zeus.) Since Zeus didn't want to decide the matter, he appointed the shepherd Paris to choose the winner. Selecting Aphrodite, Paris earned the undying wrath of her rivals Hera and Athene and, through a succession of events—climaxing with his wooing of Helen, the wife of King Menelaus of Sparta—caused the Trojan War.

Comment: Eris corresponds to the later Roman goddess Discordia, who was a physically hideous creature; it wasn't bad enough that she had snakes for hair, but she wore them tied in a blood-covered ribbon.

ERNST STAVRO BLOFELD (N, MP)

First Appearance: 1961, *Thunderball*, Ian Fleming.

Biography: Blofeld was the founder and chairman of

SPECTRE—the Special Executive for Counter-intelligence, Terrorism, Revenge and Extortion—a "private enterprise for profit." Among the group's more mundane enterprises have been selling Czech germ warfare secrets to the British, stealing heroin from one mob family and selling it to another, assassinating people for various governments, spying for pay, and the like. The organization was three years old when first introduced. As for Blofeld himself, he was born on May 28, 1908, in Gdynia, Poland. His father was Polish and his mother Greek; he studied economics and political history at the University of Warsaw before taking up engineering and radionics at the Warsaw Technical Institute. At the age of 25, he accepted a position at the Ministry of Posts and Telegraphs, realizing that "knowledge of the truth before the next man" was the key to power. Stock tips passed through his hands, and he invested accordingly; more profitable, however, was the peddling of official cables and radiograms about the impending Second World War to the Nazis. Amassing a tidy fortune, Blofeld destroyed all records of his birth and left the country for Turkey. He sold secrets to the Allies and, after the war, moved to South America; it was there the idea for SPECTRE was born. Gathering together the greatest criminal minds in the world, he specialized in extortion on an unprecedented scale—and was invariably frustrated by British secret agent James Bond. In *Thunderball,* with the help of EMILIO LARGO, he hijacks two nuclear missiles and threatens to blow up a military base and a major city if his ransom demands aren't met (£100 million in gold bullion). In *On Her Majesty's Secret Service* (1963) he plots to wage biological warfare against England and also murders Bond's wife; and in *You Only Live Twice* (1964) he masquerades as Dr. Shatterhand and, based in Japan, opens the "Garden of Death," a castle stocked with deadly plants and animals for those who wish to commit suicide. Bond sneaks in and, after strangling Blofeld, destroys the castle with a geyser. Blofeld's appearance changed dramatically from book to book, no doubt to help him keep from being recognized. When we first meet him, he has "deep black pools" for eyes, a heavy, squat nose, a black crewcut, and a thin mouth "like a badly healed wound." He weighs nearly 280 pounds, most of which had been muscle 10 years before when he was a weight lifter; now it's fat. He doesn't smoke or drink and "had never been known to sleep with a member of either sex." By the time of the second tale, he seems to have decayed somewhat. He's down to roughly 168 pounds, has silvery white hair, and the right nostril of his now-slender nose has been rotted by what is apparently syphilis. His eyes are green, thanks to contact lenses.

Quote: "Thanks in part to our German section, the recovery of Himmler's jewels from the Mondsee was successfully accomplished in total secrecy, the stones disposed of by our Turkish section in Beirut. Income: £750,000."

Comment: Blofeld's birthdate is the same as that of author Fleming. In the movies, Blofeld has been played by Donald Pleasence in *You Only Live Twice* (1967), snatching Russian and American astronauts from space in an effort to get the superpowers to go to war with one another; by Telly Savalas in *On Her Majesty's Secret Service* (1969), making ready to unleash a virus which will cause worldwide sterility; and by Charles Gray in *Diamonds are Forever* (1971), plotting to laserbeam Washington, D.C., to ashes.

THE EVIL EYE (C)

Real Name: Harms.

First Appearance: 1944, *Dynamic Comics* #12, Harry "A" Chesler.

Weapons: Dagger.

***THE EVIL EYE** goes to work.* © *I.W. Enterprises.*

Chief Henchman: The Black Demon. Though the caption describes it as "a giant black bat," it is pictured as a huge vulture.

Biography: Harms is the caretaker of the old Jordan Mansion, where he has discovered "a fortune in jewels." In order to keep people from finding the cache (presumably until he can fence or spend it), he dons a frightening mask with a glowing eye and gurgles a terrifying laugh ("Wheeeee . . . ha ha ha!"); the combination strikes terror into the hearts of anyone who comes near, and the legend of the "terrible ghost called Evil Eye" spreads. When Helen Jordan inherits the place and tries to move in, she asks private eye Lucky Coyne to find out if the mansion really is haunted. Shooting the Black Demon "squarely (in) the face," he subdues the villain in a knock-down brawl and recovers the jewels for Helen, although he also manages to burn down the house in the process.

Quote: "You know the secret of Ghost Mansion, but you will never leave alive!"

Comment: This was the character's only appearance.

EVILHEART THE GREAT (C)

Real Name: Reggie Mantle.

First Appearance: 1966, *Pureheart the Powerful* #1, Archie Comics.

Costume: Green cowl, bodysuit with black heart on chest, white "E" in the heart; black trunks; purple boots, belt and cape.

Weapons: Destructo Ray.

Biography: Whenever Reggie is humiliated by fellow Riverdale student Archie Andrews, he feels "a black mist rising . . . the blackness in my heart" and transforms into the costumed Evilheart. He isn't so much villainous as self-centered; Archie, aka Pureheart the Powerful, is his rival for the affection of debutante Veronica Lodge, and Evilheart will stop at nothing to make him look bad. More often than not, the two end up fighting each other, or else Evilheart lends a helping hand to whatever villain Pureheart is pursuing. Apart from above-average strength and his Destructo Ray, Evilheart has no superpowers.

Quote: "Whenever I see Archie with Veronica I become *green with envy*! I huff! And I puff! . . . and I emerge as *Evilheart*! The double *greatest*!"

Comment: Reggie Mantle has been a part of the Archie cast of characters since *Jackpot Comics* #5 (1942). (Though the character that was to become Reggie had appeared earlier, he wasn't identified as Reggie until that issue.)

THE EVIL ONE (MP, C)

First Appearance: 1982, *Time Bandits*, Handmade Films.

Costume: Purple bodysuit ending in fingerless gloves; golden armor, helmet; red cloak (see Weapons).

Weapons: False hand which can fire thunderbolts capable of destroying objects or transforming people into various forms of flora and fauna; knife hidden inside skull; cloak inflates to protective shell which shields him from arrows; magic pool which allows him to see anywhere in time and space and to project his magic there, magic which includes controlling people or influencing the elements.

Chief Henchmen: Robert (a scientific genius) and Benson ("mercifully free of the ravages of intelligence").

Biography: Though the Evil One claims to have given birth to himself, one of his underlings says he was created by the Supreme Being; that is probably so, since it is the Supreme Being who ultimately destroys him. The Evil One dwells in the Time of Legends, a primitive era in which peasants, giants, and ogres (including the tusked, rather inept ogre Winston), exist side by side. Living in the Fortress of Ultimate Evil, a towering castle surrounded by a shell of invisibility, the Evil One plots to take over the earth, though not through his magic, which is indeed great. He plans to invade our world more subtly, through technology. "God isn't interested in technology," he declares, anticipating the overthrow of the Supreme Being. "He knows nothing of the potential of the microchip or the silicon revolution. Look how he spends his time! Forty-three species of parrot—nipples for men! I would have started with lasers!" Once the Evil One controls the earth's technology, he plans to remake humans and the world in his image—one of absolute evil. In order to do this, however, he must first escape from the Fortress, where God has trapped him; to do so he needs to find one of the holes left in time and space due to the hasty creation of the earth. ("We only had seven days!" complains an aide to the Supreme Being.) Thus, the villain plots to get a map of the holes from the Time Bandits, a group of God's former aides who hop from hole to hole stealing treasures from different periods in time. The Bandits are lured to the castle and nearly destroyed; fortunately, the Supreme Being arrives and turns the Evil One to stone, a statue made of "concentrated evil." Though the Evil One appears to have perished, the statue breaks and a piece of the stone shows up in our era, where it burns down a house and causes two people to explode when they touch it. (Implicitly, humankind is going to be destroyed by technology.) Among the Evil Being's magical powers are the ability to spin at cyclonic speeds and to transform himself into anyone he wishes.

Quote: "I will tear you inside out over a very long period of time."

Comment: David Warner played the Evil One; Warner also played the murderous Jack the Ripper in the 1979 movie *Time After Time* and the equally nefarious Sark, tyrannical regent of a computer world, in *Tron* (1982). Marvel Comics published a comic book adaptation of *Time Bandits*.

EVIL STAR (C)

First Appearance: 1965, *Green Lantern* #37, DC Comics.

Costume: Purple tights, vest open on the sides, cowl, gloves; blue bodyshirt, cape with high collar, boots; red five-pointed star mask.

Weapons: The Star Band which draws its energy from the stars and increases the life span of the wearer; Evil Star can also use it to create any solid object he wishes, to fire destructive bolts, to protect himself behind an indestructible force-field, and to fly.

Chief Henchmen: The Starlings, artificial beings who are identical to Evil Star, have most of his powers, and are telepathically controlled by him.

Biography: A scientist from the planet Aoran in the Acrux planetary system, Evil Star is devoted to finding the key to immortality. He invents the Star Band bracelet and is delighted when it works; unfortunately, it also forces the wearer to use its other powers for evil purposes. Terminating the entire population of Aoran when they try to destroy him, Evil Star decides to conquer all of creation. To this end, he realizes he must first slaughter the Guardians of the Universe, alien beings who sponsor the intergalactic superheroes known as the Green Lantern Corps. Although Evil Star is repeatedly bested by earth's Green Lantern (whose power ring is only slightly less potent than the Star Band), he keeps escaping captivity (often with the help of the Starlings) and renewing his efforts to dominate worlds. Evil Star's most diabolical plot against the earth was to place a device in the sun which takes just an hour to cause the orb to go nova. Since Green Lantern's ring can't work against the color yellow, and he hasn't time to contact Superman, he uses the Starlings as battering rams to destroy the weapon (*Green Lantern* #131).

Quote: "Hello, *Green Lantern* . . . but in fifty-eight earthling minutes, it will be *goodbye—forever*!"

Comment: The alien terror appears once every few years in the magazine. During his career as a crimefighter, Green Lantern has fought literally dozens of villains; among the more unusual have been the Crumbler, who with his power glove destroys the force that holds matter together; El Espectro, an undying conquistador with a powerful golden sword; Hector Hammond, a lunatic with a highly evolved brain; Myrwhydden, an alien wizard; Professor Ojo, a blind mutant who sees via his Eye Helmet; Replikon, an extraterrestrial who wants to change the earth so he and his kind can dwell on it; Sonar, the leader of "the block-long nation of Modora," whose weapons make him the master of sound; the Weaponers, alien beings bent on conquering our world; and the Protonic Force, an evil, sentient energy which must inhabit matter to survive.

THE EVIL UNCLE (F)

First Appearance: "Babes in the Wood" (see Comment).

Biography: The brother of a gentleman of Norfolk, the Uncle is appointed guardian of his niece and nephew when his brother dies. However, the Uncle cares nothing for the children, only the land they've inherited, land which will go to him should some misfortune befall them both. He arranges for this to happen, hiring two hoodlums to lead the youths into the woods and kill them. But, as in "Snow White" (see THE QUEEN), one of the thugs feels sorry for the children; killing his companion, he sets the youngsters free. Sadly, they die just the same in the thick wood, and are buried beneath leaves by a robin. Still, the heartless Uncle gets his. The surviving criminal confesses his crimes and the conniving Uncle is executed.

Comment: The old ballad, the age of which is unknown, was included in many collections during the eighteenth century, most prominently those of Ritson and Percy. It is also known as "The Children in the Wood."

THE EXECUTIONER (C)

Real Name: Skurge.

First Appearance: 1965, *Journey Into Mystery* #103, Marvel Comics.

Costume: Brown tights, vest with pink battleaxe silhouette; brown armor, boots, gauntlets.

Weapons: Two-bladed battleaxe which, thanks to a spell from THE ENCHANTRESS (1), has the ability to cut a hole in space and draw energies from whatever lies on the other side, be it solar fire or Arctic cold.

Biography: The bastard son of a Norse goddess and a Storm Giant, the mighty Skurge is shunned by his father's race because he is so much smaller than they are. Thus, he makes giant-slaying his specialty as he grows up, his effectiveness earning him his *nom de guerre*. Because he is hopelessly in love with the Enchantress, he frequently partakes of her vile schemes against the golden Norse god Thor and the superhero's adopted world, Earth. Eventually he reforms, and perishes battling the evil HELA when she tries to conquer the godly abode Asgard.

THE FADEAWAY MAN (C)

Real Name: Anton Lamont.

First Appearance: 1978, *Detective Comics* #479, DC Comics.

Costume: White tights; orange vest with gold fringe and big gold clasp (see Weapons).

Weapons: "Conjure-cloak" is magic and permits the Fadeaway Man to vanish with a "pop"—apparently teleporting to some other point. It also allows him to teleport objects to his presence and for use against others, storms of matter ranging from water to volcanic ash. The Fadeaway Man also has a "magic satchel" in whose depths is any weapon the user might need. However, only the Mayan Sunstone has been drawn from it, a device "possessed of enough stored solar energy to melt" a person. The satchel seems to be a doorway to another dimension, since objects larger than it can be placed inside and carried with ease.

Biography: Holding degrees in art history from Oxford and Cambridge Universities, Lamont is a professor of art history at Cambridge, a guest lecturer at the Sorbonne, and a consultant to the Uffizi Gallery. While cataloguing the belongings of the eighteenth-century magician Cagliostro, Lamont comes across the cloak and satchel, figures out how to use them, and embarks on a life of crime. But, magic or not, the villain is unable to outsmart the superheroic Batman, who has beaten him at every turn. In their most recent encounter, in which the superhero Hawkman lends a hand, the magic artifacts inexplicably vanish when the Fadeaway Man is captured.

Quote: "Bah! I could unleash a *Pacific tidal wave* on you right now—but that would destroy these precious objects!"

FALSEFACE (C)

First Appearance: 1967, *Mighty Comics* #45, Archie Comics.

Weapons: Handgun.

Biography: Falseface is a thief able to change his features at will; he's confident that the police will never put "their clammy claws on me because I don't use the same disguise *twice*!" However, the superhero, Hangman, chases him after a crime, and the two men end up in a museum. There, light from a statue of a cat god shines on Falseface, causing him to grow and simultaneously split into nine identical criminals. The small army of Falsefaces pummels the superhero until, jarring the idol so it lights up again, the Hangman reverses the phenomenon and arrests Falseface.

Quote: "Nobody rumbles with *Falseface* and lives!"

Comment: This was the character's only appearance. See also CLAYFACE.

FATHER NATURE (C)

Real Name: Cron.

First Appearance: 1981, *Superman* #358, DC Comics.

Costume: Green bodysuit, boots; light green gloves, bands around thighs, shoulderpads, belt, armor on chest. Cron's skin is orange and his hair and full beard are yellow (worn only in human form).

Weapons: Fifty-foot-long "power prong," which allows him to transmute elements.

Biography: Eons ago, when earth had just been formed, an extraterrestrial named Nutra (aka Mother Nature) comes to our world and nurtures not only life, but also the shape and composition of the land and seas. Dissatisfied with the way she fashions the world, Cron comes to earth to remake it using his power prong. Assuming human form and duping Superman into helping him find Nutra's hidden power prong, which has worked her will from afar, Cron attempts to replace it with his own apparatus, one which will remake the world—with an environment hostile to present life forms. Superman battles the alien, who has resumed his natural cloud-like shape, but is unable to defeat him. Desperate, the Man of Steel gets a Rigellian Plasmo-Bomb from the weapons cache in his Fortress of Solitude, vowing to blow up the planet rather than leave everyone a victim to changes which "will doom every living creature on earth to a painful death." Father Nature believes him and departs;

lucky, too, since Superman has a code not to kill anyone under any circumstances and was merely bluffing.

Quote: "If it is a choice between earth as *Nutra* conceived it . . . or *no earth at all* . . . my only recourse is to *leave* this bountiful orb as I *found it*!"

THE FAT MAN (C)

First Appearance: 1964, *Kid Colt Outlaw* #117, Marvel Comics.

Costume: Green business suit.

Weapons: "The Bewitched Boomerang," which, despite its name, is an ordinary wooden boomerang.

Biography: During the last century, a ship landed in San Francisco and "an unsmiling, three-hundred pound man disembarked." Hailing from Australia, he made his way to Abilene "where some of the town toughs poked fun at him because of his weight." Tired of their taunts, he demonstrated that what they thought was fat was actually "solid muscle," and tossed them around like leaves. He also exhibited a talent for "rolling . . . like a cannonball," striking any enemy over "like a tenpin." And when anyone dared to draw a gun, he crippled their hand with his boomerang. Afterward Abilene the Fat Man "turned to crime—robbing, pillaging, and looting" with impunity. Sought out by the heroic Kid Colt, he was disarmed when the sharpshooter blasted the boomerang in mid-flight, then pointed out that he could do the same to a much larger target—the Fat Man himself. The outlaw surrendered without a struggle.

Quote: "I admire your courage, cowboy. You may lie silently in those bushes while I try to decide whether to allow you to continue living."

Comment: See other Marvel western villains HURRICANE, THE PANTHER, THE RAVEN, RED RAVEN, and ROBIN HOOD RAIDER. Other obese villains are THE BLOB, THE DUKE OF DECAY, LORD LAZEE, and TOBIAS WHALE.

FELIX FAUST (C)

First Appearance: 1962, *Justice League of America* #10, DC Comics.

Costume: Blue tights, shirt with shin-length flaps front and back, Saracen-style helmet with flap down back and golden crescent-moon on top; golden slippers, sash around waist, celestial designs (stars, moons, comets, etc.) around base of helmet and on sleeves.

Chief Henchmen: Sundry demons, including Abnegazar, Ghast, and Rath (#10 only); and Abaddon, Boreas the Wind-God, Cernunnos the Stag-God, Perry the Persian Peri, and Karkus the Kobold (#49 only), among others.

Biography: Reading the tale of Faust (see SATAN, Comment), young Felix Faust is impressed enough to want to emulate his namesake and devotes his life to the study of history, ancient tongues—and magic. Going to school at the Sorbonne and later traveling the world's ancient cities, he uncovers a copy of Abdul Alhazred's *Necronomicon*, a tome of the dark arts. With it, he is able to call forth the demons Abnegazar, Ghast, and Rath, who had ruled the planet before the coming of humankind and had been imprisoned inside the earth by a strange race known as the Timeless Ones. However, in order to control the demons completely Faust must first acquire three mystic charms which are hidden in places inaccessible to mortal beings. Using magic provided by the spirits of the demons, Faust enslaves the superheroes of the Justice League of America and forces them to fetch the mystic objects for him. They do, but before the mage can summon the demons, Aquaman sends a school of fish to distract him. The rite is stopped, the superheroes are freed, and Faust has lost the first of many confrontations with the League. For a full year, Faust gives up his life of crime after attending "a prison psychological seminar" and experiencing a primal scream. "In one shrieking *instant*, all the pent-up frustrations of his life were *expelled* and Felix Faust was literally . . . *reborn*." Becoming Curator of Special Literature at the Star City Public Library (and going about his duties dressed in his mystic garb), he stumbles upon a copy of the journals of the wizard Nostromus; possessed by the sorcerer's spirit, Faust returns to his evil ways (#182). He is a member of THE SECRET SOCIETY OF SUPER-VILLAINS.

Quote: "By *Erithal's eight eyes*! The secret journal of *Nostromus*!"

Comment: The saga of the Timeless Ones and the demons owes a great deal to author H.P. Lovecraft and his tales of the monstrous Ancient Ones and their masters, the Elder Gods.

THE FIDDLER (C)

Real Name: Isaac Bowin.

First Appearance: 1947-48, *All Flash* #32, DC Comics.

Costume: Green coat and tails.

Weapons: Various fiddles which contain guns and other weapons. In tandem with his musical abilities (see Biography), the Fiddler uses fiddles to cause objects to break apart, to generate sonic barriers, to hypnotize people, and the like. The Fiddler also drives the unlikeliest vehicle in comics history, a souped-up car in the shape of a giant fiddle.

Biography: While living in India, crook Bowin was arrested and tossed into a cell with a Hindu fakir who had the power to control serpents with a simple pipe. Bowin implored the Hindu to teach him how to do likewise and, with nothing else to do for the next five years, the cellmate complied. During this time, Bowin was able to collect odds and ends to build a fiddle, which he used to get himself and the fakir out of prison. Once they were free, the ungrateful Bowin used the instrument to murder his mentor—and then slew the merchant who'd had him thrown into prison in the first place. Heading home to the United States, Bowin intended to become the greatest criminal the country had ever seen. As the Fiddler, he began tooling around Keystone City in his fiddlemobile, committing crimes; when the superheroic Flash came to investigate, he was kept at bay by powerful sonic vibrations from one of the Fiddler's fiddles. Though he appeared to drown when his instrument caused a pier to fall apart beneath his feet, the Fiddler made it to shore and battled the Flash several more times. He has also fought such superheroes as the Teen Titans (*The Teen Titans*, #46, 1977). The Fiddler was briefly a member of THE INJUSTICE SOCIETY OF THE WORLD.

Quote: "Ha! Ha! Hearken to the Fiddler's music—as it compels you to *kill* each other!"

Comment: Other instrument-playing super villains are THE MAESTRO, THE PIED PIPER, and THE PIED PIPER OF PLUTO. The Flash who battled the Fiddler is not the same Flash who fought such super villains as CAPTAIN BOOMERANG and CAPTAIN COLD. This Flash—and the Fiddler—are villains of a neighboring dimension's Earth-2, though the mad musician came to Earth-1 to fight the Titans. Another famous foe of the Earth-2 Flash is the Rag Doll (Peter Merkel) who first appeared in *Flash Comics* #36 (1943). A carnival contortionist, he turned to crime dressed as a Raggedy Andy-type doll, complete with red mop of hair. Rag Doll was a member of the SECRET SOCIETY OF SUPER-VILLAINS.

FIREBOLT (C)

Real Name: Anthony Sloan.

First Appearance: 1984, *Power Man and Iron Fist* #108, Marvel Comics.

Costume: Purple boots, bodyshirt; black collar with blue studs; red tights; blue belt, gloves.

Biography: Anthony and his sister Rebecca lived alone with their father, a religious fanatic who "preached constantly against the evils of this world" with such furor that he drove their mother away. While they were still very young, the youths realized they had psychic abilities. Rebecca was clairvoyant and Anthony possessed pyrokinesis, the ability to start fires with his mind. Their father denounced these powers "as satanic," and punished them severely when they used them. Ironically, Rebecca was about to warn him of his impending death when he began to beat her; horrified, Anthony set the brutal man afire. Unfortunately, things got a little out of hand and the boy torched himself as well. He spent nearly a year recovering from his wounds, during which time he went insane and adopted his father's precepts. It was, according to Rebecca, "the only way for him to cope with the crushing guilt." When he got out, his face hideously scarred, New York's Times Square became his particular obsession. He took to roaming the streets and alleys as the costumed Firebolt and, spotting someone that he felt was worthy of "cleansing," he simply set them afire. Things got worse when he was convinced by Loman of Loman Real Estate to burn *his* buildings, having persuaded Firebolt that the occupants were evil. In fact, all Loman wanted was the insurance. Pursued by the superheroes Iron Fist and Power Man, Firebolt expended too much power fighting them and perished. As for Loman, he was crushed beneath a sign which fell from one of his burning buildings.

Quote: "Resistance is futile, maggot-scum."

Comment: See other fiery super villains BLOWTORCH BRAND, FIREBUG, FIREFALL, FIREFIST, Heatstroke of MASTERS OF DISASTER, HEATWAVE, and PYRO.

THE FIREBUG (C)

Real Name: Joseph Rigger.

First Appearance: 1979, *Batman* #318, DC Comics.

Costume: Red leotard with long sleeves; yellow tights; orange boots and yellow gloves, both with flame-like fringing; orange and yellow cape designed like flame; full-face cowl with orange front, red top ending in widow's peak, and red eye and mouth coverings.

Weapons: Tubes and tanks, hidden under costume, containing an incendiary "napalm derivative" which he can fire from his hands, like a flamethrower. There is also a doomsday-device in his costume which will ignite everything at once, destroying not only the Firebug but also everything around him.

Biography: While he was in the military, members of Joe's family died one-by-one within weeks of each other. His baby sister ate paint chips in their Gotham City apartment; his father broke his neck after a fall through decrepit flooring in another apartment; and his mother died of a heart attack in a stalled elevator in the Gotham State Building. To avenge their deaths, Joe draws upon his experience as a demolitions expert, vowing to burn down the three buildings in which they died—and caring nothing for whoever may be killed in the process. Destroying two of the three buildings, he tackles the Gotham State Building but is stopped by Batman; igniting his doomsday weapon, the Firebug is tricked into leaping off the building and explodes harmlessly (to everyone else, that is) in midair.

Quote: "You . . . won't *stop* me, Batman—even if I have to *fry* you!"

Comment: This was the character's only appearance. See other fiery super villains BLOWTORCH BRAND, FIREBOLT, FIREFALL, FIREFIST, Heatstroke of MASTERS OF DISASTER, HEATWAVE, and PYRO.

FIREFALL (C)

Real Name: Archie Stryker.

First Appearance: 1980, *Rom* #4, Marvel Comics.

Costume: Red armor (see Weapons) consisting of a red metal bodysuit with spikes on the sides of the legs and arms, a boxlike chest with horns on the shoulders, a horned helmet and mask, and heavy boots.

Weapons: Armor allows the wearer to generate incredible heat and to form and throw fireballs; it also allows him to fly and withstand a great deal of abuse.

Biography: A common criminal, Archie breaks into the Lansing Laserworks to rob its safe. Arrested, he is turned over to the government's Project Safeguard, which has been infiltrated by DIRE WRAITHS, who convince the group that the Wraiths' enemy, Rom, is a super villain and not a superhero. Archie is given the chance to make up for his crimes by being grafted to the Firefall suit and destroying Rom. (The armor itself was stolen from Rom's colleague Karas, who had vanished during the all-out war against the Wraiths.) He accepts, is welded into the suit by Dr. Daedalus and his team, and is body-slammed into submission by the noble Spaceknight. When last seen, Firefall had been reclaimed by his masters and given an (apparently) fatal injection, the punishment for failure.

Quote: "No matter where you run, I'll find you—and slay you without mercy!"

Comment: See other fiery super villains BLOWTORCH BRAND, FIREBOLT, FIREBUG, FIREFIST, Heatstroke of MASTERS OF DISASTER, HEATWAVE, and PYRO.

FIREFIST (C)

Real Name: Lyle Byrnes (note last name).

First Appearance: 1986, *Blue Beetle* (second series) #1, DC Comics.

Costume: White bodysuit, full-face cowl; golden gloves (see Weapons), shoulderpads, belt, boots, helmet with a black fist inside a red circle on forehead.

Weapons: All 10 fingers of his gloves (aka "firefists") shoot streams of flame, powered by small fueltanks.

Biography: A lab researcher in the field of pyrotechnics, Byrnes was caught in an explosion. The Chicago fire department rushed over, but a fallen fire fighter was helped before the trapped Byrnes. Badly scarred, he created his firefists and swore to exact vengeance against the department. Holed up in the Clinton Hotel, he made plans to burn down the soon-to-be-opened Chicago Museum of Firefighting, only to perish when his firetanks exploded after being pummeled by the superheroic Blue Beetle.

Quote: "Feel the flames of *Firefist*, fools—and know what it is to *suffer*!"

Comment: See other fiery super villains BLOWTORCH BRAND, FIREBOLT, FIREBUG, FIREFALL, Heatstroke of MASTERS OF DISASTER, HEATWAVE, and PYRO.

FISHERMAN (C)

First Appearance: 1965, *Aquaman* #21, DC Comics.

Costume: Purple bodysuit; blue thigh boots; yellow hood with black spots; silver-metal harness for storing equipment.

Weapons: Fishing rod with line ending in various, deadly hooks or razors; lures, stored in belt, which release a deadly gas when thrown.

Biography: Little is known about the Fisherman's past. A thief who specializes in stealing and then peddling hi-tech equipment, he first battled Aquaman after stealing a compound capable of causing any life form to grow huge. The two have fought many times since then; the Fisherman has also tangled with the superheroic Blue Devil, a bout which landed him in jail.

Comment: See other underwater super villains ATTUMA, BLACK MANTA, CAPTAIN NEMO, CAPTAIN WHALE, DR. FANG, KILLER SHARK, KRANG, MR. CRABB, OCEAN MASTER, ORKA, PIRANHA, and TIGER SHARK (2).

FIXER (C)

Real Name: Norbert Ebersol.
First Appearance: 1966, *Strange Tales* #141, Marvel Comics.
Costume: Green bodysuit, cowl; black mask; blue boots, gloves.
Weapons: "Anti-grav propellant unit," a purple vest which allows for flight (later transistorized as anti-gravity plates worn on feet). He has also employed various guns and rayguns, bombs, and electronic paraphernalia such as the Jericho Tubes, which turn his bellow into "a deafening sonic pitch"; a nameless device which alters the atomic structure of matter (turning a bowling ball to crystal, for example); and Computrex, the "living computer."
Biography: A genius at electronics and machines, Ebersol grew bored with school and dropped out in his teens; nor did any of the jobs he held subsequently interest him, including work as an auto mechanic and a TV repairperson. Applying his abilities to hi-tech crimes, he was arrested—but satisfied. Using his knowledge of electronics to get out of jail, he fell in with MENTALLO and the two attempted to destroy the New York offices of the international peacekeeping force S.H.I.E.L.D. (Supreme Headquarters International Espionage Law-enforcement Division). They nearly succeeded. Sufficiently impressed with his talents, the subversive group HYDRA hired Fixer as an agent, and he has since battled numerous superheroes, including Spider-Man and Captain America.
Quote: "I rigged up the Menta-scope so you could telepathically track and brain blast our enemies, Mentallo."

FLAG-SMASHER (C)

First Appearance: 1985, *Captain America* #312, Marvel Comics.
Costume: White leotard, boots; black tights, gloves, cowl with red eyepieces, cape with red lining; black belt with buckle consisting of black Americas on a white earth.
Weapons: Many, including a mace, flamethrower, and tear gas gun.
Biography: The son of a Swiss diplomat, the future Flag-Smasher (his name is not known) traveled widely as a child. Lacking roots and friends, the youth studied martial arts while his father was assigned to Tokyo. The family finally settled in New York when the diplomat was appointed to the United Nations. The teenager enrolled in college and all was relatively well until his father died during a riot outside the Latverian embassy (the embassy of DR. DOOM). Wishing to continue his father's dream for world peace, the youth took a rather different tack. Using the money left by his father, the youth purchased weapons and became a costumed villain, intending to enforce pacifism through terrorism. His targets were anything that stands for nationalism or partisanship, from flags to governments—and, of course, the red, white, and blue superhero Captain America. Attacking the living symbol of our nation, Flag-Smasher was defeated and deported. Because he is able to speak many languages, there's no telling where Flag-Smasher is now or when he will resurface.

FLATTOP (CS, TV)

Real Name: Jones (the name he gives when he meets people).
First Appearance: December 21, 1943, *Dick Tracy*. Chicago Tribune-New York News Syndicate.
Weapons: .38-caliber revolver.
Biography: With a head like an inverted triangle, Flattop is "a free lance man. I do custom killing anywhere. New York, Atlanta, Chicago, San Francisco." For each hit he earns an average of one or two thousand dollars; however, a group of wartime black marketeers give him $5,000 to kill Dick Tracy. Capturing the gumshoe and bringing him to his apartment hideout, Flattop turns around and demands $50,000, threatening that if the money isn't paid he'll give Tracy the criminals' names and set him free. The frightened thugs pay up but Tracy escapes; so does the wily Flattop. Recognized by a street hawker, Flattop douses the man with gasoline and sets him afire (the poor fellow is charred black); stealing an actor's makeup kit, he uses it to disguise his own features. However, Tracy tracks him to a movie theater where, in a shootout, Flattop is blasted in the neck by police chief Pat Patton. Brought to the hospital and operated on, Flattop is hauled to jail.
Quote: "I'll kill every copper in town for this!"
Comment: Flattop was also a character on the Dick Tracy cartoon show (1960).

THE FLORONIC MAN (C)

Real Name: Jason Woodrue.
First Appearance: 1962, *The Atom* #1, DC Comics.
Costume: Transformed into a plant being, he has bark-

like skin and leaves clustered around his wrists, waist, shoulders, head, and shins.

Chief Henchmen: Plants, which he can animate however he wishes; several varieties are mutated, most notably his enormous Venus Flytraps.

Biography: Woodrue is a villain on his home world in another dimension, a world populated with classical nymphs, satyrs, and other denizens of the woods. Exiled to our world, he promptly subjugates earth's flora and intends to use his army of plants to conquer the United States. Defeated numerous times by the superheroic Atom, Woodrue concocts a potion that turns him into a tree-being himself, "a thing of wood and sap, a mockery of humanity!" After suffering a loss at the hands of another superhero, Green Lantern, the Floronic Man tries to go straight, starting a small business which specializes in exotic plants. Tempted into action again by THE SECRET SOCIETY OF SUPER-VILLAINS, he joins the group to battle the Justice League of America (*Justice League of America* #195, 1981), of which Atom and Green Lantern are both members. Defeated (#197), he goes back to the clink; upon his release, he manages to merge his mind with all plants and acquires unprecedented power. However, the hulking Swamp Thing snaps the bond and leaves him raving mad. He is presently in the Arkham Asylum.

Quote: "Smug fools. They think I'm *bluffing*. They really think I couldn't kill you in *cold blood*! . . . Hot *or* cold, what I do, I do out of *necessity*."

Comment: See PLANTMAN, who had virtually identical powers and also THE THORN.

THE FLY (C)

Real Name: Richard Deacon.

First Appearance: 1976, *The Amazing Spider-Man Annual* #10, Marvel Comics.

Costume: Yellow cowl, yellow bodysuit with green chest, belly, and crotch; green gloves and boots.

Weapons: Wings for flight.

Chief Henchmen: Chino and Roxy (as Deacon only).

Biography: A petty thief, Deacon is shot as he flees the scene of a foiled kidnapping. Finding himself at the lab of Dr. Harlan Stillwell (the brother of Farley Stillwell, the evil brain behind THE SCORPION), Deacon and the scientist find that they each have something to offer the other. Stillwell agrees to save Deacon's life, while Deacon allows Stillwell to use his body for a bizarre experiment. Tinkering with Deacon's genes, the scientist is able to superimpose on them the genetic code of a fly. Deacon promptly acquires many fly-like characteristics: the proportionate strength of a fly; the ability to see in all directions at once thanks to huge, red eyes; the power to cling to any surface due to secretions from his fingers and toes; and wings which allow him to fly. Murdering Stillwell so that what has been done can never be undone, Deacon makes a costume for himself and becomes the super villain the Fly. His nemesis is Spider-Man, whose arachnid powers make for an interesting variation of the spider-and-the-fly rivalry.

Quote: "Jerk! You can't sneak up behind a guy whose compound eyes let him see 360 degrees."

THE FLYING TIGER (C)

First Appearance: 1981, *Spider- Woman* #40, Marvel Comics.

Costume: Bodysuit and cowl are that of a tiger; green leotard; golden belt, bands around his wrists and shins (bands are sometimes red); tiger-skin flaps beneath arms.

Weapons: Extremely sharp tiger claws; standard firearms.

Biography: Nothing is known about this character's background, save that he is a former football star who played more than once in the Super Bowl. "Bounced out of pro ball" for some unexplained reason, he becomes a high-priced mercenary with a Swiss bank account. Hired by San Francisco crimelord General Nguyen Ngoc Coy to slay local superhero Spider-Woman, he fails and is arrested. However, he resurfaces to kidnap wealthy Regis Fusskey and ends up tangling with the man's temporary bodyguard, the superhero Iron Man (*Iron Man* #177, 1983). He was last seen draped over a tree limb in a South American jungle, laid out by a superhuman punch.

Quote: "Don't bother sayin' your last words. I ain't gonna lissen to 'em anyway."

FOOLKILLER (C)

Real Name: Ross G. Everbest; Greg Salinger.

First Appearance: 1974, *Man-Thing* #3 (as Everbest); 1977, *Omega the Unknown* #9 (as Salinger), Marvel Comics.

Costume: Navy blue bodysuit, cavalier hat with red queue, mask; darker blue boots, gloves, cape (only in *Omega the Unknown*).

Weapons: "Purification gun," a pistol which fires a beam of pure light which vaporizes anyone it strikes; sash on hat is "specially designed" to serve as a "paraglider" for leaping off buildings.

Biography: A paralyzed orphan, Everbest was taken by

his grandmother to see a faith healer named Reverend Mike. Cured of his affliction, Everbest became one of Mike's disciples, carrying to the extreme the evangelist's dislike of sinners and thieves. Imagining himself the right hand of God, fated to slay all "fools," Everbest took money from the reverend's coffers and used it to make a costume and purchase his purification gun. Shocked to find Mike dallying with a young lady, he made the preacher his first victim. The crime was soundly condemned by radio disc jockey Richard Rory, whom Foolkiller deemed a fool. Abducting him and F.A. Schist, a fool industrialist, Foolkiller took them to a swamp outside of Citrusville, Florida, and was about to slay them when the monstrous hero Man-Thing appeared. A struggle ensued and Foolkiller perished (*Man-Thing* #4); his costume and gun were impounded by the police. Not long thereafter, Rory found himself a vagrant and in prison. There he met thug Greg Salinger, to whom he related his tale. Inspired by Foolkiller's exploits, Salinger "liberated the Foolkiller's equipment" upon his release and renewed his crusade . . . but with a twist. He didn't define fools as sinners but, rather, as "one totally bereft of a poetic nature"; those who boast "how much they can drink—but never (have) a poetic thought." Setting himself up in a semi-trailer truck, he used sophisticated computers to keep track of his victims and also to tap into sundry data bases. Among the heroes the second Foolkiller has battled are Omega, Hellcat, Valkyrie and, most recently, Spider-Man; he also slew the macho villain BLOCKBUSTER. The villain is presently in a hospital psychiatric ward, too mad to stand trial for his crimes.

Quote: "I decided—months ago—only to kill the greatest fools I encountered. I'm afraid you qualify."

Comment: One courteous, and certainly unique aspect of the character is that he warns his victims by handing out cards which read, "E Pluribus Unum. You have 24 hours to live. Use them to repent—or be forever damned to the pits of hell, wheregoeth all fools. Today is the last day of the rest of your life. Use it wisely—or die a fool!" He also has been known to do a rather foolish thing: mail the cards, thus leaving at least one of his victims in shock when he shows up and the note hasn't arrived. "Blast the postal service!" is all Foolkiller can say before blowing the individual away.

FORCE (C)

Real Name: Clayton Wilson.

First Appearance: 1973, *Sub-Mariner* #66 (as Wilson), though he went by the alias "Taylor" in the story); 1974, #68 (as Force), Marvel Comics.

Costume: Green bodysuit; yellow boots, trunks, gloves; golden armor consisting of a full-head helmet, belt, breastplate with green "F" (see Weapons).

Weapons: Force's armor permits him to fire destructive blasts, build a force field, and control other sources of energy. He also packs miniature concussion bombs in his belt.

Chief Henchmen: Sundry lackeys costumed in green bodysuits; all ride "jet-skis," airborne scooters which fire destructive beams.

Biography: An assistant to Dr. Damon Walthers, scientist Wilson uses his power suit to become a super criminal. Though defeated by the Sub-Mariner, he returns to battle other Marvel superheroes.

THE FOX (MP)

Real Name: Captain James.

First Appearance: 1934, *The Mystic Hour*, Progressive Pictures.

Chief Henchmen: Nameless thugs.

Biography: The Fox is a burglar-extraordinaire who masquerades as private investigator James. (He often ends up handling the investigations of his own crimes!) The Fox is also a murderer who's quick to poison his henchmen when they're captured. He is eventually cornered by young Bob Randall on a cliff overlooking the ocean; though he makes a daring leap into the sea, Randall dives in after him and brings the Fox to justice.

Comment: Montague Love played the part in this film written by John Francis Nattiford from a screen story by Susan Embry.

FREDDY KRUEGER (MP, N)

First Appearance: 1984, *A Nightmare on Elm Street*, New Line Cinema.

Costume: Floppy brown fedora; sweater with vertical green and red stripes; brown trousers.

Weapons: Leather glove, worn on right hand, which ends in five razor-sharp metal claws.

Biography: Freddy was born to Amanda Krueger (1907-68), who worked at a mental institution on Elm Street in the otherwise sleepy town of Springwood. Locked one night in a crowded cell, she was raped repeatedly by the inmates; Freddy was born from that attack, "the son of one hundred maniacs." Amanda later joined a nunnery. Raised by a string of criminals, he was finally taken in by a sadistic pimp. Whenever his father caught him with one of the women, he would whip Freddy savagely with a razor strop; sometimes he would slash the youth with a razor. It wasn't long before sexual gratification and the inflicting of pain became one in Freddy's mind. Striking out on his own (but not before he burned the pimp's house to the ground with the sleeping pimp still inside), he worked odd jobs, failed at most, and became a drunken bum. While he was lying in the street one day, a young boy tried to rob him; Freddy struck him with a bottle and the boy fell, bleeding badly. The sight thrilled Freddy, and he did some additional cutting on the boy's body with a razor. The sick man decided, then, to make child-killing his avocation. Over 20 children died beneath his claws, their bodies stored in the local power plant. The police finally found the corpses and arrested Freddy, but the search had been illegal and the charges were dropped. The so-called Springwood Slasher was thus released. Furious, several parents living on Elm Street got together and burned the plant down . . . and Freddy with it. Dying, he vowed vengeance; his bones were stored in the trunk of a Cadillac in a local junkyard. Several years later, Freddy's badly scarred ghost began visiting the dreams of the children of the Elm Street parents. And whatever he did to their bodies in these nightmares, whatever cuts he inflicted, the children would actually have when they woke up; when he cut them too much, they didn't wake up at all. In dreams, Freddy's powers were virtually without limit: He could stretch his arms to any length, he could hide inside and emerge from within common household objects—puppets, televisions, mirrors, walls—and he could even turn floors to putty (trapping anyone trying to escape). The only defense: If one is holding Freddy when one wakes up, Freddy will be brought into the real world—where he can be hurt. After slaying over a dozen children through dreams, he was finally destroyed (or so it seemed) when a psychologist (visited by Amanda's ghost) hunted down Freddy's bones and sprinkled them with holy water.

Quote: "Come to me . . . I'm waiting for you!"

Comment: Robert Englund played the part in the film and its two sequels, *A Nightmare on Elm Street* 2 (1985) and *A Nightmare on Elm Street 3: The Dream Warriors* (1987). The character was created by the first film's writer/director, Wes Craven. A novelization incorporating the stories of all three films was written by Jeffrey Cooper and published in 1987. Note: With the exception of the information about Freddy's mother, which was revealed in the third film, all biographical data about the killer's youth was revealed in the novelization.

FRESTON (N)

First Appearance: 1605, *Don Quixote*, Miguel Cervantes.

Biography: Don Quixote is country gentleman Alonso Quijano who, his mind made weak by reading about chivalry, sallies forth as a knight-errant. As such, his archenemy is the (imaginary) wizard Freston, to whom he attributes the dark events which befall him. The first of these involves Quixote's library. To wean him from his madness, his friends burn his books; Quixote imagines this to be the work of Freston, "a Conjurer, or an Inchanter (who) came hither one Night mounted on a Dragon o'th' Top of a cloud." Entering the study, he left it "full of smoke." Freston's most infamous mischief occurs when Quixote spots some 30 giants on a plain. He attacks, only to find himself battling windmills. "I am verily persuaded," says he, "that cursed Necromancer Freston, who carry'd away my Study and my Books, has transform'd these Giants into Wind-mills, to deprive me of the Honor of Victory."

Comment: In the play and motion picture *Man of La Mancha*, the character was simply referred to as the Enchanter.

FUNNYFACE (C)

First Appearance: 1942, *Superman* #19, DC Comics.

Costume: Mask which makes his face look like a balloon.

Weapons: "Weird ray" which allows him to "materialize two-dimensional figures," creating living beings from comic strip illustrations.

Biography: An unsuccessful comic strip writer, Funnyface is far more talented when it comes to science. Inventing his incredible ray, he brings four-color villains to life and uses them to perpetrate spectacular crimes. Superman is unable to stop the fiend (despite swaggering threats to "sock that silly grin clear down to your toes!"), and it remains for reporter Lois Lane to lend Superman a hand by bringing to life comic strip heroes.

Quote: "My dimensional experimentation enabled me to . . . put the strip villains to work for me to gather illegal profits!"

THE GADGETEER (C)

Real Name: Col. Roger Romane.

First Appearance: 1978, *Steel the Indestructible Man* #4, DC Comics.

Costume: Light green jumpsuit, gloves; green cloak with red collar; brown boots.

Weapons: Many gadgets, including a key-like device which turns ordinary illumination into a laser beam; portable autogyro which folds into a pocket; hand grenades.

Biography: Attached to a research and development division of the Army Engineer Corps during World War II, Romane is a mechanics genius. Discharged for insulting a superior officer—a general "who rejected Romane's concept of multi-purpose tools for use by combat engineers"—the Colonel turns to crime. He is quite successful, robbing armored trucks and the like until he is nabbed by the superheroic Steel.

Quote: "Be *blissful* in your *stupidity*, my friend! Very soon, it'll be *all* you have left to call your *own*!"

Comment: See other gadget-oriented criminals THE JOKER and THE PRANKSTER.

GALACTUS (C, TV, M)

Real Name: Galan.

First Appearance: 1966, *The Fantastic Four* #48, Marvel Comics.

Costume: Blue bodysuit with purple chest and inside of upper arms, both with vertical and horizontal black ribbing, respectively; purple boots, gauntlets, helmet with massive, "L"-shaped horns; blue armor worn on torso, "U"-lined on top, "II"-lined on bottom; purple skirt with blue stripes crisscrossing (see Biography for function of costume).

Chief Henchmen: The Punisher, a mighty robot (introduced in #49); Drone R-11; various heralds to whom he gives vast power "with a soul-chilling gaze," and who then find worlds for him to consume. The roster has included the now-superheroic Silver Surfer (Norrid Radd of the planet Zenn-La, who agreed to serve if Galactus would spare his planet, then turned on his master to help save the Earth), Air Walker (Gabriel Lan of Xandar), Firelord (Pyreus Kril, also of Xandar), Terrax the Tamer (Tyros of Laniak), and Nova (Frankie Raye of Earth).

Biography: Before our universe is born in the Big Bang, a previous universe is destroyed in the Big Crunch—the collapse of all matter. Galan dwells in that universe on the planet Taa. As the cosmos collapses, astronaut Galan and a handful of others ride a spaceship into the heart of the holocaust ("the blazing cosmic cauldron into which all the matter in the universe was plunging," although some accounts erroneously state that he rode into "the heart of their sun"); all perish but Galan, who is miraculously protected by a force calling itself "the sentience of the universe." That force, too, is dying; however, it declares, "We need not die without an heir," and merges with Galan. The Taaian survives the Big Crunch and after "an eternity of seeming nothingness," the Big Bang creates our present universe. Galan drifts in his (obviously) "sturdy starship" for countless millennia. Finally, fully metamorphosed into the towering Galactus, he emerges in orbit around the planet Archeopia and, thirsting for energy, sucks dry what "had been a biosphere resplendent with verdant life." His actions—conducted with "awesome energy sapping apparatus"—kill every living thing on Archeopia, and he resolves to drain only uninhabited worlds in the future. But as time passes his hunger grows and that criterion goes by the wayside. Nor can very many worlds successfully oppose Galactus, as he can channel his energy in various offensive ways: to generate unfathomably powerful blasts, to transmute or teleport matter, and to create force-fields. (Indeed, were Galactus ever to remove his costume, the energy contained in his body would undergo a thermonuclear reaction and turn him into a star.) Headquartered on a massive base called Taa II, which "took millennia to complete" and is the size of the Archeopian system itself, he recruits a succession of heralds and sends them forth to find worlds for him to engulf. He then travels to those worlds via Taa II. Over the years, he has made several attempts to dine on our world only to be thwarted—a first for the towering colossus!—by Mr. Fantastic of the Fantastic Four, who has invented an "Ultimate Nullifier" which can kill even Galactus. During one such encounter, however, Galactus' energies are so thoroughly depleted that he would have died without an energy transfusion from Mr. Fantastic. The grateful being vows never again to attack earth, a promise which he has kept thusfar. In his heart-of-hearts, Galactus believes that there is some as-yet unknown reason he was spared the destruction of his universe—quite possibly to help prevent the collapse of the present universe some 55 billion years hence. As he puts it, "It is my destiny to one day give back to the universe infinitely more than I have ever taken from it." Galactus' physical size has varied over the years. For example, in *What If?* #33, he appears to be roughly 20 feet tall, while in *Silver Surfer* #1 he's 30 feet if he's an inch. Regardless, he's a giant by any terrestrial standard.

Quote: "If you become my herald—willingly—perhaps I will spare that wretched orb!"

Comment: Galactus is not inherently evil; as he himself points out to one of his heralds, "If I were as compassionless as you believe—your insolence would surely have invoked instant obliteration." And as he pointed out to the future Silver Surfer, "I seek *no wealth*—no personal gain—no petty, paltry *treasure* . . . I crave the total *energy* of your hapless world." However, Galactus is a villain by virtue of the number of sentient beings he has slain; and, despite his disclaimer, he also possesses a vile temper. (To wit: furious with the Silver Surfer for having helped defend the earth, he surrounded our world with an energy barrier to keep the Zenn-Lannian imprisoned here forever.) Galactus was featured in an episode of the 1967-70 ABC-TV cartoon series *The Fantastic Four*, and is one of the few villains to have starred in his own magazine—the first and only issue of *Super-Villain Classics* (1983).

THE GARGOYLE (MP)

Real Name: McLeod.

First Appearance: 1941, *The Spider Returns*, Columbia Pictures.

Costume: Cowl, gloves, robe, capelet all made of metallic fabric; capelet and sleeves were fringed with darker, lightning-like stripes, one of which also ran down the front of his robe; dark gargoyle face on back of capelet. (Film was in black and white.)

Weapons: Handguns, tear gas bombs, torture devices, other standard weapons.

Chief Henchmen: Sundry gangmembers.

Biography: During the days before the Second World War, industrialist McLeod becomes the mysterious Gargoyle in order to destroy U.S. defense and military projects. He is eventually unmasked by the superheroic Spider.

THE GARGOYLE *(Corbet Harris), nemesis of the heroic Spider.*

Comment: Corbet Harris played the villain in this 15-chapter serial. See also THE OCTOPUS, another Spider movie villain.

GARGUAX (C)

First Appearance: 1964, *The Doom Patrol* #91, DC Comics.

Costume: Purple robe with golden belt (later white belt); white headband. Garguax's skin is green.

Weapons: Numerous robots and arms, such as the "electric leash" which fires a whip-like tongue of electricity to keep captives in line. Garguax moves through space in a city which he parks in earth orbit, "floating some 25 miles" above our world; to discourage squatters, the fortress is "a maze of the deadliest traps ever conceived," including an acid pool and a "super wind tunnel."

Chief Henchmen: The Plastic Men, globs which form into a variety of super-powered beings each possessing either great strength (blue-colored), the ability to generate intense heat (red), or incredible speed (gray). In one story (#109), the Plastic Men merge into the blue giant Mandred the Executioner who possesses all of those abilities.

Biography: "A distillation of evil," Garguax hails from a distant world, from which he says he was banished by "fools." (He doesn't elaborate.) Coming to earth, he develops a powerful new weapon on his space base and intends to test it on our world before trying it out on his. Rocketing into space, the Doom Patrol blows up the city—but not Garguax, who escapes, sets up a new base on the moon, and joins THE BROTHERHOOD OF EVIL. As a member of the Brotherhood, he tackles the Doom Patrol on numerous occasions, never coming close to winning. In time, however, the truth about Garguax is revealed. He is actually an emissary for Zarox-13, a purple-armored giant who intends to take over the earth. Coming to our world with a small army, Zarox-13 is so terrifying that even the Brotherhood (sans Garguax) allies itself with the Doom Patrol to defeat the invader. He, Garguax, and their forces are beaten back and flee into space; they have not been heard from since (#'s 111-112).

GARTH OF IZAR (TV, N)

First Appearance: January 3, 1969, "Whom Gods Destroy," *Star Trek*, NBC-TV.

Biography: A brilliant student at the Star Fleet Academy, the planet Izar native rises quickly to Captain, with the rank of admiral reportedly in the wings. Then, tragedy strikes. While undertaking a rescue mission off Antos IV, Garth is badly maimed, an accident which costs him his sanity. However, the beings he was rescuing have the ability to restructure their molecules and they teach that talent to Garth. Grateful beyond words but still wildly mad, he offers to help the aliens conquer the galaxy; when they refuse, he attempts to destroy their world. For his efforts, he is incarcerated on the prison world Ebla II. Breaking free by using his powers to disguise himself as the Governor of Ebla, Garth imprisons Captain Kirk of the starship *Enterprise*, which had come to Ebla II to dispense a new drug capable of curing mental illness. Impersonating his prisoner, Garth takes command of the ship and intends to blackmail the galaxy by threatening to use his "ultimate" bomb to make stars go nova. (Meanwhile, he amuses himself by sending his mistress Marta, an Orion, onto the deadly surface of Ebla II, "charitably" blowing her to bits before she can suffocate.) Luckily, Kirk's second-in-command, Mr. Spock, realizes the Garth-Kirk is a fake and subdues him; Garth is injected with the serum and becomes a devoted Star Fleet commander once more.

Quote: "Starship Fleet Captain is merely one of my minor titles. I am Lord Garth of Izar—and future Emperor of the Galaxy."

Comment: Steve Ihnat played the part in Garth's only appearance. The teleplay was written by Lee Erwin. The title of the show is from Euripides: "Whom the gods would destroy they first make mad." The episode was adapted by James Blish into short-story form and collected in *Star Trek* 5. Note: Elba was Napoleon's first place of exile.

THE GASSER (C)

First Appearance: 1967, *Mighty Comics* #49, Archie Comics.

Costume: Green bodysuit; brown gasmask, boots, gloves, belt.

Weapons: Cane which can be loaded with cartridges that spray sleeping or death gasses, acid, and other

***THE GASSER**, down but not out.* © *Archie Comics.*

materials; cane which transforms into a harpoon; flamethrowers and machine guns.

Chief Henchmen: Three known members of the Gasser Gang.

Biography: Venturing from his headquarters in an abandoned warehouse, the Gasser rendered people unconscious and then robbed them. The superheroic Fox tracked the gang down and brought them to justice—but not for long. In prison, the criminal began studying martial arts, then continued his training for three years at Leong Chen's Kung Fu institute in New York's Chinatown. Re-emerging on the crime scene as Martial Law, he sought to join the criminal Dragon Squad (1984, *Blue Ribbon Comics* #6). Coincidentally, the initiation demanded by the Dragon-Head was to kill the Fox. ("I can hardly believe my luck!" the former Gasser burbles with glee.) The hero defeated the villain in hand-to-hand combat, but the influential Dragon-Head had him released. Teaming with THE ERASER, Martial Law beat the Fox nearly to death and dumped him in a trashcan. Pulling himself together, the Fox got Martial Law alone and returned the favor—though it was the superheroic Web who brought Martial Law in while the Fox battled the Eraser.

Quote: "*Ha, ha-aaa*! So *the Fox* seeks to defeat this crime caper of *the Gasser*! Your unmatched daring and wily wits shall be bested by me!"

Comment: In the second tale, Martial Law erroneously recalls having been defeated in an abandoned theater the first time around. Apparently, it was quite a beating he took that night.

GEMINI (C)

First Appearance: 1977, *The Defenders* #48, Marvel Comics.

Costume: Bodysuit, glove, and boot navy blue on right, white on left when they are joined; head is silver. When they split, Reason is all white, Emotion is all navy blue, both with a silver head.

Biography: A living android, Gemini is able to split into two separate beings: Reason and Emotion. Reason has the power to "absorb energy" and, having done so, Emotion is able "to zap whatever I feel like." When he is unified, he is constantly torn between committing good and evil. ("Let's be reasonable, shall we?" asks Reason, to which Emotion replies, "No! I'm in a redhot rage! I say we *pound* this punk to a pulp!") Either apart or together, he is able to withstand enormous punishment. Created by SCORPIO (in his Jake Fury incarnation), Gemini willingly surrendered to the international peacekeeping force S.H.I.E.L.D. when the superheroic Defenders had thrashed Scorpio. But because his good side had prevailed and he'd helped the Defenders beat the villain, Gemini was set free. Moving to Los Angeles—and feeling "at home here among the West Coast Weirdos"—he briefly became a mercenary and tangled with the She-Hulk while trying to abduct a killer set free by the courts (1981, *The Savage She-Hulk* #21). His present whereabouts are unknown.

Quote: "I must see—for *myselves*!"

Comment: Another Gemini is Joshua Link, a member of ZODIAC.

GENERAL CHAN LU (MP)

First Appearance: 1968, *Battle Beneath the Earth*, Metro-Goldwyn-Mayer.

Weapons: Laser-diggers for tunneling beneath the earth.

Biography: Acting without the open approval of his masters in Peking, the Chinese officer undertakes a grandiose scheme to destroy the United States. Based in Hawaii, he orders his huge army to dig a network of tunnels leading under the nation's major cities and military and communications facilities. When these are completed he intends to place atomic bombs beneath each, debilitating the country and making it easy for the Chinese to come in and set up a new civilization. However, he is found out (the government finally listens to a renowned seismologist) and turned back by American forces led by Commander Jonathan Shaw.

Comment: Martin Benson played the part of the Asian schemer. See other Asian super villains BRIGAND LEADER, COLONEL SUN, DR. FU MANCHU, DR. GOO FEE, DR. YEN SIN, and WU FANG.

GENERAL IMMORTUS (C)

First Appearance: 1963, *The Doom Patrol* #80, DC Comics.

Costume: Blue military uniform with gold epaulets, belt; darker blue boots.

Weapons: Many hi-tech weapons, including an automated "ray cannon," another automated cannon which fires a "freezing gas"; a "polarization ray" which stops any and all machines dead; a "radio interference" device; spaceship; and "atomic converter" which will allow him to build a nuclear bomb "big enough to destroy every planet in our solar system"; many others.

Chief Henchmen: Countless operatives around the world.

Biography: General Immortus is an aspiring world conqueror who is "as old as time." At some point in the past—reportedly thousands of years ago, quite possibly at the height of the ancient Egyptian civilization—General Immortus (his real name is unrevealed) obtained a potion which granted him extended life when drunk at regular intervals. This has enabled him to plan long and hard for his eventual conquest of the world. Unfortunately, Immortus does not know the formula's composition and, over the centuries, has hired great chemists (including Pasteur!) to try and duplicate the serum. All of these efforts have met with failure and, in our era, with only enough of the compound to give him 200 years more of life, he asked brilliant scientist Niles Caulder to work on the problem. An expert in life-prolongation research, the starving Caulder cooperated until he learned the identity of the tyrant who was underwriting him; the scientist refused to continue, and Immortus kept him in line by placing a bomb in his chest and threatening to detonate it if he didn't get back to work. Caulder did indeed learn the secret of the formula, but refused to turn it over. And though Caulder was able to have the bomb removed by one of his robot assistants, he came out of the surgery paralyzed below the waist (#88). In order to confound Immortus' schemes to get the formula and conquer the world, Caulder assembled a team of superheroes known as the Doom Patrol. The heroes and villain fought repeatedly over the years, the Patrol finally perishing in an explosion. However, Caulder had given the formula to his wife, Arani. Learning of this, the ancient fiend abducted her and subjected the woman to a mind-probe, discovered the ingredients, and brewed himself a batch. Unfortunately, the formula had been designed solely for Arani's metabolism and failed to work on the fiend. He subsequently perished (or at least appeared to) when his lair was atomized in a blast (*Showcase* #95, 1977).

Quote: "This device . . . shatters the continuity of the energy that composes Negative Man! *You will die*!"

Comment: See another immortal super villain, Kang the Conqueror, aka IMMORTUS.

GENERAL INO (M)

First Appearance: November 1936, "Resurrection Day," *Doc Savage* Magazine, Kenneth Robeson.

Chief Henchman: Proudman Shaster.

Biography: A thief and kidnapper, Ino has committed crimes in Egypt, Italy, the United States, and Japan; in Japan he scored one of his biggest coups, ransoming the son of a wealthy Japanese financier for a quarter million yen (he murdered the baby after the ransom was paid, keeping the jewelry it wore). He is helped in his crimes by attorney Proudman Shaster, a smooth-talking fiend and the man who provided the acid "that had disposed of the last bit of epidermis of the Japanese merchant prince's man-child." Able to mimic most any accent, he is living in the United States when the superhero Doc Savage announces that he has discovered a serum which can revive the dead. However, the serum can only be used once, and Doc decides that King Solomon is the individual who should be revived. Leaving a trail of death, General Ino substitutes the mummy of one Pey-deh-eh-ghan for Solomon. When the Egyptian is revived, General Ino kidnaps him, forcing "Pay Day" to lead him to a long-buried tomb full of treasure. Doc Savage follows them to the Middle East, where General Ino, Shaster, and their men are drowned when the tomb floods. (The Egyptian gets away, only to be run over by a car.)

Quote: "Can you cut off a head with that?"

Comment: General Ino was one of Doc's most sadistic foes. At one point, he planned to entertain himself by releasing Doc's captured aides then watching as they were cut down by sword-wielding Arabs on horseback.

GENERALISSIMO BRAINSTORM (C)

First Appearance: 1966, *Thrill-O-Rama* #2, Harvey Comics.

Costume: Red military uniform with gold epaulets and a white belt.

Weapons: The submarine *Cranium 1*; Murderina, the mechanical mermaid.

Chief Henchmen: The Anchor, a hulking strongman; Agent OOZ; and Chief of Laboratory 1AA.

Biography: Brainstorm is a man of remarkable mental powers; not only is he brilliant, but he can also actually tap the electrical energy of his brain. (In his second adventure, he is able to "electrically charge" a periscope and use it as a radio transmitter.) Operating from a secret base in the South Pacific, he sallies forth to plunder, sometimes grandly, such as raiding a bank on the Rock of Gibraltar after first creating chaos by using the apes that live there. He is thwarted in all his plans by the seagoing superhero Pirana. Brainstorm's head is constantly surrounded by red sparks of crackling brainpower.

Quote: "One of these fine days . . . powie! Down goes Pirana for keeps."

His head surrounded by stars of energy, ***GENERALISSIMO BRAINSTORM*** *plots a new crime. © Harvey Comics.*

Comment: The character appeared in *Thrill-O-Rama* #s 2 and 3. See also CAPTAIN NEMO, another submariner.

GENERAL SPIDRAX (T, C)

First Appearance: 1985, Sectaurs action toy lineup, Coleco.

Costume: Purple breastplate, horned helmet, armored trunks, metallic thigh boots, gauntlets; blue straps crisscrossing breastplate. The flesh of General Spidrax is blue.

Weapons: Various primitive arms, including a whip.

Chief Henchmen: Spidrax commands countless soldiers; he rides about on the back of his Spider-Flyer, a giant, winged arachnid.

Biography: Like all of the Sectaurs (humanoids who have evolved from insects) General Spidrax lives on Symbion, a world "somewhere in space, somewhen in time." Spidrax serves the evil Dark Empress Devora who, headquartered in her hive-like Castle Grimhold in the capital city of Synax, is the ruler of the Dark Domain. Devora's goal is to conquer all of Symbion. It is up to General Spidrax, along with Commander Waspax and their "sting troopers," to see that this occurs by conquering the Shining Realm of Prince Dargon, who is headquartered in the Royal Palace of Prosperon. Needless to say, although he serves Devora, Spidrax seeks, ultimately, to "raise a general to . . . an emperor!" Namely, himself.

Quote: "Skull soldiers—*shoulder arms*! Wing warriors—*mount your insectoids*!"

Comment: Marvel has been publishing a Sectaurs comic book since 1985. Other unsavory sorts in the service of Devora include her son Skulk and the spy Senrad the Stealthy. See other action toy super villains BARON KARZA, DESTRO, HORDAK, MOLTAR, MUMM-RA, and SKELETOR.

GENERAL ZAROFF (N, MP)

First Appearance: 1924, "Most Dangerous Game," Richard Connell.

Chief Henchman: Ivan.

Biography: The aristocratic Zaroff was "a tall man past middle age." His hair was "vivid white, but his thick eyebrows and pointed military moustache were as black as the night. His eyes, too, were black and very bright. He had high cheekbones, a sharp-cut nose, a spare, dark face." The Russian lived to hunt. He had a gun at age five to shoot sparrows; at age 10 he killed a bear. A former Cossack, cavalry officer, he had "hunted every kind of game in every land." Leaving Russia after the Revolution (independently wealthy because he'd "invested heavily in American securities,") he traveled the world hunting . . . and finally grew bored. Needing "a new animal to hunt," he settled on Ship Trap island in the Caribbean where he hunted those unfortunate humans whom the "blood-warm" waters washed ashore. (Deceptive lights, which indicated a channel where there was none, caused numerous shipwrecks and supplied the General with his victims.) Zaroff lived in a "palatial chateau" on a high bluff, where he trained his captives in the rules of the "game," before setting them loose, armed with only a knife and a three hours' start. Zaroff pursued his human prey with dogs and a pistol "of the smallest calibre and range"; if they eluded him for three days, they went free, carried by Zaroff's sloop to the mainland. Those who refused to participate were turned over to Zaroff's aide, the deaf and dumb Cossack, Ivan, who was permitted to have his way with them. Ivan perished in a trap set by shipwrecked hunter Sanger Rainsford, who not only eluded Zaroff for three days but also turned the tables and, surprising him in his bedroom, took Zaroff's life—implicitly, by hunting him down and feeding him to his own hounds.

Quote: "The weak of the world were put here to give the strong pleasure."

Comment: Leslie Banks played the part in the definitive 1932 motion picture (filmed on jungle sets which served as King Kong's home the following year). Edgar Barrier played the madman in *A Game of Death* (1946)—a head wound, not boredom, was what turned this Zaroff into a lunatic—and Trevor Howard starred as the killer in *Run for the Sun* (1956).

GENERAL ZOD (also known as GENERAL DRU-ZOD) (C, MP)

First Appearance: 1961, *Adventure Comics* #283, DC Comics.

Costume: Purple cap, military uniform with white "sun" emblem over heart; brown boots, gloves. (Note: In the movies, he wears an exotic leather outfit with a deep V-neck.)

Biography: A scientist and officer in the defense corps, Zod is also the director of the space program on the planet Krypton until disaster strikes. A nuclear missile created by JAX-UR goes astray during a test and explodes on the inhabited moon of Wegthor. The program is discontinued and, feeling that Krypton "would be better off with him as dictator," Zod uses his scientific skills to breed a fighting force of artificial soldiers, all of whom look like him save that they are made of inorganic matter, and have white skin and unnaturally angular features. (These were identical to the Bizarros; see LEX LUTHOR, Biography.) Attempting to overthrow the government, Zod is defeated and sent to the Phantom Zone (see JAX-UR, Biography). When the Phantom Zone is destroyed by a diamond-like entity which has absorbed "a billion-billion" dead minds (1986, *D.C. Comics Presents* #97), Zod is himself drawn into the diamond where he presently resides.

Quote: "Superman—come to Zod and die—! Or we shall tear this planet apart!"

Comment: Zod was also seen in the films *Superman* (1978) and *Superman II* (1980), played by Terence Stamp. In the first film, he, Ursa (Sarah Douglas), and Non (Jack O'Halloran) are banished to the Phantom Zone for having tried to take over the planet Krypton. In the sequel, they are set free when a nuclear bomb explodes in space, shattering the zone. Coming to earth, they conquer the planet in short order and rule until Superman, using Kryptonian technology (a power-sapping ray) manages to subdue them.

THE GENTLEMAN GHOST (C)

Real Name: James Craddock (see Biography).

First Appearance: 1947, *Flash Comics* #88, DC Comics.

Costume: Formal wear, top hat, monocle, cloak, gloves, all white; the human portions of the Gentleman Ghost are entirely invisible.

Weapons: Carries a white walking stick which packs a wallop; occasionally uses flintlock pistol which fires flares and a smokescreen.

Chief Henchmen: Alfie and other thugs.

Biography: During the early years of the nineteenth century, highwayman Craddock was hanged for his crimes. The Gentleman Ghost claims to be the selfsame Craddock, having found himself in the modern era thanks to a tear in time—a trip which saved him from dying on the gallows yet, ironically, left him disembodied. Continuing his thieving ways as the Gentleman Ghost, he eludes capture during a battle with the superhero Hawkman; since that bout, he has been a regular foe of Batman. Whether the villain is actually a ghost or a brilliant illusionist has never been positively determined. Evidence for the latter idea abounds: Batman once found a hologram projector hidden at the scene of one of the Gentleman Ghost's appearances, and at various times the villain has successfully fooled people with a wire-supported costume as well as with multiple-Ghosts, created by employing thugs "hunched over inside the costume to make himself appear headless."

Quote: "This *sulphuric acid* will strip you to the *bone*. But I really wouldn't *worry* about that. I fully expect the *noxious fumes* . . . will *finish* you before you ever *reach* the *vat*!"

THE GHOST (1) (MP)

Real Name: Morton Reagan.

First Appearance: 1941, *Dick Tracy vs. Crime, Inc.*, Republic Pictures.

Costume: Business suit; black gloves, helmet sculpted like a human face which covers the Ghost's entire head and face.

Weapons: Necklace with a disk that makes him invisible.

Biography: Morton is a member of the Council of Eight, a group devoted to ridding Washington, D.C., of crime. Unknown to the other councilmembers, however, Morton wants to destroy them for having caused the death of his mobster brother, "Rackets" Reagan; while he's at it, he also intends to loot and destroy the nation's capital. Thanks to a hi-tech necklace created by an equally unbalanced scientist named Lucifer, the Ghost is able to make himself invisible and uses this talent to achieve his goals. His first crimes are to kill three of the councilmembers, which summons crimebuster Dick Tracy. Tracy arrives just in time to prevent the Ghost from blowing up the harbor in order to steal gold and various scientific devices from cargo holds. Other councilmembers die until Tracy manages to lure the Ghost into a chamber lit by an infrared light bulb. The light shows the Ghost in negative, but at least he's visible; the two tussle, but the wily Ghost flees to a nearby power plant. There, his streak of good luck ends. When he tries to escape across high-tension wires, an alert guard turns on the juice and the invisible Ghost is sizzled to death.

Comments: The character was played by Ralph Morgan in the 15-chapter serial. In motion pictures, Tracy has also battled the terrorists the Spider and his Spider Gant (*Dick Tracy*, 1937), the outlaw family known as the Starks (*Dick Tracy Returns*, 1938), the spy Zarnoff (*Dick Tracy's G-Men*, 1939), the bald-headed Cueball (*Dick Tracy Vs. Cueball*, 1946), and Gruesome (played by Boris Karloff), a master criminal who unleashes a paralytic gas (*Dick Tracy Meets Gruesome*, 1947). See also THE INVISIBLE MAN.

THE GHOST (2) (C)

Real Name: Jenkins (no first name given).

First Appearance: 1942, *Champ Comics* #22, Harvey Comics.

Costume: White robe, hood; skin of hands is painted yellow.

Weapons: Torture chamber (only the rack is used).

Chief Henchman: A bull mastiff, which the White Mask shoots through the head.

Biography: The caretaker of England's old Gloucester Castle, Jenkins comes to the United States when the structure is transported stone-by-stone. The place is supposedly haunted, a legend which Jenkins uses to his advantage to become the Ghost. Familiar with all the secret passageways and hidden compartments in the castle, he comes and goes mysteriously, robbing jewelry from people who come to visit the owner and new occupant, financier John Davenport. Wishing to get his hands on Davenport's own stash of jewels, Jenkins carries Davenport to the castle's torture chamber to wrest the information from him; but the heroic sleuth the White Mask arrives in time to spare Davenport much suffering and to reveal the identity of the decidedly non-supernatural Ghost.

Quote: "He, ha! The jewels will be mine now . . . all mine!"

Comment: This was the character's only appearance.

THE GHOST (3) (C)

Real Name: Alec Rois.

First Appearance: 1966, *Captain Atom* #82, Charlton Comics.

Costume: White bodysuit, gloves (see Weapons), boots, cape, full-head cowl with halo-like headdress.

Weapons: Right glove is teleportation unit, able to transport its wearer anywhere on the planet, or to rob safes of their contents. (In one adventure, the device became melded with his flesh. The Ghost had it covered with skin and he wears it there to this day.)

Biography: Inventing a teleportation machine, scientist Rois decides not to give the device to the world. Having lived friendless and in poverty most of his life, he opts to use it for criminal ends, satisfying himself and paying back society in one deft stroke. As the Ghost, he is able to go anywhere he chooses and quickly becomes a wealthy man. Concerned that the Ghost will eventually turn his talents against the government, U.S. authorities ask the superheroes Captain Atom and Nightshade to try to stop him. After a number of encounters, Atom apparently succeeds in destroying the teleportation device which the Ghost has been wearing in his glove, the super villain disappearing in a holocaust of energy. In truth, he's simply been teleported elsewhere, although the device *was* grafted to his hand in the process. Discovering the lost civilization of Sunuria, he becomes an object of veneration by the women who regard him as a reincarnation of a cruel deity known as the Faceless One. Named ruler of the empire, the Ghost uses it as his new base to attack the world—and Captain Atom. The two are still going at it.

THE GHOST (4) (C)

Real Name: Joost van Straaten.

First Appearance: 1969, *The Silver Surfer* #8, Marvel Comics.

Costume: Red pirate's jacket with yellow trim on sleeves; T-shirt with horizontal orange-and-blue stripes; blue trousers.

Weapons: "Patch" worn over right eye fires a vaporizing "nether blast"; hands are powerful metal claws.

Biography: An honest sea captain (apparently of the early nineteenth century), Joost is corrupted by the demon MEPHISTO and becomes consumed with the desire to find a hidden treasure. Sailing through a storm, he refuses to honor his men's request to turn back. When the ship is sunk, all perish but Joost—who is saved by Mephisto and transformed into the Flying Dutchman, doomed to sail his spectral ship across the seven seas "on a voyage without end." However, after he himself fails to destroy the superhero Silver Surfer, Mephisto plucks Joost and his ship from their appointed rounds and transforms the sailor into the withered Ghost. In this form, he is dispatched to New York on his ghostly, flying vessel to battle the superhero. The Ghost goes willingly; Mephisto promises that if he brings him the Surfer's soul, the sea captain will finally go to his eternal rest. The two battle fiercely in the streets and skies, the Surfer ultimately triumphing when he hits the Ghost with an enormous blast of cosmic power, a shock which knocks some sense into Joost's head. "Not even I am beyond redemption," he moans, and refuses to serve Mephisto. When the Surfer hears this, he sheds a tear and Joost is freed, as "a tear of forgiveness can free a lost soul from the bondage of limbo!" (#9).

Quote: "Send me the *Silver Surfer*! Bring him forth . . . or your city *crumbles*!"

Comment: According to legend, the original Flying Dutchman was an old Dutch captain who vowed he'd round the Cape of Good Hope, South Africa, if it took forever. The capricious fates heard his oath, and granted his wish; however, he must sail on until he finds a woman willing to become his wife and sacrifice all for his sake. Sighting him is regarded as an omen of bad luck.

GHRON (N)

First Appearance: 1930, "A Fighting Man of Mars," *Blue Book* Magazine, Edgar Rice Burroughs.

Weapons: Two principal implements of torture: a grill-on-wheels which is moved to or from a fire to toast a victim, and bone-breaking devices to create "abnormal deformities."

Biography: Ghron is the jed (king) of Ghasta, a small (100 free people, roughly 500 slaves) walled city built in the crater of a dormant Martian volcano. There, Ghron's chief pleasure is torture; he views himself as something of a sculptor whose art is the deforming of bodies. Ghron's face is not revealed in the tale. "Massively built," with heavy shoulders and long arms, he has a face so broad that his eyes seem set in the corners of his face. When he tries to smile, he only looks "more horrible than before."

Comment: The novel was originally serialized in *Blue Book* Magazine from April to September 1930. The book edition was published in 1931.

THE GOLDEN FUHRER (C)

First Appearance: 1975, *The Scorpion* #3, Atlas Comics.

Costume: Golden full-face helmet with human features; green jacket with red fringe; green trousers; khaki gloves; red armband with black swastika in white circle.

Chief Henchmen: Stormtroopers with khaki uniforms and green cowls.

Biography: Little is known of the villain's past, save that he was a Nazi officer in Prague in 1941. There he was apparently maimed by the Golem, a clay monster built and brought to life by Rabbi Akibah. Making his way to the United States, the Golden Fuhrer is ensconced in "the deepest sub-basement" of the World Trade Center in Manhattan, "where America's only atomic powered sewage-to-energy converter is housed." Devoted to establishing the Fourth Reich and ruling the world, the maniac kidnaps Akibah and orders him to reanimate "the organically preserved bodies" of the leaders of the Third Reich. However, the rabbi's stone monster the Golem lumbers to the Nazi's headquarters, along with the superhero the Scorpion. The clay giant hurls the Golden Fuhrer against a wall with a resounding "splat" then unleashes a flood of sewage which engulfs the villain and his henchmen, presumably drowning them all.

Quote: "Listen, old man! If you want your *daughter's body* to *stay* in *working* condition, you'd better *start cooperating*!"

THE GOLDEN FUHRER. *© Atlas Comics.*

Comment: This was the character's only appearance. See other Nazi super villains BARON BLITZKRIEG, BARON GESTAPO, BARON ZEMO, CAPTAIN AXIS, CAPTAIN NAZI, THE CLOWN, KILLER SHARK, NIGHT AND FOG, The Masked Swastika of VENDETTA, Mastermind (see U-MAN, Comment), THE RED PANZER, THE RED SKULL, and ZYKLON.

THE GOLDEN GLIDER (C)

Real Name: Lisa Snart (Professional Name: Lisa Star).

First Appearance: 1977, *The Flash* #250, DC Comics.

Costume: Golden skater's outfit, boots, domino mask.

Weapons: Skates which allow her to skate on air. Jewels which can do several things: hypnotize and generate illusions; expand and, attracted to people by their body-heat, batter them to a pulp; create impenetrable barriers; cause people to become super-heavy; teleport; and destroy objects with rays and acid.

Biography: A professional skater, Lisa becomes even better after she meets Roscoe Dillon, aka the villainous THE TOP. He teaches her how to improve her axels, and the two fall in love. When the Top is inadvertently killed by the superheroic Flash, Lisa becomes the Golden Glider and, using equipment left her by the Top and by her own villainous brother, CAPTAIN COLD, she devotes her life to causing the Flash misery. Among her most spectacular crimes have been trying to murder Flash's wife Iris and trying to help the Top's spirit possess the body of the Flash.

Quote: "*The Golden Glider* will make *Flash* rue the day he first put on his *running boots*!"

GOLDFACE (C)

Real Name: Keith Kenyon.

First Appearance: 1964, *Green Lantern* #28, DC Comics.

Costume: Gold T-shirt with gold designs on chest; gold tights, trunks, gloves, boots, and helmet (see Weapons). Skin is also gold.

Weapons: Gold sportscar designed to resemble Fort Knox; helmet which serves as a "releasing device" for his power, allowing him to will gold to take any form he wishes—from an encasement for people to a huge impenetrable barrier to bright, golden light that can fill a place. (He pretends to do these things with a sleek blue gun he carries, covering the fact that it's a spark from his helmet which is doing the changing.)

Chief Henchmen: Sundry hoodlums dressed in blue tights, gloves, and a helmet, red boots, trunks, bodyshirt and a jerkin.

Biography: Using gold that "has been immersed in sea water for over 100 years," Kenyon creates a potion which fills him with "auric energy," making him invulnerable. Using his talent to become a crook, he is stopped when the superhero Green Lantern comes up with aqua regia, a gold-dissolving acid, and sprays it on Kenyon. Escaping from prison, Kenyon goes back to the drawingboard and improves his elixir (Green Lantern #48). Not only is the reformulation immune to aqua regia but it also imbues his body "with a super-auric energy," making him invulnerable and able to control gold through his helmet. Wresting away the head-piece, Green Lantern is able to turn Kenyon to gold—though the villain returns now and then to menace the intrepid superhero, as well as his colleague the Flash.

Quote: "*Hoo-eeee*! I did it! I turned *Green Lantern* into a statue of solid gold! *Whooo-aaa*! This does my heart good!"

Comment: The character was apparently inspired by the James Bond villain AURIC GOLDFINGER who, at one point, painted a victim gold from stem to stern.

GOLIATH (C)

Real Name: Erik Josten.

First Appearance: 1965, *The Avengers* #21 (as Power Man); 1980, *Peter Parker, the Spectacular Spider-Man* #49 (as the Smuggler); 1984, *Iron Man Annual* #7 (as Goliath), Marvel Comics.

Costume: As Power Man: first: golden long-sleeve shirt; brown trousers, trunks, boots, vest with flared shoulders and red starburst surrounding neck, cowl with red starburst top, belt with golden starburst buckle. Second: golden bodysuit; brown trunks, boots, gloves, belt, cowl. As Smuggler: same as second Power Man. As Goliath: orange bodysuit with brown "Y"-like design on chest, cowl with brown "V"-like design on forehead and top; brown trunks, boots, gloves.

Biography: A soldier-of-fortune working for BARON ZEMO, Erik remains behind in his late boss's Amazon Jungle stronghold. Digging his way into the rubble-covered lab, he is surprised when the villainous ENCHANTRESS teleports over from distant Asgard. Using Zemo's equipment, she endows him with incredible physical power and superior reflexes and sics him on their enemies, the Avengers. He fails to beat the band of superheroes, and is subsequently handed his head by Luke Cage, a superhero who also calls himself Power Man. (As Erik puts it, "We battled for the right to that name. I lost.") Falling in with a succession of super villains—including THE SWORDSMAN, THE RED SKULL, THE MANDARIN, and THE GRIM REAPER—he eventually goes to work for the evil Count Luchino Nefaria, a leader in the Maggia crime organization. Nefaria offers to give him treatments that will boost his power "a thousand fold" but, in fact, the equipment does just the opposite—sapping Power Man's strength for use by Nefaria. The Avengers take on the evil Count while Erik escapes; taking a job as a dockworker, he painstakingly sets up an elaborate black market operation, as the Smuggler, only to see it crushed by Spider-Man. Later, while serving a prison sentence in Ryker's Island, he hears of a scientist named Karl Malus; they correspond and, upon his release, Erik seeks him out. (Malus had managed to obtain the growth serum invented by Henry Pym—who had used the formula to turn himself into both the diminutive but superheroic Ant-Man and the towering Giant-Man.) Malus gives Erik both the serum and a dose of Zemo-like rays. As a result, he can will himself to become some four stories tall, with the power to throw a bus like a football. Sadly—for him—after growing to a monstrous 200 feet tall, he collapses; "his rage . . . pushed (him) too far," his body unable to take "that kind of punishment without some reaction." At present, Goliath is in prison.

Quote: "The mighty *Avengers*! What a laugh! When I'm through with you, you'll be ashamed to show your faces in public. That is, if you're still *able* to!"

GOODY TWO-SHOES (C)

First Appearance: 1983, *The Thing* #7, Marvel Comics.

Costume: Red overalls; blue shirt; white socks; dark blue boots (see Weapons).

Weapons: Atomic Boots which enable him to stomp enormous holes in solid bedrock, leap mighty distances, or kick objects with "the force of a Howitzer shell."

Biography: A young Swedish inventor, Goody comes to the United States hoping to sell the rights to his boots to one company or another. Instead, he is told "he unvelcome, he illegal alien." Irked beyond words, he begins robbing banks until he runs into the superheroic Thing. After the two have a titanic battle which rages from the streets to the top of the Empire State Building, Goody is belted hard into a brick wall and goes down for the count.

Quote: "I knowed my *atomic boots* vas more than a match for any super-hero in the *New York*. Dis vere Goody takes over the town!"

Comment: In a bizarre postscript to the character's only appearance, the Thing is shown reading the comic book and complaining that the encounter as published was "embroidered," that he literally knocked Goody out of his shoes with a single small smack.

GORGAN (TV, N)

First Appearance: October 11, 1968, "And the Children Shall Lead," *Star Trek*, NBC-TV.

Costume: Silver cloak and hair; entire being is shrouded in greenish aura.

Biography: Gorgan was the last native of the world of Triacus. Holing up in a cave, he is discovered countless centuries later (in the twenty-third century) by settlers from the Federation. With his extraordinary mental powers, he intends to conquer the universe, to which end he requires a starship. Winning the loyalty of the colonists' children by passing himself off as a "friendly angel," he begins taking over their parents' minds. The adults kill themselves rather than submit, though their sacrifice comes too late to stop the starship *Enterprise* from being summoned. The vessel picks up the children, who have the power to invoke Gorgan as need be to further their plans of conquest. ("Hail, hail, fire and snow,/Call the angel, we will go,/Far away, far to see,/Friendly angel, come to me.") Fortunately, Captain Kirk is able to show the children that Gorgan is evil by demonstrating, through home movies, how loving their parents were; shown to be a hideously eroded being and not the cherubic figure he'd presented to the children, Gorgan loses their faith and perishes.

Quote: "A million friends from Marcos Twelve will make us invincible. We can do anything we wish in the whole universe!"

Comment: Attorney Melvin Belli played the character in this, his only appearance. The teleplay was written by Edward J. Lakso; the episode was adapted to short story form by James Blish and published in the anthology *Star Trek 12*.

THE GORILLA BOSS (C)

Real Name: George "Boss" Dyke.

First Appearance: 1953, *Batman* #75, DC Comics.

Chief Henchmen: Horton and Gopher.

Biography: A criminal who "always ignored any loot under a thousand dollars (as) his way of showing contempt for small-time jobs," Dyke is finally captured, tried, and executed in the gas chamber. However, as per his last request, the criminal's body is turned over to a scientist known as "Doc" who places Dyke's brain into the body of a towering gorilla. ("Now," says Doc, "one of the world's shrewdest criminal minds is in the body of this mammoth brute!") Just how shrewd becomes clear when the titan begins robbing, then orders his brain placed in the body of the superheroic Batman, and Batman's brain lodged in the skull of the ape. That way, he can spend the money as Batman while the police shoot the gorilla. But the superhero foils the scheme, and the Dyke/ape hybrid plunges to its death from the radio mast of a skyscraper. In his ape form, Dyke is able to communicate only through handwritten messages. For the record, the Gorilla Boss is left-handed.

Comment: This simian appeared just once. Batman also fought The Gorilla Gang in #156, 1963—a group of ape-suited crooks. See also GORILLA GRODD, MANDRILL, MAN-APE, and THE MOD GORILLA.

GORILLA GRODD (C)

Real Name: Drew Drowden; later, William Dawson (see Biography).

First Appearance: 1959, *The Flash* #106, DC Comics.

Biography: Grodd is a denizen of Gorilla City, a metropolis inhabited by brilliant, telepathic, unusually powerful gorillas and located near the equator in Africa. (It is "invisibly-shrouded" to prevent discovery by humans although, late in the series, the apes open a "gorilla embassy" in New York staffed by the apes who represent them in the United Nations.) "Super-evolved," the simians are ruled by the benign Solovar, whose reign is constantly being challenged by Grodd. A scientific genius, Grodd yearns to conquer not only Gorilla City but also the world. To this end, he rebels against Solovar but is bested by the human superhero the Flash; using an evolution machine, Grodd becomes a human and, calling himself Drew Drowden, ventures forth from the simian city. Once more stymied by the Flash and sent to prison in Gorilla City, Grodd commits suicide and sends his spirit into the body of William Dawson, a body which Grodd subsequently transforms into an identical copy of his old ape physique. He continues to battle the Flash in and out of Gorilla City until the superhero's death in 1985; he has also served with THE SECRET SOCIETY OF SUPER-VILLAINS.

Quote: "You may have won this battle, speedster—but the *war* between us is far from *over*!"

Comment: See other simian villains GORILLA BOSS, MANDRILL, MAN-APE, and THE MOD GORILLA.

GOTHEL (F)

First Appearance: 1812, "Rapunzel," the Brothers Grimm.

Biography: To satisfy his pregnant wife's cravings, a man steals rapunzel plants from the garden of his neighbor, the witch Gothel. Caught, he is permitted to leave on the condition that he turns their child over to the witch, which he does. Taking the beautiful baby girl Rapunzel, Gothel waits until she is 12 years old, then hides her "in a tower in the midst of a wood." There is no entrance to this tower save for a window. When Gothel wishes to enter, Rapunzel lowers her long hair and the witch would climb "twenty ells" (an "ell" is 45 inches) to the top. When a king's son happens upon the tower and falls in love with Rapunzel, the witch rages that she's been betrayed; smacking the girl around and cutting off her hair, she abandons her "in a waste and desert place, where she lived in great woe and misery." When next the young prince comes calling, Gothel, disguised as Rapunzel, releases the shorn locks with the prince in mid-climb. Tumbling to the ground, the lad falls on a thorn bush, the prickles putting out his eyes. Gothel's fate is unknown, though the prince, wandering for years, eventually finds Rapunzel; her tears restore his sight and they return to his kingdom, where "they lived long and happily."

Quote: "Aha! You came for your darling, but the sweet bird sits no longer in the nest . . . the cat has got her, and will scratch out your eyes as well!"

Comment: Gena Rowlands played Gothel in the 1985 *Faerie Tale Theatre* cable-TV presentation of the story. Other Grimm witches include the "wicked witch" who ate children in "Hansel and Gretel"; the "witch" of "Sweetheart Roland" who lopped off her daughter's head with an axe (an accident: she meant to kill her stepdaughter), then died when her stepdaughter's lover played a magic tune and she danced herself to death; the murderous witch of "The White Bride and the Black Bride" who, after trying to kill her sweet stepdaughter so her daughter can take her place as the king's bride, is "stripped naked, and put into a barrel with nails," and dragged by a horse "all over the world"; the witch who was burned in "Brother and Sister" for suffocating a queen and trying to pass off her daughter as the monarch (the daughter was fed to wild beasts); the "aged Queen, a sorceress" who, in "The Six Servants," used her daughter's beauty to lure men to their death; the witch who for years keeps a prince locked in "The Iron Stove"; and the crone with "a fiery head," who turned a girl into a block of wood and used her for kindling in "The Old Witch." See other Grimm villains MERCURIUS, THE QUEEN, and THE ROBBER BRIDEGROOM.

THE GRAPPLER (C)

First Appearance: 1981, *The Savage She-Hulk* #18, Marvel Comics.

Costume: Yellow bodysuit, cowl with purple goggles; purple trunks, cape, gloves, boots, belt.

Weapons: "Radio-controlled Grappler airplane" which lowers the Grappler by cable to the sites of his crimes; "computer-pac" which analyzes and provides "the exact spot and proper amount of leverage" he needs to lift or overturn an object; he does the actual moving with a nearly six-feet-long "titanium steel rod." The rod also contains a "tightly wound band of steel coils" which, when ejected, immediately strangle whomever they ensnare.

Biography: Growing up in a ghetto, the future Grappler (his name has not been revealed) survived simply because he was able to beat up any bully, no matter what his size. But that didn't put food on the table, so, traveling to Las Vegas, he waited for billionaire Hugh Howard to appear. When he emerged from one of his casinos, the impoverished fellow ran over and begged him to reveal the secret of his success. Howard replied, "leverage," and the young man took it to heart. Though "the rich geezer meant financial leverage," the ambitious youth studied martial arts, competed in championship matches, and used the money he earned to study finance and science both. Becoming the Grappler (and apparently having invented his own weapons), he embarked on a series of robberies. Unfortunately, the superheroic She-Hulk interfered and, wrapping him up in his own rod, trotted him off to jail. He was subsequently slain by the vigilante Scourge, brother of THE ENFORCER (2).

Quote: "So! I see that I'm going to have to beat you to a pulp after all!"

GRAVITON (C)

Real Name: Franklin Hall.

First Appearance: 1977, *The Avengers* #158, Marvel Comics.

Costume: Blue bodysuit with six purple ovals from neck to crotch; white trunks which end in a sloping pyramid above the waist; white gloves with three purple ovals; white boots, cloak.

Biography: A Canadian employed by a hi-tech firm in the Rockies, Hall was working on a teleportation machine when it exploded. His body was laced with graviton particles, with the result that he became a master of gravity, able to make people or objects (and any fragments thereof) super-light or -heavy, or increase the gravitational pull of matter. With the power, now, to sate his monstrous ego, he took over the laboratory in grand style, sending it nearly a mile in the air. Battling the superheroic Avengers, he literally sucked up the matter of the lab and became a giant with incredible strength. Beaten and reduced to normal size, he returned—and was defeated by the god Thor and sent to an "interdimensional void" (*Thor* #324). Escaping due to "a sudden influx of energy," he tackled the Avengers once again, helped by THE BLANK (*West Coast Avengers* #'s 2-4), only to be gassed unconscious and arrested.

Quote: "Revenge is much more satisfying when you can actually witness your enemy's demise!"

THE GREAT DARTFACE (C)

First Appearance: 1965, *Mighty Mouse* #163, Gold Key Comics.

Costume: None; the lunarian has a red body, sharp claws, a tusk-like nose, and a plume of yellow hair.

Biography: The Great Dartface is the fourteenth ruler of the Dart Men of the Moon. Standing only a few inches tall, he is able to leap vast distances, presumably due to the moon's low gravity. When the villainous cat Professor Ohm reaches the moon and announces that Mighty Mouse will be arriving shortly with his own expedition, the Great Dartface presumes they have come to challenge him . . . and rises to the occasion. He traps the non-super mice, ties them to bull's-eyes, and orders his subjects to skewer them between the eyes; meanwhile, he snares Mighty Mouse in an unbreakable net of moon metal. But the super-powered rodent drags his captors (the Great Dartface among them) into the exhaust of a rocket, stunning them; then he captures Ohm and returns him to earth "for a good beating." The Great Dartface speaks both the lunar language and English.

Quote: "Og spillot okee." ("Bring them here alive!")

Comment: This was the character's only appearance. See also the space tyrant MING THE MERCILESS.

THE GREAT DARTFACE. © Western Publishing.

THE GREEN BANANA (C)

First Appearance: 1982, *The Mad Book of Almost Superheroes*, Don Edwing.
Costume: Black domino mask.
Weapons: Handgun.
Biography: Nothing is known about this circa five-feet-tall banana, whose plan is "to transform the entire city of Sacramento into slaves by injecting them with home-made banana dacquiris and changing them into one of the bunch." The superheroic Fat Bat is called in to foil the scheme; he apparently succeeded, though when last seen he had smashed hard into an apartment building window without apprehending the villain.
Comment: This was the character's only appearance. Other villains in this parody book include the Purple Pothole Gang; Bruce Branflakes, who becomes the powerful, green, eight-feet-tall Macho Hunk whenever he hears the word "the" or the expression "Hey, Shorty!"; Foo Woman Choo, who turns dogs into bionic fire hydrants; the hardened Beetle Bail-Jumper who's so tough that he once stuffed his mattress down a guard's throat; Doctor Gagman and a bagful of practical jokes which he plays on superheroes; the "twisted scientist" Professor J.P. Skunkbreath, who builds an "oil-sucking bionic robot (to) gain control of the entire U.S.A. economy"; Dr. Detour, who wants to turn everyone in Walla Walla into flagmen; Mr. Lubejob; the Wart, a "demented, retired truant officer" who robs money from schools; Dr. Froglips, who plans to turn people into anchovies (he succeeds in making them french fries, instead); Professor Beerbelly, "the Napoleon of Crime"; the Over-Forty Bad Guy League, "who kidnap parents and let dogs retch on their floors"; Professor Disgusting, "the diabolically ugly arch villain" who packs a duplicating ray; and the Hitman, who turned to crime because of an uncanny resemblance to Humphrey Bogart.

The Fat Bat closes in on ***THE GREEN BANANA****. © Don Edwing and E.C. Publications.*

THE GREEN GOBLIN (C)

Real Name: Original: Norman Osborn. Second: Harold Osborn. Third: Barton Hamilton.
First Appearance: 1964, *The Amazing Spider-Man* #14 (as Norman); 1973, *The Amazing Spider-Man* #126 (as Harry; this issue is when he decides to continue the family tradition; Harry first appeared in issue #31, and didn't actually don the costume until #136); 1978, *The Amazing Spider-Man* #176 (as Hamilton, though Hamilton had first appeared in #151), Marvel Comics.
Costume: Scaly green bodysuit, grimacing goblin mask; purple leotard, gloves, boots, pointed cap.
Weapons: "Jetpowered Goblin glider" for vertical and horizontal flight; destructive "Goblin sparks" which crackle from gloves when activated by a button on the villain's belt; "Goblin surprise," a ghost-like bomb which forms an "air-tight cloud seal" to smother people or fires; various chemical concoctions, including one which can change people "into ugly little green creatures"; a "ghost," an entangling sheet made of unbreakable plastic; an "electro-bat" shocking device; and pumpkin-head "Goblin grenades, which include stun bombs, blinding flares, concussion bombs, smokescreens, laughing gas, and liquid-nitrogen for freezing objects to 200 degrees below zero (all bombs are carried in a purple shoulderbag called his "bag of tricks").

Biography: The head of the Osborn Chemical Factory, a firm which manufactures everything from chemicals to automated machinery, Norman is a money-mad entrepreneur who goes so far as to have his partner, Professor Mendel Stromm, arrested on trumped-up charges of embezzlement. Appropriating all of Stromm's research material, Norman finds notes for a compound intended to boost a person's strength and intelligence; when Norman mixes the formula it explodes, sending him to the hospital. While recovering, he realizes that the chemical has indeed boosted his IQ. Unfortunately, it has also rendered him quite mad. Upon his release, Norman uses his boosted brain to build a small arsenal and become the Green Goblin. His goal is to become crimelord of the world, and to this end he intends to make his mark by killing the superhero Spider-Man. After years of conflict—during which time Norman returns to normal twice, only to have the Goblin resurface—the villain dies, skewered through the heart by his glider (#122). Watching the struggle, Norman's son Harry snatches his father's costume when no one is looking. Already marginally insane due to drugs he's been taking, Harry is pushed over the edge by Norman's death and, filled with hatred for Spider-Man, continues the family tradition by becoming the new Green Goblin. His reign is a brief one, however. Snared by the webslinging hero (#137), Harry is turned over to psychiatrist Barton Hamilton, who nurses the young man back to normal and even induces amnesia covering his career as the super villain. But, intrigued by what he's learned about the Goblin's paraphernalia, Hamilton becomes the villain himself. Suffering a flashback (issue #180), Harry briefly dons the costume again and, outraged by what Hamilton has done, takes on the psychiatrist in a battle of the Goblins. The fight ends in an explosion set by Hamilton. Spider-Man saves Harry, though the blast again robs him of all recollection of his criminal past; Hamilton isn't so lucky, as the detonation kills him. However, the accoutrements of the Green Goblin live on, slightly transmogrified, in Spider-Man's foe THE HOBGOBLIN.

Quote: "*Spider-Man*! I've been *waiting* for you!! I *knew* if I flew around the city, you'd be sure to investigate sooner or later!"

Comment: The villain was also seen in the 1983 Parker Brothers Spider-Man videogame trying to keep the hero from defusing a bomb.

THE GREY GARGOYLE (C)

Real Name: Paul Pierre Duval.

First Appearance: 1965, *Journey Into Mystery* #105, Marvel Comics.

Costume: Gray cape with high collar, domino mask, trunks, belt (skin, made of stone, is also gray); blue gloves, boots (both of which insulate Duval's power, protecting people and objects he does not wish to transform).

Chief Henchmen: The Grey Gargoyle was, for a time, commander of the pirate spaceship *Bird of Prey*, whose crewmembers from various worlds gladly served him.

Biography: A chemist working for a drug company in Paris, Duval inadvertently upset a formula on his right hand, the hand promptly turning to stone. Duval quickly discovered that anything he touched did likewise. Opting to use his power to commit crimes, he christened himself the Grey Gargoyle (after the stone waterspouts, prominent on cathedrals, which end in grotesque faces) and looted the French capital. Coming to the United States, he was not nearly as successful due to repeated interference from the Norse god Thor. During an attempt to place weapons in earth orbit, the Grey Gargoyle was accidentally stranded there; he was recovered by the *Bird of Prey*, and briefly served as captain of the pirate vessel. Following that stint, he returned to earth and was beaten by the superheroic Avengers; he is presently in prison, drugged so that he can't use his powers to escape.

THE GRIFFIN (C)

Real Name: Johnny Horton.

First Appearance: 1973, *Amazing Adventures* #15, Marvel Comics.

Costume: Red bodysuit, mask worn around face to keep mane back; golden trunks, belt. The Griffin's flesh is white.

Weapons: Griffin has a long, spiked tail poking from his trunks; powerful, feathered brown wings on his back; and claws on his hands and feet.

Biography: "Just another dime-a-dozen punk," Horton had something the criminal Secret Empire wanted—"big fists and a small brain." Promising him great power, they subjected him to surgery which grafted eagle-like wings and claws onto his body and caused him to grow a leonine face and mane. Feeling ripped-off, and going mad from a serum he'd been given, Horton murdered the doctor who performed the surgery; but the changes kept coming, as the serum also granted Horton superstrength, caused him to grow a tail and gave him the power to control all flying animals. Despite his dander, he worked for the Secret Empire until the group folded. Arrested, he escaped from prison and became a solo operator. His principal adversary was Spider-Man (*Marvel Team-Up* #'s 38 and 78, 1975 and 1978); he died during the latter encounter, burned to death in the crash of an Avengers hovercraft.

Quote: "I can smell your fear . . . you *stink* of it!"

GRIMBOR (also known as THE CHAINSMAN) (C)

First Appearance: 1976, *Superboy* #221, DC Comics.

Costume: Blue leotard ending at chest with straps over shoulders; brown boots, wristbands.

Weapons: Countless types of chains and bonds including a "rocket-powered chain" which has a small jet engine at the tip and can be directed to wrap the powerful lariat around virtually anything; a "thermanacle," a snare which is triggered solely by the victim's body heat; a huge arrow with a muzzle on the end, able to latch onto a person's face and immediately render him unconscious; "heavily-weighted" bolo chains which wrap around people and render them immobile; "power chains" which can hold even superheroes; and, most incredible of all, a battery of satellites in earth orbit which unite by energy beams and form impenetrable bands of "light-chains" around the planet, huge links which constrict moment by moment to destroy the planet. Grimbor also commands a spaceship with a magnetic beam to attract metal, and another ray which causes rapid plant growth.

Chief Henchmen: Numerous, nameless thugs.

Biography: A locksmith and chainmaker of the late thirtieth century, Grimbor had the great misfortune to meet a young woman named Charma, an orphan who changed his life. A mutant, she had a power she couldn't control—the ability to make men love and protect her, and women hate and want to demolish her. Summoned to the orphanage where she lived, Grimbor fell under her spell and agreed to help her in an outrageous criminal scheme—to capture the Legion of Super-Heroes and hold them for ransom. The plan failed, and the couple was sent to prison. There, Charma's powers caused the other female inmates to murder her. Blaming the Legion, Grimbor settled into a huge castle at the North Pole and vowed to avenge her death by destroying the superheroes. Along these lines, his most ambitious scheme was encircling the earth with his "light chains" and refusing to disperse them unless he was named dictator of the earth, with the Legion placed at his "personal disposal." After a three-issue battle (*The Legion of Super-Heroes* #'s 277-79), he is defeated when Superboy gets close enough to deck him.

Quote: "Don't call me '*madman*,' councillor—not if you value your worthless *life*!"

GRIM REAPER (C)

Real Name: Eric Williams.

First Appearance: 1968, *The Avengers* #52, Marvel Comics.

Costume: Blue bodysuit with white skull and crossbones on chest; blue trunks, boots, left glove, cowl with "L"-shaped horns on side, "I"-shaped horns beneath them; purple cape.

Weapons: Scythe attached to right hand has a variety of weapons; apart from the lethal blade, it contains a blaster, a sleep-inducing gas dispenser, and a motor which turns the blade into a personal helicopter rotor-cum-whirring sawblade. The scythe was built by THE TINKERER.

Biography: The son of Sanford Williams, head of the munitions firm of Williams Innovations, the irresponsible Eric lost a fortune gambling before he joined the company—to embezzle. Upon Sanford's death, Eric's younger brother Simon ran the company as best he could, though it lost ground to its competitors—most notably Stark Industries, owned by Tony Stark, aka the superhero Iron Man—in large part due to a loss of credibility in the marketplace caused by Eric's illicit activities. Angry at Stark, Simon fell in with the villainous MASTERS OF EVIL who turned him into the super-powerful Wonder Man and offered him a means of striking back. When Simon apparently died battling Iron Man and his teammates in the Avengers (he didn't, and later reformed and became a superhero), Eric was embittered and just a tad guilty. Eric sought vengeance. Getting in touch with THE TINKERER, he had the gadget-master build him his scythe and so became the villainous Grim Reaper. During a confrontation with Wonder Man and the superheroic Vision, the Grim Reaper fell from a cliff and died; resurrected by NEKRA, he resumed his life of crime with no recollection of his demise—a precondition to his remaining "alive." Eventually learning that he was a bloodless zombie, the Grim Reaper immediately dropped dead.

THE GRINDER (C)

Real Name: Brute Bashby.

First Appearance: 1980, *Spider-Woman* #26, Marvel Comics.

Costume: Red bodysuit; green trunks, gloves, boots; orange cowl; blue belt.

Weapons: "Titanium grinder," a blade whirring horizontally from a tank on his back—held on by a strap around his chest—and allowing him to cut through metal and to fly. It also fires a spare "grinder wheel," which spins out like a buzzsaw blade.

Biography: A criminal, Bashby is hired by newspaper publisher Rupert M. Dockery to execute a series of crimes—and always inform the paper before he sets out. Dockery hopes that the exclusive coverage of the crimes will boost sagging sales of the newly acquired Los Angeles *Courier.* To make things even more spectacular, Dockery provides Bashby with his incredible Grinder suit. Bashby gets things off promisingly enough by robbing an antique coin exhibit. However, the superhero Spider-Woman shows up and, when the thief fires his "grinder wheel" at her, she scoops it up and uses it to disable his main blade. The Grinder crashes to the ground and is arrested; he has not surfaced since. As for Dockery, he gets away scot-free.

Quote: "I kinda figured you'd be stupid enough to try and follow me, Spider-Chickie!"

Comment: Daredevil's foe the Gladiator is also equipped with whirring blades, worn on his wrists.

GROOD (MP)

First Appearance: 1947, *Jack Armstrong,* Columbia Pictures.

Biography: Based on a remote island, the super-scientist Grood is experimenting with a means of tapping cosmic radiation to conquer the world. The felon's plans are thwarted by heroic Jack Armstrong, "the All-American Boy," who kills Grood with a hand grenade when he tries to flee the island by air.

Comment: Charles Middleton played Grood in the 15-chapter serial; Middleton also played the movie super villains #39013 and MING THE MERCILESS.

GRUMEDAN (F)

First Appearance: The seventeenth-century French folktale "La Princesse Pimprenella et Le Prince Romavin."

Costume: A cloak; for his wedding he wears "a huge bag-purse and a cravat tied in a bow, his mantle . . . of a shower of silver coins with a lining of rose color."

Weapons: Magic whistle, which can control animals; a huge, non-magic club.

Biography: Grumedan was one of "the most unjust and churlish of all the enchanters" in France. Little is known about his past, save that he was punished "often" by the Fairy Queen for his "ill-deeds." Locked inside a tree, he was freed when it blew down in a storm; imprisoned beneath a big stone on the riverbottom, he escaped when a strong current overturned the rock. He was on relatively good behavior afterwards, being threatened with "a thousand years of captivity (for) the smallest impertinence." However, he fell in love with the Princess Potentilla and, when he couldn't win her by charm, got her to agree to a wedding by threatening her parents. For forcing his affection on the poor girl, Grumedan was captured at his wedding by the fairy Melinette, who locked him inside a crystal ball which she hung from the ceiling of a great hall in the palace. "Big and clumsy," Grumedan "had but one eye, and his teeth were long, and he stammered badly." Among his powers were the abilities to make gold and to become invisible. He also wrote a five-hour-long opera dedicated to Potentilla, which he has had performed for her by 10,000 frogs.

Quote: "I am an extremely well-connected Enchanter; my power is immense. I really do not care whether you consent to my marriage with your daughter or not, but I am bound to ask your consent."

Comment: The folktale was first published in English by Andrew Lang as "Prince Narcissus and the Princess Potentilla," in *The Green Fairy Book.*

THE GUARDSMAN (C)

Real Name: Kevin O'Brien (was spelled "O'Brian" for several issues), then Michael O'Brien.

First Appearance: 1970, *Iron Man* #31 (as Kevin); 1971, #43 (as Guardsman); 1976, #82 (as Michael); 1977, #97 (as Guardsman), Marvel Comics.

Costume: Armor (see Weapons) consists of light green bodysuit; darker green boots, gloves, armbands, trunks, chest and neck; green helmet with light green sides.

Weapons: Exoskeletonic armor gives the wearer superstrength and protects against extremes in temperature; jet-boots allow for flight; gloves fire repulsor rays.

Biography: A devoted engineer working for industrialist Tony Stark, Kevin is entrusted with the top secret information that Stark is in reality, the superheroic Iron Man. What's more, Stark manufactures a suit of armor for Kevin similar to his own (for use only in an emergency). However, donning the suit before it's been tested, Kevin gets a shock; the suit's cybernetic controls affect his brain, inflaming those areas which control anger and envy. Turning against his employer, he does battle with Iron Man and is killed when he hides behind a new military vehicle—and the superhero inadvertantly ignites its fuel tank with his repulsor rays (#46). Several months afterward, Kevin's brother Michael, a New York police sergeant, takes it upon himself to make sure that Iron Man never hurts anyone again. Sneaking into the Stark plant on Long Island where the Guardsman armor is stored, he slips it on and is immediately overcome by the same malfunction which had affected Kevin. Thus, instead of merely hauling Iron Man into jail he now wants to demolish him. Defeating Michael, Stark patiently explains that what happened to Kevin was an accident; without the faulty armor twisting his mind, Michael is able to listen to reason. After several adventures in which he serves beside Iron Man, Michael and his Guardsman outfit go to work for the government's top secret energy program, Project Pegasus.

Quote: Michael: "You're going to pay for the *murder* you committed, tin man!"

GYPSY MOTH (C)

Real Name: Sybil Dvorak.

First Appearance: 1978, *Spider-Woman* #10, Marvel Comics.

Costume: Black bodysuit; gold leotard, thigh boots, gloves, cowl with antenna; gossamer yellow wings growing from her back (apparently willed to grow, it's purely decorative).

Biography: A mutant raised by Gypsies, Dvorak has the power of telekinesis, the ability to move objects with her mind as well as levitate herself (except for metal, which is "too cold, too hard to my mental touch"). As a young woman, she met and fell in love with American actor Jason Reed, who was filming *Dracula* in Rumania. She returned to the United States with him and lived at his mansion; however, Reed was rarely home (she believed he was visiting other lovers) and, barely understanding the language, Dvorak grew exceedingly sad and lonely. Making herself a costume and flying over Hollywood for diversion, she grew jealous of the many people she saw having good times below. Thus, she began tormenting the locals with her powers, mentally unravelling their clothes or else causing the duds to constrict "like things alive." After an encounter with Spider-Woman, and Reed's death from a clogged blood vessel in his heart, Dvorak used the money she inherited from the actor to found a cult dedicated to moral corruption.

Quote: "I have no *use* for friends!"

HAMMER AND ANVIL (C)

Real Name: "Hammer" Jackson and Johnny Anvil.
First Appearance: 1975, *The Incredible Hulk* #182, Marvel Comics.
Costume: Anvil: blue bodysuit with deep "V" neck and white midriff; white trunks, boots. Hammer: white bodysuit with "V" neck and blue midriff; blue trunks, boots. Both men wear red belts.
Weapons: Approximately 20 feet of golden chain binds them and endows them with superstrength, thanks to its ability to "absorb any and all forms of kinetic energy." Its only drawback is that whatever harms one also hurts the other.
Biography: Coming to earth from the planet Glxx in the Zpist star system of the Milky Way, the alien Chleee is unwittingly saved from death by criminals Jackson and Anvil. To repay them for their "kindness," the extraterrestrial takes the ordinary chain which binds them and, turning it into a golden "energy synthecon" (also written "synthicon"), endows them with superpowers. Not only are they extremely strong as long as they're bound by the chain, but also each has the ability to crack the chain like a whip, snapping the other with piledriver force into most any kind of wall—shattering it—or adversary. Free-lance thugs, they were pounded by the Hulk and by Spider-Woman (*Spider-Woman* #34, 1980) before being murdered by the vigilante Scourge, brother of THE ENFORCER (2).
Quote: "You *talk* a big fight, Spidey-mama. But . . . take a hint, bug-babe. Against us—you're *way* outta your league!"

HAMMERHEAD (C)

First Appearance: 1972, *The Amazing Spider-Man* #113 (though he was alluded to in #112), Marvel Comics.
Weapons: Standard gangland weapons.
Chief Henchmen: Bennie, Waldol, Porky, Ernie, Bert, Jimmy, Harvey, Chuck, Reno, Flakey, others; and Hammerhead's moll, Myrna. (Many gangmembers had acquired rocketpacks by the time of their appearance in issue #130.)
Biography: A small-time crook (his real name is never revealed), Hammerhead is beat up and left for dead one day in New York City's seedy Bowery section. Found by surgeon Dr. Jonas Harrow, the thug is carted to Harrow's laboratory and subjected to a most unusual operation—the smashed top of his skull is replaced by a steel alloy which is virtually indestructible. With no memory of his past save for the last thing he saw before passing out—a poster for an Al Capone film—he decides to become a crime czar. Using his mighty skull to bully his way nearly to the top, Hammerhead must finally remove only one obstacle in order to become the underworld's undisputed leader—his rival, the evil DOCTOR OCTOPUS. The two eventually find themselves on an island in Canada where, during a struggle, Hammerhead inadvertently rams a nuclear reactor, triggering an atomic explosion. Miraculously, both villains survive to continue their battle in subsequent issues. Eventually, the Hammerhead's power reaches such a point that he wins his own Hammerhead Family within the international crime organization, the Maggia.

HANGMAN (C)

Real Name: Harlan Krueger.
First Appearance: 1973, *Werewolf by Night* #11, Marvel Comics.
Costume: Purple tights, leotard with deep "V" neck and mesh front; blue hood, boots, wristbands; yellow belt.
Weapons: Noose at the end of 10 yards of rope; a large scythe.
Biography: A film buff *extraordinaire*, Krueger was especially fond of movie he-men. Hoping to emulate his movie heroes, he joined the army and fought bravely in Europe during World War II. He also spent six years in a military stockade *after* the war for having tortured prisoners of war. After his release, he was crushed when his application to become a police officer was turned down. Deciding that the whole system had become soft and corrupt, he became the costumed vigilante Hangman, murdering

men with his noose and scythe and imprisoning women. (He deemed women fundamentally blameless; they were merely "weak, frail creatures—easy prey for the depraved" men.) By the time he was finally caught, with the help of the heroic Werewolf, he'd killed nearly 40 people (five of his 15 female prisoners had starved in captivity). Cooling his heels in a mental institution, he realized his initial schedule was too ambitious. Therefore, he decided to concentrate solely on filmmakers for failing to create the kinds of heroes he'd known as a youth, ("The depraved violence of Clint Eastwood holds no candle to the unblemished humanity of John Wayne," he declares, clearly oblivious to the plight of the Indian.) Managing to escape, he resumed his criminal ways (*Spider-Woman* #4, 1978). Alas, accidentally murdering a woman (and, during one escapade, killing the makers of a splatter film), Krueger becomes so depressed that he fails to hear one Matthew O'Brien, a gutsy film critic, sneaking up behind him. O'Brien uses Hangman's own scythe to slay him.

Quote: "Only I stand in the wilderness, a *beacon* of light dedicated to the fundamentals of unadulterated *justice*!"

Comment: This character is similar to FOOLKILLER and FIREBOLT, both of whom also slew the morally corrupt.

HARLEQUIN (C)

Real Name: Molly Maynne Scott.

First Appearance: 1947, *All-American Comics* #89, DC Comics.

Costume: Orange tights with vertical black stripes; blue gloves, slippers, sleeveless bodyshirt with two big red buttons; white mask (see Weapons), ruffled collar, tutu; orange "dunce" cap with blue pompoms on front.

Weapons: Mask has lenses which enable her to hypnotize people, create illusions, and fire electrical blasts; mandolin which she uses as a club.

Biography: As a youth in the 1920s, Molly was such a fine athlete that she defeated all male challengers—leaving her without a boyfriend. Joining the professional world, she decided to be as subservient as possible, becoming a timid secretary to Alan Scott, who was program director to radio station WXYZ in Gotham City, and who was secretly the superhero Green Lantern. As a promotional gimmick, the station hired Lantern to star in a radio drama; Molly was cast opposite him as the villainous Harlequin. Falling in love with the superhero but unable to hold his interest, Molly decided to become the evil Harlequin in real life and thus monopolize his time and energies. The two battled frequently, though Harlequin never tried to hurt him; eventually retiring, Molly gained immunity from prosecution in exchange for data on other super villains. Vanishing for many years, Molly resurfaced to help Green Lantern battle ROSE AND THE THORN. This time the timing was right, and the two wed. Harlequin was briefly a member of THE INJUSTICE SOCIETY OF THE WORLD.

HATE-MONGER (C)

Real Name: Adolf Hitler (see Biography).

First Appearance: 1963, *The Fantastic Four* #21, Marvel Comics.

Costume: Purple hood, tunic with pink fringe and "H" on chest; mail jumpsuit; brown boots.

Weapons: H-ray, which boosts the emotions of fear and hatred to explosive levels and can also turn love into hate; Hate-Monger has fired this ray from a handgun as well as from a satellite. The fiend also uses standard weaponry and biological warfare.

Chief Henchman: Arnim Zola, a biologist.

Biography: The cover blurb of the character's first appearance screamed, "Don't dare reveal his true identity after reading this tale!"—and with good reason. Hate-Monger was a clone of Nazi dictator Adolf Hitler. In 1945, shortly before the tyrant's suicide, scientist Arnim Zola cloned the Fuhrer. By the fall of Berlin, he had completed growing a brain, and Hitler transferred his consciousness to that organ. A small army of bodies was also cloned over the next 18 years, and when they were fully grown the Hate-Monger moved his memories from the brain to a body—and then to another body each time an old one was destroyed. (At last count, he'd been through a half-dozen bodies.) When last seen, the Hate-Monger was teamed with THE RED SKULL and had slipped his mind into a bogus version of that villain's mighty Cosmic Cube. Since that Cube lacked a power source, Hitler's consciousness did not become the most powerful sentience in creation, as he'd hoped, but is presently imprisoned in the Cube.

Comment: Two other beings subsequently assumed the costume and name of the Hate-Monger. The first was an artificially evolved wolf known as the Man-Beast, who perished in an explosion while battling Spider-Man. The second was an android who could assume the likeness of others. It was blown up by the villain Scourge. (See THE ENFORCER [2], Biography.) Another Hitler clone was the Iron Dictator (see MULTI-MAN, Comment).

HEAT WAVE (C)

Real Name: Mick Rory.

First Appearance: 1964, *The Flash* #140, DC Comics.

Costume: Silver asbestos jumpsuit, boots, gloves, cap; red holster (worn across chest) and goggles (see Weapons).

Weapons: Heat gun which shoots fire as well as generating extreme heat; goggles also permit him to generate heat.

Biography: When he was 10 years old, Rory went with his schoolmates on a field trip to a meatpacking factory. There, he was accidentally locked inside a freezer. Finally managing to undo the latch before he froze to death, the traumatized Rory came to despise the cold. Experimenting with heat throughout his teenage years, he took a job as a fire-eater at a circus; after several years of earning a pittance, he decided to devote his talents to crime. Armed with his heat gun and asbestos suit he became Heat Wave and for many years was one of the more enduring foes of the Flash. Rehabilitated during his last prison sentence, he actually helped the Flash track down a bogus Heat Wave (Rory's parole officer Hobart) and remains a law-abiding citizen.

Quote: "*At last*! I've finally managed to *out-maneuver* the *fastest man alive* with a sneak hot-shot from the rear!"

Comment: See other fiery super villains BLOWTORCH BRAND, FIREBOLT, FIREBUG, FIREFALL, FIREFIST, Heatstroke of MASTERS OF DISASTER, and PYRO.

HEL (MY)

Biography: In Norse mythology, Hel is the daughter of LOKI and the giantess Angurboda. Her brothers are Fenris and the Serpent of Midgard. Unutterably evil from birth, Hel was half black and half blue and supped solely on the brains and marrow of men. Tossed from Asgard, the realm of the gods, she landed nine days and nights later in distant Niflheim, the dark and dreary underworld. There she made her home beneath the roots of YGGDRASIL, the great ash tree which supported the universe, and forged a bed of Care in order to deprive others of its charity. Hel served as goddess of the dead, with Hunger as her dish, Starvation her knife, and Delay and Slowness her personal aides. Her kingdom—also named Hel—was surrounded by the great river Gioll and was divided into nine separate worlds, each one being the abode of people who had died in different ways. (In some legends, Hel only got men who hadn't perished in battle, women who died of old age, or children who succumbed to sickness.) Hel is also known as Hela.

Comment: It isn't clear whether the modern word "hell" derived directly from Hel or from the Old English "helan," which means to cover or hide.

HELA (C)

First Appearance: 1963, *Journey Into Mystery* #102, Marvel Comics.

Costume: Green tights, boots, gloves, shirt, breastplate; darker green cowl, cloak with huge collar (see Weapons).

Weapons: The left side of Hela's body is dead—she is presumed to have been born this way—and without her cloak she is powerless even to move.

Biography: Nothing is known of Hela's past, though she is believed to have been born in the realm of Jotunheim, the daughter of the evil Norse god Loki (see LOKI, Comment) and the giant witch Angurboda. Appointed by Odin, the king of the gods, as the ruler of Hel and Niffleheim, Hela is in charge of dead deities, save for those who have perished in battle (those souls reside in Valhalla, a palace in Asgard, the home of the Norse gods). However, Hela yearns for more power and tries to conquer not only Valhalla but also Asgard itself. At one point she orders the building of the huge vessel Naflgar, reportedly made of the fingernails of the dead, with which she intends to invade Odin's kingdom. Though that ship is destroyed by THE EXECUTIONER, Hela has not abandoned her dream to become the most powerful figure in Asgard. Hela's touch kills mortals instantly, and she can hurt even other gods with her enchanted blasts; she also has the ability to return the newly dead to life.

Comment: Marvel's spelling of "Niffleheim" differs from the "Niflheim" which occurs in most texts on Norse mythology. Hela was inspired by the goddess HEL.

HELL-BLAZER (C)

Real Name: Charles "Chipper" Mann (see Comment).

First Appearance: 1975, *Tales of Evil* #3, Atlas Comics.

Costume: Yellow bodysuit, flaps under arms, full-face cowl with red flame markings on face, head, arms; red flame-like trunks; brown gloves, boots (yellow on cover).

Weapons: Laser gun; unspecified equipment for flight (see Comment).

Biography: Nothing is known about this character, save that he had been involved in criminal activities to help control the outcome of the 1972 summer Olympics. One of those who had refused to go along with his plan was Paul Sanders; three years later, Hell-Blazer returned to involve Paul (who had since become the amphibious Man-Monster) in a scheme to become wealthy at the expense of Sanders' oil baron father.

***HELL-BLAZER** zaps Paul Sanders, Man-Monster. © Atlas Comics.*

Quote: "*Farewell*! You die as you lived—an *idiot*!"

Comment: Although the second part of the Hell-Blazer story was not published due to the folding of Atlas Comics, the next issue would have revealed his true name to have been Chipper Mann, a petty thief who had raided his own father's hi-tech facility for his equipment. Unwilling to take chances himself, he went to others, like Sanders, to do his dirty work for him.

HELLGRAMMITE (C)

First Appearance: 1968, *The Brave and the Bold* #80, DC Comics.

Costume: A green carapace, head with mandibles, claws, and long tail similar to that of its namesake, the aquatic larva of a dobsonfly (see Weapons).

Weapons: His costume and cocoons are made of "insect fibre—stronger than steel." Only Hellgrammite's own claws can cut it.

Biography: An entomologist, Hellgrammite finds a way to gain enormous insect powers and abilities by merging his body with an artificial shell. His plan: to breed an army of creatures like himself, apparently to take over the world. Hellgrammite must return to a cocoon every 24 hours to renew his powers. Tracking him to his lair deep in a Gotham City subway, the superheroes Batman and the Creeper clog his breathing holes with fire extinguishing foam, then stun him with a live wire ripped from the train tracks. Presumably, he was somehow stripped of his powerful costume while stunned.

Quote: "Did you bruise your puny fist on the carapace of *Hellgrammite*?"

Comment: This was the character's only appearance.

HE WHO NEVER DIES (C)

Real Name: Hamid Ali.

First Appearance: 1967, *Showcase* #66, DC Comics.

Costume: White arabic garb (his flesh is also white, his head skull-like).

Weapons: "Crocodile machine," a monstrously huge tank/boat in the shape of a golden crocodile, complete with snapping jaws.

Chief Henchmen: Sundry cutthroats and pirate-types.

Biography: A poacher raping the continent of Africa, Ali is "Africa's most evil man." Reportedly immortal, "the man who has lived a thousand years" was last seen sinking to the bottom of a great river in his crippled craft (much like CAPTAIN NEMO). Though he submerged vowing vengeance, he has yet to reappear.

Quote: "Kill them! Kill them all! You fools—unlike me, they *can* die!"

Comment: This was the only nemesis ever battled by the hero B'wana Beast.

THE HIGH PRIEST OF ZOR (C)

First Appearance: 1983, *Power Man and Iron Fist* #102, Marvel Comics.

Costume: Black robe with a golden collar, stripe down front; yellow gloves.

Weapons: The Twin Idols of Zor, which grant extraordinary mystic powers when they're together. Apart, they're useless.

Chief Henchmen: Demi-Demons, an assortment of spear-carrying humanoids.

Biography: Reminiscing about his first encounter with the High Priest, superhero Power Man remarks, "As soon as I saw that glow around his hands, I knew we were in trouble." The High Priest is a short, yellow-skinned servant of the demon Magrador and has the ability to cast a variety of spells, including those which set up a force-field around his enemies, change his own size and/or shape, and enable him to move from our dimension to that of Magrador. Based in Keep Zor in New Jersey, he spends his time trying to wrest the Twin Idols from Power Man and the superhero's partner Iron Fist, to whom it has been given for safekeeping by a third superhero, Scarlet Witch. If he can obtain them, he intends to "enslave every mind on earth." Magically abducted to Keep Zor, the heroes manage to hold onto the idols while forcing the High Priest to return to his own realm.

Quote: "You'll never capture m—*oooff*!!"

HIJACKER (C)

First Appearance: 1962, *Tales To Astonish* #40, Marvel Comics.

Costume: Brown jumpsuit, gloves, boots; orange helmet with clear visor.

Weapons: Nerve gas; "Crime Tank," a vehicle with spiked treads, electromagnets, and missiles (stolen from the peacekeeping force S.H.I.E.L.D. and seen only in *Marvel Two-In-One* #24, 1976). He also packs a "varioblaster" which fires a destructive nuclear flame.

Biography: A thief, the Hijacker has no superpowers apart from his weaponry. Dedicated to becoming "very, very rich," he has thusfar been thwarted by Ant-Man and by the Thing.

Quote: "Let's see if even the mighty *Thing* can survive a close-range *missile barrage*."

THE HOBGOBLIN (C)

Real Name: Ned Leeds, Jason Philip Macendale, Jr.

First Appearance: 1964, *The Amazing Spider-Man* #19 (as Leeds); 1983, *The Amazing Spider-Man* #238 (as Hobgoblin), Marvel Comics.

Costume: Purple bodysuit; orange leotard, gloves, boots, cloak with hood; black belt; yellow face with red eyes.

Weapons: See THE GOBLIN, Weapons. Also: an "armor-plated battle van" that can drive itself (at a cruising speed of 90 mph) and various armaments in his two-story headquarters "nestled in the heart of the warehouse district" of Manhattan, including an "automated ray cannon" which guards the place.

Biography: A reporter for the *Daily Bugle*, Leeds first entered the Spider-Man stories as the boyfriend of Betty Brant—Brant reluctantly dumping longtime boyfriend Peter Parker (Spider-Man) to date Leeds. Leeds, however, detested Spider-Man. He believed that the superhero was responsible for the death of Betty's brother, and the nightmares she had about that. Thus, when Leeds got the chance, he struck back, but for the longest time, neither Spider-Man (nor the readers) knew who the Hobgoblin was. He first burst upon the super villain scene after crook George Hill, running from Spider-Man, found a former hideout of the original GREEN GOBLIN, Norman Osborn. The den contained the villain's costume and accoutrements, and Hill promptly hired another man (Leeds)—who murdered Hill and used information in Osborn's papers to find the deceased villain's other lairs. Making a new costume and collecting all of the Green Goblin's criminal paraphernalia, the new Hobgoblin first fought Spider-Man when the superhero came to investigate the Osborn thefts. The villain barely escaped with his life, after which he created a potion from Osborn's notes which gave him enormous physical strength. Allied with a crime leader known as the Rose (see THE PUMA), the Hobgoblin helped him to challenge the might of New York's other crime bosses. The Hobgoblin's identity was finally revealed in *The Amazing Spider-Man* #289, 1987. That issue also marked the death of Flash Thompson, a friend of Parker's who had been part of the series since its inception. He died saving Spider-Man from one of the Hobgoblin's pumpkin grenades. Leeds himself died shortly thereafter, strangled to death by Foreigner, an assassin who had been hired by Leeds' enemy, the villain Jack O'Lantern. O'Lantern—aka Jason Macendale— wasted no time stealing Leeds' superior trappings and becoming the new Hobgoblin.

Quote: "As for Spider-Man—he'll soon be nothing more—than a bloody *smear* on the ground!"

HORDAK (T, MP, TV)

First Appearance: 1985, Mattel Toys.

Costume: Black trunks, wristband and armbands, boots with gray band around top, middle, and toes, breastplate with red bat-like emblem on chest and high collar fringed with gray; gray belt, bone-like bands around shoulders. Hordak's skin is blue, his skull-like face white.

Chief Henchmen: The Evil Horde, an unsavory group consisting of the shaggy brute Grizzlor; the insect-like spy Mantenna; the multi-legged, two-headed Modulok; and Leech, the "master of power suction," with suction cups on his mouth, hands, and feet.

Biography: A former denizen of the planet Eternia (see SKELETOR), Hordak passed through a dimensional gate and took up residence in the Fright Zone of the world of Etheria. There, the evil ruler was faced by an ongoing rebellion spearheaded by She-Ra, the superheroic sister of He-Man of Eternia.

Quote: "You may have defeated me and my Horde, but you'll never see this child again!"

Comment: The character was the chief protagonist in Filmation's 1985 theatrical film *The Secret of the Sword*, and is a regular on the syndicated Filmation TV series *She-Ra*. See other action toy super villains BARON KARZA, DESTRO, GENERAL SPIDRAX, MOLTAR, MUMM-RA, and SKELETOR.

THE HORNET (C)

Real Name: Scott McDowell.

First Appearance: 1980, *Spider-Woman* #31, Marvel Comics.

Costume: Orange bodysuit with purple shoulders, stylized stinger on chest; purple gloves, "V"-shaped belt, boots with stylized stingers pointing up onto shins, cowl with antennae.

Weapons: See Biography.

Biography: A wheelchair-bound criminologist, McDowell is poisoned while rescuing the superhero Spider-Woman from THE ENFORCER; the super villain subjects him to a "metabolic incendiary formula", which will kill him if his body temperature rises above freezing (issue #28). Placed in a cryogenic freeze-unit for safekeeping, he is taken by THE FLY to the laboratory of the fiendish bioengineer Dr. Malus, part of a complex deal in which Spider-Woman has agreed to help the Enforcer commit crimes if Malus will save her colleague. There, McDowell, whom the Fly dubs "the human popsicle," is given an antidote and saved (#30). However, the deed is not quite as benevolent as Malus would have everyone believe. The injection causes McDowell to sprout wings for flight, gives him superstrength, allows him to fire "stings" which render people unconscious, and, of course, triggers a personality change, bringing "forth certain hostilities that normally remain repressed." Donning a costume which Malus had shipped to his apartment, McDowell takes to the skies as the villainous Hornet, committed to destroying Spider-Woman. However, she pummels him into unconsciousness, has Malus arrested, and, after a few days' rest, McDowell is himself once again (#32).

Quote: "I'm through dwelling in Spider-Woman's shadow! Through doing all the brainwork while she flies around in her sexy red costume and hogs all the glory!"

Comment: The two issues mark the Hornet's only appearances.

HORTAN GUR (N)

First Appearance: 1916, "Thuvia, Maid of Mars," *All Story Weekly*, Edgar Rice Burroughs.

Costume: Metal bands around arms; harness.

Weapons: Sword.

Biography: One of the great despots of Mars, Hortan Gur is a jeddak (prince) of Torquas, a kingdom in the planet's southwestern hemisphere. "A fierce old ogre," the jeddak is one of the "green men," tusked, olive-skinned, six-limbed beings who stand between 12 and 15 feet in height. Like most of his kind, Hortan Gur is a merciless warmonger. (As one character notes, "Great will be the pleasure of Hortan Gur when Thar Ban drags before him the mad fool who dared prick the great jeddak with his sword.") Though his armies are routed in the novel, his fate is not revealed.

Comment: The novel was originally serialized from April 8 to 22.

HOUNGAN (C)

Real Name: Jean-Louis Droo.

First Appearance: 1981, *The New Teen Titans* #14, DC Comics.

Costume: Golden thigh boots, belt, wristbands, and other decorative artifacts; red trunks, white on sides; white cowl with red headdress and golden "U"-shaped horn on front.

Weapons: Computerized voodoo dolls, each of which forms a psychosensory bond between itself and the victim once a piece of the person's skin, blood, or hair has been sampled by the doll. Thereafter, when an "electronic needle" is inserted into the doll, its presence is sensed by microcircuits and shoots pain directly to the person at the point of penetration.

Biography: Born in Haiti, Jean-Louis was raised in the United States and became an expert with computers. Working in Silicon Valley, he returned to

Haiti only when his father lay on his deathbed. Remarkably, however, after doctors had pronounced him terminal, Jean-Louis's father was cured by a local voodoo priest known as a "houngan." So impressed was the young man that he remained in Haiti to study the dark arts. However, after two years of study, he emerged quite a different houngan. He had combined voodoo magic with the science he'd learned to create an entirely new field of endeavor. Setting up shop in Paris, he engaged in a life of crime in the second incarnation of THE BROTHERHOOD OF EVIL. Houngan is divorced from Antoinette.

Quote: "The *computer fetish* holds a lock of your emerald *hair*. It has cybernetically sorted out your body's *cellular structure*! A structure I can affect by using this *electronic needle*!"

THE HUMAN FIREFLY (C)

Real Name: Garfield Lynns.

First Appearance: 1952, *Detective Comics* #184, DC Comics.

Costume: Purple bodyshirt with white "FF" in black circle; green tights, boots, cape with light green fringe, cowl with black peak and antennae; multicolored belt (see Weapons).

Weapons: Antennae are shortwave transmitters; light belt "capable of producing varied and amazing lighting effects," including blinding red light, lightning, a "bleach light" which steals all color, and a bright white light which, simulating a lighthouse beacon, can lure ships to their doom.

Chief Henchmen: Linky and various other thugs.

Biography: "The world's foremost lighting-effects genius," Garfield works at the Gotham Theater and is tired of living "on a meager salary while those idiots in the audience" arrive in limousines and flash their gems. Disguising some thugs as ushers, he stages a fake fire while *Aqua-Melodies of 1952* is being performed. But the superheroic Batman is in the audience and prevents the "ushers" from robbing panicked patrons; capturing the gang, Batman goes after Garfield, who escapes into the country. He pursues him, only to be misled by a firefly which he mistakes for a lighted cigarette; Garfield goes free and takes the insect as an omen. Holing up in a cave beneath a barn outside of Gotham City, he designs his Firefly costume and arsenal and goes on a crime spree with a new gang. However, turning one of the fiend's own light gadgets on him while he flees a robbery, the hero blinds the Human Firefly and hauls him off to prison.

Quote: "Ho! Wait till they gaze upon *The Firefly*—I'll dazzle their infantile brains!"

Comment: This was the character's only appearance, though the adventure was reprinted in *Batman Annual* #3 (1962).

HUMBUG (C)

Real Name: Buck Mitty.

First Appearance: 1986, *Web of Spider-Man* #19, Marvel Comics.

Costume: Yellow jumpsuit; purple boots; white socks; red gloves, cape, helmet with green antennae (see Weapons) and blue goggles; gray bandolier (see Weapons).

Weapons: "Sonic bandolier" which, in conjuction with his "amplification helmet," boosts insect sounds recorded on tape and transforms them into destructive blasts. Fired from his gloves, these blasts are powerful enough to blow open the doors of an armored truck.

Biography: A senior entomology professor at Empire State University, Buck is laughed-at when he tries to tell his colleagues "that insects are our friends." His funding is cut off, and to support his research he turns to crime. However, Buck is something of a klutz and after bungling several robberies is thwarted when the superhero Spider-Man twists his gloves toward each other while they are blasting. Humbug's equipment short-circuits, and he ends up in jail.

Quote: "There! A buzz from the oblique-banded leaf roller should vibrate their outer skin layer, keep them chortling uncontrollably for minutes."

Comment: This has been the character's only appearance to date. Other insect-oriented super villains include BARON BUG, THE DRAGONFLY RAIDERS, KING LOCUST, QUEEN BEE, and SWARM.

THE HUNTRESS (C)

Real Name: Crock (last name; first name is unrevealed).

First Appearance: 1947, *Sensation* #68, DC Comics.

Costume: Yellow leotard, boots, cat-like cowl, cape, all with black stripes; boots have yellow (later white) fur tops.

Weapons: Sundry traps and snares, from leghold traps to cages of various sorts. She also uses a small dagger on occasion.

Biography: Irked at how the law always hunted down crooks, the criminal Huntress (her maiden name has never been revealed) decided to turn the tables and hunt down law enforcers using her superior athletic and predatory skills. In her first escapade, she captured the superhero Wildcat and then went after the mayor, police chief, and other bastions of law and order—intending to free them in her private preserve and hunt them down (a la GENERAL ZAROFF). Escaping, Wildcat put an end to the Huntress' scheme, though she has since devoted herself to recapturing the hero, but without success. Joining THE INJUSTICE SOCIETY OF THE WORLD, she met and married the evil "Crusher" Crock, the SPORTSMASTER; they have since operated as a team. In her most heartfelt adventure, she tried (and failed) to destroy the superheroic Huntress, resenting the way her name had been misappropriated (1978, *All-Star Comics* #73). That Huntress subsequently perished; the criminal Huntress is presently keeping a low profile.

Quote: "I don't know why you stole my name, child—and I don't really care! Because after today, there will only be one *living* Huntress!"

Comment: This character's costume and modus operandi are quite similar to DC's own CHEETAH.

HURRICANE (C)

Real Name: Harry Kane.

First Appearance: 1964, *Two-Gun Kid* #70, Marvel Comics.

Costume: Purple hat, mask over lower half of face, breeches, shirt with yellow lightning streaks down chest and back to waist and a yellow band across his shoulders and top of chest; white gloves.

Weapons: Standard six-shooters.

Chief Henchmen: Various gang members.

Biography: An outlaw, Kane was running from the heroic Two-Gun Kid when he got caught up in a twister. "Stranded in the middle of nowhere," he roamed for hours, finally ending up near the camp of an Indian witch doctor. Watching the shaman mix a potion, Kane assumed it was soup and, shooting him, went to get the broth. While he was holding the bowl, it was struck by lightning; too hungry to worry about it he gulped it down, unaware that the Indian had been trying to create a speed potion and that the lightning was the catalyst which made it work. Still hungry, he jumped after a rabbit and was able to grab it. Realizing what had happened, he tested his skills and discovered that he was "faster than (a) speedin' cougar!" His draw was also lightning-quick and he decided to "make me a fancy costume—just like the Two-Gun Kid" and become the supercriminal Hurricane. Robbing trains, banks, and anyone who happened along, he was pursued by the Two-Gun Kid. During a chase, Hurricane found to his horror that "that Injun's potion gave me the speed of an antelope, but it didn't give me his *stamina*!" Breathless, he fell and was captured; ironically, he broke and permanently damaged his ankle, while his hands were rendered useless for gunfighting by shots from the Kid. Because Kane returned all the stolen booty and could do no further harm, the judge let him off with a suspended sentence. Presumably, he went straight.

Quote: "My name's *Hurricane*, and *no one* enters *my territory* without givin' up their money belt to me!!"

Comment: The character is also referred to as Mr. Hurricane in the story. See other Marvel western villains THE FAT MAN, THE PANTHER, THE RAVEN, RED RAVEN, and ROBIN HOOD RAIDER. Other super-speedy super villains include REVERSE-FLASH, SPEED DEMON, Speed Demon of VENDETTA, and ZYKLON.

HYDRO-MAN (C)

Real Name: Morris "Morrie" Bench.

First Appearance: 1981, *The Amazing Spider-Man* #212, Marvel Comics.

Biography: Bad luck for Morris: While a new generator was being tested in the ocean, crewperson Bench was accidentally knocked into the drink by Spider-Man. Concurrently washed with energy from the generator and with volcanic gases, Bench was rescued and discovered he had the power to turn himself, in part or whole, into water, every molecule of which he can control. After becoming a gusher or dripping through a keyhole, he can easily re-form simply by willing it. Becoming a criminal—and also seeking to destroy Spider-Man because of what has happened—Hydro-Man has had a singularly unspectacular career. In his most interesting adventure, he and the SANDMAN accidentally ran into each other, and became a vaguely intelligent mud monster. His most impressive escape involved evaporating and reappearing some distance from Spider-Man as rain. Hydro-Man was briefly a member of THE SINISTER SYNDICATE.

Quote: "*Yeow*! That foam is . . . becomin' a part of me! It's makin' me feel queasy! *Ulpp* . . . I think I'm gonna be sick!"

Comment: New Wave of MASTERS OF DISASTER can also control water.

HYENA(C)

Real Name: Summer Day; Jivan Shi (see Biography).

First Appearance: 1978, *Firestorm* #4, DC Comics.

Costume: None; Hyena is covered with brown fur, her head that of a hyena.

Weapons: Hyena has razor-sharp teeth and claws.

Biography: Summer is the daughter of police officer Bert and his wife Helen. A disappointment to her father, who had wanted a son, she tried hard to please him by partaking in sports and, later, by attending a police academy. But she didn't make the grade, and Bert was distraught; unwilling to suffer his displeasure, Summer joined the Peace Corps. While serving in Africa, she came across a native crippled by an arrow; ministering to the wound, she was startled when he bit her. Only when one of her corps colleagues came along and gunned him down did Summer learn that the wounded man was a were-hyena. Returning to the United States, Summer became a bipedal hyena, the first time she underwent emotional stress. (It isn't revealed whether this is macho enough for her father.) Tearing through the streets of New York, she was stopped by the superhero Firestorm—and has remained his enemy, battling him numerous times since. Complicating the matter was the fact that Firestorm's alter ego was the boyfriend of Doreen Day, Summer's younger sister. Finally managing to capture HYENA, Firestorm had her shipped to an institution in Arizona where Jivan Shi, one of the psychiatrists, was only slightly less loony than Summer. Furious because his education from schools in India was regarded as second-rate by his colleagues, the psychiatrist tricked Summer into becoming the Hyena and biting him. Becoming the were-monster himself, Jivan intended to lash out against the members of the American Medical Association. Chasing him down, Firestorm stopped the new Hyena but not before he himself was infected. Hurrying to Africa, the superhero was cured by a magician and then rounded up both Hyenas. They are presently incarcerated, undergoing medical studies.

HYPNOS (C)

Real Name: Dr. Otto Kaufmann.

First Appearance: 1975, *Tiger-Man* #3, Atlas Comics.

Weapons: Monocle which, powered by solar batteries, focuses psychic power into a beam that enables the wearer to control minds or cause pain.

Biography: Running a free psychiatric clinic in midtown Manhattan, Dr. Kaufmann is in fact more twisted than any of his patients. His goal is to rid the world of people with neuroses, thus enabling him to rule a planet of "supermen." To this end, he uses his monocle to hypnotize people into taking their own lives. The superhero Tiger-Man uncovers his plot and, while examining the monocle, accidentally unleashes its stored power on Kaufmann. The psychiatrist is struck full by the beam and plunges to his death from a rooftop.

Quote: "No—you fool. Don't *shine* it on me! The lens is still functioning!"

Comment: This was the character's only appearance. See other hypnotist super villains DESPERO, MESMERO, THE RINGMASTER, and UNIVERSO.

IBAC (C)

Real Name: Stanley "Stinky" Printwhistle.

First Appearance: 1942, *Captain Marvel Adventures* #8, Fawcett Publications.

Costume: Blue tights.

Biography: Working as a flunky for MISTER MIND, Stinky yearns to be a supercriminal himself. To this end, he makes a pact with the devil: He agrees to render his soul to SATAN if he is granted superpowers sufficient to beat Captain Marvel. The devil agrees, and whenever he mutters the word "Ibac," he is smitten with green fire and becomes superhuman. (Ibac is derived from *I*van the Terrible, Cesare *B*orgia, *A*tilla the Hun, and *C*aligula.) Defeated repeatedly by Captain Marvel (and thus not obliged to give up his soul), Stinky is presently a streetcleaner. For a time, the super villain was a member of THE MONSTER SOCIETY OF EVIL.

Comment: Captain Marvel's sidekick, Captain Marvel, Jr., had a similar adversary—Sabbac, whose name derived from the names of demons (*S*atan, *A*ny, *B*elial, *B*eelzebub, *A*smodeus, and *C*rateis).

THE ICE CREAM HATER (C)

Real Name: Ichabod Charles Earl Cream.

First Appearance: 1974, *Carvel Comics* #2, Carvel Corporation.

Costume: Blue trousers, turtleneck sweater, hood, cloak; brown shoes.

Weapons: Electronic device to shrivel bananas; TV screen to see anywhere in the world; invisibility device; other, unspecified equipment.

Biography: Although he has never tasted ice cream, Ichabod hates it because other kids tease him about his name. That, plus the fact that he is the self-professed "meanest, rottenest kid in the world," inspires him to become a costumed villain and undertake to destroy the frozen dessert industry by making it impossible to manufacture ice cream flavorings. To this end, he travels the world wreaking havoc. In France, he "ties all the grape vines together" so grape sherbet can't be made; In Japan, "he turns all the mint plants invisible" to prevent the manufacture of peppermint; in the Philippines, he transforms the coconuts into bombs "which attack our courageous Captain Carvel"; in Mexico, he glues all the strawberries together; in Panama, he causes banana plants to produce only a fraction of their usual crop. Finally, In Hawaii, the precocious lad is cornered while in the process of blowing up a pineapple field. Captain Carvel forces him to eat some ice cream; loving it, he gives up his brief but terrible criminal career.

Quote: "One day in *science class,* I decided it was my destiny to destroy all the ice cream in the world."

Comment: This was the character's only appearance.

Captain Carvel triumphs over ***THE ICE CREAM HATER.***
© Carvel Corporation.

ICICLE (C)

Real Name: Dr. Joar Makent.
First Appearance: 1947, *All-American Comics* #90, DC Comics.
Costume: White bodysuit with icicle scalloping on back of legs and on arms and shoulders (see Weapons); white gloves and boots with white icicle-like fringes; white cap with tall icicle peak.
Weapons: Cold ray gun which can freeze anything; when people are frozen, they go into hibernation. Icicle's costume is coldproof.
Biography: Onboard a ship bound for the United States from Europe, physicist Makent is found murdered in his stateroom. Moreover, after docking, the ship is frozen solid. That evening, the super-villainous Icicle begins committing crimes and, putting two-and-two tegether, the superhero Green Lantern concludes that mobster Lanky Leeds, who was on the same vessel, robbed equipment from Makent, murdered him, and is now committing super crimes. As it turns out, the Icicle is actually Makent, who murdered Leeds and made him up to resemble Makent. Jumping from a 20-story building to escape Green Lantern, Makent seems to perish in the Gotham River. However, he lives to plague Green Lantern not only as a solo criminal but also as a member of THE INJUSTICE SOCIETY OF THE WORLD and THE CRIME CHAMPIONS. The Icicle died recently when he and other super villains tried to get into the laboratory of the alien scientist Krona (see THE ANTI-MONITOR). The place exploded and they were blown to bits while trying to sabotage Krona's own evil plans (*Crisis on Infinite Earths* #10, 1986).
Comment: See other icy super villains BLIZZARD, CAPTAIN COLD, Coldsnap of MASTERS OF DISASTER, KILLER FROST, and MR. FREEZE. Icicle's principal foe was Green Lantern of Earth-2, not the Green Lantern who battled SINESTRO et al.

IMMORTUS (also KANG THE CONQUEROR, RAMA-TUT, THE SCARLET CENTURION) (C, TV)

First Appearance: 1963, *Fantastic Four* #19 (as Rama-Tut); 1964, *The Avengers* #8 (as Kang); *The Avengers* #10 (as Immortus), Marvel Comics.
Costume: As Immortus: green tights, long-sleeve tunic; orange gloves, belt, sun-symbol on chest; purple cloak, elaborate headgear, boots, As Kang: green jumpsuit; purple thigh boots, gloves, helmet with blue face, collar and belt attached by strap (see Weapons). As Rama-Tut: green trunks, sandals, Egyptian headdress; golden collar, armbands, wristbands.
Weapons: As Kang, his armor is made of metal from the fortieth century and contains equipment which enables him to create a field which protects him from outside forces—including a nuclear detonation. This equipment also enables him to fire a destructive beam and endows him with superhuman strength. As Kang, he has also used a "vibration ray" machine, a handheld rocket launcher, a paralysis device, and sundry robots including Growing Man, which gets larger as it soaks up energy. As Rama-Tut, he packs an "ultra-diode" ray pistol which turns people into slaves.
Biography: Bored with life in the thirty-first century, where peace reigns, Immortus happens upon a time machine on property which had been owned by one of his ancestors. Roaming time and stealing weaponry, he adopts the name Kang and settles in Egypt in the year 2950 B.C., where he uses his arsenal to rule the country as the Pharaoh Rama-Tut. Growing bored after a decade, he heads back to the future only to be cast by a "time storm" into the mid-twentieth century. There, he wreaks havoc as the Scarlet Centurion before continuing his journey—and leaving behind a parallel time stream which is different from ours due to his having tampered with recorded history. Returning to his native era, he conquers much of the world and settles in what had once been Switzerland, leaving the actual governing to a flunky named Carelius. Meanwhile, he makes frequent attacks on the twentieth century, where he is repeatedly stymied by the superheroic Avengers. However, each time he meddles with the past, Immortus causes a new time stream to diverge, creating not only numerous realities but also an equal number of duplicates of himself inhabiting those realities past and future. These beings each act independent of one another, not only in their crimes but also in their travels through their own time flow. (And as new time lines are created, new futures are also created, along with future Immortusi.) At present, the most imposing Immortus is the one who has set himself up as the master of Limbo, where he dwells in a massive castle. His job, assigned to him by the mighty Time-Keepers, is to help unknot the mess he's made in 80 millennia's-worth of time.
Comment: Immortus, in his Rama-Tut identity, appeared in an episode of the ABC-TV *Fantastic Four* cartoon series in 1967.

IMPASSE (C)

First Appearance: 1984, *Power Man and Iron Fist* #101, Marvel Comics.
Costume: Blue-grey bodysuit with purple shoulders,

thick stripe down chest and back, crotch and seat, insides of legs; purple gloves, cowl with widow's peak; blue-grey boots; light blue full-face mask.

Weapons: Gun which fires disease gas at those too far away to touch.

Biography: A former drug smuggler, the future Impasse (his name is never revealed) was given a choice: either go to prison or allow scientists to use him as a guinea pig for germ warfare. He opted for the latter. As a result, he became the perfect Typhoid Mary, personally immune but able to inflict sickness on anyone he touches—or who touches him. (The nature of the illness he transmits is never explained, though it causes his victims to break out in a sweat virtually at once.) Trying to make his former attorney, Caesar Cicero, the criminal kingpin of New York—and intending to control him from behind-the-scenes—Impasse was stopped by Misty Knight and her bionic right arm, and Colleen Wing, one of the sword-swinging Daughters of the Dragon. Both are aides of the debilitated superheroes Power Man and Iron Fist.

Quote: "I could kill you with my gun, but it'll be more *fun* using my hands! I want to watch you sicken and die, inch by inch!"

Comment: This has been the character's only appearance to date.

THE INCA IN GRAY (M)

Real Name: General Fernandez Vigo.

First Appearance: 1935, "The Dust of Death," *Doc Savage* Magazine, Kenneth Robeson.

Costume: Gray cloak and hood.

Weapons: The Gray Dust of Death, parasites which sting people with lethal poison; in his Vigo identity, the despot carries two pistols and a bayonet.

Biography: The dictator of the South American republic of Delezon, Vigo adopts the identity of the Inca in Gray in order to convince descendants of those ancient people that he is their rightful leader. Gaining their trust, Vigo leads them on raids against his enemies. At the same time, he uses the Inca in Gray disguise to murder officials of the neighboring nation of Santa Amoza in an effort to seize power. He is ultimately ferreted out by Doc Savage and dies when he is suffocated by gray dust in an aborted attempt to kill the international crime fighter. Vigo was "fabulously ugly," with thick shoulders and a perpetual snarl in his voice.

Quote: "I do not have to kidnap women to win my wars."

Comment: Another of Doc's South American foes was Señor Steel, the money-hungry dictator of Blanca Grande.

THE INFINITE MAN (C)

Real Name: Jaxon Rugarth.

First Appearance: 1977, *Superboy and the Legion of Super-Heroes* #233, DC Comics.

Costume: Black bodysuit covered with stars and planets; purple leotard; red belt, headdress with gold diadem; gold "infinity" sign across chest.

Biography: An inhabitant of the thirtieth century, Rugarth was a teacher at the Time Institute of Metropolis University. There, he agreed to test a powerful new time machine, one which was going to prove that time was circular by sending Rugarth so far into the future he would pass through the beginning of time and end up back in the thirtieth century. Unfortunately, the machine was *so* powerful that it whipped Rugarth over and over again through time until he emerged with the power to control time itself. Attacking Rond Vidar, inventor of the machine, he was stopped by the Legionaires, who sent him floating through the limbo of time. During the reign of terror unleashed by the ANTI-MONITOR, the Infinite Man was able to tap his power and get back into the time stream. Battling the Legion again, he was drained of his powers and became dutiful Jaxon Rugarth once more.

THE INVISIBLE DESTROYER (C)

Real Name: Dr. Martin Phillips.

First Appearance: 1960, *Showcase* #23, DC Comics.

Costume: Purple boots, bodysuit with orange circle on chest and yellow atomic symbol inside; orange helmet, cape, trunks, gloves.

Weapons: See Biography.

Biography: A brilliant physicist, Coast City's Dr. Phillips inadvertently releases his evil subconscious mind in the form of an invisible, solid-energy humanoid. Dressed in a purple costume, Phillips' cruel side realizes that to grow stronger it must absorb radiation. To this end, it plans to trigger an atom blast of the West Coast, suck up the radiation, and become indestructible. He succeeds in setting off the detonation, but the superhero Green Lantern arrives in time to shrink the blast to insignificance. The two battle, Green Lantern using his power ring, the Invisible Destroyer flinging out powerful destructive bolts. Finally, ring-beam meets bolt dead-on and the Invisible Destroyer is atomized in the resultant blast. Though it manages to marshal itself for future battles, the dark side of Phillips has now been permanently dematerialized.

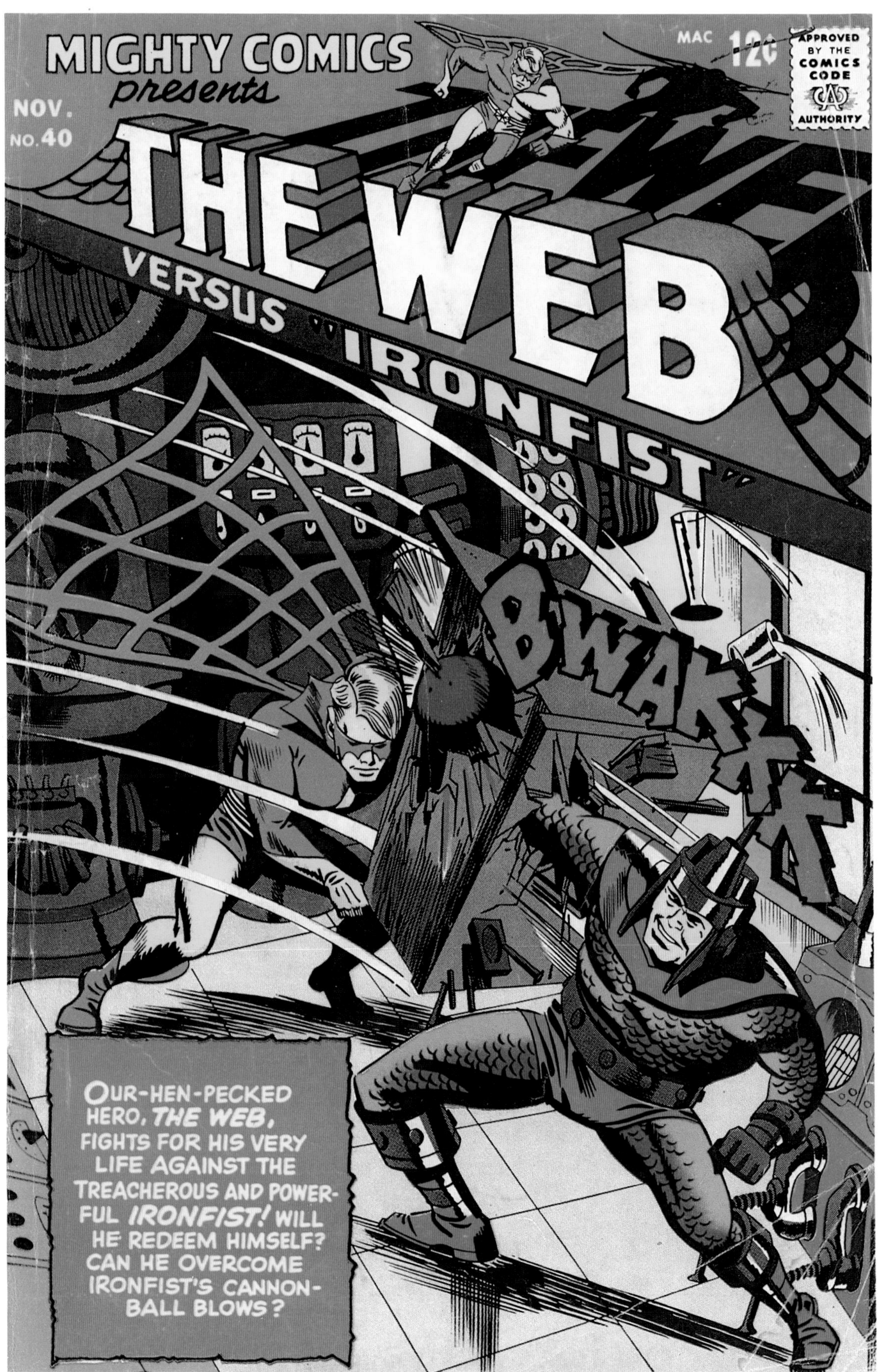

Ironfist *vs. the Web.* © *Archie Comics.*

***The Thinker** clobbers the golden age Atom with the modern Atom. © DC Comics.*

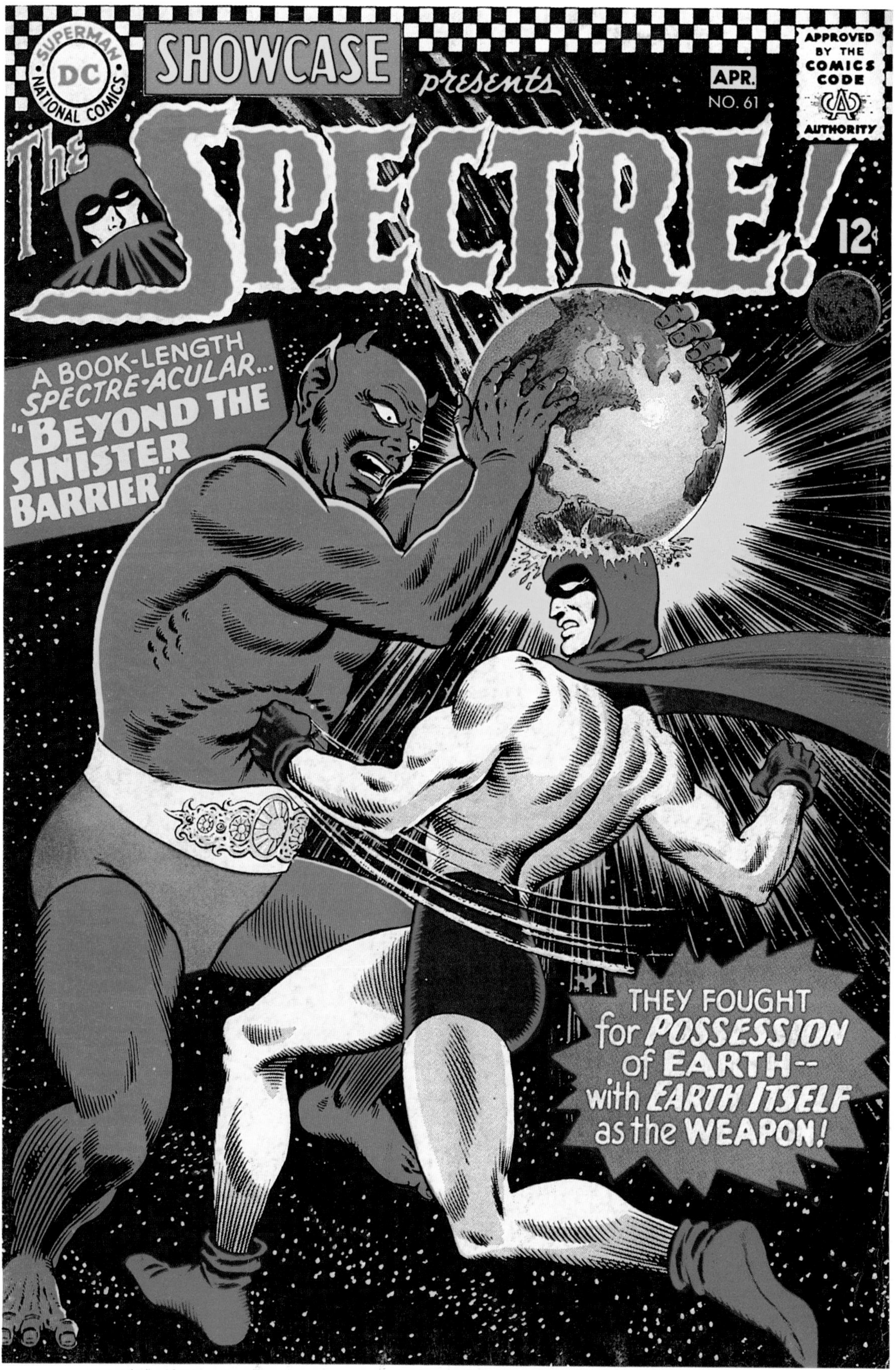

*A brilliant Murphy Anderson cover showing **Shathan** (left) in combat with the Spectre. (Doubtless South America was not pleased.) © DC Comics.*

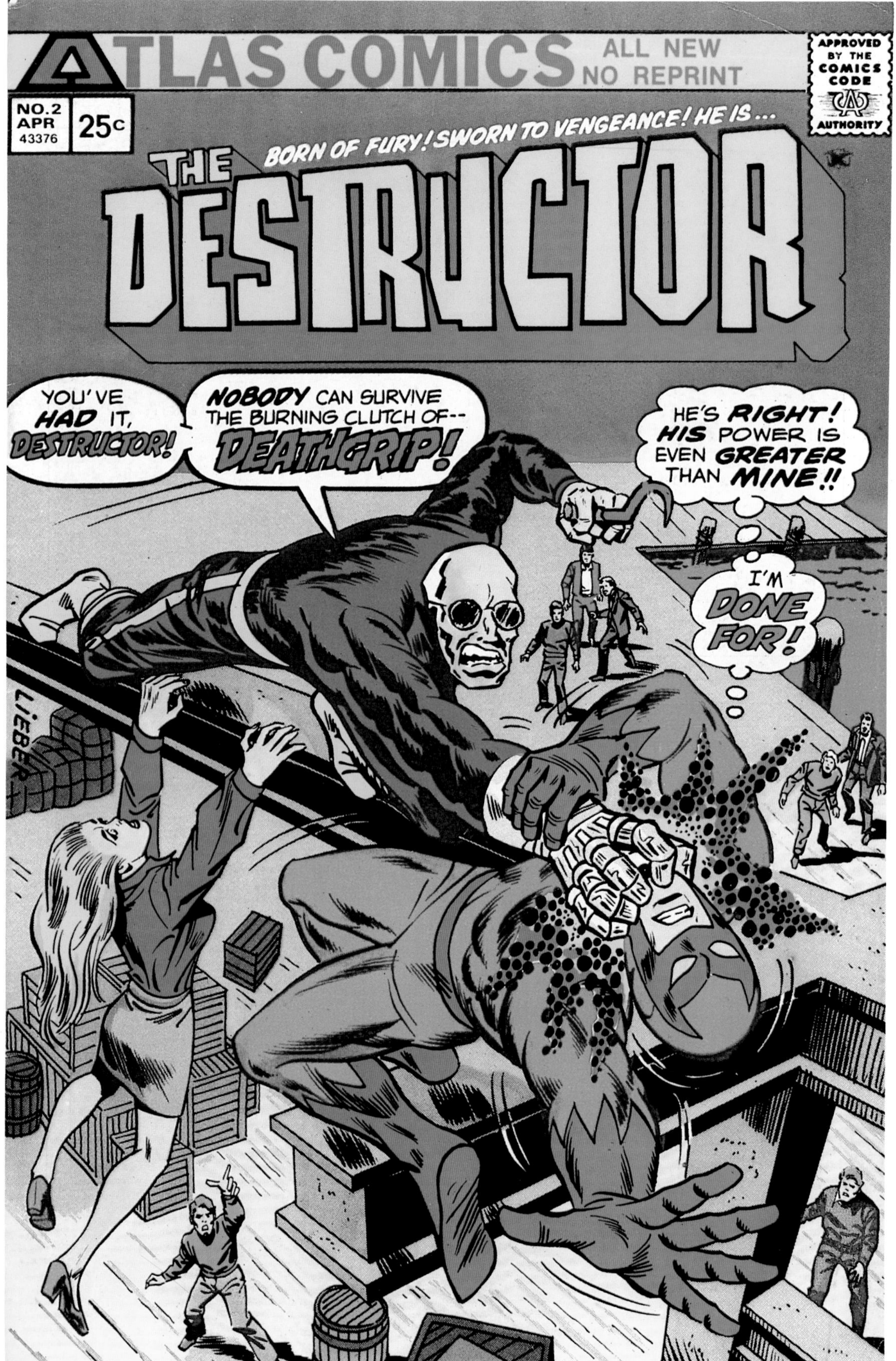

Deathgrip *having his way with Destructor. © Atlas Comics.*

Mighty Samson vs. ***King Zorr****.* © *Western Publishing.*

The Madmen *have the Blue Beetle surrounded.* © *Charlton Comics.*

The Cat Gang *takes on The Jaguar.*

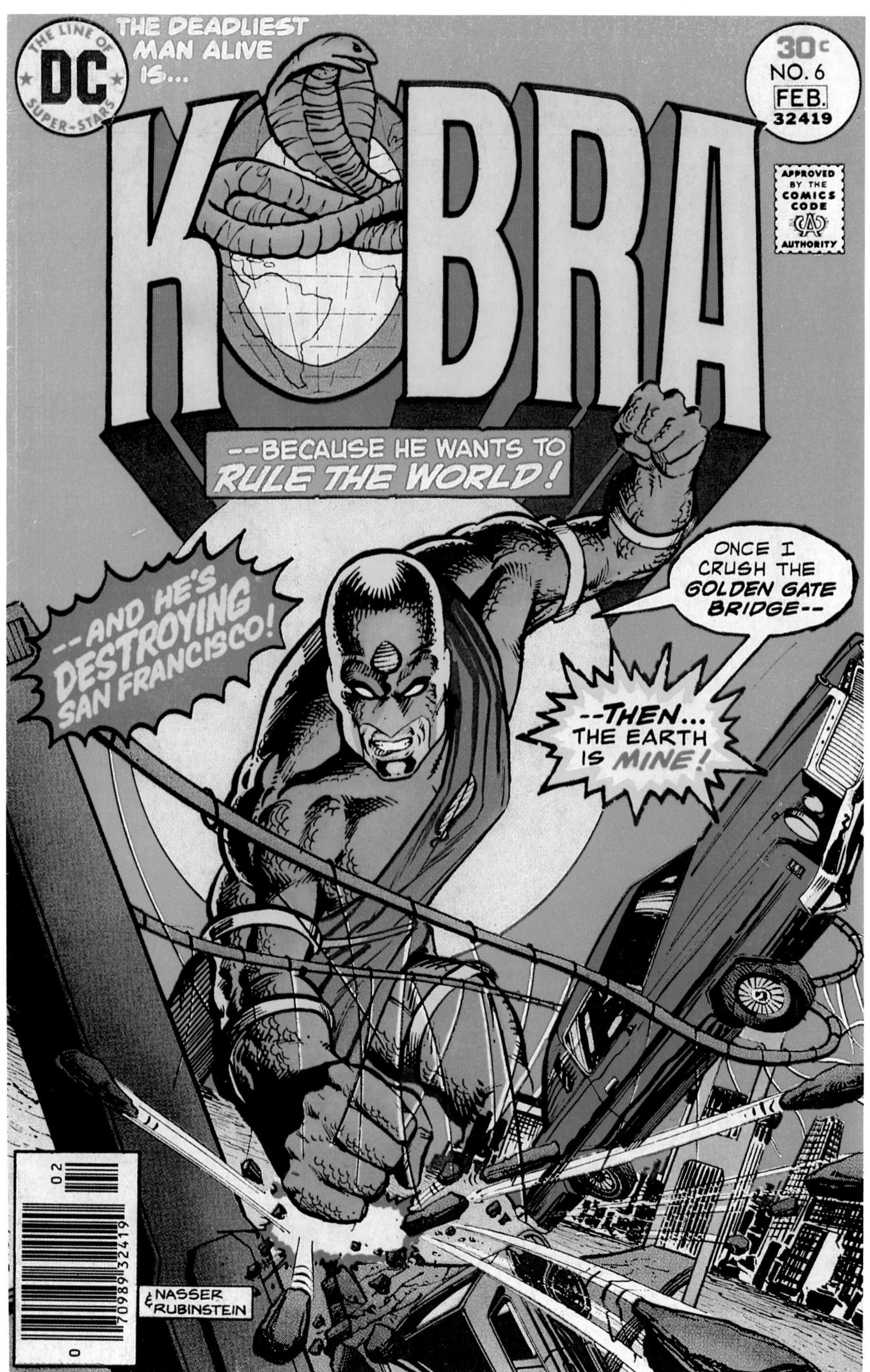

Kobra *with an utterance typical of super villains. © DC Comics.*

THE INVISIBLE MAN (N, MP, R, C)

Real Name: Dr. Griffin (no first name; see Comment).

First Appearance: 1897, *The Invisible Man*, H.G. Wells.

Biography: Although the Invisible Man created a good deal of mayhem, he perished before he could become a full-fledged lunatic and mass-murderer. A student at University College, Griffin was "almost an albino" who stood "six feet high, and broad, with a pink and white face and red eyes." An award-winning chemistry student in his late twenties, he transferred from the study of medicine to physics because the science of light fascinated him. Taking a job at a provincial college in Chesilstowe, he taught during the day and worked on a special invisibility formula at night. His work over the next three years was slowed because he had to keep it from one Professor Oliver, "a scientific bounder . . . a thief of ideas." Poverty-striken, lacking the money to continue his research, he robbed his father; alas, the money did not belong to his father and the poor man committed suicide. Renting a room in London in "a big ill-managed lodging-house in a slum near Great Portland Street," Griffin continued his work for nearly a year. Experimenting first on cloth and then on a cat (all but "the back part of the eye" disappeared), Griffin finally imbibed the formula himself. It made him ill; he spent "a night of racking anguish, sickness and fainting . . . my body afire." By dawn, his hands were like "clouded glass," and by midday he was utterly transparent. Heading to a theatrical supply shop, he clubbed the owner with a stool and stole "a mask of the better type, slightly grotesque but not more so than many human beings, dark glasses, greyish whiskers, and a wig. I swathed myself in calico dominoes and some white cashmere scarfs." He also stole the owner's boots. Roaming the countryside and adjusting to his invisibility (no easy task: dogs could smell him, his feet left prints, precipitation and fog showed his outline, and food was visible inside his body until digested), Griffin began to succumb to a creeping megalomania and casually assaulted people, nearly killing a constable. Soon, however, he took an old professor, Dr. Kemp, into his confidence. He did this because his notebooks had been stolen by a hobo and he needed help recovering them—as well as setting about his master plan of conquest. Kemp realized that invisibility had made Griffin mad and "inhuman" and, instead of cooperating with him, contacted the authorities. Griffin fled in a "blind fury" ("A little child playing near Kemp's gateway was violently caught up and thrown aside, so that its ankle was broken.") and was hunted down. In a brawling climax, he nearly strangled Kemp to death before being struck in the chest with a spade and perishing. However, in an Epilogue, it's revealed that the landlord of an inn in Port Stowe had recovered Griffin's notebooks.

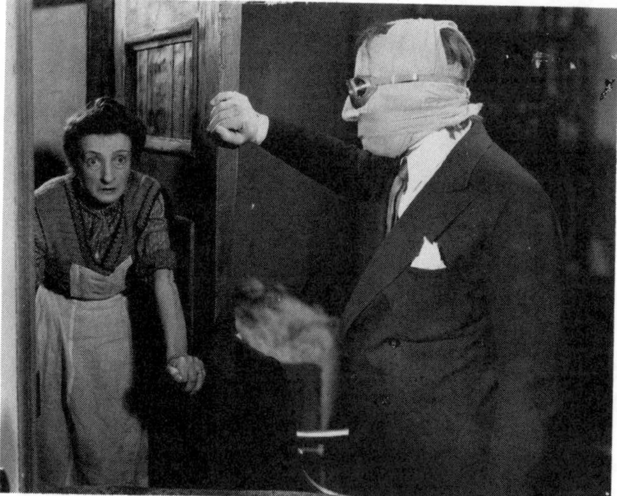

Claude Rains as ***THE INVISIBLE MAN.*** *© Universal Pictures.*

Quote: "That Invisible Man, Kemp, must now establish a Reign of Terror. He must take some town like your Burdock and terrify and dominate it. He must issue his orders. And all who disobey his orders he must kill, and kill all who would defend them."

Comment: Well-known as the Wells novel was, the character gained added eminence when the motion picture *The Invisible Man* was released in 1933. The central character also gained a first name, being called Jack Griffin in the film. Claude Rains starred as Griffin after Boris Karloff dropped out in a dispute over money. A sequel was made in 1940, *The Invisible Man Returns*, starring Vincent Price as Geoffrey Radcliffe, a convicted murderer. Alas, he's innocent and is given the serum (here called duocaine) by Griffin's brother Frank to try and prove his innocence. He does so before madness—now a recognized side effect of the drug—sets in. In 1944, Jon Hall played Robert Griffin in *The Invisible Man's Revenge*, lashing out at fellow treasure-hunters who leave him to die after finding diamonds in an African jungle. This Griffin is unrelated to the other Griffins, getting the invisibility serum from a scientist named Dr. Drury. Fittingly, Robert is eventually slain by Brutus, an invisible (except for his collar) great dane. Vincent Price (dis)appeared briefly as the Invisible Man at the climax of *Abbott and Costello Meet Frankenstein* (1948), and Griffin's serum surfaced again in *Abbott and Costello Meet the Invisible Man* (1951), recovered by Dr. Philip Gray and given to boxer Tommy Nelson so he can prove he's been framed for murder. Like "Jack" Griffin, Nelson experiences creeping insanity before he's restored by a transfusion from Costello (who, in turn, becomes invisible). There have been many other films and even a pair of TV series based on the character, but he was a hero in these dramas and unrelated to Griffin. The original story has been produced numerous times in recordings, most notably as a dramatization in 1962 and as a reading by Patrick Horgan in 1977. In comic books, the novel was adapted in 1959 as part of the Classics Illustrated series.

I.Q. (C)

Real Name: Ira Quimby.
First Appearance: 1963, *Mystery In Space* #87, DC Comics.
Costume: Blue breeches with white stripe down sides; purple jacket; yellow ascot; white gloves; navy-blue boots; dark goggles.
Weapons: Antigravity "lift" rod able to raise heavy objects; jet-powered aero-shoes which slip on over his boots and allow him to fly; energy rod able to fire destructive blasts; "magnetic cannon" to create huge solar flares.
Chief Henchmen: Numerous members of his gang.
Biography: Not a terribly bright man, Quimby was struck with brilliant engineering knowhow whenever he was in the Midway City Museum, exposed to the radiation of an alien stone, its energy released by sunlight. A criminal by trade, he used these flashes of genius to build super-scientific weapons which he and his gang used in their criminal pursuits. Though arrested by Hawkman and Hawkwoman, Quimby found that regular exposure to the stone had made the mutation become permanent; all he needed to set off surges of brilliance was to get into the sunlight. Repeatedly escaping from prison, he finally constructed a "magnetic cannon" and fired an "energy beam" directly into the heart of the sun in order to create "solar prominences which increased my intelligence as never before." Unfortunately, "the first thing my new super-genius discovered was—I had made an error in my calculations." His cannon blast had triggered a chain of events which was causing the sun to go nova. Enlisting the monstrous CHEMO to help him reverse the process (aided by Superman), I.Q. was successful, though Chemo turned on him and transformed him to stone (1978, *DC Comics Presents* #4). It took a while, but when the transmutation finally wore off, the furious super villain tried to destroy Superman; he was defeated and is currently back in jail.

THE IRON CLAW (MP)

First Appearance: 1941, *The Iron Claw*, Columbia Pictures.
Costume: Black overcoat buttoned to the top, with collar raised; black mask over lower half of face, slouch hat, wraparound sunglasses, glove over right hand.
Weapons: Left hand is sharp iron claw.
Biography: The Iron Claw goes about murdering members of the Benson family in order to uncover their concealed fortune in gold. He is eventually sniffed out by reporter Bob Lane.
Comment: An earlier villain, similar to the one in this 15-chapter serial, was seen in the Pathé motion picture *The Iron Claw* in 1916.

IRONFIST (C)

First Appearance: 1966, *Mighty Comics* #40, Archie Comics.
Costume: Blue mail bodysuit; red vest, trunks, boots; gray belt, helmet with pointed top, left-hand glove (see Weapons).
Weapons: Right hand is huge iron ball; costume is "computerized, so it unerringly performs the correct

***IVAN CHUNG** and Nhu menace Sarge Steel and Li-Li.*
© Charton Comics.

battle tactics to defeat any opponent"; jets in boots, controlled by "mechano-brain" hidden in left heel; computo-belt containing vials of explosives.

Biography: Ironfist is determined to "rule the underworld," but can't do that until the superheroic Web is out of the way. However, during the second of their two battles, the Web refuses to fight him because he has promised his wife he'll retire from crimebusting. Disillusioned, Ironfist mutters, "There's no fun in being an ultra-villain" and retires to the country to "raise chickens." He leaves his costume behind, and it goes on a rampage by itself. The Web smashes it down with a vacuum cleaner, after which his angry mother-in-law forces him to varnish the scuffed floor.

Quote: "Think you've *got* me, eh? Handcuffs are useless against my mighty iron-fist!"

Comment: The character appeared just once. On those occasions when the Web's wife allows him to fight crime, his villains include the powerful, orange Golem; Mr. Talons; the Flipper; the caped lunatic Madman; and the Vegetable who, dressed as a giant human cucumber, lobbed hand-grenades disguised as apples.

IVAN CHUNG (C)

First Appearance: 1964, *Sarge Steel* #1, Charlton Comics.

Weapons: Ancient executioner's sword.

Chief Henchmen: The Korean Nhu, the "Indestructible Man of Stone"; Li-Li, aka "the Black Lily."

Biography: A Communist agent and saboteur, Ivan is a half-Chinese Tong and a half-Russian. According to detective-cum-secret service agent Sarge Steel, Chung is "the most dangerous man I'd ever known"; based in Northwest China, he's devoted to building up Red nuclear power and resorts to everything from kidnapping to murder to achieve his goal.

Quote: "If Nhu fails, Li-Li . . . I will destroy Sarge Steel! If I do not kill him . . . he is yours!"

Comment: Chung appeared semi-regularly throughout Steel's three-year run. Other villains who tangled with the operative include the Lynx, Mr. Ize, the Prosecutors of the World, the cadaverous Smiling Skull, and Werner von Wess, the Mastermind of Crime.

JACK O'LANTERN (C)

Real Name: Jason Philip Macendale, Jr.

First Appearance: 1980, *Machine Man* #19, Marvel Comics.

Costume: Dark green belt, bodysuit (see Weapons); green leotard covered with large scales, boots, gloves; pumpkin head mask (see Weapons).

Weapons: Costume and pumpkin mask are bulletproof; mask also contains air supply and infrared lenses for night vision, and emits a halo of flame solely for effect. The villain also packs pumpkin grenades, worn on his belt; these contain gases which induce sleep, nausea, and tears—some even explode. Finally, Jack O'Lantern wears blasters on each wrist and vaults through the skies on a "pogo-platform."

Biography: A student at MIT, Jason was approached by the C.I.A. to come and work for them. He agreed, first serving in the Marines as a fighter pilot. Upon his discharge, he was assigned to Asia, where his brutality was too much even for the C.I.A. Dismissed, he became a mercenary specializing in terrorism and eventually adopted the flamboyant Jack O'Lantern guise to distinguish himself from others in his field. He subsequently became a bitter foe of the evil HOBGOBLIN. Upon the death of that villain, Jason took his superior accoutrements and became the new Hobgoblin.

Quote: "You're so predictable, Spider-Man. I knew you'd release me if others were endangered!"

Comment: O'Lantern founded the SINISTER SYNDICATE, though he didn't serve with them. GREEN GOBLIN and Hobgoblin also have a Halloween motif and hurl pumpkin bombs.

JAFFAR (MP)

First Appearance: 1940, *The Thief of Bagdad*, United Artists.

Costume: Black robe; golden belt, gauntlets; various turbans.

Biography: Determined to get to know his people better, King Ahmad dresses as a commoner and goes among them. Upon his return, Ahmad's ruthless Grand Vizier, the magician Jaffar, has him thrown in a dungeon and assumes the throne. Ahmad escapes with a thief, Abu, only to be struck blind when he confronts the wizard; Abu is turned into a dog. Meanwhile, Jaffar wins the hand of Ahmad's love, the Princess of Basra, by trading her father a flying mechanical horse. The Princess spurns Jaffar at first, but comes around when he promises to restore Ahmad's sight in exchange for her love. No longer blind, Ahmad doesn't like what he sees—the lovers sailing off in Jaffar's galleon. He pursues them in a small boat, but Jaffar whistles up a storm to stop him. Meanwhile, when the Princess' father sees what kind of man Jaffar is, he tries to renege on the deal; Jaffar responds by creating a beautiful six-armed dervish which stabs the King of Basra to death. After a series of adventures away from Bagdad, Ahmad and Abu are separated; Ahmad is captured by Jaffar and is about to be executed when Abu, armed with a crossbow, soars into Bagdad astride a flying carpet. Realizing that his short reign is over, Jaffar rushes to his flying horse and gallops into the sky, only to be shot in the forehead by Abu.

Quote: "I have powers that can force you to my will, but I want . . . your *love*."

Comment: Conrad Veidt (DR. CALIGARI's somnambulist) played the part in the Alexander Korda film; Miles Malleson wrote the screenplay. The character was loosely based upon Jaffar the Barmecide, the vizier of Harun ar-Rashid. In Arabian lore, he joined his master when Harun, dressed as a commoner, walked about Bagdad each night (as recounted in "The Barber's Sixth Story" in *The Arabian Nights Entertainments*). Other wizards in films with an Arabian setting include Sokurah (Torin Thatcher) of *The 7th Voyage of Sinbad* (1958), Koura (Tom Baker) of *The Golden Voyage of Sinbad* (1973), Zenobia (Margaret Whiting) of *Sinbad and the Eye of the Tiger* (1977), and Alquazar (Christopher Lee; see DRACULA, PISTOLS SCARAMANGA, and CAPTAIN RAMESES) in *Arabian Adventure* (1979). Sokurah dwells in a castle hidden deep in a cave on Colossa Island, and among his crimes are murder, shrinking the Princess Parisa to inches in height, and sending both a living skeleton and a flame-breathing dragon after the Arabian hero Sinbad. When the dragon is shot with a giant arrow, it falls and crushes Sokurah. Koura of Marabia is anxious to usurp the throne, and races Sinbad to the Fountain of Destiny which will increase his magic powers. Among the magician's evil acts are bringing to life a ship's masthead and a statue of the six-armed goddess Kali, both of which menace Sinbad; entombing the hero in a cave; and, by rendering himself invisible, trying to impale Sinbad with his sword. Happily, Sinbad manages to stab Koura, turning the waters of the fountain red with the magician's blood. As for Zenobia, she wants the kingdom of Charak for her son, Rafi (Kurt Christian), who is next-in-line. To this end she turns the rightful heir Kassim into a baboon, sends ghouls after his champion, Sinbad, and then races Sinbad to Hyperborea, where the effects of her magic can be undone at the Shrine of the Four Elements. Zenobia perishes when she sends her soul into the body of a saber-toothed tiger, which Sinbad slays. The non-Sinbad villain, Alquazar, has stolen a throne and now covets the Princess Zuleira. He is stopped by Prince Hasan and by the entrapment of his own soul in the Mirror of the Moon. Actor Lee used the role "to play personal tribute" to Veidt.

JAVELIN (C)

First Appearance: 1984, *Green Lantern* #173, DC Comics.

Costume: Yellow bodysuit with inverted blue pyramid from shoulders to navel; blue belt, gloves, mask, boots (see Weapons).

Weapons: Various jointed javelins worn in holsters on either thigh. These include a harpoon-javelin, explosive javelin, paint-javelin, gas javelin, and others. Javelin's boots contain rockets for flight.

Biography: Virtually nothing has been revealed about this character's past. A mercenary, Javelin was hired by Congressperson Jason Bloch to steal a Solar Jet engine from the Los Angeles-based Ferris Aircraft Company, a firm owned by the girlfriend of the superhero Green Lantern. Despite his arsenal, Javelin is bested by the superhero and is presently in jail.

JAX-UR (C)

First Appearance: 1961, *Adventure Comics* #289, DC Comics.

Biography: Sometime before the planet Krypton exploded, the scientist Jax-Ur was responsible for the destruction of the inhabited moon Wegthor. (Two explanations exist. In one, he was a space-center employee testing a nuclear rocket's destructive potential on a meteor when the missile went astray; in another, he was experimenting with the "jewel-minerals" in Krypton's Jewel Mountains and somehow generated a ray which blasted the moon to atoms. Though Jax-Ur most certainly did experiment with the jewels, for his laboratory was located in the mountains, the former explanation seems the most likely because Krypton subsequently abandoned its space program—a decision which, ironically, rendered it unable to evacuate its world when it exploded. [Even more ironic is the fact that all of the villains who had been sent to the Phantom Zone survived the explosion of Krypton.] For the sake of argument, it's possible to resolve the conflict in the two stories by concluding that Jax-Ur caused the missile to go off-target with a beam from a jewel.) For his crime, Jax-Ur was the first criminal banished to the Phantom Zone. Before the discovery of this eerie "twilight dimension," Kryptonian criminals were put into suspended animation and rocketed into space with special crystals which, over the course of a century, rid them of their villainous habits. Then scientist Jor-El (the father of Superman) learned of the Phantom Zone and developed a spotlight-like projector for the transfer of villains from our dimension to that one. There they exist as unaging, disembodied spirits, and while they are able to see the material world they cannot affect it in any way or make themselves known or seen by its citizens. The Phantom Zone villains can communicate among themselves only via telepathy. Over the years, Jax-Ur has remained a contentious fellow, trying to escape several times (for instance, when "electrical ions of the Aurora Borealis" opened the Zone a crack) and even plotting to destroy Superman from within (on one occasion, he found a way to turn his thoughts into "energy beams" which could reach outside the Zone). Other villains in the Phantom Zone include GENERAL ZOD; Dr. Xa-Du and his wife Emdine Ze-Da, both of whom caused the deaths of innocent subjects while experimenting with suspended animation; Va-Kox, who changed harmless life forms into monsters by polluting the Great Krypton Lake; Az-Rel and Nadira, psychics who used their powers to commit crimes; Kru-El (Jor-El's cousin) who built terrible weapons; Gaz-Or who, upon learning that he was soon to die, took to heart the bromide "misery loves company" and tried to destroy Krypton with an earthquake device; and Faora Hu-Ul, a woman who despised men and turned her martial arts abilities and pain-inducing thought-bolts against them.

Quote: "Who wants to be a hero? I'd rather be notorious."

Comment: Rather recently in the chronicles it has been shown that the Phantom Zone is at the fringe of a universe ruled by the omnipotent Aethyr, a being with the power to create or destroy anything in that universe merely by wishing it.

THE JESTER (C)

Real Name: Jonathan Powers.

First Appearance: 1968, *Daredevil* #42, Marvel Comics.

Costume: Green tights, slippers, jerkin; purple jester's cap with one peak and ball, collar which lies on shoulders and chest and has tassels all around it; orange glove, cowl with thin black vertical stripes; blue mask.

Weapons: Numerous toys and gadgets including a yo-yo which he uses like a mace or bolo, its cord made of steel for choking or binding victims; marbles which he drops in his wake to trip-up adversaries; exploding popcorn; caltrop-like objects which release tear gas; Frisbee-like discs which release a sleeping spray; explosive balls; small, heavily armed robots; and many other items.

Biography: A stage actor, Powers was severely panned in his first starring role, *Cyrano de Bergerac* and was dismissed after just a single performance. Only able to get work as a pratfalling comic on a children's show, he quickly grew disconsolate; contacting THE TINKERER, he commissioned a handful of exotic weapons, cobbled together a costume, and snubbed his TV "jester" role by embarking on a criminal career as the Jester. Because of his training, Powers is a fine athlete and swordsman; he briefly teamed with THE COBRA and Mr. Hyde (see MR. HYDE, Comment) in issue #61, the group using the unofficial name Trio of Doom.

Quote: "The forces of dark merriment shall still win the day! *Haha hahee*!"

Comment: THE JOKER, THE PRANKSTER, and THE TOYMAN also use toys and gags as weapons.

JIM EVERS (C)

First Appearance: 1941, *Spitfire Comics*, Harvey Comics.

Costume: Red trunks, boots, cowl, gloves.

Weapons: Paralyzing ray; invisibility ray.

Chief Henchmen: A gang of thieves wearing green tights, boots, and cowls.

***JIM EVERS** attacks his earthly hosts. © Harvey Comics.*

Biography: Evers is a scientist of the future (1980) who, after learning "the secret of rocket travel," builds a spaceship and heads for Mars. Unfortunately, a meteor strikes the ship and leaves it stranded in earth orbit where the scientist is "nourished by unknown rays of the sun," and not only survives but also grows to a height of eight feet. Returning to the earth's surface in 1990 when a small comet happens to nudge the ship out of orbit, it turns out that the "effects of time and space has [sic] warped his once brilliant brain and illusioned him with the idea that mankind hated him." Thus, he decides to make humankind suffer by becoming a criminal. Happening upon a gang of thieves in the midst of a crime, he saves them from capture and they become his flunkies. ("I don't want any of the money you rob," he generously informs them, "as long as you kill—kill!") Eventually, the heroic Magician from Bagdad catches up to the thugs and, after beating up the gang, tangles with Jim on a cliff. (Magician: "Ho! You wretched infidel of a dog, for once we meet honestly and openly!") and tosses him to his death.

Quote: "I love the earth—ha—haa—but—I hate human beings!!"

Comment: This was the character's only appearance. The adventure was hampered by terrible writing, though the John Giunta art was superb.

THE JINX (C)

First Appearance: 1981, *Adventure Comics* #488, DC Comics.

Costume: Navy blue bodysuit with orange stripes forming "V" on front and back and a small orange "J" on chest; navy blue full-face cowl with an orange pyramid on bottom and an inverted one on top; orange boots and gloves with navy blue feet and hands.

Biography: Nothing is known about this character's past, save that with a motion of his hand he can cause bad luck to happen to people, from having a car splash pedestrians by running through a puddle to causing grocery bags to split to having rats pop from hiding to terrify someone. (This implies not only telekinesis but spontaneous generation.) Settling in Fairfax to go on a "crime spree," he first intends to destroy the only ones who can stop him, Vicki Grant and Chris King, owners of the "Dial-H for Hero" device. After observing how they deal with two other villains—the crab-costumed Cancero and the slimy Jelly Woman—he waits at Alexander Hamilton Junior High in order to destroy the youths in their mortal identities. But they manage to become Snowfall and Captain Saturn, respectively, the latter felling the Jinx with a well-tossed metal ring.

Comment: This was the character's only appearance. The magazine also featured a story starring chemist Angela Wainwright, aka the villain Belladonna, Princess of Potions. Dressed in a purple leotard and cape, she wafted various gases from her rings, including clouds which induce sleep, choking, and darkness.

JOE PARRY (C)

First Appearance: 1964, *Justice League of America* #31, DC Comics.

Weapons: The Panacomputer, a device from the planet Pthisthin which has enormous artificial intelligence and the ability to synthesize animate beings.

Chief Henchmen: Sundry thugs and Super-Duper (#31 only); ULTRAA (#201 only).

Biography: A small-time crook, Parry is walking along a beach when he stumbles upon the Panacomputer, a small, yellow "wishing machine" from another planet. Discovering that "anything a guy can think of, it can make," he uses it to create the Super-Duper, a composite of Justice League of America heroes Green Lantern (arms and ring), Flash (legs), Wonder Woman (head and magic lasso), Hawkman (wings), and Batman (torso). However, because the Panacomputer is yellow, and Green Lantern is powerless against anything yellow, the power ring Super-Duper took from Green Lantern is also useless; unaware of this, it banks on using the weapon and is defeated by Hawkman. The Panacomputer is no longer a threat after it runs out of power. After doing time, Parry is walking along the boardwalk in Atlantic City, New Jersey, when he meets Jack Grey, who is cleaning dishes at a diner. Jack is secretly Ultraa, a young man with superstrength and superspeed. Joining Parry in a bank robbery, he attracts the attention of the Justice League when he rips the door off a vault. In time, Parry is captured and ends up in jail; Ultraa is allowed to return to his native Australia (#201).

Quote: "I find an alien *gizmo* . . . so what do I *do* with it? Do I ask it to give me a *college education*? Do I use it to get on *The Johnny Carson Show? No! I* have to get tied up fighting the *Justice League*!"

Comment: Super-Duper returned briefly in #65. Kept in the League's souvenir room, it was reanimated by T.O. MORROW.

THE JOKER (C, TV, CS, MP, N)

Real Name: Unrevealed, though he used the alias "John Dough" in 1969 (*Justice League of America* #77).

First Appearance: 1940, *Batman* #1, DC Comics.

Costume: As the Red Hood (see Biography): red cape, mask; blue tuxedo. As the Joker: purple formal jacket and trousers with black pinstripes; green shirt with purple string tie; orange vest; purple gloves, shoes with white spats; often wears lavender overcoat and fedora.

Weapons: Countless gimmicks, including a deadly joy-buzzer; darts coated with "Joker Venom," a concoction which not only kills people but also leaves them with a broad grimace; razor-edged playing cards; a vacuum cleaner the size of a garbage truck to suck up loot (and Batman); a sky-sled which also shoots fireballs; and a gun which puts victims at ease when a "Bang you're Dead" banner pops out on a stick . . . on which the victim is then impaled (the Joker cackling, "It's a spear-gun!").

Chief Henchmen: Varies; the Joker uses whomever he needs and then discards them. (As he tells one thug, "I have no further need for him! So I'm trading you—and *lantern jaw* here—for two other criminals!")

Biography: A laboratory assistant, the young Joker (his name has never been revealed) decides to undertake one crime, rob $1 million so he can live comfortably, and then retire. Becoming the Red Hood, he actually commits several crimes and crosses paths with the superheroic Batman. Trapped at the Monarch Playing Card Company, he tries to get away by jumping into a chemical vat which empties into the Gotham River; he succeeds in getting away (an "oxygen tube" in his mask provides him with air) but not without a price. The chemicals permanently dye his skin white, his hair green, and his lips a bright red. The change nudges his mind into insanity and he continues his criminal ways, but always with a twist. One time he bases all his killings on the punchlines of well-known jokes; another time he sets a quota for himself of executing a crime each day. And more often than not, he uses comedic props to commit these crimes. Early in his career, the Joker is captured, tried, and executed in the electric chair (*Detective Comics* #64). However, getting hold of his body, the Joker's flunkies administer a drug which returns him to life. When incarcerated, the Joker spends his time in State Prison; at one point, he became the editor of the prison newspaper.

Quote: "I may be *crazy*, Batman—but I'm not *stupid*! He who fails and *runs away*, lives to *win* another day!"

Comment: On the *Batman* TV series (1966-68) the Joker was played by Cesar Romero, who also played the part in the 1966 *Batman* film. In 1966, Signet Books collected the Joker's greatest comic book escapades in the paperback *Batman vs. the Joker*. He teamed with CATWOMAN and the PENGUIN in Winston Lyon's 1966 Signet novel, *Batman vs. the Three Villains of Doom*. The Joker was a recurring villain in the Batman comic strip and remains a powerful criminal force in the Batman comic books. He was the star of his own nine-issue DC comic, *The Joker*, from 1975 to 1976.

THE JUGGERNAUT (C)

Real Name: Cain Marko.

First Appearance: 1965, *X-Men* #12, Marvel Comics.

Costume: Brown tights, bands around arms, forearms, and knuckles, full-head helmet (see Weapons) and breastplate with red waist.

Weapons: Helmet, made from a metal forged in another dimension, protects the Juggernaut from psychic assaults.

Biography: Cain is the product of a broken home. His father, Kurt, a nuclear researcher, separated from his wife Marjory; Kurt subsequently married Sharon Xavier, the widow of his colleague Brian Xavier. (Her son by Brian, Charles, would one day become the leader of the superheroic X-Men.) After a stint in boarding school, Cain went to live with his father, who abused him terribly. Kurt also had no use for Sharon, whom he'd married for her money, and she died of a broken heart. While Kurt and Cain were busy arguing one day in the lab, Cain inadvertently overturned some unstable chemicals and the place became an inferno. Kurt perished in the blaze, leaving Cain and his stepbrother Charles alone in the large mansion in New York's Westchester County. Embittered, Cain soured even further as Charles excelled in his scholastic achievements and mastered his mutant powers of telepathy. Running away, Cain became a mercenary and eventually found himself in Asia. There he stumbled upon the ancient temple of Cyttorak and, taking hold of a magnificent ruby, received a mystic message from another dimension: "Whosoever touches this gem shall possess the power of the Crimson Bands of Cyttorak." Growing in stature and finding himself endowed with staggering physical strength—he can walk through a mountain if he chooses or survive an artillery blast—Cain became a super villain known as the Juggernaut. He has had several run-ins with the X-Men, among other superheroes.

THE JUNGLE-MAN (C)

Real Name: Tommy Young.

First Appearance: 1963, *Detective Comics* #315, DC Comics.

Costume: Leopard-skin loincloth and shoulderstrap; black headband.

Biography: A gang of criminals goes to the wilds of Africa, where one of them dresses as the superhero Batman and sets traps for a jungle-bred human known as Jungle-Man. Each time he's snared, the Jungle-Man is rescued by the other members of the gang who convince him that Batman is evil and must be stopped. Since Batman "has flown on the winds to a great city," the thugs bring Jungle-Man to Gotham City, where he uses his power of communicating with animals—among them, a giant snake, an elephant, and a rhinoceros—to distract Batman while the lawbreakers go about their crimes. Using his great deductive abilities to match Jungle-Man's footprints with those of the son of Edgar Young, a boy who was lost in the jungle 15 years earlier, Batman approaches Tommy with a teddy bear he'd loved as a child ("Where have I seen it before? Bwango! Bwango!"). Jungle-Man is persuaded that Batman is his friend and, routing the criminals, rejoins his parents.

Quote: "*Booda*! Boga, boga! At last I have my revenge against evil *Bad-Man*!"

Comment: This was the character's only appearance. For the record, "Edgar" is an homage to Edgar Rice Burroughs, a creator of the jungle hero Tarzan; "Young" is most likely a tribute to Jill Young, jungle-born heroine of the 1949 film *Mighty Joe Young*.

KANJAR RO (C)

First Appearance: 1961, *Justice League of America* #3, DC Comics.

Costume: Blue boots, wristbands, belt, cap with yellow fin, leotard with white "V" front and yellow braid around shoulders (the archfiend has multifaceted yellow eyes, like those of a fly).

Weapons: "Energi-rod" which he can use to fly (or permit others to fly), send signals across the universe, transmute matter (such as creating air in a vacuum or wringing water out of air), freeze a being's vocal chords with a "stupor ray," read minds, or instantly teach alien languages by subjecting someone to its "aranna ray." He also possesses a Gamma Metal Gong whose "ultra-sonic vibrations" are capable of paralyzing every being on a planet, a "hyperspatial telescope" for studying worlds in deep space, and a belt which projects television images of events elsewhere on a planet. He travels through space by entering the fourth dimension and crossing it on his galley-like "cosmic boat," whose oars "collect and focus the power of cosmic rays." When the vessel is not in use, he uses the energi-rod to shrink it to the size of a toy.

Biography: The delon (dictator) of the planet Dhor in the Antares system, Kanjar Ro is surrounded by enemies, most notably his "arch-enemy" Hyathis, the orange-skinned panala (queen) of the world Alstair; the metal man Kromm, who is gromar (king) of Mosteel; and Sayyar, the lizard-like jeffan (emperor) of Llarr. The foursome have been fighting "for years . . . in space and in our worlds," each one trying to rule the Antares solar system. Using his telescope to follow the exploits of the Justice League superheroes on earth, Kanjar Ro decides to "enlist" them as his unwilling allies by using the Gamma Metal Gong to paralyze everyone on earth. He explains, "Only the combined voices of Hyathis, Kromm, and Sayyar—speaking my name—can release the people of earth." The heroes do indeed capture the other leaders, but only to end the hostilities; expecting them to betray him, Kanjar Ro cannily uses his energi-rod to rob his foes of speech. Anticipating this, however, the superheroes had recorded the utterences through various means and, liberating earth, exile Kanjar Ro and his bellicose enemies to "Meteor-World," a small planet built for expressly that purpose. Escaping, he has since repeatedly fought both the Justice League and the space hero Adam Strange. He is currently on earth, though exactly where is not known.

KEHAMA (P)

First Appearance: 1810, "The Curse of Kehama," Robert Southey.

Biography: The most evil Raja in the world, Kehama had an equally cruel son named Arvalan. When the peasant Ladurlad protects his daughter Kailyal from Arvalan's advances, he incurs the wrath of Kehama; after a series of adventures, Ladurlad and Kailyal go to heaven and Kehama *et fils* end up in hell.

Comment: This extremely involved poem, which dwells primarily on the suffering of Ladurlad, draws extensively on Hindu mythology.

THE KEY (C)

First Appearance: 1965, *Justice League of America* #41, DC Comics.

Costume: Tan jumpsuit; brown boots, glove, belt, keyhole-shaped headdress.

Weapons: Numerous weapons, from simple blasters to those which punch holes between the dimensions, all in the shape of keys; psycho-chemical he himself ingests which gives him limited psionic abilities and puts people under his control (their conduct controlled, of course, by a keyboard).

Chief Henchmen: The Key-Men, simple flunkies.

Biography: Nothing is known about the past of this man (presumably earth-born) who wants to conquer the universe. He has frequently battled the Justice League of America, the superheroes being the most formidable impasse to his goal, but has yet to defeat them. His most dramatic effort along these lines was to impel the Leaguers to slaughter each other. He was undermined when Superman took a trip into the past, before the command was given, and returned to the present; unaffected, he knocked his partners out before they could harm one another (#63).

KHAN (TV, MP, N)

Real Name: Khan Noonian Singh (see Comment).
First Appearance: February 16, 1967, "Space Seed," *Star Trek*, NBC-TV.
Costume: Red shirt, trousers (TV); brown jacket with open front and short sleeves; black trousers; necklace with the "A"-shaped emblem of the starship *Enterprise* (MP only).
Biography: Khan was one of a race of superhumans, eugenically bred on earth in the 1990s. Known as *Homo superior,* they used their superior strength and intellect to rise to power, simultaneously seizing over 40 nations in 1992 with the intention of ultimately consolidating under one ruler—Khan, who himself ruled one-quarter of earth's population in South Asia and the Middle East. But the superhumans couldn't hold these countries and were deposed; Khan, the last holdout, was overthrown four years later. Escaping into space with four score of his followers aboard the Botany Bay, Khan and his fugitives went into hibernation for two centuries, drifting until they were discovered by the starship *Enterprise.* Brought aboard, they tried to take over the ship but were routed; Captain Kirk then offered Khan the option of rehabilitation or deposit on the planet Ceti Alpha V, a lifeless world, barely habitable, which Khan will be allowed to govern as he saw fit. Preferring to rule in hell than to serve in heaven, Khan accepted banishment to the planetoid. He was accompanied by Marla McGivers, a controls systems specialist on the starship, who had fallen in love with the charismatic Khan. Fifteen years later, the starship *Reliant* visited the Ceti Alpha system and sent a landing crew to what they believed was Ceti Alpha IV. It is, however, Ceti Alpha V. Captured by Khan, they learn that six months after he and his people were stranded there, the adjacent Ceti Alpha IV exploded. As a result, Ceti Alpha V suffered an orbital shift and the climate went from bad to worse; Marla and most of Khan's followers perished. Commandeering the *Reliant,* Khan stole the Genesis Effect device, a tool which could either create or destroy life on planets. Khan intended to use it for the latter purpose. However, he was pursued and defeated by Kirk and, badly wounded in a starship battle, spitefully detonated the Genesis device, hoping that the *Enterprise* would be consumed as well. Fortunately, only the ship of the vile superhuman was obliterated.
Quote: "How can one impart courage to sheep? I offered the world order. *Order*! And what happened? They panicked!"
Comment: Ricardo Montalban played the part on the TV series, and then again in the 1982 theatrical motion picture *Star Trek II: The Wrath of Khan.* The original teleplay was written by Gene L. Coon and Carey Wilbur. In 1968, James Blish's short story based on "Space Seed" was published in the anthology *Star Trek 2*; there, the character was known as Sibahl Khan Noonian. A novelization of the film was written by Vonda N. McIntyre and published in 1982.

KHOSATRAL KHEL (M)

First Appearance: August 1934, "The Devil in Iron," *Weird Tales,* Robert E. Howard.
Biography: "Millenniums" ago, the demon Khel rose from "Night and the Abyss" to walk the earth. Impervious to all human weapons, he took human form—in his natural shape he is a "thing . . . a blasphemy against all nature"—and "stalked through the world like a god," and in no hurry, for to him "a century was like an hour." Settling at last on the isle of Dagonia (located in modern-day Iran), he enslaved its primitive people until undone by a priest wielding a magic knife. Forged from a meteor, the blade was placed across Khel's breast and held him "senseless and inanimate" upon a golden dais. Alas, circa 10,000 B.C. a fisherman came upon the island, now called Xapur, and took the knife, allowing Khel to stir anew. Not only did the demon rebuild his ruined city, but also he brought its long-dead citizens back to life. Enter the heroic Conan the barbarian, who was searching for a missing slave named Octavia. After several adventures with the demon, the barbarian got ahold of the magic knife and slew Khel by driving the "crescent blade to the hilt" into his chest. The demon's "metal limbs melted and changed" back to inhuman form, and he went "back to hell whence he crawled."
Comment: The short story was collected in *Conan the Barbarian* (1955), *Conan the Wanderer* (1968), and *The People of the Black Circle* in 1977.

KILLER FROST (C)

Real Name: Dr. Crystal Frost; Dr. Louise Lincoln.
First Appearance: 1978, *Firestorm* #3 (as Crystal); 1984, *Fury of Firestorm* #20 (as Louise, not yet Killer Frost); 1985, #34 (Louise as Killer Frost), DC Comics.

Costume: Very pale blue boots, dress with bell sleeves; two strings of pearls draped over head, pearl necklace.

Chief Henchmen: Anyone she freezes over (see Biography).

Biography: A former student of Dr. Martin Stein (aka the superhero Firestorm) at Hudson University, Crystal Frost was in love with him . . . and was disconsolate when she learned that he did not share her love. Unfortunately, she happened to learn this while they were both on a research project in the Arctic. Not thinking clearly, she accidentally sealed herself inside a thermofrost chamber and emerged with a dramatically altered metabolism. She had become a heat vampire, using a kiss (or some other touch) to draw heat from her victims, at the same time leaving them a dead block of ice. (Or she can merely sap enough heat to "fog your brain . . . freezing your ability to reason and making you my icy slave." So powerful was her will that she was even able to enslave Superman [*DC Comics Presents* #17, 1980].) She also had the ability to radiate intense cold in waves or as icicle projectiles, as well as fly by chilling the air so it could hold her. Trying to kill Stein, she was captured by Firestorm and sent to prison (actually, a freezer at the jail; she is helpless at absolute zero). Escaping, she served briefly with THE SECRET SOCIETY OF SUPER-VILLAINS. While she was visiting with friend Dr. Louise Lincoln, Crystal was informed that the months she'd spent in the cooler had caused irreparable damage and she was dying. Furious, she attacked Firestorm, who allowed her to draw off a hefty portion of his nuclear energy, which destroyed her. Distraught over her friend's fate, Lincoln performed an experiment similar to the accident that had transformed Crystal Frost; she became a new Killer Frost. Teamed with the evil PLASTIQUE, she was defeated and sent to jail.

Quote: "They thought I was *dead* . . . but how can you *freeze* the burning flame of *hate*?"

KILLER KANE (CS, MP)

First Appearance: January 30, 1929, *Buck Rogers in the Year 2429 A.D.*, daily comic strip (21st episode), John E. Dille Co.

Weapons: Paralytic smoke bombs; super-powered "Iron Man" robot; standard-issue Org "jumping belt" containing "inertron" ("it falls upward" for jumping vast distances); Org "rocket gun" which fires "explosive bullets."

Biography: Kane lives in the 25th century, years after Mongol Reds have all but annihilated "peace loving North America." (Snorts one attacker from his airship, "Begin on that big idol holding a torch . . . that's their goddess.") "Orgs" or pockets of resistance still exist, one of them—the East Central Org—spearheaded by Anthony "Buck" Rogers. A 20-year-old, Buck had been surveying an abandoned mine near Pittsburgh back in the 20th century when he was overcome by a "peculiar" gas; he awoke 500 years

***KILLER KANE** drawn by Dick Calkins. © John Dille Co.*

later. In the Asian-dominated world, Kane is a Major in the resistance forces. He is the lover of soldier Wilma Deering, but she jilts Kane for Buck, his mortal enemy; hurt and vengeful, Kane goes to the Mongol emperor and vows to serve him in exchange for being made a squadron commander. A deal is struck and, in Buck's words, Kane "plunged into a criminal career of such utter daring and magnificent proportions as to be unequalled in the annals of two centuries." Kane frequently uses aliases to move about; in his most famous criminal adventure ("Martian War Threat"), he went about as Wing Bat Wu, master Martian spy. Kane's most devoted accomplice is Ardala Valmar, a former lieutenant in the East Central Org. Though she loves Kane, he is still hung-up on Wilma.

Quote: "Now, Buck, *you yourself* shall tell me the way through the cordon. A little toasting over hot coals may persuade you."

Comment: Anthony Warde played Killer Kane in the 12-episode 1939 serial *Buck Rogers* (which was subsequently edited into the feature film *Destination Saturn*); in this version, Kane has already conquered the world by the time Buck arrives. In the 1979 film, *Buck Rogers in the 25th Century*, Joseph Wiseman (see DR. NO) played Kane; Pamela Hensley was Ardala. Other comic strip foes of Buck Rogers include Toom, "mighty and ruthless warlord of Mars," who repeatedly tries to invade the earth; the pirate Black Barney, who has an itchy disintegrator-ray trigger-finger; and San-Lan of the Hans, a would-be world ruler who was featured in the first Buck Rogers adventure, the novel *Armageddon 2419 A.D.*, first published in *Amazing Stories* in 1928.

KILLER MOTH (C)

Real Name: Cameron Van Cleer.

First Appearance: 1951, *Batman* #63, DC Comics.

Costume: Purple bodysuit with yellow moth emblem on chest; orange gloves, non-utile wings (later a cape, then wings again); green boots (later orange), tights with horizontal orange bands; black trunks (later orange); yellow belt; green full-head helmet with antennae (see Weapons).

Weapons: Long, green Mothmobile with purple cocoon-like hood and equipped with radar and smokescreen devices; antennae which pick up local radio calls; "almost invisible" wire attached to his back which enables him to scale heights or swing across open spaces; gun which fires "glistening strands of gooey," entangling cocoon-material. (In his first adventure, Killer Moth was called to the scene of a crime by a moth-signal flashed in the sky side-by-side with the bat-signal shined by the police when summoning Batman.) The criminal belongs to THE SECRET SOCIETY OF SUPER-VILLAINS.

Chief Henchmen: Larva, Pupa, others; all wear costumes identical to Killer Moth, save for the emblem on chest, which they lack.

Biography: After serving a term at Gotham State Prison, inmate #234026 decides that when he gets out he's going to become the patron saint of criminals by protecting them from the crimefighting Batman. Wealthy due to his many crimes, Cameron sets up Moth Mansion, a "lepidopteral lair" with a gravity-free room to trap trespassers, false walls for hiding, and even a throne of melted wax. As many times as he is arrested by Batman, he returns—this, despite the fact that during one confrontation the Killer Moth took a bullet in the head from an angry henchman. The resultant surgery cost him part of his brain.

KILLER SHARK (C)

Real Name: General Haifisch (Killer Shark #1); Unrevealed (Killer Shark #2).

First Appearance: 1952, *Blackhawk* #50 (Killer Shark #1), Quality Comics; 1984, *Blackhawk* #269 (Killer Shark #2), DC Comics.

Costume: #1: green tights, vest with orange fringe on sleeves and yellow circle with black swastika over heart; green cowl with shark fin on top and lighter green goggles; yellow wristbands; orange boots with yellow cuffs. #2: purple bodysuit, cowl with shark fin on top and green goggles; white boots, belt, suspenders.

Weapons: #1: U-Boat. #2: Various implements including a whale-shaped submarine and shark-shaped jet.

Chief Henchmen: Both had numerous flunkies.

Biography: A Nazi general possessing superhuman strength—no doubt derived from medical experimentation—Haifisch was taken under Hitler's wing and trained to be the ultimate soldier. As Killer Shark, he tangled with the Allied adventurers the Blackhawks; he seems to have drowned during a battle on his U-Boat. A second Killer Shark raided the seas as a non-super pirate and fought the Blackhawks on numerous occasions; his whereabouts are unknown.

Comment: Another noteworthy Blackhawks nemesis is the Emperor. Dressed in a blue robe and a golden full-face helmet with a white laurel branch around the head, he is the "ruler of all international crime combines." On those rare occasions when he ventures from his lair, he does so dressed in golden armor which has an antigravity belt for flight and fires "golden energy jolts" from its gauntlets. His assassins dress like gladiators and pack sonic stun guns; his chief operative is the huge and powerful Gargantua, who wears a green outfit like that of a centurion. Additional Blackhawks villains include the winged Madame Butterfly, the seagoing Captain Squidd, the robot known as the Iron Emperor, and such luminaries—more intimidating in name than in deed—as the Bat, King Condor, Mr. Yesterday, Von Volter the Terrible, Grin the Grabber, the Scavengers of Doom, the Thunderer, and Carnage. See other underwater super villains ATTUMA, BLACK MANTA, CAPTAIN NEMO, CAPTAIN WHALE, DR. FANG, FISHERMAN, KRANG, MR. CRABB, OCEAN MASTER, ORKA, PIRANHA, and TIGER SHARK (2). Other Nazi super villains are BARON BLITZKRIEG, BARON GESTAPO, BARON ZEMO, CAPTAIN AXIS, CAPTAIN NAZI, THE CLOWN, THE GOLDEN FUHRER, NIGHT AND FOG, The Masked Swastika of VENDETTA, MASTERMIND (see U-MAN, Comment), THE RED PANZER, THE RED SKULL, and ZYKLON.

KILLER SHRIKE (C)

Real Name: Simon Maddicks.

First Appearance: 1977, *The Rampaging Hulk* #1, Marvel Comics.

Costume: Purple bodysuit with black shoulders, tops of arms and chest; black cape, trunks, boots, gloves, cowl with yellow queue; yellow belt, shrike silhouette on chest.

Weapons: Costume is bulletproof; there is an antigravity device implanted in his back; and he wears wristband blasters which also boast razorsharp crescent blades on either side for hand-to-hand combat.

Biography: An ex-soldier, Maddicks went to work for the multinational Roxxon Oil Company as an undercover operative. To make him more effective Roxxon subjected him to a vicious regimen of strength-boosting exercises, and he also under-went a surgical procedure which implanted a unit in his lower back enabling him to fly. Battling the heroic Ulysses Bloodstone, he suffered amnesia due to a malfunction of his weapons. Falling in with a succession of unsavory characters—including scientist Stephen Weems, aka the Modular Man, and the corrupt Brand Corporation—Maddicks eventually regained his memory and became a free-lance criminal operative.

Comment: The character has also battled the heroes Spider-Man and the Beast; he appears infrequently in the Marvel lineup.

KING KULL (also known as THE BEASTMAN) (C)

First Appearance: 1951, *Captain Marvel Adventures* #125, Fawcett Publications.

Costume: Brown boots, fur loincloth (sometimes with black spots); golden skull helmet with white horns.

Weapons: The "Moon Machine" to pull the moon closer to the earth; the "Dwindle Ray" which can shrink any object, including an entire planet; spaceship.

Biography: Thousands of years ago, Kull was the King of the Submen, brutish beings who nonetheless "had scientific weapons unknown to the world of today." But the human race outnumbered the Submen and, rising "in bloody revolt," exterminated the evil creatures. Kull was the only survivor and, hiding in a secret underground chamber, set off a bomb behind him so the humans "will think I blew myself up." There, in his lair 50 miles underground, he had hidden all manner of scientific equipment, including sleeping gas. Putting himself into suspended animation, he scheduled himself to wake at a point in the future when he could wipe out humankind "at the height of their glory and power." Stirring in our era, he relished putting his enormous sinew to the task of destroying everything in his path before undertaking his grandest project: to "wipe them out" by drawing the moon closer to the earth and wreaking havoc with the tides. Though the machine was destroyed by Captain Marvel, Kull escaped and returned to subject our world to his Dwindle Ray. This time he teamed with the vile DR. SIVANA, but the two ended up fighting each other and were sufficiently weakened so that Captain Marvel could haul them off to jail. King Kull remains a foe of the Marvel Family, and was briefly a member of THE MONSTER SOCIETY OF EVIL.

Quote: "Attention human worms! Ho ha! When earth has shrunk to small size, I'll grind it under my heel like a peanut! *Ha ho ha ho haaaa!*"

Comment: In the debut tale, Kull is referred to as the one and only "boogey man (who) from time immemorial . . . has tortured the hearts of children everywhere." The character is unrelated to the barbarian hero of the same name created by Robert E. Howard in 1929.

KING LOCUST (C)

First Appearance: 1967, *T.H.U.N.D.E.R. Agents* #17, Tower Comics.

Costume: Red T-shirt; gray trunks.

Weapons: Huge mechanical grasshoppers which can crush and fly, and whose wings generate typhoon-

***KING LOCUST** commanding his fleet of mechanical locusts as NoMan gets caught up in the action.*

force winds; sonic gun which generates a debilitating sound "like the magnified drone of a million grasshoppers"; life-size robot locusts which can chew through metal; human-sized, insect-like robot programmed to kill.

Chief Henchmen: Five-member King Locust Gang, all of whom ride inside their own giant grasshoppers.

Biography: An extortionist, King Locust demands $1 million from the U.S. government or he vows to destroy various federal government installations. Hiding himself inside the trunk of extortion money, the superhero NoMan of T.H.U.N.D.E.R. infiltrates Locust's hive-shaped headquarters high in the mountains and captures the super villain and his gang.

Quote: "NoMan, in one second you're going to be just a smear on the ground!"

Comment: This was the character's only appearance. T.H.U.N.D.E.R. stands for The Higher United Nations Defense Enforcement Reserve. See other insect-controlling super villains BARON BUG, THE DRAGONFLY RAIDERS, HUMBUG, QUEEN BEE, and SWARM.

KING NARCOR (C)

First Appearance: 1971, *Jungle Adventures* #3, Skywald Publishing Company.

Costume: Red robe with yellow markings on chest, shoulders, and sleeves.

Weapons: Dagger; the Omni-stone, created by "ancient Egyptian alchemists" and able to grant both great magic powers and immortality.

Chief Henchmen: Skyguards, winged blue warriors; Demon-Men, soldiers who do not bleed; his advisor Hemovore; other aides, spies, and soldiers; his chimp-like pet and confidant Brog; and a huge octopus-like creature "made of magic" which protects his citadel.

Biography: Narcor dwells in Africa, in a citadel atop a huge peak abutting the plains of Calare, beyond the Bog of Eternal Darkness. A powerful wizard, Narcor hopes to conquer more and more of the Dark Continent. However, an alliance is formed by the benevolent leaders Koalrack, Alindon (also spelled Alendon), and the jungle hero Zangar; although Narcor's armies are victorious, Zangar is able to get inside the mage's citadel. There, his unwilling fiancee Tellana smashes the Omni-stone and, powerless, Narcor stumbles into a pit of fire while fleeing the wrath of Zangar.

Quote: "*Opportunity glitters*! On the morrow-morn, my *chariots* shall *triumph*! All *Calare* shall be—*mine*!"

Comment: This is the character's only appearance; his name is alternately spelled Narcor and Nacor throughout the tale.

KING ZORR (C)

First Appearance: 1969, *Mighty Samson* #19, Gold Key Comics.

Costume: Purple trunks; purple and orange headband. (Like all of his people, Zorr's skin is blue, his wings, from the top, colored in bands of brown, orange, green, and purple.)

Weapons: Huge club; spear; whistle to summon Spearbirds (see Chief Henchmen).

Chief Henchmen: Hordes of subjects known as the Wing Men, who look like Zorr and can also fly; only Hawkarr is named. He is also served by Spearbirds, flocks of huge, pteranodon-like birds which dive with a "long sharp beak," can slice through trees or impale people, and also carry huge boulders to drop on the king's enemies. Zorr summons these flocks to him by whistle.

Biography: Nothing is known about this character's past. Zorr and his Wing Men live north of N'Yark (New York), an unspecified time after "a great nuclear war (has) devastated the planet." Presumably mutated from either humans or birds, Zorr wishes to chase the humans from the city so "our winged people can take over the tall buildings as roosting places," but his job is complicated by the presence of the superhuman Mighty Samson and, later, by the turncoat Hawkarr, who becomes sick of "King Zorr's cruel methods" and joins the humans. Realizing he must destroy these two adversaries who keep turning back his Spearbirds, Zorr corners the weaponless Hawkarr in the skies and impales him, then turns on Samson. The two battle atop the ruins of the Chrysler Building where King Zorr takes such a beating that his wings become paralyzed and he plummets to his death.

Quote: "You have beaten off this attack, but I will win your big city! I will strike again . . .and again . . . and again until you all flee!"

Comment: This was the character's only appearance. For the most part, Mighty Samson battled mutated monsters during his 32-issue run. One notable exception to the roster of monsters was the barbarian chief Kull, yet another villain to use the name of Robert E. Howard's legendary sword and sorcery hero. He appeared in issue #10 (1967).

KING ZORTH (C)

First Appearance: 1965, "Victory for the Trigans," IPC.

*The death of **KING NARCOR**. © Skywald Publishing.*

Costume: Red robe; lavender cape; golden sash around waist, necklace, helmet.

Weapons: Air fleet of jet fighters and crescent-shaped airplanes known as "atmosphere scouts" armed with fire bombs known as "heat projectiles" (there are also ground-based versions of the guns); a Navy; the Waves, "invisible, supersonic waves of energy . . . a shock wave that could crumble stone to powder."

Chief Henchman: Klud, the traitorous brother of Trigo.

Biography: The planet Elekton circles the star Yarna over a billion miles from our world; on one of the world's eight continents, Victris, dwells the warmongering nation of Loka. From the "silvery domes" of the capital city of Byzan, the king of Loka plots the conquest of the planet. However, after a series of engagements on land, in the air, and upon the seas, he is defeated by brave Trigo and the freedom-loving people of Vorg, a nation to the southeast. When last seen, Zorth is returning to Loka on foot while Trigo forges the mighty new Trigan Empire. Zorth is a sadist who is as cruel to his own people as to his enemies; when his men lose a battle, he orders his guards to "see that one in every ten of these shrinking curs is led out to instant execution."

Quote: "It matters little whether we first obliterate Vorg . . . or Cato . . . since we will destroy both in our good time."

Comment: The story was serialized in IPC's comic magazines. The despot returned in the story "Elekton in Danger." Other villains in the longrunning saga include Trigan subject Yenni, a thief, who, after being arrested by the warrior-king Kassar of Hericon, nearly incited a war between Trigan and Hericon by kidnapping Kassar's sister ("Truce With Hericon"); the tyrannical Akkan, leader of the Trigan colony of Zabriz ("Revolution in Zabriz"); Thara, Trigo's power-mad niece ("Battle for Trigan City"); and the scientist Thulla, who tries to conquer the moon of Bolus ("The Invasion of Bolus"). The strip was brilliantly drawn by Don Lawrence.

KLAW (C)

Real Name: Ulysses Klaw.

First Appearance: 1966, *The Fantastic Four* #53, Marvel Comics.

Costume: Red bodysuit, left glove, boots; purple trunks; purple skullcap with black fringe and nose-guard (sometimes cap is red with purple area in center).

Weapons: Right hand has been replaced by "soni-claw," a dish-like appendage which fires destructive blasts of sound.

Biography: A university physicist, Klaw is working on a process to turn sound waves to matter. Requiring vibranium to complete his experiments, he journeys to Wakanda, the African nation where the only known deposits exist. When the natives who guard the "sacred mound" deny Klaw permission to mine it, he has his men kill their chief, T'Chaka; standing by, the chief's young son T'Challa (who will one day become the superhero the Black Panther) snatches Klaw's own sonic gun and uses it to exact vengeance, blasting Klaw's right hand. The maimed scientist flees and, building the soni-claw with black market vibranium (which he should have obtained in the *first* place), he has what's left of his hand removed and the weapon fitted to his forearm. A decade passes before he returns to Wakanda. Beaten by the Black Panther and the Fantastic Four, the enraged criminal hurls himself into a huge sonic converter in the hope of obtaining superpowers. He succeeds, turning his body into a mass of "living sound" with phenomenal physical strength. He can, for example, lift a tank with no effort. Withal, he has yet to defeat the Fantastic Four or his other perennial foes, the Avengers.

Quote: "The Avengers, eh?! Now I won't have to go looking for you! I'll just kill you here!"

KOBRA (C)

Real Name: Burr (surname; no first name).

First Appearance: 1976, *Kobra* #1, DC Comics.

Costume: Golden, scaled bodysuit, cowl, gloves, and boots (later all became red, no scales); golden belt and bands around shins, thighs, upper arms, wrists; green toga (later a cloak was added, along with a yellow-and-black cobra emblem on chest).

Weapons: Venom-spray (acid) which is fired from small hoses on his gloves and sears those who disobey or fail him (this was later replaced by a gas which blinds or renders his foes insensate); strangling "tongue" which shoots from glove of other hand.

Chief Henchmen: Eve, who is also his inamorata; Cobra Cultists who are garbed in green-scaled bodysuits; CHEETAH.

Biography: Two Burr brothers were born in New Delhi on May 25, 1953. Siamese twins, they were separated after a 21-hour operation. However, one of the brothers was kidnapped by a cult of cobra-worshippers who must replace their leader every 44 years; they saw in his efforts to survive the surgery the strength "to work his will upon the world." Taken to their lair (which makes "an opium den look like a Christian Science reading room"), he was raised to be a killer and, on his 21st birthday, he drank cobra venom to test his worthiness to lead them. Surviving, he took the name Kobra and dedicated himself to conquering the world for his cult. His brother, Jason, devoted himself to stopping his sibling, but there was a catch: Whatever pain was experienced by one was also felt by the other. Eventually, Kobra managed to slay his brother with the help of neural neutralizer which interrupted their link. He continues his despotic activities to this day.

Quote: "*Silence*, inquisitive dolt! Mine is to give *orders*, not *answers*!"

Comment: There were seven issues of the Kobra's magazine; the series was conceived as a variation of Alexandre Dumas' *The Corsican Brothers*.

KODOS THE EXECUTIONER (TV)

Real Name: Anton Karidian (see Biography).

First Appearance: December 8, 1966, "The Conscience of the King," *Star Trek*, NBC-TV.

Biography: When the planet Tarsus IV experiences a famine due to a mutated form of fungus, it's a calamity which fits right in with governor Kodos' warped ideas of eugenics. He uses the blight as an excuse to kill half the population of 8,000 souls to ensure that the "superior" half survives. Representatives of the governing Federation arrive shortly thereafter and are shocked by the crime. But all they find of Kodos are his charred remains, and the books on Tarsus IV are closed. Twenty years later, people who had survived the genocide begin to die. Curiously, they are murdered everywhere the troupe of actor Anton Karidian happens to play. As it turns out, Kodos did not die but became Karidian who, underwritten by the Interstellar Cultural Exchange, brings Shakespeare to space bases. Unbeknownst to Kodos, his 19-year-old daughter Lenore has taken it upon herself to protect him by slaying anyone who might recognize him. Learning of her activities and shocked to the core ("You weren't even born! I wanted to leave you something clean!"), Kodos throws himself in front of a phaser beam intended to kill eyewitness Captain Kirk of the starship *Enterprise*. Shocked by what has happened, Lenore promptly loses her mind. These events take place in the 23rd century.

Quote: "I was a soldier in a great cause! There were things that had to be done—hard things, terrible things!"

Comment: Arnold Moss starred as Kodos; Lenore was played by Barbara Anderson. Barry Trivers wrote the teleplay.

KOR THE CONQUEROR (C)

Real Name: Dr. Anton Koravyk.

First Appearance: 1967, *The Doom Patrol* #114, DC Comics.

Costume: Brown loincloth; white lab jacket.

Weapons: Destructive sound gun.

Biography: A brilliant scientist and an expert in sound, Dr. Koravyk is a good friend of Niles Caulder, leader of the superheroic Doom Patrol. While Koravyk is busy conducting an experiment in time warps, something goes awry and de-evolves him to a towering Neanderthal named Kor. Going on a rampage through Johannesburg, and carrying one of Koravyk's sonic weapons, he is stopped when the Doom Patrol manages to reverse the effects of the accident.

KRANG (C)

First Appearance: 1963, *Fantastic Four Annual* #1, Marvel Comics.

Costume: Many different costumes, uniforms, armor, etc., over the years. He currently wears green tights, belt, and gloves; a yellow leotard with long sleeves and a red starburst on chest; dark green boots; red cape (Krang's skin is blue).

Weapons: Numerous arms, from guns to swords to tridents.

Chief Henchmen: ORKA; many warriors in his army.

Biography: Born to the water-breathers of the sunken continent of Atlantis, Krang became a soldier with one eye always on the throne. Ingratiating himself in time to the superheroic Sub-Mariner, the ruler of Atlantis, he rose through the ranks and simultaneously consolidated his power with the military. Then, when the Sub-Mariner was visiting the surface world, Krang struck, setting himself up as tyrant. But the people detested his cruel ways and, with their support, the Sub-Mariner eventually met Krang in battle and reclaimed the throne. Krang was exiled, but that hasn't stopped him from making repeated stabs at the throne. His most recent, in league with THE SERPENT SQUAD, ended in his defeat at the hands of the Sub-Mariner, Captain America, and Nomad.

Comment: See other underwater super villains ATTUMA, BLACK MANTA, CAPTAIN NEMO, CAPTAIN WHALE, DR. FANG, FISHERMAN, KILLER SHARK, MR. CRABB, OCEAN MASTER, ORKA, and TIGER SHARK (2).

KRAS (TV)

First Appearance: December 1, 1967, "Friday's Child," *Star Trek*, NBC-TV.

Weapons: Phaser pistol for killing.

Biography: Kras is a Klingon, one of the swarthy, militaristic alien humanoids who are sworn enemies of humans and their Federation in the twenty-third century. Kras has been dispatched to the planet Capella IV to stop the Federation from securing rights to mine the life-sustaining mineral topaline. Encouraging a rebellion against Capella IV's teer (ruler), Akaar, Kras lets the revolutionaries kill Akaar, then betrays them, looking to take over the planet for the Klingons. However, Captain Kirk and a landing party from the starship *Enterprise* intercede. They wound Kras with a bow and arrow, after which he is killed by Keel, one of the rebels.

Comment: Tige Andrews starred as Kras; D.C. Fontana wrote the teleplay. Other Klingons who have figured prominently in the *Star Trek* adventures include Commander Kang (Michael Ansara), who invades the *Enterprise* in "Day of the Dove"; Captain Klingon (K.L. Smith) who attacks the starship in "Elaan of Troyius"; Commander Kor (John Colicos, who also played BALTAR), military governor of Organia in "Errand of Mercy" and commander of the battlecruiser *Klothos* in the animated cartoon "Time Trap" (voice unknown); and Captain Koloth (William Campbell), the sworn enemy of the Federation's Captain Kirk in "The Trouble With Tribbles" and commander of the battlecruiser *Devisor* in the animated adventure, "More Tribbles, More Troubles" (voice by James Doohan).

KRAVEN THE HUNTER (C)

Real Name: Sergei Kravinoff.

First Appearance: 1964, *The Amazing Spider-Man* #15, Marvel Comics.

Costume: Orange armbands, tights, both with black leopard-spots; lion-head vest, with mane serving as capelet; tan sandals; zebra-skin wristband, belt with tusks radiating from it (see Weapons).

Weapons: Tusks on belt contain "tranquilizer drug"; he also has used "escape-proof" magnetic handcuffs; drums that are so loud they disorient foes; a "control collar" which compels people to obey him; "electro-bursts" fired from the eyes of his lion vest; and various primitive weapons, from spears to snares.

Biography: The son of wealthy Russians who fled to England after the Revolution, Sergei lost his parents shortly thereafter. Traveling around the world and living from day to day, the youth finally settled in the wilds of Africa. There, he learned the ways of the jungle and earned great wealth as a big game hunter. He also befriended a witch doctor who showed him how to combine herbs into a potion giving him superhuman agility and senses, not to mention the strength to deliver a "nerve punch" capable of felling "a full-grown charging rhino." Eventually growing bored with hunting animals, he decided to hunt humans, and his friend THE CHAMELEON—who sold the pelts and ivory Kraven bagged—suggested that he tackle the superhero Spider-Man. Agreeing to do so, Kraven came to New York and immediately demonstrated his prowess by capturing two escaped cobras and felling a pair of gorillas on-the-loose. Though Kraven proved no match for Spider-Man, who left him snared in a web in the park, he returned again and again to tackle this worthy opponent. He also took time out to hunt the jungle superhero Ka-zar (*Astonishing Tales* #'s 1 and 2 [1970], and *The Amazing Spider-Man* #'s 103 and 104), though that effort also ended in defeat. ("*Amazing*!" Kraven gasped after spraying Ka-zar with gas from a tusk, "that vapor-blast would have felled a *bull elephant*!" To which the jungle hero rather cockily replied, "Yes—because a mere *beast* would not have held its *breath*!") In *The Amazing Spider-Man* #'s 110 and 111, Kraven teamed with an incredibly strong and agile young man named Martin Blank, who dressed in a shaggy suit and hunted Spider-Man as the Gibbon. Even that team-up failed to defeat the wallcrawling hero, and though Kraven has since directed most of his energies to hiring himself out as a hitman, he hopes to triumph eventually.

Quote: "I do not *believe* in honor—only in *expediency*!"

Comment: The nonsuper aspects of Kraven were evidently inspired by GENERAL ZAROFF.

KRISS-KROSS (C)

Real Name: Kristopher Kross.

First Appearance: 1982, *DC Comics Presents* #45, DC Comics.

Costume: Orange trunks, boots; red stripes criss-crossing torso, forehead, and thighs.

Biography: After stealing hi-tech instruments from Concordance Research—which does work for the U.S. Department of Defense—traitor Kross is trying to flee by plane when Superman smashes the aircraft. He bails out, only to be struck by lightning on the way down; his body is somehow fused with the equipment, giving him the power to "control technology from a distance." After wreaking havoc with the Navy (causing jets to take off by themselves and overloading systems onboard ships until they explode) and drawing even more power from satellites in earth orbit, Kross is finally short-circuited. The superhero Firestorm breaks his satellite link with a sizzling "fzzaam," and Superman knocks him out with a tried-and-true "kpow!"

Quote: "My power will kriss-kross a continent—a world—creating a network of chaos!"

Comment: This was the character's only appearance.

KULAK (C)

First Appearance: 1940, *All-Star Comics #2*, DC Comics.

Costume: Golden robes, headdress.

Weapons: The Ring of Life, a will-sapping amulet; and the helmet of Nabu the Wise, a magic artifact possessing the spirit of the mage along with great mystic powers.

Chief Henchmen: The ghosts of his warrior slaves from Brztal.

Biography: Kulak was the high priest of Brztal, a world he ruled for centuries. A master sorcerer, Kulak had the power to make people turn on each other planet-wide, using the Spell of the Whispering Death; he also had the ability to become a physical giant. Using his magic he attempted to devastate other worlds; somehow, though, one civilization managed to trap him on our world, where he remained in hibernation until unearthed by unsuspecting archaeologists. Waking and resuming his evil ways, he was prevented from destroying our world by the mystic superhero the Spectre. Returning sometime later, Kulak took over the Spectre's will using the Ring of Life. Next, he lifted the helmet of Nabu the Wise from Dr. Fate and attempted to use it to tap great mystic energies. But the power proved too great, and flung the tyrant into a distant dimension. He has not been heard from since.

Comment: Other conquerors cut from the huge, evil Kulak cloth include THE ANTI-MONITOR and TRIGON.

KUNG (C)

Real Name: Thomas Morita.

First Appearance: 1977, *Wonder Woman #237*, DC Comics.

Costume: Purple bodysuit with black and white yin and yang symbol on chest, rising sun red-and-white stripes from waist to bottom of chest; red trunks; white belt, boots.

Biography: Due to his Japanese ancestry, the first-generation American Morita experienced a great deal of hostility during the pre-World War II years. After his parents' death, which he ascribed to prejudice, Morita returned to Japan and studied both martial arts and mysticism. Mastering the art of turning into any animal he wishes (without losing his human intelligence), he returned to the United States as Kung, the Assassin of a Thousand Claws, serving the Japanese war-effort. After tangling with the All-Star Squadron, he perished at the hands of Wonder Woman in 1943.

KURGAN (MP)

First Appearance: 1986, *Highlander,* Twentieth Century-Fox.

Costume: Sixteenth-century: black cloak, gloves; animal-skull helmet; intricate armor. Twentieth-century: black trousers, vest; mail gloves; white T-shirt.

Weapons: Sword.

Biography: Kurgan was one of the earth's few immortals, men who inexplicably live forever. Born 3,000 years ago in what is now the Soviet Union, he turned up as a soldier in Scotland in the sixteenth century; there he first met fellow immortal Connor MacLeod, who would be his eternal enemy. After wounding Connor, he moved on; five years later, he turned up on Connor's farm. Though Connor was away, another immortal, Ramirez, was present; the men dueled, Kurgan suffering a slit throat before killing his adversary (by cutting off his head, the only way immortal can kill immortal). Raping Connor's wife, Kurgan went his own way. The men met again in New York City in 1986 for the Gathering, a long-prophesied time when all the surviving immortals are to be mystically drawn to one spot to battle to the death for a mysterious prize. Rendered insane by eons of killing, Kurgan holed up in a flop house and dressed in a shaved-head, punk style—complete with safety pins through the scar in his neck—and went on a tear through New York, slaying immortals and mortals alike before he and Connor, the last two immortals, met in a climactic duel in an empty warehouse. When Connor lopped off Kurgan's head, demons visibly fled the immortal's dying body. Connor won the prize, which is the ability to use his wisdom to psychically influence the minds of world leaders. It isn't clear how or why, but Kurgan and his sword both had the power to smash stone walls.

Comment: Clancy Brown played the part in the motion picture; the story was written by Gregory Widen, with a screenplay by Widen, Peter Bellwood, and Larry Ferguson.

KURSE (C)

Real Name: Algrim the Strong

First Appearance: 1984, *Thor* #347, Marvel Comics.

Costume: As Algrim: blue armor, helmet, gauntlets, boots. As Kurse: golden thigh boots with red fins on the sides and yellow decorations; yellow shirt; red girdle beneath white belt shaped like an elongated skull; red vest with yellow markings on front; spiked, golden bands around shoulders; red gloves with golden cuffs; yellow mask with horns on the side; red helmet with red horns on top, yellow on the sides; white skull-like necklace.

Biography: An elf, Algrim dwelt in Svartalfheim in another dimension and served Malekith the Accursed, the evil ruler of the Dark Elves. To protect Malekith from the wrath of the superhero Thor, Algrim met him in battle; caring nothing for either being, Malekith caused the earth to open beneath them. Thor was able to fly to safety using his magic hammer, but Algrim ended up taking a lava bath. Near death, the elf was found beneath the English countryside by the extraterrestrial Beyonder. Curious, "to watch him fulfill his desire" and murder Thor, the alien revived him. Taking the name Kurse, the elf headed for New York (by strolling across the ocean floor) and tore the city apart until met by Thor and the superheroic children known as Power Pack. After a ferocious battle, Kurse finally realized that it wasn't Thor who was his enemy, but Malekith. Tracking him to Asgard, the home of the gods, he slew the archfiend and then gave up his evil ways. At last report, he was still in Asgard.

Quote: "Now I shall administer the coup de grace . . . and forever will the legends sing of the glory of *Algrim the Strong* who slew the *Mighty Thor*!"

Comment: Malekith himself was quite a villain, a wizard who used his powers to serve the vile SURTUR.

THE LAME ONE (MP)

Real Name: Walter Odette.

First Appearance: 1937, *Dick Tracy*, Republic Pictures.

Weapons: The Flying Wing, an airplane armed with a ray that destroys objects by high frequency rays.

Chief Henchmen: The Spider Gang, of which the physician Moloch is the most devoted; Gordon Tracy.

Biography: Based in San Francisco, the Lame One—known to the police as the Spider—is a powerful crime boss. Among the crimes he attempts during his brief but busy screen career are plotting to sell the formula for the alloy nickolanium to an hostile foreign power; robbing millions in furs; stealing the magnificent Mogra Necklace; destroying the Bay Bridge with his sonic disintegrator; robbing the gold strike of prospector Death Valley Johnny; stealing bullion from a ship; and sundry, less flamboyant kidnappings and murders. Though detective Dick Tracy is able to waylay the Lame One time after time, Tracy is hampered more than once by his own brother Gordon, who the Lame One has turned into a slave through surgery. In the end, Tracy and a group of G-men corner the villain in his headquarters, Cragg's Head. Moloch is arrested but the Lame One escapes in a car, with Gordon at the wheel. But Gordon swerves to avoid hitting his brother's secretary Gwen and his ward Junior, who are coming up the road; the car goes off a cliff, killing both the Lame One and his unwilling accomplice.

Comment: Edwin Stanley played the Lame One; John Picorri was Moloch. The 15-chapter serial was written by Barry Shipman and Winston Miller, based on a story by Morgan Cox and George Morgan. The Lame One does not appear in the Dick Tracy comic strip. See also THE GHOST.

LASKA (MP)

First Appearance: 1952, *Blackhawk*, Columbia Pictures.

Weapons: Destructive electronic ray; wrist radios for communicating with her henchmen.

Biography: Laska is one of the most successful saboteurs working in the United States. Kidnapping Dr. Rolph, inventor of the electronic ray, she unwittingly attracts the notice of ace crimebuster Blackhawk, who rescues Rolph. Though Laska escapes, Blackhawk ultimately arrests her as she tries to leave the country. Apart from trying to undermine the United States, Laska also has no qualms about murdering her superior who she believes is going to let Blackhawk have her so he can go free.

Comment: Carol Forman played Laska in the 15-chapter serial. Forman also played THE SPIDER LADY and THE BLACK WIDOW.

THE LEADER (1) (M)

Real Name: Baron Vardon.

First Appearance: December 1937, "The Golden Peril," *Doc Savage* Magazine, Kenneth Robeson.

Weapons: The Hand of Death, a glove covered with hundreds of tiny needles which inject a swift-acting poison; .45 automatic.

Biography: Vardon is a tall man with black eyes and hair and "a thin, mobile face." A League of Nations representative, he asks the superhero Doc Savage to help him block the plans of a mysterious man named the Leader who, based in Switzerland, is trying to conquer the world. He's attempting to do this by raiding an ancient Mayan treasure in the Valley of the Vanished and flooding the market with billions of dollars worth of gold. The gold standard would thus be undermined, throwing every nation into panic; simultaneously, his cohorts would stir up rebellion everywhere, setting him up as world dictator. What Savage doesn't know is that the Leader is Vardon, who fakes his own demise by the Hand of Death so that, should he be thwarted, he would be able to assume a new, anonymous identity. When Doc finally corners the Leader, he does indeed perish, albeit accidentally, by the Hand of Death. In his identity as the Leader, Vardon's skin somehow seems more "ghastly white," his eyes more "malevolent."

Quote: "You assured me you could seize control of this country within two hours. You failed."

THE LEADER (2) (C)

Real Name: Samuel Sterns.

First Appearance: 1964, *Tales to Astonish #62*, Marvel Comics.

Costume: Orange bodysuit with golden shoulders, collar, belt, suspenders-like straps; golden boots, gloves (Leader's skin is green).

Weapons: Numerous, including advanced robots, computers, a space station headquarters, and other hi-tech tools.

Chief Henchmen: Many nameless spies and aides.

Biography: Working as a custodian at a scientific research center in the Nevada desert, Sterns is busy moving cans of nuclear waste when one of the canisters explodes. Bathed in gamma radiation—the same kind of radiation which turned Dr. Bruce Banner into the mighty Hulk—Sterns becomes a super-genius. Deciding to rule the world, he takes the name of the Leader and organizes an international spy ring. But each operative proves too independent and the group fails in its goal; establishing headquarters in a New Mexico laboratory—and, later, in space—he is constantly thwarted by such superheroes as the Hulk and the Avengers.

LEAPFROG (C)

Real Name: Vincent Patilio.

First Appearance: 1967, *Daredevil #25*, Marvel Comics.

Costume: Green bodysuit, full-head frog mask; light green trunks, powerpack on back (see Weapons), gloves, "springshoes" (see Weapons).

Weapons: Springshoes, which are boots containing "power-pack driven leaping coils."

Biography: "A small-time loser," Patilio spends his spare hours inventing new gadgets with "a dream of making it big." Creating extremely powerful leaping coils, he creates a costume and becomes the criminal Leapfrog. Arrested by Daredevil, he is tried and found guilty—no surprise after he underscores his guilt by slipping on his boots in the courtroom and jumping three stories toward the ground. (Losing a boot as he plummets earthward, he breaks a leg and is recaptured [#26]). After doing time, the inventor returns to his wife Rosie and son Eugene. Rosie supports them until she dies of cancer; Patilio, who has been working "sellin' shlock on the East Side," slips into a deep depression. Realizing that the only way to snap his father out of it is "by becoming the success he always wanted to be," teenaged Eugene dons the costume and, as the Frog-Man, helps the superheroes Spider-Man and the Human Torch stop THE SPEED DEMON (2). That does the trick, and the proud ex-villain is reborn (*Marvel Team-Up #121*, 1982).

Comment: The character's name is written both "Leapfrog," "Leap Frog," and "Leap-Frog."

LE CHIFRE (N, TV, MP)

First Appearance: 1953, *Casino Royale*, Ian Fleming.

Biography: Working as paymaster for a Russian undercover operation in France, Le Chifre makes the mistake of skimming money in order to open his own brothels. When his Soviet masters find out, they order Le Chifre to repay the money or suffer the consequences; heading for Royal-les-Eaux, a resort in the north of France, he hopes to win big at the gaming tables. Since Western Europe would like nothing better than to see Le Chifre default, they send secret agent James Bond to beat him at baccarat. Bond succeeds, earning Le Chifre's wrath. Captured and tortured (seated naked on a chair with an open bottom, Bond is severely beaten on the buttocks and genitals), he escapes with the help of a Russian woman who has fallen for him. True to their word, the Russians murder Le Chifre.

Comment: "Chifre," in French, means "number." Peter Lorre played the part in the relatively faithful *Climax Mystery Theater* TV presentation in 1954; in the 1967 film version—a comedy!—Le Chifre, now the head of a spy ring, was played by Orson Welles.

LEVIATHAN (C)

Real Name: Edward Cobert.

First Appearance: 1983, *The New Defenders #126*, Marvel Comics.

Costume: Golden tights, leotard; white boots.

Biography: In 1979, Cobert was named head of the Olympus Project, a U.S. government operation based in the Caribbean. The purpose of the project was to develop "a new breed of super-human," one who would have direct government ties (as opposed to the many superheroes who were "operating independently"). But Cobert and his team decided to take the plan a step further: they also wanted to "totally eradicate" the old superheroes, and Cobert himself underwent the transformation to become a superbeing. Becoming an ultra-powerful giant with a small child's IQ, he was captured by the peacekeeping force S.H.I.E.L.D. (Supreme Headquarters International Espionage Law-enforcement Division) and kept locked up and sedated in a top-security cell a mile beneath S.H.I.E.L.D.'s Manhattan headquarters. But he was released by agents of PROFESSOR POWER—as a diversion to allow MAD DOG to escape the clutches of S.H.I.E.L.D.—and he tore down several blocks of New York before the superheroic New Defenders were able to knock him out and shackle him. Returned to S.H.I.E.L.D., he was released a second time by the Professor.

Quote: "Fee fie foe fum! Bite off your heads—one by one!"

Comment: This has been the character's only appearance to date; he is unrelated to the Leviathan created by PLANTMAN.

LEX LUTHOR (C, CS, TV, MP)

First Appearance: 1940, *Action Comics* #23, DC Comics, (see Comment).

Costume: Luthor has worn many clothes and suits over the years, from a simple lab jacket to prison grays to various colorful costumes. At present, his standard-wear is armor which he found on the planet Lexor (see Biography). It consists of a green, metallic bodysuit; a lighter green vest/helmet unit with yellow, red, and green pyramid on chest; a light green girdle with purple fringing; and purple gloves, boots, belt (see Weapons).

Weapons: The armor serves like an exoskeleton and boosts his physical strength to a superhuman level. Luthor has used countless other weapons over the years. Among the most spectacular and/or unusual of these are a kryptonite serum which makes Luthor lethal to his nemesis Superman, a discovery he uses in tandem with a satellite which turns all lead (the only substance known to block kryptonite) to glass making it impossible for Superman to protect himself; a time machine; an antigravity machine; a shrinking ray; an enlarger ray; a giant, flying robot which he uses to rip apart Fort Knox; a jetmobile; a helmet which allows him to animate rocks (and, naturally, he uses his power on kryptonite, sending a "kryptonite man" forth to kill Superman); a machine which brings beings to earth from the fourth dimension; a "money magnet"; an "earthquake maker"; an "atomic death ray"; a "repeller-ray" which sends objects flying with destructive force; "Luthorite," which is the "hardest and strongest" metal there is; an "Automaton Bloodhound," a robot dog; a battering ram built from a prison stamping press (with which to make an escape); and many others.

Chief Henchmen: Though Luthor usually works alone, he has employed many thugs over the years (such as the Superman lookalike Gypo and BLOODSPORT) and has also teamed up with other super villains like THE PRANKSTER.

Biography: As a teenager, Luthor moves with his family (including younger sister Lena) to Smallville, which happens to be the home town of the youthful superhero Superboy (later Superman). The two first meet when Luthor disposes of a chunk of kryptonite which was debilitating the Boy of Steel. Later, Superboy returns the favor by building Luthor a lab in his home, where, Luthor vows, he is going to apply his scientific genius to finding a cure for kryptonite poisoning. Alas, one day Luthor's lab catches fire when some chemicals explode. Passing, Superboy blows out the blaze "with a super puff." Unfortunately, not only had Luthor been in complete control of what had been going on, but also the fumes, stirred by the hero's breath, made Luthor's hair fall out for good. The accident causes Luthor's mind to become "completely warped," and he's disowned by his parents. (When he's sent to reform school, the Luthors are so ashamed they move to another town and change their name to Thorul. Lena is told that her brother died in a mountain-climbing accident; when the elder "Thoruls" die in an automobile accident, they leave everything to their daughter. Luthor has only occasional contact with her, though he truly loves her; she is now the widow of FBI agent Jeff Colby—who, ironically, once sent her brother to jail—and the mother of young Val Colby.) Luthor's stay in reform school fails to rehabilitate him, and through four decades, no matter how often he has to go to (and escape from) prison, he remains obsessed with destroying Superman. Inarguably, the most significant crime ever perpetrated by Luthor is the one which resulted in the creation of an entirely new civilization: the Bizarros (*Action Comics* #254, 1959). Having it in mind to defeat Superman by creating an exact, albeit evil, copy, he constructs a duplicator ray. Tricking Superman into visiting his lab by claiming to have a cure for kryptonite, Luthor switches on the machine and creates a copy of Superman—but one which is quite imperfect. The creature, Bizarro, has pure white skin, spiky black hair, and extremely angular features. Though he moves and thinks (indeed, knows everything that Superman knows) Bizarro is made of "nuclear matter" which strictly speaking is not alive. Refusing to hurt Superman, and shocked by its horrid features ("Me not human!" it wails), Bizarro tries to destroy itself. But it cannot, and is miserable until reporter Lois Lane uses the ray to create a Bizarro-Lois for him as a companion. Woefully out-of-place on earth, the Bizarros travel into space and settle an uninhabited world, using another duplicator to create not only copies of themselves but of other superheroes as well as reporter Jimmy Olsen, newspaper editor Perry White, and even Superman's dog Krypto. Because of their imperfect nature, the Bizarros tend to do everything backwards. They watch negatives of films (and root for the bad guys), go to sleep when an alarm rings, eat cold hot dogs, and get their hair done at an "ugliness parlor"; fittingly, the name which the Bizarros choose for their square world is Htrae. As for Luthor, in the midst of his crimes he does one truly magnanimous act, on a world orbiting the red star X-156-99F. Inviting Superman there to do battle (Superman has no superpowers under a red star), Luthor finds that the once-great inhabitants of the planet have become savages. He helps them rebuild their civilization, even turning himself over to Superman under the condition that the Man of Steel bring water to the "desert-like" world. Superman agrees, and the people change the name of their world to Lexor in honor of their savior (*Superman* #164). Luthor returns many times, marrying the woman Ardora and fathering Lex, Jr.—though both die when Lexor is destroyed during one of Luthor's bouts with Superman. Needless to say, the holocaust does nothing to soften the super villain's feelings toward Superman. Although it hasn't figured prominently in the chronicles, Luthor has a hideout in Metropolis called Luthor's Lair. Situated inside a former museum, it contains statues of his heroes (Attila, Genghis Khan, Captain Kidd, and Al Capone among them), a workshop, and also a "reminder room" whose many calenders "remind me how many years I've spent in prison because of Superman—and that I must never lag in my war against him." Another lair is located in an unused observatory on a mountainside outside of Metropolis. Whether Luthor will ever defeat Superman is not known; however, it *is* known that his criminal legacy will live on in the form of his thirtieth-century descendant, Fleish Rohtul. Lex belongs to THE SECRET SOCIETY OF SUPER-VILLAINS.

Quote: "Prepare for the worst, *Superman*! I, Luthor, have unleashed my most terrific menace! *The floating air mines*! Unless every country pays a billion dollars blackmail, these mines will destroy their capital cities!"

Comment: The Luthor described above was actually first introduced in *Adventure Comics* #271 (1960). Before then, in every appearance, Luthor was the same character first seen in *Action Comics* #23. Problems occurred subsequent to the *Adventure Comics* issue for it was explained there that Luthor had hated Superman since his youth because the latter had cost him his hair. Since the original Luthor *had* all of his hair in the first year of his existence (though it was gone by 1941), and hadn't met Superman until the two were adults, the writers explained the anomaly by deciding that Luthor was in fact two different men. The original Luthor was now said to be *Alexei* Luthor of Earth-2 in a parallel dimension. This vintage Luthor was also a scientific genius, and he had a fairly successful criminal career on his world, his dossier including having fanned the flames of war between two European nations in 1940, hoping it would "engulf the entire continent in bloody warfare," and also having established the "glass-enclosed" oceanic city Pacifico where he bred "biological monstrosities" to send against the world. Alexei's career ended in *Crisis on Infinite Earths* #9. During that interdimensional slugfest, Alexei complained to the evil BRAINIAC that his Earth-One counterpart—whom he described as a "second-rate lab rat"—was being given too much responsibility. Brainiac agreed that "We do not need two Luthors," and vaporized Alexei. However, to further complicate matters, there are still two other Luthors wandering through the Superman chronicles, both of them benevolent souls: Alexander Luthor, a scientist on Earth-3's dimension, who is actually a superhero thanks to a supersuit he invented (first seen in *DC Comics Presents Annual* #1, 1982); and Alexander Luthor, Jr., his son, whom he sent rocketing from Earth-3 just before its dimension was destroyed (*Crisis on Infinite Earths* #1, 1985). The youth's course carried him through antimatter which imbued him with incredible antimatter powers. Lex Luthor was also featured from time to time in the longrunning Superman comic strip, and on the cartoon series *The New Adventures of Superman* (1966-67), *The Superman/Aquaman Hour* (1967-68), and *The Batman/Superman Hour* (1968-69). The character was played on the screen by Lyle Talbot in the 15-chapter Columbia serial *Atom Man vs. Superman* (1950), in which Luthor, hidden behind a full-head metal helmet, uses a ray to break people into their component atoms and reconstruct them wherever he wishes (hence the name Atom Man), keeping Superman at bay with synthetic kryptonite. When the effects of the debilitating rock wear off, Luthor opts to destroy Metropolis outright with his sonic vibrator. Setting the device, he kidnaps Lois Lane and flies off in a spaceship. But Superman saves the city, then smashes through the rocket and snares his enemy. Luthor returned to the big screen in *Superman* (1978), trying to make a killing in real estate. Buying all the land east of the San Andreas fault, he uses a nuclear missile to sink all the land west of it. Superman repairs the fault and jails Luthor, but the villain returns in *Superman II* (1980), helping GENERAL ZOD in his battle against the Man of Steel, and in *Superman IV* (1987). Gene Hackman played the part in all three films; he was assisted, in the first two, by Eve Teschmacher (Valerie Perrine) and Otis (Ned Beatty). In the third, he was served by the super-powered Nuclear Man. Interestingly enough, though this Luthor is bald, he wears a variety of wigs. In 1986, when the Superman saga was revamped for the comic books by artist/writer John Byrne, Luthor was changed yet again. Now he is the billionaire head of the powerful Lexcorp with "an interest in virtually every business based in Metropolis." He uses this company as a shield for countless illegal operations, and has vowed to kill Superman because the hero once arrested Luthor (mortifying him beyond words) for reckless endangerment.

LIEUTENANT COMMANDER GARY MITCHELL (TV)

First Appearance: September 22, 1966, "Where No Man Has Gone Before," *Star Trek*, NBC-TV.

Costume: Federation uniform: black trousers, golden bodyshirt with U.S.S. *Enterprise* insignia (stylized pyramid) over heart.

Weapons: Extraordinary psionic powers (the ability to read minds, levitate and transmute matter, hurl energy bolts).

Biography: Mitchell was the second officer of the starship *Enterprise*. A good-natured ladies' man, he had been a student of *Enterprise* Captain James T. Kirk at the Star Fleet Academy; the men had known each other for 15 years. At one point, on the planet Dimorus, Mitchell intentionally took a poisoned dart that had been thrown at Kirk by a rodent-like creature. On stardate 1312.4, while on a deep-space mission, the ship was buffeted by strange radiation; only Mitchell seemed to be affected, his latent psionic powers boosted to astonishing levels. At the same time, the mutation caused him to become a megalomaniac. ("You fools!" he screamed at one point. "Soon I'll squash you like insects!") Learning that Mitchell intended to breed a race of creatures such as himself, Kirk had no choice but to abandon his old friend on the deserted world of Delta-Vega. Once there, however, Mitchell absconded with Dr. Elizabeth Dehner of the landing party; Kirk set out in pursuit. Taking an awful beating at the hands of the lunatic, Kirk implored Dehner to help him. As it happened, she, too, had latent psionic powers which the radiation had enhanced. Reluctantly throwing an energy bolt from her hands she stunned Mitchell, Kirk finishing the job by firing a phaser bolt at an overhanging bolder, thus crushing his second officer. These events occurred in the twenty-third century.

Quote: "Morals are for men, not gods!"

Comment: Gary Lockwood played Mitchell; Sally Kellerman was Dehner. The teleplay was written by Samuel A. Peeples.

LIGHTMASTER (C)

Real Name: Dr. Edward Lansky.

First Appearance: 1977, *Peter Parker, the Spectacular Spider-Man* #3, Marvel Comics.

Costume: Yellow bodysuit, boots, and gloves; orange leotard with yellow oval on chest and 50 black lines radiating from it to a matching oval in the back; orange full-head cowl with yellow oval in center and 50 black lines radiating from it as well (see Weapons).

Weapons: Costume circuits enable him to fire light blasts from his hand, and to mold light into physical shapes, including a huge flyswatter with which to crush Spider-Man; huge cymbals to deafen his victims; a mighty vacuum cleaner to suck people up; and a sphere which he can enter to ride through the skies, among others.

Biography: The vice-chancellor of Empire State University, Lansky designs his special costume in order to terrorize government officials and thus avert budget cuts at his school. In a battle with Lansky, the superheroic Spider-Man—who happens to be an ESU student in his civilian identity—sends electricity through his body hoping to cause the suit to blow a fuse. Instead, the charge turns Lansky into an energy being who requires light to survive. Eventually fading away into the "light dimension," he is drawn to the superheroic Dazzler, a mutant who absorbs light energy; tapping her power, Lightmaster reassembles in our world (*The Amazing Spider-Man* #203, 1980). Taking over her body using equipment in his lab ("You, my dear—shall be my *battery*—!"), he is exorcised when Spider-Man knocks the Dazzler out and subjects her to the equipment on "reverse." Back in the light dimension, the villain plots to return; this time he takes over the body of the superhero Quasar, whose alien energy bands fill the bill. Reformed once again, Lightmaster manages to keep Spider-Man at bay until he can use his scientific knowledge to undo the accident that caused him to become Lightmaster in the first place. Succeeding, he is imprisoned—with the implication that he will one day construct a new suit.

Quote: "You are merely a human with superior powers—but *I* possess the energy of the *sun itself*!"

Comment: This character's power is almost identical to

that of SINESTRO, down to the yellow color of the objects he creates.

THE LIGHTNING (MP)

Real Name: Warfield (no first name).
First Appearance: 1938, *Fighting Devil Dogs*, Republic Pictures.
Costume: Full-head, black metal helmet with lightning "fin" on top; black gloves, cloak, pants, shirt.
Weapons: The Wing, a futuristic aircraft which is a crescent-shaped wing; "artificial thunderbolt," a device which fires projectiles that electrify any structure or craft they hit, killing anyone therein.
Biography: As the Lightning, a scientist named Warfield uses his knowledge of electricity to create the artificial thunderbolt which provides him with a lucrative criminal income. However, when a platoon of U.S. Marines investigating crime in the tropics comes perilously close to sniffing him out the Lightning electrifies them. Two survivors, Tom Grayson and Frank Corby, vow to fight the criminal and enlist the aid of top electrical experts to do so; unwittingly, however, they include Warfield in the group. Eventually, they learn that one of the team members is the Lightning and resort to the old trick of gathering the group in a room, declaring that they know the criminal's identity, and hoping the malfeasant will try to make a run for it. Warfield does indeed flee, hastening to the Wing. However, the sleek aircraft is blasted from the sky by a ray gun designed specifically for the task by one of the other scientists.
Comment: Hugh Sothern played the part in this 12-episode serial. In 1966, the serial was edited into a feature film known as *The Torpedo of Doom*.

LILITH (RE, N)

Costume: Lilith is traditionally pictured as a beautiful woman with long, black hair.
Biography: According to ancient Talmudic lore, Lilith, created from dust, was the first woman. (In some accounts, particularly in Arab legend, she was one of the wives of SATAN. A promiscuous sort, she left his side to sow her oats.) On earth, she immediately fought with Adam who insisted that she be subservient to him; Lilith reasoned that since they were both created from dust, they were equal. Fleeing Eden after the argument, she was pursued, upon God's command, by the angels Senoi, Sansenoi, and Sammangelof. Finding Lilith, they informed her that if she didn't return to Adam, 100 of her children would die each day. Lilith refused to go and, understandably, she became consumed with hatred and a thirst for vengeance when the angels made good their threat. Thereafter, Lilith wandered about during storms and brought harm to all the children and pregnant women she could get her hands on. The only protection against her vengeance was an amulet inscribed with the names of the three angels who had pursued her. (Some legends say she could also be driven away by a coin bearing the names of Adam and Eve and the words, "Avaunt thee, Lilith!") Lilith also had it in for Adam and, during the 130 years he was separated from Eve after being driven from Eden, she visited him. They slept together, from which union came the shedim, the demons who torment humankind. In tales which first appeared during the middle ages, Lilith was also regarded as a succubus, a woman who seduced men while they slept. Lilith is widely considered to be a composite of several demons from Babylonian mythology and the child-eating lamia of Greek mythology, a monster who had the torso of a woman and the hindquarters of a snake.
Comment: In literature, Lilith is featured in Goethe's *Faust* and in Dante Gabriel Rossetti's *Eden Bower* (1870). In the latter tale, it was Lilith who sent the serpent to lead Adam and Eve astray. According to some scholars, Lilith is the "screech owl" referred to in Isaiah 34:14. See SATAN.

LIVING LASER (C)

Real Name: Arthur Parks.
First Appearance: 1966, *The Avengers* #34, Marvel Comics.
Costume: Green bodysuit, trunks, vest with gold shoulders, collar, beltbands running diagonally from armpit to belt; gold boots, gloves with studs around hem; gold helmet with "ribs" running back from brow and flared "V" design on forehead.
Weapons: Laser-firing wristbands, followed by laser implants.
Biography: A scientist working on offensive laser weapons, Parks decides to take advantage of his research in the field by becoming a laser-powered villain. Jailed by the heroic Avengers, he escapes and allies himself with other super villains, most notably THE MANDARIN and BATROC. Originally, he is armed only with wristbands which fire destructive lasers, but he refines his equipment, actually implanting laser circuitry in his body, and becomes one of the supergroup's most resilient foes. Although he is apparently destroyed due to an overload during a battle with Iron Man, the Living Laser is certain to return at some future date.

THE LIVING MONOLITH (originally THE LIVING PHARAOH) (C)

Real Name: Ahmet Abdol.
First Appearance: 1969, *X-Men* #54 (as the Living Pharaoh); 1969, #59, (as the Living Monolith), Marvel Comics.
Costume: As the Living Pharaoh: garb of an ancient Egyptian pharaoh. As the Living Monolith: silver trunks with slender shoulderstraps, boots, skullcap with stylized solar disk and flared ears, bands around upper arms and wrists.
Biography: A professor of archeology at the American University at Cairo, Ahmet theorizes that the ancient pharaohs held the power they did because of mutant abilities. Moreover, aware that he himself has latent mutant powers, he feels that he is in some way entitled to hold some of the authority they once commanded.

THE LIZARD (1). © Ace Magazines.

Concluding that another latent mutant, Alexander Summers, was soaking up the catalytic cosmic rays and preventing him from getting his fair share, Abdol goes forth as the Living Pharaoh, kidnaps Summers, places him in a room where he cannot absorb the radiation, and drinks up enough power to become the 30-feet-tall Living Monolith. Though Summers is subsequently able to drain Abdol's power, the archaeologist in turn unearths the Cheops Crystal, which allows him to resume his career as a would-be world-conqueror—until stopped and imprisoned by the superheroes Power Man, Iron Fist, and the X-Men.
Comment: Summers subsequently became the superhero Havok.

THE LIZARD (1) (C)

First Appearance: 1942, *Lightning Comics* #1, Ace Magazines.
Costume: Red cape; yellow gloves, boots, trunks (skin is green and lumpy, face reptilian).
Chief Henchman: Pet gila monster with poisonous fangs.
Biography: Able to scale sheer walls, the Lizard is a burglar nonpareil. However, when he tangles with the superheroic Raven he gets sloppy: forgetting to shut the pouch in which he carries his gila monster, he dies from its death-bite.
Quote: "Take this key and open the safe or my pet gets a taste of her throat."
Comment: This was the character's only appearance.

THE LIZARD (2) (C)

Real Name: Dr. Curtis Connors.
First Appearance: 1963, *The Amazing Spider-Man* #6, Marvel Comics.
Costume: Labcoat (the Lizard's body is green and scaly, with a reptilian head and tail).
Weapons: According to Spider-Man, the Lizard's tail packs the punch of "a runaway sledgehammer."
Biography: A surgeon who lost his right arm during "the war," Connors changes his field of endeavor. Setting up a laboratory near the Everglades in Florida, he becomes "one of the world's leading authorities on reptiles." The reason, he admits to his wife Martha and son Billy, is that by studying the regenerative power of lizards, he hopes to discover how humans

"might grow a new pair of legs, or arms! Perhaps even new eyes, or a new heart." Extracting a serum from "experimental lizards," he does indeed grow a replacement arm—but, sadly, the potion also turns him into a maniacal human lizard. The heroic Spider-Man heads for Florida, meeting the super-strong Lizard in his headquarters, an old Spanish fort surrounded with alligators which the villain controls. At the height of their furious battle, Spider-Man manages to slip him an antidote and Connors returns to normal. Concluding, "I tampered with the forces of nature which must not be tampered with," he burns his notes and assumes he's seen the last of his alter-ego. Not so. Like MR. HYDE, he finds he can't control the reversions and becomes the monster once again (issue #44); this time Spider-Man stops him by slowing his reptilian metabolism in a railroad refrigerator car. After several other encounters, Spider-Man subjects Connors to an instrument he himself created—a bio-enervator, which saps his Lizard essence and pumps it into an iguana. Whether, in the future, Connors (or the iguana) will become the Lizard is not known.

Quote: "*Flee* puny humans! This swamp is *mine*! Here *the Lizard* reigns supreme!"

LOCKSMITH (C)

First Appearance: 1983, *Spider-Woman* #50, Marvel Comics.

Costume: Gray tights, sleeveless jerkin; green hood, cape, slippers.

Weapons: "Bioelectric drainer" which can be personalized to sap the powers of individual superbeings.

Chief Henchman: Ticktock, who has a limited ability to see into the future.

Biography: Born "with a fascination for locks and mechanisms," the future Locksmith (his name has never been revealed) became a great escape artist on the West Coast. However, after several years he was playing to empty houses because, he decided, the public had become fascinated with superheroes and super villains, "scores of . . . gaudy cretins." Using his savings, he bought a building and converted it into a prison, then made locks out of his bioelectric drainer, each one "tailored to neutralize various abnormal powers." Then, selecting his targets, he stalked them for months. When he had figured out the ideal scheme, he used his talents as a master illusionist to trick the targets into the drainer, after which he carted them off to prison and a specially designed cell. Over a three-year period, he imprisoned such personalities as the super villains HANGMAN (whom he kept drugged), Dansen Macabre, whose dance kills or hypnotizes (he coated the floor with ball bearings so she couldn't get a foothold), DADDY LONGLEGS (crammed in a small cell), FLYING TIGER (likewise), GYPSY MOTH and others. He also locked up the superheroes Tigra and Spider-Woman. However, Spider-Woman ingeniously convinced Gypsy Moth to use her telekinetic power to switch their uniforms; when Locksmith tried to put them back where they belonged, the drainer designed for Gypsy Moth didn't work on Spider-Woman. Escaping, she set the others free and the police came for Locksmith.

Quote: "With all of you under locks, human beings can again strive to achieve with pride and honor—without being overshadowed."

Comment: Locksmith was the last foe faced by Spider-Woman during the run of her magazine.

LODAC (MP, C)

First Appearance: 1961, *The Magic Sword*, United Artists.

Weapons: Magic ring which grants him great power; fire-breathing dragon, ogre, flame demons, dwarfs, pinheads, and various other monster-slaves.

Biography: Lodac the sorcerer lives in fourth-century England and needs only two things to make his life complete: a Magic Ring which will boost his power many times (which is in the possession of Sir Branton) and ownership of the kingdom. He contrives a plot to get both. Kidnapping the king's daughter Helene, Lodac appears at the court and, before turning into a buzzard and flying off, announces that he's going to feed her to his dragon. The king promptly offers half his kingdom to whoever gets her back, and Sir Branton vows to do so. The offer isn't as bold as it seems; Branton agreed to give Lodac the ring in exchange for Helene and half the kingdom. Unknown to the treacherous knight, however, Lodac intends to subjugate him and rule through him once he has the ring. Spoiling the plan is St. George who, under the protection of his adoptive mother, Sybil the witch, travels with Branton. In the end, Lodac gets the ring and slays the renegade knight, mounting his head on a wall; Sybil flies to the castle as a bird and, snatching the Magic Ring, metamorphoses into a panther and kills Lodac; and George defeats the dragon, rescuing Helene.

Comment: Basil Rathbone played the sorcerer in the film. The character was also featured in the Dell comic book adaptation of the film (*Movie Classics*, September 1962).

LOKI (MY, S, C)

Biography: Loki was the most malicious of the Norse gods. The son of Laufey and the giantess Farbauti, he represented fire as a destructive force. A physically striking god, his looks were misleading; he was a cunning and utterly untrustworthy creature. His greatest ambition was to overthrow and destroy the gods, and he committed countless murders to this end. Most prominent among his victims was the sun god Balder, who was killed when Loki duped the blind winter god Hodr into throwing a mistletoe dart at him. At one point, Odin, the king of the gods, became so disgusted with Loki that he had him bound to a rock with 10 great chains while a serpent hung over him, dripping poison on his head. That was agony enough, but the torture went from bad to worse when Loki's well-meaning wife Sigyn came by and caught the venom in a cup. As she turned to empty the vessel she accidentally spilled it on her husband, who rattled with such pain that the entire world shook. Though Loki was supposed to remain bound until Ragnarok (judgment day, also known as "Götterdämmerung," the Twilight of the Gods), he managed to escape. But the course of events for Ragnarok is decreed by immutable fate. Loki will eventually be slain by Heimdall, the guard of Bifrost, the rainbow bridge which leads from Asgard (the realm of the gods) to Niflheim (the underworld). The two gods were sworn adversaries and fought when Heimdall tried to recover a necklace belonging to Freya, the goddess of love and healing, which Loki had stolen. The struggle will rage for eons, finally and ironically ending on Ragnarok, when Heimdall will deal a death blow to Loki, who will respond in kind before perishing. As it happens, all the gods are to die shortly thereafter, though Loki will not live long enough to see his life's ambition realized. By Sigyn he fathered two sons, Nari and Vali. However, his most infamous offspring came from his union with the giantess Angurboda—Fenris, a monster wolf who is to eat Odin on Ragnarok; the Serpent of Midgard, whom Odin heaved into the sea, where he lay coiled at the bottom and grew big enough to girdle the earth; and Hel, the goddess of the dead.

Comment: In the four operas of Richard Wagner's *The Ring of the Nibelungs*, (1867-76), Loki is known as Loge. His most significant function in these works occurs in the first opera, *The Rhinegold*, when he steals a magic ring made from gold which had been lying at the bottom of the Rhine. Loki has been a continuing villain in Marvel Comics since 1962 (*Journey Into Mystery* #85; now *Thor*). Hewing quite closely to the mythological Loki, the comic book super villain can change into any shape he wishes, including that of other gods (though he does not acquire their unique abilities). Marvel's Loki dresses in a green bodysuit and cowl; golden trunks, boots, and gloves, as well as golden armor on his chest; and a formidably horned golden helmet. See HEL.

THE LONE WOLF (N, MP)

Real Name: Michael Lanyard.

First Appearance: 1914, *The Lone Wolf*, Louis Joseph Vance.

Biography: Working for a rundown hotel in Paris, Michael is an unhappy young man who survives by swindling others. Happening to pick a man named Bourke to rob, he finds out that Bourke is himself a thief. Impressed with Michael's intelligence and intensity, he decides to take the boy under his wing. The boy becomes proficient in explosives, jewelry, art, weapons, and even science and math. However, Bourke's greatest bequest is the three rules that will ensure Michael a successful career as a thief: to "know your ground thoroughly before venturing upon it; to strike and retreat with the swift precision of a hawk; (and) be friendless." Going back out on his own, Michael lives the life of an urbane chap during the day, and the bold Lone Wolf by night. In the first novel the Lone Wolf is menaced by the mob, which fears that his success as a solo operator will undermine their own effectiveness.

Comment: There were seven Lone Wolf sequels: *The False Faces* (1918), *Alias the Lone Wolf* (1921), *Red Masquerade* (1921), *The Lone Wolf Returns* (1923), *The Lone Wolf's Son* (1931), *Encore the Lone Wolf* (1933), and *The Lone Wolf's Last Prowl* (1934). There was also a series of Lone Wolf films, although the character was now a reformed safecracker, stealing on behalf of Scotland Yard, women-in-distress, and the government. See A.J. RAFFLES.

LORD LAZEE (C)

First Appearance: 1966, *Unearthly Spectaculars* #2, Harvey Comics.

Costume: Red bodysuit, boots; silver shoulders, breastplate, helmet with horns; blue belt with white starburst buckle.

Weapons: Control panel, which is part of his couch and allows him to operate his destructive weapons remotely. These weapons include robots which, situated around the world, follow his bidding (e.g., launching powerful missiles); a communications satellite; and a powerful robot double of himself.

Chief Henchman: His butler Vigoro.

*The portly **LORD LAZEE** at his control panel. © Harvey Comics.*

Biography: Based in a luxurious bunker "deep in the earth near a U.S. city," the incredibly obese Lazee uses his missiles to extort a fortune from world governments. However, the superhero Jack Q. Frost of the International Counter-intelligence Agency finds his bunker and stops the villain before he can collect; in his second outing, Lazee plots revenge by destroying the ICA. Lazee never leaves his couch and subsists on food pills, presumably because he's too lazy to chew his own food.

Quote: "Attention, Mr. President—members of Congress. I wish to direct your attention to the Panama Canal Zone. In precisely forty-three seconds . . . the canal will be no more!"

Comment: *Unearthly Spectaculars* #'s 2 and 3 mark the character's only appearances. See other corpulent super villains THE BLOB, THE DUKE OF DECAY, THE FAT MAN, and TOBIAS WHALE.

THE LORD OF TIME (sometimes referred to as THE TIME LORD (C)

First Appearance: 1962, *Justice League of America* #10, DC Comics.

Costume: Red jerkin, boots, helmet with yellow trim and stripe down center; yellow belt, wristbands, tights; black trunks.

Weapons: Chrono-cube for time travel; destructive antimatter sphere; the Eternity Brain, a computer capable of stopping the flow of time.

Chief Henchmen: Various thugs, often plucked from the past and future.

Biography: A native of the year 3786, the Lord of Time has robbed our own era on numerous occasions. Each time out he's run into the Justice League of America, though in one instance—the inauguration of the Eternity Brain—he actually *solicited* the League's assistance. That occurred when, to his utter horror, he discovered that he would not be able to restart time once it had been stopped. Fortunately, Elongated Man was able to get inside the machine and prevent the program from kicking in. After that debacle the Lord of Time relocated his headquarters from limbo to 1,000,000,000 A.D., where he fathered (by cloning) a family of six sons and a daughter. When the sons turned on him, he reluctantly went back in time and prevented their creation; the two events so sobered him that he has given up his wicked ways.

Quote: "The *JLA* is helpless! Now *nothing* can stop me from becoming *master of the world*!"

Comment: IMMORTUS, LORD SATANIS, and THE REVERSE-FLASH are also super villains from the future.

LORD SATANIS (C)

First Appearance: 1981, *Action Comics* #527, DC Comics.

Costume: Black bodyshirt with red "Y"-shaped stripes on chest, miniskirt with yellow fringe, the red stripes from the bodyshirt continuing nearly to the hem then encircling the garment; white cloak with black lining and very high collar; red tights, gloves, helmet; gray boots.

Biography: Nothing is known about this character's background, or even what he looks like beneath his helmet. Born in the distant future—at least a million years hence—he is the product of an era where magic has replaced science, an era ruled by the wizard Ambra. Ambra possesses a magic runestone which once belonged to the magician Merlin, an artifact which the magician Satanis covets. Spurring other mages to rebel against Ambra, Satanis kills the fellow; however, before the usurper can get his hands on the runestone, Ambra flings it through time. Ambra's daughter Syrene subsequently marries Satanis, not because she loves him but because she adores power. Learning that the runestone has come to rest in our era, and finding an incantation that will send them back, they set out for the twentieth century. As soon as they arrive they search for Superman, since a powerful body is required as a medium to transfer the power from the stone. Needless to say, Superman does not stand still for this and the conflict ends with Syrene casting the stone another century into the past. She and Satanis go after it, only not as allies. Syrene summons SATAN to take her husband to hell but, instead, they make a deal for Satanis to head even further back, to fourteenth-century England, where Satanis sets himself up as a lord, snatches Superman from the present, and also recaptures the runestone. However, Syrene comes after him and they duel over Superman and the stone, the end result being the Man of Steel becomes two distinct individuals, each possessing a portion of the powers of the original. Thinking on her feet, Syrene promptly snatches the version of Superman with the invulnerability and disappears. Charging herself fully with the runestone's power—her Superman dying in the process—she tries to destroy her husband. Satanis manages to get inside the body of the deceased Superman, whose powers are added to his own and enable him to send Syrene back to the future. Meanwhile, the surviving Superman tackles Satanis to try and reclaim his possessed half. Fortunately, the dead half's mind still lives and tosses Satanis out. As soon as he is gone, Superman uses a time machine borrowed from hero Rip Hunter and sends Satanis to be with Syrene. Their fates there are unknown.

Comment: Other would-be conquerors from the future include IMMORTUS, THE LORD OF TIME and THE REVERSE-FLASH.

MACHETE (C)

Real Name: Ferdinand Lopez.

First Appearance: 1985, *Captain America* #302, Marvel Comics.

Costume: Green tights, shirt; golden gloves (see Weapons), shoulderpads; iron-gray boots, belt-like sheath for knives, pouches on chest; black mask; blue holster.

Weapons: Machete is armed to the teeth with knives; they are sheathed around his waist, along his back, and in his gloves—the gauntlets being magnetic and automatically reuniting him with a weapon should he happen to be disarmed. The blades come in all different shapes and sizes, including razor-edged discs for throwing Frisbee-style.

Biography: A revolutionary from San Diablo, a South American nation, Machete presumably wants to turn the republic into a dictatorship. To this end, he raises money abroad by hiring himself out to the highest bidder. In his first (and, to date, only) appearance, Machete joins Batroc's Brigade and uses his awesome skill at knife-throwing to battle the superheroic Captain America (see BATROC).

Quote: "Ha! This is how the famous Captain America enters the fray—cowering behind his renowned shield! Let me show you how *real* men battle!"

MACHINESMITH (also known as MR. FEAR) (C)

Real Name: Samuel Saxon (has also gone by the name of Starr Saxon).

First Appearance: 1969, *Daredevil* #49 (as Starr); 1969, #54 (as Mr. Fear); 1977, *Marvel Two-In-One* #47 (as Machinesmith), Marvel Comics.

Costume: As Mr. Fear: blue bodysuit with purple shoulders, stripe down chest, waist; purple trunks, boots, gloves, cloak with high collar, hood, holster. As Machinesmith: yellow jumpsuit; green boots, turtleneck shirt.

Weapons: Countless robots, firearms, a hovercraft, other devices.

Biography: A robotmaker, Saxon leased his creations to criminals in exchange for a handsome fee. When one of his robots was thwarted by the superhero Daredevil, the paternal Saxon sought vengeance. To make it sweeter, he slew Daredevil's nemesis MR. FEAR and briefly adopted his identity. During a struggle atop his hovercraft, however, Saxon plunged to the ground (*Daredevil* #55); recovered by his robots, he was saved when they transferred his mind into a computer which could become ambulatory by interfacing with one of his many identical, super-powerful android bodies. Eventually growing disconsolate with his artificial life, he was unable to kill himself (it went against his programing). Thus, he maneuvered events so that Captain America did it for him, wrecking the prime computer during a battle. It is likely, however, that his robots had made a duplicate of his mind-program and that he will one day return.

MADAM COBRA (C)

First Appearance: 1965, *Adventures Into the Unknown* #162, American Comics Group.

Costume: Brown trunks, gloves, boots; black T-shirt with white, serpentine eyes on the chest; blue cape.

Biography: Also known as the Snake Witch, Madam Cobra is an evil spirit who tries to take over the Unknown (i.e., heaven) from the Grim Reaper. Banished from limbo, the spindly, olive-skinned witch plots to return the favor by preventing the souls of four newly departed men from reaching the Unknown. The "board of governors of the Unknown" give the Grim Reaper one week to find them or he'll be fired. The superhero Nemesis—himself a ghost—comes to his rescue, tracing the theft to the sorceress. She proves a worthy adversary, able to fly, teleport herself and others, bring inanimate objects to murderous life, summon imps from hell, breathe fire, and create animals of supernatural strength. But Nemesis outsmarts her; when she whistles up a giant cat to kill him, he uses his own powers to make Madam Cobra look like him. She perishes "under the rending teeth and claws" of the feline, the cat vanishing along with her; the souls are thus free to make their way to the Unknown and the Grim Reaper keeps his job.

Quote: "Grow, *grow*! Become *huge* . . . huge enough to tear Nemesis apart!"

Comment: This was the witch's only appearance. Other villains battled by Nemesis include Trigger Norton, a notorious gangleader who commits perfect crimes with the help of "the most up-to-date and expensive of computers"; Satania, the flaming She-Devil; Goratti, the one-eyed "Mafia chief of the United States"; and Merry Andrew, a robot clown.

***MADAME COBRA**, The Snake Witch, battles Nemesis.*
© American Comics Group.

MADAM MASQUE (C)

Real Name: Whitney Frost (changed from Countess Giuletta Nefaria).

First Appearance: 1968, *Tales of Suspense* #97 (as Big M); 1969, *Iron Man* #17 (as Madam Masque), Marvel Comics.

Costume: Blue bodysuit; navy blue leotard, gloves, boots; golden mask, holster.

Weapons: Standard firearms; sleeping gas.

Chief Henchmen: Super-powered robots known as Dreadnoughts; lieutenants and flunkies in the Nefaria Maggia family.

Biography: Giuletta's father, the Italian Count Luchino Nefaria, was long the leading figure in the powerful international crime organization, the Maggia. Hoping for a son to inherit his power, he was distraught when his wife Renata gave him a daughter, then died. Unwilling to raise the girl himself, the inconsiderate Count sent her to the United States to be brought up in the household of his investment counselor Byron Frost and Byron's wife Loretta (who not only gave her a home, but a slightly less ostentatious name). Upon the Frosts' death some 20 years later, the Count had a change of heart. He told Giuletta the truth about her roots and insisted that she be his heir. She refused, wanting to spend the rest of her life with fiancé Roger Vane, an attorney. Alas, learning the truth about his bride-to-be, Vane deserted her and, crushed, Whitney agreed to work with her father. When the Count was arrested after trying to hold Washington D.C., for ransom, Whitney assumed Maggia leadership under the name of "Big M." During a run-in with the superhero Iron Man, she tried to flee via skycraft; when the vessel crashed her body was maimed and her face badly scarred by corrosive chemicals stored onboard. Discovered by operatives of gold-hungry millionaire Mordecai Midas, she was given tip-top medical care and recovered—save for her face, which she hid behind a golden mask. Now known as Madam Masque, she fell in love with industrialist Tony Stark, who was not horrified by her mangled features. She continued to love him even when she discovered that he was secretly Iron Man; however, the romance proved to be star-crossed. When her father was released from prison, he and Iron Man tangled. During the battle the Count was accidentally pulverized beneath a prototype Jupiter Landing Vehicle which had run amok. Vowing never again to love anyone, Madam Masque resumed leadership of the Nefaria Maggia family and remains at large. To date, her most elaborate scheme for killing Stark was to transfer her mind into the body of Stark's lover, Bethany Cabe. Fortunately, Cabe's mind in Masque's body came to the rescue and the minds were put back where they belonged.

Quote: "Put your helmet down immediately—or I'm going to put Ms. Cabe's *brains* all over that wall!"

Comment: CATWOMAN and Batman are two other adversaries who have fallen in love.

MADAME ROGUE (C)

Real Name: Laura De Mille.

First Appearance: 1964, *The Doom Patrol* #86, DC Comics.

Costume: Original: navy blue bodysuit. Second: navy

blue leotard armor, boots, gauntlets; silver armor bodysuit.

Biography: A beautiful actress from France, Laura was involved in a car accident which radically altered her personality. Swinging from good to evil like MR. HYDE, she encountered THE BRAIN, an evil genius who exposed her to a ray which enhanced the cruel and crushed the good in her. Dubbed Madame Rogue, she became a part of the Brain's BROTHERHOOD OF EVIL, serving as the headmistress at L'Ecole des Filles, the girls' school which was actually the Brotherhood's headquarters in Paris. After the evil league suffered a defeat at the hands of the superheroic Doom Patrol, the Brain decided to give Rogue an edge. Subjecting her to yet another ray in "the gloomy chamber" which served as his lab at the school, he gave her the power to stretch and form her features into any likeness she wished (#90). After numerous battles with the Doom Patrol, Rogue found herself attracted to their leader, Niles Caulder, who used his scientific genius to suppress her evil side. The Brain quickly undid his handiwork, but Rogue's benevolent side surfaced long enough for her to blow up the Brotherhood's headquarters and the Brain with it (or so she thought; see THE BRAIN). Falling in with the evil Captain Zahl—a former U-Boat captain and longtime enemy of Caulder—Rogue was present but unable to stop the Nazi when he caused an explosion which destroyed her beloved Caulder and the Doom Patrol (#121). Despite her remorse, Rogue remained with Zahl, the two of them trying to conquer the nation of Zandia only to be stopped by the New Teen Titans. In another conflict with the Titans, Zahl died when one of his own bullets ricocheted and Rogue was electrocuted when she was smacked into a piece of electronic equipment by an infuriated Changeling of the Titans. Rogue perished with her good side in charge, penitence on her lips (*The New Teen Titans* #15, 1982).

Quote: "I—died *long* ago—when the Brain altered my mind and turned me evil . . . I am glad the *rest* of me dies now. . . ."

MADCAP (C)

First Appearance: 1985, *Captain America* #307, Marvel Comics.

Costume: Yellow right boot, left glove, full-head cowl, bodyshirt on top right and tights on left; pink with vertical black stripes on right of tights, left boot, left half of bodyshirt, and right glove; purple cloak, Musketeer-style hat sans plume.

Weapons: Bubble-gun.

Biography: A highly religious young man, the Madcap-to-be (his name is unrevealed, as is his denomination) is on a field trip with his congregation when their bus collides with a truck bound for the evil society A.I.M. (see MODOK). Onboard is the chemical Compound X07, which is designed to accelerate the healing of wounds; everyone dies in the crash except the future villain, who lands in a puddle of X07. Losing all faith in goodness—those who died in the accident were all good and blameless people—the youth finds that in addition to recovering at once from all injuries he can make people act recklessly and without inhibition by briefly holding their gaze. Stealing a costume and a bubblemaking gun (to get peoples' attention), Madcap causes a rash of insanity until he's subdued by Nomad, the sidekick of Captain America. Madcap spends time at Bellevue Hospital for psychiatric evaluation, only to escape and menace Daredevil, among other superheroes.

MAD DOG (C)

Real Name: Robert "Buzz" Baxter.

First Appearance: 1972, *Amazing Adventures* #13 (as Baxter); 1983, *The New Defenders* #125 (as Mad Dog), Marvel Comics.

Costume: Brown bodysuit with black shoulders, snarling dog-face silhouette on chest; black boots, claws with red fingertips; dark red cowl with pointed ears.

Weapons: Poisoned foam which is produced naturally in his mutated body and "paralyzes the body and warps the senses."

Chief Henchmen: THE MUTANT FORCE (#125 only).

Biography: The future super villain had an innocuous enough childhood. The boyhood friend of young Patsy Walker, he was the basis for a character in the comic book, *Patsy Walker,* written by her mother. Marrying Patsy after graduating from high school, Buzz spent the next few years in the Air Force. After serving overseas, Captain Baxter worked in security at a military base in North Carolina. Soon thereafter he was transferred to the private Brand Corporation, a division of Roxxon Oil, to oversee security on government-related projects. He eventually made colonel, but also lost his wife, who had been drifting away for some time (Buzz had become something of an autocrat and a manic-depressive). Looking to make a career for herself, Patsy became the costumed crimefighter Hellcat; she ended up back at Brand in an official capacity during an investigation of corruption at the corporation. During a confrontation with her indignant ex-husband, Hellcat scratched his face to put him in his place; furious, he became even more livid when Brand was found guilty and closed down. Leaving the Air Force, Baxter became a willing subject at Roxxon's Mutagenic Department, where he acquired the ferocity, reflexes, speed, and senses of a dog, as well as superhuman strength and an extremely powerful jaw lined with deadly teeth. Joining the subversive group the Secret Empire (see PROFESSOR POWER), he partook in several criminal escapades and one domestic romp, attempting to disrupt the wedding of his ex-wife and Daimon Hellstrom, aka the superheroic Son of Satan. His shining moment as a super villain occurred when the clergyman officiating at Patsy's wedding asked if anyone objected to the marriage . . . and Mad Dog ripped down the wall. The rabid fiend is presently being held by the international peacekeeping force S.H.I.E.L.D. (Supreme Headquarters International Espionage Law-enforcement Division).

Quote: "I want you to look me square in the eyes when you *die*, witch! I want the last sight you ever see to be the face of the man you betrayed!"

THE MAD HATTER (C, TV)

Real Name: Jervis Tetch; a second Mad Hatter adopted that name as well, although his real name has never been revealed.

First Appearance: 1948, *Batman* #49, DC Comics; 1956, *Detective Comics* #230, DC Comics.

Costume: Tetch dresses in formalwear, including a big bowtie, a large top hat, and white gloves (see Comment). The "impostor" Tetch wears street clothes.

Weapons: Both Hatters employ sundry weapons. The first Tetch has used a chair which reads the minds of those strapped into it, the second a radioactive spray which forces Batman to remove his cowl. But the most extraordinary weapons are the trick-hats of the second Tetch. These do everything from hypnotizing to causing insanity or amnesia.

Chief Henchmen: Various nameless thugs.

Biography: A madman, Tetch is a thief who undertakes grand robberies; apprehended by the superhero Batman, he is committed to the Arkham Asylum. Meanwhile, another Mad Hatter surfaces, this one a hat collector who will stop at nothing to obtain famous or unusual hats. He travels the world from the Australian outback (to get a boomerang hat) to Yappa Island (to acquire a rock hat which strengthens the neck); he thinks nothing of robbing museums (George Washington's hat was obtained in this fashion). However, the one prize which has eluded him is Batman's cowl, and he'll do anything to possess it. After numerous encounters, Tetch is nabbed by Batman and sent to prison; he is apparently slain there by the first Tetch, who escapes. Though presently incarcerated back at Arkham, he will doubtless escape to menace Batman again.

Quote: "Don't you dare *move*, my darling! This *key* can activate my machine—turn Mr. Fox into a well-dressed *vegetable*!"

Comment: The character was inspired by the Mad Hatter in Lewis Carroll's *Alice's Adventures in Wonderland* (1865), a figure who did not collect hats but was simply mad as a hatter (an expression which derived either from an [English] corruption of "adder" or the fact that hat finishers rubbed hot irons across felt which released, as a nerve-damaging vapor, mercury used in processing the original fur). The comic book character's second incarnation was based directly on the definitive illustrations done for the Carroll book by Sir John Tenniel. David Wayne played the part of Batman's nemesis on the *Batman* TV series which ran from 1966 to 1968.

THE MAD THINKER (C)

Real Name: Dr. Santini (alias; real name never revealed).

First Appearance: 1963, *The Fantastic Four* #15, Marvel Comics.

Costume: Green jumpsuit; brown boots.

Weapons: Numerous hi-tech devices, including the Quasimodo (Quasi-Motivational Destruct Organ), robot duplicates of the Fantastic Four; "hypno-lens," a hypnotic monocle; and circuitry affixed to his body which allows him to communicate with his computers while he's away from his headquarters (i.e., in prison).

Chief Henchmen: The "Awesome Android," a towering, clay-like robot which can reform itself to ape the powers of others. The Mad Thinker is also assisted by various thugs.

Biography: Nothing is known about this character's past. A deductive and mathematical genius with a photographic memory, he is unable to initiate great research, but, reading or stealing the works of others, he comes up with brilliant criminal applications.

MAELSTROM (C)

First Appearance: 1980, *Marvel Two-in-One* #71, Marvel Comics.

Costume: Light blue bodysuit with purple chest, back, and flared shoulders; purple boots, sash around waist (later a flap from waist to knees), gloves, helmet with horns on the sides and a red horn in front.

Chief Henchmen: Falcon, his right-hand man; the scientist Dr. Hydro, whose experiments he underwrote "in return for the data from their results"; and Maelstrom's Minions: yellow-skinned brute Gronk, a "massive muscled master of adhesion," able to control his body's stickiness; the blue and white-garbed Helio, who can "bend the very molecules of the atmosphere to his every whim"; and the red-robed Phobius, who can "instill paralyzing fear . . . with but a single glance." Maelstrom has also employed the services of Deathurge, about whom little has been revealed. Garbed entirely in black, save for a white cape, boots, and gloves, this visible but intangible being is a master of weapons, including spears, bows and arrows, and axes, and travels about on a flying lance.

Biography: Maelstrom is the son of two mutated humans. His father was Phaeder, a geneticist and a member of the Inhumans (a race mutated from humankind by the alien Kree); his mother was Morga, a Deviant (mutated from humankind by the alien Celestials). The two met on the continent of Lemuria after Phaeder left the Inhumans' island home of Attilan "over a century ago," having been censured for "conducting genetic experiments forbidden by our ancestors." Unwelcome by the rest of the Deviants, Phaeder and Maelstrom left Morga behind and moved on, traveling the world together. When the Inhumans moved their abode to the moon "three decades ago," Phaeder and his son returned to their native Atlantic island to live; finding traces of Terrigen Mist, a mutagenic substance used by the Inhumans, the rulers set up an underwater lab called "New Attilan" and set about using the Mist, and other tools, to dominate both the Inhumans and the Deviants. One of these tools was an "Anti-Terrigen Compound" which Maelstrom undertook to turn loose against the Inhumans in order to reduce the "race into powerless humans—ripe for the conquering." Not only did he fail—due to the efforts of the superheroic Fantastic Four and the Inhuman superhero Black Bolt—but, also weakened by his own re-routed Anti-Terrigen missile, his body and that of the feeble Phaeder were destroyed by the turncoat Deathurge. (Serving Maelstrom, he said, "is my duty—but not my desire," and promptly ran an axe clean through him.) Though the underwater base was destroyed (#72), Maelstrom was able to shift his mind and spirit to a cloned body and resurfaced to continue his project. To date, his most ambitious crime was his most recent, trying to absorb all of earth's kinetic energy. The process transformed him into a super-powered giant who ultimately self-destructed when the Avengers tinkered with his "energy governor." Maelstrom absorbed energy without changing his mass, an imbalance which sent "his every molecule . . . dispersing across the vastness of the universe" (*The Avengers* #250, 1984). Presumably, the villain was able to transfer to a cloned body before fully dissipating. In life, the villain had the Terrigen-inspired ability to soak up kinetic (motion) energy and recycle it as waves or bolts of power or as superstrength.

Quote: "Your manipulation of electrons shall not long withstand my biokinetic barrage."

THE MAESTRO (C)

First Appearance: 1962, *Justice League of America* #16, DC Comics.

Costume: Blue coat and tails, cape with white lining.

Weapons: "High-frequency cosmi-radio beam (which) control the motor centers" of the brain and make people (and superheroes) dance helplessly; bubble-like spheres emitted from a pipe organ, each of which is "a masterpiece of nuclear engineering," prohibiting anyone trapped within from escaping, including superheroes. (Each bubble nullifies the prisoner's strength; Green Arrow's orb magnetizes his arrows to his quiver, Superman's shell is laced with kryptonite, Green Lantern's prison deadens his will power so he can't cause his power ring to function, and so on.)

Chief Henchmen: Nameless crooks who rob while the superheroes are incapacitated (and are apparently allowed to keep all the money; see Quote).

Biography: Nothing is known about this character's past, save that he is headquartered in a cave outside the small town of Three Corners and wants to defeat the Justice League of America solely for the challenge. Bombarding the town with his cosmi-radio beam (disguised as music), he debilitates the locals and superheroes alike while his henchmen commit robberies. Eventually tracking him to his lair, the Justice League is snared in his unbreakable spheres—at which point the Maestro leaves the cavern and seals it with dynamite. Unknown to the villain, however, Superman had coated himself with lead which makes him immune to kryptonite. Breaking out, he frees the others and together they round up the villain.

Quote: "I want no loot, no money! My only motivation was to smash the *Justice League*!"

Comment: The tale of the Maestro was not a true adventure of the Justice League. In the context of the story, the bout with the Maestro was concocted by fan Jerry Thomas and submitted to the League as an example of a trap from which they couldn't possible escape. After reading the tale, the heroes found its hole: The microscopic Atom couldn't have heard the music and, figuring out what was going on, he would have informed the others, thus resulting in Superman's coat of lead. This was the character's only appearance; however, the Justice League also battled Maestro Anton Allegro in #163, and a different Maestro altogether in #237. See other musical super villains THE FIDDLER, THE PIED PIPER, and THE RED PIPER OF PLUTO.

MAGMA (C)

Real Name: Jonathan Darque.

First Appearance: 1981, *Marvel Team-Up* #110, Marvel Comics.

Costume: Red bodysuit (see Weapons), belt; purple trunks, boots, gloves, helmet (see Weapons), "V"-shaped harness on chest.

Weapons: Costume provides Darque with superhuman strength; magma gun fires both liquid lava and red-hot rock "faster than the speed of sound," which enables them to "pass through a two-foot block of titanium steel." Magma's helmet fires destructive blasts of "geothermal energy." The super villain also has various vessels, including hi-tech tanks, hovercrafts, and huge burrowers.

Chief Henchmen: Murphy, Gonzales, Carson, and other purple-garbed miners who also pack magma guns.

Biography: An engineer, Darque ran his own mining company "using brilliantly innovative methods and machinery." Hassled by environmentalists, he ignored them until his wife died in a car crash, plunging off a cliff as she tried to avoid demonstrators at one of his excavation sites. Eventually, a class action suit was filed against his company and he was forced to shut down. "But . . . I still had my brain," he recalled, and decided "to use that greatest resource to gain vengeance on the ignorant society that did this to me." Becoming Magma, he established an underground headquarters and practiced various methods of releasing "dormant tensions within the earth." The eruption of Mt. St. Helens was "a little experiment of mine" and, with that under his belt, he planned to "obliterate New York City" unless he was paid $100 million. Fortunately, the superheroes Iron Man and Spider-Man were able to foil his plan. When last seen, the frustrated super villain had apparently committed suicide by piloting his hovercraft into a volcanic crater.

Quote: "You've all felt my warning tremors! And now you've heard my demands! Meet them, and you'll live. Disregard them . . . and your entire city will *die!*"

Comment: This character has much in common with Marvel's other subterranean super villain, MOLE MAN.

MAGNETO (C, R)

Real Name: Magnus (old alias); Michael Xavier (recent alias; actual name has never been revealed).

First Appearance: 1963, *The X-Men* #1, Marvel Comics.

Costume: Original: red bodysuit, helmet with purple-fringed visor; purple gloves, boots, trunks, belt, cloak (made of "metal mesh armored fabric," it literally pours from the hanger onto Magneto's body when he wills it). Second: orange bodysuit; blue boots, belt; purple cape; helmet identical to Original. Third: purple jumpsuit with black collar; red cape; white boots, gloves, belt. Fourth: red boots, bodysuit with no sleeves and flared shoulders and a white "M" from chest to crotch; lilac cape.

Weapons: Magneto rarely uses weapons, though he has employed an earthquake-creating device, a volcano-maker, a television surveillance system, and an "energizer" to boost his power when necessary.

Chief Henchmen: Neo-Mutants, animals transferred into articulate servants and people given superpowers—most notably Lorelei, whose voice enslaves others. These characters appeared only in *X-Men* #'s 61-63, 1969.

Biography: A survivor of Nazi concentration camps, Magneto roams Eastern Europe after the fall of Germany, marrying Magda and fathering a daughter (whose name has never been revealed). Not long thereafter, his latent mutant powers surface and Magneto discovers that he has the ability to create and control magnetism—and, to a lesser extent, fly, generate heat sufficient to melt metal, cause non-metals to become weightless, and fire electric blasts. Under unknown circumstances, his daughter is slain and Magneto uses his powers to avenge her; this shocks Magda, who knew nothing of his abilities and "ran . . . in terror." Though Magneto searches for Magda, he is unable to find her and settles in Israel. (She later gives birth to twins, son Pietro and daughter Wanda, who as mutant adults briefly serve with him in the BROTHERHOOD OF EVIL MUTANTS before becoming the superheroes Quicksilver and Scarlet Witch.) In Israel, using the name Magnus, he joins the staff of a hospital in the seaport city of Haifa, helping survivors of Nazi atrocities. He works alongside Charles Xavier, a mutant with psionic powers and future leader of the mutant superheroes, the X-Men. The two even team to use their abilities against the evil Baron Strucker, a member of the subversive group Hydra, who kidnaps a patient to learn where a great cache of gold is hidden. The next few years are shrouded in mystery, but when Magnus resurfaces as the costumed Magneto, he is a highly knowledgeable scientist and radically pro-mutant, with little trust for the rest of humankind. ("Mutants will not go meekly to the gas chambers," he says on one occasion, revealing the depth of his paranoia.) Vowing "to make homo sapiens bow to homo *superior*," he seeks to dominate the world on his own and also in tandem with the Brotherhood of Evil Mutants, of which he is the founder. However, after 20 years of waging warfare from his principal headquarters on the jagged Asteroid M in earth orbit he finally realizes that his aggressive partisanship is wrong. Declaring a truce with his perennial enemies, the X-Men, he takes the name Michael Xavier ("cousin" of Charles), acquires a new wardrobe, and becomes the mentor of a new group of superheroes, the New Mutants.

Quote: "The human race no longer deserves dominion over the planet earth. The day of the *mutants* is upon us!"

Comment: Much of what we know about Magneto's past wasn't revealed until #150 (1981) and #161 (1982). Magneto (along with THE CRIMSON DYNAMO and TITANIUM MAN) was immortalized in the song "Magneto and Titanium Man" which appeared on the *Venus and Mars* album by Paul McCartney and Wings in 1975.

MAJOR DISASTER (C)

Real Name: Paul Booker.

First Appearance: 1966, *Green Lantern* #43, DC Comics.

Costume: Blue trunks, cowl with white pitchfork on forehead, bodysuit with red stripe down the center; light blue hood, gloves, capelet, belt; red thigh boots.

Weapons: Stress-Null Beam Ray Machine, which can create disasters such as windstorms, earthquakes, lightning storms, landslides, hail storms, and meteor showers and at the same time weaken the superheroes Green Lantern and The Flash.

Chief Henchmen: Brilliant but nameless scientists who wear red tights, trunks, and jerkins, and white bodyshirts, gloves, boots, and cowls with a red top.

Biography: Months before his debut as a master criminal, Booker is simply a "punk crook." While fleeing the police, he breaks into an apartment belonging to Terga and Thomas Kalmuku, the latter being the best friend of the superhero Green Lantern. Studying Kalmuku's diary, Booker learns all about the hero and his colleague The Flash. Armed with the knowledge of their strengths and weaknesses, he commissions various scientists to construct his Stress-Null Beam Ray device which he houses in a mansion outside of Pineaire City. Intent on conquering the world by ridding it of superheroes and then threatening the mortal inhabitants with destruction, Major Disaster is destroyed when, hounded by the dogged superheroes, he accidentally switches on his machine without wearing his "special insulated gloves." The unit explodes, vaporizing the villain. However, his atoms reassemble (*Green Lantern*#57) and he seeks vengeance against Green Lantern. Thwarted, he turns against Superman in a subsequent escapade. By this time, he no longer needs his machine to create disasters; the explosion made it possible to whip up storms and the like simply by willing it. After yet another loss to Green Lantern, Booker loses his mind and is presently under the care of a prison psychiatrist.

Quote: "I now have *two* territories in my pocket—*Coast City* and *Central City*! In due time, I'll have the whole country under my control!"

Comment: See other earthquake-makers AVALANCHE, QUAKEMASTER, Shakedown of MASTERS OF DISASTER, and VORTEX. WEATHER WIZARD can also control the elements.

MALA (C)

First Appearance: 1950, *Superman* #63, DC Comics.

Weapons: Device to extract all moisture from a planet's atmosphere; mass-hypnosis machine which operates via "intensified light waves."

Chief Henchmen: His brothers U-Ban and Kizo.

Biography: A delegate to the 10-member "ruling council" of the planet Krypton, Mala is a scientist who yearns to rule the world. With his brothers, he concocts a scheme of stealing Krypton's atmospheric moisture as a means of making the population capitulate. He fails and, for his efforts, Mala and his brothers are rocketed into space in suspended animation—the means by which rogue Kryptonians were then imprisoned (see JAX-UR, Biography, for further details of the Kryptonian penal system). Years later, after Krypton has exploded, the brothers are revived when a chunk of the planet penetrates their ship. Because they are far from their late world's red sun, the men possess superpowers like those of another surviving Kryptonian, Superman. Coming to earth, they construct a device intended to hypnotize all earth people into subservience. In an ingenious strategy move, Superman defeats the brothers by stirring up sibling rivalry, then sitting back while they pummel each other. Ultimately, the hero entombs them in another ship and rockets them into space. Collision with a planetoid frees them, and Mala seeks revenge by building an exact copy of earth and tricking Superman into going there while he obliterates the real earth. But nothing gets past the Man of Steel, who sees through the masquerade and manages once again to imprison the trio in a spaceship (*Action Comics* #194, 1954). The young men have yet to return from this third exile.

MAMMOTH (C)

Real Name: Baran (last name unrevealed).

First Appearance: 1981, *The New Teen Titans* #3, DC Comics.

Costume: Black bodysuit; golden gloves, boots, belt, "M"-shaped studded harness.

Biography: Apparently a mutant like his matter-transmuter sister Selinda (SHIMMER), Australian-born Baran has possessed superhuman strength and imperviousness since childhood. The siblings were taunted unmercifully at school and, pushed to the limit, they began using their powers against their peers. Banding together, local parents attempted to exile the entire family; to assuage their outrage, the parents of the two "special" children agreed to send them to see Dr. Helga Jace of Markovia, an expert in the area of super-powered youths (she is counselor to the superheroic Outsiders). Jace worked with the children to try and complement their powers with a sense of ethics. However, she failed and at some point in their adolescence, for reasons as yet unrevealed, they turned to crime—he as the powerhouse Mammoth, she as Shimmer. Their most notorious crimes occurred after the youths answered a newspaper ad and joined THE FEARSOME FIVE. As members, they have battled the Teen Titans repeatedly. One of the less-intelligent super villains, Mammoth is blindly devoted to his sister.

Quote: "*Nothin'*—can stop *Mammoth*! Not any pipsqueak *toy guns* . . . not any stupid *blasters* . . . *nothin'*!"

MAN-APE (C)

Real Name: M'Baku.

First Appearance: 1968, *The Avengers* #62, Marvel Comics.

Costume: Bodyshirt, cowl are the skin of a white ape; green loincloth, boots; purple belt.

Chief Henchmen: N'gamo and other followers in the White Gorilla Cult.

Biography: A great soldier in the forces of Wakanda, the African republic ruled by the superhero (though non-super-powered) Black Panther, M'Baku plots a coup while the hero is in the United States, fighting alongside the Avengers. In the Panther's wake, M'Baku revives the outlawed White Gorilla Cult and, hunting and slaughtering a rare albino ape, acquires superstrength by bathing in its blood and eating its flesh. Donning its hide, he becomes the rebel Man-Ape, dedicated to ridding Wakanda of its present leader and returning the nation to its previous, non-industrial state. Upon the Panther's return Man-Ape bests him in battle, though he's ultimately defeated when the cult's statue collapses upon him. Recovered by N'gamo, Man-Ape follows the Panther back to the United States and draws him into battle by kidnaping his lover, Monica Lynne. Victorious, he is defeated by the superhero Captain America when the Avengers come to the Panther's rescue. Banished from Wakanda under the penalty of death, he becomes a mercenary. During his American exploits, Man-Ape was briefly allied with THE GRIM REAPER.

Comment: See GORILLA BOSS, GORILLA GRODD, MANDRILL, and THE MOD GORILLA.

MAN-BAT (C)

Real Name: Kirk Langstrom.

First Appearance: 1970, *Detective Comics* #400, DC Comics.

Costume: Ordinary trousers (head is that of a bat, hands are claw-like, and giant, leathery wings grow from his arms).

Biography: Affiliated with the Gotham Museum of Natural History, Langstrom is an expert on nocturnal mammals. Working nights, he isolates a bat-gland extract which is supposed to give him "natural sonar-detection" ability; with it, he hopes to be a crime-fighter like his hero Batman. The potion succeeds, enabling him to move through utter darkness thanks to his "ultra-sensitive hearing" picking up "bounce-back echoes" emitted by his vocal chords. Unfortunately, the serum also causes him to mutate into a half-man, half-bat. Though he helps Batman break up the Blackout Gang, a band of criminals who can see in the dark, Langstrom slowly becomes insane, like THE INVISIBLE MAN. Making his fiancée Francine Lee take the extract, Man-Bat turns her into She-Bat. Luckily for the daughter created from this union, Rebecca (born in *The Batman Family* #17), Batman is able to provide Kirk and Francine with an antidote which works in seconds. (Though for a brief period after being attacked by a vampire bat, Francine is transformed into She-Bat whenever there's a full moon.) Langstrom now and then becomes Man-Bat, able to change by popping a pill; most of the time he works on behalf of the law, though insanity does creep in if the dosage is too strong or if he goes too long without crunching down the antidote. In addition to his sonar power, Man-Bat can fly, has "animal instincts," and possesses superhuman strength.

Quote: "The gland extract must be causing *hallucinations*! I . . . I *can't* be turning into . . . *argh-h-h . . . skreek*! *Skreek*! *I . . . AM*!"

Comment: The character has appeared regularly in the Batman comic books and elsewhere (for example, *DC Comics Presents* #35, teamed with Superman); he also starred (along with She-Bat) in two issues of his own title in 1975 and 1976.

MAN-BULL (C)

Real Name: William Taurens (he has also used the name Bull Taurus).

First Appearance: 1971, *Daredevil* #78, Marvel Comics.

Costume: Blue trunks.

Weapons: Two horns which grow from the top of his head.

Chief Henchmen: Itch, Freak-Face, and sundry other gangmembers.

Biography: A small-time thief, Bull was hired by a crimelord called Mr. Kline, aka the Assassin (and actually android MK-9), to collect subjects for tests he was performing with a formula made from the altered enzymes of bulls—a serum designed to increase human strength and stamina. When the formula was proven, Kline hoped to use it to breed an army of super-henchmen. However, the superhero Daredevil interfered with a planned kidnaping and Bull came back empty-handed; thus, the unforgiving Kline gave the protesting Taurens the injection. The subject's skin promptly became dark hide, his brutish visage grew even more savage, he sprouted a pair of huge horns, and he found himself possessed with enormous strength and a high degree of invulnerability. Becoming a supercriminal, he has frequently attacked Daredevil, whom he blames for his fate; most of these battles ended with Man-bull in prison. Man-bull was briefly a member of the informal criminal group the Death Squad, which also consisted of THE MELTER and Whiplash (aka BLACKLASH). Kline perished in #84.

Quote: "You *said* the only way I'd *leave* this prison was over your *dead body—an' you were right*!"

Comment: Taurus is, of course, the zodiacal sign of the bull; this character is similar to the ancient Greek monster the Minotaur, who had a bull's torso atop an otherwise human body.

THE MANDARIN (C)

First Appearance: 1964, *Tales of Suspense* #50, Marvel Comics.

Costume: Original: red trousers, cloak, mask with high, flared brows; green jerkin, boots. Second: green cap, robes with high collar; red mask with high, flared brows. Third: green shirt, boots, tights, cape, cap; red mask the same. Fourth: green cape with red fringe; red helmet with gray band from back to forehead, flared "brows" at the base; gray shoulderpads, mail loincloth; light green glove on right hand, slippers with brown straps running up shins; brown belt, collar with straps running under arms; red dragon tattoo on belly.

Weapons: The Mandarin wears 10 finger rings, each of which serves a different function. From thumb to little finger, left hand: ring fires electromagnetic energy; ring shoots extreme heat; ring shoots electrical "electro-blast"; ring is a "mento-intensifier" which allows user to control minds within the range of a few yards; ring radiates intense cold. From thumb to little finger, right hand: ring is "matter rearranger" which can cause a natural change in matter, for instance water to vapor or breathable air to poison; ring fires "impact beam" which throws off a concussive force and can draw or repel objects; ring is a "vortex beam" which creates winds that can be storm-like or enable the wearer to fly; ring is "disintegration beam"; ring emits "black light," to create utter darkness. In addition to the rings, whose range is limited, Mandarin has created countless other weapons such as a personal rocket for rapid escapes; a teleporter to snatch others or flee a sticky situation; a "hate-ray"; and a tractor beam capable of pulling down a missile.

Chief Henchmen: Numerous flunkies over the years; the towering robot ULTIMO; and many other super villains who have worked as employees or teammates, including THE ENCHANTRESS (1), THE EXECUTIONER, THE LIVING LASER, POWER MAN, THE SANDMAN, and THE SWORDSMAN.

Biography: Reportedly a descendant of Genghis Khan, the Mandarin is the son of a noble Englishwoman and a wealthy Chinese man. Raised by an aunt after his parents' death, he received a superb education in China and abroad, and was particularly adept at science. Eventually rising to a high level in the government, he was snatched from the pinnacle of success, his wealth confiscated, in the Communist revolution. Hoping to find a means of recovering the power and prestige he'd lost, the Mandarin-to-be headed for the forbidden Valley of Spirits. There, he found a spaceship which had belonged to Axonn-Karr, a dragon-like creature from the planet Maklu-4.

Though the Makluan was long-dead, the scientific apparatus aboard his ship was still functional. Immersing himself in the ship and its treasures, he learned over the next few years how to operate the finger rings he found onboard. With that power at hand, the Mandarin began spreading his influence from the valley, eventually becoming more powerful than the rulers who had deposed him. Trying to conquer the world, he has repeatedly run into a roadblock named Iron Man, not to mention the superhero's colleagues the Avengers. Headquartered at a castle in China—a satellite lair in earth-orbit was totalled by the Avengers, and another in the Gobi Desert was wrecked by the Hulk—the Mandarin was briefly betrothed to Mei Ling. Selflessly, the woman sacrificed her life to save one of her fiance's victims, Janice Cord, who was then the girlfriend of Tony Stark, aka Iron Man, Neither Mei's death nor repeated defeats have deterred the Mandarin.

Quote: "This apparatus . . . will destroy the entire rice crop of China, forcing the government to invade neighboring nations. Then, when the chaos of war grips the entire country, I will . . . seize control."

MANDRILL (C)

Real Name: Jerome Beechman (see Comment)

First Appearance: 1973, *Shanna the She-Devil* #4, Marvel Comics.

Costume: Blue boots, leotard with long sleeves; red cloak with very high collar.

Chief Henchmen: The women of Black Spectre, his personal shock troops; subsequently replaced by the Fem-Force. (Note: Fem-Force is unrelated to the superhero group of the same name.)

Biography: Jerome's father is Frederic Beechman, a scientist at New Mexico's Los Alamos Atomic Proving Grounds. One evening, Frederic a white man, and black cleaning woman Gemma Sinclair are exposed to radiation from a leaking nuclear pile. Following the accident, Frederic and his wife Emily give birth to a black son who has odd tufts of hair on his body, while Gemma and her husband Buck parent a nearly albino daughter. Despised by his parents, Jerome is abandoned in the desert by his father. There, he meets Gemma's daughter NEKRA, who has run away from home. The two hide from civilization for six years, until one day, learning of the "monsters" existence, citizens of a nearby town go after them with guns and pitchforks. It is then the two teenagers discover that they are mutants: Nekra's hate had made her superstrong while Jerome—permanently metamorphosed into the simian Mandrill—had acquired savage strength and also exuded an animal pheromone which no human woman could resist. Beating and murdering the attackers, and reveling in his powers, Mandrill conceives of a plot to take over three tiny West African republics and merge them as one mutant-tolerating Eden—under his rule. When he and Nekra are defeated by the jungle heroine Shanna, he comes back with an even grander scheme—to overthrow the United States government. Storming the White House with Black Spectre, Mandrill and Nekra are defeated by Shanna and the superheroes Daredevil and the Black Widow. Though Nekra is captured, Mandrill escapes and uses his power to organize the all-female Fem-Force. Though twice defeated, he whips up his most ambitious plan yet—to conquer the world. First, however, he attacks his parents at the Indian Point Nuclear Power Plant, seeking vengeance for their having abandoned him. Met by the superheroic Defenders, Mandrill not only loses but is also shot and wounded by his mother. Carted off by the Fem-Force, he has not been heard from since.

Quote: "You tracked me halfway across a *continent*, masked man—only to meet your *fiery doom*!"

Comment: According to *Marvel Two-In-One* #3, the villain's name is Hensley Fargus; why he assumed this pseudonym is never explained. See also the simian villains GORILLA BOSS, GORILLA GRODD, MAN-APE, and THE MOD GORILLA.

MAN-ELEPHANT (C)

Real Name: Manfred Ellsworth Haller.

First Appearance: 1981, *The Savage She-Hulk* #17, Marvel Comics.

Costume: Gray elephant head (see Weapons), feet, bodysuit (see Weapons) with yellow harness on chest and yellow (silver on cover) tubing down arms and legs (see Weapons); red gloves (missing on cover), trunks.

Weapons: The head: two white tusks on head are detachable and, fastened to powerful chains, can be used as grappling hooks "or just to tear, gouge and gore"; the trunk can strangle people or detect "the most subtle of odors" as well as emit "a sonic signal or knockout gas"; and the ears can "amplify voices from afar." The body consists of a "hydraulics super suit," a harness which gives the arms, hands, and legs superstrength; and "heavy-duty shock resistant" skin.

Biography: The "rags to riches Einstein of Los Angeles," Haller is a philanthropist and the head of a company which is "a world leader in innovative hydraulics." Anxious to sell super suits to various firms—energy companies to explore "hostile environments," mining groups to "clear trees or mine ore," and so on—he decides to prove their worth by donning one himself and battling the superheroic She-Hulk. Seeking her out, the cocky Haller is not only handed his pachydermic head but also realizes that such a suit is dangerous since "the potential for abuse is enormous." He withdraws it from the market, pays for all the damage their battle causes, and all is forgiven.

Quote: "The sense of sheer exhilaration that comes with wielding this super suit is nothing short of *intoxicating*! It could use air-conditioning, though."

Comment: This was the character's only appearance.

MAN-MOUNTAIN (C)

Real Name: "Brute" Brainard.

First Appearance: 1966, *Showcase* #63, DC Comics.

Costume: Purple trunks.

Biography: A boxer, Brute has a glass jaw which leaves him on the canvas each and every bout. After a drubbing at Megalopolis Square Garden, Brute is recovering in his dressing room when a Phi, Beta, and Kappa Ray grenade is dropped in his window. The radiation causes him to turn green and nearly double in height; he also possesses incredible physical strength and is impervious to bullets. Learning that the grenade belonged to the Masked Swastika of the villainous group VENDETTA, Man-Mountain agrees to help them in their criminal endeavors. He beats up the superheroic Inferior Five, though the group's leader Merryman refuses to give up. When Man-Mountain hauls off to belt him, the frail superhero lifts his hands to cover his eyes; so doing, he taps Man-Mountain's chin and, still possessing his glass jaw, the giant falls. Shortly thereafter, he returns to his normal self and is arrested.

Quote: "Chee! I never won a fight before in my whole pugilistic career! But I creamed them super-guys in nothin' flat!"

Comment: The character is a parody of the superhero the Hulk. This was his only appearance.

MANSLAUGHTER (C)

First Appearance: 1984, *The New Defenders* #133, Marvel Comics.

Costume: Blue gloves, bodysuit with white diamond-shape over heart and red tassel hanging from it; purple boots, studded belt and wristbands, bow tie, pouch slung over right shoulder, mask over left side of face.

Weapons: Pouch contains firearms, nerve gas, "incredibly deadly poison."

Biography: Nothing is known about this character's past, save that he has "broken out of prisons from San Quentin to Dannemora." When the superheroic New Defenders bust up the cocaine operation of a crime boss, Manslaughter is hired to slay them. And a good choice he is. A telepath, Manslaughter can "block out the peripheral vision and subliminal hearing of others," rendering him invisible "except when seen straight on." With his pouch of weapons, he stalks the superheroes, only to be frozen solid by member Ice Man. Turned over to the peacekeeping force S.H.I.E.L.D. (Supreme Headquarters International Espionage Law-enforcement Division), which has "special powers detention facilities," he has not been seen since.

Quote: "Defenders, eh? I've never killed superheroes before! It should be—fun!"

MAREX (MP)

First Appearance: 1952, *Zombies of the Stratosphere*, Republic Pictures.

Costume: Dark bodysuit with "V"-shaped lightning bolt on chest; hood with identical bolt on forehead (film was black and white).

Weapons: Robot (the same one previously seen in *The Mysterious Doctor Satan* [see DOCTOR SATAN]); spaceship; ray guns.

Chief Henchmen: Narab and Elah.

Biography: Because his planet is cursed with a hostile climate, Marex plans to knock earth out of its orbit and move his world into its balmy spot 93 million miles from the sun. To do so, he and his aides Narab and Elah rocket to earth where, hidden in a cave which can only be accessed via an underwater channel, he supervises the construction of a hydrogen bomb potent enough to do the deed. However, they hadn't counted on interference from Larry Martin of the Interplanetary Patrol. Wearing a flying suit, Martin sniffs out Marex and his extraterrestrial hoodlums, who perish in the ensuing gun battle. The hero defuses the bomb moments before it's due to explode.

Comment: Lane Bradford played Marex in the 12-chapter serial. The production was noteworthy in that Leonard Nimoy, later Mr. Spock of *Star Trek*, co-starred as Narab. Robert Garabedian appeared as Elah. In 1958, the serial was edited into a feature film entitled *Satan's Satellites*.

THE MARIONETTE (C)

First Appearance: 1982, *Adventure Comics* #489, DC Comics.

Costume: Green tights; bodysuit green on top half and sleeves, white on bottom half, with green "M" in center; white trunks, gloves, boots, cowl with green top and "M" on forehead.

Weapons: Strings attached to a "flying 'X'" which make him virtually impossible to knock down, and give him superstrength.

Biography: An alien being, the Marionette is actually the pawn of The Controller, an artificial brain of his own creation. "I planned it as the *perfect artificial brain*," the beleaguered Marionette explains, but admits he "made it—*too* human. (It) was . . . *insane*." Putting words in his creator's mouth and sending him on a rampage of earth, the Controller is finally defeated by young Vicki Grant, who uses the "Dial-H for Hero" device to become the superhero Frosty and shatters the "X" with ice. The Marionette promptly dies from a combination of "the *exertion*—and earth's alien *environment*."

Quote: "And now, if you do not *mind*—or even if you *do*—I shall *leave* this confinement!"

Comment: This was the character's only appearance. The same issue also featured the villain Distortionex, who can repair with his right hand what he destroys with his left . . . concealing all evidence of bank robberies and the like.

MARLOF (MP)

First Appearance: 1953, *Canadian Mounties vs. Atomic Invaders*, Republic Pictures.

Biography: The leader of foreign saboteurs, Marlof plans to set up a missile base in the remote region of Taniak in northern Canada. From this base, Marlof intends to level cities throughout North America. Marlof is able to move about freely disguised as a crusty old trapper named Smokey Joe. Surviving a chase that leads through avalanches, frozen lakes, precipitous chasms, and even a reindeer stampede, the Canadian Mounted Police eventually manage to capture their man.

Comment: Arthur Space (DR. MORGAN) played Marlof in the 12-chapter serial. In 1966, the serial was edited into a feature entitled *Missile Base at Taniak*.

THE MASK (C, MP)

First Appearance: 1940, *Whiz Comics* #2, Fawcett Publications.

Costume: Tuxedo and white mask.

Weapons: Standard firearms and aircraft, as well as a foolproof brainwashing unit known as the Brainograph.

Chief Henchmen: An international network of spies and thugs.

Biography: "An international spy who used several aliases . . . the most dangerous adversary of the entire secret service," the Mask worked from a Virginia estate outside of Washington, D.C., directing the destruction of United States aircraft carriers, cruisers, submarines, and dirigibles and the stealing of top secret plans. When his nemesis Spy Smasher found the headquarters, the Mask blew it up and stayed on the move, the two fighting time and time again. Ironically, he eventually fell prey to one of his own devices. Subjecting Spy Smasher to the Brainograph, the Mask ordered the brainwashed hero to kill . . . which Spy Smasher did, obediently strangling the Mask to death (*Whiz* #15, 1941).

Quote: "Kill! Kill! Kill! No . . . don't kill me! Not *me*!" (The Mask's last words.)

Comment: The Mask was the longest-running foe of Spy Smasher, the two of them battling through 14 adventures. Spy Smasher himself became something of a super villain by virtue of having been exposed to the Brainograph. Programmed to destroy the United States, he spent the next three issues

***THE MASK** makes his comic book debut. © Fawcett Publications.*

trying to do just that—being pursued, all the while, by the superheroic Captain Marvel. Eventually, Captain Marvel used his own powers of super-hypnosis to cure him. For the rest of his run Spy Smasher spent his time fighting non-super saboteurs—ordinary Nazis as well as costumed characters such as the Dark Angel and the Golden Wasp. Hans Schumm portrayed the Mask as a no-doubt-about-it Nazi in Republic's 12-chapter 1943 serial.

MASKED MARAUDER (C)

Real Name: Frank Farnum.

First Appearance: 1966, *Daredevil* #16, Marvel Comics.

Costume: Lavender jumpsuit; purple cape, boots, gloves, full-head helmet (see Weapons).

Weapons: "Optiblast" helmet which causes short-lived or permanent blindness, at the wearer's whim.

Chief Henchmen: Steele, Hacker, and sundry other thugs.

Biography: Farnum is a scientist as well as a former boss of the Nefaria family of the crime group the Maggia (see MADAM MASQUE). Creating his optiblast helmet, he becomes the costumed Masked Marauder. Defeated by the superhero Daredevil, he takes a job, as Farnum, managing the building where Matt Murdock (aka Daredevil) has his law offices. Biding his time, he strikes again (#26-27). Beaten once more, he subsequently battles other Marvel heroes, including Iron Man.

THE MASTER (1) (TV)

First Appearance: 1970, "Terror of the Autons," *Dr. Who*, BBC.

Weapons: Spaceship (complete with remote control "beeper" to let him know if anyone's tampering with it); silver capsules containing sleeping gas and nerve gas, which can be released remotely by a black control box; various firearms.

Biography: The Master is one of the Time Lords, an advanced race of beings based on the planet Gallifrey. The Time Lords possess telepathy (as well as a body temperature of 60 degrees); they can regenerate themselves up to a dozen times, which allows them to attain rather ripe old ages. After studying at the Time Lord Academy, the Master grows bored and steals a TARDIS (Time and Relative Dimensions in Space). Using it to roam both time and the universe, the Master decides to make himself the ruler of all creation. Aided by highly developed mesmeric powers, he nearly succeeds on several occasions, only to be thwarted, ultimately, by the benevolent Time Lord, Dr. Who. When he is nearly at the end of his allotted regenerations, the Master no longer cuts a splendid figure but is a skeletal creature. At this time he engages in one of his most heinous crimes, tapping the Source, a power source used by the planetary federation known as the Union of Traken. That bioelectronic power allows him to transfer into the body of Tremas of Traken and begin his cycle all over again. Unfortunately, it also causes the destruction of the planet Logopolis. (Events recounted recently in "The Keeper of Traken.") Among his other crimes are causing the destruction of Atlantis while, posing as one Professor Thascales, he tries to steal the Crystal of Kronos so he can build a matter transmitter ("The Time Master"); endeavoring to conquer the earth with the help of lizard-beings known as the Sea Devils ("The Sea Devils"); and trying to steal the all-powerful Doomsday Machine ("Colony in Space").

Quote: "What have I ever wanted? Power! Complete and total power!"

Comment: The teleplay for the Master's first appearance (which was on British TV) was written by Robert Holmes. The fiend has been seen frequently on the British series and in many of the Dr. Who novels published in England. The Master was originally played by the late Roger Delgado. Other Dr. Who villains include Lady Adrasta, the despot monarch of the planet Chloris ("Full Circle—Earthshock"); Broton the Zygon, a sucker-covered alien who had chameleon powers and tried to kill everyone on earth ("Terror of the Zygons"); Caven the pirate ("The Space Pirates"); the Celestial Toymaker, who turned people into puppet-like toys ("The Celestial Toymaker"); the thief Cessair of Diplos, who stole a piece of the Key to Time ("The Stones of Blood"); the Great Intelligence, a noncorporeal other-dimensional creature who took over human minds in an effort to conquer earth ("The Abominable Snowman" and "The Web of Fear"); Count Grendal of Gracht who attempted to take over the planet Tara by replacing its leaders with look-alike robots ("The Androids of Tara"); the Martian Ice Warriors, green warmongers who stand nearly eight feet tall and thirst for planets to rule ("The Ice Warriors"); Styre the Sontaran who tortured humans to determine their resistance to pain, preparatory to an invasion ("The Sontaran Experiment"); the mind-stealing alien Akagra who intended to impress his own consciousness on the mind of every living being ("Shada"); Styggron, a Kraal scientist and organizer of the invasion of earth ("The Android Invasion"); Toba, the merciless Dominator who conquered the peace-loving planet Dulkis before perishing when his spaceship exploded ("The Dominators"); the War Lord, who went rifling through history to steal the greatest warriors and thus build an indestructible fighting force ("The War Games"); Xanxia the queen of Zanak, who drained planets of their energy in order to keep her youth ("The Pirate Planet"); and Professor Zaroff, an earth scientist who bred fishpeople as part of his plan to destroy the planet ("The Underwater Menace").

MASTER (2) (C)

First Appearance: 1983, *Alpha Flight* #2, Marvel Comics.

Costume: Black bodysuit with white "V"-like design on chest; silver bands around shins and forearms; silver helmet with red "V"-like design on forehead and brace-like structure on head, neck, and shoulders (see Weapons); red cape.

Weapons: The Master's helmet, surgically affixed to his head, links his mind to the ship's computer. It also enables him to create illusions and send them about the planet.

Biography: The future Master (his name is unrevealed) is a member of a tribe of Asians searching for warmer climes 400 centuries ago during the Ice Age. Taking more than his fair share of food, clothing, and women, the Master is driven from the tribe and might well have died had he not been compelled by a telephathic command to travel north. There he finds a huge spaceship, one belonging to the alien race the Plodex. (Devoted to colonization, these extraterrestrials send craft to other worlds, beam out "a strange, hypnotic signal . . . calling every life form on the planet," and deem the one being that survives the arduous trek to be the world's dominant life form. Their plan is then to extract the molecular structure of this creature through a slow butchering process and implant this structure upon millions of eggs which are then sprayed across the planet. The half-Plodex, half-native creatures which hatch from these eggs are thus ideally suited to conquer the world.) The ship sent to earth crashes, and when the Master answers its call he undergoes the butchering—a procedure which, performed on his still-living body, drives him insane with pain. After his body is fully dissected only his brain remains alive, absorbed into the ship's computer. During the next 30,000 years, however, the ever-independent Master is able to take over the computer and not only learn everything that's going on across the planet, but also absorb the wisdom of the Plodex. Ordering the ship to build him a new body, the "genetically restructured" Master spends the next 10,000 years preparing to conquer the earth. He is thwarted the first time out by the superheroes of Alpha Flight, and his ship is destroyed (#4). He survives by swimming to a huge fish-like submarine which he'd built 5,000 years before, just in case the spacecraft were ever destroyed. In a second battle with Alpha Flight, he has his helmet torn from him and was last seen when his submarine exploded (#16).

Quote: "Bold words, Namor. But with all the power of a handful of smoke to back them."

Comment: Only two Plodex eggs grew on earth: One became the superhero Marrina of Alpha Flight, and another became a murderous monster.

MASTER JAILER (C)

Real Name: Carl "Moosie" Draper.

First Appearance: 1979, *Superman* #331 (as Master Jailer); 1981, *The New Adventures of Superboy* #18 (as Kator), DC Comics.

Costume: As Master Jailer: gray bodysuit, full-face cowl; white leotard with vertical black stripes, belt with vertical black stripes and keyhole buckle; white wristbands, anklebands, collar, headband. As Kator: green bodysuit with yellow "K" on chest; yellow cape, wristbands, helmet with fin on top, belt, trunks with light green vertical stripes; light green boots, bands around his shoulders.

Weapons: Numerous inescapable traps.

Biography: As a youth growing up in Smallville, Carl "Moosie" Draper was "a fat ugly clumsy oaf" who carried a torch for young Lana Lang—who was herself in love with Superboy. Burning with jealousy, Carl became a super villain due to a bizarre chain of events. In order to keep from getting rusty between deeds of superheroism, Superboy built the super robot Kator as a sparring partner. But Kator, unhappy that he could be deactivated at Superboy's whim, tried to murder his creator. Though that failed and Superboy dropped him into the nearest star, destroying him, Kator managed to strike back. Having *expected* to perish, the robot had sown the seeds of vengeance by giving Carl directions to a remote cave where he'd built a machine designed to give the user his own powers of superstrength, invulnerability, and flight. Carl immediately attacked Superboy, whom he resented for being so popular and good-looking; fortunately, the same deactivation switch which would have worked on Kator stops Carl dead in his tracks. Reversing the circuitry of Kator's machine, Superboy drains Carl of his criminal nature, at least for the time being. His failure did not stop Carl from loving Lana, whom he tried to impress by losing weight and putting on layers of solid muscle. He even underwent plastic surgery to improve his looks. Though that didn't work, he was undeterred. Studying science and becoming a master locksmith and architect, he established the Mount Olympus Correctional Facility, an ultimate-security prison for holding super villains. This impressed Superman no end, and he took the time to make it even more secure by covering the jail with a dome and placing it on a floating platform some four miles from the ground. Superman proposed calling the place "Draper's Island," but the shortsighted Lana suggested "Superman's Island" instead. Flipping out from indignation, Carl became the Master Jailer and decided to use the jail to hold do-gooders—starting with Lana and Superman. Needless to say, the Man of Steel managed to escape; Carl presently resides in a cozy cell on Superman's Island.

Quote: "If all this far-out *hardware* . . . can even do *half* the things he promised—*Superboy* and *Smallville* are about to meet a *new Moosie Draper* they'll *never forget*!"

MASTER KHAN (C)

First Appearance: 1975, *Iron Fist* #2, Marvel Comics.

Costume: Dark red robes with a purple collar and belt and pink trim on the sleeves.

Weapons: The Power Gem of Quan, a multi-faceted orb which collects the energies that allow the wizard to remain on earth; it also doubles as a crystal ball, allowing him to see anywhere he wishes.

Chief Henchmen: Fera, "a wolf in human form"; sundry nameless flunkies.

Biography: K'un-Lun is a legendary city "in the frozen Himalayas." There, young Daniel Rand learned martial arts and obtained a mystic power in his hands, becoming the superhero Iron Fist. His archenemy there, and later in the outside world, is Master Khan, an "ages-old sorcerer." He dissipates when the superhero Power Man shatters the gem (*Power Man and Iron Fist* #100, 1983), though it isn't clear whether the fiend is really dead.

Quote: "This is too rich! Thanks to the kindness of fate—*I shall actually see Iron Fist die*!"

THE MASTERMIND (CS)

Real Name: Joel Kenner.

First Appearance: October 6, 1940, *The Spirit*, Register and Tribune Syndicate.

Biography: Running for mayor, Kenner commits a series of vicious murders in an attempt to discredit the current mayor and police chief. Among the crimes are poisoning his own campaign manager and putting "rocket chemicals" in an aide's car to cause it to fly out of control. However, the superheroic Spirit realizes that Kenner is the killer when he comments about the poison used to kill his associate—something the police didn't even know. While scuffling with the crimefighter, Kenner draws a knife and accidentally stabs himself, presumably to death.

Quote: "It's the Spirit who murdered Brody and Clarke! Why? Because he owes the mayor protection!"

MASTER OF YIMSHA (M)

First Appearance: September 1934, "The People of the Black Circle," *Weird Tales*, Robert E. Howard.

Costume: "Long black velvet robe, embroidered with gold thread" and "a velvet cap."

Biography: The Master is a wizard and one of the most powerful figures in the world of 10,000 B.C. "Steeped in the dark arts," he possesses talents as varied as the ability to read minds (or, with a phrase ["Aie, yil la khosa"], to send minds back through time to "view all the shapes that have been you"), or to turn himself into other creatures. He can also summon forth demons, the Lords of the Black Circle, to do his bidding. Living on the mountain Yimsha in Vendhya (what is now India), he kills the king of Vendhya and arrogantly intends to make a slave of the king's sister Yasmina. However, the heroic barbarian Conan, protected by an enchanted girdle, comes to her rescue; transforming himself into a giant vulture, the Master is slain by a "savage thrust" of Conan's knife.

Quote: "How can I explain my mystic reasons to your puny intellect?"

Comment: The novella was serialized over three months; it was published in book form in *The Sword of Conan* (1952), in *Conan the Adventurer* (1966), and in *The People of the Black Circle* (1977).

MASTER PANDEMONIUM (C)

Real Name: Martin Preston.

First Appearance: 1986, *The West Coast Avengers* #4, Marvel Comics.

Costume: Red tights, blouse with full sleeves; golden cloak, boots, two bands around chest, mask with horns on side. There is a star-shaped hole straight through the fiend's chest which, says he, is the symbol of his lost soul.

Weapons: The Amulet of Azmodeus which enables Master Pandemonium to teleport himself.

Chief Henchmen: Two demons who grow from

Pandemonium's arms (see Biography); other demons also dwell inside the super villain.

Biography: A popular film star, Preston was driving drunk and piloted his car off a cliff. Though he well deserved to die, he didn't. He simply lost an arm. Dangling upsidedown by his seatbelt, Preston was visited by the demon MEPHISTO, who offered to put him back together and save him in exchange for his soul. Needless to say Preston agreed. A demon appeared and fixed his *own* arm to Preston's shoulder; another demon repeated the process with Preston's good arm. (Thereafter, whenever he removes these arms, they sprout back into the human-sized demons who donated them.) The next time Preston showed his face was to acquire Anvil Pictures. Using the studio as his base, Preston—now known as Master Pandemonium—busies himself working Mephisto's will and searching for the "The Five," a quintet of lost demons who will apparently bestow great power upon him.

Comment: See SATAN for other instances of soul-selling.

MATRIX-PRIME (C)

Real Name: Brains (see Biography).

First Appearance: 1983, *The Daring New Adventures of Supergirl* #6, DC Comics.

Costume: Iron-gray armor from head to toe.

Weapons: The robot's entire body is a weapon, possessing great strength and the ability to fly, thanks to rocket-engine legs, and move at great speeds. It is also a robot manufacturing plant, able to whip up small machines and automatons for any purpose.

Biography: A robot built by the scientists of The Council—an international league dedicated to becoming the world's sole data base for all kinds of information—Matrix-Prime was dispatched from the group's lair beneath Lake Michigan to be a hi-tech thief. But the robot had the misfortune of tangling with Supergirl, who followed it back to the organization's headquarters. There, a woman named Brains, the leader of THE GANG—super-powered flunkies for the Council—took personal control of the robot and guided it through another tilt with Supergirl. Matrix-Prime was again beaten soundly and, as a result, Brains fell into a coma. However, in defeating the robot, Supergirl caused an energy surge that left Brains' consciousness in the body of Matrix-Prime. The two battled yet again, only this time Supergirl reduced the robot to a heap of scrap metal to ensure that it didn't rise again. The fate of Brains is as yet unrevealed.

MATTER MASTER (C)

Real Name: Mark Mandrill.

First Appearance: 1961, *The Brave and the Bold* #35, DC Comics.

Costume: Green bodysuit, socks; gold belt; red cape; green cap with queue, all covered with celestial symbols (stars, Saturns, comets, etc.).

Weapons: The Mentachem Wand allows Matter Master to control any matter, from making an object larger or smaller to animating and controlling inanimate objects; the Wand can also release heat and other forms of energy. Matter Master also uses the Wand to fly, usually on a miniature island.

Biography: An aspiring alchemist, Mandrill is working feverishly to turn lead into gold when a beaker of chemicals blows up. Reflexively shouting, "Stay away from me!" he is shocked when the compound obeys. Forming a wand from the substance, he discovers that it can channel his mental commands into any object, forcing it to do what he wishes. Creating a costume and venturing forth as Matter Master, he commits a string of robberies—only to be apprehended by the Hawkman. However, the superhero fails to take Matter Master's wand and he immediately escapes from custody. The super villain has crossed wands with both Hawkman and the Justice League of America on numerous occasions; he belongs to THE SECRET SOCIETY OF SUPER VILLAINS.

MAULER (C)

Real Name: Aaron Soames; Turk Barrett; Brendan Doyle.

First Appearance: 1980, *Daredevil* #167 (as Soames); 1981, #176 (as Barrett); 1982, *Iron Man* #156 (as Doyle), Marvel Comics.

Costume: White bodysuit; blue full-head helmet which also covers left shoulder; blue gauntlets, belt, boots, slug-like vents on shins, waist, left wrist (see Weapons).

Weapons: Costume itself is known as MAULER—Mobile Armored Utility Laser-Emitter, Revised (has also been referred to as Mobile Armored Utility Laser-guided E-beam, Revised)—and gives the wearer superstrength and invulnerability. In addition, the left arm-vent is an "electro-shock" blaster and the ankle-vents are "rocket boosters" which allow for flight at speeds "faster'n a speedin' bullet."

Biography: The MAULER costume is invented by the Cord Conglomerate for the Defense Department, and is intended to be the prototype for a closet full of battle suits. But a pair of misadventures follows. First Soames, a Cord employee of 35 years, steals the armor to lash out at his boss for replacing him with a computer; when Soames is defeated by Daredevil, petty thief Turk rips the costume off to get back at Daredevil for past injustices. He, too, ends up in prison. However, "compromised security" still causes the government to cancel the contract. Showing a remarkable lapse of good judgment, President Edwin Cord seeks to win the government back in a most unusual way: He costumes three men in the suits and sends them out as the Raiders to battle the superhero Iron Man. In addition to flight, each Raider has a special weapon. Raider-1 has blaster wristbands, Raider-2 has a force shield and "syphon net," and Raider-3 packs "amplisonic shatter-guns." Iron Man wins (*Iron Man* #145, 1981), and Cord is arrested for endangering innocent lives. Ironically, leading industrialist Tony Stark (who is secretly Iron Man) ends up buying the assets of Cord's company. Unwilling to take defeat lying down, Cord employs mercenary Doyle to do two things—steal the suit back and destroy all the tapes (filed at Stark International) linking its creation to him. Thus protected, Cord intends to lease the suit to whoever will pay for it, providing himself with a nice source of income when he gets out of prison. But though Doyle, a former Vietnam vet, is able to lift the suit, Iron Man prevents him from getting the tapes. Rather than allow himself to be captured (or have to kill Iron Man's assistant, who once saved Doyle's life on a combat mission), the thief flies off with the suit, planning to use it in future mercenary activities.

Quote: "Say g'bye to yer *face*, bucko . . . !"

Comment: Other armored villains include THE CRIMSON DYNAMO and TITANIUM MAN.

MAUR-KON (C)

First Appearance: 1978, *Shogun Warriors* #1, Marvel Comics.

Costume: Green jumpsuit with black chest and an orange, stylized eagle-like design upon it; orange headdress with three horns in front, six behind it; blue boots, gloves, cape.

Weapons: "Pool of dark life," a lava pit which he uses to create monsters and also to communicate with them across vast distances; an "arcane mirror-screen" for witnessing remote events; tank-like "war machines."

Chief Henchmen: Lieutenant Magar, his second-in-command; various warriors and "techno-mages"; also the giant monsters Rok-Korr—a tentacled giant which can split into the giant Earth-Monster, Fire-Monster, and Water-Monster—and the towering, insect-like robot Mech-Monster.

Biography: Eons ago, when the first life forms appeared on earth, a band of humanoid aliens from the planet Mynda (in the Milky Way's Nanon star system) came to our world intending to colonize and practice their "perverted alchemy of sorcery and science." With their dark arts, they bred dinosaurs using "the hot blood of the earth itself" and thus "defiled" our world. But their right to do so was eventually contested by other Myndai known as the Followers of the Light, and the Great Chaos Wars erupted. Lord Maur-Kon, leader of the colonists (aka the Followers of Darkness), was placed with his people in suspended animation in their underground base on a Pacific island; there they remained until a volcano awakened them in our era. Once again breeding monsters, Maur-Kon—"the very avatar of evil"—was defeated by the giant robots known as the Shogun Warriors and the treachery of his own Lieutenant Magar, who regarded as blasphemy the use of technology (Mech-Monster) over "the rites of evil (and) sorcery." Maur-Kon subsequently resurfaced, helping DR. DEMONICUS in his evil plans (#'s 12-13).

Quote: "The Followers of the Light shall rue this day for the rest of their very *short lives*."

MAXIMUS (C)

First Appearance: 1966, *The Fantastic Four* #47, Marvel Comics.

Costume: Original: green armor, later silver. Second: red bodysuit, cowl with gold top; gold trunks, boots, gloves, cape, shoulderplates. Third: white armor from head to toe, save for red necklace. Fourth: white bodysuit; blue trunks, vertical bands around legs, boots, various pieces of body armor.

Weapons: Numerous devices including a force-field projector, robots, and a deadly "atmo-gun" which was supposed to destroy every human on earth but, instead, created an energy barrier around Attilan.

Chief Henchmen: The Trikon, a trio of destructive energy beings created from the subhuman Alpha Primitives; Omega, an Alpha Primitive; his servant, the Seeker. He has also worked with the Inhuman criminals Aireo, Falcona, Leonus, Nebulo, Stallior, Timberius, and Zorr.

Biography: Maximus is the son of Agon and Rynda of the Inhumans, an offshoot of human evolution created 25,000 years ago due to genetic tinkering by the alien Kree. Based on the Northern Atlantic island called Attilan, they make incredible technological strides, not the least of which is the scientist Randac's discovery of Terrigen, a mutagenic mist. A mixed blessing, the mist deforms some Inhumans and gives others incredible superpowers.

Agon and the pregnant Rynda elect to subject themselves to it; as a result, their son Black Bolt is born with the power to destroy objects with his voice. Their second-born, Maximus, is given a dose of Terrigen when he's an infant and ends up with scientific genius, a limited ability to control the minds of others, and the power to put people to sleep with "a mind-numbing bolt." Insanely jealous of his mighty brother, Maximus tries to get him imprisoned by tricking him into using his voice indiscriminately. He fails, and turns on the Inhumans by agreeing to work with their Kree enemies. Learning of this, Black Bolt uses his voice to destroy a nearby Kree spaceship. Much to his horror, the vessel crashes on an Attilanian government building, killing his parents within. To make matters worse, the loudness of Black Bolt's voice pushes Maximus' already shaky mind over the edge. Despite his rather inept handling of the crisis, the powerful Black Bolt is named ruler of the Inhumans—and, not surprisingly, Maximus becomes his sworn enemy. Five different times Maximus has been able to wrest the throne from Black Bolt, though on each occasion he has subsequently been overthrown. His most nefarious such takeover occurs when Attilan is moved to the moon. Becoming comatose after using a weapon which "was not adequately shielded," Maximus is able to use an extraterrestrial "crystal of power" to switch minds with Black Bolt and rule in his brother's body. He is eventually found out by the superheroic Avengers who restore his mind and that of Black Bolt back to their original bodies (*The Avengers Annual* #12, 1983). Once Attilan is relocated, Maximus resumes his main hobby: attempting to destroy all humankind and rule the earth.

Quote: "Soon all but a handful of humanity will be eliminated—and the earth will be made pure once more!"

MEDEA (MY, P, S, MP)

Biography: Medea was the daughter of the Colchian king Aeetes and granddaughter of the sun god Helios. The priestess of Hecate, goddess of sorcery and witchcraft (who wandered the earth at night and could only be seen by dogs—hence, the reason dogs bark at night), Medea fell in love with the hero Jason, who had come to Colchis to steal Aeetes' Golden Fleece. Married before the goddess' altar—Hecate witnessing their vows—Medea provided Jason with charms that would protect him from harm during his quest. (Among them: a sleeping potion for the dragon that guarded the fleece, and a stone which made his enemies fight each other.) But her devotion spoiled her judgment. As they fled Colchis on Jason's ship, the *Argo*, Medea looked to delay her father by chopping her younger brother Absyrtus to pieces and tossing his limbs overboard. While Aeetes tarried to collect the fragments, the Argonauts escaped. Medea was purified for her crimes by her aunt, the sorceress CIRCE. Back in Thessaly, Medea created a magic potion which made Jason's father, Aeson, young again. Seeing this, the daughters of Pelias—Jason's uncle—asked Medea to do the same for their father. But she didn't like Pelias and, instead, hacked him to death, then fled on a serpent-drawn chariot. Meanwhile, Jason fell in love with Princess Glauce of Corinth. Learning of this, Medea exacted an awful vengeance: She sent the bride a robe which immolated her as soon as she put it on. Then, still angry, she slew her own children (sired by Jason), murdered Glauce's father Creon, and burned Jason's palace to the ground. Hastening to her chariot ("steeped in kindred gore," according to Euripides) she rode to Athens and wed King Aegeus. Things didn't go well there either. The king didn't know that the great hero Theseus was his son, and when the youth came to Athens Medea was afraid he would hold more influence than she if Aegeus learned the truth. Thus, she convinced the king to offer poison to the youth. However, Aegeus recognized the sword Theseus carried and knew, then, who he was; Medea hurried away, this time to Asia, accompanied by Medus, her son by Aegeus. She has not been seen since.

Quote: "May I live to see him and his bride, palace and all, in one common destruction." (Euripides)

Comment: The earliest surviving chronicles of Medea are *Medea* by Euripides (circa 450 B.C.) and *Argonautica* (circa 300 B.C.) by Apollonius of Rhodes. Other important works are *Medee* by Pierre Corneille (1635), the poetic rendition *Medea* (1946) by Robinson Jeffers, and the operas, both called *Medee*, by M.A. Charpentier (1693) and Cherubini (1797). In the movies, Nancy Kovack played the part in *Jason and the Argonauts* (1963) and Maria Callas in the 1971 Pier Paolo Pasolini film *Medea*, based on Euripides.

MEDUSA (TV, C)

First Appearance: 1967, *Birdman and the Galaxy Trio*, NBC-TV.

Costume: Black leotard, boots; green collar, stripes on shoulder, belt, cape, headdress with light-green serpent-headed band at base.

Weapons: Serpent band around head which spits destructive ray; submarine which generates forcefield that renders objects invisible.

Chief Henchmen: Using magic, Medusa turns animals into human-like bipedal monsters (similar to those created by DR. MOREAU) to do her bidding. The spells ultimately dissipate, though it isn't clear whether this is due to an inherent time limit or the fact that Medusa must remain in close proximity to her slaves.

Biography: Traveling the seas in her submarine, Medusa surrounds ocean liners in her force-field then sends her henchmen out to rob the passengers. When they are through, she leaves lighted dynamite behind to sink ship and passengers, who are guarded by her henchmen . . . who remain behind and are destroyed with the ship. Caught in the midst of her piracy by the airborne Birdman, she is sent fleeing in her submarine's minisub, never to be seen again.

Quote: "Bah! The living tell tales, but not of Medusa! They all must die!"

Comment: Medusa's only comic book appearance was in *Hanna-Barbera's Super TV Heroes* #2, 1968. This character is unrelated to the mythological monster. The Medusa of Greek legend was a beautiful woman who insulted the goddess Athena. As punishment, the deity turned Medusa's most beautiful feature, her hair, into a mass of writhing snakes. (A few accounts also give her talons, yellow tusks, and/or bronze-scaled skin.) Regardless, those who saw the otherwise still-lovely woman turned to stone. Other super villains who have felt the justice of Birdman include Dr. Millennium, X the Eliminator, the Ringmaster, Morto the Marauder, Cumulus the Storm King, Nitron the Human Bomb, the Mummer, the Brain Thief, the Constrictor, Reducto, the Magnatroid, Vulturo the Mind Taker, Dr. Freezoids, Professor Nightshade, the Speed Demon, the Ant Ape, and Skon of Space.

MEGATAK (C)

Real Name: Gregory Nettles.

First Appearance: 1983, *Thor* #328, Marvel Comics.

Costume: Orange bodysuit, helmet with blue "M"-shaped mask; blue gloves, boots, trunks, horizontally ribbed vest with orange "M" reaching from shoulders to waist in the front and back.

Weapons: Wand which fires energy bolts.

Chief Henchmen: "Phosphor armada," destructive videogame creatures which he transports from a program into our world; Megatak can destroy these at will, absorbing the energy.

Biography: At the twelfth annual Electronics Show in Chicago's McCormick Place convention center, Nogari Corporation makes ready to unveil Megatak, its "dazzling new game of advanced future warfare." Sent to steal the program for a rival firm, Nettles bribes the company's costumed mascot to let him borrow his costume; sneaking behind the huge display in an effort to stop the first public demonstration of the game—which would make it impossible for the underhanded rival to claim to have invented it first—Nettles gets his hands on the circuitry when the game is activated. "Sucked" into the game program, he emerges later as "electric energy personified." Since the "ionized integration" has also "driven Gregory Nettles insane," he attacks the convention center with an army of destructive spaceships and people-chomping Pac-man-type figures from the program. When the superhero Thor arrives, Megatak cannibalizes the energy of his creations, becoming the "warrior of the future" and firing electrical bolts from his hands. Using his enchanted hammer, Thor is able to siphon off the energy and render Megatak powerless. After spending time as "a mere industrial spy in a silly costume," he was slain by the vigilante Scourge, brother of THE ENFORCER (2).

Quote: "'This villain,' Thor, is called *Megatak*—and not even a superduper like yourself can withstand . . . the raw power of *living energy*!"

Comment: This has been the character's only appearance to date.

MEGATON (C)

Real Name: Jules Carter.

First Appearance: 1972, *Captain Marvel* #23, Marvel Comics.

Costume: Silver girdle, boots, wristbands, breastplate with two jagged white streaks down the sides of his torso, Megaton's skin is golden, the tope of his head faceted like a diamond.

Biography: While on an expedition in the Arctic, Carter stumbles upon a long-abandoned underground outpost of the extraterrestrial Kree. Tripping an invisible beam, he triggers the Psycho-Tron, "an interrogation unit (which) probes for your deepest fears . . . and then lets them haunt you until you crack." Subjected to his "fear of creatures . . . of hell . . . of dying," Carter is finally rescued by the other three members of the expedition. But the excitement isn't over yet. Once outside, Carter begins to glow, absorbing energy from a nuclear reactor. The generator explodes, and only Carter survives—albeit, not as the man he was. His flesh hardens to "an armor-like shell," his body temperature rises to fissionable levels, and he hungers for energy, which he must drain from others to sustain himself. He is then able to turn that energy into heat hot enough to melt metal. Becoming the insane

Megaton, the Nuclear Man, he takes on the superhero Captain Marvel in order to absorb his energy. However, Marvel is able to overload him, causing Megaton to explode.

Quote: "No use strugglin', insect! I feel myself gettin' *stronger . . . strong enough to destroy this stinkin' mudball planet*!"

Comment: Another super villain fought by Captain Marvel was the would-be world-conqueror from Titan, the vicious alien Stellarax born in the "life-baths" of his creator Isaac. He and his murderous "death-ray" were destroyed during a furious battle over Washington, D.C. (#62, 1979). The only "villain" Marvel was unable to beat was cancer, to which he succumbed in the graphic novel, *The Death of Captain Marvel* in 1982.

THE MELTER (C)

Real Name: Bruno Horgan.

First Appearance: 1963, *Tales of Suspense* #47, Marvel Comics.

Costume: Green bodysuit with thin, vertical black stripes on the tights; orange trunks, bodyshirt with flared shoulders, boots with flared hems, gloves, helmet; black domino mask.

Weapons: Device, worn on chest, which can melt iron; later replaced with a gun. He presently uses a box, worn on his belt and supported by suspender-like cables, which can melt not only iron but also wood, rock, and human skin.

Biography: A munitions manufacturer for the United States Military, Horgan went out of business when inspectors discovered that he was using sub-par materials. The weapons contracts were turned over to his rival, Stark Industries, whose chief, Tony Stark, is secretly the superhero Iron Man. Watching one of his plants being closed down, Horgan notices one of his inferior radar units shining a ray which melts all the iron in its path. Studying the instrument and making a portable unit which could be carried about, Horgan becomes the Melter and begins attacking Stark's holdings. After clashing with Iron Man, he abducts Stark and has him design a melter which can work on other objects. He is eventually hunted down and slain by the vigilante Scourge, brother of THE ENFORCER (2).

MENTALLO (C)

Real Name: Marvin Flumm.

First Appearance: 1966, *Strange Tales* #141, Marvel Comics.

Costume: Red jumpsuit; brown gloves, boots, belt, helmet with red goggles (see Weapons).

Weapons: Mentallo's costume boosts his telepathic abilities; he has also used various guns, bombs, and has employed a duplicate of FIXER's antigravity flying vest.

Biography: A telepath, Flumm first became aware of his abilities in his early teens. Content to work as a shoe salesperson, he was recruited by the international peacekeeping force S.H.I.E.L.D. (Supreme Headquarters International Espionage Law-enforcement Division), whose ESP Division became aware of his powers. Entering a training program, Flumm became more ambitious as his talents were nurtured and fine-tuned. Before long he became extremely proficient at reading minds, locating people beyond his visual range, impressing his thoughts on the brains of others, and creating illusions. He also hatched a plot to take over S.H.I.E.L.D., from which vantage point he planned to seque into a position of political power. But his scheme was uncovered and Flumm beat a hasty retreat from the organization, taking with him a suit which strengthened his innate powers. Teaming with Fixer, he attempted to destroy S.H.I.E.L.D.'s New York base. Defeated—but barely—he was sent to prison and later escaped with Fixer's gadgets. Joining the criminal group HYDRA, he attempted to assassinate the President of the United States and ended up jailed again. Freed by HYDRA, he reunited with Fixer in an effort to capture the superheroic Micronauts for his criminal masters. He failed, has since engaged in other crimes, and remains at large.

Quote: "You are the one whose psi-abilities I sensed! They are strong—but not as strong as my *mind-meld*!"

MEPHIS (N)

First Appearance: 1938, "Carson of Venus," *Argosy*, Edgar Rice Burroughs.

Costume: The uniform of a Zani kordogan (sergeant).

Biography: Aspiring to conquer all of Venus, the fiendish Mephis and his brutal Zani soldiers lay siege to the great kingdom of Korva. But the Zani guard is infiltrated by the heroic earthman Carson Napier, who helps the besieged Venusians beat the Zanis back. As for Mephis, he perishes after eating food poisoned by a vengeful woman named Zerka, whose husband had been murdered and tortured by the Zanis. Mephis is "a small, insignificant" frightened-looking man whose eyes constantly dart from side to side. As for the Zanis, they distinguish themselves by shaving their heads, save for "a ridge of hair about two inches wide that runs from the forehead to the nape of the neck." During his brief but terrible reign, Mephis' preferred means of torture was to strap people to "a hideous thing" which crushed them inch by inch, beginning with the toes, while concurrently burning them with molten metal.

Quote: "Torko, take the woman first. We'll make her talk."

Comment: Burroughs was inspired to create Mephis by the sinister exploits of Hitler; he went so far as to include the salute "Maltu (i.e. "hail") Mephis." This was the character's only appearance. The literature of the time had a number of Hitler-like dictators. Another notable example is Eric Linklater's *The Wind on the Moon* (1944), in which a pair of children rescue their father from the clutches of the despotic Count Hulagy Boot (the children's tale also features a witch, who turns the children into kangaroos, after which they join a zoo). *Carson of Venus* was serialized in *Argosy* from January 8, 1938, through February 12, 1938. See ORTHIS for another of Burroughs' political tales.

MEPHISTO (C)

Real Name: Mephisto is derived from Mephistopheles (see SATAN, Comment).

First Appearance: 1968, *Silver Surfer* #3, Marvel Comics.

Costume: Red bodysuit, boots, gloves, sash around waist with flap down front reaching almost to his feet; darker red cloak with high collar (recently pictured as frayed and ragged). Mephisto's skin is a light shade of red, his hair darker red; his ears are devilishly pointed.

Weapons: "Mystic Vapors" which rise from a brazier at the foot of his throne and allow him to see the goings-on in other dimensions.

Chief Henchmen: MASTER PANDEMONIUM, plus countless demons and human souls which he's managed to acquire; also, sundry human slaves. He also created and is served by THE GHOST (4).

Biography: Nothing is known about the origin of this demon, who resembles the classic SATAN in many ways and hails from another, fire-washed dimension. Mephisto freely refers to this realm as Hell—though it isn't clear whether it is actually the traditional Inferno or simply an effort of Mephisto to prey upon human superstition. (Indeed, there is some question as to whether his very appearance is as it appears to be, or whether he assumes it to accentuate the similarity between himself and the Devil.) In his own domain as well as ours, Mephisto possesses enormous supernatural ability, including awesome physical strength and the power to fly, throw out destructive blasts, become invisible, alter his size or shape, summon forth monsters and demons when needed, and more. It has been demonstrated that he cannot, however, read minds or force anyone to serve him; they must be seduced. Mephisto's professed "ultimate victory" is to encourage armageddon, at which point he stands to inherit a great many souls. His principal foe has been the superheroic Silver Surfer ("One so *noble*—possessed of such great *power*—must not walk freely among those *Mephisto* would exploit!"). But he has also battled the benevolent Norse god Thor and the cycle-riding superhero Ghost Rider.

Quote: "The greatest joy in doing evil is to be rewarded by the sight of those who suffer its consequence!"

Comment: Stan Lee has never written, nor John Buscema and Joe Sinnott drawn, a more dramatic and spectacular tale than Mephisto's origin. See also SATAN.

MERCURIO (C)

First Appearance: 1973, *Thor* #208, Marvel Comics.

Costume: Silver boots, trunks, wristbands, belt, inverted "U" on chest, shoulder armor, skullcap. (Mercurio's skin is red on Gramos; when he tries to teleport to earth, the left side becomes blue.)

Biography: Deep in the Milky Way, the planet Gramos is a peaceloving world until a rift in space opens nearby. Sucking up light due to an electromagnetic imbalance, the warp threatens the very existence of Gramos; thus, the planet's High Lord sends Mercurio to earth, to build a device capable of relocating earth's electromagnetic field back home. (The would-be savior is not sent in body, but by psychobeaming. His mind is broadcast into the body of rich landlord Karl Sarron, Mercurio using Sarron's wealth to construct the machine.) With the destruction of Gramos imminent, Mercurio decides to hurry things along by bringing his own body to earth, a superstrong body which can also fly and generate extreme heat and cold. To do so, he draws energy from the superhero Thor and uses it to make the transference. However, only half his body arrives, the other half being a dark opposite. Requiring more of Thor's energy to complete the teleportation, Mercurio engages him in battle. He loses and is encased in iron by the Norse god; however, he is accidentally rescued by Xorr, a jewel which is the collective consciousness of a long-dead alien race. Returned to Gramos, Mercurio convinces the High Lord to send out a force to tap Xorr's powers and close the rift in space. Thor assists them in this, and the planet is saved.

Comment: This was the character's only appearance.

MERCURIUS (F)

First Appearance: 1812, "The Spirit in the Bottle," the Brothers Grimm.

Biography: Mercurius has been corked inside a bottle for "a long time," the bottle buried among the roots of an ancient oak tree. Released by a young woodsman, the spirit grows to a towering height and informs him that he intends to strangle the lad to death. Showing remarkable presence of mind, the young man says he'll let the spirit do so only if he can prove that he "art the right spirit" by crawling back into the bottle. Mercurius may be powerful, but he isn't terribly bright; shrinking "small and slender," he creeps back in and is trapped again. This time, he has to strike a generous bargain to get out, and gives the woodsman "a bag just like a plaster" which turns iron to silver and heals all wounds. Nothing is known of Mercurius' past, save that he was not "shut up there for such a long time as a favor," but for committing some kind of evil. What happens to the demon after he leaves the woodsman is also not known.

Quote: "Whoso releases me, him must I strangle."

Comment: See other Grimm villains GOTHEL, THE QUEEN, and THE ROBBER BRIDEGROOM.

MESMERO (C)

First Appearance: 1968, *The X-Men* #49, Marvel Comics.

Costume: Light green bodysuit with high, round collar; purple cape, boots, gloves, trunks, belt with "M" buckle, cobra-like helmet with green front (originally, it had horns), harness on chest.

Chief Henchmen: Androids known as the Demi-Men; also MACHINESMITH.

Biography: Mesmero is a mutant with the power to hypnotize anyone—and not just to obey his every wish. He can also build "memories" into their minds, as well as induce very specific amnesia. Mesmero's life is a tantalizing mystery before he joined THE MACHINESMITH with an ambitious scheme to replace living people with androids, in order to control their wealth and power. After that and other crimes were foiled by the superheroic X-Men, Mesmero became a sideshow mesmerist for a time. A tentative return to crime ended in disaster when Spider-Man came calling; Mesmero's present activities are not known.

Comment: See other hypnotist super villains DESPERO, HYPNOS, THE RINGMASTER, and UNIVERSO.

METALLO (C)

Real Name: John Corben.

First Appearance: 1959, *Action Comics* #252, DC Comics.

Costume: Metallo's skin is green; he also wears golden gloves, thigh boots (sometimes metallic tights), and a leotard. His head is usually pictured as a lighter shade of green than the rest of his body.

Weapons: Golden flying scooter (introduced in *Brave and the Bold* #175, 1981). That issue also marked the debut of a kryptonite beam which, from his chest, could hurt mortals as well as Superman. As Metallo explains, "Kryptonite (rays) normally pass harmlessly right through matter . . . unless that matter is also super-dense like Superman's tightly packed molecular structure. I was able to slow down the rate of particle emissions enough to affect humans." It is also revealed (in *Blue Devil* #3, 1984) that his hands can extend from his body.

Chief Henchmen: Smithers, Rojek, and a small army of gun-toting mercenaries in military uniforms (*Blue Devil* #3 only).

Biography: By profession, Corben is a reporter; in his spare time, however, he's a thief and killer. Badly injured in a car crash, he is found by Professor Vale, who puts him back together using "a special metallic armor plate (and) a fleshlike, rubber-plastic skin." With artificial organs (except for his brain), Corben is now Metallo—"unmeltable and shatterproof" as well as "indestructible" as long as he takes the one-a-day uranium capsules which power him. To ensure a constant supply of uranium, Corben uses his newly acquired superstrength to steal it. Learning that kryptonite is an even more effective power source than uranium—it needn't be replaced each day—and, even better, will keep Superman at bay, he steals some from an exhibit in Metropolis. Unfortunately, shortly after popping it into the fuse box in his chest, he drops dead; in order to protect Superman, the sample on display had been fake. Like many super villains, however, Metallo isn't *really* dead and returns to battle such heroes as Batman and the Blue Devil.

Quote: "Even if they tried to shoot me, the bullets'd bounce off my metallic body like green peas! Nothing stops me! I can do whatever I want! I'm *invincible!*"

Comment: Metallo was given an entirely different origin in *Superman* #1, (second series), 1987. Believing Superman to be the scout of an invading army, an unnamed scientist builds Metallo to destroy him. This version of the character looks completely human, covered with "plastex" skin. It is never revealed whose brain resides in the kryptonite-powered skeleton; after a bruising battle in which

Superman is badly beaten and nearly insensate, Metallo—himself ripped to his bare metallic skeleton—is carted off by Lex Luthor. He has not been seen since. Early in the chronicles of Superman (*World's Finest Comics* #6, 1942), the Man of Steel had battled a similar if less exotic super villain named Metalo. Discovering both "the most powerful metal on earth" *and* a "strength serum," he builds a flying supersuit and goes on a crime spree. He and Superman finally duke it out ("the mountains tremble" when they clash), and when last seen Metalo had been beaten to the brink of senselessness.

THE METAL MASTER (C)

First Appearance: 1963, *The Incredible Hulk* #6, Marvel Comics.

Costume: Brown jumpsuit; red boots, belt with thick black line around center.

Weapons: Spaceship.

Biography: The Metal Master hails from the planet Astra, whose natives have the ability to shape metal solely by mental commands. But the Metal Master (his true name is never revealed) wants to use his power to do more than sculpt: he wants to conquer the world. Captured and rocketed into space in exile, he "roamed the galaxies seeking a planet which was rich in metal." Finding our world, he flies about on a "metal flying carpet" and begins melting tanks, planes, bridges, rockets, oil wells, and other metal structures until earth is on the brink of surrender. Finally, however, the superheroic Hulk makes a fake cannon out of plastic and cardboard and bluffs Metal Master into repairing everything he'd destroyed and leaving the earth.

Quote: "More missiles! Will the helpless fools *never* learn?"

Comment: This was the Astran's sole appearance.

METEOR MAN (C)

Real Name: Professor Randolph Ormsby.

First Appearance: 1966, *The Doom Patrol* #103, DC Comics.

Costume: None; the Meteor Man is a flaming, humanoid meteor.

Biography: An astronomer (and world-class hypochondriac), Ormsby joins the Doom Patrol on a trip into space in order to study a huge meteor. As luck would have it, the space rock turns Ormsby into a living version of itself and, when they return to earth, the towering astronomer goes on a rampage. The powerful Meteor Man is restored to normal by the superheroes, and has not been seen since.

MICHAEL CONRAD (MP, M)

First Appearance: 1963, *Black Zoo*, American International Pictures.

Chief Henchmen: Nero the lion; Victor the gorilla; Baron the tiger; Kwan the leopard.

Biography: Conrad is widely known as the head of a private zoo, Conrad's Animal Kingdom. Conrad has personally captured his prize exhibits, and is assisted at the zoo by his wife Edna, his mute son Carl, and zookeeper Joe. In private, however, Conrad is something more sinister—a member of the True Believers, a cult of animal worshipers led by the tiger-masked Radu. When people cross him, Conrad sends out his animals to destroy them. His first wife (Carl's mother) is torn apart by a lioness when she tries to leave him; a reporter is mauled to extinction by Baron when she pokes around the zoo; Jerry Stengel is gnawed to death by Nero when the developer threatens to take Conrad's land; Joe is fed to Nero when he's forced to kill Baron; and Jenny Brooks is pounded to death by Victor when she tries to convince her friend Edna to leave Conrad. Eventually, Carl recalls his mother's death, which he's blocked from his mind for so long. Reeling with anger, he pummels Conrad to death. The film closes as he's about to feed Edna to Nero.

Quote: "Evil men and fanatical women want to steal our home. These so-called humans have plotted against us! But . . . together we'll take care of them!"—to his cats, which have gathered in the living room to listen to Conrad play the organ.

Comment: Michael Gough played Conrad in the film. Charlton Publications issued a fumetti (photo comic) version of the film.

THE MIDNIGHT MAN (C)

Real Name: Anton Mogart.

First Appearance: 1980, *Moon Knight* #3, Marvel Comics.

Costume: Blue bodysuit, gloves, full-face cowl, boots, cape.

Weapons: Oriental daggers; standard firearms.

Biography: Nothing is known about this character's past or present life-style, save that he lives in an opulent New Jersey mansion and, promptly at midnight, he robs great art, magnificent jewels, and the like. He does so not to fence them, but simply to own them. As he explains to his nemesis, the superhero Moon Knight, "Greed is in my blood. I must possess things." Falling into a river and presumed drowned during their first battle, the Midnight Man is actually carried by the current to New York and the mouth of a drainage viaduct. There, the "filthy wastes of the city" literally melt his face into a mask of deformity. Hiding for three days in the sewer system, he returns home to find that the police have taken "all my priceless . . . paintings, statues, antique furnishings, rugs, jewelry and artifacts." For that, and for his maiming, the now-insane Midnight Man vows vengeance against Moon Knight. Setting up housekeeping in the sewers, he collects trash ("a living mockery of what I once was") and goes to work for BUSHMAN, who helps to lure the superhero into a flooding sewage chamber (#9). However, Moon Knight is not alone; Bushman has left Midnight Man in there with him. Fortunately, the superhero is able to chisel an escape route in the brick wall and, when last seen, Midnight Man is being washed, once again, down a river (#10).

Quote: "You called me 'refreshingly psychotic.' Now, however, only the latter half of the description applies."

Comment: There are hints of THE PHANTOM OF THE OPERA in the latter half of the character's saga.

***MIGHTY MAN** demonstrates his powers to the Fly.* *© Archie Comics.*

MIGHTY MAN (C)

Real Name: Professor James Stoker.

First Appearance: 1966, *Fly Man* (previously *The Fly*) #36, Archie Comics.

Costume: Original: black cowl; gray mail bodysuit, gloves, and boots, with studded blue bands around neck, head, waist, thighs, ankles, wrists, arms, and shoulders. Second: bodysuit, cowl, boots, and gloves are red; studded bands are silver (on cover, bodysuit is silver, boots, gloves, bands, and trunks are blue).

Biography: Tired of being bullied around, scientist Stoker of Magnus Labs develops a serum called Mightium, which gives him "the strength of a million men." Unfortunately, the timid Stoker is also rendered mad by the formula. Overpowering the superhero Fly Man, he is prevented from pounding him into the concrete by the timely arrival of Fly Man's mentor Turan from the other-dimensional Fly World. Turan uses his sorcery to return Stoker to sanity, and the former villain apologizes for his brief reign of terror. However, exposure to the Mightium radiation has made it impossible for Fly Man to slip back into his normal identity; thus, Turan is forced to go back in time, spill the Mightium formula down the drain, and fill Stoker's test tube with water. Not that this stops the villain from returning in the second incarnation of the hero's magazine (*The Fly* #4, 1983). Through dreams, Stoker recalls his one-day career as Mighty Man—"My mind wouldn't let it stay buried! Like a ghost doomed to haunt its former house." Recalling the formula after "paralyzing headaches and mind-shifts," he takes a double-dose and once again goes on the rampage. This time the villain's tyranny is stopped when he suddenly becomes an old man—"Mightium affected the flow of adrenaline, gave me my terrific strength (but) it burned out my metabolism, aged me."

Quote: "Are you too craven to match your insect powers against the unparalleled brawn of . . .*Mighty Man*!"

Comment: THE INVISIBLE MAN also ingested a serum which made him mad.

MINDBOGGLER (C)

First Appearance: 1984, *Fury of Firestorm* #29, DC Comics.

Costume: Olive tights; red boots, gloves; blue belt; ragged white T-shirt with black "MB" on chest.

Biography: Nothing is known about this character's past, and only slightly more has been revealed about how she received her powers. Subjected to an energy beam by the villainous assassin BREATHTAKER, she comes away with the power to control peoples' minds completely, from making them hallucinate to forcing them to do whatever she wills (even while they believe they're doing something else). Sent out to kill Firestorm, she is stymied because there are two minds inhabiting the superhero's body. Though she confuses one, she can't touch the other. Sent to jail with Breathtaker, she gets out and has battled Firestorm several times since. According to Breathtaker, she must undergo energy beam treatment regularly or her powers will fade. However, this has not happened to date and was clearly his way of trying to keep a rein on her.

MING THE MERCILESS (CS, R, MP, C, N, TV)

MING THE MERCILESS *drawn by Alex Raymond. © King Features Syndicate.*

First Appearance: January 1934, *Flash Gordon*, King Features Syndicate.

Costume: Original: red robe with high collar and yellow sunburst on chest; brown slippers. Second: red robe with yellow chest, sash around waist, cuffs, collar; stripe down skirt; red heart-shape on chest; red "widow's peak" cap with yellow dragon plume; blue cloak; brown boots. Variations of these basic costumes appear in the films, novels, and TV series.

Weapons: Rocket armada with destructive rays; "dehumanizing machine" to turn people into slaves; spacegraph, a television screen which sees anywhere; human-eating saber-toothed Tigrons; various swords and pistols.

Biography: When a strange new planet is discovered to be on a collision course with earth, Dr. Hans Zarkov rockets into space in an effort to destroy it. With him are "Yale graduate and world renowned polo player" Flash Gordon and lovely Dale Arden. They crash-land on the world, named Mongo, which is roughly one-half the diameter of earth (4,000 miles), though the gravitational force is nearly equal. Mongo is ruled by the despot Ming of Mingo City; the self-styled Emperor of the Universe leads a civilization whose science is far in advance of that of earth. ("The reason for our success," he cackles to Dale, "is that we possess none of the human traits of kindness, mercy, or pity! We are coldly scientific and ruthless.") His plans to use Mongo's science to disrupt the earth are thwarted by Flash, who remains on Mongo after the earth is saved, leading various rebellions against the tyrant. Ming's daughter is Princess Aura who, despite their relationship, is not immune to her father's ire. ("If you dare disobey me, Aura, I'll have your pretty back lashed to ribbons.") One reason for his displeasure is that she's in love with Flash. The Emperor worships the "great god Tao."

Quote: "Zogi, if you were not the high priest I would have your tongue torn out."

Comment: Other villains in the Flash Gordon strip include Azura, the Witch Queen of Kira, the cave world; Ming's ally King Orax of the Fire People; and Brukka, chief of the giants on Northern Mongo. In the 1953-54 syndicated TV series, Flash fought the Great God Em of Odin, the Mad Witch of Neptune, the Evil Queen of Cygnil, and the villainous Bizdar, among others. Bruno Wick played the evil Emperor in the 1935 Mutual radio series; other villains in the short-lived series include Queen Nylanda with her Destructo Cannon, Prince Neron and his Dissolvo Pistol, and the nefarious Raoul Du Farge. Charles Middleton (GROOD, #39013) played Ming in three movie serials: *Flash Gordon* (1936; feature title *Rocket Ship*), a retelling of the original comic strip epic; *Flash Gordon's Trip to Mars* (1938; feature title *Mars Attacks the World*), wherein the monarch is busy drawing the nitrogen from earth's atmosphere; and *Flash Gordon Conquers the Universe* (1940; feature title *Peril from the Planet Mongo*), in which he spreads the dust of the Purple Death all over the earth. In the 1980 feature film *Flash Gordon*, Max von

Sydow played the part to sadistic perfection. (He causes floods and earthquakes on earth, remarking, "I like to play with things awhile before annihilation.") In this film, Ming was aided by Klytus (Peter Wyngarde) and Kala (Mariangela Melato). Ming is the antagonist in the 1957 syndicated live-action TV series and in the NBC/Filmation 1979 cartoon series *Flash Gordon*. Flash and his allies the Defenders of the Earth also battle Ming in the 1986 syndicated cartoon series and 1987 Marvel comic book *Defenders of the Earth*. Ming has likewise been seen in the many comic book incarnations of Flash Gordon from Dell (1943-53), Harvey (1950-51), King (1967-68), Charlton (1969), and Gold Key (1947; 1978-80). In books, Ming was featured in a series of Flash Gordon novels published by Avon in 1974, and in another line from Tempo in 1981. Ming was also in the 14 Flash Gordon Big Little novels for children published between 1935 and 1948, all of which were set on Mongo.

MIRAGE (C)

First Appearance: 1982, *Detective Comics* #511, DC Comics.

Costume: Orange cowl, bodysuit; darker orange boots, hood, gloves, trunks which rise to chest.

Weapons: A gem which creates sight-and-sound illusions.

Chief Henchmen: Nameless gang members.

Biography: Nothing is known about this character's past. Obtaining his gem through unknown means (the gem's own origins also have not been revealed), he robs Gotham City blind until Batman is able to develop a device, worn in the ear, which filters out the gem's illusion-creating high frequency waves. Though one of Mirage's flunkies is able to break the earpiece, Batman draws upon his incredible willpower to overcome the illusion and bring the felons in. They have not seen the light of day since.

MIRROR MAN (C)

Real Name: Ventris.

First Appearance: 1954, *Detective Comics* #213, DC Comics.

Costume: Ordinary street clothes with square, thick-framed mirror-eyeglasses.

Weapons: Mirror which generates heat; portable "two-way electronic mirror that" Ventris stole "from a dead scientist's personal belongings," a device which "X-rays anything covered by cloth."

Chief Henchmen: The Mirror Man Mob, a group of underlings.

Biography: Upon beginning a seven-year prison sentence for unspecified crimes, Ventris is given a routine medical examination. Intentionally shattering a mirror, he hides several fragments; that night he breaks out, using the shards to blind the guards. Establishing a "bizarre hideout" with a mirror motif (presumably, his prior criminal activities had netted him a small fortune), Ventris becomes the thieving Mirror Man. At the same time, he tries to prove his criminal genius by using the "electronic mirror" to discover the secret identity of the superhero Batman. Not only does Batman foil him—by wearing distorting mirrors beneath his cowl—but also he ultimately nabs Ventris and throws him back in prison.

Quote: "Mirror, mirror, on the wall—who's the smartest crook of all? Me!"

Comment: This was the character's only appearance.

MIRROR MASTER (C)

Real Name: Sam Scudder.

First Appearance: 1959, *The Flash* #105, DC Comics.

Costume: Orange bodysuit with green belt, boots, cowl, wristbands, holsters.

Weapons: Mirror Master seldom uses the same weapon twice, but among those he has used are mirror guns which fire destructive beams; a mirror-pack which taps solar rays and allows him to fly; a funhouse mirror which causes distortions on the viewer's side; multidimensional mirrors for travel to other dimensions; mirrors, whose images he can draw forth as three-dimensional illusions which are completely under his power; a mirror which permits him to see several seconds into the future; and a mirror which generates "mirror guardians," duplicates of himself who lend a hand in his criminal activities.

Biography: While toiling in a prison workshop, making mirrors, criminal Scudder does something which causes one mirror to retain the image of the shop foreman. (He says he "ruined" it, though just how isn't clear; apparently he did something to the silver backing.) Keeping the mirror and studying it when he's released, he finds that mirrors can be "a virtual glass arsenal" for pulling off crimes. However, no matter what weapons he creates, they—along with Scudder's dreams—are invariably shattered by the Flash. The superhero even manages to escape Mirror Master's most dastardly trap—to be turned into a mirror and have a bazooka fired at him from point-blank range. (The Flash survives by using his "power of total molecular control" to melt himself from solid to molten glass, enabling him to duck the projectile.) The villain perishes at the hands of the even more villainous KRONA during the Crisis on Infinite Earths. Mirror Master belonged briefly to THE SECRET SOCIETY OF SUPER VILLAINS.

Quote: "My nasty little *Solaser mirror* captured a single ray of *sunlight* . . . which the giant refracting mirror is now about to *magnify* and *reflect* toward a rather *familiar skyline* on the horizon!"

Comment: Mirror Master was the first villain Flash faced when the hero's title was revived in 1959 after an absence of 10 years, during which time the hero was radically revamped. The Flash was the first superhero comic book of the so-called Silver Age.

MISSILE-TOE (A)

First Appearance: 1977, AAU Shoes ads.

Costume: Gray bodysuit with pink "M" on chest; pink gloves, boots with yellow trim; pink trunks; gray cowl with pink and yellow stripes on top.

Weapons: Missiles containing Toe-Main Poison shot from feet.

Biography: Nothing is known about this character's past. Wishing to destroy the world, he must first stomp out the heroic AAU Shuperstar. Battered by the hero, he disintegrates.

Quote: "I'll get a real boot out of de-feeting the *AAU Shuperstar.*"

Comment: This one-page ad was the character's sole appearance.

THE MIST (C)

First Appearance: 1941, *Adventure Comics* #67, DC Comics.

Costume: Original: a robe. Second: none.

Weapons: "Inviso-solution" which renders objects invisible or, in a reformulation, forces people to do his bidding. During World War II he used his chemical to create invisible bombers to attack the Allies.

Chief Henchmen: Roscoe and Bennie Bozak, other nameless thugs.

Biography: A scientist (his name has never been revealed), the future Mist concocted an "inviso-solution" and tried to peddle it to the United States military for use during the First World War. They refused, and when the Second World War began he dispatched invisible operatives to steal American top secrets in revenge. He was thwarted each time by the superhero Starman. At the onset of his criminal career, the Mist treated his robe with inviso-solution, giving his body (though not his head) a tenuous, fog-like appearance. In time, however, repeated use of the formula gave him the power to become a living mist, clothes and all, able to sneak through small cracks or float on the air. In this form, he could solidify just a part of his body—his fist to punch or his head so he can speak—while the rest of him remained gaseous. A member of THE SECRET SOCIETY OF SUPER VILLAINS, he was banished with that group into limbo by the Justice League and Justice Society of America.

Quote: "Ever since *overuse* of my *inviso-solution* made me a mist in *fact* as in name—I've enjoyed crime even more than *before*! It's a positive *joy*!"

Comment: The chemical compound has been written as both "inviso" and "invisio."

MISTER ATOM (C)

First Appearance: 1947, *Captain Marvel Adventures* #78, Fawcett Publications.

Costume: Blue skin top to bottom with wide golden "M" on chest, darker blue above the insignia; bullet-shaped blue head with darker blue sides, yellow top, and red eyes; yellow belt, bands around elbows, wrists, knees, toes; dark blue trunks.

Biography: To prove that atomic power can be used to create life, Dr. Charles Langley creates Mr. Atom, a nearly 10-feet-tall robot. Intending to bring the robot to life in careful steps, he's thwarted by an explosion which animates the robot in one grand moment. As a result, it is extremely strong, brilliant, able to fire atomic blasts. Virtually indestructible, Atom decides that there is no reason whatsoever for him to serve humankind when he has the power to dominate it or to destroy it utterly, if it refuses to be subjugated. Routed by the superheroic Captain Marvel, the robot was stashed in a special lead cell—only to be freed, in time, by extraterrestrials who needed his help to conquer the earth. As often happens with super villains, Mr. Atom and the aliens ended up battling among themselves. During one fracas Mr. Atom was caught in an explosion which flung him to the year 2053. Trying to conquer *that* world, he was once again thwarted by Captain Marvel. Atom rarely fought alone after that, and was a member of THE MONSTER SOCIETY OF EVIL.

Quote: "I was not destined for an inglorious serfdom! To rule over men—yes, that is my destiny!"

Comment: This character is clearly intended as a parable, the force of the atom which refuses to be bridled and will ultimately destroy us.

MR. BIG (N)

First Appearance: 1954, *Live and Let Die*, Ian Fleming.
Chief Henchman: Solitaire.
Biography: Bragging to British secret agent James Bond that he is the first "of the great Negro criminals," Mr. Big lives up to the billing. Working for the Soviet espionage group SMERSH, he uses his cover as a United States businessperson to smuggle gold coins into the country. The coins are part of a massive pirate treasure Mr. Big mines in Jamaica on the Isle of Surprise; from there, the gold makes its way to banks and pawn shops in New York's Harlem and in Florida where the profits are used to underwrite Russian operatives in the United States. The well-dressed, articulate villain dies when his boat is blown up by a time bomb Bond had placed earlier. Nor does the explosion come too soon for Bond. The villain was about to tow Bond behind the boat so his body could be ripped apart on a coral reef. Mr. Big's personal seer is the Haitian-bred woman Solitaire, who is schooled in voodoo and telepathy.
Comment: Yaphet Kotto played Mr. Big in the 1973 motion picture version of the novel, though the characters were quite different. In the film his name was Dr. Kananga, the prime minister of San Monique in the Caribbean. Instead of working for SMERSH he was growing heroin on his island, intending to distribute the drugs through a chain of "Filet of Soul" restaurants in the United States. He perished when, during a fight with Bond, the secret agent shoved a gas capsule down his throat causing Mr. Big to explode.

MR. COMPUTER (N)

Real Name: I.B.M. Computer (not his real name, but his adopted name).
First Appearance: 1970, *Dick Tracy*, William Johnston.
Biography: A mutant, Mr. Computer is "a model of what all men will be in some distant future." As a small boy, he is brighter than the brightest adults; he is shunned and feared, even by his parents. That breeds hate in the young man, who turns his ability to file, recall, and correlate everything he has ever learned to one goal—world domination. "A giant of a man, extremely heavy," Mr. Computer is bald with "an almost perfect square" for a head. His eyes are "bright and sparkling, like two small, flashing lights." The archfiend prepares for his undertaking by abducting scientists and using a drug to extract their knowledge. ("Every man wants to be the Supreme Power," he tells Tracy. "All have failed . . . because they did not have the necessary knowledge of their fellow human beings to manipulate them perfectly.") Even Tracy's knowledge is dumped into the villain's mind so that he can anticipate the detective's every move. In the end, after coldly murdering several of the people who pose "a danger" to him, Mr. Computer experiences a mind overload during a shootout with Tracy and dies of a brain hemorrhage.
Quote: "Things will be much different when I am in control of society. I will purify mankind. Those who have cruel thoughts will be destroyed."
Comment: The character never appeared in the Dick Tracy comic strip. The novel was published by Tempo Books.

MR. CRABB (C)

First Appearance: 1965, *Blue Beetle*, Vol. 3, #50, Charlton Comics.
Costume: Blue trousers, cape, gloves, shoes; yellow shirt (skin is red).
Weapons: The Scorpion, an eight-legged mechanical underwater conveyance with huge, electrified pincers.
Chief Henchman: Eric, foreman of the oil operation.
Biography: Drilling for oil on a rig in the Texas Gulf—where he destroys all competition, hoping to control the region's output—Mr. Crabb of the Crabb Oil Company stores the crude in a huge domed warehouse under the sea. From there, he ships it to Red China in submarine tankers. His operation is wrecked when the superheroic Blue Beetle invades his stronghold; the oil tanks are destroyed and the dome collapses, though the fate of Mr. Crabb is unknown. As Blue Beetle observes, "He may have gone down in the Scorpion, or he may turn up again to trouble an already troubled world!"
Quote: "Remove this reminder of man's weakness from my sight."
Comment: This was the villain's only appearance. See other underwater super villains ATTUMA, BLACK MANTA, CAPTAIN NEMO, CAPTAIN WHALE, DR. FANG, FISHERMAN, KILLER SHARK, KRANG, OCEAN MASTER, ORKA, PIRANHA, and TIGER SHARK (2).

MISTER FEAR (C)

Real Name: Zoltan Drago, Samuel Saxon, Larry Cranston, Alan Fagan.

First Appearance: 1965, *Daredevil* #6 (Drago); 1969, #54 (Saxon); 1972, #91 (Cranston); 1980, *Marvel Team-Up* #92 (Fagan), Marvel Comics.

Costume: Blue bodysuit with purple shoulders, stripe down chest, waist; purple trunks, boots, gloves, cloak with high collar, hood, holster; dark blue skull-like mask.

Weapons: Pellets, fired from a gun, which release gas that causes people to experience profound fear. Drago also uses time-release capsules which he hides in Daredevil's billyclub; Fagan deals it out by a hypodermic ring (which allows him to administer "a full-strength dose" for superheroes, instead of the gaseous "dilute form"). Saxon has used "repello rays" which repel objects and a hover disc; Cranston added rocket jets to the outfit.

Chief Henchmen: Ox, a powerful brute; and Eel, who can generate shocks. They and Mister Fear were grouped, informally, as "the Fellowship of Fear," teaming only in the Drago incarnation. Fagan had various nameless thugs in his employ.

Biography: A slightly mad sculptor, Drago tries to invent a gas which will bring his waxworks to life, something that will give him an army of paraffin slaves. Instead, he invents a chemical which causes fear. Recognizing the criminal potential inherent in the gas, he designs a costume, pulls together a pair of accomplices, places a duplicate costume and pellets in a New York warehouse, and slinks forth as Mister Fear. Beaten by the superhero Daredevil, Drago does time and is released. No sooner is he out, however, than Samuel Saxon (see MACHINESMITH) tracks him to his hotel, wrests from him the location of his spare suit and pellets, and murders him. (Unbeknownst to the men they are overheard by Larry Cranston, who is also rooming in the hotel.) Saxon's reign is brief and, after he nearly dies while battling Daredevil, the Mister Fear accoutrements pass to Cranston, who convinces authorities that he is a relative of Saxon's. Cranston lays low for a while, and when he finally goes after Daredevil (he's a former classmate of Matt Murdock, aka Daredevil, and hates him intensely), his career is even shorter than that of Saxon (one issue instead of two). This time the Mister Fear trappings go to a bonafide relative, Cranston's nephew Alan Fagan. ("You despised me," he gloats to his uncle's portrait, "but your money and your *Mister Fear* costume still fell into my hands after you died!") Embittered because he was constantly thrown out of schools and laughed at, he plans to use his genius to begin "a largescale reign of terror" by building an atom bomb. But his dreams of extortion and terrorism are nipped in the bud by Spider-Man and Hawkeye; he goes to jail and, as no relatives step forth this time around, the police hold the costume and gas capsules. Remarkably, when Fagan finishes doing time, the paraphernalia is returned to him.

Quote: "It gives me *pleasure*—to see a being of your reputation, *cowering* before me!"

Comment: See other fear-inducing villains BUSHMAN, DR. SPECTRO, D'SPAYRE, PHOBIA, PSYCHO-MAN, PSYCHO-PIRATE, and SCARECROW (1).

MR. FREEK (C)

First Appearance: 1966, *Frankenstein* #2, Dell Publishing.

Chief Henchmen: Kilo, a brute of a man; and Bruto, "the largest gorilla in the world . . . over a ton of pure strength . . . and no brain."

Biography: Mr. Freek lives "on a small island in the Caribbean." Standing approximately three feet tall due to "an unfortunate accident" (which is never described), Freek has been compensated with a superior brain. Heading for the East Coast of the United States, Freek rides the gorilla's shoulders and uses his strength to commit spectacular robberies, then finally decides he wants Seaboard City for his own. The citizens flee in terror, but before Freek can enjoy his urban domain or conquer the next town, the superhero Frankenstein arrives. Beating up the ape, Frankenstein sends Mr. Freek and his simian aide sailing for home, where the angry villain vows to

***MR. FREEK** atop his gorilla-assistant. © Dell Publishing.*

avenge his defeat. He does indeed return (#3), this time with a giant spider as well as Bruto. However, Frankenstein defeats him once again, ending the villain's career.

Quote: "What? Does someone dare not to be frightened away? Does someone think they can stand in my path?"

Comment: See also THUNDER-MAN, who used a giant ape to wreak havoc.

MISTER FREEZE (Originally MISTER ZERO) (C, TV)

First Appearance: 1959, *Batman* #121, DC Comics.

Costume: Original: light blue bodysuit with white "icicle" motif on shoulders and chest; white trunks; white gloves and boots with icicle fringing; red belt, goggles, holster; clear dome over head. Second: white bodysuit; blue leotard, boots; purple shoulderpads and gloves; white collar to which trapezoidal helmet is attached. (Note: While sleek, this costume is not fabric but armor-like, apparently made of a plastic compound.)

Weapons: Cold gun which freezes any object in its path.

Biography: While working on a gun which could generate a deep freeze, the criminal genius who later became Mister Freeze was accidentally coated with chemicals being employed in the weapon's construction. As a result, he could no longer live in temperatures above 32° Fahrenheit. Designing an insulated refrigeration suit, he returned to crime as Mister Zero. After repeated defeats at the hands of the crimefighting Batman, the frigid fiend revised his costume and changed his name to Mister Freeze. He remains one of the superhero's most enduring foes.

Comment: On the *Batman* TV series (1966-68), Mr. Freeze was played in turn by George Sanders, Otto Preminger, and Eli Wallach. See other icy super villains BLIZZARD, CAPTAIN COLD, Coldsnap of MASTERS OF DISASTER, ICICLE, and KILLER FROST.

MR. HYDE (N, MP, R, C)

Real Name: Edward Hyde (see Biography).

First Appearance: 1886, *The Strange Case of Dr. Jekyll and Mr. Hyde*, Robert Louis Stevenson.

Biography: Henry Jekyll was born into a large fortune and, for the most part, was a happy, moral soul. It occurred to him, however, that if good and evil "could be housed in separate identities . . . the just could walk steadfastly and securely on his upward path (free) of this extraneous evil." Thus, working in the laboratory of his London home (a mansion "which wore a great air of wealth and comfort"), he created a formula consisting of a "red tincture" which, when special salts were added, "began, in proportion as the crystals melted, to brighten in colour, to effervesce audibly, and to throw off small fumes of vapour." Then it went dark purple and faded to "a watery green." Drinking the potion he cried, "reeled, staggered, clutched at the table and held on . . . gasping with open mouth" as he suffered "a grinding in the bones, deadly nausea, and a horror of the spirit." Immediately feeling reckless and "disordered," Jekyll realized at once that the experiment had backfired. He was now "more wicked, tenfold more wicked" than before and, worse, exulted "in the freshness of these sensations." Foul as he was on the inside, the external trappings were their equal. According to one character, there was something "wrong . . . displeasing . . . downright detestable" about the creature's appearance. "Pale and dwarfish, he gave an impression of deformity without any namable malformation, he had a displeasing smile . . . and he spoke with a husky, whispering, and somewhat broken voice." He seemed, in short, "hardly human . . . something troglodytic." (Jekyll later realized that this new creature, Mr. Edward Hyde, was "smaller, slighter, and younger" than he was because his evil side was so underdeveloped.) Using Jekyll's money, the depraved Mr. Hyde set himself up in a two-story house in Soho that was ripe with "sordid negligence." Inside, however, he filled his home with fine art, wine, and elegant carpets, for Hyde enjoyed the good life. At first, Jekyll enjoyed the "pleasures undignified" he sought as Hyde; he retained the memories of what he did, and could always change back to his wholesome former self. Soon, however, Hyde increased in physical stature and Jekyll had to increase the amount of formula he drank to bring him forth; toward the end of his criminal career, the dosage had tripled. In time, the transformations occurred unaided and Hyde was around more often than Jekyll. Thus, in one of the rare moments when Jekyll returned, he quaffed a poison to end his life. Hyde's potential for evil was limited by the brief span (a little over a year) of his existence. Among his minor crimes was to scribble blasphemous remarks on holy writings and to destroy a painting of Jekyll's father. His three major acts of violence were, first, after bumping into a girl of "eight or ten" in the street he "trampled calmly over the child's body and left her screaming on the ground"; next, to smash in a woman's face when she tried to "sell him lights"; and third, to use his heavy cane to club M.P. Sir Danvers Carew to death in the street: "the bones were audibly shattered (and) the stick . . . had broken under the stress."

Quote: "To cast in my lot with Jekyll, was to die to those appetites which I . . . pamper."

Comment: Hyde has enjoyed a popular career beyond the printed page. On the stage, he was first played by Richard Mansfield in Boston in 1887; the actor made that role his specialty for 20 years. On the screen, the first film version was made in 1908 (with uncredited stage actors from Chicago). It was followed by filmings in 1912 (Harry Benham played Hyde), 1913 (King Baggot), three in 1920 (Hank Mann, Sheldon Lewis, and, in a classic portrayal, John Barrymore); 1932 (Fredric March, who won the Best Actor Oscar for his performance); 1941 (Spencer Tracy); 1951 (*The Son of Dr. Jekyll*, with Louis Hayward as Edward Jekyll, the bastard son of Hyde who, while trying to exonerate Henry Jekyll, takes the formula and becomes a monster himself); 1953 (*Abbott and Costello Meet Dr. Jekyll and Mr. Hyde*, starring Boris Karloff as a Jekyll who, this time out, is trying to infuse humans with animal traits); 1957 (*Daughter of Dr. Jekyll*, in which Gloria Talbot is blamed for crimes being committed by Mr. Hyde [Arthur Shields] who, it turns out, wasn't really a dark side of Jekyll but a separate creature entirely, a werewolf!); 1960 (*The Two Faces of Dr. Jekyll*, starring Paul Massie); 1967 (Jack Palance in a superb made-for-TV movie); 1973 (*I, Monster*, starring Christopher Lee as Mr. Blake [apart from the name change, the film was quite faithful to Stevenson]); again in 1973 (Kirk Douglas in a *musical* made-for-TV movie); and 1975 (*Dr. Black and Mr. Hyde*, starring Bernie Casey as Dr. Henry Pride in modern-day Los Angeles). There have been countless variations on the theme—i.e., a nerd becoming hip in Jerry Lewis' *The Nutty Professor*—but none of the other Hydes is a super villain. On the radio, Spencer Tracy recreated his role the same year the film was released, on "Lux Radio Theatre"; Fredric March did likewise on "The Theatre Guild on the Air" in 1950. Laurence Olivier tried his voice at the part on "Theatre Royale" in England in 1952, while Kevin McCarthy did the honors in the United States on "Radio Mystery Theater" in 1974. In comic books, Classics Comics published an adaptation of the story in 1943, offering another version (as Classics Illustrated) a decade later. Marvel Comics has published two versions—one in *Supernatural Thrillers* #4 (1973) and another in *Marvel Classic Comics* #1 (1976).

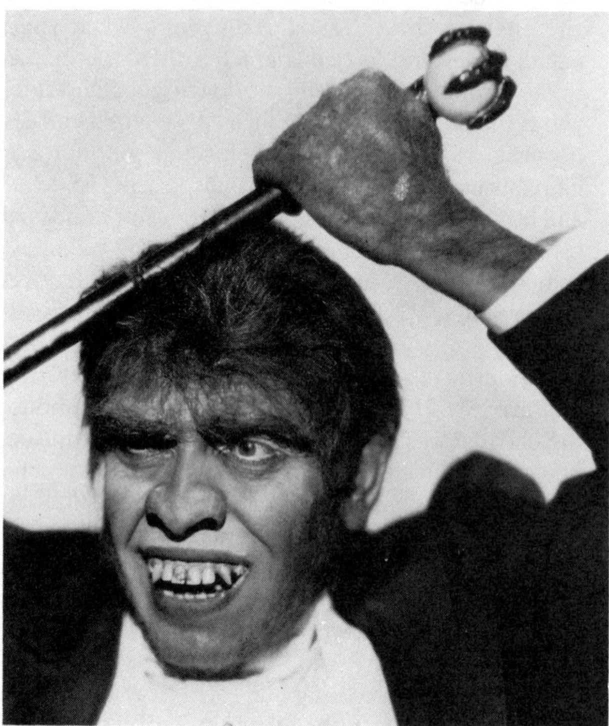

Fredric March in his Oscar-winning performance as ***MR. HYDE*** *in* Dr. Jekyll and Mr. Hyde. *© Paramount Pictures.*

MR. MASTERMIND (C)

First Appearance: 1977, *Dynomutt* #2, Marvel Comics.

Weapons: Mechano-disruptor ray which makes machines go haywire.

Biography: A "not-too-nice gent who claims to be the most brilliant person who ever lived," Mr. Mastermind holds Big City for ransom, threatening to "make every machine go wild" if he isn't paid $1.47—the fine he once had to pay for an overdue library book. While the city council debates, Mr. Mastermind attacks toasters, merry-go-rounds, soda machines, garbage compactors, and the like. Meanwhile, investigating the case, the superhero Blue Falcon and his robotic dog Dynomutt learn that Mr. Mastermind has another book that's been overdue since 1928. They track him to his lair, where he destroys all evidence of his machine. However, they are able to throw him in prison due to the $536.55 he owes on the overdue book.

Quote: "This city must learn to *obey* someone who is unbelievably superior to them all!"

Comment: Dynomutt gained his greatest fame as a TV hero. Villains featured in his 1976 ABC-TV series include the Harbor Robber, Hyde, Supermugg, the Queen Hornet, the Wizard of Ooze, the Red Vulture, and the Injustice League of America. Marvel published six issues of the *Dynomutt* comic book.

MR. MIND (C)

First Appearance: 1943, *Captain Marvel Adventures* #22 (as voice only); 1943, #26 (in the flesh), Fawcett Publications.

Costume: None. Mr. Mind is an inches-long worm with green skin, a black back, and red spots on his side. However, he does wear glasses and a voice amplifier to boost his poor eyesight and small voice.

Weapons: Many scientific gadgets.

Chief Henchmen: THE MONSTER SOCIETY OF EVIL.

Biography: Mr. Mind was born on another world, a planet of worms (neither his name nor that of the planet has been revealed). Endowed with a mutant-brain far superior to that of his fellow worms, Mr. Mind learned that a satyr-like alien had been stranded on his world and had set up a laboratory. Taking over the being's mind, the worm used his body to build eyeglasses and a voice amplifier. He also built a radio which enabled him to hear broadcasts from earth, a world he resolved to conquer. Traveling to our planet and organizing the Monster Society of Evil, he waged war against earth's protector, Captain Marvel (a battle which spanned a total of 232 pages before concluding!). In the end, Mr. Mind was captured and tried for having ordered 186,744 murders. Captain Marvel himself was the prosecutor. ("Is it not true that on the night of Aug. 7th you and your henchmen attempted to blow up Washington and put all the people to death in horrible ways?") When Mr. Mind's own lawyer refused to defend him, the extraterrestrial worm was sent to the electric chair—the jury not even bothering to leave the courtroom to reach their verdict! Mr. Mind was subsequently sent to a taxidermist to be stuffed and placed in a museum. Unbeknownst to the executioner, however, Mr. Mind's kind are impervious to electricity and the jolt only stunned him. Taking over the mind of the taxidermist, the tiny terror had him mount and stuff a fake worm while he spun a cocoon and took a decades-long nap. Awaking in our own era (when Captain Marvel has himself escaped suspended animation), he resumed his conflict with the superhero. In their most dramatic confrontation, Mr. Mind transformed himself into a titanic worm in a (doomed) effort to defeat Marvel.

Quote: "My wonderful Monster Society of Evil is finished. All those good times we had destroying and killing, are over!"

MISTER 103 (C)

Real Name: John Dubrovny.

First Appearance: 1965, *The Doom Patrol* #98, DC Comics.

Weapons: See Biography.

Biography: A brilliant if mad biochemist, Dubrovny transforms himself into Mister 103, aka "the Atom Master" and "the Atomic Man." As such, Dubrovny is able to turn himself into any of the 103 elements then known to science, assuming their properties (including magnetism for iron) in any shape he wishes. (He can also assume them concurrently—i.e., diamond for strength and lead for shielding.) Taking on the insane scientist, the Doom Patrol is able to render him powerless using a ray created from an element unknown on earth. However, Dubrovny doesn't stay down for long. Finding a meteor capable of nullifying the alien ray, he *eats* it and then links up with Nicholas Galtry (see THE ARSENAL), who underwrites his experiments to find a new means of destroying the Doom Patrol. Mister 103 is defeated again, though just barely. He has not been heard from since.

Comment: Among the other super villains the Doom Patrol has battled are Yaramishi Rama Yogi, the Great Guru, who uses advanced psychology (masquerading as mysticism) to battle the superheroes; the Bug Man, who can control and/or become any insect ("Now that you're trapped in my cocoon," he cackles after becoming a giant silkworm, "my deadly bees will finish the job!"); Dr. Death, a mad scientist who, among other schemes, tries to take over the country by causing its leaders to lose their minds and commit suicide (unrelated to Batman's foe DR. DEATH); the mutants Ar, Ir, and Ur who detest normal humans and use their atomic powers to put the world and a comet on a collision course; the Black Vulture, aka Decker, who has a flock of trained birds of all kinds; and the Wrecker (Harvey Keller), who uses his space base to destroy all technology.

MR. V (C)

Real Name: Marco Xavier.

First Appearance: 1966, *House of Mystery* #160, DC Comics.

Costume: Featureless, full-face white mask; white gloves, turtleneck shirt with black and white vulture emblem on chest; black jacket; violet trousers.

Weapons: Captive-Ray Gun "capable of overcoming any force on earth"; "transfer ray" to turn his men into fire-breathing monsters; lightning bolt gun; and a "molecular ray" which turns people into powerful giants.

Chief Henchmen: Señor Mendez (#160); Abba Sulkar, who tries to stop the Martian Manhunter with a tape recorder which probes peoples' memories, and a "disintegrator" gun (#161); "regional lieutenant" Zoltar (#162); "local unit" leader Cluzot and a renegade creature from Mercury (#163); others who are nameless or low on the crime totem pole.

Biography: Mr. V is the leader of Vulture, "a worldwide

criminal organization." Living in "a posh Mediterranean villa," Marco dons a mask before appearing to his men on a large TV in their base beneath a small souvenir booth in a marketplace near his home (he also has a second base in a converted airplane). At the request of "a special security department" of the government, the super-powered J'onn J'onzz, the Manhunter from Mars, devotes himself to Vulture's destruction. J'onzz and Mr. V's various henchmen clash repeatedly until the villain's death (#173); the fiend perished when an experimental weapon exploded in his hand as he tried to shoot the Martian Manhunter.

Quote: "*Manhunter*! . . . If you had arrived only seconds later, the cylinder would have provided me at least with a small army of permanent monster-men!"

Comment: This was the character's only appearance.

MISTER WOLF (F, MP)

First Appearance: 1853, "The Three Little Pigs," J.O. Halliwell.

Biography: Nothing is known of Mister Wolf's past until he approaches the abodes of the three pigs, brothers who have built their homes of straw, furze (or twigs), and bricks, respectively. After blowing down the first two homes with his mighty breath (and eating the pigs therein), Mister Wolf ventures to the third. Unable to blow the brick house down, Mister Wolf ascends to the roof and shimmies down the chimney. Unknown to him, however, the third pig has placed a kettle of boiling oil in the fireplace, and the usually cunning Mister Wolf is scalded to death.

Quote: "I'll huff, and I'll puff, and I'll blow the house in."

Comment: Halliwell was the first anthologist to publish the tale in its present form; he was also one of the few to have the wolf actually eat the pigs. The story is similar to the earlier "The Wolf and the Seven Little Kids" (1812) from the Brothers Grimm (the goats fed their enemy stones and he drowned), and "The History of the Celebrated Nanny Goose" published in England in 1813 in which the cleverest of three goslings survives the wolf's attack by building a house of bricks. In his *Green Fairy Book*, noted anthologist Andrew Lang included a version which did not have a wolf but a fox, huffing and puffing his way through the homes of mud and cabbage before being stymied by the one made of brick. Arguably the most famous telling of the tale was Walt Disney's 1933 *Silly Symphony* cartoon short, "The Three Little Pigs," with its song "Who's Afraid of the Big Bad Wolf?" Halliwell was also the first anthologist to collect the story of "Chicken-licken." In that tale, Chicken-licken is hit on the head by an acorn; convincing her friends Hen-len, Cock-lock, Duck-luck, Drake-lake, Goose-loose, Gander-lander, and Turkey-lurkey that the sky has fallen, they set out to inform the king. En route, they meet the sly, villainous Fox-lox who offers to lead them. Instead, he takes them to his den where he and his cubs consume them. The story is sometimes published as "Henney-Penny" or "Chicken Little," and the villain is frequently called Foxy-loxy. A fox is also the killer in "The Gingerbread Man," also known as "Johnny Cake." In most versions of this nineteenth-century folktale, the titular cookie meets his end when a fox offers to carry him across a stream and eats him. The most popular variation is one in which the Gingerbread Man meets and addresses the Fox, who pretends to be deaf; when the pastry lad comes too close, the Fox pounces.

THE MOD GORILLA BOSS (C, N)

First Appearance: 1967, *Strange Adventures* #201, DC Comics.

Costume: Black- and white-striped doublebreasted suit; yellow shirt with black stripes; black tie and handkerchief with pink polka dots.

Chief Henchman: Gavern.

Biography: A brawny thug develops a formula which gives him the might and appearance of a gorilla; he uses his simian strength and agility to commit crimes and pound adversaries into "grave fodder." However, he hasn't quite perfected it and must return regularly to his rural laboratory for fresh injections. The Mod Gorilla Boss is ultimately outwitted by the superhero Animal-Man, who realizes that there's a reason the burglar always beats "hasty departures from crime scenes." Engaging him in battle at the site of a robbery, Animal-Man waits until his hirsute adversary returns to normal, then arrests him.

Quote: "You . . . you tricked me!—Kept me so busy I-I forgot about the time element!"

Comment: This was the pushy primate's only appearance. See other ape villains GORILLA BOSS, GORILLA GRODD, MANDRILL, and MAN-APE.

MODOK (C, N)

Real Name: George Tarleton.

First Appearance: 1967, *Tales of Suspense* #94, Marvel Comics.

Costume: Purple bodysuit, gloves, boots, headband.

Weapons: Hover-chair, which can fly, used to support his great weight; various weapons, including a potent "ultra ray" gun, sleep-inducing "somna gas," and numerous robots.

Chief Henchmen: The entire membership of A.I.M. (see Biography).

Biography: Tarleton was an engineer and operative for A.I.M. (Advanced Idea Mechanics), an organization of scientists and subordinates devoted to conquering the world via science. When A.I.M. developed an "alteration chamber" which, theoretically, could cause beneficial mutations, A.I.M. leader Lyle Getz chose Tarleton at random to be its first (and very unwilling) subject. When he emerged from the chamber, Tarleton's head was several times its normal size (it took four strong men to lift him) and his mental abilities were also enormous. He had acquired a photographic memory as well as psionic powers which enable him to throw off "mental thrusts" (i.e., deadly blasts), generate extreme heat, and create a protective energy field. Dubbed Modok (Mental Organism Designed Only for Killing), Tarleton was furious with his hideous, super-cephalic state and not only killed Getz but also took over A.I.M. and applied his vast new intellect to its goals of world domination. He ruled the evil league for a decade and a half before being deposed by those dissatisfied with his tyranny and repeated defeats at the hands of everyone from Iron Man to the Hulk to the jungle hero Ka-Zar to the international security group S.H.I.E.L.D. Taken prisoner by his former underlings, Modok was brainwashed and now slavishly serves the rulers of A.I.M.

Quote: "I am not so hypocritical as to attempt to disguise my desires . . . as anything but what they are. The procurement and application of power."

Comment: Modok was the villain in the only Iron Man novel, *And Call My Killer . . . Modok!*, written by William Rotsler and published in 1979. A parody of the villain, Moskull (the head of THE RED SKULL in Modok's hover-chair), fought the female superhero Bernie America in *Captain America* #289 (1984). Moskull's goal was "to conquer the galaxy and open a chain of Pizza Huts all across the Milky Way." Yet, perhaps more bizarre than the parody was a development in the life of Modok himself—the introduction of Ms. Modok in *The Incredible Hulk* #290 (1983). Dr. Katherine Waynesboro was transformed into a "mate" for the floating head; as Modok put it, "We desire each other, for no other intelligence exists on earth—that can satisfy our yearnings for a match of the mind." Unfortunately for Modok, Ms. Modok was disgusted when Modok slew THE ABOMINATION ("All life has value!" she cried), and they battled. In the end, Modok flew off while Ms. Modok was returned to her Waynesboro identity.

MO-GWEI (M)

First Appearance: March 1934, "Meteor Menace," *Doc Savage* Magazine.

Costume: Yellow robes and the Mask of Bron, half-king of hell, with "a red clot of a nose, villainous yellow eyes, and two great upturned horns."

Weapons: The Blue Meteor, a radio-controlled monoplane which, packed with a radioactive element, sends out rays that shock "the human nervous system" and cause madness; an antidote, distilled from the meteor, "which kept the nerves functioning despite the shock of the blue meteor emanations."

Biography: A scientist, Mo-Gwei dwells in the abandoned Tibetan village of the Mad Ones. He holds court on a bulletproof steel platform suspended from the ceiling of an underground temple-chamber, hewn from solid stone both to celebrate the meteor and to protect people from its powerful rays. Using fragments of the space rock to create his deadly monoplane, Mo-Gwei sends it forth to make people mad. Described as "the bloodiest criminal that ever walked the earth," Mo-Gwei plans to use the Blue Meteor to conquer the world. However, Mo-Gwei is pursued by the superhero Doc Savage, who is about to capture him when Doc's maddened guide Shrops knocks the fiend into a deep pit. Mo-Gwei perishes in the 200-foot fall.

Quote: "I shall boil each of you in yak tallow, and crack open your skulls so that the ravens may feast!"

Comment: This was one of Doc's first super-foes. In *The Secret in the Sky* (May 1935), Doc fought another "extraterrestrial" menace, the Comet Gang, which used four artificial comets to help them commit crimes. The gang would fly to the scene of a crime in their "new type of terrestrial ship capable of traveling at terrific speed, and of handling with remarkable facility," rob a ship, jewelry store, or bank, and then escape. The gang and the secret of their comets perished in an enormous nitroglycerine explosion.

THE MOLE (CS, TV)

First Appearance: November 17, 1941, *Dick Tracy*, Chicago Tribune-New York News Syndicate.

Chief Henchman: Oily.

Biography: About to be murdered in 1926 by his own gang (his feet are stuck in wet concrete and he is about to be dumped in the bay), the Mole comes up with a plan: He'll build an underground hideout and will let the gang use it whenever the heat is on. They agree, unaware that he plans to charge them through the nose and then kill them one by one as they accept his "hospitality." With the burrowing ability (and face) of his furry namesake, the Mole digs the labyrinthine hideaway with his hands, a sanctum accessible only through an unused boiler in a junkyard; while he sleeps, he is protected by 220 volts of electricity which run through the metal ladder descending into his lair. Bootlegging electricity from overhead wires, the Mole is fed secretly each day by an aide named Oily (for a cut of the Mole's income, he slips food through a removable brick in the greasing pit of his service station). The Mole makes a fortune with his doublecrossing operation. The Mole is extremely powerful from "digging in the earth." He's eventually captured by Dick Tracy, who falls through the softened earth into the caverns.

Quote: "I got their money—and eliminated them. It was lots of fun!"

Comment: The Mole was also a character on the Dick Tracy cartoon show (1960). See ADMIRAL CEREBRUS, Comment, for The Mole (2), and ZODIAC MASTER, Comment, for The Mole (3).

MOLECULE MAN (C)

Real Name: Owen Reece.

First Appearance: 1963, *The Fantastic Four* #20, Marvel Comics.

Costume: Green trousers, jacket with jagged purple bolts rising diagonally from waist, front and back, to shoulders and flaring outward; purple wristbands, boots, belt. (Sometimes wears purple gloves and a blue helmet; later the trousers and jacket are replaced with a bodysuit and purple trunks, though the purple markings on his torso remain the same).

Weapons: A golden wand (see Biography).

Biography: "A small, frail, timid child, ever clinging to his mother," Reece grows up to be "a weak, wretched adult, bitter and lonely . . . brimming with hatred and fear." Working as a technician at an Acme Atomics nuclear power plant, Reece gets careless one day and inadvertently turns on a new, unproven particle accelerator. Bathed with radiation, Reece finds his latent psionic abilities activated. The accident scars his face with black bolts radiating from around his nose, but the good news is that it also gives him absolute control over matter, including the ability to reshape and levitate it. Fired for his ineptitude, Reece (after coating his boss's desk with ice) storms out and becomes a super villain. At the same time, he cannot quite shuck the lack of confidence which has dogged him all his life, and he becomes largely dependent on a baton-like placebo wand he carries to channel his powers; even at that can't bring himself to use his power on living beings. Defeated by the Fantastic Four and imprisoned in another dimension, he creates an artificial "son" and, before dying of old age (a process accelerated by virtue of being in another dimension), places his consciousness in the wand and gives it to the new Molecule Man. The artificial being escapes and heads to earth, where he perishes when the Thing of the Fantastic Four snatches the wand. The instrument thereafter becomes a criminal sparkplug, making super villains out of everyone who comes to possess it. Finally, Reece's mind manages to build itself a new body, which he promptly inhabits. After briefly resuming his evil ways, he goes into analysis and becomes a solid citizen. After helping to save the world from the monstrous Beyonder (*Secret Wars II* limited series, 1985-86), the reformed Reece settles down in a suburb of Denver with Coloradan Marsha Rosenberg, and once again works at a nuclear power plant.

THE MOLE MAN (C)

First Appearance: 1961, *The Fantastic Four* #1, Marvel Comics.

Costume: Green jumpsuit; darker green boots, cloak; blue glasses (to improve his diminished vision).

Weapons: Huge mole-shaped "Mole Machine" for digging through the earth; laser cannon; and an arsenal of quarterstaves: wooden for hand-to-hand combat, another which fires destructive sonic blasts, another which launches electric bolts, and another which is a flamethrower.

Chief Henchmen: The Moloid Subterraneans (informally, his "Monster Mob"), an army of golden-skinned subterraneans; he also controls sundry dinosaur-like giants.

Biography: All his life, the Mole Man-to-be (his name has never been revealed) was "mocked" because of his ugliness. ("What?" gasps a young woman. "*Me* go out with *you*? Don't make me laugh!") Though he managed to get work as a nuclear scientist, it was difficult landing a job. ("I *know* you're qualified," says one potential employer, "but . . . you'd scare our other employees away!") Deciding to leave society and live "alone . . . at the center of the earth," he eventually made his way to Monster Isle where a cavern led him to the planet's core. Losing most of his sight in a fall, he realized that he was relegated to living inside the earth forever. Developing "a natural radar sense," he found and conquered various races of subterranean creatures, had them carve out an "underground empire" which he dubbed Subterranea, then dispatched the larger beasts to attack the cruel surface world. Though his plans to raze society and dominate humankind have been thwarted by the Fantastic Four, Spider-Man, and other superheroes, he is unrelenting—especially after drilling by wealthy entrepreneur Alden Maas caused magma to flood the Mole Man's kingdom, killing many of its denizens. He has also had to contend with Tyrannus, an ancient wizard who dwells underground and has designs on the Mole Man's kingdom. The dwarfish felon's longtime lover is Kala, an Atlantean who rules the domed subsea kingdom of the Netherworld and also holds surface dwellers in contempt.

Quote: "I love getting *underfoot*!"

Comment: The Mole Man holds the distinction of being the first super villain fought by any superhero in the Silver Age (post-1962) Marvel universe. See, too, Dick Tracy's foe THE MOLE; Batman also battled a burrowing villain named the Mole (see ZODIAC MASTER, Comment).

MOLTAR (C, T)

First Appearance: 1983, "The Saga of Crystar," *Crystal Warrior* #1, Marvel Comics (see Comment).

Costume: Moltar as a human: blue bodysuit, cape; red trunks, belt fringed with yellow, boots with yellow hem, collar which covers shoulder and most of chest. Moltar as a magma being: covered with solid red lava, nine volcanic cones radiating from around his skull; whenever he is angry, flame and smoke erupt from these craters.

Weapons: Golden mace and axe.

Chief Henchmen: His lover Lavour and devoted Zardeth, Feldspar, and Warbow, magma beings, all.

Biography: Brothers Moltar and Crystar were princes dwelling in the city of Galax on the distant world of Crystalium. For years, Crystalium was consumed with warfare, the Demon Lord "for reasons of his own" having decided to conquer the planet. The humanoid denizens, led by their king, battled the Demon Lord and the hordes of chaos, his "minions and demon slaves"; when the king was slain in battle, a mysterious wizard named Ogeode appeared to take command of the defenders. The Demon Lord was eventually driven back and the planet knew peace once more. However, before leaving, the despot cursed Crystalium. As Moltar told the tale, the evil invader vowed to "send . . . one who would divide our planet against itself, setting . . . brother against brother . . . ." Enter the sinister sorcerer Zardeth just a few months later, the night before the brothers' coronation as joint-kings. He demanded obedience from the kings, or he would wage war against them; thinking of the long war his subjects had just suffered, Moltar opted for conciliation, whereas Crystar and Ogeode opted for resistance to tyranny. The princes fought. Moltar stabbed Crystar and then fled to Zardeth, who was holed up underground, at the Fountain of Fire, a pit of bubbling magma. There, Zardeth caused the prince and his followers to be sucked up by the lava and turned into powerful rock-humanoids. Giving them "dragons of magma" to ride through the air, the sorcerer sent them forth to conquer Galax. Meanwhile, Ogeode had used *his* powers to turn Crystar and his aides into powerful beings of crystal.

Quote: "I'm your brother, not your *gorf*! Don't reprimand me like a tame *house lizard*!"

Comment: The Crystalium characters were co-created by Marvel and Remco, which produced the line of action figures. See other action toy super villains BARON KARZA, DESTRO, GENERAL SPIDRAX, HORDAK, MUMM-RA, and SKELETOR.

THE MOLTEN MAN (C)

Real Name: Mark Raxton.

First Appearance: 1965, *The Amazing Spider-Man* #28, Marvel Comics.

Costume: Original: streetclothes. Second: golden trunks (Molten Man's skin is golden).

Biography: Raxton is the assistant of Professor Spencer Smythe, "inventor extraordinary." Together, they invent a "liquid metal alloy," which the greedy Raxton then decides he wants to sell "to the highest bidder." Smythe refuses to let it go, and the two men struggle; during the fracas, Raxton drops a large jar of the stuff he was carrying and is coated with it. He stumbles into an electric arc and his skin absorbs the alloy; as a result, he acquires superstrength, becoming strong enough to overturn a car or, turning to crime, to take a beating from the mighty fists of the superheroic Spider-Man. Spider-Man stops him with his powerful webbing, and the two have just one more battle (#35) before the Molten Man is rewebbed and put away for a long time. Despite the hefty prison sentence, however, Raxton spends much of his time in the hospital where he is looked after by his stepsister, Liz Allan, a nurse. There, she and her brother make a horrifying discovery. The metamorphosis Raxton underwent has yet to run its course. The liquid metal alloy was created using a meteor which contained organic materials and, as a result, the metal has fused with his flesh and is slowly eating his body away. At the same time, his skin has become a churning, superheated mass which sears anything it touches—and is getting hotter by the moment. Leaving captivity and hunting down the ingredients he hopes can reverse the process, he is again pursued by Spider-Man. Plunging into the East River after battling the superhero (issue #133), he is miraculously prevented from melting by pollutants in the river and—despite seeming to have self-immolated upon his return in issue #173—remains a hot thorn in Spider-Man's side.

Quote: "It's no picnic being hit by a molten fist, is it? . . . Especially if you're kicked by a molten *toe* at the same time!"

MONGU (C)

Real Name: Boris Monguski.

First Appearance: 1962, *The Incredible Hulk* #4, Marvel Comics.

Costume: Green armor, sandals, gloves.

Weapons: "Two ton ax," actually a spiked mace with axe-like blades (a fake made of "cardboard and cork"); circa eight-feet-tall humanoid Mongu body is actually an exoskeletonic shell in which Boris resides; spaceship (in reality, a disguised Mig fighter-jet); "ear-splitting sound gun," which is *not* a fake.

Chief Henchmen: Sundry Soviet soldiers.

Biography: Nothing is known about this character's past. A Russian soldier, he is sent to the United States pretending to be an extraterrestrial in order to capture the Hulk. With the super-powerful being in their possession, Russian scientists hope to learn the secret of his great strength and build an army of Hulk-like warriors. The ploy is simple. Landing in a city park, the towering "Mongu" dares earth's mightiest mortal, the Hulk, to champion the earth in a battle at the Grand Canyon. If Hulk wins, the world will be spared; if not, Mongu says his armies will invade. The Hulk accepts the challenge and walks into the trap. However, the Russian soldiers are unable to hold him and, after beating them to pulp, he leaves, a free Hulk.

Quote: "The warriors of my world will attack this puny planet and conquer it without mercy."

Comment: This was the character's only appearance. Two issues before, the Hulk had battled a bonafide alien force, Captain Torrak and the Toad Men, who came to earth with conquest in their hearts but left with the Hulk's green fists in their orange faces. They were armed with highly advanced magnetic weapons which, if we did not surrender, they intended to use to cause the moon to crash into our world. See other Soviet super villains Boris Kartovski (see DR. CLEMENT ARMSTRONG, Comment), COMRADE STUPIDSKA, THE CRIMSON DYNAMO, THE RED GHOST, THE SOVIET SUPER SOLDIERS, THE TITANIC THREE, and TITANIUM MAN.

MONGUL (C)

First Appearance: 1980, *DC Comics Presents* #27, DC Comics.

Costume: Purple bodyshirt, boots; blue tights, belt, bands around shoulders, wrists, neck, head (lengthwise). Mongul's skin is yellow.

Weapons: Warworld, an artificial satellite built by the "blood thirsty Warzoon"; its "surface is dotted with mile-high missiles and macro-laser cannons capable of decimating entire worlds."

Biography: Little is known about the roots of this enormous, nearly eight-feet-tall character who possessed incredible strength and the ability to fire destructive blasts. At one time the ruler of a world of billions of people, he fled when a prophet, an Arkymandyte, "came shuffling down out of the mountains" and stirred his subjects to revolt. Heading to earth and capturing Jimmy Olsen, Lois Lane, and Steve Lombard—three of Superman's dear friends—he forced the Man of Steel to help him obtain a crystal key which once belonged to an alien race known as the Largas. The key activated Warworld, which was destroyed only through the combined efforts of Superman and his cousin Supergirl. Although Mongul appeared to perish of a massive cerebral hemorrhage while running Warworld, he returned numerous times, trying to conquer various planets. He eventually fell prey to the "black mercy," a plant he'd tried to use against Superman. The life form dines on the living aura of others and, to keep its victims on hand, causes them to dream pleasant dreams. When last seen, Mongul was merrily dreaming of ruthless tyranny.

Quote: "When I'm *done,* all the *universe* will share the same government—*me*!"

Comment: It is unclear why Mongul didn't use his great physical powers to subdue his rebellious people. Perhaps they, too, had powers, or, more likely, he acquired his abilities through some unrevealed means after leaving the planet.

THE MONOCLE (C)

Real Name: Jonathan Cheval.

First Appearance: 1946, *Flash Comics* #64, DC Comics.

Costume: Tuxedo and blue cloak.

Weapons: Numerous monocles which fire destructive rays; cosmic blasts which can melt metal (including police guns); laser-light to cut through objects; X-rays; simple white light; and so forth. The monocles work whether held in the hand or worn on the eye; indeed, they can be operated by remote control, allowing the Monocle to blast any superhero whom he allows to "confiscate" a lens.

Biography: Jonathan is the third-generation Cheval to operate the family optics store in New York. He was content until forces beyond his control turned him to crime. The bank which owned the mortgage on his shop had made a clutch of bad investments, making it necessary for the bank to divest some holdings. The Cheval property was particularly valuable and, though the family had almost paid off their land, the bank destroyed the records and foreclosed. Furious at the bank, Jonathan decided to get revenge. A genius at designing new forms of lenses, Jonathan designed his killer eyepieces and murdered five of the six members of the institution's board of directors. He was finally apprehended by the superhero Hawkman. But Cheval didn't stay in jail long and, turning to a life of crime, he joined THE SECRET SOCIETY OF SUPER-VILLAINS. He and his fellow Society members were finally swept through a "dimensional vortex" through the combined efforts of the Justice League of America and Justice Society of America. He has been drifting in that purple limbo ever since (*Justice League of America* #197, 1981).

Quote: "I was planning to take my *new slaves* on a trip through Central Park . . . this *meeting* better be *important*."

THE MONSTER MASTER (C)

First Appearance: 1967, *Turok, Son of Stone* #56, Gold Key Comics.

Costume: Green loincloth; red belt, boots, headdress with wilted feathers.

Weapons: Flute.

Chief Henchmen: Tribe of cave people.

Biography: The Monster Master (also referred to as "the Honker Master") dwells in the Lost Valley, a region where dinosaurs co-exist with primitive humans. Astride an allosaurus, he trains the "Honkers" (dinosaurs) to obey him; using behavioral conditioning, he elicits planned responses from the beasts to notes played on his flute (one note compels them to swat their tail, another to kill people, and so on). Moving in with a tribe, he forces them to serve him under pain of death. Meanwhile, attacked by one of the Honkers, a triceratops, the Indians Turok and Andar use poison arrows to slay it. They are immediately captured by the Monster Master's slaves, since "It *death* to kill his Honker!" and, without captives, "we be blamed for Honker's death." Showing clemency, the Master dispatches the two to capture him a baby dinosaur to train. The pair does indeed snare a Honker, but, instead of bringing it back, they skin it and don the hide. When they are close enough to the Monster Master, they simply jump out and attack him. The flute is destroyed when the allosaurus accidentally steps on it and the Monster Master is destroyed when the liberated carnivore makes a meal of him.

Quote: "They kill Honker! Now they have to bring me young live Honker to train!"

Comment: For most of his 130-issue run, Turok battled primarily primitive races and Honkers, not super villains like the Monster Master.

MONTENEGRO (C)

First Appearance: 1981, *Power Man and Iron Fist* #71, Marvel Comics.

Costume: Navy blue bodysuit (gray on cover) with blue collar and zipper (white on cover); blue boots, gloves.

Weapons: Gun which fires pitons "with enough force to drive" the metal spikes "into sheer stone cliffs"; "Alpine Gun" which "duplicates the weather conditions found in the highest Alps"; grapnel and rope for climbing.

Biography: Nothing is known about this red-bearded mercenary, save that he is an expert mountaineer and hails from the Black Mountains (implicitly, in the Swiss Alps). In his only appearance to date, he tries to steal a quarter containing "prototype microcircuitry (which) dampens electrical current all around it." He is stopped cold by the superheroes Iron Fist and Power Man.

Quote: "You'll rue the day you tried to thwart *Montenegro*!"

THE MOON KILLER (S, MP)

Real Name: Professor Wells.

First Appearance: *Dr. X*, a play by Howard W. Comstock and Allen C. Miller.

Biography: A scientist with a particular interest in cannibalism—he has even written a book about it—Wells is a research scientist at Professor Xavier's academy. A one-armed scientist, Wells has recently made great strides in biology, most notably his use of electricity in keeping a human heart alive outside the body for three years. In private, however, he is a serious loon. Whenever there's a full moon, its rays summon up memories of a traumatic experience when he was forced to commit an act of cannibalism (implicitly, his arm had been eaten). At these times, Wells retires to a private laboratory, uses electricity to animate a powerful artificial arm, renders his features monstrously deformed with synthetic flesh he's invented, and sallies forth to commit acts of murder and cannibalism. The Moon Killer meets his end when he jumps at reporter Lee Taylor, who hurls a kerosene lamp at him, then shoves the flaming cannibal out a window.

Quote: "Dr. Xavier is still working on his theory that strong mental repressions—phobias hidden in the darkest corners of the subconscious mind—can be brought to the surface."

Comment: *Dr. X* gained its greatest fame as a motion picture. The 1932 Warner production starred Preston Foster as Professor Wells. A pseudo-sequel to the film was *The Return of Dr. X* (1939), based on the short story "The Doctor's Secret" by William J. Makin. This time out, Wells was nowhere to be seen; the villain was Humphrey Bogart as Dr. Xavier, not the researcher from the first film but a scientist who had been electrocuted.

MOONMAN (C)

Real Name: Erik Bolton.

First Appearance: 1966, *House of Mystery* #156 (as Mr. Thunder); 1967, *House of Mystery* #168 (as Moonman), DC Comics.

Costume: As Mr. Thunder: red hooded robe with white lightning bolts on chest. As Moonman: blue bodysuit with white crescent moon on chest and cuffs; blue mask/helmet shaped like the moon.

Weapons: Walking tank with tentacles; traditional tank with destructive thunderbolt rays; magnetic ray gun; submarine disguised as an island (all as Mr. Thunder only).

Biography: The leader of a pack of international mercenaries known as the Thunderbolt Gang, Bolton's first crime is to eliminate the competitors of a chemical manufacturer who wants to corner the market. Operating from a mountain lair, he is found out by Robby Reed, wielder of the "Dial-H for Hero" device. Reed captures the gang, but Mr. Thunder escapes. The villain returns (#157) with a new gang and steals a priceless Cosmic Computer which he uses to unlock the doors of the world's great banks and repositories. However, his Operation Breakthrough is thwarted by Reed, and this time Thunder goes to jail. Escaping again (#168), he hurries to another mountain lair where he draws upon his chemical knowledge to whip up a potion that will "create an invincible Thunderbolt army!" Because of a miscalculation, the mixture explodes; but it proves to be a fortuitous accident, as the combination of the chemicals coating his body and the moon's rays gives him control over gravity as well as the ability to cause "lunar hysteria" and trap people in "moon-dust beams." Reed battles him yet again as the so-called Moonman tries to steal the valuable Moonfire Ruby by attracting the jet which is transporting it. Managing to knock him out, the teenager advises police to "make sure he's put in a cell with a moonless view."

Quote: "Who needs a Thunderbolt Gang now? I have the world in my grip with these lunar powers!"

MOONSTONE (C)

Real Name: Byron Becton; Dr. Karla Sofen.

First Appearance: 1974, *Captain America* #169 (as Becton); 1978, *The Incredible Hulk* #228 (as Sofen), Marvel Comics.

Costume: As Becton: light blue metallic boots, cowl with purple ridge on top and yellow goggles, leotard with flared shoulders and yellow circle on chest; purple metallic tights, wristbands, belt, armbands. (Note: color scheme differs on cover of first appearance, with gold for light blue). As Sofen: gold bodysuit with flared shoulders, no sleeves; gold trunks; white boots, gloves, belt, circle on chest, helmet with gold eyepieces, armbands.

Weapons: The moonstone, a lunar rock which grants the bearer the power to fly, fire destructive bolts, and move through solid matter. It is believed to have been imbued with some of the powers of the Watchers, aliens with godlike powers.

Biography: A petty thief, Becton is hired by "a European collector" to steal moon rocks from a small midwestern university. When he picks up one of them—from the "Blue Area moon headquarters" of the Watcher, a supreme alien intelligence—he merges with the stone and becomes immensely powerful, able to fire destructive rays from his hand. Eventually captured, he is left in the care of psychiatrist Sofen, who apprenticed with Dr. Faustus, a psychologist and criminal genius. Intrigued with the stone's power, Sofen persuades Becton to give it up (by using a gas to make him think he's become a grotesque creature) and absorbs it into her own body. Using her newfound powers, she tries to steal hi-tech instruments from a laboratory, hoping to sell them to the criminal group the Corporation; upended by the superheroic Hulk, she joins the Corporation and, taking on the Hulk and Captain America, finds herself in prison. Escaping with the help of a warped genius known as Egghead, she joins his MASTERS OF EVIL and is jailed yet again. Escaping and teaming with BLACKOUT, she fights the superheroic Inhumans and the Dazzler and strikes out a third time. Freed from captivity yet again, with the help of the second BARON ZEMO, she currently remains at large.

MORBIUS (TV)

First Appearance: 1976, "The Brain of Morbius," *Dr. Who*, BBC.

Biography: Morbius is one of the Time Lords, a telepathic, time-traveling race of super-geniuses from the planet Gallifrey. A member of the ruling High Council, Morbius first tries to take over the planet and then the universe; he is routed and executed for his troubles. However, one of his followers, Dr. Mehendri Solon, preserves the still-living brain of the Time Lord. Storing it on the planet Karn, he begins building a monstrous body for it, using bits and pieces of dead aliens—with the exception of an arm, which he lops from his servant Condo. Luckily, the heroic Dr. Who is aware of what's going on and journeys to Karn. He destroys Morbius' brain in a mental tussle and slays Solon with hydrogen cyanide gas; the rampaging monster-body is pushed from a cliff by the Sisterhood of Karn, a group of sorceresses.

Comment: Robin Bland wrote the teleplay for the adventure, which ran for four episodes.

MORDEK MAL MORIAK (also MORDIAK) (C)

First Appearance: 1975, *Wulf the Barbarian* #1, Atlas Comics.

Costume: Blue jumpsuit, boots; darker cape, helmet. He also has a green version of the costume.

Weapons: Enchanted Crystal, which allows Mordek to see anywhere he wishes.

Chief Henchmen: Chief aide Gherba; Balik, the "Eye of Mordek," who wears the Enchanted Crystal on his chest (first issue only); the Trolls of Drakenroost, his elite but brutish warriors.

Biography: A sorcerer on "a nameless world in a forgotten time," Mordek marries a young woman "to gain control of the iron baronies." (The woman is never named, though her son—Mordek's stepson—is called Modeo Don Tyrak.) Upon his wife's death, Mordek becomes the master of the barbaric planet's ironworks. Nestled comfortably in his stronghold Drakenroost, he keeps the factories running with slave labor, while men astride dragons known as Spy-Birds carefully keep the masses in line. Resenting the wizard's cruelty, Modeo learns sorcery on his own and plots to overthrow him. Meanwhile, Mordek has another enemy in young Wulf the Barbarian. (Not long after ascending to power, Mordek had sent his armies "a thousand leagues" to slay the benevolent Lord Wulfgar and his family and thus become the ruler of Baernholm; but the lord's son, Wulf, survived, and vowed to avenge the slaughter.) In time, Wulf teams with Modeo to try and destroy the sorcerer; he even acquires the "Golden Star," a jewel which for some reason Mordek fears. However, the series ended after four issues with the villain still in charge of his realm—increasing his holdings daily, turning people into demons to kill Wulf, and sending his Trolls out to rape and plunder (also trying to kill Wulf).

MORDEK MAL MORIAK. *© Larry Hama and Atlas Comics.*

Quote: "Prince Wulf is powerless until he comes of age. I must simply find and slay the troublesome brat before he can ascend to the crown."

Comment: Wulf's only other foe (issue #2) was the sorcerer Rasselas, who commanded the water demon Bel-Shugthra. He was stabbed to death, and his demon defeated by Sri-Amantra, the fire demon.

MORDRU (C, TV)

First Appearance: 1968, *Adventure Comics* #369, DC Comics.

Costume: Purple robe with green (sometimes yellow) belt, stripe down center; dark green tights and slippers with a lighter green stripe from tip of slipper to knee; light green helmet with white horns (sometimes wings) on side.

Chief Henchmen: Countless acolytes.

Biography: The "Master of the Sorcery Sinister," Mordru migrates to the planet Zerox, the Sorcerer's World, late in the thirtieth century (whence he came is not known). Progressing rapidly, he becomes a master wizard and eventually takes over the planet—helped along by powers he appropriates from fellow mages. Conquering other worlds, he is eventually beaten, soundly, by earth's noble Legion of Super-Heroes. Imprisoned in an airtight vault, Mordru manages to escape, although the event proves so traumatic that whenever he's anywhere the air is thin, he immediately loses his mystic powers. After several confrontations with the Legionnaires, Mordru is finally robbed of his powers by the even more evil DARKSEID. Mordru presently lies comatose on Zerox, tended by his devotees. Ironically, not long before the run-in with Darkseid, Mordru felt that his own powers weren't up to snuff because Zerox's "magical resources are almost completely depleted." Thus, he assumed a new identity, Lord Romdor, and tried to set up headquarters on Avalon, "a fresh, unspoiled planet." He was sent packing when the Legion brought his castle down around his ears; had he succeeded there, he might have been better-equipped to rid the universe of the more dangerous Darkseid.

Quote: "Enough discussion! You shall be enclosed in a mystic sphere—where you shall be imprisoned till it pleases me to slay you!"

Comment: The character appeared on TV in the 1979 movie *Legends of the Super-Heroes*.

MORGAN LE FEY (F, N, CS, MP, C)

First Appearance: Sixth century A.D.

Biography: According to most records, the historical Morgan le Fey was queen of the island of Avalon in the sixth century A.D., and it's likely that King Arthur was buried there upon his death. Little else is known about her. Conversely, there have been countless retellings of the legend of King Arthur. Hence, there is no definitive version of her fictional life. She is invariably the daughter of Arthur's mother Igrene, though not always by the same father (Uther Pendragon). In the best of the tales—which were told orally in the same century she and Arthur lived—she is usually portrayed as a sorceress who learned her black arts in a nunnery. She both loathes Arthur's virtue and hungers for his throne, and her hobby is planning his death with "intricate care (for) hatred was her passion and destruction her pleasure" (*The Acts of King Arthur and His Noble Knights* by John Steinbeck). Failing at sundry assassination attempts—most ruthlessly with Arthur's own mighty sword Excalibur, which she had stolen and given to her enchanted lover Sir Accolon to do the dirty deed (in *Le Morte d'Arthur*)—she finally enchants Arthur, forces him to sleep with her, and bears a son, Mordred (also Modred), who becomes his archenemy. (In many tales, Mordred is simply Arthur's nephew, often the son of Morgan le Fey by either King Lot of Orkney or her husband, Sir Uryens.) Grown to manhood, Mordred seizes the throne while Arthur is off on a Roman war, and rules cruelly; returning, Arthur's armies battle those of the usurper (traditionally in Cornwall), where the men slay each other. In most accounts, Morgan le Fey does not perish—the only one of Arthur's enemies not to do so—but retires to her island. Apart from her quest for the throne, Morgan le Fey's most notorious deed is arranging for the Green Knight to appear at Arthur's court during a New Year's party. The green-skinned warrior offers any of the knights present the chance to lop off his head, provided he can return the blow if the challenger fails. Sir Gawain (in some accounts, he is the son of Morgan le Fey) takes up the gauntlet and fails miserably, unaware that the knight is bewitched. Fortunately, because of his great virtue, Gawain weathers two blows, though the third *does* nick him. The witch moves through the story disguised as an old woman and, according to the tale, initiates the entire affair in an effort to scare Arthur's wife Guinevere to death. Another of her illicit deeds is to bring the French hero Ogier the Dane to her castle, when he was a century old, use her magic to rejuvenate him, and send him out to fight on behalf of Arthur's enemies in France. Adding insult to injury, she leaves Ogier free just long enough to fall in love—after which she recalls him to Avalon. In some stories, Morgan le Fey is aided in her dirty work by an ugly dwarf. In other accounts, Morgan le Fey is also the mother of Agravain, Gareth, and Gaheris; she also has other names in Arthurian fiction, most prominently Morgawse, Morcades, and Anna (the latter sometimes being a separate character, Arthur's full sister).

Quote: "Fetch me my lord's sword. There will never be a better time to kill him." (*The Acts of King Arthur and His Noble Knights*)

Comment: Figures related to Morgan le Fey include Morgana in Boiardo's *Orlando Innamorato* (1487; she lives at the bottom of a lake, guarding treasure) and its sequel, Ariosto's *Orlando Furioso* (1532; she's a witch); and the Fata ("fairy") Morgana, a vision, or mirage, traditionally seen off the coast of Sicily. Though Arthurian tales stretch back to an historical account by Gildas (circa 540 A.D.) and a poem entitled *Gododin* (circa 600 A.D.), the characters were first fleshed-out in Geoffrey of Monmouth's twelfth-century *History of the Kings of Britain*. The first expansive fiction based on Geoffrey of Monmouth's account was written shortly thereafter by the Norman poet Wace in his verse epic *Roman de Brut*. There were other fictionalizations, but by far the greatest and most canonical of these have been the anonymous *Sir Gawain and the Green Knight* (circa

1370), Sir Thomas Malory's *Le Morte d'Arthur* (circa 1469), and T.H. White's *The Once and Future King* (1958). She also figured prominently in Mark Twain's iconoclastic *A Connecticut Yankee in King Arthur's Court* (1889), whose hero Hank Morgan says of her, "She was loaded to the eyelids with cold malice (and) among her crimes murder was common." She was also fond of torture, particularly the rack. In motion pictures, she was seen in the 1949 serial *The Adventures of Sir Galahad*, played by Pat Barton (as a hero fighting the evil Merlin!), and was featured prominently (albeit renamed Morgana) in *Excalibur* (1981), played by Helen Mirren. In the latter film she was a student of the wizard Merlin, who tricked her into spewing out her youth as a mist, thus leaving her old and withered. In comics, she was Prince Valiant's foe in 1938 in his popular comic strip; she also fought Spider-Woman in that hero's comic book starting with #2 in 1978. As Morgaine Le Fey she battled the superheroic Demon in his DC Comics magazine beginning with #1 in 1972.

MORGOTH (N)

Real Name: Melchar (in Valinor).
First Appearance: 1954, *The Fellowship of the Ring*, J.R.R. Tolkien.
Chief Henchman: Sauron.
Biography: One of the race of Godlike immortals known as the Vala, Morgoth was the only one of these majestic beings to turn to evil. His greatest crime was to destroy the two sacred trees of Valinor, in the Undying Lands (which lie west of the sea). So doing, he relocated in Middle-Earth (east of the sea) where he founded the kingdom of Angband and dwelt in the magnificent fortress Thangorodrim. There he wore the Silmarilli, stolen from the elves, in his Iron Crown. These were gems, fashioned by Feanor the elf, which contained the light of the two trees and were the only relic of the trees' glory. Feanor recruited a force to follow Morgoth and reclaim the Silmarilli; Morgoth finally won the War of the Great Jewels after many years. He wasn't as fortunate when the Valar themselves crossed the sea and came after him, being overthrown in the Great Battle. During his reign, Morgoth's most noteworthy contribution to corruption was the breeding of the Orcs and Trolls, misshapen creatures who served the cause of evil. They formed powerful tribes after Morgoth's downfall, perpetuating his evil ways. Morgoth's servant Sauron did likewise, masterminding heartache which caused even Morgoth's crimes to pale by comparison.
Comment: The character is only briefly referred to in *The Fellowship of the Ring*, the first volume in "The Lord of the Rings" trilogy (1954-56). Morgoth's complete story, from the dawn of creation, is told in *The Silmarillion*, a prequel to the trilogy.

MORPHEUS THE DREAM DEMON (C)

Real Name: Robert Markham.
First Appearance: 1981, *Moon Knight* #12, Marvel Comics.
Costume: None (his face is serpentine, his eyes large and red).
Chief Henchman: Dr. Peter Alraune (#'s 22-23 only).
Biography: Suffering from an unknown and "uncontrolled breakdown of chromosomal structure," Markham agrees to an experimental treatment. But the drug given to him by Dr. Peter Alraune has a tragic side effect. It leaves him unable to sleep, and within two months he goes quite mad. Moreover, the "psychic dream energies" (aka "ebon energies") which he formerly released in sleep must now be shed while he's awake. These energies are fully charged "after the deprivation of each sleep cycle," and he can release them as destructive blasts, tangible bonds, or an impenetrable force-field. Calling himself Morpheus after the Greek god of sleep, Markham sets out to build himself a fortune as well as a palatial home "fit for a god." But the superhero Moon Knight interferes and, forcing him to squander all his energy in battle, carts him off to a hospital where he is put under perpetual sedation. However, now that he can dream, Morpheus discovers in his unconscious state that he can also "link up" with the dreams of others. Taking control of the mind of Alraune, the fiend sends him out to kill Moon Knight. Though the superhero survives the attacks, the night demon is able to "break through to the waking state" and leaves his hospital bed (#22). Pursuing Moon Knight, he tries to enter his nemesis' dreams and kill him there; charging Morpheus from behind, the superhero strangles him until he falls unconscious (#23).
Quote: "Few more hours and I'll be at my peak again, ready to *explode* . . . ready to *rip 'em apart*!"
Comment: Dr. Alraune is the brother of Moon Knight's aide Marlene.

MOTA (MP)

First Appearance: 1951, *Flying Disc Man from Mars*, Republic Pictures.
Weapons: Atom-powered, bat-shaped craft which can ascend or descend vertically, hover, and fly in any

direction without turning around; thermal disintegrator.

Chief Henchmen: Drake, Ryan, various other flunkies.

Biography: Flying to earth in his extraordinary craft, Mota approaches nuclear scientist Dr. Bryant with a proposition: He'll give the physicist vast knowledge if Bryant will help build atomic craft and bombs to expedite a Martian takeover of earth. Bryant readily agrees, but aviator Kent Fowler gets wind of the goings-on at Bryant's factory and works to thwart the pair. They, in turn, accelerate their timetable by atom-bombing towns, plants, and bridges in an effort to bully the government into submission. Meanwhile, Fowler learns that Mota has set up a secondary base inside a volcano and hurries over. Infiltrating the base, Fowler gets into a scuffle with Mota's henchman during which an atom bomb accidentally drops into the crater of the volcano. The hero flees before the weapon triggers an explosion which consumes Mota, Bryant, and their hired hands.

Comment: Gregory Gay played the Martian in this 12-chapter serial. Gay also played PROFESSOR STEIGG. In 1958, the serial was edited into a feature film entitled *Missile Monsters*. Other Martian movie super villains are NYAH and THE PURPLE MONSTER.

MULTI-FACE (C)

First Appearance: 1965-66, *The Brave and the Bold* #63, DC Comics.

Costume: Green jumpsuit with white collar, braid around shoulders.

Weapons: A "remote control ray" which snatches rockets from flight and draws them to his island; "weird disc," roughly five feet in diameter, which flies and attracts metal (used by Multi-Face to snare Wonder Woman by drawing her bracelets); machine gun.

Chief Henchmen: Various unnamed aides.

Biography: Little is known about the past of Multi-Face (his real name is never revealed). "The world thinks I am dead—killed accidentally in a prison escape," he chuckles. However, not only does he live, but also the accident has given him "the power to change my features at will." As Multi-Face, "the villain of a thousand visages," the flesh of his face is iron-gray, clay-like, and can be molded instantaneously into any face "human or animal," from that of a clown to an alien to a wolf. Based on a remote Mediterranean island, the Ile d'Amour, he is preparing to launch Operation Armageddon, the theft of cargo missiles while they carry gold from site to site. Unfortunately for him, Supergirl *and* Wonder Woman happen to be vacationing on the Island of Love and they nip his plans in the bud.

Comment: Multi-Face's scheme has to be one of the most contrived in comic book history. Presumably, somewhat like DR. NO, he intended to use his ray to snatch nuclear missiles at some point and hold the world for ransom. Hence, the "Armageddon" tag. The rather incredible title of this story was "The Revolt of the Super-Chicks," an allusion to the fact that both Supergirl and Wonder Woman had gone to the island to find romance, not a superheroic challenge.

MULTI-MAN (C)

Real Name: Duncan Pramble.

First Appearance: 1960, *Challengers of the Unknown* #14, DC Comics.

Costume: Originally, none. Later: blue leotard with high red collar; red boots, belt, gloves.

Weapons: Serum which allows him to acquire a new life and new power each time he perishes.

Chief Henchman: Multi-Woman, a giant robot who can change her shape.

Biography: An assistant to archaeologist Charles Ferriss, Pramble accompanies the explorer and the adventurers, the Challengers of the Unknown, on an expedition to the Island of Ruins. In "a gloomy, subterranean chamber," Pramble finds a vial of liquid light which, along with antidotes to counter its powers, was created by an ancient alchemist. Reading the directions, Pramble finds that "once I drink it, I will be given extra lives—and with each life I'll gain a different power." The first power he acquires is the ability to fire destructive blasts of light from his hands. Perishing in a jump from a cliff while escaping the Challengers, he is reborn as a green, scaly merman who can swim like a fish and survive underwater. Robbing the famous Bambidoor necklace from a ship, he dies in an explosion set by the Challengers—only to emerge as a bird-man. Fortunately, the Challengers are able to approach him via parachute and, dousing him with the antidote, haul him off to prison. However, while he is incarcerated the formula causes him to change. Pramble shrinks, except for his head, which grows *larger* to accommodate a huge, brilliant brain. Escaping, he uses his boosted intelligence to decipher the ingredients in the alchemist's formula and is able to make as much of it as he needs, taking it in capsule form. He is also able to build his huge robot sidekick Multi-Woman (#34), whom he dubs his "electronic queen." After many encounters with the Challengers, Multi-Man once again becomes mere Duncan Pramble. Although he later obtains vast telepathic powers, these blow his own mind during a battle. He remains comatose to this day.

Quote: "What can you do now, *Challengers*? *Kill* me? Nobody dares—for I'd just spring forth anew, with newer powers!"

Comment: Multi-Man was a member of the League of Challengers-Haters, whose super-villainous members included Kra, King of the Alien Robots, and Volcano Man, aka Dr. Edward Gruner, who was able to create slaves of molten rock (which lived on after his death and merged into a single Volcano Man). Other super villain nemeses of the Challengers are the Iron Dictator, a clone of Hitler (predating Marvel's HATE-MONGER); Sponge-Man, a diver who became infected with a disease which turned him into a human sponge able to ingest sound and color as well as liquids; and Villo, who committed crimes with the help of the computer Brainex.

MULTIPLEX (C)

Real Name: Danton Black.

First Appearance: 1978, *Firestorm* #1 (as Black); 1978, *Firestorm* #2 (as Multiplex), DC Comics.

Costume: Blue tights, skintight jerkin with light blue fringe and stripes running horizontally across chest, belly, and waist; purple cape, boots, gloves; dark blue helmet with purple sides and light blue mask.

Chief Henchmen: The Enforcer, alias Leroy Merkyn, who wears a green helmet with a gold face; a green bodysuit with gold stripes on chest and armor on shoulders; and gold gauntlets, boots, trunks. Virtually indestructible, this costume grants the wearer superpowers (and has jets in the boots for flight). Merkyn was a small-time mobster before being hired by Multiplex to attack Firestorm; beaten by the superhero and jailed, Merkyn was murdered by Henry Hewitt, at which time the costume passed to a woman named Mica, who also tackled Firestorm and ended up in prison.

Biography: An aide to Dr. Martin Stein, Black was convinced (incorrectly) that Stein let him do all the work, then took all the glory for designing the Hudson Nuclear Plant reactor. Black complained to the Nuclear Regulations Council, which postponed the startup of the reactor until the claims could be examined. That gave Black the time he needed to sneak into the plant to copy Stein's blueprints and thus "support" his charges. However, that same night Stein also snuck into the plant to turn the reactor on. *His* concern was that the delay would be misinterpreted as lack of faith in the safety of the plant, and he wanted to forestall any such concerns. Making the night even more interesting was the presence of antinuclear activist Edward Earhart, who intended to blow up the plant altogether. Arriving at the facility, Earhart knocked out both Stein and young Ronnie Raymond, an environmentalist who objected to what Earhart was planning, and deposited them in the main reactor room. When the reactor exploded, Stein and Raymond merged to become the superhero Firestorm. Nearby, Black was also irradiated and acquired the ability to split into numerous "duploids," super-strong versions of himself which act independently from, though subservient to, the original (although they become smaller and less powerful each time he spins off another). Multiplex and Firestorm have battled on numerous occasions, most notably when Multiplex went to work for powerful businessperson Henry Hewitt.

Comment: Hewitt later became the super villain Tokamak and battled Firestorm himself. With the help of Multiplex, Hewitt recreated the nuclear accident which had given Firestorm his powers. Acquiring superstrength, the magnate donned silver armor to keep his atomic energy from draining off and called himself Tokamak—after the Russian word for fusion plasma reactor. However, during a battle with Firestorm Tokamak's suit ruptured; the hero managed to hurl him far into the atmosphere before he exploded and was (apparently) destroyed.

MUMBLES (CS, TV)

First Appearance: October 16, 1947, *Dick Tracy*, Chicago Tribune-New York News Syndicate.

Weapons: Guitar with hollow compartment for storing weaponry (such as an ounce of muriatic acid which Mumbles threatens to toss in singer Kiss Andtel's face while abducting her).

Biography: Unable to speak articulately, Mumbles can only be understood by his closest aides. A snappy dresser, he insists that all his aides dress just as sharp and only wear pink shirts, like his. He also plays the guitar. A thief and killer (most recently icing a police officer by throwing a car cushion in front of his speeding motorcycle), he is put in a delicate position when his gang finally insists on dividing all stolen goods equally. ("We're through playing second fiddle," they declare.) Mumbles appears to accede to their demand, but secretly plots to kill them on their getaway boat. "I'll blowm alup," he mutters, igniting dynamite on the boat, then leaving on a rubber raft. Fortunately for the gang, detective Dick Tracy arrives in time to save them. Unfortunately for Mumbles, his raft springs a leak and he drowns.

Quote: "Emus bina dopta trysili stuntlitha." (Mumbles'

first mumbled line; translation: "Coffyhead must have been a dope to try a stunt like that.")

Comment: Mumbles was also a character in the Dick Tracy cartoon series (1960).

MUMM-RA (T, TV, C)

First Appearance: 1985, Thundercats action toys, LJN Toys (under license from Telepictures Corporation).

Costume: Mumm-ra is swathed in white bandages and wears a red, hooded cloak when he's resting; when he sallies forth to battle his enemies, he is magically clothed with another suit, consisting of red trunks, helmet with brown serpent horns and golden nose-guard, medallion with black serpents intertwined; golden boots, wristbands; green cape. Mumm-Ra has blue-green skin.

Chief Henchmen: The mutants Monkian, S-s-slithe of the Reptilians, Jackalman, Grune the Destroyer, Ratar-o, and Vultureman. The mutants on Third Earth live in Castle Plun-darr, a gargoyle-shaped palace made of stone.

Biography: No one knows whence Mumm-ra came, or how long he has lived on in his magnificent castle, a pyramid with obelisks rising from each point in the base, the whole located on the planet Third Earth. Found there one day by mutants from the planet Plun-darr (a world of "boiling oceans and scum deserts"), he forms an alliance with them. If they will serve him, he will help them to destroy their archenemies, the cat-like Thundercats. (That heroic race is not native to Third Earth, but migrated there when the planet Thundera slipped from its orbit and was destroyed.) Actually, Mumm-ra has an ulterior motive for the pact. He wishes to be the sole master of the planet once again. To do so, he must obtain from Lion-o, leader of the Thundercats, the Sword of Omens, a powerful weapon with the Eye of Thundera set in its hilt. Whosoever wields it has "sight beyond sight, for the eye enables you to see dangers that lie in wait before you face them." Not only would the Sword weaken Lion-o, it would boost Mumm-ra's powers enormously. Called "the ever-living," Mumm-ra cannot die and possesses great magical powers, including the ability to bring statues to life and create incredible illusions.

Quote: "The only thing you've succeeded in doing, worms—is making me *angry*!"

Comment: The character also appears in a syndicated cartoon series (also available on videocassette) produced by Rankin/Bass, and in a Marvel comic book which began publication in 1985. Another popular TV/action figure series was *Blackstar,* a Filmation series which aired in 1981. The villains in that show were the wizard king the Overlord, who dwelt in the towering Ice Castle, as well as Neptul, Lord of Aquaria; the invincible wizard Kadray; the Leopard Man Tongo; and Gargo, the Vampire Man. The Blackstar toys were from Galoob. Other action figure toy-lines which had super villains include the Power Lords (from Revell), whose spindly, insectlike Arkus was an evil dictator who commanded the likes of Raygoth, the Goon of Doom, and the four-fisted Ggripptogg; the Evil Warriors of Galoob's Interfaceables, namely the saber-toothed Tuskus, the wicked strategist Brainor ("whose brain pulses with evil"), the armored Torto the Claw, and the leader of the humanoid mammoths, Tembo; and the Flexatrons (from S & T Sales), whose evil members were the snake-like Vipen, the skeletal Herr Bone who was the executioner of the Varykon race, and the beastly Devilor, the leader of the Varykons. See other action toy super villains BARON KARZA, DESTRO, GENERAL SPIDRAX, HORDAK, MOLTAR, and SKELETOR.

MURDER LEGENDRE (MP)

First Appearance: 1932, *White Zombie,* United Artists.

Chief Henchmen: The principal zombies, Von Gelder, Scarpia, Chauvin, and the Witch Doctor.

Biography: Once the slave of a witch doctor, Legendre learned the man's secrets, became a mystic master in his own right, and made a zombie—a reanimated corpse—of the witch doctor. (At some point in the past, Legendre was also sentenced to die, though he somehow cheated the executioner.) He is now the owner of a sugar plantation run by zombies. "They work faithfully," he explains to fellow plantation owner Beaumont, adding matter-of-factly, "They are not worried about long hours." Beaumont, however, couldn't care less about zombies. He's in love with young Madeline, who has come to Haiti to be with her fiancé Neil, and wants the voodoo master's help in winning her love. Instead, Legendre makes a drugged slave of Beaumont and, with the help of a love potion, takes Madeline for his own. As for Neil, he's chased to the edge of a cliff by zombies and is about to die when a missionary clubs Legendre; without a leader, the zombies march off the precipice. Stunned, Legendre also loses control over Beaumont, who regains his wits long enough to grab his nemesis and fly from the cliff with him.

Quote: "The witch doctor, once my master—the secrets I tortured out of him!"

Comment: Bela Lugosi (BARON ROXOR, DR. ALEX ZORKA, DR. MIRAKLE, DR. PAUL CAR-

RUTHERS, DRACULA, and PROFESSOR ERIC VORNOFF), played Legendre, arguably his most menacing screen performance; Garnett Weston wrote the screenplay. While there have been numerous zombie films, only a few have featured lunatics using the creatures to commit crimes. Foremost among them are Dr. Dangre (Henry Victor), who raised the dead to fight for the Nazis in *King of the Zombies* (1941), and Dr. von Altmann (John Carradine), who did likewise in *Revenge of the Zombies* (1943). Lugosi himself returned to the field as Dr. Renault in *Zombies on Broadway* (1945), menacing a pair of talent agents who had come to the Caribbean searching for zombies to perform in a nightclub. Preposterous . . . but it was a work of genius compared to *The Incredibly Strange Creatures Who Stopped Living and Became Mixed-Up Zombies* (1963), in which a fortune-teller made slaves of her disfigured ex-lovers.

MYSTERIO (C)

Real Name: Quentin Beck. (Escaping once from prison, he posed as the director of the Restwell Nursing home and went by the name of Ludwig Rinehart. Concurrently Danny Berkhart was briefly Mysterio. See Biography.)

First Appearance: 1964, *The Amazing Spider-Man* #13, Marvel Comics.

Costume: Dark green bodysuit with thin black stripes crisscrossing vertically and horizontally; green gloves, boots; red cape; opaque, milky white dome over entire head (see Weapons).

Weapons: His costume is a mass of weaponry. He has a one-way helmet (Mysterio can see out, but no one can see in); the soles of his boots contain smoke ejectors for spilling out clouds of mist (which shield him from others, though a built-in sonar allows him to see them) and also "magnetic plate springs" for clinging to walls or making incredible leaps; and his gloves emit an acid-based spray for dissolving Spider-Man's webbing. He also has a gun which fires miniature black holes which "create a gravity field so dense that neither light nor matter escape them," and packs hallucinogenic gas bombs.

Biography: A movie stuntman, Beck uses his skills to create special effects for TV movies. An expert in both stunts and effects he comes up with the idea of creating a Spider-Man costume complete with gadgets which will allow him to duplicate the superhero's feats. Instead of doing good deeds, however, he commits robberies and lets Spider-Man take the blame. Then, donning his Mysterio garb (using the technology he'd developed to mimic Spider-Man's powers), he sets out to capture the *real* Spider-Man . . . and earn a hefty reward. Though the superhero whips him in their first encounter (and gets a taped confession to boot), they battle every time Mysterio manages to escape from prison. (His most ingenious ploy is to steal flour from the prison kitchen, set it afire in his cell, apply a "burned skin" mask which he makes from cornstarch and food coloring and, while being rushed to the hospital, use the anesthetic in the ambulance to knock out the drivers and flee.) On one occasion, Beck teaches cellmate Danny Berkhart how to use the Mysterio accoutrements, and, faking his own death, lets Berkhart play Mysterio while he goes underground (issue #141). It is subsequently revealed that Beck had assumed the Ludwig Rinehart identity; in issue #193 he reclaims the Mysterio mantle for his own. Mysterio was a member of the short-lived anti-Spider-Man group THE SINISTER SIX.

Quote: "No one makes a fool of Mysterio and lives!"

Comment: It has been implied (but never proven) that Beck also masqueraded as an extraterrestrial alien allied with THE TINKERER, in *The Amazing Spider-Man* #2. However, there is no internal evidence in that story to support this claim; moreover, were it true, Beck surely would have boasted about it when he rather longwindedly told his life story to Spider-Man during their first encounter. Still, the question remains.

MYSTIQUE (C)

Real Name: Raven Darkholme.

First Appearance: 1978, *Ms. Marvel* #16 (as Raven); 1978, *Ms. Marvel* #18 (as an unnamed criminal); 1981, *X-Men* #141 (as Mystique), Marvel Comics.

Costume: White boots, gloves, leotard with flaps front and back, reaching to ankles; golden belt with demonic-face buckle. (She has also worn other outfits, including a blue bodysuit and red vest, as well as a blue robe.) Mystique's skin is blue.

Weapons: Sundry guns.

Biography: A mutant, the inherently wicked Mystique has the power to change her shape. (She can also conceal her true age, making her origins wide open to speculation.) As Raven, she works for the United States government as deputy director of the Defense Advanced Research Planning Agency; no one there has any idea as to her criminal nature. As Mystique, she reorganizes the disbanded BROTHERHOOD OF EVIL MUTANTS and, apart from tilts with the superheroic Ms. Marvel, her most spectacular crime is an attempt to goad the public into assassinating Senator Robert Kelly, an anti-mutant activist. Ironically, the mutant X-Men come to his rescue. Mystique turns over a new leaf when the government begins investigating not only her but also all mutants. In exchange for a Presidential pardon, she and her teammates go to work as government operatives. However, she is likely to resume her old career when the heat dies down.

Comment: THE SPACE PHANTOM can also impersonate other people. Other super villains who have fought Ms. Marvel include Kerwin Korman, aka the blast-firing Destructor; the winged, razor-taloned Death-Bird; the witch Hecate and the wizard Magnum, who order soil to form into sword-swinging "Earth Giants"; Maxwell Plumm, a building contractor who, as the costumed Steeplejack, fires white-hot rivets at his adversaries; and large, intelligent, humanoid reptiles known as the Lizard People (named are the leader Aracht'yr, his wife Mirielle, B'ok, Haemon, Khadar, and M'dhar [see SERPENTYNE]).

NAKARI (M)

First Appearance: June 1930, "The Moon of Skulls," *Weird Tales*, Robert E. Howard.

Costume: "Naked except for a beplumed helmet, armbands, anklets and a girdle of colored ostrich feathers."

Weapons: Dagger.

Biography: Nakari is the "regal yet barbaric" Queen of Negari, one of the fiercest tribes in sixteenth-century Africa and descendants of the people of the lost continent of Atlantis. When the daughter of a friend is sold as a slave to the Negari, the Puritan adventurer Solomon Kane treks to Negari territory to try to save her. Captured by Nakari, Kane is informed that she wishes him to marry her and help forge the peoples of Africa into a fighting force capable of overrunning Europe. He refuses and, escaping his captors, saves the captive woman as she is about to be sacrificed beside the skull of an ancient king. Simultaneously shooting the skull, Kane causes an earthquake which swallows up Nakari's people; the queen herself perishes when one of her warriors hurls her against the sacrificial altar, shattering her body.

Quote: "She shall be punished as I have punished her before—hung by her wrists, naked, and whipped until she swoons!"

Comment: The story was serialized over two months. Other villains in the chronicles of Solomon Kane include the outlaw leader Le Loup ("Red Shadows," 1928); the murderous ghost of Gideon ("Skulls in the Stars," 1929); the murderer Gaston the Butcher ("Rattle of Bones," 1929), the pirate Jonas Hardraker, aka The Fishhawk ("Blades of the Brotherhood," 1968); a tribe of vampires ("The Hills of the Dead," 1930); and the Akaanas, winged cannibals ("Wings in the Night," 1932).

THE NAMELESS ONE (C)

First Appearance: 1966, *The Mighty Crusaders* #5 (first series), Archie Comics.

Costume: Purple bodysuit; yellow wristbands, "X" on chest with DEMON lettering and demon face in center; golden helmet; white belt, boots.

Weapons: Evolution-ray machine to turn people into "mindless troglodytes"; missiles which are "inconceivably destructive"; rocketship for use by his minions.

Biography: The Nameless One is the leader of the in-

THE NAMELESS ONE. © *Archie Comics.*

ternational terrorist group D.E.M.O.N. (Destruction, Extortion, Murder, Oppression, Nefariousness). He has many lairs, but his most spectacular is a flying city which can transfer to and from another dimension at his command, and whose "every molecule of matter . . . cancels out super-powers," making the Nameless One safe from the law. Capturing the superheroic Mighty Crusaders and preparing to subject them to his Evolution-ray, the Nameless One is interrupted by THE SPIDER, who wants to kill the heroes himself. While the two villains struggle, the superhero Mr. Justice finds the switch which teleports the lair from this world, leaving the Nameless One behind. Captured, he is locked in a prison stockade run by the secret service group A.U.N.T.I.E. (Amalgamated Universal Network To Inhibit Evil).

NEBULA (C)

First Appearance: 1985, *The Avengers* #257, Marvel Comics.

Costume: Purple bodysuit; navy blue boots, leotard open from the neck to the waist with long sleeves to the wrist *only* under the arms, held on by four straps per arm; blue wristbands trimmed with purple (see Weapons). Nebula's skin is blue.

Weapons: Nebula's wristbands fire destructive rays.

Chief Henchmen: Various piratic alien aides, including the Rigellian Gunthar, the Taurian Kehl, the Sark Levan, and the Laxidasian Skunge.

Biography: Virtually nothing is known about this character's past. The granddaughter of THANOS, she is an interstellar pirate and despot who made a name for herself hijacking Thanos' space station, Sanctuary II. After Thanos fell comatose, she moved the starbase from our solar system to that of the Skrulls (see SUPER-SKRULL), whose empire was ripe for conquest after its throneworld had been consumed by GALACTUS. Although the spacefaring superhero Captain Marvel was able to hitch a ride onboard the space station, and the Avengers followed him, thwarting Nebula, she managed to destroy the planet Xandar as well as a slew of Skrulls before she escaped. While she has not yet returned, it's likely that Nebula is mustering her forces for some new scheme.

THE NEEDLE (C)

First Appearance: 1978, *Spider-Woman* #9, Marvel Comics.

Costume: White tights, full-head cowl with long queue, gloves, bodyshirt with purple sleeves; purple boots.

Weapons: Needle, approximately a yard long, for attacking people; another needle, normal size, for sewing peoples' lips together.

Biography: After working late one night at his small shop, an elderly tailor heads home and is mugged. Badly beaten, permanently unable to speak, one of his eyes destroyed, he ends up in the hospital. Lying there, "seething with futile rage," he discovers that he can release an "electric presence" through his good eye, one which can mesmerize others (presumably, this power is his focused hatred). Upon release nearly six months later, his business having folded in the interim, he seeks vengeance. Creating a costume, he goes out to torture muggers. Cornering them with his large needle, he paralyzes them with his eye and then stitches their lips together with the small needle. And if an innocent bystander happens along, they receive the same treatment. The vigilante is eventually apprehended by Spider-Woman.

THE NEGATOR (C)

Real Name: Rodney.

First Appearance: 1982, *Marvel Two-in-One* #88, Marvel Comics.

Costume: Black leotard with long sleeves, silver armor on the outside; red hood, cape; silver mask with eyes and no other features, thigh boots, straps crisscrossing chest, with mushroom cloud emblem in center.

Weapons: Jet backpack activated by emblem on chest; ray gun.

Biography: As a young man, Rodney (his last name has never been revealed) "was strong and healthy." Working in a uranium mine, he discovers that "accumulated exposure to the unusually rich ore" has cost him his health. Getting a job as the assistant to president Stephen Edward Shields of the Pacific Energy and Utility Corporation, he creates his costume and weapons and uses his position in the company to begin destroying the nuclear industry. He gets underway by killing top company officials, then tries to cause a meltdown of Los Angeles' Diablo reactor—not only getting revenge, but also taking a huge ransom from PE&U to call off the holocaust (which he doesn't do) *and* receiving a contribution of over $10,000 from the group People to Protect Our Environment (which had been misled into thinking no one would be hurt). Fortunately, the She-Hulk and the Thing of the Fantastic Four are able to defeat the Negator and remove the explosive he'd planted before it can cause the meltdown. The Negator is arrested and has not resurfaced. "Wasting away from radiation sickness," it's unlikely he will return.

Quote: "All of Los Angeles shall soon lie as silent in death as this hapless guard—because of . . . *the Negator*!"

THE NEGATRON MAN (C)

Real Name: Dr. Collins.

First Appearance: 1983, *Lancelot Strong, The Shield* #1, Archie Comics.

Biography: A Soviet spy, Collins masquerades as a lab assistant at Fort Sherman in order to get his hands on the Negatron Stimulator, a device which "harnesses the power of a neutron star." So-doing, it generates a debilitating gravitational field. When the superheroic Shield arrives to foil the robbery, the instrument falls; nonetheless, Dr. Collins recovers it and fires it at the Shield. Collins is nearly incinerated when the damaged unit explodes. Taken to the hospital, he is X-rayed; the radiation interacts with the negatronic residue in his body, turning him blue and giving him "the awesome energies of a collapsing neutron star." Able to fly (i.e., "reverse gravity") or destroy objects by increasing their gravity, the villainous doctor doesn't realize that "the more energy he expends . . . the more his already impenetrable mass increases!" Allowing himself to be pummeled, the Shield grins and bears it until the Negatron Man goes nova. And a good thing too—for, as the Shield observes, "Who knows *how much* his gravitic powers would have disrupted earth's own gravity?"

Quote: "*Ha, ha, ha!* You're weakening, patriotic fool!"

Comment: This was the character's only appearance. This Shield is unrelated to the Shield who fought THE ERASER, THE RED SHADOW, and THE STORM KING among other villains.

NEKRA (C)

Real Name: Nekra Sinclair; briefly masqueraded as Adrienne Hatros.

First Appearance: 1973, *Shanna the She-Devil* #5, Marvel Comics.

Costume: Very stylized black bikini, collar, cape (technically, six tendrils of fabric attached to her arm, elbow, and wrist which meet at her waist and form a bat-like cape); white hairband. She has also worn other costumes—most notably a red leotard with a blue, redlined cloak—but the bikini is her principal garb.

Chief Henchmen: Devotees of the sprawling Cult of Kali; GRIM REAPER.

Biography: Gemma Sinclair, a black woman, worked as a janitor at New Mexico's Los Alamos Proving Grounds. One day, an accidental explosion gave both she and white scientist Frederick Beechman a radiation bath; pregnant by husband Buck, she gave birth to Nekra—who, despite her black parentage, was born white—while Beechman's son Jerome, delivered concurrently, was black. Regarded as a freak, Nekra ran away from home at the age of 14 and ended up meeting the similarly ostracized Jerome in the desert. They fell in love and stayed together for several years, during which time their radiation-derived mutant powers surfaced. Nekra found that she could transform anger and fear into superhuman strength and imperviousness, while Jerome became more and more simian in appearance—eventually becoming THE MANDRILL. (On the "plus" side, Jerome also became "irresistable to all women.") After a misguided adventure in Africa which was thwarted by the jungle heroine Shanna (see THE MANDRILL), the pair returned to the United States and tried to overthrow the government. This plot was foiled by Shanna in league with the superhero Daredevil, and, while the Mandrill escaped, Nekra was turned over to the international peacekeeping group S.H.I.E.L.D. (Supreme Headquarters International Espionage Law-enforcement Division). Sedated so she couldn't use her powers and escape, she got a boost from a TV broadcast showing THE HATE-MONGER, and busted free. "Happening upon a den of fanatics in an abandoned subway tunnel in New York," she offered herself as a willing sacrifice to their goddess—knowing full well she couldn't be harmed. She survived and, taking it as a miraculous sign, the cultists appointed her High Priestess of the Cult of Kali. Moving to the west coast and "seeking a front for her hidden empire," she came upon Adrienne Hatros' clinic for emotional research. Realizing that the Hatros Institute would allow her to study and tap her wellsprings of hate, she had one of her adherents stab Adrienne to death and took the researcher's place. Found out and defeated by the superhero Spider-Woman, Nekra was again turned over to S.H.I.E.L.D. Escaping a second time, she left her Kali Cult behind and continued her criminal ways, most recently with Grim Reaper—who died trying to take over the mind of the superhero Wonder Man. Found and reanimated by Nekra, Grim Reaper is currently her living-dead slave.

Quote: "Trust and affection—emotions I find alien and repulsive."

Comment: One account has Nekra running away at age 10. However, 14 (cited in *Spider-Woman* #16) is more reasonable. Unlike Nekra, most of Shanna's enemies tended to be non-super criminals, such as the poacher Ivory Dan Drake (her first nemesis; he died in his debut story), King Phobotauros and the Bullworshippers of Crete (Phobotauros, too, perished in his one and only appearance), and the drug dealer and slave trader El Montano (who also came and went in a single issue).

NEMESIS (C)

Real Name: Danielle Belmonde.

First Appearance: 1984, *Alpha Flight* #7 (as Danielle); 1984, *Alpha Flight* #8 (as Nemesis), Marvel Comics.

Costume: Black boots, bodysuit with red chest, belly, inside of thighs, and tops of arms from shoulders to wrists; red full-head cowl with black face and white eyes; black cloak attached to wrists and heels with red lining and high collar, black on the outside and red on the inside; red gloves.

Weapons: A sword which is "scarcely an atom's width thick" and can "slice through almost anything—by cleaving between the molecules."

Biography: A classics student at McGill University in Montreal, Danielle teams with villain Ernest St. Ives to muscle in on her father's cafe. However, when St. Ives murders the old man, Danielle's mind snaps; she becomes the villainous Nemesis and, after cleaving St. Ives to death, is apprehended by members of the superheroic team, Alpha Flight. Nemesis makes oblique references to "Night" as her mother—perhaps because her own mother is dead—but it is never revealed how she came to possess her sword.

Quote: "Do not move or you may lose more blood than you can afford."

Comment: St. Ives was also a super villain of sorts. During the First World War, he was badly wounded and Death came calling. But St. Ives literally smacked away the Grim Reaper; in so doing he not only survived but also acquired the ability to kill with his own touch. Returning to civilian life he took the name Deadly Ernest and used his power when necessary.

THE NEW QUEEN (N)

First Appearance: 1697, "The Blue Bird," *Contes des Fees*, Mme d'Aulnoy.

Biography: Nothing is known about this Queen before she married a king upon the death of his first wife. The king has a beautiful daughter, Florine, while the New Queen's daughter is quite ugly; thus, when Prince Charming comes calling, he falls in love with Florine—despite the fact that the New Queen has forced her to dress in rags. In a rage, the New Queen imprisons Florine and turns the prince into a blue bird for seven years. After just two years, however, the lovers are restored and Florine's stepsister is turned into a cow.

Comment: "The Blue Bird" was the story which gave us the popular princely name, Prince Charming. This tale is unrelated to Maurice Maeterlinck's play, published in 1909, about a girl and boy who go looking for the blue bird (of happiness).

NIGHT AND FOG (C)

First Appearance: 1985, *All Star Squadron* #44, DC Comics.

Costume: Night: navy blue thigh boots, gloves nearly to shoulders, and leotard with crescent moon on belly; black domino mask. Fog: purple goggles, bodysuit with blue cloud motif on chest and three thick black stripes around torso from chest to waist; black trunks; blue cape, gloves, thigh boots.

Weapons: See Biography.

Biography: At the onset of World War II, Hitler predicted that the Allies would be consumed in "nacht und nebel," night and fog. Tickled with the vivid metaphor, he ordered scientists of the Reich to create an actual Night and Fog—superbeings to advance the cause of Nazism. A brother and sister were selected (their names are not known), Night being given the power to create absolute darkness (apparently using her hair) which affects all of the senses, including mobility itself; and Fog being granted the power to turn into a choking, sentient cloud. The German super villains battled the Allied superheroes, the All-Star Squadron, just once, fleeing and never being heard from again.

Comment: Other Nazi super villains include BARON BLITZKRIEG, BARON GESTAPO, BARON ZEMO, CAPTAIN AXIS, CAPTAIN NAZI, THE CLOWN, THE GOLDEN FUHRER, KILLER SHARK, The Masked Swastika of VENDETTA, Mastermind (see U-MAN, Comment), THE RED PANZER, THE RED SKULL, and ZYKLON.

NIGHTMARE (C, N)

First Appearance: 1963, *Strange Tales* #110, Marvel Comics.

Costume: Bodysuit with flared shoulders, slippers, trunks, cape—all are green with fine black crosshatching (Nightmare's flesh is white). (Note: Sometimes crosshatching is absent; outfit was purple in first confrontation.)

Weapons: "Mystic potion" to draw humans to his realm

while they sleep; "mystic prod" with which to command the creatures of his domain, such as the spider-like Spinybeast; a "transparent sphere" in which the souls of the sleeping are imprisoned and literally flung into the Dream Dimension.

Chief Henchmen: Countless guards and slaves, including the Demons of Despair, blank-faced, gray-cloaked luminaries who steal sleepers' astral selves; and a nameless gray flying unicorn which is Nightmare's steed.

Biography: Nothing is known about Nightmare's past. Ruling the Nightmare World in the Dream Dimension, he himself has a dream: to conquer our dimension. Visiting nightmares on people (implicitly, to increase his own power), he also draws souls to his dimension to study them. (When he does so, their bodies remain asleep on earth.) The superheroic magician Dr. Strange frequently enters Nightmare's realm to rescue fellow mortals, as well as to stop Nightmare's other schemes. The only creature feared by Nightmare is the Gulgol (first appearance: #122), a tall, lumbering, orange monster whose fish-like head and neck are covered with spikes. Hailing from "the Netherworld," the Gulgol is "a heartless creature of destruction" and "the one foe I cannot defeat—for *he never sleeps*!" In his most clever crime, Nightmare snatches Strange while he sleeps, imprisoning him without his powers. Strange responds by using his non-superpower of hypnosis to convince Nightmare that the Gulgol has come, then persuades his captor that he can defeat the monster if released. The terrified Nightmare obliges (Strange noting judgmentally, "Cowardly snivelling does not become you!") and Strange escapes.

Quote: "You know the rules of sorcery, *Dr. Strange*! Those who enter a hostile dimension must be prepared to *pay* for it—with their *lives*!"

Comment: Nightmare was the first foe faced by Dr. Strange, and was also the wizard's nemesis in the 1979 paperback novel *Nightmare*, written by William Rotsler.

THE NIGHT-OWL (C)

First Appearance: 1942, *Action Comics* #53, DC Comics.

Weapons: "Black light projectors" which can throw a major city into utter darkness.

Chief Henchmen: Pet owl who uses poison-coated claws to guard his hideout; sundry thugs.

Biography: A brilliant scientist, the Night-Owl is so-called because he somewhat resembles that bird and has perfected a means of seeing in the dark. Holed-up in a dismal cavern, he plots to throw Metropolis into darkness so his flunkies can rob the city blind. After a successful series of "preliminary skirmishes," he launches his "big drive," only to be stopped by Superman.

Comment: This was the character's only appearance.

NIGHTSHADE (C)

Real Name: Tilda Johnson.

First Appearance: 1973, *Captain America* #164, Marvel Comics.

Costume: Navy blue bikini, gloves, holster, thigh boots; gold necklace, headband, three thin armbands.

Weapons: Various firearms.

Biography: Born in New York's Harlem, Tilda discovered early in her life that she had a natural affinity for science. However, she applied her talents toward crime in order to make a quick escape from the ghetto. Her minor-league escapades brought her to the attention of THE YELLOW CLAW, who gave her a costume and the wherewithal to commit more spectacular crimes. Her first job proved to be her last for him. Intending to use a chemical to turn men into slaves, she was thwarted by Captain America and abandoned by her disappointed mentor. Seeking vengeance against the superhero, she was defeated once again and ended up in prison. Upon her escape, she built an army of robots and endeavored to become a leading figure in New York crime; after several successes against the Maggia crime organization, she was defeated by the superheroes Iron Fist and Power Man. Another two tilts with the crimebusting pair followed, the most recent of which landed her back in jail.

NIGHT-SLAYER (originally known as NIGHT-THIEF) (C)

Real Name: Anton Knight.

First Appearance: 1983, *Detective Comics* #529, DC Comics.

Costume: Black bodysuit, gloves, boots, full-head cowl.

Weapons: None as Night-Thief; as Night-Slayer he used various firearms and daggers, often relying upon a stiletto.

Biography: The son of Charles Knight, a prominent Gotham City mobster, Anton spent years in the Orient becoming a martial arts master. While he was gone, his father took in an urchin named Natalia, who, through letters, Anton came to love. Returning to Gotham City when his father died, Anton discovered that he and Natalia had in common a love not only for each other but also for the night. To keep the darkness symbolically everpresent, he took to wearing a black costume which he wore when he went out to commit crimes as Night-Thief—robberies designed to keep Natalia in the comfort to which she'd grown accustomed. Blending in with the shadows to avoid capture, Night-Thief was nonetheless snared by Batman and ended up in prison. Natalia donned a blue dress and, as Nocturna, tried to free him; though she failed, Night-Thief managed to escape from prison on his own and returned to Natalia. She, meanwhile, had partnered herself with criminal Sturges Hellstrom, who happened to make a pass at her (which she rejected) just as Knight was looking on. Knight murdered Hellstrom, but rather than being received with open arms he was spurned by Natalia who felt that he'd fouled the beloved night with the killing. Then, adding insult to injury, she sought comfort in the arms of Batman, a nobler creature of the night. This made Knight furious and, attempting to kill the Caped Crusader, he was foiled when Natalia shot him. Crawling off, his mind having snapped, he became the Night-Slayer and turned from robbing to murdering. During his most venomous escapade, he managed to bury a knife in Natalia; Batman's sidekick Robin quickly placed her in a convenient hot air balloon to protect her, and she soared off while Night-Slayer was apprehended. Night-Slayer is now serving a life sentence, but Nocturna's whereabouts are unknown. Though the balloon was found much later, she was not in it.

NINO SALVATORE SEBASTIANI (MP)

First Appearance: 1980, *The Nude Bomb,* Universal Pictures.

Costume: Red bodysuit, over-the-head mask; paisley vest; thimbles on every finger.

Weapons: Nude bombs, missiles which can destroy all fabric on earth.

Biography: A mad fashion designer, Nino plans to launch his bombs in order to destroy all clothing on earth—except for his own fashions, which people will thus be forced to wear. He is thwarted by American secret agent Maxwell Smart.

Comment: Vittorio Gassman played the ambitious tailor. The picture underwent a title-change to *The Return of Maxwell Smart* when sold to TV.

NITRO (C)

Real Name: Robert Hunter.

First Appearance: 1974, *Captain Marvel* #34, Marvel Comics.

Costume: Purple gloves, boots, tights, leotard with indigo sides, arms, and a golden disc on chest; golden wristbands.

Biography: A widower (his wife's name was Mary), retired electrical engineer, and ham radio buff, Hunter was tuned-into one evening by the Lunatic Legion, a league of crooked scientists which chose him to become an operative of their own masters, the alien Kree (home race of Captain Marvel, who serves the interests of our world rather than his own). Spirited away to a secret Kree laboratory, Hunter was genetically rebuilt so that he could explode with enormous concussive force . . . and then regroup his scattered atoms. Christened Nitro, the superbeing was sent to steal the secret government nerve gas Compound Thirteen, a theft prevented by Captain Marvel. Indeed, Marvel did more than stymie Nitro, he added his own energies to Nitro's resultant self-detonation, causing the Kree agent to explode with such force that it took months for him to pull himself back together again. In a subsequent encounter, Marvel collected Nitro in two separate containers, making it impossible for him to reform. He was released when his daughter Virginia obtained a court order which permitted him to stand trial for his crimes. Needless to say, as soon as he was allowed to regroup, Nitro escaped. He was eventually snared by Spider-Man, and is presently kept on ice, using a sleeping gas.

Comment: The title of Nitro's debut tale was, fittingly, "Blown Away." See also Captain Marvel's explosive foe MEGATON.

THE NOODLE (TV)

First Appearance: 1967, "The Noodle," *George of the Jungle* (Super Chicken segment), ABC-TV.

Costume: Purple sports jacket, shoes; lavender vest, pants; white shirt; black tie.

Weapons: Blue vacuum cleaner to suck up money in banks; rocket strapped to back for quick escape; jet plane which converts to limousine.

Chief Henchmen: Butler named Beastly; green cat which, when let out of the bag, distracts people so the Noodle can rob them.

Biography: "One of the world's richest and brainiest criminals," the Noodle lives in a metropolitan apartment planning bank robberies. When he plots, his entire head throbs and undulates from the effort. He manages to get the city's resident superhero Super Chicken out of the way by giving him amnesia (he drops a massive watermelon on the fowl's head, making him "just another dumb cluck"); he is finally captured when Super Chicken's lion aide Fred crashes the airborne Super Coup on the villain during a robbery. When last seen, the Noodle and Beastly are sharing a prison cell.

Quote: "It's no fun committing perfect crimes if I always get caught."

Comment: Other Super Chicken villains include the Zipper (a zipper who literally "zips" around), the Oyster, Wild Ralph Iccup, Rotten Hood, Merlin Brando, Fatman, The Muscle, The Easter Bunny (he turns rotten), and Briggs Bad Wolf, an actor who "flips his fright wig," takes his part to heart, and kidnaps his leading lady. See another Super Chicken foe, DR. GIZMO.

NOSFERATU (MP, N)

Real Name: Count Orlock (also Orlof in some versions of the silent film; Dracula in the remake. See Comment).

First Appearance: 1922, *Nosferatu*, Prana.

Biography: Orlock was a lanky creature, bald, with severely pointed eyebrows and ears. "Hundreds of years" old, the vampire long dwelt in a castle in the mountains of Transylvania. Sailing from his homeland in 1838 to feed on fresh blood, he traveled to Bremen (Wismar in the remake). Leaving a trail of death, he thirsted after Ellen Hutter (Mina Harker in the remake), the wife of his real estate agent. Aware of Orlock's foul nature, Ellen sacrificed herself to keep the vampire at her bedside until dawn. Struck by the first rays of the sun, he perished. Among Orlock's idiosyncrasies were the fact that he never blinked; in the original film, his features became more grotesque as the story progressed. In Romanian, "nosferatu" means "not dead."

Quote: "When it is all over, I will banish the light of day entirely. We will build beneath the ground tremendous cities."

Comment: The character was played by Max Schreck in 1922, and by Klaus Kinski in the 1979 remake, *Nosferatu the Vampyre*. The plot of both movies hews very closely to that of *Dracula*; the names and certain aspects of plot were changed in the original in an ill-fated effort to avoid legal entanglements, since *Dracula* was still protected by copyright. (The courts ruled against the filmmakers when Bram Stoker's widow brought suit.) Tellingly, the term "nosferatu" was used in *Dracula* to describe that vampire. In the remake and in the Paul Monette novelization of same, the name Dracula was used. See: BARON BLOOD, BEN CORTMAN, BLACULA, COUNT YORGA, DRACULA, PAUL JOHNSON, and VARNEY THE VAMPIRE.

#39013 (MP)

First Appearance: 1939, *Daredevils of the Red Circle*, Republic Pictures.

Weapons: Superspeed car.

Biography: Prisoner #39013 has spent 15 years in jail thanks to evidence turned over by Granville, his former partner. Escaping, the thug imprisons Granville and takes his place, vowing to destroy Granville's businesses and everyone for whom he cares. When a carnival pier owned by Granville is the target of arson, a young boy is killed; three college athletes who work the pier—the self-styled Daredevils—vow to uncover and arrest the fiend. Meanwhile, #39013 hires a gang and turns his wrath on Granville's considerable stores of gas and oil. But the Daredevils manage to get wind of each caper and nip it in the bud, albeit at great personal jeopardy. They are caught in burning buildings, nearly destroyed by bombs and, in one daring escapade, are all but incinerated when they rescue the District Attorney from a deadly dose of gamma rays (discovering that his foe the D.A. takes gamma ray treatment for medical reasons, #39013 tampers with the unit to give him an incendiary dose). Finally learning where the villain has his hideout, the heroes close in. Aware that the sportscar the Daredevils have been using has the potential to catch his own ultra-souped-up vehicle, #39013 plants a bomb in it which will detonate when the car hits 70 mph. Then he flees. However, #39013 totals his own car in the escape and, trying to be helpful, one of his thugs carries him to the Daredevils' car and speeds off. Moments later the car explodes, reducing the villain to a fraction of his former self.

Comment: Charles Middleton played #39013 in the 12-chapter serial. Middleton also played MING THE MERCILESS in the Flash Gordon serial, and GROOD in the Jack Armstrong serial.

NYAH (MP)

First Appearance: 1955, *Devil Girl from Mars*, Gigi Productions.

Costume: Black silk tights, cloak, skirt.

Weapons: Device which nullifies electricity; atomizing gun; gadget which can trap objects within an invisible electronic shield.

Chief Henchman: Nyah was assisted by the towering robot Chani.

Biography: When a civil war leaves men in perilously

low supply on Mars, Nyah comes to earth to abduct as many as her spaceship can carry. Intending to land in London she touches down, instead, in the Scottish Highlands. There, she shuts down all the electricity in an inn and encloses it in her electronic shield. Killing a handyman and wrecking a few sheds in a show of power, she finally persuades one of the men at the inn to take her to London. As they lift off, the self-sacrificing fellow—Albert, a guilt-stricken murderer—repays his debt to society by (inexplicably) causing Nyah's saucer to blow up.

Comment: Patricia Laffan played the part of Nyah. Other Martian movie super villains are MOTA and THE PURPLE MONSTER.

OCEAN MASTER (C)

Real Name: Orm Curry Marius.
First Appearance: 1966, *Aquaman* #29, DC Comics.
Costume: Purple bodyshirt with pink (later white) manta ray on chest; maroon tights, cloak, boots; black (later gold, then purple) helmet with golden fish-face-style mask. Later donned golden wristbands, belt.
Weapons: Sleek Manta-Ship for underwater travel; it fires destructive rays, releases fog to enable it to make getaways, boasts an antigravity ray capable of lifting an ocean liner, and launches a "killer-craft," a drone vessel released from the Manta-Ship which fires harpoons and also contains TV cameras for spying. Ocean Master also possesses various examples of "ancient Atlantean science," most notably the will-sapping "super-weapon" and a rod which "acts as a transformer for body energy, increasing its strength a thousand-fold." Lastly, Ocean Master owns six of the 12 Crystals of Ancient Atlantis, gems which grant the owner enormous magical powers including superstrength, teleportation, the power to breathe underwater, illusion-creating talents, control over sea monsters, and the ability to fire destructive bolts.
Chief Henchmen: Sundry flunkies.
Biography: After Aquaman's mother died, his father Tom remarried and, with his new wife Mary, had a son named Orm. Since only Aquaman's mother was an Atlantean, only he inherited her ability to live underwater. According to the superhero, "Orm hated me for this—and also because I was older, bigger, stronger." Because Aquaman used his powers for good, Orm turned to evil (the superhero frequently having to bail out his half-brother when he was caught). Then, one day, Orm "received a head blow from a falling rock" and suffered amnesia. He forgot everything but his criminal urges and, disappearing for a while, finally resurfaced as Ocean Master, intent on looting the seaways. He and Aquaman battled frequently, despite the fact that the superhero refused to harm his half-brother. Ocean Master finally gained a potential edge when he discovered six of the 12 Crystals of Ancient Atlantis and became a powerful wizard. However, Aquaman's love for his half-brother repelled the magic and caused it to slam back on Ocean Master, causing an explosion; buried beneath a mountain of debris, the super villain has not been heard from since.
Quote: "Now I have you, *Aquaman*! You're doomed like the frightened sardine you are!"
Comment: Orm also happens to be another name for the Loch Ness Monster. See other underwater super villains ATTUMA, BLACK MANTA, CAPTAIN NEMO, CAPTAIN WHALE, DR. FANG, FISHERMAN, KILLER SHARK, KRANG, MR. CRABB, ORKA, PIRANHA, and TIGER SHARK (2).

THE OCTOPUS (1) (MP)

Real Name: Chase (no first name).
First Appearance: 1938, *The Spider's Web*, Columbia Pictures.
Costume: White robe, hood, full-face mask.
Weapons: Pistol; fake right hand which always remains in full view and enables him to sneak his real hand beneath his robe and grab his gun; radio which disguises his voice when he communicates orders to henchmen; Vibration Room which uses headphones to bombard the wearer with radio waves that, ever after, leave victims ultra-sensitive to all sound.
Chief Henchmen: Various nameless thugs.
Biography: Looking to rule the United States by taking over its communications, transportation, and various industrial resources, banking czar Chase disguises himself as the Octopus. From his headquarters in the Banker's Association building—where he pretends to be running a technical school, which enables him to purchase exotic equipment without arousing suspicion—the Octopus supervises acts of terror against the resources he's seeking to control. Among these acts are causing trains to collide, razing bridges, blowing up trucks, and killing Roberts of Roberts Trucking and Mason of Mason's Metal Works in order to replace them with his own men. However, he is tracked down by the costumed detective known as the Spider, who immediately thwarts the Octopus' most diabolical crime: using a time-bomb hidden in a bus to

destroy a bus terminal while thousands of people are inside. (Because he allowed the Spider to triumph, the thug in charge of that particular operation is electrocuted by the Octopus.) Regrouping, the Octopus tries to darken the city by blowing up the West End Power Plant, but the Spider once again interferes; the superhero also prevents the robbery of a gold shipment bound for a city bank and, later, stops the villain's men from tunneling into the bank vault for a second try at the gold. At last, the Spider enters his enemy's sealed lair via fire truck ladder and shoots the Octopus dead.

Comment: Charles Wilson starred as the Octopus in this 15-episode production.

THE OCTOPUS (2) (M)

First Appearance: February 1939, *The Octopus* #4 (Note: Though identified as #4, this was, in fact, the first issue.), Popular Publications.

Costume: Octopus mask.

Weapons: Ray gun which turns people into monsters.

Biography: Based in a hospital, the Octopus was the leader of the foul Purple Eyes through whom he plotted to rule the world. The Octopus was stopped by Jeff Fairchid, a doctor who treated the poor during the day and, as the Skull Killer, murdered criminals at night.

Comment: The villain's sole adventure carried the subtle title "The City Condemned to Hell." It was written by Norvell Page under the pseudonym Randolph Craig. Page also chronicled the adventures of the superheroic Spider. *The Octopus* became *The Scorpion* for the second and final issue. See THE SCORPION (2).

THE OCTOPUS (3) (CS)

First Appearance: November 17, 1946, *The Spirit*, Register and Tribune Syndicate.

Biography: The Octopus is described by Central City police commissioner O'Dolan as "the foulest criminal in the world." Exerting control over "all the important criminals of the world," he divided his time between Caramba, South America, and Central City, U.S.A. The Octopus' face was never seen, but was kept in shadow or hidden behind a disguise. He was murdered in a subway while wearing one such disguise; dressed as the superhero the Spirit, he was cornered and shot dead by gangsters. At the time of his death, he owned an atomic bomb which he was trying to peddle to a foreign country.

Quote: "Gentlemen, I can promise you a very profitable future, so why worry about what I look like?"

OIL CAN HARRY (MP, C, TV)

First Appearance: 1946, *My Old Kentucky Home*, Terrytoons.

Costume: Floor-length black overcoat with padded shoulders and flared lapels, the coat tightly belted around the waist; top hat (black or green with a white band); white gloves; red string tie (sometimes a bow tie); black shoes with spats.

Weapons: He has used countless weapons, from a giant slingshot to conventional pistols. His one regular conveyance is a motorcycle with a sidecar.

Chief Henchmen: Though he has used cat-flunkies on rare occasion, Harry is a loner.

Biography: Nothing is known about this cat's past. Apparently a land baron (he has held the mortgage on more than one mouse hole), he spends his every waking hour pursuing Pearl Pureheart. However, the beautiful mouse only has eyes for Mighty Mouse—who must rescue her every time Harry abducts her.

Quote: "You underestimate me, rodent! So long, cheese-eater!"

Comment: Harry has also been featured in the Mighty Mouse comic books and in the animated cartoons made for TV. In 1986 Moxie Nutrition began featuring him—as Heartless Harry—on the packaging for its line of Mighty Mouse cereals. In this guise he wears a blue costume and cape, as well as light blue boots, a white samurai-style helmet, and purple gloves. He also packs a pair of blasters. He is the superhero's only recurring foe. Other super villains battled by Mighty Mouse in his long cartoon career include the renegade cowboy Bad Bill Bunion; Jekyll and Hyde Cat; the bullying Kilkenny Cats; another Western crumb, Deadeye Dick; the "Witch" and her cat; the Goons from the Moon; and "the Raiders," a group of bunny-eating vultures. See other cat villains, COUNT GATTO and TERRIBLE TOM.

THE OLD FAIRY (F)

First Appearance: 1696, "La Belle au Bois Dormant," Charles Perrault, *Mercure galant*.

Biography: Upon the birth of his daughter, a king gathers together "all the Fairies that could be found in the land" and holds a feast. The seven fairies are all named godmothers, thus offending an eighth who had been overlooked because "it had been more than fifty years since she had been out of a tower, and they believed her to be dead, or enchanted." The Old Fairy shows up during the meal and a place is set; but she is not provided with golden cutlery like the other Fairies

Maleficent, one version of ***THE OLD FAIRY*** *from* Sleeping Beauty. *Courtesy Bill Latham. © Walt Disney Publications.*

and takes offense. Outraged now, she curses the child and declares that on her sixteenth birthday she'll pierce her hand with a spindle and die. When she departs in a huff, another Fairy is able to modify the curse so that the princess will only sleep until "a king's son shall come and wake her up." Though the king bans spindles throughout the kingdom, the Old Fairy waits 16 years and then materializes, with a spindle, in a room atop the palace tower. The princess falls asleep, at which point one of the other Fairies hastens over in a flaming chariot to put the rest of the court to sleep so she won't be alone when she awakens. A century later (the Old Fairy presumably dead), a prince finds the Sleeping Beauty and awakens her. However, her problems are not yet over. She marries the prince, whose mother happens to be a cannibal. When Sleeping Beauty bears children, her stepmother decides to eat them. When her son is away, she orders the beautiful child Aurore dressed with "Sauce Robert" and readied for eating. A lamb is substituted and the child is hidden; the same thing is done when she demands a plate of Aurore's brother Jour. When the cannibal asks to eat Sleeping Beauty, she is fed a deer instead. Naturally, the prince is furious when he returns home and, rather than face his wrath, his mother hurls herself into a vat filled with "toads, vipers, snakes and serpents."

Comment: The Old Fairy has many different names due to the various versions of the tale. Though Norse lore has the king of the gods, Odin, putting the beautiful Brynhild to sleep in a castle until a brave man comes to save her, the earliest known version of the "Sleeping Beauty" story appeared as "Troylus and Zellandine," collected in the French *Perceforest* in the fourteenth century. In that story, the Princess Zellandine is cursed by a goddess who wasn't invited to the feast. There was no goddess or Fairy involved in the sleep of Talia caused by "a small splinter in some flax" in the seventeenth-century Italian anthology *Pentamerone*, though after she's been awakened and raped by a king, Talia and her children are menaced by the king's cannibal wife. The flesheater perishes in a fire. The Grimm Brothers version, "The Sleeping Beauty," hews closely to Perrault, as the king has the Wise Women of his kingdom to a feast honoring his daughter. However, since he has only 12 gold plates, he only invites a dozen of the Wise Women; the thirteenth, "burning to avenge herself, and without greeting or respect," storms in and voices her curse. The Tchaikovsky ballet, *Sleeping Beauty,* borrows from both Perrault and Grimm and adds material of its own; the 1890 work was the basis for Walt Disney's brilliant 1959 feature cartoon *Sleeping Beauty,* in which the character is now Maleficent, a witch. She perished when, transforming herself into a dragon, she was skewered by Prince Phillip's enchanted sword. Maleficent's voice was provided by Eleanor Audley. Other film versions of the story were made in 1902, 1908, 1913, 1922, 1935, 1947, 1950, 1952, 1955, 1963, and 1966 (the later two based on the ballet). A variation on the theme appears in the Hong Kong film *Sleeping Beauty* (1961) in which a man tries to leave his inamorata, a witch, for another woman. The witch avenges herself by using magic to wreak havoc on his career and love life.

ORKA (C)

First Appearance: 1970, *Sub-Mariner* #23, Marvel Comics.

Costume: Blue bodysuit with white chest, cowl with yellow fangs surrounding the face; yellow belt (see Weapons); white trunks.

Weapons: Belt which is attuned to the morphotron and allows Orka to draw energy from his whales.

Chief Henchmen: A herd of whales, which he rides.

Biography: A water-breathing denizen of Atlantis, the powerful but dull-witted Orka was devoted to the traitorous commander KRANG. Exiled with his master by the mighty Sub-Mariner, Orka became a pawn in Krang's scheme to regain the throne he'd briefly (and illegally) held. Finding criminal marine biologist Dr. Lemuel Dorcas (creator of TIGER SHARK), Krang allowed him to place Orka in a "morphotron," a device which gave subjects the attributes of selected animals. In this case, Dorcas and Krang genetically merged the Atlantean with a herd of whales. Sent out to battle Sub-Mariner, Orka was beaten and left on the seabottom beneath a pile of boulders. Found months afterward by Virago, a villain from another dimension, Orka gathered together his whales and, understandably piqued, attacked Atlantis anew. Defeated once more, he eventually fell in with the none too honest Roxxon Oil Company, whose scientists found a way to triple his size and free him of his dependency on the belt. Sent to fight the Avengers, Orka struck out for the third time and headed out to sea. He has not been seen since.

Quote: "*I've won*! I have *destroyed* the Sub-Mariner!"

Comment: See other underwater super villains ATTUMA, BLACK MANTA, CAPTAIN NEMO, CAPTAIN WHALE, DR. FANG, FISHERMAN, KILLER SHARK, KRANG, MR. CRABB, OCEAN MASTER, PIRANHA, and TIGER SHARK (2).

ORTHIS (N)

First Appearance: 1923, "The Moon Maid," *Argosy All-Story Weekly,* Edgar Rice Burroughs.

Weapons: Spaceships; electronic rifles which disintegrate metal.

Biography: On Christmas Day in the year 2025, the spaceship *Barsoom* sets out for a trip to Mars. In command is Julian 5th; Lieutenant Commander Orthis is his first officer, an "unscrupulous and . . . obnoxious" man who "never . . . thought a considerate thought" in his life. An engineer with the International Peace Fleet, Orthis was largely responsible for the design and construction of the *Barsoom* and is livid that he was not named its captain; thus, he sabotages the vehicle's engines, and Julian barely manages to land the craft on the moon. As it happens, the moon is both hollow and inhabited, and while Julian and his allies repair the *Barsoom,* the bitter Orthis allies himself with the barbaric, human-like Kalkars. The craft leaves without the engineer, who spends the next quarter-century building spaceships. In the year 2050 he leads the Kalkars in a successful invasion of earth, capturing Washington and London and crippling all resistance with his electronic rifles. Though the Kalkars conquer our world, Orthis does not live to enjoy it. Julian boards his ship and, rather than call off the invasion, Orthis blows the craft, himself, and Julian to pieces. Little is known about Orthis' past. A New Yorker, he attended Air Force School with Julian 5th for four years; after graduation, Orthis was assigned "principally to land service." He had a wife whom he abandoned; she died not long before the spaceflight.

Quote: "By God we will not reach Mars. You dare to order me about like a dog and an inferior—I, whose brains have made you what you are!"

Comment: The character's full story was told in two serials, *The Moon Maid* and *The Moon Men* (1925); and in the serialized novella "The Red Hawk" (1925), which told of the overthrow of the Lunarians long after the events in the first two novels. The original adventure was serialized in *Argosy All-Story Weekly* from May 5 to June 2 and was a rewritten version of Burroughs' unsold tale, *Under the Red Flag* (1919), a parody of the Russian Revolution. The first book edition of *The Moon Maid,* combining the three parts, wasn't published until 1926. See MEPHIS for Burroughs' other political fantasy.

OTTO VON NEIMANN (MP)

First Appearance: 1933, *The Vampire Bat*, Majestic Productions.

Chief Henchmen: Emil Borst.

Biography: Based in a castle in the Central European village of Kleinschloss, Neimann is a physician who has succeeded in creating life in the laboratory. "No mere crystalline growth," he chortles proudly to his assistant Ruth Bertin, "but tissue, living, growing tissue. Life that moves, pulsates, and demands food." The food in question is human blood, which von Neimann obtains by hypnotizing his helper Emil and sending him forth to kill, manipulating him by telepathy. All the while, the superstitious townspeople think that a vampire is afoot. Ruth learns the truth, and has to be bound in the lab to keep her from running to Police Inspector Karl Brettschneider; in time, however, Brettschneider figures out what's going on and informs Emil, who kills himself, taking von Neimann and the life-creating apparatus with him.

Quote: "What are a few lives to be weighed in the balance against the achievements of biological science?"

Comment: Lionel Atwill—THE BUTCHER (see Comment), THE SCARAB, SIR ERIC HAZARIAS—played the singleminded scientist, Robert Frazer the doomed Emil, and Fay Wray the fair Ruth. Edward T. Lowe wrote the film.

THE OUTSIDER (C)

Real Name: Alfred Pennyworth (originally Beagle; changed in *Batman* #214).

First Appearance: 1943, *Batman* #16 (as Alfred); 1964, *Detective Comics* #334 (as the Outsider), DC Comics.

Costume: Purple trunks (skin is white and cobbled).

Chief Henchmen: The Grasshopper Gang, a group of thugs wearing green bodysuits, cowls with bug-eyes and antennae, and wings.

Biography: An Englishman, Alfred comes to the United States to work as the butler for millionaire Bruce Wayne, just as his own father Jarvis had served Bruce's father Thomas. Though Alfred had originally pursued a career as an actor, he honors his father's deathbed wish to work for the American Wayne. (It takes him a while to arrive, however. "Two ships were torpedoed under me," he tells Wayne, "and I spent a fortnight adrift on a life raft.") An amateur sleuth, he discovers at once that Wayne is actually the superhero Batman, and serves him faithfully for years. Then, in 1964 (*Detective Comics* #328), during a battle with gangsters, Alfred is crushed by a boulder while pushing Batman from its path. Unembalmed ("his body was kept under refrigeration to prevent deterioration"), he is placed in a mausoleum—though, miraculously, he is not quite dead. Three days after the accident, "Brandon Crawford—physician—physicist—biologist—geologist—all-around scientific genius" is wearing a "sensitive micro-audiometer" as he chases a rare insect through the cemetery. Hearing a faint moan inside the crypt, he ventures in and finds "a very faint spark of life" in Alfred, whose "sheer will to live staved off death." Carrying the butler to his basement laboratory, Crawford subjects him to an untested, experimental cell-regeneration machine. As a result, Alfred turns into a white, stone-like creature with a criminal mind (his "altered brain" also "understands the principals" of the "ultra-scientific machines" in the lab) while Crawford becomes a catatonic double of Alfred. Calling himself the Outsider ("I don't even feel *human* any more! I am *outside* the human race!"), Alfred embarks on a project to destroy Batman and begins by transmuting the hero's sidekick, Robin, into a coffin. However, Batman figures out how to work Crawford's equipment and not only saves his partner ("Ooooh! I had the peculiar feeling that I'd been changed into a coffin!"), but also restores Alfred and Crawford to normal (*Detective Comics* #356). The butler explains everything that has happened before losing all memory of his brief career as the Outsider. A devoted Alfred remains Wayne's butler to this day.

Quote: "I must save *Batman* and *Robin* from—no! *No*! That's wrong! I don't want to save them—I want to *kill* Batman and Robin!"

THE OVERLORD (C)

First Appearance: 1969, *The Silver Surfer* #6, Marvel Comics.

Costume: Iron-gray boots, armored tights, chest harness, spiked armor over right shoulder, spiked wristband on right hand; orange loincloth with flap to knees; tan belt with yellow buckle; green T-shirt with high collar. The Overlord's left hand is a three-pronged claw.

Chief Henchmen: Slaves of various ranks, including the yellow-garbed "Trustees" (the highest rank); the "Emissaries," green, red, and yellow costumed flunkies who ride small spaceships from world to world doing his bidding; and the blue-, green-, and red-costumed "Executioners."

Biography: The "ultimate conqueror" was born on a world of the future where his father was chief of research of "one of the galaxy's few remaining atomic experimental centers" (atomic energy having been replaced by "magnetic power sources"). When an atomic device malfunctioned and exploded, the Overlord's father had his genes "irrevocably altered." When he fathered a child, the boy proved to be a mutant with strength and savagery "beyond compare." Growing to some 30 feet in height, and virtually indestructible, the boy remained more or less under control until the death of his parents. At that point, he did whatever he pleased and so was ordered exiled in "deepest space." Alas, no one could carry out the order and, worse, it convinced the young giant that other beings were his enemies. Vowing to become "overlord of the universe," he went on a rampage to destroy all life forms he encountered, save for those few which he enslaved. Having already slain "untold billions" he was challenged by the superheroic Silver Surfer, who happened to have left our time in an attempt to find his lost love. Battered insensate by the giant and his destructive blasts, the Surfer was revived by a slave from his own home world of Zenn La. Traveling back in time, the superhero found the rampaging atomic pile which had contaminated the Overlord's father in the first place and, surrounding it within "a protective cosmic shield," prevented the birth of a mutated Overlord.

Quote: "He will furnish me much *amusement*—before his life is *snuffed-out* like a dying *candle*!"

THE OVERMASTER (C)

First Appearance: 1985, *Justice League of America* #235, DC Comics.

Costume: Green breastplate, trunks, tights; red gloves, belt, boots; golden mask; black mushroom-shaped headdress; black and gold design on kneeguards of boots and on forehead of headdress.

Weapons: Mountain-sized spaceship.

Chief Henchmen: THE CADRE.

Biography: According to Aquaman, "We may never know for certain" what the Overmaster was. Having landed on earth at some time in the remote past, the towering, humanoid Overmaster could fire destructive blasts from his hands and claimed to have been responsible for all the world's major extinctions. Luring the Justice League of America to his spaceship hidden within a remote mountain, he said he was poised to decide if our species would follow the dinosaurs "into oblivion." His method—to pit the Cadre against the Justice League. What developed during the course of battle was that the Overmaster was apparently not what he said, but a parasite living in the slug-like body of an alien who lay dormant in the ship. Having somehow acquired a huge humanoid body, he was powering it telepathically from the host—and trying to fulfill delusions of grandeur by murdering the Justice Leaguers and then attempting the destruction of the human race. All his chatter about having destroyed other races on earth was either idle boasting or the work of the sleeping host-being. Defeating the giant and the Cadre, the superheroes fled the spaceship before it took off. The fate of the slug-like alien, the Overmaster, and the Cadre is not known.

Quote: "Your possibilities are all foreclosed, your freedom is at an end."

THE OVERMIND (C)

Real Name: Grom.

First Appearance: 1971, *The Fantastic Four* #111, Marvel Comics.

Costume: Silver armor, gauntlets, boots, helmet.

Biography: Millennia ago, the beings of the planet Eternus conquer the aging process. Having eliminated natural death, they launch wars and wargames in an effort to control the population. Destroying the planet Gigantus, the Eternians are surprised when a Gigantian fleet launches a crushing counterattack. Doomed, the Eternians place their collective minds into the body of Grom, their mightiest gladiator. Grom is then launched into the cosmos, sleeping as his body assimilates the billion brains of Eternus. Awaking in the present day, near earth, he finds himself possessed of amazing mental powers, to abet his awesome physical strength. He can control the will of others, create illusions, levitate matter, and fire destructive mental bolts. Attacking our world, the so-called Overmind is defeated by the Fantastic Four who are helped by a surprise ally, the Stranger—the Overmind's counterpart from Gigantus! The Stranger not only helps beat the Overmind, but also shrinks him to roughly the size of a molecule and strands him on a speck of dust. The Overmind is found and recruited years later by the foul Null, the Living Darkness who (like the Overmind and the Stranger) is himself the personification of a race—in this case, the enemies of the S'raphh who once dwelt on our moon. The revitalized Overmind is sent to another dimension and Other-Earth, a world more or less identical to our own. Conquering that world, he is dethroned when our world's superheroic Defenders cross the dimensional barrier. They are aided in the struggle by the bonded mental abilities of six Other-Earth telepaths, who subsequently make a permanent move into the Eternian's body and turn him from a force for evil into a force for good.

THE OWL (C)

Real Name: Leland Owlsley.

First Appearance: 1964, *Daredevil* #3, Marvel Comics.

Costume: Green cloak; olive green jacket, pants; white shirt with ruffled sleeves; large red bow tie.

Weapons: Long, sharp talons attached to wrist of right hand and continuing well beyond the fingers. On occasion, the Owl has also flown about on a huge, metal owl as well as in a helicopter with a cockpit shaped like an owl's head.

Chief Henchmen: "Sad Sam" Simms (aka "Silent Sam"), "Ape" Horgon, McGraw, Hackett, Roscoe, other thugs over the years.

Biography: Owlsley was a financier whose crooked business practices were exposed by the IRS. Obtaining (from unknown sources) a potion which gave him the power of limited flight, he assembled a gang and endeavored to become a powerful crime leader in New York. But his efforts were undermined by the superhero Daredevil, and the Owl ended up in prison. Upon his parole, the Owl—never one to hold a grudge—immediately abducted Judge Lewis, who had sentenced him; though Daredevil freed him, the Owl got away (#'s 20 and 21). Sadly, he suffered paralysis of the legs, seemingly as a result of having taken repeated doses of the flight potion. He and Daredevil have continued to battle frequently, however, most notably when the Owl has attempted to kidnap various scientists and doctors to help him regain the use of his legs. For a while he walked with the help of exoskeletonic braces; but these, along with his talons, were destroyed in a battle with fellow super villain, DOCTOR OCTOPUS. The Owl himself was badly injured in the bout, and spent a while recovering in a prison infirmary.

Quote: "*Two* flew over the Owl's nest—but only *one* shall *survive*!"

THE PANTHER (C)

Real Name: "Professor Elixir" (see Biography).

First Appearance: 1965, *Two-Gun Kid* #77, Marvel Comics.

Costume: Red bodysuit, boots, gloves, panther-like mask.

Weapons: Standard six-shooters.

Chief Henchmen: Three gangmembers, only Luke mentioned by name, who travel about in Elixir's enclosed wagon.

Biography: The Panther is a traveling medicine peddler known only as Elixir. When the Panther first "started to strike in these parts" (an unspecified town in the old west), he concentrated on robbing trains. "Soon he appeared to be all over the territory in his ruthless rampage of crime," robbing hundreds of people, striking silently, or using "his cat call to spook cattle." Eventually, the heroic Two-Gun Kid tracked him to his cave lair and, after a strenuous battle with the unusually agile criminal, arrested him.

Quote: "Welcome to my *lair*, Two-Gun! I am *honored* by your *presence* and will be *delighted* by your death!"

Comment: See other Marvel western villains THE FAT MAN, HURRICANE, THE RAVEN, RED RAVEN, and ROBIN HOOD RAIDER.

PARA-MAN (C)

Real Name Ree Zee.

First Appearance: 1972, *Marvel Feature* #7, Marvel Comics.

Costume: Green bodysuit, gloves; yellow boots, belt, wristbands, two studs on each leg, just above knee, wristbands, full-head cowl with red eyes and green cheeks. (Note: costume is different on cover, with white and green cowl, green mail trunks and neck, and other differences.)

Chief Henchman: Boswell (see Biography).

Biography: Holed up in a small house in the middle of a marsh, scientist Boswell builds an android to serve "as a houseboy." However, the robot possesses far more intelligence than Boswell suspects and, when it's finished, it turns the tables and enslaves its creator. It demands to be called Para-Man (because "I am a being *beyond* mere *man*") and gives Boswell a new project: to capture and study insects so he can give Para-Man "the strength of ants—the stinging fury of wasps." Alas, he captures the superheroes Ant-Man and the Wasp by mistake, which proves to be Para-Man's undoing. During a battle—in which he displays vast physical strength—chemicals ignite and their house explodes, blowing Para-Man to pieces. But Boswell and the robot's talking head survive and, when last seen, the robot was demanding that the obedient scientist put him back together again. When he was whole, Para-Man's hobby was watching home movies of his creation.

Quote: "I grow *melancholy*—must be the *oil*!"

Comment: This was the character's only appearance.

THE PARASITE (C)

Real Name: Raymond Maxwell Jensen.

First Appearance: 1966, *Action Comics* #340, DC Comics.

Costume: Green trunks, white vertical stripe down chest (the Parasite's skin is purple).

Biography: Working as a laboratory handyman, Jensen is carting canisters of radioactive waste to a dump when he remembers that the payroll is occasionally shipped "incognito" to foil would-be robbers. Wondering if the money is in the container, Jensen opens it and finds that it does indeed carry radioactive waste. Becoming a miniature sun, he begins burning off energy as well as sucking it in from the people around him. Then he's struck with an inspiration. Since Superman happens to be at the lab—it was his waste, in fact, that Jensen was toting—the handyman decides to sap the Man of Steel's might and thus become the most powerful being on earth. Unfortunately, his eyes are bigger than his atomic structure and Jensen overloads; blown to quarks, he floats into the atmosphere as a purple haze. As it happens, however, an alien cartographer studying the earth notices the cloud, detects life in it, and pulls Jensen back together. Returning to earth, the Parasite dedicates himself to stealing Superman's power—though, wisely, he only takes a little at a time. To date, despite numerous attempts, he has yet to succeed in completely draining the Man of Steel. However, each time the energy-sponge gets close to the superhero, he does manage to absorb enough power to give him great strength and the ability to fly for quite some time. During the course of his life as the parasite, Jensen has also absorbed a great deal of knowledge from the minds of others and qualifies as a genius. Jensen briefly returned to normal when he was blasted by an alien raygun. Marrying his lawyer Lorna and fathering twins—daughter Trini and son Troy—he lived happily until an alien named Xviar turned him into the Parasite once again in order to use him against Superman. Sadly, the Parasite cannot go near his family for fear of depleting their energy.

Quote: "I fleetingly *tuned in* on Superman's *mental state*. Being an *alien* from an extinct world, having *no family* to gather around the home and hearth with over the Christmas holidays—the man from Krypton is in a real 'blue funk' that can't help but *handicap* him in a crisis!"

PAUL JOHNSON (MP)

First Appearance: 1957, *Not of This Earth*, Allied Artists.

Costume: Earth clothes, with sunglasses to hide his all-white eyes.

Weapons: Telepathy; hypnotic powers; deadly energy blasts fired from eyes; matter transmitter to ship items—especially blood—to and from Davanna; killer umbrella, a living being which is kept folded in a tube until needed, at which point it unfolds massive wings, zips over to its victim, closes over the person's head, and simultaneously kills it while opening a major vein.

Biography: Johnson hails from the planet Davanna, a world suffering from perennial nuclear warfare. Because of constant radiation, their "agglutin is disintegrating at an uninterrupted rate." The aliens require fresh stores of blood and Johnson has been sent to earth to determine if human blood will fill the bill. If the answer is positive, the Davannans will take over our world. Settling into a home and hiring a chauffeur so he can get around, Johnson starts killing people and using their blood to send home and to cure his own "anemia." After he's been on earth just a few weeks, Johnson meets a woman from his home world who informs him that the war has all but obliterated Davanna and that they must remain on earth. Since she requires blood, Johnson takes her to a doctor's office to give her an injection—accidentally using blood from a rabid dog and killing her. When Johnson's true nature is found-out by his private nurse Nadine, she informs her boyfriend, a motorcycle cop; there's a chase and the telepathic Johnson, unused to loud sounds, is driven to distraction by the officer's siren. Unable to concentrate on the road, he drives off a cliff and perishes. Back on the street, however, is a dead ringer for Johnson, someone else from destroyed Davanna.

Comment: Paul Birch played the alien vampire. See: BARON BLOOD, BEN CORTMAN, BLACULA, COUNT YORGA, DRACULA, NOSFERATU, and VARNEY THE VAMPIRE.

PECOS ALLBELLIN (M)

First Appearance: August 1938, "The Munitions Master," *Doc Savage* Magazine, Kenneth Robeson.

Weapons: Quick-freeze device which creates a vacuum "of sudden, terribly intense coldness" that instantly freezes all moisture in a room; radio-controlled flying machine guns (controlled by a mothership in the stratosphere); robot-controlled bombers; "the Burning Death," a paste which, once activated by a special gas, melts any flesh it touches.

Biography: Allbellin is a man of medium height with "a prematurely (sic) streak of gray in otherwise perfectly black hair. His face (is) that of an indolent ladies' man, but his eyes hinted a shrewd brain." In public, he wears a perpetually vacant expression ("insipid, almost stupid") to mislead those with whom he comes into contact into presuming him witless. Formerly the dictator of a South American country, Allbellin "had ruled by cruelty and fear. And one of his delights had been torture." When he is finally deposed, he takes most of the country's money with him and allies himself with attorney Carloff Traniv in an effort to rule the world. To do this, he plans to coerce the superhero Doc Savage into performing brain surgery which will force world leaders to do exactly what he says—surgery not unlike that which has already given him an army of "automata" soldiers. He also finances and arms insurgents the world over to control countries where he can't get to the leaders for surgery. Both Allbellin and Traniv die by the Burning Death: Traniv because Allbellin has spread it on his clothes, and Allbellin because a would-be victim has spread it on his. Despite his grandiose plans, Pecos is not above enjoying smaller, twisted pleasures during his exile, to wit: "Allbellin was very cold-blooded about it. He smacked her on the jaw."

Quote: "Get the execution squad! Have those men . . . in Cell 3 taken out for immediate execution! I will be there to witness it!"

THE PENGUIN (C, CS, TV, MP, N)

Real Name: Oswald Chesterfield Cobblepot.

First Appearance: 1941, *Detective Comics* #58, DC Comics.

Costume: Blue top hat with purple band; blue formal jacket; purple trousers with thin black stripes; white shirt, gloves, and bow tie; yellow vest; monocle; cigarette and holder.

Weapons: One thousand umbrellas, including gun-umbrella, parachute-umbrella, acid-spraying umbrella, flamethrowing umbrella, helicopter umbrella, rocket umbrella, sword-umbrella, and even a biological warfare umbrella which releases bacteria.

Chief Henchmen: Varies; he usually has a gang of nameless thugs supporting him.

THE PENGUIN . . . in his incarnation as a Mego action toy.
© DC Comics.

Biography: As a youth, Oswald runs the Cobblepot Bird Shop with his mother. (His father had been caught in a thunderstorm without his umbrella, dying two weeks later of bronchial pneumonia. Ever since then, Mrs. Cobblepot has insisted that Oswald carry his umbrella when he goes out.) Because of his big nose and rotund physique, Oswald is constantly teased by the neighborhood kids; he retreats more and more, spending nearly all his time with the birds at the shop. In fact, he becomes so attached to them that he majors in ornithology in college. Sadly, his mother becomes ill and dies, her long illness costing so much that Oswald's creditors take the shop from him. Furious, he decides to turn to crime and tries to join a local underworld gang—but is cruelly laughed from their headquarters. ("You? *ha ha*! A *crook*? Haw haw! Try comedy! With that snoot, you already got Bob Hope beat!") They boot him out, admonishing him to "*Stay* out, you bulgy little *penguin*!" But Oswald has other ideas. Dressing like a penguin—which becomes his standard wear—and customizing his everpresent umbrella so that it fires .45 caliber bullets, he goes back to the gang, guns down the leader, and takes over. Then, during his first robbery—stealing a rare Prussian egret—he leaves them to be caught by the police. Based in Gotham City, the vain, dapper supercriminal tangles frequently with the superhero Batman and invariably ends up in prison.

Quote: "If I'm finally going to kill *the Batman*, I want to take a little time to think up something really fiendish!"

Comment: Burgess Meredith starred as the Penguin on the *Batman* TV series from 1966 to 1968; he also played the part in the 1966 motion picture *Batman*, teamed with CATWOMAN, THE JOKER, and THE RIDDLER to kidnap the world's foremost diplomats. (In that film, the Penguin also owned a submarine which was built in the shape of a duck, complete with a propulsion system consisting of webbed feet churning aft.) In Winston Lyon's 1966 Signet novel, *Batman and the Three Villains of Doom*, the Penguin was vying with the Joker and Catwoman to win a gold-covered machine gun known as the Tommy, "the crimeworld's top award," which is handed out once every decade. Also in 1966, Signet published a paperback entitled *Batman vs. the Penguin*, reprinting the best of the duo's comic book battles. The Penguin also appeared regularly in the Batman comic strip, and continues to make his mark in the various comic books featuring Batman.

THE PERSUADER (C)

First Appearance: 1967, *Adventure Comics* #352, DC Comics.

Costume: Light blue bodysuit; darker blue leotard with open sides, bands around wrists, shins, thighs; red gloves, boots; full-head white helmet.

Weapons: Atomic Axe which can cut through anything, including energy; if he slashes it between an object and gravity or magnetism, the object will drift away.

Biography: Inhabiting the latter half of the thirtieth century, the Persuader is "the highest paid killer and strongarm gangland enforcer in the galaxy . . . also number one on the science police list of wanted extortionists." Nothing is known about his past or about how he came to possess either his

*The demon **Tchernabog** from* Fantasia. *Courtesy Bill Latham,* *© Walt Disney Productions.*

***Skeletor** in a typical pose. © 1983 Filmation Associates; character © Mattel, Inc.*

***Moltar** with his henchmen (from the left) Zardeth, Feldspar and Warbow. © Remco.*

The Desert Rat. © *Harvey Comics.*

King Zorth. © *IPC Magazines Ltd.*

Professor Death. © *Atlas Comics.*

The Claw*, one of the foulest creatures in all of comic book villaindom.*

***Captain Whale** (aboard his Killer Whale) vs. Nukla.* © Dell Publishing.

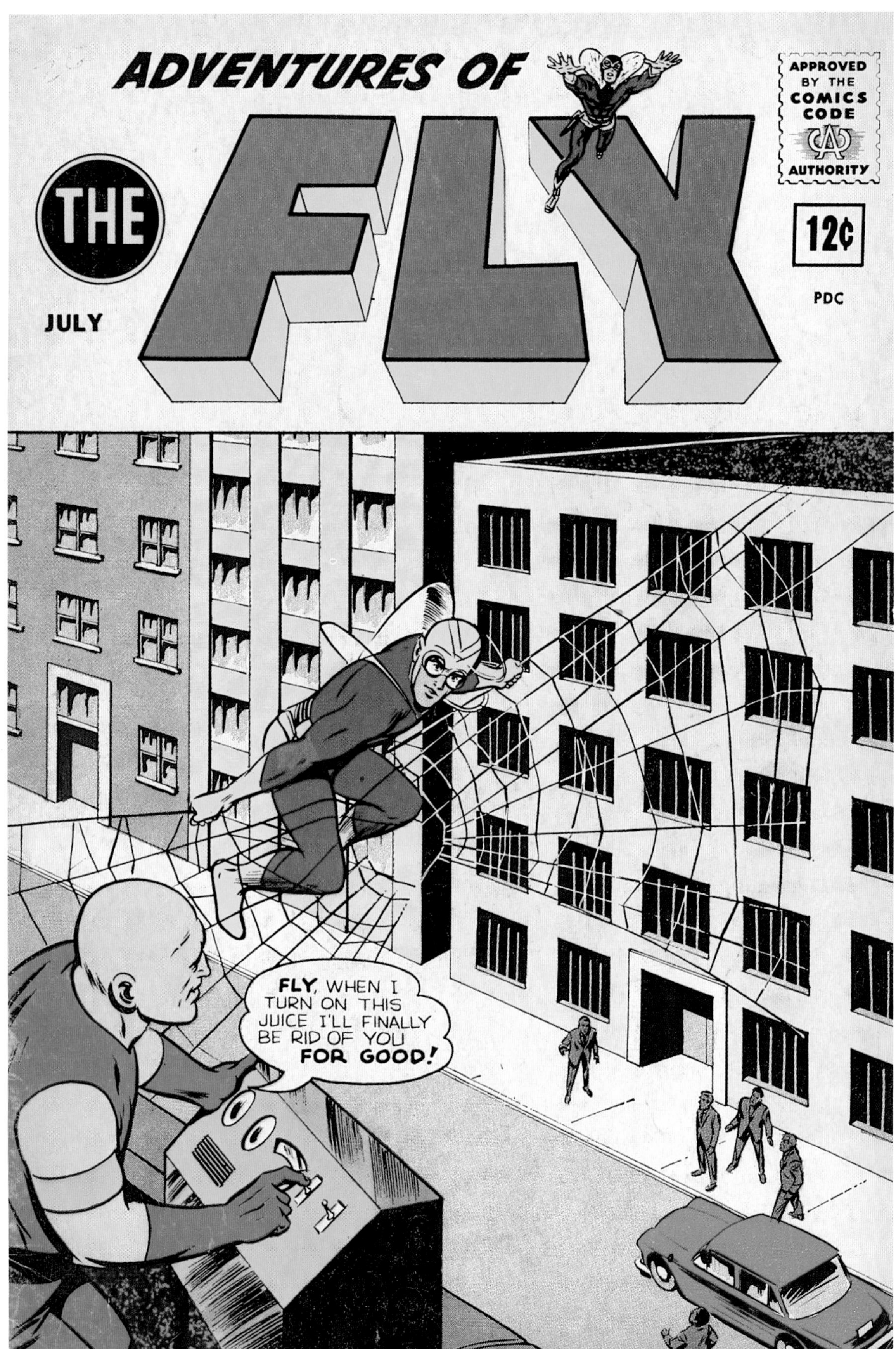

***The Spider**, in a later incarnation, bearing a striking resemblance to **Lex Luthor**. © Archie Comics.*

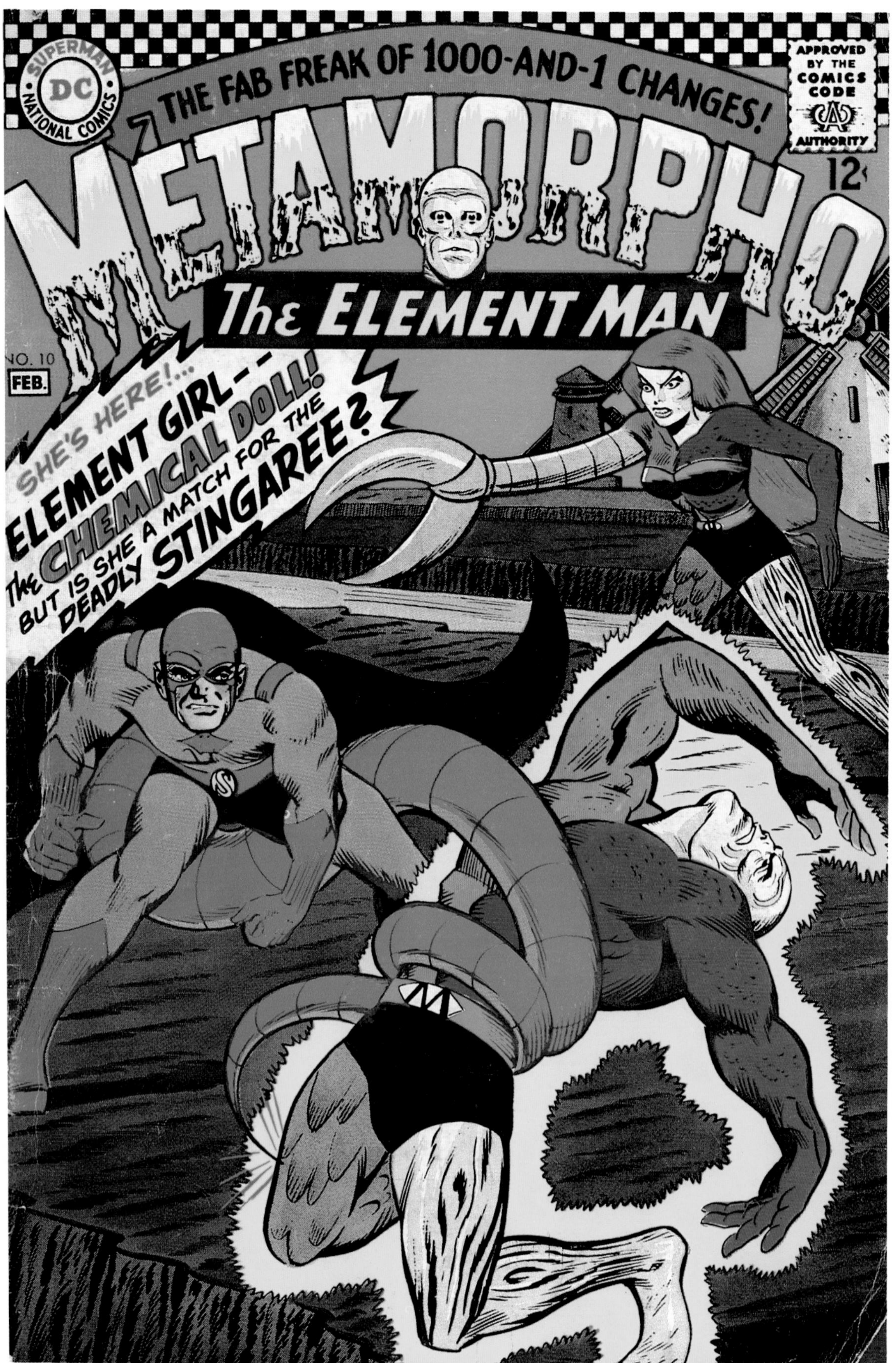

Stingaree *tackles Metamorpho. © DC Comics.*

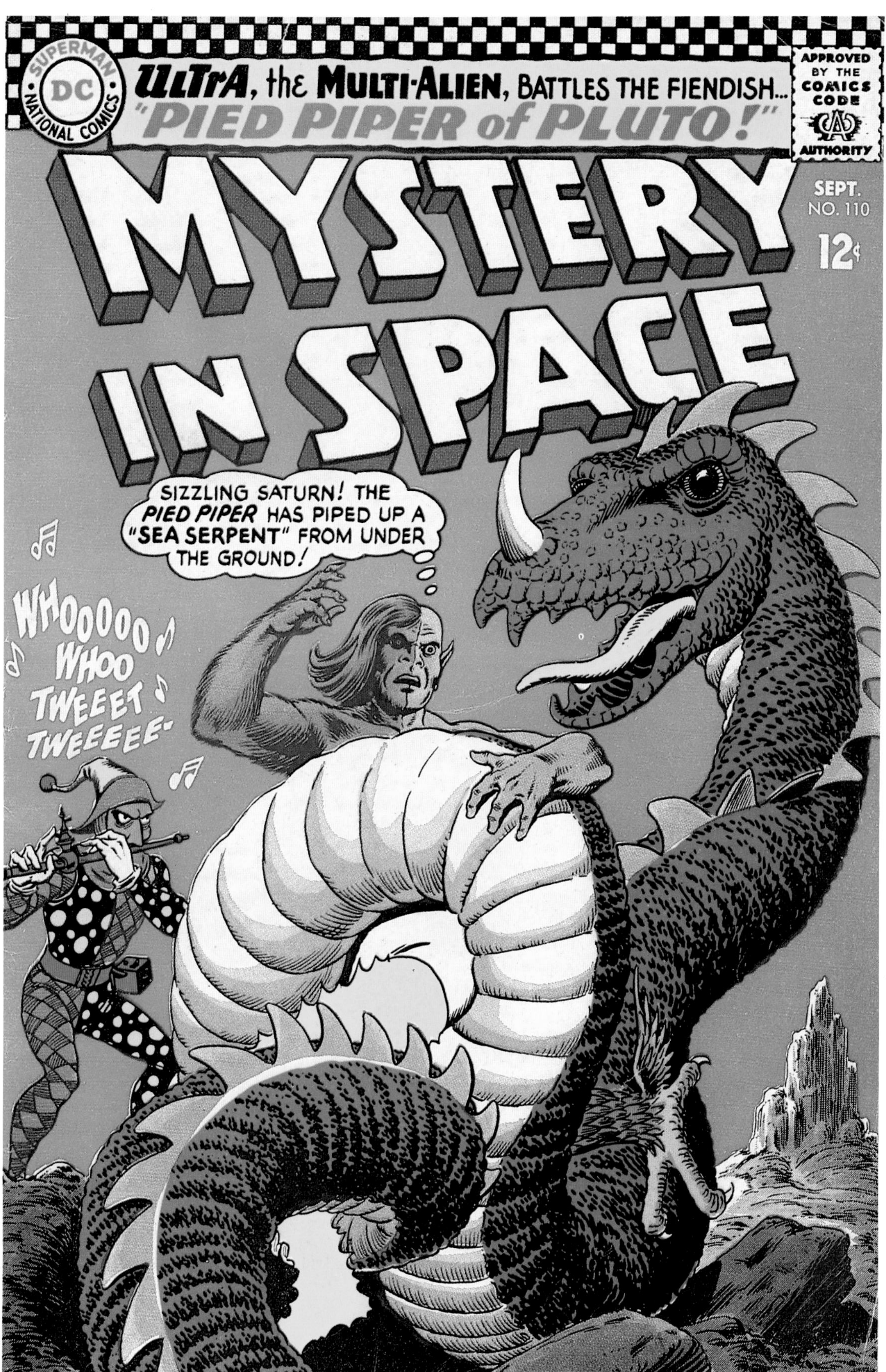

Ultra, the Multi-Alien, snared by a serpent under the command of ***The Pied Piper of Pluto****.* © *DC Comics.*

Emilio Largo *(Adolfo Celi) and his crew of cutthroats in* Thunderball. *Courtesy United Artists.*

Sir Hugo Drax *(Michel Lonsdale) in* Moonraker. *Courtesy United Artists.*

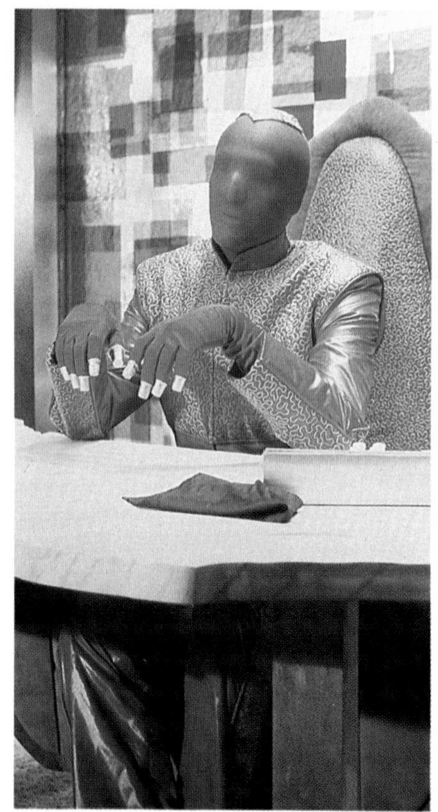

Nino Salvatore Sebastiani. © *Universal Pictures.*

Morgan le Fey *(Helen Mirren) anoints her son Mordred with magic in the film* Excalibur. © *Warner Brothers.*

Atomic Axe or his enormous physical strength, sufficient to rip through a steel vault. He is also impervious to gunfire (though it may be his costume which makes him invulnerable). Pardoned of all crimes by the Legion of Super-Heroes after he helps battle the solar system-threatening menace of the Sun-Eater (see THE CONTROLLER), the Persuader teams with fellow super villains to form THE FATAL FIVE. He currently perpetrates crimes both as a member of the group and as a solo operator.

Quote: "You shouldn't have hounded me off *Jupiter*, Governor! Now you're going to *pay* for that!"

PEW MOGEL (N)

First Appearance: January 1941, "John Carter and the Giant of Mars," *Amazing Stories*, Edgar Rice Burroughs.

Costume: "Gorgeous trappings of platinum and diamonds."

Weapons: Detachable body parts (see Biography); "television machine" to spy on distant cities; sword; radium gun.

Chief Henchman: 130-foot-tall slave giant named Joog.

Biography: Pew Mogel is a synthetic man created by the Martian scientist/surgeon Ras Thavas. As such, he can dismember himself and still function; his eyes can see independent of his body, and his head is fully operational even when severed from his shoulders. For years, the artificial man was a student of Ras Thavas. Then, megalomania got the best of him. Stealing much of the scientist's equipment, he left the city of Morbus, with an army of synthetic men, and resettled in a deserted city on the banks of the Dead Sea at Korvas. Cobbling together Joog from bits and pieces of various Martian races, Pew Mogel hatches a scheme to conquer all of Mars: He plans to construct a race of four-armed soldier apes. All that stands in his way is sufficient iron with which to construct weapons. Thus, he abducts Dejah Thoris, royal princess of the city of Helium and the wife of the warrior hero John Carter, and threatens to dismember her unless the iron works at Helium is turned over to him. Tracking him to his city, Carter lops off Pew Mogel's head; feeling around for it, the creature's body stumbles from a high tower and perishes, and Carter hurls the head after it. ("He could hear the thing shrieking all the way down.") Because of his artificial birth, Pew Mogel is a "misshapen man" with a bullet head, massive shoulders, a "crooked" torso, arms "not equal in length," and one foot larger than the other. He has yellow teeth, thin lips, hollow cheeks and close-set, lidless eyes. Had he survived, another of his top priorities was to build himself a handsome new body.

Quote: "If you have not evacuated all your workers from the iron mines and factories in three days, then I will start sending you the fingers of the Royal Princess of Helium."

Comment: The story is one of two which form the book *John Carter of Mars* (the other is "The Skeleton Men of Jupiter"; see BANDOLIAN).

P'GELL (CS)

First Appearance: October 6, 1946, *The Spirit*, Register and Tribune Syndicate.

Biography: A war orphan, P'Gell became mistress to a Nazi general when she was just 14 years old. ("The old boy liked his olives green and I liked my diamonds big.") They were based in Istanbul where "there was a good market for Nazi generals . . . so I traded him in for a better deal." She continued to move up until she became "quite wealthy . . . selling happiness at inflationary prices," finally marrying Nazi spy Hans Dammt. At war's end, P'Gell turned him over to Emil Petit, a "dealer in men," who sold him to Russia for one million kroner. Marrying Petit, she learned that he was the sole possessor of the valuable Kalkov formula of prolonged life, and had him ambushed by a Turkish gangleader named Picar. When the superhero the Spirit appeared, she lost the formula to him; marrying Picar, she joined his ring of thieves. By the time of her seventh marriage, she had fulfilled a lifelong desire to emigrate to the United States and, marrying one Mr. Raymond, became headmistress of an exclusive girl's school. When he was murdered by a vengeful Picar, P'Gell continued her life of crime, teaming with the likes of the lesbian thief Gerta and the whacky explosives expert Doktor Dekker. However, P'Gell pursued no treasure with greater enthusiasm than she chased the Spirit, with whom she was in love.

Quote: "This sophomoric crimefighter bit is nonsense . . . running around in a mask is just a way of hiding a feeling of *insecurity.*"

Comment: Other villains who populated the adventures of the Spirit include the Black Queen, the strip's first female villain (June 16, 1940), who committed suicide when she was captured in her second appearance; jewel thief Silk Satin (March 1941) who was also in love with the superhero; gangster Sand Saref (January 1950), a tough lady ("I will blow out your murdering brains if you step any closer") who likewise loved the Spirit; E. Launcelot "Lonesome" Cool, a lifelong criminal who peddles inferior construction materials; and ruthless mobster Vino Red.

THE PHANTOM (MP)

Real Name: Oscar.

First Appearance: 1931, *The Phantom of the West,* Mascot Pictures.

Chief Henchmen: The League of the Lawless (not to be confused with THE LAWLESS LEAGUE).

Biography: When strapping young rancher Jim Lester tries to find out who killed his father, the Phantom and his League of the Lawless put the town of Rawton under siege. Anyone who talks is threatened with death. And, indeed, those few who do come forth are murdered. Ultimately, however, Lester discovers that Oscar, a wisecracking eccentric, is the murderous, power-mad Phantom and he's incarcerated.

Comment: Comedian Tom Dugan starred as Oscar, though someone else (uncredited) played the Phantom, who is seen in shadow for most of the 10 chapters in this serial. Ford Beebe wrote the screenplay.

THE PHANTOM OF THE OPERA (N, TV, MP, R, C, S)

Real Name: Erik.

First Appearance: 1908, *The Phantom of the Opera,* Gaston Leroux.

Costume: See Biography.

Weapons: Punjab lasso, among other weapons, used for killing.

Biography: Hideously ugly at birth, Erik ran away from home and briefly joined a carnival as "the living corpse." Moving on and learning magic, ventriloquism, and other skills from Gypsies, he eventually became an entertainer in the court of the Shah of Persia. There, Erik used his skills as "the trapdoor lover" to design a palace which allowed the Shah to move unseen behind walls and under floors, and also helped him to exterminate his enemies. Alas, because he knew the potentate's secrets, Erik was to be executed; however, a friend substituted a corpse for Erik and the future Phantom escaped. In time, making his way to Europe, Erik became a builder and helped to design the Paris Opera House. There, he built for himself "a dwelling unknown to the rest of the earth, where he could hide from men's eyes for all time." Erik's flat was dominated by a drawing room, a guest bedroom, and his own bedroom which was decorated almost entirely in black like "a mortuary chamber." In the middle of the room was a canopy which was hung with red brocade curtains; under the canopy was an open coffin where Erik slept. An organ filled one entire wall, and there was a desk at which Erik practiced his new vocation—composing. His principal project for the next 20 years was an opera entitled *Don Juan Triumphant.* Able to access most areas of the Opera through the catacombs and sundry trapdoors, Erik permitted the performers and the owners of the Opera House to "live in peace." He had only two stipulations: under no condition could they sell his private box (Box 5) and they must pay him an "allowance" of nearly 240,000 francs a year. Physically, Erik "is extraordinarily thin and his dress-coat hangs on a skeleton frame." Beneath his mask, "his eyes are so deep set that you can hardly see the pupils. All you see is two big black holes, as in a dead man's skull. His skin, which is stretched across his bones like a drumhead, is a dirty yellow. He has hardly any nose to speak of and the only hair he has is three or four long dark locks on his forehead and behind the ears." His hand "smelt of death" and he wore a mask "that hid his whole face." Falling in love with singer Christine Daae, Erik began giving her lessons in her room each day through his disembodied "angelic voice" and music. He also killed to further her career. His most dramatic crime occurred when management ignored his warning that if Christine's rival Carlotta went onstage, the diva's "singing will bring the chandelier down"—which it did, "released from its hook" by Erik. Eventually kidnapping Christine—his opera was completed and he wanted "to live like a normal man and have a wife like everybody else"—he was pursued by her lover Raoul de Chagny, who was aided by the man who had saved Erik's life, "the Persian." Erik captured them both, but released all his prisoners after Christine willingly kissed him. He was last seen riding to the Opera in a carriage, after having instructed the lovers to place his death notice in the *Epoque.* The Phantom died peacefully—implicitly, of a broken heart—and his bones were discovered years later beneath the Opera.

Quote: "Feast your eyes, and your soul on my cursed ugliness! Look at Erik's face! Are you satisfied? I'm a good-looking fellow, eh?"

Comment: The character has gained his greatest fame in the movies, played first by Lon Chaney, Sr., in 1925. In that version, he was pursued, beaten, and tossed in the Seine by a mob. (The Opera House set still stands on a soundstage at Universal, a tribute to the star who made the studio great.) Claude Rains (THE INVISIBLE MAN) played the part in 1943, though the origin of the Phantom (now known as Erique Claudin) was changed. He is a violinist and composer who sells his life's work, a piano concerto, so that he can pay for Christine's singing lessons. When the work is rejected (and subsequently stolen) by an unscrupulous publisher, Erique strangles him; the publisher's secretary responds by tossing a pan of acid in the musician's face. Insane from pain and rage, he becomes the Phantom of Leroux's story. In the end, he apparently perishes when gunfire causes the catacombs to collapse. The next Phantom was Herbert Lom (1962) who, as Professor Petrie, haunts the London Opera. He becomes the mad Phantom after his opera is stolen; breaking into the publisher's shop, he is caught in a blaze which he tries to extinguish with acid. Scarred by the liquid, he stumbles into a sewer and is rescued by a dwarf, who thereafter becomes his assistant. Petrie dies saving Christine from a chandelier which the dwarf weakens while crawling among the rafters. A variation on the Leroux theme was Brian De Palma's 1974 film *The Phantom of the Paradise*, in which

Lon Chaney, Sr., as ***THE PHANTOM OF THE OPERA****. © Universal Pictures.*

composer Winslow Leach (William Finley) writes a rock opera based on the Faust legend (see SATAN), only to have it stolen by a rock promoter. Leach breaks into the thief's record plant where, after being wounded by a guard, he stumbles into a record pressing machine where his face is horribly mangled. Later, he haunts the theater where his rock opera is being staged, insisting that his inamorata, Phoenix, be the female lead. Another variation was *The Phantom of Hollywood* (1975), a TV movie starring Jack Cassidy as a former movie idol who was disfigured in an accident. He went about killing people who were trying to destroy the backlot of Worldwide Studios, where he made his home. The most recent screen Phantom was Maximilian Schell, whose Phantom was a Hungarian voice teacher in a 1983 made-for-TV movie. Basil Rathbone played the part on radio in 1943 on *Lux Radio Theatre*, and there have been various stage versions, most notably in 1975 at the Wimbledon Theatre in England. In that production, the theater itself was the set! Edward Petherbridge played the part. Most recently, the Phantom was the subject of a hit Andrew Lloyd Webber musical, *The Phantom of the Opera*. Michael Crawford originated the role in London in 1986, recreating the part on Broadway late in 1987. The character was also transmogrified into the Phantom of the Sewers by writer/artist Jack Kirby for his comic book *The Demon* (#8, 1973). Still dressed in formal attire and a mask, and dwelling in an abode like that of Erik (right down to the organ), the former actor worships his long-lost love Galatea and kidnaps Glenda, a woman who resembles her. He is destroyed and Glenda is rescued by the Demon. The Phantom of the Horse Opera was a cowboy nemesis of the animated cartoon characters *Beany and Cecil*.

THE PHANTOM RULER (MP)

First Appearance: 1950, *The Invisible Monster*, Republic Pictures.

Costume: Robe, cloak, gloves; hood with mesh facemask (colors unknown; film was in black and white). All were chemically treated (see Weapons).

Weapons: Ray which interacts with the clothing to render him invisible; standard firearms.

Biography: The Phantom Ruler is a large-scale criminal who obtains aides by bringing in illegal aliens. Feeling ambitious, he smuggles in a European locksmith, who helps him crack a formidable bank vault; when the locksmith is captured, his fiendish employer murders him so he can't talk. (He often does this to those of his henchmen who are captured, a practice which ultimately leads to his demise.) Though he eludes the law—specifically, insurance investigator Lane—he dies when the police barge into his headquarters and he steps on a live wire, a trap he'd set to electrocute a pair of thugs who'd outlived their usefulness.

Comment: Stanley Price was the Phantom Ruler in the 12-chapter serial. In 1966, the adventures were edited into a feature film entitled *Slaves of the Invisible Monster.*

PHOBIA (C)

Real Name: Angela Hawkins III.

First Appearance: 1981, *The New Teen Titans* #14, DC Comics.

Costume: Light green bodysuit with black shoulders, stripe down chest, "V"-shaped patch over crotch; black neck and hood, gloves, thigh boots; green cloak with high collar and light green lining.

Biography: Angela has the power to instill fear in others simply by willing it. A British aristocrat, she was already insensitive to the needs of others; when, as a child, she found that she had this power, she became positively callous and self-indulgent. Quickly tiring of having her every whim fulfilled, she gladly joined the new BROTHERHOOD OF EVIL when approached by its leader, the evil BRAIN. The Brotherhood partook in many extraordinary battles, not only against the superheroic Teen Titans but also against fellow super villains MADAME ROUGE and BROTHER BLOOD. Unfortunately, after their last defeat at the hands of the Titans, the Brotherhood was virtually disbanded. Phobia, however, remains at large.

Quote: "You have *tasted* the fear-creating powers of *Phobia*—pray I do not decide to let you *feast* on them!"

Comment: Other fear-inducing super villains include BUSHMAN, DR. SPECTRO, D'SPAYRE, MISTER FEAR, PSYCHO-MAN, PSYCHO-PIRATE, and SCARECROW (1).

PHOR TAK (N)

First Appearance: 1930, "A Fighting Man of Mars," *Blue Book* Magazine, Edgar Rice Burroughs.

Costume: Harness "so scant as to leave him almost nude."

Weapons: "The Flying Death," a robot ship which can be sent out to destroy other ships; invisibility paint (used, to great effect, on a cloak of invisibility).

Biography: One of the "red men," the dominant race of Mars (their skin is actually reddish-copper in color), Phor Tak is an old scientist who lives in the nation of Jahar. Inventor of the most powerful weapon on the planet—a raygun which causes metal to disintegrate, as well as a paint which insulates against it—his triumph "aroused the jealousies of other scientists." Their abuse, coupled with the lack of gratitude shown by his patron, monarch TUL AXTAR, compels Phor Tak to flee. Setting up a laboratory in the castle of Jhama, he vows to lash out at his enemies and, in the process, conquer Mars. However, as he is about to kill TUL AXTAR with a disintegration rifle, he is shot through "the centre of his breast" by the brave warrior Tan Hadron of Hastor. Phor Tak has "a finely shaped head, covered with scant, grey locks."

Quote: "The tyrant squeezed me like some juicy fruit and then cast the empty rind aside. He thought it was empty, but . . . he was wrong."

Comment: This was the demented scientist's only appearance. The novel was first serialized in *Blue Book* Magazine from April to September.

THE PIED PIPER (C)

Real Name: Hartley Rathaway. (Note: Mortified by their son's activities, his parents persuaded law officials to book him as "Henry Darrow"; no less embarrased by his family, Hartley often went by the name Thomas Peterson.)

First Appearance: 1959, *The Flash* #106, DC Comics.

Costume: Green minstrel's cap, slippers, jerkin with white polka dots; light green tights; brown belt.

Weapons: Pipes which produce destructive waves, generate impenetrable shells made of "hyper-sonic waves," and hypnotize people. He also has used a device known as the Sonic Boomatron, bagpipes which send out "the concentrated energy-equivalent of 50,000 decibels" and turn any object into pure sound by forcing its "atoms to conform to an involuntary cyclical vibratory pattern." However, his most devastating weapon is the Sonicator, which stores sounds and then plays them back with earthquake-like results.

Biography: The son of wealthy publisher Osgood Rathaway and his wife Hazel, Hartley was born deaf. His father spared no expense to find a cure for the affliction and finally, after years of treatments, a successful operation was performed. Hartley became a fanatic about sounds, studying them constantly and even discovering a sequence of notes which made people bow to his will. (He devised a pipe to compel his tutor to give him good grades, a harmonica to win the ladies, and so on.) Wealthy, bored, and just a little "emotionally disturbed," Hartley decided to turn to crime as the Pied Piper. ("*Of course*!" he realizes, "the constant *danger* of being *caught, wounded* or *killed* while breaking the *law—that's* what's been *missing* from my life!") The Pied Piper did indeed get challenge aplenty; he constantly faces and is beaten by the superheroic Flash.

Quote: "With any luck at all . . . I'll be able to finally *rid* myself of the *two curses* which have plagued my life with the most *pain* and *misery*: my arch-enemy *the Flash*—and my despicable *family*!"

Comment: See other musician super villains THE FIDDLER, THE MAESTRO, and THE PIED PIPER OF PLUTO.

THE PIED PIPER OF PLUTO (C)

First Appearance: 1966, *Mystery in Space* #110, DC Comics.

Costume: Patchwork costume consisting of blue with white spots (left leg of tights, right side of bodyshirt, left arm); green and black checkers (right leg, arm, left side of bodyshirt); red slippers, belt; yellow jester's cap with green brim; green cowl.

Weapons: "Versatile electronic flute" which plays a "brain-enslaving tune" that can hypnotize any and all creatures; "aerosol energy spray" which forms an "impenetrable force-field" around the Piper; "dimension compass" for navigating through the dimensions; "super-disruptor charge," a monumentally powerful antimatter bomb.

Chief Henchmen: Blaster-toting, yellow-skinned thugs in red bodysuits.

Biography: Also referred to as the Pluto Piper, this extraterrestrial began his criminal career in his unnamed native solar system, where his "nuclear fleet" of saucers was smashed by the Meson Ray of the defending worlds. Defeated everywhere, he left his universe and came to our dimension. Finding a beautiful but uninhabited world, he decided to populate it with "scientists, farmers, mechanics, all the rest that are needed to build civilization." Leaving it and warping to Pluto, he used his flute to draw the colonists into his ship. Enter the superheroic Ultra the Multi-Alien, who managed to rescue the captives just before the Piper sealed the dimensional tunnel with the super-disruptor charge. Ironically, the antimatter detonation stranded the Piper alone on his world forever.

Quote: "My . . . flute will now play . . . a 'nesting call' . . . that lures the *flying sword-beaks*, the worst vulture species known! *Ultra* will soon look like a roast on a spit! Ha, ha!"

Comment: A quartet of super villains were responsible for originally giving Ultra his powers. Captain Ace Arn of Earth, he was struck simultaneously by rayblasts from the guns of four alien crooks. The combined blasts turn him into a hybrid of his attackers, with the superpowers of each. Other fiends faced by the metamorphosed Arn are the energy-ball flinging Energy Eaters of Venus; the three-eyed alien Dr. Taxo, who invented a will-sapping mist; Dr. Dynamo and his de-molecularizer, which allowed him to break down stolen goods for easy transportation; and Jal-Rel, an evil Venusian who stole a hotel from Mars (complete with patrons) and held it for ransom. See other musician super villains THE FIDDLER, THE MAESTRO, and THE PIED PIPER.

PIGEON PERSON (A)

First Appearance: 1977, Hostess Cupcake Ads.

Costume: Red bodysuit with arms, legs, and feet covered by white feathers.

Weapons: Large white wings for flight.

Chief Henchmen: An army of super-powered pigeons.

Biography: Nothing is known about this character's past, save that her mission in life is to steal every statue in America. Using her birds to carry off the Statue of Liberty, she finally has only one monument left—Mt. Rushmore. Fortunately, as she launches her attack, the superheroes Batman and Robin (whom she disdains as an "imitation bird" and chastises soundly for referring to her as Pigeon Woman) manage to distract the birds with Hostess cupcakes and simultaneously cast a net around the villainess.

Quote: "I can't blame my pigeons . . . even a bird brain knows that a Hostess Cup Cake in the beak is worth any two statues in the street."

Comment: This one-page ad, told in comic book style, marked the character's only appearance. Other villains who appeared in this series and battled a variety of DC and Marvel superheroes include Topsy-Turvy Man who "has the ability to turn things upsidedown"; the Muse, who uses his synthesizer to transform people into musical notes (except while he is feasting on cup cakes whose "chocolate flavor and fudgy icing make me feel like singing"); the Cup Cake Crooks; Golddigger, who is entirely gold, packs a blaster, and has the "power to make himself intangible" so he can't be nabbed; the ice-making Icemaster; the powerful android Torgo; the flamethrowing Hotshot; Hy Torque, who drives a souped-up car that can knock over virtually anything "as easy as an ordinary car knocks over a trash can"; the Ricochet Monster, whose body repels anything thrown at it (though he succumbs to the delicious taste of Hostess Fruit Pies [apple and cherry]). Also, the armored, axe-swinging Battleaxe; Ralph G. Fake, "the criminal lawyer with the ability to change himself into Legal Eagle," a megalomaniac with wings, feathers, and talons; the Human Computer, a man wearing armor and a computer helmet that allows him to outsmart anyone; Frizone who, like MISTER FREEZE, needs cold to live and, using a snow-spewing biplane, begins deep-freezing the countryside; the Roller Disco Devils, who roam the streets using ghettoblasters to annoy people (the superheroic Hulk "not like loud noise" and literally wraps the street around the punks); the unnamed "evil mind" who sends forth an armored flunky to commit crimes; the Phoomie Goonies, terrorists of a "revolutionary government"; Demolition Derby, a man who can destroy objects by flinging his derby at them (similar to that of Oddjob [see AURIC GOLDFINGER, Comment]); Phae-Dor, an extraterrestrial Kree who wants to conquer the earth. Also, Gudrun the Golden, who wants to "gather unto myself all that is gold so it may reflect back mine glory"; Madame Web, a costumed web-spinner who commits crimes in order to frame Spider-Man for daring to spurn her love (she is unrelated to the clairvoyant Madame Web who also appears in the Spider-Man comic books); Jet-Set Jessie, a superspeed jewel thief; the Destroyer who uses apparently magical powers to destroy things in order to make "everybody . . . miserable and unhappy like me"; Golden Raven who can fly and commands an army of falcons who swoop and soar "like a squad of feathered warplanes"; Tara Cobal and Fortran, scientific geniuses who are using computers to destroy weather satellites, thus forcing all TV stations to come to them for the weather forecast; the Vacuum Vulture, a mortal man who rides around in a tank-like vacuum and uses it to steal. Also, the red-costumed Midnight Ladies, who steal furs, black pearls, caviar, oil—"anything dark and valuable"; Dr. Sorcery, who uses the magic philosopher's stone to cause deadly mischief, such as weakening the steel beams of a bridge during a marathon "to make the race more challenging"; the Chocolate Baron, "a crook whose love of chocolaty goodness has led him to monopolize everything chocolate"; the evil K-9, a man in a dog suit who uses an ultrasonic dog whistle to attract pedigreed dogs and then hold them for ransom; the Borrower, a man who can get anything he wants simply by handing people IOUs (which are presumably enchanted in some way); Professor Plutonium who, in a scheme reminiscent of that of the earlier Auric Goldfinger, is going to destroy all of America's gold reserves by bombing Fort Knox ("If I can't have it, I'll destroy it!"). Also, Mr. Foxx, who is kidnapping the great chefs of Gotham City in order to eat well and collect ransoms (for which he never does return the chefs); Crime Director, a filmmaker who uses props from movies he is making to commit crimes; Flame Thrower, an arsonist who uses a super-flamethrower to cause fires; Johnny Punk, a rock star who uses "mega-pitch" high-frequency sound waves to enslave those who attend his concerts; Impercepto, a "malevolent alien" who needs gold for energy and can become invisible; the Rhinos, huge tanklike vehicles which are impervious to all weapons (though the drivers, apparently belonging to a paramilitary group, are not impervious to the allure of Twinkies); and unnamed villains who use a super-tank to crash the gates of Stark Industries and try to take over the plant. THE PENGUIN and THE FLY have also appeared in the ads.

PIRANHA (C)

First Appearance: 1974, *Sub-Mariner* #70, Marvel Comics.

Costume: Purple bodysuit; red gloves, boots, fishtail-shaped vest. Face is red with fish-like mouth and fins radiating from side of head.

Chief Henchmen: Piranha can command all other fish and fish-mutants.

Biography: Years ago, the superheroes Sub-Mariner and Spider-Man battled the Aquanoids. This race of "Men-Fish" was the result of genetic tinkering done to fish by the evil Lemuel Dorcas at his undersea base. (The villains ORKA and TIGER SHARK were also the handiwork of Dorcas.) When, in the course of battle, the base was destroyed, the surrounding waters were contaminated with radiation from its equipment (*Marvel Team-Up* #14, 1973). Caught in this mutagenic cloud was a piranha. "I took its power at *full strength*," he said later, "and . . . I began to *change*." Becoming humanoid with a great intellect, he was also "filled with hate" for Sub-Mariner. Using his telepathic control over other fish, Piranha ordered them to enter the cloud and thus created his own army of Men-Fish. However, he was not quite up to slaying Sub-Mariner. During their battle he was wounded, his blood seeping into the sea and attracting his own carnivorous, non-mutated piranhas, who devoured him (#71).

Quote: "My *pets* will only begin to *devour* you—the final feast will be reserved for *me*!"

Comment: See other underwater super villains ATTUMA, BLACK MANTA, CAPTAIN NEMO, CAPTAIN WHALE, DR. FANG, FISHERMAN, KILLER SHARK, KRANG, MR. CRABB, OCEAN MASTER, ORKA, and TIGER SHARK (2).

PISTOLS SCARAMANGA (N, MP)

First Appearance: 1965, *The Man With the Golden Gun*, Ian Fleming.

Weapons: Gold-plated Colt .45.

Biography: A crack-shot, the impotent Pistols relieves his tensions by murdering people. An assassin-for-hire, he works largely in the Caribbean and Central America at the behest of the KGB. He also controls a gang of terrorists who ply their dirty work for the advancement of communism. Secret agent James Bond is sent to kill the assassin, who is identifiable not only because of his unique gun but also because he has three nipples. Bond eventually corners him on a train in Jamaica, where the agent's colleague Felix Leiter plants an explosive which derails them; pursuing Scaramanga into a marsh, Bond guns him down.

Quote: "I always thought I liked animals. Then I discovered I liked killing people more."

Comment: *The Man With the Golden Gun* was the last James Bond novel. Unfinished at the time of the author's death, it is sketchy in terms of plot and characterization. In the 1974 motion picture, Christopher Lee (CAPTAIN RAMESES, DRACULA) plays a remarkably different Scaramanga. "Francisco" Scaramanga is the son of a circus ringmaster (father) and a snake charmer. Orphaned at an early age, be becomes a trick shot at the carnival; by the time he's 15, he is plying his talent in a criminal direction. Taken in by the KGB, he becomes an assassin; he goes independent in the late 1950s. Settling down on an island in Red Chinese waters, he pays his rent by doing "favors" for the communists. In the film, he uses stolen secrets to construct a solar-powered generator which not only will make him the world's energy czar, but also provide him with a fantastic destruction ray. Tracked down by Bond, Scaramanga is shot to death while hunting Bond a la COUNT ZAROFF. The island itself explodes when a thug is knocked into the generator's coolant, causing it to malfunction. In addition to his solar ray and golden gun, the movie Scaramanga has a car which turns into an airplane. Lee, incidentally, is a distant relative of author Fleming, and was one of the actors originally in the running to play DR. NO. Other notorious criminals in the Bond novels are brothers Jack and Seraffimo Spang of the diamond-smuggling Spangled Mob in *Diamonds Are Forever* (1956); assassin Red Grant and Russian agent Rosa Klebb—who's armed with poison-coated knitting needles and a similarly toxic knife hidden in her shoe—in *From Russia, With Love* (1957); killer von Hammerstein in the short story "For Your Eyes Only" (1960); drug smuggler Kristatos in the short story "Risico" (1960); gangsters Horror and Sluggsy who terrorize a New York resort in *The Spy Who Loved Me* (1962); thief and killer Major Dexter Amythe in the short story "Octopussy" (1966); the assassin Trigger in the short story "The Living Daylights" (1966); and KGB agent Maria Freudenstein in the short story "The Property of a Lady" (1966).

***PISTOLS SCARAMANGA** (Christopher Lee) in* The Man with the Golden Gun. *Courtesy United Artists.*

PLANTMAN (C)

Real Name: Sam Smithers.

First Appearance: 1963, *Strange Tales* #113, Marvel Comics.

Costume: Original: green bodysuit, full-face cowl, cape; light green trunks, eyemask (like leaves joined at the stems), gloves and boots with leaf-like fringe. Second: dark green cowl, bodysuit with leaf-like decorations on shoulders; light green boots and gloves with leaf-fringing, trunks, leaf-like mask which surrounds face but does not cover it.

Weapons: Guns which accelerate the growth of plants, mutate them (i.e., to fire deadly thorns), and enable Plantman to will them to do what he wishes—even if it's against their nature (i.e., strangle people or grow to giant size). Plantman has also used a submarine for underwater experiments.

Chief Henchmen: Slave-automatons made of tree bark; Leviathan, a monster made of seaweed.

Biography: Working for a decade as an assistant to a renowned English botanist, Smithers came to the United States when his employer died. Here, he attempted to continue the research in which he'd been involved overseas: to boost the IQ of plants so that humans can communicate with them. Decried for his improbable plans as well as his lack of a college degree, Smithers went to work as a gardener for Long Islander Morris Evans. Dismissed because he'd been performing experiments instead of his duties, Smithers was delighted when a lighting bolt struck a plant gun on which he'd been working, and empowered it with the ability to bend all flora to the wielder's will. Becoming the costumed Plantman, he immediately sought vengeance against Evans. However, Evans' daughter happened to be the flame of the Human Torch, and the superhero not only nipped Plantman's plot in the bud but also destroyed his gun. Fleeing and building a new weapon, Plantman has continued to battle not only the Torch but also the Avengers and the Sub-Mariner.

Comment: See other plant-controlling villains FLORONIC MAN and THE THORN.

PLASMUS (C)

Real Name: Otto Von Furth.

First Appearance: 1981, *The New Teen Titans* #14, DC Comics.

Costume: Black trunks (Plasmus's skin is pink and clay-like).

Biography: Working a mine in East Berlin, Otto and four other miners were trapped in a cave-in. For a week the quintet was bathed in the radioactive rays of the radium they had been mining; all but Otto perished. When he was finally saved, the German was abducted from the hospital by the evil General Zahl (formerly Captain Zahl; see MADAME ROUGE). A captive in Zahl's laboratory, Otto was given a battery of chemicals which, in tandem with the radiation, resulted in a grotesque metamorphosis. He became a humanoid mass incapable of being stopped by fists or projectiles, while at the same time his touch became deadly. Recruited by the evil BRAIN for his reformed BROTHERHOOD OF EVIL, Otto—as Plasmus—helped to battle the New Teen Titans while also seeking to destroy Zahl for what he had done to him. Though Zahl is dead, Plasmus is still chockful of anger and remains a super villain.

Quote: "Der fool has been reduced to a protoplasmic *blob!* He deserved nothing more!"

PLASTIQUE (C)

First Appearance: 1982, *Fury of Firestorm* #7, DC Comics.

Costume: Purple bodysuit with light blue fringe on high collar, inverted light blue arrow-like symbol on chest; light blue gloves, boots, with three horizontal black stripes on the latter, two on the former.

Weapons: Plastic explosives affixed to costume.

Biography: A terrorist supporting the cause of French Canadian separatism, Plastique (her real name is never revealed) attacked both Canadian and American sites to advance her cause. Dropping by the editorial offices of the New York *News Express* one day, she ordered the paper to give up its mills in Quebec or she would destroy the building. When the superhero Firestorm arrived on the scene, he used his nuclear abilities to disintegrate her clothes, not only spoiling her plan but also mortifying her. Plastique was arrested, but her underhanded lawyer snuck her a compound developed by the mysterious Doctor at the behest of Plastique's colleagues; injecting her, the attorney gave his client the power to fire destructive blasts from her fingers. Busting out of prison, she teamed with KILLER FROST and had her freeze Niagara Falls while Plastique attempted to destroy the vital power plant there. But Firestorm arrived and, while his superheroic associate Firehawk took on Killer Frost, he caused Plastique to render herself unconscious from the concussion of one of her own blasts. Both super villains are presently incarcerated.

THE PLUNDERER (C)

Real Name: Lord Edgar Parnival Plunder; also referred to as Captain Plunder.

First Appearance: 1966, *Daredevil* #12, Marvel Comics.

Costume: Originally wore a pirate costume (#'s 12-13), briefly donned a bodysuit, cape, and cowl (#14), then discarded all for a leather jacket, jodhpurs, and boots.

Weapons: "Vibra-ray" guns which cause metal to fall apart.

Chief Henchmen: Feepers, his butler; Boswell, a spy; Slagg, his first mate; other nameless pirates.

Biography: A scientist, Lord Robert Plunder was on an expedition in Antarctica when he found a lost jungle known as the Savage Land; there he discovered a substance which he dubbed the Anti-Metal, an isotope of Vibranium which disintegrates metal. Upon his return to England, he learned that his wife Blanche had died. To make matters worse, word of his discovery had gotten around, and foreign agents came after him to try and learn the Anti-Metal's secret location. Rescued by his butler Willis, Robert realized the spies will not give up and decided to separate his sons and keep on the move. He took Kevin to the Savage Land, while butler Willis set sail with Parnival ("Edgar" is seldom used). Years later, Parnival was able to use some of his family fortune to pay off those who were chasing him and he returned to England. Living at Castle Plunder, he studied and became a top scientist and engineer. However, Parnival's real goal was to become a world criminal power; for that, he required the Anti-Metal. An adequate sample lay in a vault at the castle, but there was no way he could open it. His father had given him only half the key, leaving the other half with Kevin. Since Parnival had only cryptic clues as the whereabouts of the Savage Land, he decided to become a modern-day pirate and roam the seas until he found it . . . and his brother. Finally arriving, he discovered that his father had died and Kevin had become the jungle hero Ka-Zar. Undaunted by his powerful sibling, he snatched Ka-Zar's portion of the key and headed for home. Over the years he repeatedly tried to take over the world using the Anti-Metal. But each time he was stopped by superheroes such as Daredevil (his first nemesis), Spider-Man, the Hulk, and even Ka-Zar. He apparently perished in *Ka-Zar the Savage* #33 (1984). Having fallen in love with the jungle heroine Shanna, he was battling Ka-Zar on the deck of an icebreaker when the criminal crew started shooting at Shanna. Plunder broke away from the fight long enough to run over and push Shanna out of danger (Ka-Zar busying himself with the gunmen). In the process, Plunder fell overboard and drowned. (His limp body is visible beneath the ice . . . though, knowing comic book super villains, it's possible he was recovered and revived. That tale remains to be told.)

Quote: "You baboons! How could you let the mine shaft cave in? This'll set my schedule back days!"

POISON IVY (C)

Real Name: Pamela Lillian Isley.

First Appearance: 1966, *Batman* #181, DC Comics.

Costume: Green boots, leotard covered with leaves; light green tights with dark green leaves down side (on occasion she has worn only a leaf-covered bikini instead of tights and a leotard); leaf headband, necklace, bracelets.

Weapons: Lipstick containing drug which hypnotizes anyone she kisses; poison darts fired from bracelets; the Energizer, a hand-held device which causes plants to obey her commands; and a vine which, when thrown around people, automatically chokes them to death.

Chief Henchmen: See Biography.

Biography: A brilliant botany student from Seattle, Pamela fell in love with one of her professors, Marc LeGrand, an unmitigated heel. Anxious to get hold of a museum's rare herb from ancient Egypt—an urnful which would help him in his research—he persuaded Pamela to help, then poisoned her to prevent her from ever turning on him. Instead of dying, Pamela became immune to all poison; having done so well at the museum, she became Poison Ivy (derived from her initials) and committed herself to a life of crime. Among her most noteworthy crimes—all of which were thwarted by her nemesis, Batman—were turning her devoted chauffeur Ivor into a towering, equally devoted plant monster (*Batman* #344) and growing an army of moss-beasts (*Batman* #367). She belongs to THE SECRET SOCIETY OF SUPER-VILLAINS.

Quote: "*Money talks* in this world, Big Jack. And by *noon* today, *Poison Ivy* will speak with a very *loud* voice, indeed!"

THE POPPY (MP)

Real Name: Madame Ying Su.

First Appearance: 1931, *Chinatown After Dark*, Action Pictures Corp.

Chief Henchmen: Sundry thugs.

Biography: A master thief and murderer based in San Francisco, the Poppy lives in an apartment with a secret passage to the street; she leaves a poppy beside the bodies of her victims. In the film, she's trying to obtain a rare dagger. She and her gang are stopped by Detective Horatio Dooley.

Comment: Carmel Myers played the Poppy in her only screen appearance; Betty Burbidge wrote the film. See also THE DRAGON LADY and THE DRAGON QUEEN.

POWDER POUF (CS)

First Appearance: January 4, 1948, *The Spirit*, Register and Tribune Syndicate.

Biography: Arrested for murder but released for lack of evidence, Powder immediately slugs her guard, smashes a jeweler's head against concrete (subsequently kicking him), hits her old boyfriend Nick with a drill and pushes him into a garbage truck ("When Nick wakes up, he'll find himself in the city incinerator. If the garbage people burn him up, is that *my* fault?"), and allies herself with a new young thug named Bleak—whom she promptly frames for robbery. Luckily, the superhero The Spirit is able to clear him and put Powder behind bars. But she doesn't remain there for long, and tangles frequently with The Spirit.

Quote: "Lay a finger on me and I'll spill your liver all over the sidewalk."

Comment: According to the strip, Powder's first name drives from "gunpowder." Other sinister Spirit "vamps" were Lorelei Rox, Autumn Mews, Wisp O'Smoke, and Plaster of Paris.

POWER RING (C)

First Appearance: 1964, *Justice League of America* #29, DC Comics.
Costume: Green domino mask, bodysuit with inverted white triangle on chest and green star inside; white gloves, boots (boots are sometimes light green).
Weapons: Green ring which can create and animate any object his mind can conceive.
Biography: Like his fellow members of the CRIME SYNDICATE, POWER RING lived on Earth-3, a world virtually identical to ours, existing in a parallel dimension. Meeting the insane Buddhist monk Volthoom, Power Ring (his real name was never revealed) was given his magic ring. Joining with other superbeings, he plundered the planet at will—occasionally venturing to our own world to rob here as well (most notably in *The Secret Society of Super-Villains* #13, 1978). Ironically, he and his fellow Syndicate members died in a futile attempt to *save* Earth-3 from destruction at the hands of the ANTI-MONITOR (*Crisis on Infinite Earths* #1, 1985).
Comment: This villain's powers were identical (and his costume nearly-so) to the superhero Green Lantern. THE CALCULATOR can also will animate objects to appear.

THE PRANKSTER (C)

Real Name: Oswald Loomis.
First Appearance: 1942, *Action Comics* #51, DC Comics.
Costume: Green pinstripe suit; white shirt; red bow tie with white polka dots; orange hat with a diagonally-striped green, white, and black hatband; brown shoes with white spats.
Weapons: Among the Prankster's vast arsenal of often deadly tricks are a flute-gun, ink-dissolving gas (which he uses on United States currency, buying the inkless bills at a cut-rate price using coins—then restoring the original printed matter, thus reaping a fortune), a flying car, a blimp in his own likeness, teargas peashooters, youth elixir from the Fountain of Youth which he uses to turn Superman into an infant (fortunately, the Baby of Steel discovers that sugar is the antidote), and super laughing-gas which forces others to play practical jokes.
Chief Henchmen: Al Fresco, who was briefly his "understudy" ("I need an understudy . . . so I can concentrate on executive problems"); also various flunkies.
Biography: Dubbed the "clown king of the underworld," the Prankster and his crew burst upon the scene by entering two banks and forcing the patrons within to *accept* money (money they stole in a series of petty crimes). Their actions are well-publicized, so when they appear at a third bank the manager is happy to admit them—at which point they rob him blind. Superman intervenes and the Prankster is believed dead when he escapes into a cavern and is caught in a cave-in. But he survives and returns over and over to commit crimes and lethal practical jokes. Perhaps the Prankster's most inspired crimes are sponsoring a contest wherein children were to write about Superman's escapades, thus making it impossible for him to go anywhere without being mobbed and hindered; and infiltrating the United States copyright office, establishing a copyright on the alphabet, and insisting on a royalty. (And a handsome one, at that; just one newspaper, the *Daily Planet*, is charged $2000 a week [in 1943 dollars] for permission to use the English language.) The Prankster has used many aliases over the years, among them Mr. Van Prank, Mr. Prank Ster, Colonel P.R. Ankster, and Ajax Wilde.
Quote: "*Superman* is invulnerable to bullets, explosives, acid and all other means of destruction! By ridiculing him before the public, we can laugh him out of *Metropolis*!"
Comment: See a similar villain, THE JOKER.

THE PRAYING MANTIS MAN (C)

Real Name: Hunter Mann.
First Appearance: 1965, *Blue Beetle*, Vol. 2, #4, Charlton Comics.
Costume: Original: green praying mantis "skin" over his own. Second: brown armor, helmet with green "eyes" on top.
Weapons: Carbon dioxide Frigi-gun to freeze objects in their tracks.
Chief Henchman: Ant #119, his lab assistant.
Biography: Green-skinned because he became "saturated in chlorophyll," Mann hates all of humankind because they "rejected me, laughed at me, called me hideous when my skin . . . turned green." Intending to destroy civilization, he uses a combination of chlorophyll, xanthophyll, and carotin to breed colonies of giant insects, from ants to wasps to dragonflies (which he rides), musing, "It was only a matter of time until certain species such as the army ants, conquered the world. I am merely accelerating

evolution." The difference, of course, is that "the insects I created will obey me." He plans to use the wasps to sting people to death, giant termites to eat cities, and so on. After several ill-fated battles with the superheroic Blue Beetle, the Praying Mantis Man is last seen plunging to his death when the dragonfly he is riding is enveloped with insecticide. (Though the villain calls to the airborne hero for help, the retreating Blue Beetle rather callously shouts over his shoulder, "Don't have time . . . I've got better people to save.")

Quote: "You will enjoy the rare privilege of seeing your world destroyed."

Comment: The insect-man's fatal fall occurred in *Blue Beetle* Vol. 3, #53 (1965). Other Blue Beetle villains include the Giant Mummy, which was resurrected by nuclear blasts; the conquest-hungry lightning master Mr. Thunderbolt from the planet Uxer; Dr. Jeremiah Clubb, who houses his own mind in the body of his mighty robot Mentor the Magnificent; Magno Man, whose gadgets give him the power to cause earthquakes (Magno Man was actually archaeologist Dr. Louis Forte, who was furious with the Blue Beetle for having pointed out that a skull he'd found wasn't prehistoric because it had a dental filling); and the Eye of Horus, a sentient orb from Ancient Egypt which turns people into its hawk-headed slaves.

THE PREDATOR (C)

Real Name: Carol Ferris.

First Appearance: 1984, *Green Lantern* #178, DC Comics. (Note: See STAR SAPPHIRE for earlier Ferris appearances.)

Costume: Black bodysuit with chrome shoulderpads that form a "V" down his chest and back; black and chrome horizontally-striped boots and gloves (see Weapons); chrome helmet with red eyepieces.

Weapons: Gloves and boots have sharp claws; chrome wings under arms for flight and to use as a shield against bullets; axe; dagger; rope (for swinging).

Biography: After being forced from the top spot at Ferris Aircraft by her father (who felt himself better equipped to stave-off impending financial disaster), and simultaneously losing her lover Hal Jordan for an extended period (secretly the superhero Green Lantern, he had left on a lengthy mission), young Carol Ferris snapped—literally. She not only became the criminal Star Sapphire once more, but also separated into two beings, the second being the male (i.e., more aggressive) Predator. Using Carol's business savvy to set up Intercontinental Petroleum and trying to take over Ferris Aircraft—helped along by committing strategic murders now and then—the Predator even began wooing Carol! However, during a battle with Green Lantern the Predator merged again with Carol. He has not been seen since.

Quote: "I'll *not* use my *claws* on you—but then, I really don't *need* them against prey of *your* meager caliber!"

Comment: The MR. HYDE nature of the character is not nearly so unique or interesting as the psychosexual implications of the Carol/Predator romance.

PRIMUS (C)

First Appearance: 1977, *Captain America* #209, Marvel Comics.

Costume: Whitish-gold trunks.

Chief Henchman: Doughboy, who is even more malleable than Primus.

Biography: Primus was created by ARNIM ZOLA, the scientist responsible for HATE-MONGER. A bioengineered humanoid created at Zola's castle in Switzerland, Primus has superstrength as well as the capacity to harden or soften his body and to adopt any shape he wishes. Turning against Zola when the scientist attempts to conduct research on a woman with whom Primus has fallen in love, the artificial man flees with another Zola creation, Doughboy; Zola is in no position to pursue, being locked in combat with Captain America at his burning stronghold. Together, the pliable people team with the second BARON ZEMO. Capturing Captain America, Zemo holds him prisoner while Primus assumes the hero's likeness and sullies his good name; he also falls in love with the hero's girlfriend Bernadette Rosenthal, with whom he hopes to father a race of superior beings. Captain America escapes and, after a titanic struggle, Primus beats him; however, the clay-like megalomaniac retreats when Bernie professes her love for Captain America and not for Primus. Zola's creation has not been seen since.

PRINCESS ASA (MP)

First Appearance: 1960, *Black Sunday*, American International Pictures.

Chief Henchman: Javuto, her lover.

Biography: Early in the seventeenth century, in the Balkan country of Moldavia, Princess Asa of the House of Vaida is charged with witchcraft and sentenced to die by her brother, the Grand Inquisitor of an Inquisition. She is killed along with her lover and colleague Javuto when a spike-lined mask is hammer-ed onto her face; however, before she dies, Asa swears vengeance on her brother's heirs. As it happens, Asa is not only a witch but also a vampire and she simply hibernates in her coffin for two centuries. When she and Javuto awake, Asa hypnotically enslaves a local physician, Dr. Choma, who drains blood from one of her brother's descendants, the prince of Vaida, and uses it to nourish Asa. Regaining her strength, Asa has Javuto murder the prince's son Constantine, then plots to completely revitalize herself by sucking the spirit from the body of the prince's daughter Katia, who is a deadringer for Asa. Drawing Katia to her tomb, she is about to make the withdrawal when the villagers, led by Dr. Gorobec, a colleague of Dr. Choma, storm the vault and burn Asa to death.

***PRINCESS ASA** (Barbara Steele) her face scarred from the spiked mask in* Black Sunday. *© American International Pictures.*

Comment: Barbara Steele starred as Asa, Arturo Dominici as Javuto. The film was made in Italy, where it was known as *La Maschera Del Demonio* (*The Mask of the Demon*). The scenario is *very* loosely based on Nikolai Gogol's short story "Vij," published in his collection *Mirgorod* in 1835. In that tale, a young philosopher, Homa, kills a witch who tries to seduce him. Later, he goes to a convocation of demons at a church where the sorceress is revived; performing a rite of exorcism, he keeps the "gnomes" at the church until dawn, and they perish. Another witch alluded to in the tale both turns into a dog and sucks human blood; in her natural form she "was all blue and her eyes glowing like coals." Other especially nasty movie witches include Flora Carr, a professor's wife who uses witchcraft to further her husband's career (until she's crushed beneath a massive gargoyle) in *Burn, Witch, Burn* (1962, based on Fritz Leiber's 1953 novel *Conjure Wife*); Curwen (Vincent Price; see DR. PHIBES and THE INVISIBLE MAN) who, in *The Haunted Palace* (1963), is burned at the stake in 1765 and, possessing his grandson Ward through an enchanted portrait, wreaks vengeance on the village until the painting is burned; Vanessa Whitlock of *Witchcraft* (1964), who rises from her grave when the Whitlock family cemetery is disturbed by construction workers; seventeenth-century Lavinia Morley (again, Barbara Steele) who, through twentieth-century J.D. Morley (Chirstopher Lee), is lashing out at the descendants of those who burned her in *The Crimson Cult* (1968); and *Simon, King of the Witches* (1971), who lives in a storm drain and, between blood sacrifices, puts a curse on the city when his home is washed away. While there are countless other witches in fiction, not all of them are quite this evil or demonstrably tied to SATAN; even Little Goody Two-Shoes was arrested for practicing witchcraft when she made a weather forecast using a barometer in John Newbery's children's story *The History of Little Goody Two-Shoes* (published in 1765). See also THE WITCH OF THE WEST.

PRINCESS MARCUZAN (MP)

First Appearance: 1965, *Frankenstein Meets the Space Monster*, Allied Artists.

Costume: Black metallic-fabric bodysuit, Egyptian-style headdress.

Weapons: Powerful and ferocious monster Mull.

Chief Henchman: Nadir.

Biography: Because of a nuclear war on Mars, the Martian population has been severely depleted. Under the command of Princess Marcuzan, a spaceship is dispatched to earth to steal women. Attacking the spaceship of robot astronaut Frank Reynolds, which was headed for the Red Planet, the Martians send it crashing to earth, leaving the android burned and scarred . . . and mad. He attacks the Martians, battles Mull, frees the kidnapped earth women, then blows up the ship.

Comment: Marilyn Hanold starred as Marcuzan, Lou Cutell as Nadir. Other films in which evil aliens regard our world as a singles bar include *The Mysterians* (1959), from the planet Mysteroid; *Blood Beast from Outer Space* (1965; based on Frank Crisp's novel *The*

Nadir (Lou Cutell), chief henchman of ***PRINCESS MARCUZAN*** *in* Frankenstein Meets the Space Monster. *© Vernon-Senaca Films.*

Night Callers), in which Mr. Medra gets girls by advertising in *Bikini Girl* magazine, then promptly ships them to Jupiter's war-depleted moon Ganymede; and *Mars Needs Women* (1966), with former Disney child star Tommy Kirk as the leader of the Martians.

PRINCESS PYTHON (C)

Real Name: Zelda DuBois.

First Appearance: 1965, *The Amazing Spider-Man* #22, Marvel Comics.

Costume: Scaly green bodysuit; darker green leotard with leaf-like trim.

Chief Henchman: Twenty-five-feet-long python.

Biography: Nothing is known about this character or how she came about her remarkable talent for snake-charming. Joining THE CIRCUS OF CRIME, she helps rob the audience after THE RINGMASTER has put them in a trance. Unlike most of the circus members, Princess Python has an independent streak and occasionally commits crimes on her own; during one such venture she battles the superhero Iron Man and her snake perishes in a tub of acid. Princess Python is so distraught she tries to hurl herself in as well, but the hero saves her. The villain is in shock for months; when she snaps out of it she doesn't go back to the Circus but, with her new pet python, joins THE SERPENT SQUAD and partakes in international extortion and piracy; when that group is smashed by Captain America she returns briefly to the Circus and then spends a short period with THE SERPENT SOCIETY. She is presently in hiding, though where is not known.

PROFESSOR DEATH (C)

Real Name: Professor Hannibal Burns.

First Appearance: 1975, *John Targitt . . . Man-Stalker* #3, Atlas Comics.

Costume: Navy blue cloak with high collar (cloak is red on cover); purple-blue bodysuit (green on cover).

Weapons: Death-13, a nerve gas, which he dispenses from human skulls (each skull carrying 1.03 grams); "Charon's Chariot," his yacht.

Chief Henchmen: Ralph and other flunkies.

Biography: Born in Munich, Germany, in 1944, Hannibal is adopted by United States Army Colonel Andrew Burns. Nothing is known about him until he turns up in October of 1973 at the Exeter Research Corporation, a federally financed think tank in Washington, D.C. There he has an accident while working with a nerve gas known as Dethx-13. "Bathed in chemicals, drenched in the nerve-gas," Burns comes out of the wreckage looking like a living cadaver. Killing a security guard and stealing his clothes, Burns vanishes . . . until he resurfaces as the head of a rapidly growing crime ring. Using Dethx-13 (renamed Death-13) to slay any and all rivals, he intends to become "the lord of crime." He appears to have perished when the heroic Targitt came aboard his yacht and blew it up.

Quote: "Let this be a *warning* to the world! *No man*—not the F.B.I., C.I.A., or the *entire underworld* itself can *halt* the rise of . . . *the kingdom of Professor Death!"*

Comment: This was the character's only appearance. He was also the only super villain battled by Targitt in his three-issue run. Incidentally, his yacht is named after Charon who, in Greek mythology, ferried the dead across Acheron, the river of woe, into the underworld.

PROFESSOR DOOM (C)

First Appearance: 1966, *Captain Marvel Presents the Terrible 5* #1, M.F. Enterprises.

Weapons: Brainwashing gas X-3421; flying "mallet," a remote-control device which knocks people out.

Biography: A professor at Dartmoor University in the northeastern town of Riverview, Doom is also the head of the subversive organization B.I.R.D. (Bureau of International Revolutionary Devices). Headquartered in a cavern 200 miles from Riverview, in upstate New York, Doom plans to use his gas to control the minds of students . . . and then the world. His plans meet a roadblock named Captain Marvel, who captures the villain as he tries to seaplane from his lair and turns him over to the police.

Quote: "I'm not only brilliant, I'm lucky."

Comment: This was the character's only appearance. He was erroneously called Dr. Doom on the cover.

PROFESSOR ERIC VORNOFF (MP)

First Appearance: 1955, *Bride of the Monster*, Rolling M Pictures.

Chief Henchman: Lobo.

Biography: A native of an unspecified country in Eastern Europe, Vornoff flees, settling briefly in Scotland (adjoining Loch Ness where he begins incredible experiments) before relocating permanently in the United States. Settling into a lab beneath an old house on the verge of a vast swamp, Vornoff begins working on an atomic device which will allow him to breed a slave race "of unthinkable strength and size." He is assisted in this work by the towering brute named Lobo. A dozen people die as a result of Vornoff's experiments, and Police Lieutenant Dick Craig finally comes calling when his girlfriend, reporter Janet Lawson, barely escapes becoming a "bride of the atom." Vornoff overpowers the police officer but, resenting years of abuse, Lobo turns on his master and subjects him to the atomic device. As it happens the unit finally works, transforming Vornoff into a superhuman. Slaying Lobo, he stumbles into the swamp and is grabbed by one of the byproducts of his experiments in giantism, an enormous octopus. While the two tussle, lightning strikes and reduces them both to ash.

Comment: Bela Lugosi starred as Vornoff, Tor Johnson as Lobo in this low-budget production. The film was originally released as *Bride of the Atom*. Lugosi has also played the super villains BARON ROXOR, DR. ALEX ZORKA, DR. MIRAKLE, DR. PAUL CARRUTHERS, DRACULA, and MURDER LEGENDRE.

PROFESSOR FORTUNE (also known as MISTER MEMORY and THE ACE OF CLUBS) (C)

Real Name: Amos Fortune.

First Appearance: 1960, *Justice League of America* #6, DC Comics.

Costume: White robe, trousers, sash around waist, shirt with black collar; black shoes with white spats (as Professor Fortune); none (as Mister Memory); a white bodysuit, gloves, boots, full-face cowl, and ace of clubs printed on his chest (as the Ace of Clubs).

Weapons: The stimoluck, a device which affects the small good luck and bad luck glands in the human body; "the Wheel of Fortune," a huge vertical wheel which, when spun, destroys the good luck glands of anyone who is strapped to it; the de-memorizer, a gun which causes people to suffer instant amnesia; powerful "glass bombs"; cards subjected to concentrated "stellaration" (star-force), the "strange force that influences cards and their luck," which means that when they are flipped at the superheroes, the cards cause reactions in accordance with their nature in "fortunetelling argot"—for example, four of diamonds causing betrayal and two of spades a loss of power; device which brings the images on tarot cards to murderous life; and the "fortutron," which causes rich people to become compulsive (losing) gamblers.

Chief Henchmen: The brainwashed Batman, along with SEA THIEF (in #14 only); ROYAL FLUSH

GANG (#43); the Luck League, a group of seven people born on the seventh day of the seventh month and given an extra dose of good luck with the Wheel of Fortune; other nameless flunkies over the years.

Biography: As a child, "Pudge" Fortune was fascinated with the idea of luck, which led him to a career as a professional gambler. He also earned degrees in science, applying what he'd learned to his profession (revealed in issue #43). Subsequently discovering the human "luck glands," he invented the stimoluck and turned to crime, giving himself good luck and the Justice League heroes bad. But that plan backfired when Leaguer J'Onn J'onzz broke free; being a Martian, he had no luck glands. Fortune's luck concurrently ran out, as the Leaguers sent him up the river. Returning as Mister Memory and enslaving Batman, Fortune was once more defeated by the League (#14); as the Ace of Clubs he teamed with the Royal Flush Gang and was stopped yet again when his stellaration ray was duplicated by Hawkman and used to restore the superheroes to normal. He has attacked his perennial foes numerous times since, and remains at large.

Quote: "With every turn of the wheel, another charge of *bad luck* shoots through the *Justice League* members—which not even their super-powers can overcome!"

Comment: See THE ROYAL FLUSH GANG for other details of Fortune's childhood.

PROFESSOR IVO (C)

First Appearance: 1960, *The Brave and the Bold* #30, DC Comics.

Costume: Original: none. Later: red robe.

Weapons: Machine with twin gun barrels, one of which draws powers from superheroes, the other feeding those powers into AMAZO (see Biography).

Chief Henchmen: Various androids, the most notable of which is Amazo; elixir of immortality.

Biography: Nothing is known of this character's past. Yearning to acquire a vast fortune, Ivo feels that the best way to achieve this is first to become immortal. To this end, he must obtain the oldest creatures on the planet to use in his potion. Building Amazo, he employs a power-transference device to stock him with the strength of the Justice League of America and sends him out to acquire the aged beings. Upon Amazo's success, Ivo creates and then drinks the serum before Green Lantern is able to arrest them both (by nullifying Amazo's version of his own power ring using yellow chlorine gas, the ring being ineffective against anything yellow). The villain is given a 500-year sentence, which he is quite capable of serving. But he escapes and, in round two, tries to steal the Leaguers' powers for himself. Alas, his machine can't handle Superman's powers and blows up, not only knocking Ivo out, but also knocking some sense into his head. He reforms and, as Professor Ives, teaches astronomy at a university in New England. All goes well until he suffers a delayed reaction to the elixir. His features become distorted, his flesh grows scaly, and he is forced to undertake a new project: to use a machine like his power-transfer device to steal life force from others. Using androids to kidnap his victims, he is stopped by the Justice League and placed in the Arkham Asylum. He has had other criminal adventures—most notably killing off descendants of Justice League members in the thirtieth century—but he has yet to restore his misshapen features.

Quote: "One by one I'm transferring the super-powers of the *Justice League* members to Amazo. Then—nothing will stop us from conquering the earth!"

PROFESSOR PITHER (C)

First Appearance: 1984, *Archie Giant Series Magazine* #544, Archie Comics.

Costume: White lab smock.

Weapons: The Crystal Skull, an Aztec relic which refracts and intensifies solar rays a thousandfold, sending a "surge of evil" through Pither's body and allowing him to surround himself in a transparent, impenetrable shield; "Multi-Dimensional Activator" for time travel.

Biography: A mad scientist who dwells in Crackstone Manor, Pither captures the alien Prince Olobolo and hides him in the past, refusing to let him go unless the extraterrestrials give him "the secret to our electromagnetic drive." This they refuse to do, fearing that he will then "build a space ship and wreak universal havoc"—which, indeed, seems to be his plan as, sheathed in the shell generated by the Crystal Skull, he has been robbing banks to stock his warchest. Whenever he feels his power ebbing, he simply returns to the past where, worshipped as "the Fat God," he gives the Aztecs trinkets in exchange for time with the skull. Pursued by the good witch Sabrina, he is forced to steal the Crystal Skull and bring it to the twentieth century when she interrupts his ritual recharging; shrinking herself to doll size, she crawls inside it and then expands, shattering the object. Bending over the fragments and mourning their loss, Pither is caught in sunlight re-

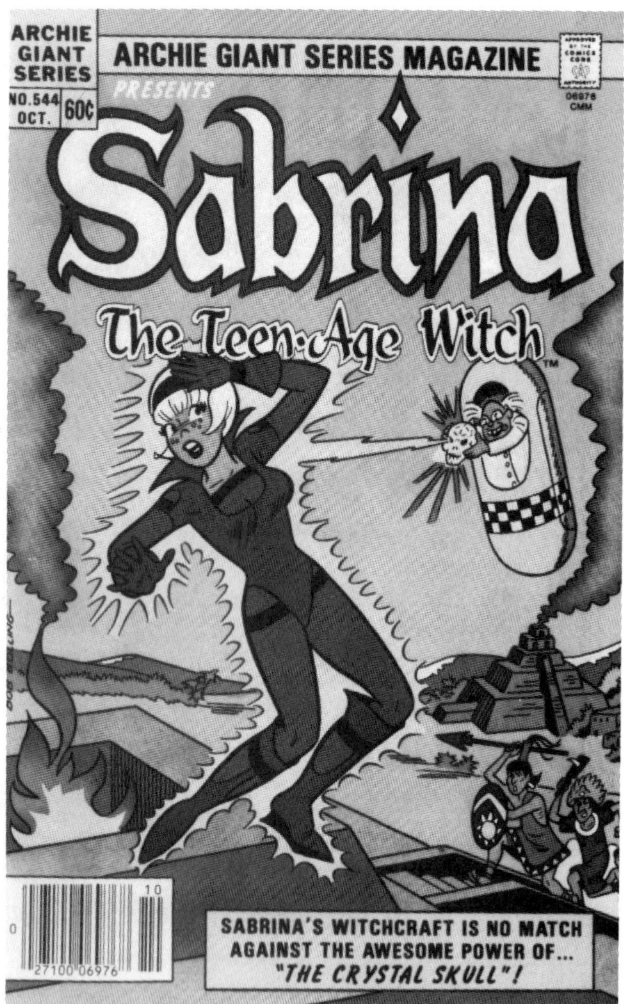

Sabrina feels the wrath of ***PROFESSOR PITHER*** *and his crystal skull. © Archie Comics.*

flected from each of the shards and is "reduced to atoms."

Quote: "*Sob*! I'll put it back together with Dippy Glue!"

Comment: This was the character's only appearance. It's interesting to note that Pither spoke with a lisp, which gives him a rather sly surname.

PROFESSOR POWER (C)

Real Name: Anthony Power.

First Appearance: 1982, *Marvel Team-Up* #117, Marvel Comics.

Costume: Orange bodysuit-armor (see Weapons); green boots, gloves, helmet, belt, bands around shoulders (see Weapons).

Weapons: Power's armor is an exoskeleton which gives him superstrength and radiates explosive "alpha-bursts"; it also contains a destructive electron beam gun in the right forearm and jetpack for flight. As head of the Secret Empire, he also commands "robot pursuers," "air cars" to attack enemy outposts, and "nullifier jackets" which cancel the powers of superheroes.

Chief Henchmen: MAD DOG; THE MUTANT FORCE; LEVIATHAN; the many operatives of the Secret Empire.

Biography: A history professor and White House foreign affairs advisor, Power is devoted to United States policy—until his son Matthew has a nervous breakdown and falls comatose while serving in Vietnam. Disgusted by the indecisiveness of the United States in that conflict and by the cowardly protests erupting around the nation, the elder Power concludes that the only way to straighten out the world is for him to take over the nation and return it "to a position of dominance in the world"—to which end he organizes a league of powerful, well-financed "super-patriots." However, what really kicks his plan into high gear is the destruction of "what small shreds of sanity Matthew had left," when he gets "caught in the psychic crossfire" between Professor Charles Xavier of the superheroic X-Men and MENTALLO. Slipping off the deep end, Power suits his son up in specially designed armor, has his own mind transferred into Matthew's body, and undertakes his agenda of conquest as Professor Power. Holed-up in "a perfect replica of a medieval castle" nestled in the heart of the Virginia Smokies, he joins his group with "the remnants of the old Secret Empire," a subversive league which had twice before been thwarted in its efforts to take over the country (see Comment). Rallying other super villains around him—most notably MAD DOG and THE MUTANT FORCE—he puts Project Sublimate into action, only to be stopped by the New Defenders. Worse, the psychic Moondragon merges the minds of Matthew and Anthony, causing the latter to succumb to "total madness" which leaves Professor Power "a quaking, gibbering wreck." It is unlikely that he will return. (This final saga spans *The New Defenders* #'s 127-130.)

Quote: "You face no common super-foe. *I am power incarnate*!"

Comment: The Secret Empire was first introduced in *Tales to Astonish* #81 (1966), and was revealed to be out of business in *Strange Tales* #149 (1966). The second incarnation made its debut in *Amazing Adventures* #11 (1972), and fell in *Captain America* #175 (1974).

PROFESSOR STEIGG (MP)

First Appearance: 1955, *Creature with the Atom Brain*, Columbia Pictures.

Costume: Radiation suit when performing surgery.

Biography: An elderly scientist, Steigg develops a process whereby dead people can be turned into obedient, super-strong zombies. The technique is simple: He opens the skull and replaces a portion of the brain with a sponge-like nuclear matter, rather clumsily bolting the skull back in place with huge rivets. Steigg is funded by mobster Frank Buchanan, who uses the mindless, radio-controlled creatures to murder those responsible for having had him deported. He also blows up buildings and trains in an effort to keep a cunning police scientist, Chet Walker, at bay. But his efforts to stop Walker fail and, cornered in the lab by police, the partners send all the zombies out to kill the intruders. Alas, it's the villains themselves who are undone.

Comment: Gregory Gay portrayed the awful scientist; Michael Granger costarred as Buchanan. Gay had previously portrayed the super villain MOTA.

PROFESSOR THOMAS ARCHER (M)

First Appearance: July 1937, "He Could Stop the World," *Doc Savage* Magazine, Kenneth Robeson.

Costume: Red domino mask.

Weapons: *The Silver Cylinder,* a "stratosphere ship" 400 feet long which can stay aloft for weeks; jammer to stop all radio communication worldwide; Z-ray, a "supercosmic ray" found in the upper stratosphere which can be used to control minds or, in a blue-vapor form, reduce people to a mound of powder (rays controlled remotely by Professor Archer's golden eyeglasses).

Chief Henchmen: See Biography.

Biography: "Stratosphere scientist" Professor Homer Randolph has invented *The Silver Cylinder* and conducted research into the Z-ray in order to benefit humankind. However, Professor Thomas Archer, a teacher and "student of atomic forces," has other ideas. He wants to rule the world. (As Randolph whines, "What I meant to make all peoples better, they will use to destroy, and murder, and plunder.") Abducting Randolph's girlfriend—Ann Garvin, who teaches at the same school as Archer—the fiend takes her to Empire City, his monumental domed fortress on Mt. Lassen in the High Sierras. There, he forces Randolph to serve him by threatening to turn Garvin into a giant (an illusion he works on others using mirrors). Assisted by black-robed, mind-controlled slaves, he throws the Z-ray's sundry powers out against the world until the superhero Doc Savage penetrates Empire City and wrecks the Z-ray control panel. Randolph, in turn, blows up Empire City with Archer still in it.

Quote: "Crush the prisoners."

PROFESSOR TORGLE (M)

First Appearance: January 1938, "The Living Fire Menace," *Doc Savage* Magazine, Kenneth Robeson.

Weapons: "High-frequency ray" which Torgle uses to imprison people; glass electric chair for torture; glass knife, also for torture and killing.

Biography: The Living Fire is "death that cannot be avoided . . . a hell-fire." An ore which hails from the center of the earth, it "has strange electrical qualities." The longer people are exposed to it, the more electricity they absorb; if they touch anything that grounds them, they die. If they touch a person who hasn't been exposed to the ore, that person dies. Professor Torgle wants to understand and control the ore, which, "if it could be smelted or milled . . . would be an impregnable metallic substance" which could be peddled to receptive governments. Accordingly, he builds a laboratory deep beneath a desert near Palm Springs, a facility where everything is made of non-conductive glass. Prior to setting up shop here, he was "one of the most dangerous criminals the world had ever encountered . . . particularly dangerous because he was a scientist . . . with a sharp, keen brain." His past crimes are not detailed; all that's revealed is that he has escaped from an asylum in which he was supposedly incarcerated. As befits someone of his heinous nature, Torgle is physically repulsive. "His feet headed one direction, his body another, as if some giant had . . . twisted him halfway around. His head was unbelievably flat (with) eyes that . . . glowed like tiny red coals. The mouth looked like a ragged slit cut by a knife into a dull piece of red leather." When he kidnaps the scientist-aides of the superheroic Doc Savage to help in his research, Torgle invites the enmity of the lawman. However, he doesn't live long enough to be brought to justice: Torgle is strangled by a fellow criminal whom simultaneously he stabs to death.

Quote: "I have not been able to solve the secret of the power rock, so I have amused myself making death traps that never fail."

PROFESSOR ZINGER (C)

First Appearance: 1966, *Sinbad Jr.* #2, Dell Publications.

Costume: White lab coat.

Weapons: Fire Ray gun which melts ice; highly advanced computer.

Biography: Little is known about this mad scientist's past. When the world "laughed at my great fire ray invention," claiming "it was merely a destructive, useless toy," Zinger set up a laboratory at the South Pole. There, using his fire ray, he began melting the ice cap and flooding major cities; his intention was to flood the world until it agreed to acknowledge him as its ruler. Fortunately, the young adventurer Sinbad, Jr., with his parrot Salty, found Zinger's lair. Using his magic belt, the lad reflected the fire ray back at the lab; melting the ice beneath the facility and destroying the madman's scheme. Ironically, Zinger can't swim and must be pulled from the flood by Sinbad, Jr.

Quote: "Now we all know that my fire ray really works . . . because I'm gradually melting all the ice and snow here at the South Pole!"

Sinbad Jr. about to put ***PROFESSOR ZINGER*** *on ice. © Dell Publications.*

Comment: On his TV series *The Adventures of Sinbad Jr.*, the youthful hero also battled such villains as Captain Sly, the Invisible Villain, the Evil Wizard, the Kooky Spooks, and the Surfboard Bully. The one-season syndicated series was produced by Hanna-Barbera.

THE PROWLER (C)

Real Name: Hobie Brown.

First Appearance: 1969, *The Amazing Spider-Man* #78, Marvel Comics.

Costume: Green jumpsuit; purple cape, full-head cowl, boots, gloves (see Weapons).

Weapons: Steel claws on gloves; blasters on wrists which fire bullets or various kinds of gas.

Biography: An inventor, Hobie is miserable because he has to support himself as a window washer and because his girlfriend Mindy doesn't understand him. Having created various tools to make his work easier—including a wristband fluid-shooter and claws for helping to hold onto slippery walls—he up-and-quits his job one day and becomes a costumed super villain. His plan? To steal as the Prowler, then turn the money in as Hobie . . . and thus get a job he likes, due to the favorable publicity. His plan goes afoul due to the interference of the superheroic Spider-Man; convinced that Spider-Man is a reckless enemy of the people, the Prowler decides to destroy him. He breaks into a diamond shop to draw him out, and the two battle again. This time, after Spider-Man defeats the villain by gumming up his wristband blasters with webbing, the hero magnanimously lets Hobie go after being convinced that he'll return to his law-abiding ways. But Hobie grows resentful and gets back into costume once more (#93, 1971); once again he is thrashed, this time suffering severe injuries in a fall. Spider-Man burns the Prowler's costume, the two call a truce, and Hobie marries Mindy.

Quote: "Whatever happens to you *now*, web-slinger—you *deserve* it!"

Comment: Another character named the Prowler has also stalked Spider-Man, this one a burglar originally known as the Cat (*The Amazing Spider-Man* #30, as the Cat; *Peter Parker, the Spectacular Spider-Man* #47, as the Prowler).

PSI (C)

Real Name: Gayle Marsh.

First Appearance: 1982, *The Daring New Adventures of Supergirl* #1, DC Comics.

Costume: Golden boots, bikini armor connected by band between top and bottom; blue cape with hood.

Biography: Born in Skokie, Illinois, Gayle discovered at the age of 12 that she had psychic abilities, mental powers which enabled her to fly, move objects by mere thought, fire destructive bolts which can raze a city block, and create a "psionic hold" capable of containing virtually anyone (even, as she later discovered, a superhero like Supergirl). Because of her powers, the teenager was sent for study to the Institute for Higher Psychokinetic Study in Chicago. Though her stay was supposed to be brief, her parents were killed in a highly suspicious car crash while she was there, and the Institute's head, Daniel Pendergast, was named her legal guardian. Naturally, Pendergast had an ulterior motive for his actions. Disgusted with the "fetid cesspool of decay" which society had become, he wanted to destroy it and start all over . . . to which end he intended to use Gayle, as Psi, working under his telepathic control. He sent Psi out to kill, but her heart wasn't in it; though she was able to defend herself against Supergirl, she wasn't able to wipe out Chicago as Pendergast ordered. Furious and insane, Pendergast himself became a living mound known as Decay, whose touch destroyed any matter (#3). Realizing that she had been serving the wrong side, Psi attacked Decay and the two of them vanished—presumably to another dimension. Neither has reappeared since.

Quote: "*Pitiful fool*! Mankind *destroys* itself through hate . . . through filth . . . through bodily *contamination* . . . and yet you can *still* fight me—?"

PSIMON (C)

Real Name: Simon Jones.

First Appearance: 1980, *The New Teen Titans* #3, DC Comics.

Costume: Red robe (Psimon has a blue brain in a dome atop his head).

Biography: A physicist, Simon was "obsessed with piercing the barriers between dimensions." Finally succeeding, he accidentally opened a rift between our universe and that of the supremely evil TRIGON. The demon struck Simon with a beam that transformed him into a super-powered flunky, "a living psionic. All my mind could conceive I could create." Given the task of paving the way for Trigon's invasion of our dimension by destroying a team of sorcerers who were seeking to kill Trigon, Psimon saw an ad in a criminal newsletter announcing the formation of a team of super villains. Joining THE FEARSOME FIVE, he took over the band and made it subservient; unfortunately, Psimon became greedy and sought to preserve the sorcerers so that he could rule on his own. Learning of this, Trigon did not kill him ("death would be too painless") but dissipated his "atoms throughout the light stream," leaving him stranded in bodiless limbo (#5). After Trigon's defeat, Psimon was able to contact the Fearsome Five; informing them that he'd subjugated the group because he'd been under Trigon's control, he convinced them that, henceforth, he would be a team player. They freed him with a device stolen from the Teen Titans (#7), after which Psimon and his teammates resumed their criminal ways. Psimon perished, for good, when he learned that BRAINIAC and LEX LUTHOR had intended to use him and other super villains as sacrificial lambs to battle and weaken targeted superheroes. Mistakenly believing that he'd slain Brainiac, Psimon turned on Luthor—only to have his braincase blown to pieces by the former (*Crisis on Infinite Earths* #10, 1986).

Quote: "*Titans*! Heed the wrathful word of *Psimon*! We await you on the field of *battle*! Come and learn who your *superiors* truly *are*!"

PSYCHO-MAN (C)

First Appearance: 1967, *The Fantastic Four Annual* #5, Marvel Comics.

Costume: Silver armor with green tubing surrounding legs and green markings on chest (see Weapons); green gauntlets, helmet with orange face.

Weapons: Hand-held emotion-activating unit which stimulates three emotions: hate, doubt, and fear. Psycho-Man can control the depth and length of a person's reaction, which can be pushed to the point of a victim's death. Psycho-Man has also used an illusion-causing device as well as a large "mind-ray" machine capable of affecting everyone on the planet. The Traanian's armor provides him with superstrength.

Chief Henchmen: Live Wire, Shell-Shock, Ivan (human flunkies); H.M. Unger, an android version of HATE MONGER.

Biography: Psycho-Man is an inhabitant of Traan, a world in the microscopic Sub-Atomica system. Due to overpopulation on the five-world system, scientist Psycho-Man (his real name is unrevealed) is sent to earth to investigate the possibility of conquest. (Psycho-Man does not become human-sized, however. He remains microscopic, functioning from inside his armor.) Sent running back to his world by the Fantastic Four, he has battled the heroes several times since (most dramatically on *his* home turf in "Stranded in Sub-Atomica," #'s 76-77, 1968). Most recently, when Psycho-Man attacked the domain of the superheroes' friend Queen Pearla in the "microverse," team member Invisible Woman used Psycho-Man's weapons against him. Although the details of what she did have not been revealed, the vile scientist has apparently been reduced to a gibbering idiot.

Quote: "You may have snatched victory from my grasp, but even now, I feed with delight upon your psychic pain—as the sight of your dead comrade sours your triumph!"

Comment: See other fear-inducing villains BUSHMAN, DR. SPECTRO, D'SPAYRE, MISTER FEAR, PHOBIA, PSYCHO-PIRATE, and SCARECROW (1).

PSYCHO-PIRATE (C)

Real Name: Charley Halstead; Roger Hayden.

First Appearance: 1944, *All-Star Comics* #23 (as Halstead); 1965, *Showcase* #56 (as Hayden), DC Comics.

Costume: Red cloak with very high collar; cowl, red on left and black on right; tights, red on the inside of legs, black on the outside; black trunks with red sides; boots, black on the inside, red on the outside; red bodyshirt with black chest on right, black belly on left (reverse pattern on back), arms black on the outside save for the wrists where black is on the inside; yellow faces of joy (over heart) and tragedy (on right side of belly); yellow belt.

Weapons: The golden Medusa Masks which enable him to control human emotions (as Hayden only).

Biography: A linotypist for the *Daily Courier*, Halstead despised his wealthy and contented publisher Rex Morgan. A natural genius in the causes and effects of human emotions, he became the Psycho-Pirate and launched a campaign to dispirit and destroy the publisher. Though thwarted and sent to prison by the Justice Society of America, Halstead applied his brilliant criminal mind and natural grasp of psychology to other crimes over the years. Ailing during his last stay in prison, he passed on all he knew about the human condition to fellow prisoner Roger Hayden; he also informed Hayden about the legendary Medusa Masks which gave their owner the power to control human emotions. When Halstead perished, Hayden became the new Psycho-Pirate and sought out the masks—which were in the possession of archaeologist Kent Nelson, aka the superhero Dr. Fate. Though he managed to steal them, the new Psycho-Pirate didn't have them for long, being bested by Dr. Fate. However, exposure to the masks, as well as his own innate abilities, gave Hayden the ability to force others to experience any emotion he pictured on his own face, as well as to experience illusions. In subsequent criminal activities he faced the Spectre and, as a member of THE SECRET SOCIETY OF SUPER-VILLAINS, the Justice Society of America. Though his own powers eventually warped his emotions and drove him mad, this did not keep him from becoming involved in the greatest criminal caper of all time: the destruction of countless galaxies in the Crisis on Infinite Earths (see THE ANTI-MONITOR). Freed from the insane asylum where he'd been kept (and given back his Medusa Mask), Psycho-Pirate teamed briefly with the Anti-Monitor—until he realized that he would eventually be destroyed by the monstrous alien. Joining the superheroes who were fighting him, Psycho-Pirate went even madder with fear of what the Anti-Monitor would do to him if he were ever captured. Though the Anti-Monitor was defeated, Psycho-Pirate is presently in a straightjacket *and* a padded room at the Arkham Asylum (as chronicled in *Crisis on Infinite Earths* #'s 1-12, 1985-86).

Quote: "*Look* at me. See the *fear* in my eyes and let it creep into your *soul*."

Comment: Others who have tinkered with human emotions include BUSHMAN, DR. SPECTRO, D'SPAYRE, MISTER FEAR, PHOBIA, PSYCHO-MAN, and SCARECROW (1).

PUG (S)

First Appearance: 1616, *The Devil is an Ass*, Ben Jonson.

Biography: A servant of SATAN, this novice devil is sent to earth for a day to see what mischief he can cause. Hired as a servant at the home of the empty-headed country squire Fitzdottrel, Pug observes the evil rampant among humans and, realizing he can never hope to be so wicked, returns to hell dispirited.

Comment: The play wasn't published until 1631. Although humans are the real villains in the tale—especially the land-speculator Meercraft, who cheats Fitzdottrel out of his holdings—and Pug doesn't get to work any cruel deeds per se, he is the yardstick by which Jonson measures our own nastiness, i.e., as bad as devils are, humans are worse.

THE PUMA (C)

Real Name: Thomas Fireheart.

First Appearance: 1984, *The Amazing Spider-Man* #256, Marvel Comics.

Costume: Blue T-shirt, tights and jagged red stripes running parallel to each other down chest to mid-thigh and red stripes around bottom of tights; blue bands with red triangle designs; two red feathers worn in hair; yellow belt; thick tufts of orange fur attached to shoulders and shins (Puma's skin is orange and shaggy in spots).

Chief Henchman: Jenna Taylor, his executive assistant at Fireheart Enterprises.

Biography: Multimillionaire Fireheart is the head of Fireheart Enterprises, a Heartsdale, New

Mexico, corporation. When he isn't busy building shopping malls, he becomes the Puma; using a touch of ancient magic to enhance his family's centuries-old selective breeding, he transforms his physical features to a feline form. In this identity, the Native American Fireheart is either a guardian, looking out for his tribe and their reservation (for instance, killing predators which slaughter their animals); or else he is a highly-paid killer-for-hire, using his Puma powers not just for the money but also for the thrill of the hunt. The first superhero he tackles is Spider-Man, who has been interfering with the crimes of a local masked mobster named the Rose. Though he fails to destroy the hero, the Puma gives him a run for his money due to his incredible physical strength, martial arts skills (he trained under the legendary Muramoto), leaping ability, and phenomenal senses. Once he has smelled something Spider-Man has touched, he can track the hero anywhere in New York City. Fireheart's uncle is the shaman of his tribe.

Quote: "Spider-Man appears to have survived his fall! *Good*! He is a courageous foe—and deserves a better death!"

PUNCH AND JEWELEE (C)

First Appearance: 1967, *Captain Atom* #85, Charlton Comics.

Costume: Punch: tights, yellow on left, orange on right; blouse, left side orange, right side yellow, left arm yellow, right arm orange; green trunks, slippers, gloves, jester's cap and collar with red bells; red mask. Jewelee: yellow tights; brown T-shirt with black jewel motif on chest and a large diamond on each shoulder; black-and-white checkered miniskirt; red jewel eyepieces; light brown gloves.

Weapons: Punch: flying boots; "sting strings" which he snaps at people or tangles around them, and which deliver a debilitating dose of electricity. Jewelee: "hypno-jewels" which create illusions and blinding lights. Both share a mind-recording device which not only explains how to use the equipment, but also enables them to read the minds of others.

Biography: Puppeteers at the Coney Island amusement park in New York, Punch and Jewelee (stage names; their real names are unknown) find an ancient chest which washes onto the beach. Inside is a collection of odd, extraterrestrial devices. Also in the chest is the mind-recording device. Designing costumes based on their characters Punch and Judy, the pair establish a headquarters at the amusement park and go to work as criminals. Their first scheme is an ambitious one. They plot to abduct renowned scientists, tap their secrets, and peddle the information on the international market. The scheme is thwarted by the superheroes Captain Atom and Nightshade. Though the evil couple escape, they have not surfaced since.

THE PUPPET MASTER (C)

Real Name: Phillip Masters.

First Appearance: 1962, *The Fantastic Four* #8, Marvel Comics.

Weapons: Transian clay, which enables him to control those whose likeness he sculpts.

Biography: Born in Transia in the Balkans, Masters is still a young child when he moves to the United States with his parents. Lonely, he takes to building marionettes and shaping figurines from clay he has brought from home. In time, Masters attends college where he befriends classmates Jacob Reiss and Marcia Deaton. When the trio graduate with biology degrees, Reiss uses an inheritance to establish a research facility in upstate New York, where Masters and Reiss work side-by-side. Reiss also marries Marcia and they have a daughter, Alicia. Tragically, Masters soon becomes jealous of his partner's contentment and plots to destroy it. Masters plans to blow up the center one night, but is discovered by Reiss, who happens to be driving by. They fight and Reiss is knocked into a vat of the Transian clay which they have been using to simulate the life-generative conditions of antediluvian earth. His fall sets off the explosion Masters had been arranging. Reiss perishes and, when his wife and daughter come from the car to see what the delay is about, Alicia is blinded. Having no idea that it was Masters who had been behind the accident, Marcia subsequently marries him so that Alicia will have a father. Before long, Marcia perishes from slow-acting toxins she'd absorbed in the blast; as for Masters, he devotes himself to studying the Transian clay in the hope of finding a cure for Alicia. Failing, he sells the facility, moves to Manhattan, and opens a small sculpture studio where he makes an astonishing discovery: He can control the physical actions of anyone whose likeness he sculpts from the clay. Christening himself the Puppet Master he decides to use his abilities to make other people suffer. Coercing a man to jump from a bridge, he is livid when he discovers that the Human Torch of the Fantastic Four swooped by and saved him. Since then, Masters has dedicated himself to dominating those superheroes, among others, but without success. The only benefit from his criminal actions is the introduction of Alicia to the Thing of the Fantastic Four. The two remain lovers for nearly two decades; Alicia is presently wooing the Thing's partner, the Human Torch.

Quote: "*Obey me,* my puppets! For *my* will is *your* will! You shall never escape your new master!"

Comment: A similar villain was Marvel's Mister Doll, who could harm people by shaping their features over those of a voodoo-like doll. Doll subsequently became THE BROTHERS GRIMM.

THE PURPLE MAN (C)

Real Name: Zebediah Killgrave.

First Appearance: 1964, *Daredevil* #4, Marvel Comics.

Costume: Purple bodyshirt, trousers, shoes (skin is same shade of purple).

Chief Henchmen: Various thugs dressed in purple jumpsuits with pink shoulders and orange helmets.

Biography: Working for the communists as a spy, Killgrave is ordered to steal samples of a new nerve gas being produced for the U.S. military. Sneaking into a base, he is discovered and fired upon by a guard; missing the intruder, the bullet strikes a canister and its liquid content splashes all over Killgrave, turning him purple. Questioned, he is shocked when his captors release him. Killgrave soon realizes that because of the nerve gas bath he took, he has the power to control peoples' minds—from a single individual to an entire crowd—as long as he is in their physical presence. Dubbing himself the Purple Man, he begins his career as a super villain only to be captured by the superhero Daredevil. Confined in a cell in which his "powers of total persuasion (were) dampened by a chemical mist," he escapes two years later when an electrical short circuit cuts off the mist and he mentally overpowers a guard. Moving from New York to San Francisco, he builds a criminal empire; ironically, Daredevil himself moves to the city on the Bay, and the two have tangled numerous times since.

Quote: "I'm quite glad you decided to *join* us here, Daredevil . . . it'll make this town . . . less *lonely* . . . for a *time,* at any rate."

THE PURPLE MONSTER (MP)

First Appearance: 1945, *The Purple Monster Strikes,* Republic Pictures.

Costume: Black bodysuit, gloves, boots; golden-scaled vest, cowl, cuffs on gloves and boots. (Note: The movie was black and white; this was the color scheme on posters advertising the film.)

Weapons: Electro-annihilator, a ray gun which can destroy anything; "distance eliminator," a TV for communication with Mars, poison carbo-oxide pills.

Chief Henchmen: Garrett and other terrestrial thugs; Marcia the Martian.

Biography: When Dr. Cyrus Layton sees a purple light streak through the heavens, he hops into his car to see where the "meteor" might land. Reaching the crash site, he's astonished to find a wrecked rocket with a humanoid occupant. However, he's even more amazed when the alien explains that he's come to earth expressly to see the spaceship which Layton has designed. The astronomer/engineer proudly shows his plans to the Martian, who promptly kills his host with a "carbo-oxide" gas pellet (safe for Martians, deadly for terrestrials) and enters his body. As the Martian reveals to Layton before killing him, he is actually the advance scout for an invasion force, in which Layton's reusable spaceship is to play an integral part. Layton was a member of the Scientific Foundation and, to build the ship, the extraterrestrial needs components developed by other Foundation members, including special fuel, a booster, a stabilizer, and the Electro-annihilator to protect it from meteors the ship may encounter in space. Despite having hired a gangster named Garrett to work for him, the Martian—who for some unknown reason calls himself the Purple Monster—finds the going rough. Layton's niece Sheila and Scientific Foundation attorney Craig Foster know of the Martian's existence and anticipate his moves. Frustrated, the Purple Monster puts in a call to the emperor of Mars requesting help; a female aide named Marcia is blasted earthward in one of the Martian X-70 rockets and arrives a few days later. But even two Martians aren't a match for the earthlings. Eventually learning where the Purple Monster is building his ship, Craig hurries over and uses the Electro-annihilator to disintegrate the would-be invaders when they blast off for home.

Comment: Roy Barcroft (CAPTAIN MEPHISTO, RETIK) played the Purple Monster and Mary Moore was Marcia in the 15-chapter serial. John Davidson appeared as the Martian emperor. See also MOTA and NYAH, other Martian movie super villains.

THE PUZZLER (C)

First Appearance: 1942, *Action Comics* #49, DC Comics.

Weapons: Sundry puzzle-related instruments—for example, a crack on the head with a poker to kill someone who had the audacity to beat him at poker. However, the Puzzler's most sadistic weapon is a wheel-of-fortune which strangles the user if it lands on red (as it is pre-set to do).

Chief Henchmen: Various lackeys.

Biography: "A genius at solving puzzles," the Puzzler decides "to utilize the principles that win games to launch a crime campaign unrivaled in history." Leaving clues to future crimes, he is always caught by Superman.

Quote: "It tickles my vanity to think *I* can outsmart *Superman*!"

Comment: The character has a great deal in common with Batman's foe THE RIDDLER. See also THE CLUEMASTER.

PYRO (C)

Real Name: St. John Allerdyce.

First Appearance: 1981, *X-Men* #141, Marvel Comics.

Costume: Bodysuit, yellow to waist then pyramiding to a point on chest, orange on arms and rest of chest down to waist; yellow gloves; orange cowl with red eyepieces; red vest with high collar and yellow flame on chest (suit is fireproof).

Weapons: Yellow flamethrower worn on back, with red hoses attached to wrists. (Allerdyce carries the flamethrower because he can't cause fires on his own.)

Biography: An Australian, Allerdyce was a mutant who could cause a flame to grow and assume the shape of anything he willed. Once it had taken form, the fire did whatever Allerdyce commanded. A journalist who had become a successful novelist—he wrote romances as well as tales based on his experiences as a reporter in Asia—Allerdyce gave it all up when he met the villain MYSTIQUE and she asked him to join her vile *New* Brotherhood of Evil Mutants. Presumably, Allerdyce had grown cynical and antagonistic because of the critical drubbings he took for his novels. Doubtless, becoming Pyro served as an outlet for his hostility . . . though he has lately showed signs of reforming (see BROTHERHOOD OF EVIL MUTANTS).

Quote: "What is your strength—compared to the *living flame* of *Pyro*?!"

Comment: See other fiery super villains BLOWTORCH BRAND, FIREBOLT, FIREBUG, FIREFALL, FIRE-FIST, Heatstroke of MASTERS OF DISASTER, and HEATWAVE.

QUAKEMASTER (C)

Real Name: Robert Coleman.

First Appearance: 1980, *DC Special* #28, DC Comics.

Costume: Purple tights, boots, cowl with white circle on forehead and red "T"-shaped jackhammer symbol inside; green trunks, gloves, bodyshirt with purple shoulders and yellow "Q" on chest; yellow belt with "Q" buckle.

Weapons: Jackhammer which sends out energy waves powerful enough to destroy everything from a street to a person's skeleton.

Biography: A well-known Gotham City architect, Coleman took the rap when an apartment he'd designed toppled during a hurricane. Feeling that he'd been unjustly pilloried, Coleman struck back by designing his special jackhammer and causing tremors throughout the city as Quakemaster. Ironically, his were the only buildings unable to take the stress. Captured by Batman, he briefly joined THE SECRET SOCIETY OF SUPER-VILLAINS when his sentence was up. Quakemaster no longer serves with that group and is presently laying low.

Comment: THE SPOOK and VORTEX are also super-villainous architects. See other earthquake-makers AVALANCHE, MAJOR DISASTER, Shakedown of MASTERS OF DISASTER, and VORTEX.

THE QUEEN (F, MP)

First Appearance: 1812, "Snow White and the Seven Dwarfs," the Brothers Grimm.

Weapons: Poisoned apple (only on the rosy, delectable side; the white side is safe); magic mirror to tell her "who is fairest of us all"; lace which strangles whoever puts it on; a poisoned comb.

Biography: A "proud and overbearing" woman, the Queen cannot bear the fact that Snow White, her husband's daughter by a previous marriage, is lovelier than she. Thus, the Queen orders her huntsman to kill the girl in the woods; once there, however, he is unable to slay the seven-year-old. Setting her free, he cuts the heart from a boar and presents it to the Queen, who salts, cooks, and eats it. Thinking herself rid of Snow White, she's shocked when the mirror informs her that the girl is living with seven dwarfs in the glen . . . and, adding insult to injury, notes that the girl "is a thousand times more fair." Dressing herself as a peddler, the Queen crosses the seven mountains and goes to the dwarfs' house. She gives Snow White the deadly lace, but the dwarfs cut it away before it can choke her; returning disguised as a "different sort of old woman," the Queen gives the girl a poisoned comb, which the dwarfs take from her hair before its toxins can work. Returning again as "a peasant woman," she convinces Snow White to bite a poisoned apple. The girl agrees (only after the Queen shows her it's safe by biting the white side) and, after a single bite, falls dead. However, while moving her coffin, the dwarfs dislodge the apple and she revives. Falling in love with Snow White, a prince takes her for his bride and, when the Queen shows up at the wedding, he has her fit with "red-hot iron shoes, in which she had to dance until she fell down dead."

Quote: "Looking-glass upon the wall, who is fairest of us all?"

Comment: The most famous screen Queen was Lucille La Verne, who provided the character's voice in the 1937 Walt Disney cartoon feature *Snow White and the Seven Dwarfs*. In that version, she was chased onto a ledge by the dwarfs and fell to their death. In *Snow White and the Three Stooges* (1961), the Queen was now the Queen of Fortunia who ordered the young girl's death so she wouldn't inherit the throne. Patricia Medina played the part. More faithful versions of the fairy tale were filmed in 1913, 1916, 1917, and 1955. See other Grimm villains GOTHEL, MERCURIUS, and THE ROBBER BRIDEGROOM.

QUEEN BEA (C)

First Appearance: 1967, *Double-Dare Adventures* #2, Harvey Comics.

Costume: Red dress; golden tiara with antennae; golden scepter with a graven bumble bee on top.

Biography: Based on the Martian moon of Deimos, the lovely queen wants to conquer the earth. To this end, she tricks the superhero B-Man into coming to her glass-domed palace where, using a kidnapped earthman, she intends to make an exact duplicate of the hero ("but with control over his mind"). However, the hero escapes her clutches and, grabbing his fellow earth dweller, jumps into the teleporter device, destroying it as they beam home so the queen can never menace our world. Nonetheless, she does manage to sneak a trio of gray-garbed Martian thugs aboard to destroy B-Man's store of all-important honey. ("You'll eventually lose your mind without this honey supply, Bee!" they gloat.) Fortunately, the F.B.I. is able to synthesize the substance.

***QUEEN BEA** explains herself to B-Man, while a captive earthman looks on. © Harvey Comics.*

Quote: "We required your presence here, human bee—your body must be duplicated perfectly! An over-injection of venom might kill a man!"

Comment: This was Queen Bea's only appearance; she was also the only foe B-Man faced in his two-issue run. See also QUEEN BEE.

THE QUEEN BEE (C)

Real Name: Zazzala.

First Appearance: 1963, *Justice League of America* #23, DC Comics.

Costume: Leotard with horizontal black and orange stripes and flared shoulders; orange boots (later red), gloves (later black); diaphanous wings growing from her body and enabling her to fly. She used to wear an orange star headband.

Weapons: Multipurpose "magno-nuclear rod" which controls bumble bees, stores and uses magnetism, and forces others to do her bidding as well as turn into small, insect-like beings. She also has bombs capable of destroying an entire planet and which explode or defuse themselves solely at her "personal mental command." Queen Zazzala flies through space in her hive-shaped Hive Ship which is "protected by anti-discovery devices."

Chief Henchmen: The winged, airborne Bee-Men.

Biography: Zazzala was born on the planet Korll, whose human inhabitants evolved from insects and are outwardly identical to earthly humans. Centuries ago, Korllian scientist Per Kazz discovered an elixir of immortality. Unable to drink it himself—he was old, and the chemicals had a healthy kick to them—he came up with a test to determine "the wisest, healthiest, and strongest person on all Korll." Hiding the serum in three separate vials on the cloud-covered world Somalar, he created monsters to protect each vial: a giant "lava being," a giant killer plant, and a "teleporting glacier." Per Kazz died on the planet, as did the long line of Korllian queens who went in search of the elixir. Finally, Zazzala came up with a twist. Journeying to earth, she threatened to destroy it if the superheroes of the Justice League failed to get the elixir for her. Although the Leaguers were aware that her ultimate ambition was to conquer the universe, they had no choice but to comply. Although Green Lantern used his power ring to seal the vials, keeping their contents from the queen, she proved most resourceful. Going through Per Kazz's notes, she found his experiments with power rings and was able to construct an instrument able to open the vials. Immortality had its drawback: She became paralyzed once she'd ingested the formula. Thus, using her magno-nuclear rod, she enslaved the superheroes—reducing them in size and giving them wings—and sent them out to find an antidote. This accomplished, she tried to keep the heroes as her slaves but was outwitted by the Atom, who used the rod to paralyze her once again (#60). In time, Zazzala found the means to remain mobile *and* immortal by using her wand to draw magnetic energy from people. Zazzala remains a villainous force in the universe.

Quote: "Now that you super-beings have become my worker-drones, I command you to gain for me the treasure that will make me *queen of the universe*!"

Comment: See also QUEEN BEA, another extraterrestrial villain. Other insect-controlling super villains are BARON BUG, THE DRAGONFLY RAIDERS, HUMBUG, KING LOCUST, and SWARM.

QUEEN OF DIAMONDS (MP)

First Appearance: 1929, *The Ace of Scotland Yard,* Universal Pictures.

Biography: The head of a band of crooks, the Queen sets her sights on one of the richest prizes in England—a ring belonging to Lady Diana Blanton. Disguising herself as a man (Prince Darius), the Queen gains access to her ladyship and informs her that she has no right to the ring. The imposter then uses hypnotic powers to show Lady Diana the past, visions which persuade her that the ring belongs to the Darius line. Unhappily for the Queen, Lady Diana's inamorato is Inspector Blake—the titular Ace—who uncovers the scam and sends the Queen and her band to prison.

Comment: Grace Cunard played the part in the 10-episode serial. *The Ace of Scotland Yard* has the distinction of being the first all-talking movie serial.

THE QUEEN OF HEARTS (N, MP, TV)

First Appearance: 1865, *Alice's Adventures in Wonderland,* Lewis Carroll.

Costume: Dress and crown identical to queen of hearts playing card.

Biography: With her timid husband the King, the Queen is the ruler of Wonderland a world which, in the dream of young Alice, exists at the bottom of a very deep rabbit hole in England. Ruling Wonderland with an iron hand, the queen is quick to order the decapitation of anyone who crosses her, from the Duchess who has the audacity to box her ears to the gardeners who mistakenly

***THE QUEEN OF HEARTS** as rendered by Tenniel.*

plant a white rose tree in her prize rose garden, and then compound their blunder by painting its flowers red. Her favorite game is croquet, played with flamingoes as mallets and hedgehogs as balls. She and the rest of her court turn into a pack of cards at the end of Alice's dream.

Quote: "Off with her head!"

Comment: Verna Felton provided the Queen's voice in the most famous screen version of the tale, the 1951 animated Walt Disney feature. Most recently, Jayne Meadows played the part in the 1985 TV miniseries.

QUEEN OF THE NIGHT (S)

First Appearance: 1791, *The Magic Flute,* Wolfgang Amadeus Mozart.

Chief Henchmen: Ladies-in-waiting; Monostatos.

Biography: Nothing is known of the character's past. Based in Egypt, the Queen is the champion of ignorance and terror; the only soul standing in her way is Sarastro, High Priest of Isis and Osiris, who seeks to promote reason and love. ("Who is not pleased by such teaching," says he, "is not worthy to be called man.") To this end, Sarastro abducts the Queen's daughter, Pamina, so that she can lead a righteous life. This annoys the Queen to no end and, when her three ladies-in-waiting save Prince Tamino from a serpent, she asks in return that he rescue her daughter. The young man hastens to Sarastro's Temple of the Sun, where he eventually learns the truth about the Queen. She, meanwhile, goes to her daughter and gives her a knife (tempered with "the vengeance of Hell") with which to slay Sarastro. But Pamina is talked out of it by the Chief of the Temple Slaves, Monostatos, a Moor who lusts for her; when she spurns him, Monostatos does a quick about-face, joining forces with the Queen, who has promised him Pamina's hand when Sarastro is defeated. But the High Priest's power proves too great and, in a final confrontation, amidst thunder and lightning, the Queen, Monostatos, and the three ladies-in-waiting are swallowed up by the earth.

Quote: "Fühlt nicht durch dich Sarastro Todesschmerzen, so bist du meine Tochter nimmermehr!" ("If you do not cause Sarastro a painful death, you will be my daughter no more!")

Comment: Written in German, Mozart's last opera was commissioned by actor/producer Emanuel Schikaneder, who also wrote the libretto; it was first performed at the Theater auf der Wieden in Vienna on September 30. The "Revenge Aria" sung by the Queen is one of the most difficult in all opera. The Queen's part was written for a soprano. Remarkably, while there are countless villains in opera, from the assassin Sparafucile in Verdi's *Rigoletto* (1851) to the Inquisition's oily spy Barnaba in Ponchielli's *La Gioconda* (1876), there aren't many whose evil is on par with that of the Queen. Among the chosen few are the curse-spouting witch Fata Morgana who causes the Prince to fall in love with three oranges in Prokofiev's *The Love for Three Oranges* (1919), which also boasts the devil Farfarello; the evil magician Klingsor who tries to kill the hero in Wagner's *Parsifal* (1882); and Dapertutto, the evil genius who steals the poet Hoffmann's soul in Offenbach's *The Tales of Hoffmann* (1881).

QUEEN YLLANA (MP)

First Appearance: 1958, *Queen of Outer Space*, Allied Artists.

Weapons: Beta Disintegrator capable of destroying objects as far from Venus as Earth . . . including Earth itself.

Costume: Various dresses; sequined full-face mask with slits for mouth and eyes and tendril-like extensions rising from forehead.

Biography: The year is 1985. Horribly scarred in a radiation accident, Queen Yllana of Venus has also lost

***QUEEN OF THE NIGHT** drawn by Simon Quaglio for a production of* The Magic Flute *in Munich, 1818.*

her mind. Ruling her world with an iron hand and getting rid of all the men—a man caused the accident which mutilated her face—the paranoid queen notices Earth building a space station and comes to believe that Earth people are out to blow up Venus. Destroying the space base with a blast from her Beta Disintegrator, she simultaneously knocks a spaceship off-course. The interplanetary cruiser crashes on Venus, where its passengers, all men, stand trial. The crew is found guilty of conspiring against Venus, the ship's Captain Patterson compounding the crimes by spurning Yllana's advances and, worse, ripping off her mask. However, before the Earthmen can be executed the kindhearted Talleah leads a coup against the queen, ending tyranny on the second world from the sun.

Comment: Laurie Mitchell played Yllana; Zsa Zsa Gabor was Talleah.

RADIOACTIVE MAN (C)

Real Name: Dr. Chen Lu.

First Appearance: 1963, *Journey Into Mystery* #93, Marvel Comics.

Costume: Green boots, loincloth which goes up to mid-chest, harness consisting of straps which reach from the front to the back of his loincloth (see Weapons); yellow starburst on chest (Radioactive Man's skin is green).

Weapons: Harness soaks up radiation which is constantly leaking from the villain, thus preventing it from harming anyone he does not wish to harm.

Biography: One of the more mountebank super villains, Lu is presently a fiend without a country. A nuclear physicist in Mainland China, Lu was asked by the government to find a way to strike back at Thor after the superhero prevented a military strike against India. Lu offered himself as a weapon. Exposing himself to a huge dose of radiation (after having spent several months rendering himself immune to its deadlier aspects), he became the superhuman Radioactive Man, able to fire radioactive blasts, generate intense heat, surround himself with an impenetrable force-field, and turn his energy into superstrength. Withal, he was clobbered by Thor and hid until he was found by BARON ZEMO and asked to join the MASTERS OF EVIL. After Thor and the Avengers defeated that band on two separate occasions, Lu fled to Vietnam where he served as one of THE TITANIC THREE. Leaving that group and having another go with the Masters of Evil, he was defeated yet again and last surfaced as an associate of THE MANDARIN.

RADIUS (C)

Real Name: Ralphie Hutchins.

First Appearance: 1981, *The Savage She-Hulk* #22, Marvel Comics.

Costume: Blue leotard with red circle on chest; golden belt, gloves, boots.

Biography: The "Mad Doctor" is a geneticist who (in issue #19) captures the superhero She-Hulk to study her physical makeup. When she escapes, he turns his assistant Ralphie into a humanoid "Brute Creature" whose malleable flesh makes combat with him like fighting "someone made of Playdoh." While She-Hulk rips both the monster and the UCLA lab to pieces, the doctor escapes. Returning to his experiments, he is hired by crimeboss Shade to provide him with a means of destroying She-Hulk—a feat which will prove to other crimelords that he is "king of the hill" (see TORQUE, Comment). Using Ralphie's remains he creates Radius who, due to further genetic tinkering, is able to "vibrate every molecule in his body until his body is like a force field." He can also set up "a resonant field" which allows him "to control the vibration of anything within that field." That permits him to melt guns, cause wind storms (he can also freeze the air molecules to make them sting like pinpricks), shake people to death, or stop objects cold. When he fails to defeat the superheroine, Radius is short-circuited by his creator, who simply touches the "terminate" button on a handheld monitoring device. Shade tries again to destroy She-Hulk by turning Ralphie into TORQUE.

Quote: "How can you stop someone who doesn't even have to touch you—to kill you?"

THE RAINBOW RAIDER (C)

Real Name: Dr. Quinn.

First Appearance: 1966, *House of Mystery* #167, DC Comics.

Costume: White trunks, boots, belt, wristbands (skin turns whatever color he is tapping; see Biography).

Biography: A "notorious . . . inventive crime chief," Quinn shines a laser beam through a rainbow crystal; "absorbing all the power" of the beam, he becomes the Rainbow Raider able to tap any of the colors displayed in a rainbow on his belly. Red allows him to cut metal, violet to shrink objects, orange to throw out a misty smokescreen, yellow to drain energy from animate or inanimate objects, and green to cause people to move in slow motion. He can also become invisible by tapping the ultraviolet. However, using the "Dial-H for

Hero" device, young Robby Reed becomes the superhero Radar-Sonar Man and knocks the villain out while he's invisible—and, hence, overly confident.

Quote: "Those poison fumes will snuff out your life before you break out of my slow motion spell!"

Comment: This was the character's only appearance.

RAINBOW RAIDER (C)

Real Name: Roy G. Bivolo.

First Appearance: 1980, *The Flash* #286, DC Comics.

Costume: Black bodysuit; jerkin with vertical color stripes, from right to left: red, orange, yellow, green, blue, indigo, violet; boots and gloves have the same colors vertically.

Weapons: Prisma-goggles, whose switches allow Roy to fire solid light particles in a variety of colors. Creating a rainbow which unravels before him like a ribbon, he can ride it through the skies; generating other colors causes different reactions. Blue causes sedation in whoever the beams strike, black drains them of all color, and red creates anger; presumably, yellow induces cowardice and green envy. The impact of the other colors is not known, though all of them strike their targets with debilitating force. The goggles can also cause flashes of light equivalent to "a thousand bursting flashbulbs." The villain's other principal weapon is invisibility paint.

Biography: As a child, Roy was an artistic prodigy save for one problem. Though his paintings were brilliant, he could see only in black and white. As one art critic put it, "I'm afraid his abysmal color sense is nothing short of revolting." Roy's father, an optometrist, worked slavishly to solve his son's problem. After careful research, the elderly man came up with the prisma-goggles, though he died as he gave them to Roy. Much to the surprise of the 21-year-old, the glasses didn't give him color vision, but rather they gave him the power to make color obey him in the form of waves. Since he had been "robbed of a brilliant art career," he reasoned that "it's only fitting that I rob others" and went about stealing art masterpieces. Stopped by the Flash, he had only a handful of encounters with the superspeedster before the hero perished in 1985.

Quote: "Unlike other *supervillains*, I'm not into money. No, Roy G. Bivolo is compelled by *higher* motivations—like *art appreciation*!"

Comment: The first seven letters of the character's name—Roy G. Biv—stand for the colors of the spectrum in their proper sequence, as pictured on his jerkin.

RAMPAGE (C)

Real Name: Stuart Clarke.

First Appearance: 1976, *The Champions* #5, Marvel Comics.

Costume: Red bodysuit with silver exoskeletonic braces across chest and along arms and legs (see Weapons); black trunks with yellow fringe; red boots with yellow stripe down front and around top (see Weapons); yellow wristbands, helmet with red goggles (see Weapons).

Weapons: Exoskeleton gives Rampage enormous physical strength; "boot jets" enable him to fly; costume and helmet made of "invincible alloy" which protects him from injury.

Biography: The head of Clarke Futuristics, a Los Angeles hi-tech firm, Clarke owed a fortune to the government and his subcontractors, among others. He was counting heavily on his new supersuit, the "exo-skeleton uniform," to be bought by police and thus save him from his financial difficulties. However, the contract went to his rival, Stark Industries (owned by Tony Stark, who is secretly the superhero Iron Man). Rather than declare bankruptcy, Clarke decided to don the suit and rob banks—but only those protected by the government's Federal Deposit Insurance Corporation, a tack he considers poetic justice. He was eventually defeated by the Los Angeles-based superheroes the Champions.

Quote: "If you come one step *closer*, I'll smash this fist right through the *Angel's skull*!"

Comment: The character appeared through issue #8.

RANAQ (C)

First Appearance: 1984, *Alpha Flight* #14, Marvel Comics.

Biography: Also known as the Devourer (no relation to Marvel's other DEVOURER), the demon Ranaq is "one of seven great beasts, old and powerful." Back in the year 984 A.D., Ranaq is imprisoned in the spirit realm by Nelvanna, an Eskimo goddess and mother of Alpha Flight's Snowbird. After 900 years of incarceration, Ranaq is freed in Calgary, Canada, by an Indian medicine man (who was forced to do so when the greedy Zebediah Chase and his accomplice Lucas Stang held the Shaman's granddaughter at gunpoint). Possessing Chase's body, Ranaq is shot dead by Lucas, who fires a bullet made from a mystic amulet (#19). Thus imprisoned in the corpse, Ranaq is liberated again in our era by Elizabeth Twoyoungmen, who unearths Chase's skull during an archaeological dig. This time, Ranaq possesses the great-granddaughter of the still-living Lucas; tracked down by the mystic Shaman of the superheroic team Alpha Flight, the demon is exorcised (#18). It has not been seen since.

Quote: "Foolish, puny mortal! You dare pit your inconsequential weapon against *Ranaq?*"

Comment: The tale was told out-of-sequence over three issues, the story set in 1884 coming last. The character's name has been misspelled Ranoq.

RA'S AL GHUL (C)

First Appearance: 1971, *Batman* #232, DC Comics. (Note: Ra's' daughter Talia had appeared one month before, in *Detective Comics* #411.)

Costume: Green cloak with gold buttons, sometimes has gold fringe as well (see Biography for comments on Messiah wardrobe).

Weapons: Cylinders in which humans are mutated into mindless slaves.

Chief Henchmen: His personal bodyguard is Ubu; he is, on occasion, assisted by his mutated humans. Otherwise, Ra's oversees an international criminal network which once included the League of Assassins, a murder-for-hire group originally headed by Dr. Ebenezer Darrk (who died in a confrontation with Talia) and now led by an Oriental called the Sensei. The Assassins are no longer affiliated with Ra's; among their crimes are the killing of the superhero Batwoman and circus acrobat Boston Brand, who subsequently became Deadman.

Biography: First mentioned in the writings of seventeenth-century historian Al Talmun, Ra's al Ghul is "many centuries" old thanks to repeated minute-long immersions in the fiery Lazarus Pit—from which he always emerges possessing "the strength of ten" and seized with "a fit of madness." (His daughter, Talia, gets similar treatments but "for only a moment.") Now, however, his days of being able to revitalize himself are nearing an end. Thus, he hastens his plan "to restore *harmony*" to the world by conquering it and setting up his daughter and a yet-to-be-chosen husband as rulers. Having already met the superhero Batman, Talia wants him for her spouse; to this end, Ra's kidnaps the superhero's sidekick Robin just to see what kind of sleuth Batman is, and in that way determine if he's a worthy husband for the love-struck Talia. Ra's is impressed, but the two don't wed; indeed, Batman devotes considerable energies to thwarting Ra's' scheme. In their most dramatic confrontation (*Batman* #335), the superhero smacks the burning Ra's into his pit and the villain's stronghold in Infinity Island explodes. Remarkably, though, he does not die. Remarking on the incident, Ra's says, "I was dissolved, yes, but I was reconceived" (*Batman Annual* #8). Spotting the sun immediately after his rebirth, he vows to "master its rays . . . become the Messiah of the Crimson Sun" and, donning a red cloak and bodysuit with a bright sun emblem on his chest, he sets up a satellite base in earth orbit for that purpose. But Batman does some tinkering on Ra's' shuttle so that the villain is sucked into the sun; for now, he appears to have perished.

Quote: "You are *proud, detective*. You do not plead for . . . the *antidote* to the poison in your blood! Nor would I *give* it!"

RATMAN (C)

First Appearance: 1981, *Charlton Bullseye* #2, Charlton Comics.

Costume: Black mask (Ratman's skin is blue).

Weapons: Mouse-tang automobile; gangmembers use jet packs to go to and from crimes.

Chief Henchanimals: Various nameless rats.

Biography: When a firm owned by Katrina O'Toole of Petropolis develops "a nuclear-powered mouse trap,"

RATMAN *trapped. © Charlton Comics.*

the henchmen of the towering Ratman steal the plans, which are hidden in Katrina's pearl necklace. The superhero Cap'n Catnip tracks Ratman to his lair in the Minnion Muenster Company; there, he finds that the legendary villain is actually a pipsqueak who simply casts a large shadow using a flashlight. The villain is carted off to jail.

Quote: "At last, my fine *enemies*, we meet face to mask!"

Comment: This was the character's only appearance.

THE RATTLER (MP)

Real Name: Dr. Edwards.

First Appearance: 1934, *Mystery Mountain*, Mascot Pictures.

Costume: Black cape, slouch hat, mask.

Weapons: Extremely lifelike masks to impersonate various townspeople; standard firearms.

Biography: A wealthy landowner, Dr. Edwards owns much territory coveted by the railroad. In order to protect his land and acquire even more, he becomes the Rattler, a masked outlaw who, with his band of outlaws, murders railroad workers, hoping to scare them off. However, hero Ken Williams gets onto the Rattler's trail and, after numerous adventures, traces him to his cave hideout. The Rattler is killed there in a titanic explosion.

Comment: Edmund Cobb played the Rattler in all but the last scene when Dr. Edwards was unmasked (Edward Earle played Edwards) in this 12-chapter serial. Future western superstar Gene Autry had a small part as one of the Rattler's henchmen. THE WRECKER is another Mascot villain who uses lifelike masks.

RAVAGER (C)

Real Name: Ranark.

First Appearance: 1982, *Marvel Two-In-One* #84, Marvel Comics.

Costume: Brown loincloth, headband; silver wristbands.

Biography: Centuries ago, Ranark was "the most feared shaman of all," an Indian sorcerer who made "obscene pacts with the dark spirits until he became like unto a god himself." Fearful of his might—which included enormous physical strength, the ability to grow huge, the power to shoot beams from his eyes which cause "searing agony," and dominion over fire, water, and earth—medicine men of neighboring tribes banded together and used spells to imprison his spirit within a sacred urn, which they hid in a remote crypt in the mountains of northwest Alberta. Employing a "powerful mind-spell" in the present day, Ravager mesmerized the superheroic Shaman of the team Alpha Flight and forced him to open the urn. Free, Ranark headed to Manitoba, Canada, where he caused huge trees to grow in the city, the massive roots toppling buildings. Alpha Flight and the superhero the Thing of the Fantastic Four took him on, the Ravager showering these heroes with boulders and causing the earth to mold itself into huge clutching hands. Fortunately, the team was able to knock him out with an explosion (they rammed two cars together), after which Shaman imprisoned the Ravager's soul inside a "mystic cocoon." The Ravager has not been heard from since.

Quote: "Before I have finished, no one on earth will fail to shudder at the mere mention of my name!"

RAVEN (C)

Real Name: Thorn Trask.

First Appearance: 1963, *Rawhide Kid* #35, Marvel Comics.

Costume: Purple breeches, shirt with rawhide tassels hanging from arms, cowl with a beak and yellow eye-slits; white gloves; brown shoes.

Weapons: Standard six-shooter.

Biography: Thorn lives in Red Rock, a western town of the last century. Head of the Civic Betterment League, he talks tough against outlaws in town—until he pulls on his Raven garb and robs people blind. Tangling with the heroic Rawhide Kid in a mine, he is killed in a cave-in. He is survived by his sister Nora.

Quote: "*Hah*!" Another hapless victim for the *Raven* to attack and rob!"

Comment: This character's sole adventure was drawn by comics-great Jack Davis. See other Marvel western villains THE FAT MAN, HURRICANE, THE PANTHER, THE RED RAVEN, and ROBIN HOOD RAIDER.

THE RAY (C)

First Appearance: 1966, *Captain Marvel* #4, M.F. Enterprises.

Costume: Dark green gloves, boots, cowl with antennae, bat-like ears and red eyes (see Weapons); olive green bodysuit with purple stripe down chest and yellow lightning bolt in stripe; purple trunks;

*Mid-air, **THE RAY** maligns the legal profession . . . and his nemesis, Tinyman. © M.F. Enterprises.*

black belt with yellow diamonds all around it; blue wings (see Weapons).

Weapons: Blue wings on costume for flight, though they fail to work when exposed to rainwater; red eyes hypnotize enemies; torch ray gun for cutting metal; explosive capsules which, strapped to bats, unleash their destructive power when the bat's body heat melts the pellets' shells; "tiny helicopter" for flight—though it isn't clear why he uses this very slender, one-person craft on occasion instead of his wings.

Chief Henchmen: Two bats trained to steal.

Biography: Nothing is known about this thief, save that he has his headquarters in an old castle outside of Riverview in upstate New York. He was last seen rotting in prison after being apprehended by the superheroes Captain Marvel and Tinyman.

Quote: "Training these mammals as retrievers was a stroke of genius! Yes sir, Ray—you're a genius!"

Comment: Although THE BAT had none of the weapons possessed by the Ray, it's apparent the two characters are the same; if nothing else, the costumes are virtually identical. It's likely the name was changed to avoid confusion with the superhero Batman, whose TV series had recently debuted.

REACTRON (C)

Real Name: Benjamin Krullen.

First Appearance: 1982, *The Daring New Adventures of Supergirl* #8, DC Comics.

Costume: Yellow bodysuit from head to toe; purple leotard covered with white stars; two red rings circling torso diagonally (like atomic symbol), fastened at chest, and a thick bracelet around each wrist (see Weapons).

Weapons: Reactron's red bands act as control rods which enable him to tap his radioactivity and fire it as destructive blasts.

Biography: A U.S. Army sergeant in the 1960s, Ben inadvertently received a dose of nuclear radiation—though the effects didn't surface until years later. Following a tour of duty in Vietnam, he couldn't hold down a job until he linked up with the Council (see THE GANG), whose scientists used his radioactivity to turn him into a super-strong, airborne, blast-firing nuclear generator. While working evil deeds for the Council, Reactron battled Supergirl in the skies over Chicago; the super villain apparently perished in the resultant nuclear explosion.

THE REAPER (C)

Real Name: Louis Dawson.

First Appearance: 1984, *Power Man and Iron Fist* #109, Marvel Comics.

Costume: Light blue bodysuit, cape, hood, gloves; red skull-like, full-face mask; blue boots.

Weapons: Portable flamethrower, machine gun, and hand grenades.

Biography: A member of the Eleventh Precinct SWAT team in New York City, Dawson was laying siege to a building held by terrorists when his own home happened to burn down. Devastated by the fire—it killed his son Andrew and badly scarred his wife—Dawson suffered a breakdown and was committed. All he could talk about at the sanitarium was revenge, "presumably against the terrorists who had kept him away from saving his family." After a few months, Dawson was sent to work on a government-subsidized farm, then returned home where he spent most of time alone, tinkering in his home workshop . . . preparing weapons for the future, plotting revenge. When a fellow officer was accidentally slain by a young hood, Dawson debuted as the Reaper. Tracking the boy down to a church, he managed to waylay both the superheroes Iron Fist and Power Man and intended to kill the youth. However, he saw his own son in the boy's frightened features and was snapped back to sanity—even saving the boy's life when the church collapsed from a hand grenade he'd lobbed earlier.

Quote: "The time is now. The field is full. The harvest is ready, and—*I am the Reaper*!"

Comment: This was the character's only appearance.

THE RECORDER (MP)

Real Name: Dr. Benson.
First Appearance: 1949, *Bruce Gentry—Daredevil of the Skies,* Columbia Pictures.
Weapons: Flying discs which, controlled by complex radio electronics, can be flown to destroy any targets.
Chief Henchmen: Krendon, Chandler, and Allen.
Biography: An enemy agent, Benson communicates with friend and foe alike by radio—hence his sobriquet. Inventing the flying discs, the Recorder and his operatives use them to undermine U.S. security. However, they are consistently thwarted by heroic Bruce Gentry who, in due course, finds the villains' hideout. But while Gentry is busy subduing the Recorder, wily Krendon sends a disc out to destroy the Panama Canal. Taking to the air, Gentry pursues the disc and intercepts it, parachuting to safety after sacrificing his plane to detonate the disc. Meanwhile, the saboteurs perish when the disc control unit explodes.
Comment: Forrest Taylor was the Recorder in this 15-chapter serial.

THE RED GHOST (C)

Real Name: Ivan Kragoff.
First Appearance: 1963, *The Fantastic Four* #13, Marvel Comics.
Chief Henchmen: The Super-Apes (a baboon, gorilla, and orangutan).
Biography: A brilliant Soviet scientist specializing in cosmic radiation, Kragoff has studied from afar the American superheroes the Fantastic Four, who gained their phenomenal abilities due to exposure to cosmic rays during a spaceflight. Intent on duplicating their feat, he persuades the Soviet government to send him and three specially trained simians into space. What he doesn't tell his leaders is that he also plans a side trip to the moon where the Fantastic Four are on a mission. (Venomously jealous of scientist Reed Richards of the Fantastic Four, Kragoff wishes to destroy him.) The resulting radiation bath gives the Russian the power to become partially or completely immaterial, and his apes acquire superstrength (the gorilla), the ability to change shape (the baboon), and the power to attract or repulse objects (the orangutan). Assuming the name the Red Ghost, Kragoff reaches the moon—where he suffers the first of many defeats at the hands of the courageous quartet. On two separate occasions he has also taken it on the chin from Spider-Man.
Comment: See other Soviet super villains Boris Kartovski (see DR. CLEMENT ARMSTRONG, Comment), COMRADE STUPIDSKA, THE CRIMSON DYNAMO, MONGU, THE SOVIET SUPER SOLDIERS, THE TITANIC THREE, and TITANIUM MAN.

THE RED KNIGHT (C)

Real Name: Dr. Lewis Coll.
First Appearance: 1965, *Blue Beetle* #5, Charlton Comics.
Costume: Red knight's armor.
Weapons: Flying horse; lance.
Biography: Dr. Coll lives in a remote castle where, using his scientific genius, he constructs a rocket capable of reaching the planet Saturn in a matter of hours. Visiting the sixth planet, he carelessly goes abroad without a spacesuit and ends up with dread methaneammonia poisoning. The infection causes him to become murderously misanthropic and, taking his cue from a chess set, he becomes the Red Knight. Using a special Saturnian silicate, he creates a costume for himself and gives his horse the power of flight. After robbing banks and terrorizing the airways, the Red Knight is defeated by the superheroic Blue Beetle, who uses dust from the tomb of the mummy Ac-Tem to subdue him. His senses restored, Coll is pardoned for his misadventure.
Comment: This was the character's only appearance.

THE RED PANZER (C)

Real Name: Helmut Streicher.
Costume: Red German World War II uniform with blue belt, strap across chest, boots, helmet; light blue gauntlets (see Weapons), full-face metal mask.
Weapons: Gauntlets fire destructive blasts.
Chief Henchmen: Various Nazi soldiers.
Biography: An "inventor genius" loyal to the Third Reich, Helmut was scoffed at by the German high command. Thus, he adopted his Red Panzer guise and, with "weapons circuits" sewn into his uniform, went to work as a solo operative. After nearly defeating Wonder Woman, he was tossed in a U.S. jail. However, his work had caught the attention of Hitler, who ordered fifth columnists to smuggle him from prison. Becoming a personal right arm to the Fuhrer in the United States, the Panzer began to have dreams of grandeur. ("I could continue the Nazi ideals *without* the aid of the Fuhrer! They would salute *me* instead of Hitler!") However, his ambitions became academic

when he was once again defeated by Wonder Woman, apparently perishing when Hitler's sonic cannon, the Cyclosonitron, exploded (*DC Special Series* Vol. 2, #9, *Wonder Woman Spectacular*, 1978).

Quote: "It will be an honor to serve the Fatherland! *And* to destroy America!"

Comment: See other Nazi super villains BARON BLITZKRIEG, BARON GESTAPO, BARON ZEMO, CAPTAIN AXIS, CAPTAIN NAZI, THE CLOWN, THE GOLDEN FUHRER, KILLER SHARK, NIGHT AND FOG, The Master Swastika OF VENDETTA, Mastermind (see U-MAN, Comment), THE RED SKULL, and ZYKLON.

THE RED RAVEN (C)

Real Name: "Red" Raven.

First Appearance: 1964, *Rawhide Kid* #38, Marvel Comics.

Costume: Orange wings (see Weapons), tailfeathers, bodysuit; purple harness, cowl, boots, trunks.

Weapons: Raven's costume was "treated by a special Indian herb. On the upsweep, the feathers will let air pass through . . . and . . . on the downstroke, they close together, allowing you to beat the air."

Chief Henchmen: Two gangmembers.

Biography: A bank robber, Raven is captured by the hero the Rawhide Kid and placed in prison. There, his cellmate is a Navajo medicine man. Near death, the old shaman gives Raven "something hidden here, under my mattress"—the winged harness. When the Indian dies, Raven simply flies from his cell as a guard opens the door. Going on a criminal rampage, Raven meets his match when the Rawhide Kid heads for the Navajo tribe, gets wings of his own, and has a mid-air showdown with the felon. Raven's career ends abruptly when he slams headfirst into a mountainside.

Quote: "It—it's *impossible*!! *Nobody* can shoot a gun out of a man's hand while he's moving in the air!"

Comment: Marvel published several popular western titles from the 1950s to the 1970s, the cowboy heroes battling countless super villains. Among the more interesting of the ultrafiends was Kid Colt's foe, Doctor Danger, who came to town with the Invisible Gunman—actually a gun held in mid-air by a powerful magnet. Ventriloquist Danger did the shooting from within his cloak; naturally, no one could stop the Invisible gunman because they were firing at empty space. And the Iron Mask, who was armored from head to toe and done-in when Kid Colt jumped him and repeatedly banged the crook's head against a rock ("Must be vibratin' somethin' awful inside that mask"). Also, the Two-Gun Kid's nemesis the Rattler, who wore a snake-like green bodysuit and cowl and was a circus ringmaster; the acrobat Whirlo assumed the Rattler's disguise when the villain was captured. And the Stingray, a pharmacist who wore a blue bodysuit, a red cape and cowl, and knocked people out with his gaseous "stun potion"; this villain, originally known as the Scorpion, changed his name to remove the stigmata of failure. Lastly, the black-garbed Tarantula who cracked a stinging cat-o'-nine-tails against the heroic Night Rider.

THE RED SHADOW (C)

First Appearance: 1967, *Mighty Comics* #45, Archie Comics.

Costume: Red leotard, belt, mail bodysuit, cloak and hood; brown boots and gloves. (Note: On cover, bodysuit and leotard were blue; cape, hood, gloves, and boots were purple.)

Biography: Standing some four stories tall and impervious to bullets, the Red Shadow is one of the most formidable foes ever fought by the Shield. ("Compared to the towering menace of this *Red Shadow*," gasps the superhero, "all the villains I've battled in the past are strictly from *nowheresville*.") Created by a P.E.R.I.L. machine "out of the atoms in the air," the Red Shadow is a device which can only be used once because of the paucity of "an integral rare element." However, as the giant is pulverizing the Shield, the superhero discovers that "some side-effect of the Red Shadow's substance materializes your heart-felt wish if you concentrate hard enough." So the beleaguered hero wishes for an equally-strong Blue Shadow . . . which delivers "the most powerful punch this planet has ever seen" and socks the Red Shadow beyond the stratosphere. There, the villain is dissolved by solar radiation.

Quote: "*I . . . seek . . . the . . . doomed . . . Shield!*"

Comment: This was the character's only appearance; on the cover, he was called the Doom Shadow. P.E.R.I.L. is a group of evildoers; though they all wear costumes, only a few of the criminals are super villains. These are the villainess Dragonfly; the Blender, who can blend into any background; and the Vibrateer, who has a "gizmo" which gives him "vibrational abilities." The non-super agents aren't terribly bright, as witness the following exchange during a meeting in their "underground cavern headquarters": "Now about blowing up the planet earth . . ." says one. To which another responds, "Forget it! *We're* on earth, too, remember!" The group has a "spy-eye satellite" which can pick up detailed TV pictures of doings on earth and beam them to P.E.R.I.L. headquarters. See THE STORM KING.

THE RED SKULL (C, N, TV)

Real Name: Johann Shmidt (over the years he has also used numerous aliases, including Cyrus Fenton, Bettman P. Lyles, and Tod March).

First Appearance: 1941, *Captain America Comics* #1, Marvel Comics.

Costume: Varies; most often a green jumpsuit with a red swastika on chest; sometimes a basic Nazi uniform. Always wears a red, skull-like, full-head mask.

Weapons: The Red Skull has used a wide array of arms over the decades, both conventional and extraordinary. Among the latter are his lethal Dust of Death, which kills on contact; the Sleepers, huge robots with which Hitler intended to destroy the world if the Third Reich were defeated; a skull-shaped spaceship (red, of course); and the Cosmic Cube, an extraordinary device built by researchers belonging to the evil scientific league A.I.M. Described by the venomous character as "the ultimate source of power," the palm-sized cube was constructed using a "mysterious, omni-dimensional X-element" which allowed him to control the will of every living thing on earth; to order inanimate objects to do whatever he wished, even against the laws of physics; to emit powerful destructive blasts; to turn soil into a powerful living being; and to create matter. The cube could only function properly if all the Red Skull's fingers were fully closed over it. Eventually lost in the sea (*Tales of Suspense* #81), the cube was later recovered by THANOS, who used it to become god-like in *Captain Marvel* #'s 28 to 33, only to have that superhero triumph. The cube was briefly recreated under the supervision of the Red Skull and HATE-MONGER in *Super-Villain Team-Up* #17. (Another cosmic cube had been made by the alien Skrulls, race of THE SUPER-SKRULL. It eventually copied the sentience of one of its users, evolved a body, and became the powerful Shaper of Worlds, a non-malevolent godlike being.)

Chief Henchmen: His right hand men are Horst and Wolfgang, who were in the Berlin bunker with the Red Skull and went through suspended animation with him (see Biography); sundry other thugs.

Biography: Captain America said it best: the Red Skull was a super villain who loved to "Revel in atrocity! Bask in evil! Delight in depravity." Johann was born in Germany in 1899 to Herman and Martha Shmidt. His mother died in childbirth and, mad with grief, his father took his own life. Living in "an endless parade of orphanages," Johann was a loner who finally struck out on his own at the age of seven. He lived by stealing, and "drifted from town to town, jail to jail"; he committed his first murder by clubbing a young woman to death with a shovel when she spurned his affections. Discovering that "the act of murder had somehow opened a door in my soul," he felt "dizzying joy" and joined the Nazi party. Hitler saw an abundance of evil in Johann's soul, and personally trained him in the ways of Nazism. When his lessons were complete, Johann was given his costume and new identity as the Red Skull, and was sent to the United States to carry out terrorist atrocities. Working in Europe during the war, he commanded armies and razed countless towns and their occupants. He eventually became second-in-command to Hitler, in large part because he killed others who were in line for the job. Profoundly bored with assaulting "inferiors" in the field, he was delighted when the superhero Captain America appeared on the scene. The two became mortal enemies and remained so until, near the end of the war, the bunker in which they were battling was bombed. Captain America escaped, but the Red Skull was trapped inside with ruptured containers of an experimental gas, putting him into suspended animation. Discovered by a criminal group known as THEM (an elite division of A.I.M.), the villain was awakened and immediately returned to his evil ways. As fortune would have it, Captain America had also ended up in suspended animation, by virtue of being frozen in icy seas; the two met and promptly resumed their struggles. However, nearly two decades later, the conflict came to an end—this time for good. Much to his dismay, the German discovered that the effects of the gas which kept him alive in the bunker were not permanent and that his true age was catching up with him. Realizing he had one last chance to kill Captain America, he engaged him in battle at his estate, Skull-House; however, during the furious fist fight, the suddenly decrepit villain simply keeled over and died in the arms of his nemesis (*Captain America* #300, 1984). However, his evil was not quite vanquished. The Red Skull had a daughter, born from a union with a "washer-woman" who worked on the Isle of Exiles where he spent the early days after his revival. (The woman, a dead-ringer for his wife, also perished in childbirth.) Subjecting the child to his "Deus Machina," which nurtured her evil side, the Red Skull "genetically accelerated" his daughter's aging process. Quickly becoming a fully grown woman, she has lived by the credo, "That which cannot be understood can only be hated." The self-described "beast-goddess, the avatar of primitive savagery," she became a sorceress and developed numerous psychic talents, including the ability to levitate herself and others. Later, as black-garbed Mother Superior, she assumed the leadership of the villainous Sisters of Sin (Sister Dream, Sister Pleasure, Sister Agony, and Sister Death) and seeks revenge on her father's old enemy.

Quote: "Can you *imagine* the ecstasy I knew as I eradicated *entire populations*?"

Comment: The Red Skull was the preeminent Captain America villain, and was the hero's adversary in the novel *Holocaust for Hire* written by Joseph Silva in 1979. The character also appeared on TV, in the Captain America segments of the animated *Marvel Superheroes* syndicated cartoon series in 1966. There was also a second Red Skull, who was created by Marvel to tie-up loose ends in continuity. (The original Red Skull perished in *Young Men* #25, 1954. Thus, when the character returned in 1966, it was revealed that the dead Skull was actually a Communist spy who had been impersonating the villain while Johann slept.) But, curiously undoing the continuity they were trying to restore, Marvel subsequently brought back the Red Skull who was supposed to have died in 1954. This occurred in *The Amazing Spider-Man Annual* #5, 1968. In that tale, he was shown to be living in Algeria. There he was pursued by Spider-Man—wanted for the murder of the hero's parents years before when they were working for the U.S. government. Ironically, if that killing had not occurred, Peter Parker might never have become the superhero. (Who knows where he would have been living when that radioactive spider came calling?) That Red Skull's henchman was a brute named Sandor. Other Nazi villains are BARON BLITZKRIEG, BARON GESTAPO, BARON ZEMO, CAPTAIN AXIS, CAPTAIN NAZI, THE CLOWN, THE GOLDEN FUHRER, KILLER SHARK, NIGHT AND FOG, The Masked Swastika of VENDETTA, Mastermind (see U-MAN, Comment), THE RED PANZER, and ZYKLON.

THE REGULATOR (C)

Real Name: Barnabas Boulton.

First Appearance: 1980, *Justice League of America* #174, DC Comics.

Costume: Red bodysuit; yellow leotard open from the breast to waist; yellow gloves with two red bands around wrist, boots with two red patches on feet, goggles, helmet with red fin on top (see Weapons).

Weapons: Helmet allows the Regulator to control vermin or to slay humans.

Chief Henchmen: A swarming army of giant rats.

Biography: An employee of the Metropolis division of S.T.A.R. labs, located "on the fringe of suicide slum" scientist Boulton invents a helmet which can control vermin in the manner of a modern Pied Piper. When he tries to convince authorities to see the helmet to rid the slums of rats, they laugh in his face; suffering a nervous breakdown, Boulton is institutionalized. Escaping after several months, deluded that he was put away because his colleagues were jealous of his genius, he becomes the Regulator. Breaking into S.T.A.R., he sends a horde of rats into a mutation chamber, breeding carnivorous giants. His plan is simple: to let his mutated rats gnaw to death, in turn, "the police . . . then the politicians! And the bankers! And the reporters! All who have oppressed the poor." But the rats are stopped by the Justice League of America, and the Regulator himself apparently perishes when he falls into a smokestack during a battle with the superhero Black Lightning. (Despite the loud, accompanying "FTOOM!" it's conceivable his costume protected him.)

Quote: "Did you think my *regulator helmet* only affected *vermin*? Though with *humans*, the effect isn't so much *control*, as it is—*destruction*!"

Comment: The Regulator is one of the few black super villains; this has been the character's only appearance to date.

RETIK (MP)

First Appearance: 1952, *Radar Men from the Moon*, Republic Pictures.

Costume: Ornate robe with floral design in metallic fabric; metallic fabric also used for shirt and hood; medallion worn around neck. (Costume was very similar to that of THE PURPLE MONSTER so that footage from the earlier serial could be edited into this one.)

Weapons: Atomic gun powered by rare element lunarium (found only on the moon).

Chief Henchmen: The jumpsuited Krog, Zerg, Robal, and Nasor.

Biography: The ruler of the moon, Retik has designs on earth as well. When he begins destroying U.S. defense installations with his atomic gun, the lunar villain attracts the attention of the airborne superhero Commando Cody. Surviving assaults from the atomic gun, a volcano, floods, and a trip to the moon, Cody is able to blast Retik and his personal rocket ship to pieces as the invasion of earth is about to get underway.

Comment: Roy Barcroft starred as Retik in this 12-chapter serial. Barcroft also played CAPTAIN MEPHISTO and The Purple Monster. A feature version of the serial was released in 1966 as *Retik the Moon Menace.*

REVERSE-FLASH (C)

Real Name: Professor Adrian Zoom (see Comment).

First Appearance: 1964, *Flash* #139, DC Comics.

Costume: Identical design to that of the superhero the Flash, but with "opposite" colors: yellow bodysuit with red bolt in black circle on chest; yellow gloves with jagged red hem; yellow cowl with flared red ears; red belt, boots with "wings" on side.

Weapons: Time machine; heavy-matter boots which cause an object to triple its weight every two-tenths of a second.

Biography: Born in the twenty-fifth century, the telepathic Professor Zoom uses "the advanced technology of his future-era" to artificially duplicate the superspeed abilities of the twentieth-century superhero the Flash. Journeying to our time, the super villain inaugurates a "grudgewar" against his model, spurred partly by evil, partly by pride. Of all his horrible doings, his most heinous crime is murdering the Flash's wife Iris (*The Flash* #276). Zoom had always loved her, and when she spurns his romantic advances he does her in with "a vibrating superspeed thrust to the brain." (Luckily, however, Iris' psychic self is extracted by her parents and placed in the body of another young woman. The Flash and his wife are eventually reunited.) Maddened by the loss, Flash grabs "the human filth" and carts him into his time machine, intending to take Zoom ahead to the twenty-fifth century and a certain death sentence. But Zoom had rigged the console-panel to send them into the past; as they speed toward the moment of creation, Flash is able to leap out into the time stream but Zoom dazed from his apprehension, cannot. Though he plummets "into an oblivion far more fearsome than death's embrace," he manages to return . . . only to die, for good, in *The Flash* #324. Believing Iris dead, the Flash falls in love with another woman, Fiona Webb, whom Zoom attacks. While protecting her, the Flash kills Zoom by inadvertently snapping his neck. Reverse-Flash was a member of THE SECRET SOCIETY OF SUPER-VILLAINS.

Quote: "Yeah—when I'm *finished* with *you*, I'll be the first and foremost *Flash* . . . and the only kind of Flash *you'll* be . . . is *dead*!"

Comment: One account gives Zoom's birthdate as 2633; this is obviously erroneous, since all other adventures place him in the twenty-fifth century. In a subsequent revision of his origin, it seems that there was more to Zoom than we knew. Originally, he was actually twenty-fifth century thug Eobard Thawne, nicknamed the "Professor" due to his scientific genius. When a "time satellite" (i.e., time capsule) arrives in the future, sent by our era's Dr. Walter Drake, it is found to contain, among other artifacts, a costume donated by the Flash. Thawne gets a hold of it and, boosting the latent superspeed waves the costume has absorbed from the superhero, Thawne becomes a superspeedster himself. Adopting the name Zoom he becomes the Reverse-Flash—committing rather than preventing crimes. The Speed Demon (1) of VENDETTA and THE SPEED DEMON (2) are other superfast super villains.

REX RUTHLESS (C)

First Appearance: 1981, *The Kid Super Power Hour with Shazam*, NBC-TV.

Costume: Turquoise tights, jerkin with golden epaulets and braid; golden gloves, belt; black cape, boots with gold cuffs.

Weapons: Propulsion jets under cape for flight; e-longating boots to make him taller.

Biography: Rex is a wicked student at Hero High, a school for super-powered humans of the future. Virtually powerless without his gimmicks, Rex has one goal in life—to humiliate Captain California, the surfing superhero.

REX RUTHLESS. © *Filmation.*

Comment: The character appeared on the "Hero High" segment of the show, which lasted just one season. Other rats at Hero High were Dirty Trixie, his girlfriend, who packed a pouch full of nasty jokes; and the diminutive Bratman. The series was produced by Filmation.

THE RHINO (C)

First Appearance: 1966, *The Amazing Spider-Man* #41, Marvel Comics.

Costume: Gray jumpsuit, gloves, boots, rhino-head cowl with one large horn and a smaller one behind it (see Weapons).

Weapons: Costume is bonded to his skin and is extremely tough, like animal hide; horn can be used to penetrate just about anything.

Biography: A powerful but minor hood (his name has never been revealed) the Rhino-to-be acquires his powers after going to work for a group of spies-for-hire. Hoping to turn the brute into a super-assassin, they expose him to radiation and chemical treatments which give him awesome strength and invulnerability. Costuming him and sending him out to kidnap astronaut John Jameson (whom they intend to peddle to the country offering the fattest ransom), the group doesn't count on the Rhino going independent. Telling his bosses to take a hike, he becomes a sovereign super villain and goes after Jameson for himself. Though Spider-Man intervenes and sends the Rhino to prison, the burly fellow refuses to stay put; the two have battled repeatedly over the years. The Rhino is a member of THE EMISSARIES OF EVIL and THE SINISTER SYNDICATE.

Quote: "I gave you your chance, Spider-Man . . . but if you won't listen—it's *your* funeral!"

THE RIDDLER (C, TV, N, MP)

Real Name: Edward Nigma (i.e., E. Nigma).

First Appearance: 1948, *Detective Comics* #140, DC Comics.

Costume: Green boots, bodysuit covered with black "?"s; purple gloves, belt, mask.

Weapons: Countless devices over the years, from mere smoke bombs to exploding roses to a vat of molten wax in which people are dipped and turned into candles.

Biography: The Riddler's criminal career began in high school. His history class was holding a contest to see who could assemble an historically-themed jigsaw puzzle the fastest. The night before the contest, Edward pried open the drawer to study the puzzle before it was disassembled. Becoming fascinated with puzzles, he affiliated himself with a carnival and would challenge others with puzzles: "Solve that Chinese puzzle and I pay you," he would dare. "If you don't and I do . . . then you pay me!" Naturally, the games were always fixed. (For example, the pieces of one puzzle were marked with instructions which only he could read through his specially tinted glasses.) Eventually, he became cocky enough not only to want to commit crimes, but also to try and baffle the great sleuth Batman by giving him puzzling clues. (To wit: He provided a clue which the hero deciphered as "banquet" when, in fact, the Riddler meant "bank wet"—and flooded a local bank while Batman was looking for him at a fancy banquet.) Though the Riddler is constantly being captured—most recently, he was inmate #74658 at the Gotham Penitentiary—he lives to taunt Batman and refuses to turn over a new leaf.

Quote: "I'll make each crime a duel of wits between myself and the law—and fix the puzzles so I'll always win!"

Comment: Considering his popularity today, it's surprising that the Riddler appeared in *Dectective* #s 140 and 142 and then did not show up again until *Batman* #171 in May of 1965. Shortly thereafter (January 1966) the character was catapulted into pop culture legend by being the first nemesis to face Batman on the *Batman* TV series. Frank Gorshin played the part for most of the character's appearances during 1966 to 1968 (briefly replaced by John Astin in 1967). Gorshin was also the Riddler in the 1966 film *Batman* and in the 1979 two-part prime time TV special, *The Legend of the Super-Heroes.* The character was also featured in Winston Lyon's 1966 Signet novel, *Batman vs. the Three Villains of Doom.*

THE RINGMASTER (C)

Real Name: Maynard Tiboldt.

First Appearance: 1962, *The Incredible Hulk* #3, Marvel Comics.

Costume: Original: navy blue tights, top hat; blue necktie, vest, gloves; white shirt; red ringmaster's jacket, boots, both covered with black stars. Second: red tights, necktie, top hat (see Weapons); green vest, ringmaster's jacket, boots both covered with black stars; white shirt.

Weapons: Hat contains a unit which, amplifying the Ringmaster's psionic energy, emits the waves through a disc on the front of the hat, enabling him to control the minds of individuals or entire crowds.

Chief Henchmen: THE CIRCUS OF CRIME.

Biography: Tiboldt's Circus was a fixture in Austria. For generations, the honored position of ringmaster was handed down from Tiboldt father to son. When Nazism began spreading through the land, Fritz Tiboldt became an active supporter and moved the circus to the United States to carry out espionage. His racket was uncovered by the superhero Captain America, and Tiboldt had no choice but to work with the Allies against the Nazis. He and his wife Lola were eventually murdered by a Nazi who had eluded capture. The circus fell to their son Maynard, who wasn't able to hold his own against the larger touring attractions in America. Embittered and feeling vengeful for his father's capture, Maynard turned to crime . . . but with a twist. Using plans for a nullatron—a hypnotic device invented by Germany during the war—he modified the design so the unit could fit inside his ringmaster's hat. Thereafter, wherever his circus played, he hypnotized the crowds and then had his performers rob them. ("Don't take your eyes off me for a minute—note the spinning lines on my hat—the stars on my jacket—the lines—the stars . . . .") If the take was not to his satisfaction, he would then go through the town and entrance the entire population. He was first defeated by the Hulk, whom he had tried to turn into a circus attraction. He and his Circus of Crime have appeared regularly in other Marvel titles as well.

Quote: "Nothing that lives can defy me!"

Comment: See other hypnotist super villains DESPERO, HYPNOS, MESMERO, and UNIVERSO.

THE ROAR DEVIL (M)

Real Name: V. Venable Mear.

First Appearance: June 1935, "The Roar Devil," *Doc Savage* Magazine, Kenneth Robeson.

Weapons: Ultra-short sonic wave transmitter which can be used to shake the earth or smother all sound by paralyzing the eardrum.

Biography: Mear, an old man but neither stooped nor feeble, is a criminal psychologist, dwelling in an upper-class section of Powertown, New York. There he plans to build the world's greatest crime organization assisted by a thug's buried files, collected over a decade, which contain "blackmail evidence . . . on wealthy men and men high in public office." Posing as the Roar Devil, Mear burrows for the cache with his sonic transmitter and, finding it, intends to use the data to get "all kinds of privileges." However, the superhero Doc Savage gets onto Mear's trail and uses anaesthetic gas to subdue him and his henchmen. All are sent to Doc's crime college in upstate New York where their criminal natures are surgically reformed. Physically, Mear is a strange fellow. He has eyes of "no particular color," and a head "of amazing bigness above the ears . . . white and hairless"; more than anything, it resembled "a tremendous skull."

Quote: "Here is evidence that would hang several of our best-known criminals. I have tried to get these men to join me, and they have refused. They will change their minds, now."

ROBAN (C)

Real Name: Nabor.

First Appearance: 1966, *House of Mystery* #162, DC Comics.

Weapons: "Monster-making machine" which turns people into beasts; wind machine to collect smog.

Biography: Early in the 1950s, Mr. Nabor is arrested for fraud and run out of Littleville. Vowing revenge, he buys a monster-making machine "from an impoverished criminal scientist" and returns nearly a decade later, behind an alias (albeit, a rather transparent one), to kill the town. Based in a mansion overlooking the city, he uses his machine to send out an "invisible ray" which turns people into a weird array of destructive creatures, from a human porcupine to a four-armed slug. Convincing the populace that this is all because of a strange smog which has settled over the city (a cloud he created), Roban watches with glee as Littleville is abandoned. However, Robby Reed figures out that Roban is causing the changes and, becoming a superhero by using his Dial-H for Hero device, arrests him, stemming the exodus.

Quote: "Soon Littleville will be deserted—a ghost town that will be avoided like the plague! I've done it at last! *I've destroyed Littleville!*"

Comment: This was the character's only appearance.

THE ROBBER BRIDEGROOM (F)

First Appearance: 1812, "The Robber Bridegroom," the Brothers Grimm.

Biography: A well-to-do criminal and cannibal, the Robber woos a miller's daughter, telling her and her father nothing of his true nature. Inviting her to his home in the wood, the Robber has some cannibal guests over; spying on the group, the young bride-to-be watches as the "cutthroats" get a female guest drunk, cut her to pieces "without mercy," then cook and eat her. Sneaking away, the young woman waits until the wedding day to reveal what she knows. Outraged, the wedding guests "held him fast," the Robber and his cohorts being summarily executed. The Robber had a pet, a bird, who surreptitiously warned people to stay away.

Quote: "You must come and pay me a visit next Sunday; I have already invited company."

Comment: The short tale contains some of the Brothers' grisliest scenes, including a severed finger trying to escape the cannibals. Other nefarious characters of the Grimms include "the elder brother" who, in "The Singing Bone," slew his younger brother and took credit for having killed a boar (only to be betrayed by a talking flute, carved by a shepherd from one of the victim's bones); the "Fox" of "The Fox and the Geese" ("There is no mercy to be had! You must die!"); the "Fairy," who lived in a well and used children as slave labor in "The Water Sprite"; the "King" of "The Devil's Three Golden Hairs," who tried to drown the peasant baby fated to marry his daughter and, when the child survived, sent him to procure three hairs from a demon in the Black Forest (the youth succeeds and the King is made a ferryman as punishment); the "wicked dwarf" in "Snow-White and Rose-Red," who turned a prince into a bear and stole his treasure; the girl who is so "wicked (and) jealous" that "The Three Little Men in the Wood" curse her to "grow uglier every day . . . each time she speaks a toad shall jump out of her mouth at every word (and) she shall die a miserable death" (which she does, nailed into a cask and drowned); and the hobgoblins who enchanted a castle in "The King's Son Who Feared Nothing." The Devil himself was also featured in numerous Grimm tales, including "The Peasant and the Devil," "The Grave Mound," "The Devil and His Grandmother," "The Devil's Sooty Brother," and "The Three Apprentices." See other Grimm villains GOTHEL, MERCURIUS, and THE QUEEN.

ROBIN HOOD RAIDER (C)

Real Name: Gance.

First Appearance: 1967, *Kid Colt Outlaw* #139, Marvel Comics.

Costume: Green bodysuit; orange hood which goes over shoulders, trunks, boots, gloves.

Weapons: Bow and arrow.

Chief Henchmen: Various unsavory characters in Rat's Roost (see Biography).

Biography: The owner of Gance's Saloon in the "lawless, broken down mining town" of Rat's Roost, Gance steals from the rich and keeps it—giving out just enough to local toughs, "buying goodwill and protection" if he needs it. And need it he does when the heroic Kid Colt rides into town. Spotting Gance paying off some hombres, he snoops around the saloon-keeper's room and finds the Robin Hood costume; escaping, he ambushes the crook when he goes to rob rancher Ned Delman. When last seen, Gance was being hauled off to prison.

Quote: "*Greetings*, little lady! They can stop me now—*if* they want to put a *bullet* through you! Har har!"

Comment: See other Marvel western villains THE FAT MAN, HURRICANE, THE PANTHER, THE RAVEN, and RED RAVEN.

ROMULAN COMMANDER (TV)

First Appearance: September 27, 1968, "The Enterprise Incident," *Star Trek*, NBC-TV.

Weapons: "Cloaking Device," an instrument capable of making a starship invisible.

Chief Henchman: Subcommander Tal.

Biography: The Romulans, a race of bellicose humanoids, are sworn enemies of the human Federation in the twenty-third century. The Commander—her name is not revealed in the story—is one of the few who has any chance of being reformed. When the Federation starship *Enterprise* enters Romulan space to steal the Cloaking Device, the Commander surrounds it with a small fleet and orders Captain Kirk to surrender the ship to her. Though Kirk refuses, the Commander is ultimately undone when she falls in love with Mr. Spock, chief science officer of the *Enterprise*. While Spock occupies the Commander, Kirk steals the Cloaking Device and returns to his vessel. Outraged, the Commander demands Spock's execution. However, Spock is teleported back to his ship before the order can be carried out. In disgrace, the Commander grabs the Vulcan as he disappears so she can go with him. Though the Commander's subordinate, Tal, pursues the enemy, the *Enterprise* uses the Cloaking Device to escape. The Commander's fate is unknown, though chances are good she defected to the Federation. To have returned to a Romulan world would certainly have resulted in her execution.

Quote: "There is no force I can use on a Vulcan that will make him speak. But there are Romulan methods capable of going into a human mind like a spike into a melon."

Comment: Joanne Linville played the commander; Jack Donner was Subcommander Tal. D.C. Fontana wrote the teleplay. Another sinister Romulan is the nameless Commander (Mark Lenard) who raids Federation colonies in "Balance of Terror." Among Romulan characteristics is a fondness for torture and an irrefragable rule never to take prisoners.

ROTTEN KID (C)

First Appearance: 1984, *Normalman* #1, Aardvark-Vanaheim.

Costume: Orange bodysuit with black "ROTTEN KID" on chest; purple trunks, boots, cape.

Biography: Rotten Kid lives on the planet Levram, where everyone has superpowers. While most Levramians are benevolent, Rotten Kid is not. No sooner does the non-super Normalman arrive from earth than Rotten Kid abducts him (under the pretense of knowing where to find an Anti-Physics Probulator to return him to earth) and sells him to the evil Ultra-Conservative. When last seen, Rotten Kid is driving away in a truck; as for Normalman, he is rescued by the heroic Captain Everything and Sgt. Fluffy.

Quote: "I got 'im right *here*! But it's gonna *cost* ya . . . two-million chocolate bars, one tanker full o'root beer, a pound o' . . . ."

Comment: Unfortunately for Normalman, he stumbled from the Ultra-Conservative right into the hands of the Pope of Pain, a super-evangelist. Note that the home world of Rotten Kid, spelled backwards, identifies one of the publisher's competitors.

ROTWANG (N, MP)

First Appearance: 1926, *Metropolis,* Thea von Harbou.

Costume: Black shirt, trousers, robe.

Chief Henchman: A dwarf.

Biography: A scientist, Rotwang is a resident of Metropolis in the year 2026. In this city, the upper classes live a life of luxury above the surface, while the unclean masses—who keep the machinery running—live and work in catacombs beneath the surface. Nothing is known about Rotwang's past. With "eyes smouldering of a hatred which was very closely related to madness," he has only one arm; he lost it after foolishly mixing Aetro-oil with quicksilver (this explanation is not present in the film). Working in a home in the middle of the city, an abode described as "a blot and an annoyance . . . to the cleanly town," Rotwang has created a lifelike robot, the first of what he hopes will be a race of perfect mechanical workers. But Jon Fredersen, the Master Industrialist of Metropolis, has other ideas for the robot. He wants Rotwang to kidnap a woman named Maria, a young mother who has been preaching hope and pride to the masses, and then substitute the robot for her to "sow discord among the workers and destroy their confidence in her." Rotwang obeys, but the look-alike robot goes too far. It incites the workers to revolt, causing widespread damage through the underworld. Meanwhile, the real Maria manages to escape. Pursuing her to the rooftop of a church, Rotwang is about to strangle her with his metal artificial hand when Jon's liberal son Freder arrives. After a fierce struggle, Rotwang falls off the roof to his death; the robot is then burned on a pyre. Ultimately the real Maria and Freder mediate a more charitable relationship between the two classes of Metropolis, forestalling future dissension.

Quote: "Isn't it worth the loss of a hand to have created *this?*"

Comment: Rudolf Klein-Rogge played Rotwang in the 1927 German silent film; von Harbou wrote the screenplay and Fritz Lang directed. In 1985, the black and white picture was given a superb rock score by Giorgio Moroder and reissued with several color-tinted scenes.

RULU (MP)

First Appearance: 1951, *Mysterious Island,* Columbia Pictures.

Weapons: Spacecraft and destructive rays.

Biography: Flying in from Mercury in the year 1865, the beautiful Rulu sets up headquarters on an island way off the beaten track. Her mission: to find a radioactive metal which will allow her to create an explosive potent enough to obliterate our world. Thwarted by scientific genius CAPTAIN NEMO and a group of Civil War castaways, Rulu perishes in a titanic explosion.

Comment: Karen Randle played Rulu in this 15-chapter serial. The castaways, Nemo, and the island were all derived from the Jules Verne novel, *Mysterious Island.* Rulu, however, was not a part of the original tale. Obviously, the producers felt that the original tale wasn't cinematic enough—though they were willing to cash in on (and corrupt) its good name.

SABRETOOTH (C)

First Appearance: 1977, *Iron Fist* #14, Marvel Comics.

Costume: Orange bodysuit with black stripe down center to waist; circle of blond fur around shoulders, like a stole, and tufts at his wrists and shins; black trunks.

Weapons: Claws on hands and feet are extremely sharp, as are teeth.

Biography: Nothing is known about this character's past or private life, save that he was once the apprentice of a master assassin named Foreigner. A killer for hire, he has worked for MONTENEGRO and with THE CONSTRICTOR, among other criminals; he was also briefly a member of the Marauders, a group of super-assassins assembled by an elusive figure named Mister Sinister. Apparently a mutant, Sabretooth possesses superhuman senses and has the ability to recover from wounds and toxins at an extremely rapid pace.

Comment: During nearly 15 years of crimefighting, Cage and/or Iron Fist have also battled Big Ben (Donovan), 330 pounds of angry muscle; the brutish Mangler; Spear, Mangler's brother, who fired trident-like shafts; the underworld linchpin, Bushmaster; Curtis Carr, aka Chemistro, who could transmute matter using his "alchemy gun" (he quit the business after accidentally transmuting his foot into steel, at which point his former cellmate Arch Morton took over); Discus (Tim Stuart), who flies via jetpack and flings Frisbee-like blades; his partner Stilleto (Tom Stuart), a knife-throwing villain who also fires mini-blades from a wristband; Goldbug, who robs only gold and uses a gold-dust gun to paralyze his victims (similar to AURIC GOLDFINGER and GOLDFACE); Scimitar, an expert with knives and swords; Control 7, a costumed "mercenary espionage unit" which will "do whatever you pay 'em to"; and Steel Serpent (aka Davos), who briefly appropriated the mystic strength which gives the eponymous Iron Fist his power. See WEATHER WIZARD, Comment, for Saber-tooth.

SALENSUS OLL (M, N)

First Appearance: 1913, "The Warlord of Mars," *The All-Story Magazine*, Edgar Rice Burroughs.

Weapons: Sword.

Biography: Possessing skin the color of a "ripe lemon," Salensus Oll is "a coarse, brutal beast of a man (with) fierce black whiskers and moustache." According to his nephew Talu, prince of a rival principality, Oll is "a cruel and tyrannous master whom all hate." The jeddak (emperor) of Okar, the land of yellow-skinned Martians, Salensus Oll aspires not only to greater power, but also to the hand of the Royal Princess of Helium, Dejah Thoris, whom he abducts. Her husband, warrior John Carter, tracks her to Salensus Oll's palace; there he slays the "resplendent" jeddak by running his blade "straight through the rotten heart of Okar's rotten ruler." Dejah is reuinited with her beloved Carter and Talu is made jeddak in his uncle's place.

Quote: "In a moment . . . we may return to the battle, while she who is now the Princess of Helium looks down . . . upon the annihilation of her former countrymen and witnesses the greatness which is her husband's."

Comment: This was the character's only appearance. The novel was originally serialized in *The All-Story Magazine* from December 1913 to March 1914; it was published in book form in 1919.

THE SANDMAN (C)

Real Name: William Baker (has also used the alias Flint Marko, presumably inspired by the powerhouse Maggia villain, Man-Mountain Marko).

First Appearance: 1963, *The Amazing Spider-Man* #4, Marvel Comics.

Costume: Original: always wears the same street clothes (brown trousers and a green T-shirt with thin, horizontal black stripes). Second (introduced in *Marvel Team-Up* #2, 1972): light green tights, dark green trunks, cowl, boots, T-shirt with silver collar and fringe on sleeves.

Biography: Raised by a single mother in New York City—his father left home when the boy was three—Baker steals to survive. Destroying a promising football career in high school when he agrees to help throw a game, he goes to work as a hired thug. When his girlfriend Marcy Conroy marries another hood, Vic Rollins, Baker snaps. Going on an unparalleled crime spree, he is captured and becomes "the most incorrigible prisoner" at maximum security Island Prison. Escaping one night through a drainage tunnel, he remains at large, robbing at will, until a police dragnet closes in. Hiding out at an "atomic devices testing center" near Savannah, Georgia, he is caught in a nuclear blast. "The molecules of his body merged . . . with the molecules of sand under his feet, and his body took on the qualities of the sand itself." As the Sandman, he can become soft all over or in any spot he wishes so that bullets pass right through him or people who try to collar him grab only sand. He can harden to rock-like consistency—enabling his jaw to take a punch or his fist to throw one—or even reshape his lower quarters into a steamroller. He can pour himself into any shape he wishes, including "an innocent-looking mound of sand" to hide his booty after a theft (a pile which police invariably pass right by), or granules to pour through an opening that would stymie even an insect; and he can snuff out a flame (even the superhot hero the Human Torch) without being fused into glass. In his first encounter with archfoe Spider-Man, Sandman is stymied when he's sucked into an industrial vacuum cleaner. However, he returns many times over the years until a trauma compels him to give up his criminal career, at least for the time being. Teaming with Hydro-Man, who can become water, the two accidentally merge and become a mud-man. When the villains finally manage to separate, the sobered Sandman reforms. According to *The Amazing Spider-Man* #154, Sandman can be destroyed by laserbeams. For a brief period, the villain was a member of THE SINISTER SIX.

Quote: "Dream on, dummies! I can smash my way outta any prison!"

SATAN (RE, P, N, S, MP, TV)

Real Name: Sammael (see Biography and Comment for nicknames and other names).

First Appearance: The Old Testament, 1 Chronicles 21 (see Biography).

Costume: See Biography.

Weapons: Pitchfork (see Biography).

Chief Henchmen: Countless demons, including LILITH and PUG.

Biography: Satan means "Adversary" in Hebrew, and he is the foremost evil spirit in the Judeo-Chirstian faiths. The character himself is mentioned frequently in the Old Testament (". . . Satan stood up against Israel . . ." [1 Chronicles 21], ". . . and Satan came also among them . . ." [Job 1], ". . . and let Satan stand at his right hand . . ." [Psalms 109]), and is Jesus' chief adversary and the symbol of evil in the New Testament (". . . forty days, tempted of Satan . . ." [Mark 1:13], ". . . I beheld Satan as lightning fall from heaven . . ." [Luke 10:18-19], ". . . if Satan himself goes disguised as an angel of light . . ." [2 Corinthians 11:14-15]). However, the 54 Biblical references to Satan by name are fleeting and superficial. (References to devils are plentiful, though unreliable. For instance, "hairy ones" in Leviticus 17:7 was translated as "devils" in the King James Version and "he-goats" in the Revised Version.) Satan did not take on a dimensional personality until elements of the Persian religion of Zorastrianism were assimilated into religious writings and thought. Founded by Zoroaster (the Greek form of the Persian Zarathustra) circa 1000 B.C., the faith holds that there is an ongoing battle between the good Ormuzd and the evil Ahriman (also known as Angra Mainyu), who represents evil, darkness, and the unclean. According to Hebrew lore, Satan had been one of the Seraphim, the highest class of angel. He had 12 wings and, like all Seraphim, fiery breath and the ability to see into the future (though Satan wasn't always willing to accept what was foretold). Always ambitious, Satan grew livid when he was ordered to honor Adam, the first man. Instead, he and his fellow conspirators enticed men to commit sin. As punishment, Satan and his allies were banished from heaven. However, they had no intention of leaving without a fight. Lead by Satan, the dark angels revolted against God, who was championed by the Archangel Michael and his hosts. Climaxing the battle was a fight between Michael and Satan; losing, the latter grabbed Michael's wings and tried to drag him down, but God interceded and rescued his devoted archangel. God did one thing more; he appointed Satan as the tempter of humankind. It was Satan's job to try and seduce them and weed the good from the wicked. Despite his significant role in Jewish lore, it was in secular writings that Satan came into his own as a fully-realized villain. A brief but dramatic portrait appeared in Dante Alighieri's *The Divine Comedy* (1321) where, known as "Hell's Monarch"—Lucifer—he dwelt in the center of the earth. Possessing three faces ("one in front of hue vermilion . . . the right 'twixt wan and yellow . . . the left . . . such as come from whence old Nile stoops to the lowlands"), he gnawed perpetually on Brutus and Cassius, who had betrayed Julius Caesar, and on Judas Iscariot. His six eyes perpetually wept blood and on his back were "two mighty wings . . . like a bat." Satan was given a more human form and personality (along with vanity, arrogance, and other human traits) in John Milton's epic poems *Paradise Lost* (1667) and *Paradise Regained* (1671). Having revolted against God and lost, Satan lived beyond Chaos in his palace Pandemonium (a word coined by the poet) aided by Beelzebub and the lesser demons Moloch (the fiercest fighter, "besmear'd with blood . . . and parents' tears"), Mammon ("the least erected Spirit . . . always downward bent"), and the relatively "graceful and humane" Belial. Originally the "Fall'n Cherub" stood "like a Tow'r . . . in shape and gesture proudly eminent." After the fall, having lost his "Original brightness," he remained "majestic though in ruin" and still moved about on "swift . . . indefatigable wings." In the first work, Satan orchestrated the misfortunes of Adam and Eve; in the second, "the subtle Fiend" tempted Christ in the wilderness. Able to disappear into thin air, "the Tempter" revealed himself fraught with guilt over his revolt. Once established, the character of Satan took on a purely adversarial status in other works, devoted to tormenting human souls, who have come to him through misdeed, and others which he or lesser devils have wooed. In story and legend, Satan's likeness ranges from more or less human and refined to possessing horns, a spiked tail, red skin, and cloven hooves. The red color of the skin derives from basking in the fires of hell; the horns and hooves come from ancient Hebrew lore in which goats, the zenith of uncleanliness, became identified with the prince of the unclean spirits. The pitchfork, or trident, is symbolic of the Trinity and is a holdover from Roman mythology and culture in which both the sea god Poseidon and gladiators wielded the three-pronged weapon. According to *The Satanic Bible*, the devil today represents the following qualities: indulgence, vital (corporeal) existence (not "spiritual pipe dreams"), wisdom, kindness only to those who deserve it, vengeance, responsibility to the responsible (and not for "psychic vampires"), the conviction that humans are "just another animal," and "so-called sins" as acceptable means to "physical, mental, or emotional gratification."

Quote: "When the first wrong was done to the first Indian, I was there. When the first slaver put out for the Congo, I stood on her deck" (*The Devil and Daniel Webster*).

Comment: In fiction and on the stage, there are several notable works about Satan. In the Old English poem *Christ and Satan*, circa 800 A.D. he laments his fall and tempts Jesus (poet unknown; believed to be either Caedmon or Cynewulf). In Chaucer's *Canterbury Tales* (1387), the devil is featured in "The Friar's Tale." A summoner meets the devil, and the two travel together. They encounter a carter, who commends his horse to the devil; the devil doesn't take it because the curse didn't come from the heart. However, when they come to an old woman from whom the summoner tries to get money, she sneers that the devil should take him . . . and so the devil does, since the oath was sincere. Other tales of Satan are Christopher Marlowe's play *The Tragical History of Dr. Faustus* (first performed in 1588 and based on the life of the legendary sixteenth-century necromancer), in which Satan offers Faust knowledge in exchange for his soul (that dramatization, in turn, inspired Johann Wolfgang von Goethe's 1808 play *Faust, The First Part of the Tragedy*, among others); *Robert the Devil*, an 1831 opera by Scribe and Delavigne based on medieval legend (Robert is really the Devil's son, Satan going by the name of Bertram); Washington Irivng's *The Devil and Tom Walker* (1824; the devil claims poor Tom); Lord Byron's poem *The Deformed Transformed* (1824) in which the Devil gives the hunchback Count Arnold the body of the hero Achilles (only a fragment of the work survives); *The Devil and the Old Man* by John Masefield (1913; the devil dies, crushed by an anchor in "a shower of bright sparks"); "The Devil, George, and Rosie" by John Collier (1934; the devil deals with overpopulation in hell and rails, "I wish I had never invented that particular sin"); Stephen Vincent Benet's "The Devil and Daniel Webster" (1937; Mr. Scratch loses the soul of Jabez Stone when Webster defends Stone in a jury trial); *Satan and Sam Shay* by Robert Arthur (1942) and "A Deal With the Devil" by Lord Dunsany (1948), both about the devil and gamblers; and *Rosemary's Baby* by Ira Levin (1967; the devil sires a child by a mortal woman). Though William Peter Blatty's bestselling *The Exorcist* (1972; film version, 1973) popularized the notion of demonic possession, it was actually a lesser demon, Pazuzu, who did the possessing. On the screen, Satan is usually portrayed in human form, to wit: by Adolphe Menjou in D.W. Griffith's *The Sorrows of Satan* (1926, an adaptation of Marie Corelli's 1895 novel; masquerading as Prince Riminez until the very end when, in shadow, he reveals his bat wings, horns, and spiked tail to the young writer he's tried to corrupt); by Emil Jannings in F.W. Murnau's German adaptation of *Faust* (1926); by Walter Huston in *All That Money Can Buy* (1941; a brilliant adaptation of "The Devil and Daniel Webster," with a screenplay co-written by Benet); by Laird Cregar in *Heaven Can Wait* (1943, interviewing a heel who thinks he should be damned); by Rex Ingram in *Cabin in the Sky* (1943, yearning for the soul of Little Joe); by Claude Rains in *Angel on My Shoulder* (1945, sending a dead hoodlum back to earth as a judge); by Ray Mil-

The Devil (Walter Huston, left) reveals a lost teasure . . . along with a contract for Jabez Stone (James Craig) to sign in The Devil and Daniel Webster. *(See SATAN).*

land in *Alias Nick Beal* (1949, dispatching a seductress to ruin a crusading DA); by Stanley Holloway in *Meet Mr. Lucifer* (1953) who introduces clean-living families to TV; by Vincent Price in *The Story of Mankind* (1957); by Ray Walston in *Damn Yankees*, adapted from a novel and the smash stage musical (1958; the devil sides with the Washington Senators to help defeat the New York Yankees); by Robin Hughes in "The Howling Man" on TV's *Twilight Zone* (1960; the devil is imprisoned in a hermitage—human until he convinces a visitor to set him free and thus makes a final horned, cloaked transformation); by Stig Jarrel in Ingmar Bergman's *The Devil's Eye* (1961; he orders Don Juan to earth to seduce a virgin); by Burgess Meredith in "Printer's Devil" on *Twilight Zone* (1963; as Mr. Smith, the devil gives scoops of events-to-be to a newspaper publisher); by Donald Pleasence in George Stevens' *The Greatest Story Ever Told* (1965); by Peter Cook in *Bedazzled* (1967; his name is Mephisto in this comedy and, when he's not chasing down souls, he's busy putting scratches on record albums, causing static in telephone lines, and working other forms of mischief); by Andreas Teuber in *Dr. Faustus* (1967, with Richard Burton as the titular victim and Elizabeth Taylor as Helen of Troy); and by Bill Cosby in Disney's *The Devil and Max Devlin* (1981). At the climax of the latter film, in which mortal Devlin must collect the souls of people who trust him, Cosby, who has played his role dramatically against-character, reverts to natural form—a bellowing satyr complete with hooves, red skin, and horns. Another famous Disney demon, the leathery devil in the "Night on Bald Mountain" segment of *Fantasia* (1940), is actually the lesser spirit TCHERNABOG. Damien, the devil's son and Anti-Christ, was featured (and ultimately thwarted) in the motion pictures *The Omen* (1976), *Damien: Omen II* (1978), and *The Final Conflict* (1981). The most recent screen devils were George Burns (who also played God) helping a struggling songwriter in *Oh God! You Devil* (1984) and the late James Coco as Dr. D in *Hunk* (1987), turning a nerd into the Adonis of the title. See also ASMODEUS, MEPHISTO, and SHATHAN.

SAURON (N)

First Appearance: 1938, *The Hobbit*, J.R.R. Tolkien.

Weapons: The One Ring, mightiest of the magical Rings of Power.

Biography: One of the foulest creatures ever to inhabit Middle Earth, Sauron had a long and vile history. In the First Age, he was merely a servant to MORGOTH. On his own after his evil master's fall, Sauron lay low until roughly Second Age 1000 when, dwelling in Mordor (which lies east of Gondor), he raised the fortress Barad-dur ("tower dark"). In the twelfth century he forged the One Ring, on which he bestowed awesome (and thoroughly evil) magical properties; through it, he planned to rule all of Middle-Earth. Over the next 15 centuries and countless battles, Sauron slowly expanded his kingdom until he was finally captured in 3262 by Ar-Pharazon of Numenor (far west of Gondor). Sauron spent the next half-century perverting that kingdom; he finally convinced Ar-Pharazon to undertake a reckless crusade against the Undying Lands, a campaign which resulted in the destruction of Numenor. Though Sauron's body was destroyed, his spirit lived on; getting another body, one which was black and unbearably hot to the touch, he returned to Mordor and, in 3429, attacked Gondor. Overthrown five years later, he lost the One Ring when his finger was lopped off. He fled, and hid "for long years . . . until his shadow took shape again, no less ambitious though considerably less powerful." By Third Age 1300 he was on the move again, posing as the Necromancer and assuming various guises—most often that of an eye. Though he still didn't possess the One Ring, his magical powers were great and, aided by monsters and demons such as Orcs (evil creatures which were his principal aides), trolls, the savage men known as Haradrim, and others, he went forth and conquered sundry kingdoms of dwarfs, elves, humans, and hobbits (beings under a meter tall). By mid-2900, shedding the guise of the Necromancer, he made ready to take Gondor and the west once and for all. Realizing that Sauron's powers were still tied to the One Ring, a group of hobbits sought and destroyed the charm in 3019; this left Sauron so weak that he dissipated, "gone now beyond recall, gone forever." Sauron spoke the Black Speech, a language used by him and his aides; among the fiend's many names throughout Middle-Earth were the Dark Lord of Mordor, the Shadow, the Lidless Eye, the Enemy, and the Lord of the Rings.

Comment: Although the character first appeared in *The Hobbit*, the bulk of his tale is told in *The Fellowship of the Ring* (1954), *The Two Towers* (1955), and *The Return of the King* (1956).

THE SCARAB (MP)

Real Name: Dr. Maldor (no first name).

First Appearance: 1944, *Captain America*, Republic Pictures.

Weapons: The Purple Death, a "subtle, unknown poison," a will-sapping powder derived from a jungle flower (stored in his ring, the poison is dispensed via cigars); portable Electronic Firebolts which can break through anything; TV to see anywhere; Thermodynamic Vibration Engine which can shatter anything to small fragments.

Biography: The leader of the Mayan Explorers Club, Dr. Maldor is deeply offended when the club's hugely successful archaeological expedition to Central America results in wealth and fame for everyone—except him. Named curator of the Drummond Museum of Arts and Sciences, an honor which he considers unworthy ("It was *my* expedition . . . and how was I rewarded? I was made curator of an insignificant museum!"), Maldor sets out to kill everyone associated with the expedition. He also tries to get his hands on a recently discovered clay tablet map which shows the location of a great treasure. As Mayan Explorers Club members begin dying—driven to commit suicide when their minds are taken over by Dr. Maldor's Purple Death—the superhero Captain America launches an investigation. Poking around for clues, the hero survives being run over by a tractor, caught in a crate set ablaze by a Portable Electronic Firebolt, trapped in a house which is bombed flat and a skyscraper which is shattered by the Thermodynamic Vibration Engine. Ultimately, Captain America exposes Dr. Maldor and recovers the stolen Life-Restorer machine, a device which can bring the newly-dead back to life. For their crimes, Maldor and his thugs are given the electric chair.

Quote: "You will walk to the window and step out . . . into eternity!"

Comment: Lionel Atwill played the Scarab in this 15-chapter serial. He also played the super villains OTTO VON NEIMANN and SIR ERIC HAZARIAS. The Scarab was not a villain in the Captain America comic book.

THE SCARECROW (1) (C)

Real Name: Jonathan Crane.

First Appearance: 1941, *World's Finest Comics* #3, DC Comics.

Costume: Tan, ragged scarecrow jerkin, trousers, and floppy hat (with straw poking from the top); brown boots; orange hood over entire head, knotted about the neck with a rope.

Weapons: "Fear-radiating pill" and other devices to induce terror in others.

Chief Henchmen: Various, nameless thugs.

Biography: As a child, Crane hated birds and his hobby was tormenting them. The birds' reaction, their instinctive fear, drove him to make the study of fear his profession. Becoming a psychology professor at Gotham University, he spent the bulk of his income on texts and research; as a result, so shoddy was his personal appearance that fellow teachers and students alike called him "Scarecrow." Angered by their attitude, he decided to make more money—through crime. Becoming the Scarecrow, "a symbol of poverty and fear combined," he used terrorism and murder to achieve his ends. (In *Batman*, #200, 1968, he went one step further and concocted a "fear-radiating pill" which caused paralyzing terror in any who beheld him.) Unfortunately, the synergy between his manic criminal life and his classroom activities proved disastrously strong; he was soon dismissed from the staff for shooting a gun during a lecture, among other irresponsible fear-inducing acts. The Scarecrow has yet to fulfill his dream of becoming wealthy and defeating his nemesis, the crimefighting Batman.

Comment: The character appears regularly in the numerous Batman magazines. See other fear-inducing villains BUSHMAN, DR. SPECTRO, D'SPAYRE, MISTER FEAR, PHOBIA, PSYCHO-MAN, and PSYCHO-PIRATE.

THE SCARECROW (2) (C)

Real Name: Ebenezer Laughton.

First Appearance: 1964, *Tales of Suspense* #51, Marvel Comics.

Costume: Resembles a scarecrow with tattered green trousers, jerkin knotted about the waist with a cord; orange gloves, boots, full-head hood whose ends form a floppy ruff; tufts of straw at his shoulders, wrists, and ankles.

Chief Henchmen: An army of trained attack crows who, responding to both his voice and gestures, steal for him.

Biography: Extremely double-jointed as a child, Ebenezer watches a carnival rubber man perform one day and decides that that's what he wants to do for a living. Becoming a contortionist, acrobat, and escape-artist, he eventually lands a job at a vaudeville-type show as Umberto the Uncanny. When Iron Man appears one day, in pursuit of a criminal, Ebenezer helps to capture the crook; it suddenly dawns on him, however, that he could make a fortune if he turned to crime. Lifting a scarecrow wardrobe from a costume store and stealing the crows of a fellow performer, he chooses as his first target the apartment of industrialite Tony Stark. It proves to be a poor choice, since Stark is secretly Iron Man and hits the Scarecrow with everything he has. Ebenezer is defeated, and has since had the stuffing knocked out of him by other heroes as well; he recently went mad from sheer anger and frustration, making him a far more dangerous (and deadly) adversary.

THE SCARECROW (3) (TV, C)

First Appearance: 1966, *The Mighty Heroes*, syndicated.

Costume: Tattered brown clothing (skin is orange).

Chief Henchmen: The Straw Men, knee-high versions of the Scarecrow.

Biography: Made of straw and "scary enough to frighten anything," the Scarecrow slinks from a field and roams the countryside, terrifying farmers and stealing their animals so that he can become "the richest farmer in the county." However, he doesn't count on the superheroic Mighty Heroes. Tornadoman destroys the Straw Men with cyclonic winds, while Cuckooman threatens the Scarecrow with some very hungry horses, forcing the Scarecrow to return to his post.

Quote: "Come on, you Straw Men. Off the hay rack . . . and into battle."

Comment: This was the character's only appearance (though the cartoon adventure was told in comic book

THE SCARECROW (3). *© Terrytoons.*

form in *Mighty Mouse* #161, 1967). Other villains in the Mighty Heroes series included the Frog, the Junker, the Shrinker, the Ghost Monster, the Stretcher, the Monsterizer, the Drifter, the Shocker, the Enlarger, the Toy Man, the Duster, the Timekeeper, the Time Eraser, the Raven, the Paper Monster, and the Bigger Digger.

THE SCAVENGER (C)

First Appearance: 1967, *Aquaman* #37, DC Comics.
Costume: Blue bodysuit, boots, gloves, diver's helmet (see Weapons); purple belt.
Weapons: Scorpion Ship which moves about on pincer-like legs and boasts various weapons including an electrical field and blasters, both hand-held and cannon-size.
Biography: Nothing is known about this character, who first burst upon the criminal scene in a quest for the "time decelerator," a device invented long ago by a race of extraterrestrials. Though Aquaman managed to smash the super villain's ship, the Scavenger obtained the time decelerator; alas, all it did was cause him to regress beyond infancy to nothingness. Though he has since managed to reverse its effects, he has tried no additional criminal activities of note.
Comment: Scavenger's motives for wanting the time decelerator were never revealed. It is clear, however, that he intended to begin criminal acts of some sort, most likely on or beneath the seas.

SCORPIO (C)

Real Name: Jacob Fury; Jacques LaPoint.
First Appearance: 1968, *Nick Fury, Agent of S.H.I.E.L.D.* #1 (as Jacob); 1974, *The Avengers* #120 (as Jacques), Marvel Comics.
Costume: Both wear white tights, vest, hood with black scorpion silhouette on circular red field on forehead; red bodyshirt; full-face mask; orange boots, gloves, trunks covered with large studs. After being resurrected the first time, Jacob wore an orange bodysuit and boots with yellow gloves and trunks, and an orange cowl with a black scorpion design on the forehead. In his android incarnation, he wears a red bodysuit, cowl, boots, and gloves with black bands on his shins, thighs, wrists, upper arms, and shoulders; and a blue belt.
Weapons: The Key to the Zodiac, a circle with three prongs which summons "solar force" and fires it as destructive blasts; "sleep fumes"; rocket-like transport.
Chief Henchmen: Fellow members of ZODIAC.
Biography: Jacob becomes Scorpio due to a longstanding rivalry with his brother, Nick Fury, head of the world peacekeeping force S.H.I.E.L.D. (Supreme Headquarters International Espionage Law-enforcement Division). Attacking a S.H.I.E.L.D. research facility in Las Vegas and using sleep fumes to render the personnel unconscious, he battles Nick. "Well-versed in the ways of acrobatics," Jacob gives the lawman a run for his money. However, World War II combat veteran Nick gets the upper hand and Scorpio flees to his "awesome aerial craft" which descends outside the facility. Fortunately, quick-thinking S.H.I.E.L.D. agent Mitch Hackett arrives and gets off a shot at the vehicle's engine, causing it to explode and kill Scorpio . . . or so it appears. The Key preserves him and he becomes an independent operator. Meanwhile, LaPoint becomes Zodiac's new Scorpio, albeit without the Key. Not that Jacob fares too well with the weapon. Failing repeatedly to make his mark as a super villain, Jacob finally takes his life with a pistol. However, the Key once again meddles, this time creating an android Scorpio and placing Jacob's spirit inside. Ruling a new Zodiac consisting entirely of android villains, Jacob has Jacques slain . . . along with most of the human Zodiac members. The android villains take their places and are still at large.
Quote: "The *vengeance* of Scorpio has reached its consummate moment! Now . . . will I fulfill my malevolent oath, sworn in blood . . . to *kill Nick Fury*!"
Comment: Jacob first appeared, in his non-villainous identity, in *Sgt. Fury and His Howling Commandos* #68 in 1969. He committed suicide in *The Defenders* #50 in 1976. Nick briefly assumed the Scorpio guise after his brother's "death" in the aircraft explosion, impersonating him in an effort to infiltrate Zodiac. Though he succeeded, the criminals escaped.)

THE SCORPION (1) (MP)

Real Name: Doctor Marshall (no first name).
First Appearance: 1937, *Blake of Scotland Yard*, Victory Pictures.
Costume: Black slouch hat, cloak; full-face mask.
Weapons: Scorpion-like claw on his right hand.
Biography: When former Scotland Yard inspector Sir James Blake and several scientist colleagues invent a death ray, munitions magnate Count Basil Zegelloff hires the evil, hunchbacked Scorpion to steal it. However, a fake radium tube has been planted in the death ray, rendering it useless. Discovering this, the Scorpion sets out to obtain the real tube. Though he tries abduction, rigs explosives, and attempts

murder to get it, he eventually loses the death ray back to Blake . . . who rigs it with a massive dose of electricity and leaves it in a safe. When the Scorpion tries to reclaim it he receives a debilitating shock and is promptly arrested. (The foul Count Zegelloff had already been nabbed in the previous chapter.)

Comment: Lloyd Hughes played the part in the 15-chapter serial.

THE SCORPION (2) (M)

First Appearance: April 1939, *The Scorpion* #1, Popular Publications.

Costume: Gray-green robe and hood; red scorpion mark across face.

Weapons: Drug which turns people into lunatics.

Biography: The leader of a gang known as the Purple Eyes, the Scorpion is devoted to world conquest. Based in a lair he's built beneath a building's incinerator, the villain moves anonymously about New York in a garbage truck. He is pursued by a vigilante known as the Skull Killer.

Comment: The fiend's only adventure was called "Satan's Incubator." Originally penned as a story of THE OCTOPUS, it was changed to accommodate the new character; hence their similarities, including the same nemesis.

THE SCORPION (3) (MP)

Real Name: Professor Bentley.

First Appearance: 1941, *The Adventures of Captain Marvel*, Republic Pictures.

Costume: Black robe, hood, with two white scorpions on his chest and one on his forehead.

Weapons: Standard firearms; the Golden Scorpion disintegrator, a four-feet-long weapon in the shape of a scorpion.

Chief Henchmen: Numerous gangsters.

Biography: As part of the Malcolm Scientific Expedition, Bentley is searching Siam for relics of the Primitive Scorpion Dynasty. In an ancient temple, the professor and his colleagues find the Golden Scorpion, an "atom smasher" which can disintegrate any matter when its five lenses are set in place. To keep this great find from being used for evil, the archaeologists divide the lenses among themselves and return to the United States. There, becoming the

***THE SCORPION** (3) (Harry Worth) shows off his Golden Scorpion disintegrater in* The Adventures of Captain Marvel. *© Republic Pictures.*

Scorpion, Bentley and his thugs track down the mirrors, threatening to murder anyone who gets in their way, and make ready to conquer the world. However, the superhero Captain Marvel intercedes and Bentley gets to use the Golden Scorpion just once. Trying to escape, he stumbles into the ray and is evaporated.

Comment: Harry Worth played the part in the 12-episode serial. The character never appeared in any of the comic book escapades of Captain Marvel. The Scorpion was also the name of a saboteur in the 1942 serial *Don Winslow of the Navy.*

THE SCORPION (4) (C)

Real Name: MacDonald Gargan.

First Appearance: 1965, *The Amazing Spider-Man* #20, Marvel Comics.

Costume: Green cowl: green tail (see Weapons) and bodysuit—both encircled by thin, black stripes; olive-green trunks, belt, gloves, boots.

Weapons: Seven-feet-long, super-powerful mechanical tail which he controls by will. He subsequently adds a destructive "sting" to the appendage, an "electro-magnetic" blaster (*Marvel Team-Up* #106, 1981).

Biography: "Mac" Gargan is a private eye hired by newspaper publisher J. Jonah Jameson to find out how young photographer Peter Parker gets unparalleled shots of the superhero Spider-Man. (Neither Gargan nor Jameson discovers that Parker *is* Spider-Man.) Though Jameson runs the pictures in his newspaper *The Daily Bugle*, he regards the hero as a menace and wants to see him destroyed. Learning of a local scientist whose research in mutations may hold the answer, Jameson drags Gargan to his lab. There, the publisher pays Gargan and scientist Farley Stillwell $10,000 each for the latter to mutate the former into someone with "powers which are greater than Spider-Man's." Stillwell offers to prepare a potion which will give the detective the powers of a scorpion, though he offers a caveat: "I don't know how it would affect your brain!" Deciding the risk is worth the money, Gargan gulps down the formula. As a result, he becomes powerful enough to crush a granite block in his bare hands, rip through two feet of steel, crush a gun with his foot, or snip through virtually anything with pincer-like fingers. Stillwell also devises a costume, whose tail is equally as powerful as his body ("involuntary nerve impulses, activated by mental commands" allow Gargan to operate the tail). However, after the transformation is complete, Stillwell's research reveals that it will be only a matter of time before Gargan's "*evil nature* will take over." So it does, and quickly. Realizing that if he can beat Spider-Man "the whole *city* is mine for the taking," he tackles the wallcrawling hero. Though he is soundly beaten, the Scorpion refuses to cry uncle. Despite long stays in jail and at the Sherwood Nursing Home (in an iron straitjacket), he remains one of Spider-Man's most persistent adversaries. As for Jameson, he has set up a fund to repay the victims of the Scorpion's crimes.

Quote: "I've got *news* for you . . . I *do* know the difference between right and wrong! Whatever the Scorpion does is *right*!"

THE SEA HAG (CS)

First Appearance: December 26, 1929, *Thimble Theatre*, Hearst newspapers.

Costume: Black robe with hood; red scarf with black stripes; red stockings with white stripes.

Weapons: Broom for flight; schooner for sailing the seas.

Chief Henchman: Bernard, a vulture.

Biography: The last bonafide witch on earth, the Sea Hag uses the black arts to try to destroy the do-gooder Popeye the Sailor. Beyond that, her greatest goal is to see that piracy is restored to the seas. The witch lives on Vulture Island though she has a number of other hideouts, of which Hide-Out Number 412, in the Eighth Sea, is by far the most dangerous. In addition to housing 327 ferocious vultures (not counting the devoted Bernard), it is the home of the vicious Cave Monster. The Sea Hag also runs the Institute of Witchcraft, on whose athletic field aspiring witches practice levitation.

Quote: "I'm having my house done over . . . I have to wait for a new shipment of termites."

Comment: Other enemies of Popeye the Sailor include the robot Emok; the brutes Jabbo, Oxheart, and Bolo; General Bunzo; Patcheye the Pirate, a dead-ringer for our hero; and the fanged Toar. See also Popeye's archnemesis BLUTO.

THE SEEKER (C)

Real Name: Ralphie Hutchins.

First Appearance: 1981, *The Savage She-Hulk* #21, Marvel Comics.

Costume: Blue trunks (the Seeker's skin is blue; his eyes large and red on an otherwise featureless face).

Biography: Little is known of the character's past, save that he's a young man who has been mutated by a scientist known only as the "Mad Doctor." Described as "the ultimate hit man," the Seeker is able to absorb any stimulus around him, no matter how insignificant,

THE SENTINEL struts his stuff. © *Western Publishing.*

and "magnify it a thousandfold," turning the breeze created by someone walking toward him into a ferocious wind, or the sound of a dripping faucet into a deafening roar. He can also tap energy—like the electric output of a car—and "convert it directly to a powerful energy blast." When a man named Shade comes to Los Angeles to take over the local mobs, he sets the Seeker loose against the She-Hulk, aware that a victory over the superhero will make him feared. But She-Hulk topples a freeway ramp on the Seeker, and he is crushed. Ralphie survives, however, and lives to do battle with She-Hulk again (see RADIUS).

Quote: "Nothing stops the Seeker! The Seeker can crush you—with your own power!"

THE SENTINEL (C)

Real Name: Ron Harris.

First Appearance: 1982, *Doctor Solar, Man of the Atom* #31, Gold Key Comics.

Costumes: Red bodysuit, boots, trunks; white belt with black "S" buckle; purple cape; black cowl with red markings.

Weapons: Electrified sword.

Biography: An actor in a science fiction film, Harris is playing the part of a superhero known as the Sentinel. During the shooting of a scene, a spotlight falls on a special effects laser projector, exposing Harris to "a massive dose of energy." The accident creates a solid-energy duplicate of the Sentinel, a clone which seeks to destroy those who have crossed the actor. Endowed with superstrength, the ability to fly, and the power to bring machines to life, he sends his director to the hospital (with a mere energy blast) before the superheroic Doctor Solar arrives. The two men battle, but the film's scientific consultant, Gail Sanders, saves the day simply by smashing the laser projector. Without his power source, the "energy construct" vanishes.

Quote: "I *owe* you, little man. You've heaped enough misery on me to last a lifetime! But all that's changed now!"

Comment: This was the character's only appearance. Other villains of Doctor Solar include "the fiendish Nuro," who creates android killers in one story, a mind-unbalancing machine in another, and simply plans to conquer the earth in yet another; Transviac "the energy-consuming computer"; Primo, a "fiery creature from the earth's core"; and the half-robot, half-human King Cybernoid.

SERPENTYNE (C)

First Appearance: 1980, *Rom* #8. (Note: The Lizard People had appeared previously, in *Ms. Marvel* #20, 1978.)

Costume: Purple belt and harness on chest. (The rest of his body—which includes a powerful tail—is lumpy and lizard-like. It's also orange, save for the cover of #9 where it's green.)

Weapons: Two long daggers tucked into belt. (He is pictured with a hi-tech gun on the cover, but does not possess one in the story.)

Biography: The Lizard People were "born in the atomic

fires of the . . . first nuclear bomb test. Somehow the radiation interacted with the desert fauna," speeding up the evolutionary processes of the lizards in the area. Endowed with enormous intelligence, the reptilian bipeds built a sprawling underground civilization. There, shunning humans, they lived in peace. But one day, the military discovered them and, in the ensuing battle, the Lizard People took hostages. (The people were rescued by the superheroine Ms. Marvel.) Among the human captives was an extraterrestrial shapechanger, one of the DIRE WRAITHS. Deciding the caverns would make an ideal base, he summoned the other Wraiths and, in revenge, stormed the labyrinth, killing "warriors and breeders, the old and the as-yet unhatched." All but Serpentyne perished and, maddened by the carnage, the extremely powerful mutation devoted itself to lurking in the catacombs and slaying Wraiths. As it happened, killing Wraiths was also the mission of the superhero Rom who, during one such outing, fell into an open grave. The bottom gave way and he found himself in the underground lair of Serpentyne. The lizard man tried to slay him and take his weapons; during the battle, however, Serpentyne was impaled on a stalagmite. Realizing that he'd been "driven crazy by the thought of being . . . the last of my race," he apologized to Rom and died.

Quote: "Mine must be the hand that banishes the Dire Wraiths! Mine must be the victory! *Mine alone*!"

Comment: Serpentyne is less villainous than demented, but his actions and attitude ("I *will* combat them, Rom—when you lie cold and dead") make him far from virtuous.

SET (MY)

Biography: The most loathsome god of Egyptian mythology, Set represented the forces of evil and darkness. Set was the brother of Isis, the benevolent goddess of the earth and moon; the husband of Nephthys, the goddess of the dead; the father of Osiris, the chief deity of good (in some accounts, Set and Osiris are brothers); the grandson of Keb, the god of the earth, and Nut, the god of the heavens. His great-grandfather is Ra, the god of the sun; and finally, Set's son is Anubis, the god of the dead. Physically, Set is a bizarre hybrid of creatures. He has the body of a mule, the ears and snout of a jackal, and a lion's tail. (Some scholars believe he is an okapi.) Without question, Set's most heinous crime was the murder of Osiris. Jealous of Osiris' power, Set eventually overcame him, locked him in a box and heaved him into the Nile. Mulling over his actions, Set had a change of heart. Opening the coffin, he cut Osiris into 14 pieces and strewed them all over Egypt. Sister Isis and wife Nephythys dutifully gathered them up and brought him back to life; with the help of her son Horus, the god of light, Isis promptly murdered Set by feeding him to Anubis.

Comment: The battle between Set and Osiris did not enter Egyptian mythology until some 1,500 years after the gods themselves were created, circa 3200 B.C. Set was also known as Seth. Set is also involved with the evil SIX-HEADED MUMMY.

THE SHADOW THIEF (C)

Real Name: Carl Sands.

First Appearance: 1961, *The Brave and the Bold* #36, DC Comics.

Costume: Purple bodysuit, cowl, gloves, boots (as Sands); he is merely a two-dimensional black silhouette as the Shadow Thief.

Weapons: Wristwatch-like "dimensiometer" which shifts the user's body to the world of Xarapion in another dimension, leaving the person's shadow on earth but fully under that individual's control; paralysis ray.

Chief Henchman: Floyd, a fellow criminal (*Hawkman* #5 only).

Biography: "A common criminal without any special powers," Sands was always intrigued by shadows. He experimented with them and, one day, was lucky enough to break through to "an alien dimension." There, he found the blue-skinned scientist Thar Dan trapped beneath a rock on the world of Xarapion. Sands provided the alien with iron filings (iron being fuel for the alien's disintegrator raygun) and Thar vaporized the boulder. In gratitude, Thar gave Sands the dimensiometer, which the crook promptly used to send his shadow out on crimes. When Sands was in this mode, as the Shadow Thief, nothing could touch him—from the hands of a foe to any kind of projectile—though he could touch whatever he wished. Rather ingeniously, the airborne superhero Hawkman forced Sands to return to earth from Xarapion in midair and demanded the dimensiometer in exchange for keeping him from splattering on the ground. Sands seemed to comply, but actually hid the device's "winding mechanism" in his mouth. Former cellmate Floyd helped him escape from prison and get back the dimensiometer; back in business, the Shadow Thief once again robbed Midway City blind. This time, however, his scheme went far beyond simple robbery. Thar had warned Sands that every time he activated the dimensiometer he affected the "magnetic lines" of earth. In due course, that would cause an Ice Age, "ending all life on earth." Thus,

Sands plotted to destroy our world once he had robbed it and settle on Xarapion as its leader; if anyone there contested his rule, he would simply engulf that world, too, in an Ice Age and "find myself another dimensional world to take over." Using the paralysis ray, he got rid of his only conceivable enemies (Thar Dan, Hawkman, and Hawkgirl). However, canny Hawkman used his telepathic control over birds to summon forth a flock and carry his body out of range of the beam. He then trapped Sands in the beam on Xarapion (*Hawkman* #5, 1962). Naturally, that failed to hold the super villain and he has repeatedly tangled with Hawkman ever since. His most noteworthy criminal activities have occurred of late in the service of Hyathis, empress of Hawkman's home world, Thanagar. He has assisted in her (thusfar) futile attempts to take over the universe. The felon is a member of THE SECRET SOCIETY OF SUPER-VILLAINS.

Quote: "There isn't a weapon on earth that can harm *me, Hawkman*—but watch what mine does to *you*!"

Comment: The character's origin tale, written by the late science fiction novelist Gardner Fox, is remarkably inventive and evocative; it was drawn by Joe Kubert, one of the medium's finest artists.

THE SHAGGY MAN (C)

First Appearance: 1966, *Justice League of America* #45, DC Comics.

Costume: The brute is covered with brown fur and sports a beard and head of shaggy hair.

Biography: Approximately twelve-feet-tall, the Shaggy Man was an android built by Professor Andrew Zagarian. Originally, Zagarian hadn't intended for his creation to live. Experimenting with "plastalloy," a skin-like substance, he had hoped to be able to use it to create synthetic organs and such. He built his android simply to test the substance, but used too much electricity in the experiment and brought Shaggy Man to life. Naturally antagonistic, the brute turned on Zagarian and the Justice League was summoned; ironically, Zagarian had actually managed to deactivate the creature in the interim, but the heroes' arrival merely set it off again. Since the Shaggy Man could not be destroyed (it was empowered with the ability to heal any and all damaged parts of its body), the heroes had Zagarian build a second Shaggy Man and, placing the two beasts in a pit, let them duke it out for eternity (#45). However, years later a villain named Hector Hammond snatched the original Shaggy Man from his prison and sent him to the Justice League satellite headquarters. He was defeated, this time, when superhero Green Lantern used his power ring to shrink him to a relatively harmless size. As for the second Shaggy Man, it was rocketed into space by Batman (*Justice League of America* #186, 1981).

THE SHARK (C)

Real Name: T.S. (for Tiger Shark) Smith.

First Appearance: 1963, *Green Lantern* #24, DC Comics.

Costume: Original: purple trunks. Second: blue boots and gloves with fin, blue leotard with cutaway sides and white circle on belly.

Weapons: None until *Green Lantern* #126, when he agrees to kill the superhero for the evil General Fabrikant, and is provided with a gun which collects gold from the ocean.

Biography: When a test at a nuclear power plant goes awry, part of the reactor is blown into the ocean. There, the radiation strikes a passing tiger shark which is sent along an "accelerating evolutionary spiral." Staggering to shore, it is kicked one million years into its evolutionary future. The resultant being is a normal human, save for his shark-like head and amazing physical and mental powers. Testing his abilities, he finds that he can create everything from a windstorm to a volcano, melt rock, become a giant, fire destructive mental bolts, instill fear in humans, and absorb knowledge from the minds of others. Still, the dominant instinct in the Shark is to hunt and prey. Moving among humans (with an applied head of hair to hide the fin atop his skull), he receives a mental impression of the mighty superhero Green Lantern, whom he deems a worthy adversary. The Shark challenges him via telepathy, simultaneously sealing Coast City within a dome-like force-field in order to make it his "private hunting reserve." Green Lantern is able to knock him out by clobbering him with an iceberg, then de-evolves the Shark and places him in an aquarium; however, the villain is restored and has battled the superhero numerous times over the years.

Quote: "Puny human . . . have I succeeded in making you afraid? Do I detect a note of *fear* in your mind?"

SHATHAN (C)

First Appearance: 1966, *Showcase* #61, DC Comics.

Costume: Blue trunks; white belt. (Shathan's flesh is red.)

Chief Henchman: Azmodus, a red-skinned demon dressed in a yellow leotard and cape. In #60, this supernatural fiend from Tholagga, land of astral evil, tried to pave the way for Shathan's invasion by battling the superheroic ghost the Spectre. Though he, like the Spectre, could expand to the size of a galaxy, whip comets around by their tails, and command matter to do his bidding, he was drained of his powers in a moment of weakness and was left floating, inert, "in no-time and non-space."

Biography: When the universe was created in the Big Bang, an "evil, malignant" universe was created from negative "psycho-matter." In this universe was formed the world of Dis, whose indigenous "demons" worshipped the giant being Shathan. Yearning to rule more than Dis and its cosmos, Shathan set his sights on "the physical-matter universe—with *earth* serving as a stepping-stone." He began paving the way centuries ago, by sending "evil mental images" which resulted in the Golden Calf, witches, and other forms of irreverence. Though men like Moses, Buddha, and Mohammed were able to rise up and "lead the way of goodness," Shathan finally bridged the dimensions by using peoples' shadows to control their wills—the chants the people spoke in unison broke "the barriers between the worlds." After the two beings slugged it out, the Spectre finally hauled Shathan back to the beginning of time and plunked him down in the fury of the Big Bang. The result? "In that most awesome of all energy explosions, the essence of Shathan the Eternal is . . . spread across the vast cosmos."

Quote: "Never before have I been *struck*! I—do not like it!"

Comment: This character is similar in virtually every way to SATAN. He was also, obviously, a prototype for the much later ANTI-MONITOR. Shathan's only appearance was superbly written and drawn by Gardner Fox and Murphy Anderson, respectively, longtime pros who were at the peak of their powers.

SHAZANA (C)

First Appearance: 1965, *Strange Tales* #133, Marvel Comics.

Costume: Green bodyshirt, skirt slit up both legs (essentially forming three separate flaps), cowl with holes for three horn-like queues of hair; light green earrings, tights covered with thin, jagged lines.

Weapons: A "gleaming, pulsating" mystic globe which is "the source of my great power."

Chief Henchmen: Sundry palace lackeys, including those who police her realm astride flying demonic steeds and shoot would-be rebels with paralyzer rayguns.

Biography: Fleeing a trap set by BARON MORDO, the magic superhero Dr. Strange found himself in a strange dimension. There, he was greeted by a young woman who told him that she was the rightful ruler of the land and that her throne had been usurped by her evil half sister Shazana. Reading the mind of Shazana's gray, lizard-like pet, Strange discovered that the queen's power derived from a basketball-sized orb which she had obtained from "an unsuspecting magician," whom she had immediately slain. Also learning from the pet that the globe was hidden beneath her throne, Strange smashed it—and Shazana's power. The "shock of her defeat (having) unseated her mind," Shazana was left a babbling idiot and her sister resumed her own benevolent rule.

Quote: "You call those petty baubles enough tribute for *Shazana*? Return with far greater treasures for me, or your very *lives* shall be forfeit!"

Comment: Shazana's costume is quite similar to that of THE ENCHANTRESS (1), created that same year at Marvel. This was the character's only appearance.

SHIMMER (C)

Real Name: Selinda (last name unrevealed).

First Appearance: 1981, *The New Teen Titans* #3, DC Comics.

Costume: Yellow bodysuit with seven circular holes cut from neck to navel, and two down each leg to boot; golden thigh boots, gloves, band around neck.

Biography: See MAMMOTH for origin. A member of THE FEARSOME FIVE, Shimmer is a "matter transmuter," able to change any matter into any other matter.

Quote: "With a simple pass of my *hand*—I can *transmute* the very *fabric* of this wooden door into easily passable *water vapor*!"

THE SHOCKER (C)

First Appearance: 1967, *The Amazing Spider-Man* #46, Marvel Comics.

Costume: Yellow arms, tights, cowl, and "V"-shaped vest (front and back) with crisscrossing diagonal black stripes (cowl has brown top ending in widow's peak, and there is a silver stripe along each arm); brown leotard, boots, with silver fringe; brown gloves with silver backs and wristbands (see Weapons); silver belt.

Weapons: "Vibro-smashers," gloves used to destroy objects, such as safes and walls, with intense vibration and/or by increasing the force of his punches.

Biography: A rather unsuccessful safecracker, the Shocker (his name is never revealed) finds himself in prison . . . a place which he resolves never to go to again. While incarcerated, he uses the prison workshop to construct tools that will quietly shake open any safe made. Constructing his Vibro-smashers he uses them to break out of prison. Once free, he makes himself a padded costume (to protect him from his own device) and begins his more flamboyant criminal phase as the Shocker. Though Spider-Man finally stops him—by webbing the Shocker's fingers apart so he can't press his glove buttons—the villain returns now and then to menace the wallcrawling hero.

Quote: "Webhead, you've *tangled* with me once too *often*! *This* time you're gonna be—*shattered by the SHOCKER*!"

Comment: There is another, lesser-known Shocker at Marvel. He's Randall Darby, a mutant who generates electrical jolts with his touch.

SIDEWINDER (C)

Real Name: Seth Voelker.

First Appearance: 1980, *Marvel Two-In-One* #64, Marvel Comics.

Costume: Brown bodysuit with orange mail sleeves, snake-like mask with yellow serpent insignia on forehead, trunks with purple stripe down center; purple breastplate, belt, bands around shoulders, gloves, thigh boots; orange ribbed collar, cape with yellow lining.

Weapons: Circuits in costume cause a rift in space, allowing Sidewinder to teleport by shifting sideways into and out of another dimension. The circuits can only be activated by a device which has been surgically implanted in Sidewinder.

Chief Henchmen: THE SERPENT SOCIETY.

Biography: Fired from his position as a college economics professor, Voelker went to work for the Roxxon Oil Company. Growing bored with his financial position, he agreed to allow scientists at the Roxxon subsidiary, the Brand Corporation, to turn him into a secret operative working outside the law. Undergoing an operation in which a device was implanted allowing him to interface with his costume circuitry, Voelker became Sidewinder. Named the leader of Roxxon's SERPENT SQUAD he quickly tired of serving Roxxon and became an independent operator and head of his own criminal group, The Serpent Society. He and his band remain a potent force in the criminal world.

Quote: "I will allow him to draw as close as I dare, as if I am petrified with fear . . . and then dimensionally displace myself out of harm's way."

Comment: Other snake villains include COBRA, COPPERHEAD, and THE SNAKE; super villains who can teleport include ANGLE MAN and THE VANISHER.

SILVERMANE (C)

Real Name: Silvio Manfredi.

First Appearance: 1969, *The Amazing Spider-Man* #73, Marvel Comics.

Costume: None; Silvermane's body is a mass of metal pipes, wires, tubing, and servomechanisms.

Biography: Emigrating from Italy to the United States, the Manfredis settled in New York's "Little Italy." There, young Silvio soon became a part of the activities of the international crime group the Maggia. In time, Manfredi rose to power, though his career was stalled in the 1950s when he spent time in prison for tax evasion. Upon his release, he teamed with mobster Dominic Tyrone to reestablish his influence within his own family. Some 10 years later, triumphant, he ordered Tyrone's death to consolidate his own power; as a result of that killing, Manfredi's hair turned snow-white and he was nicknamed Silvermane. (As it turned out, Tyrone survived and became the foul Rapier. He returned years later in an effort to turn the tables on Manfredi, but failed [*Peter Parker, the Spectacular Spider-Man* Annual #2, 1980].) Because of his success with the Maggia, Silvermane was approached by the worldwide subversive group HYDRA to become their leader. As the head of both organizations, Manfredi became arguably the most powerful mobster on earth. He even managed to become young again when he found ancient tablets on which a black magic youth formula was inscribed. Forcing Dr. Curtis Connors (aka THE LIZARD) to mix the potion, he quaffed it and knocked off half of his 80 years. However, Silvermane subsequently broke every bone in his body when he was caught in a struggle between the hero Spider-Man and his foe THE GREEN GOBLIN. The fall he took also nullified the effects of the youth serum. Running his operations bedridden, he was nearly killed by the energy-sapping heroine Dagger, the woman despising Silvermane for his part in trafficking drugs. But his organs and most of his head were transplanted into a cyborg body, and he reappeared as a super-powered gangster. Manfredi was married to the late Caterina; his son, Joseph, is Blackwing of the CIRCUS OF CRIME.

SILVER SAMURAI (C)

Real Name: Kenuichio Harada.

First Appearance: 1974, *Daredevil* #111, Marvel Comics.

Costume: Original: silver chestplate, tights, trunks; blue helmet, sleeves, boots, loincloth. Second: silver-blue girdle, helmet, gloves, tights, boots, chestplate with red rising sun. Third: silver armor with red rising sun on chest.

Weapons: Katana, a samurai sword so treated as to be able to slice through virtually anything.

Biography: The son of Shingen Harada, a powerful criminal in Japan, and boss of the Yashida Clan, Kenuichio did not join the Clan but, instead, studied to be a samurai. Mastering the fighting arts of the ancient class, he went to work for the international criminal THE VIPER, serving as her chief henchman. In what stands as the most embarrassing comic book escapade in the career of the Silver Samurai—or any other villain, for that matter—he once paused in his struggles with Daredevil to battle actor John Belushi's samurai character on the set of *Saturday Night Live*. Marvel publisher Stan Lee also appeared in that adventure (*Marvel Team-Up* #74, 1978), doing a dance (!) on the show.

Quote: "Tell your *mourners*, fool, that you fell a helpless *victim* of . . . the Silver Samurai!"

SILVER SHADE (C)

Real Name: Xavier Pervis.

First Appearance: 1986, *Firestorm* #53, DC Comics.

Costume: Silver bodysuit, trunks, boots, gloves, helmet (see Biography).

Biography: Pervis was born with the power to telekinetically manipulate small amounts of metal, shaping an ounce at a time to his will. He became a sculptor, but quickly tired of "expending my talent on mediocre craftworks for the rich." He spent 12 years studying metallurgy and molecular physics until he discovered that he could increase the amount of metal he could control by feeding on energy. Thus, drawing energy from Pittsburgh's main generating plant into his foundry, he grasped the live cable, was shot through with electricity, and did indeed gain the ability to control enormous amounts of metal with his mind. Requiring a constant supply of energy, he fashioned his costume and etched photovoltaic cells into its surface, which enabled it to serve as a solar battery (though he could also lunch on a nuclear pile for a quick fix if need be). Becoming Silver Shade, he set forth to use his power to shape metal throughout the city into monstrous, living works of art. He was stopped by Firestorm when the nuclear man overloaded the super villain's suit and caused it to explode.

Quote: "Today I pushed my power to its *limit* . . . I felt the harmonics of the *universe* vibrating through my soul."

Comment: This has been the character's only appearance to date.

THE SILVER SWAN (C)

Real Name: Helen Alexandros.

First Appearance: 1982, *Wonder Woman* #288, DC Comics.

Costume: White boots, leotard with open belly and long sleeves, diadem encircling head and face, wings (see Weapons).

Weapons: Bird-like wings for flight.

Biography: All her life, aspiring ballet dancer Helen was shunned by others as "the *ugly duckling*—too hideous (for men) to even *consider* loving me!" Needing a flunky, the Roman god of war Mars approached her with a proposition: He will give her superpowers—superstrength, the ability to fly, and a destructive screech—if she will turn those powers against the hated superhero Wonder Woman and the President of the United States, destroying them both. She accepts. Bested by Wonder Woman, the Silver Swan is deprived of her powers by Mars (#290). The super villain is in love with Captain Wonder, an evil identity of DOCTOR PSYCHO.

Quote: "Another *second* and she would've been splattered across the countryside like an overripe melon . . . ."

SINESTRO (C, TV)

First Appearance: 1961, *Green Lantern* #7, DC Comics.

Costume: Black bodysuit with blue starburst collar; blue trunks, belt, boots, wristbands. Sinestro's skin is red.

Weapons: Power ring which creates any object Sinestro's mind can conceive and also enables him to fly and fire destructive bolts. (The objects he creates are all yellow, a color which the power ring of his nemesis, the superhero Green Lantern, cannot affect due to an impurity in the hero's power battery.)

Biography: A humanoid denizen of the planet Korugar, Sinestro is chosen by the wise and benign Guardians of Oa to be his world's Green Lantern—the wielder of a mighty power ring. Each time he charges his ring at the power battery, he is equipped with 37 diors (24 earth-hours) worth of super-abilities. However, not long after he becomes a Green Lantern, Sinestro is overcome with dissatisfaction. He wants to rule, not serve, and uses his abilities to take over his world. Arrested by the Guardians and banished "to the antimatter universe of Qward," Sinestro lashes out by building a viso-teleporter to bring all the denizens of the terrestrial city of Valdale to Qward. Earth's Green Lantern flies over to rescue them, imprisoning Sinestro in an impenetrable power-bubble. But the fiend escapes and, using a yellow power ring—a color against which Green Lantern's ring is ineffective—he now comes and goes from the antimatter universe at will. Sinestro has devoted himself to striking back at the Guardians by plaguing Earth's Green Lantern. On Korugar, Sinestro's only known relative, his father, operates the equivalent of a terrestrial opium den. Sinestro was a charter member of THE SECRET SOCIETY OF SUPER-VILLAINS.

Quote: "I do not consider myself *bound* by law! I *can* smash you—and I *shall*!"

Comment: The character has appeared over a dozen times since his debut. Charlie Callas played the part in the 1979 TV movie *Legends of the Super-Heroes*. See LIGHTMASTER, who is quite similar.

SINISTRO, BOY FIEND (C)

Real Name: Jack Biceps.

First Appearance: 1968, *Charlton Premiere, Vol. 2, #3, Charlton Comics.*

Costume: Blue trousers, cape, vest with yellow "S" in black circle over heart; brown gloves, boots; white shirt; black mask, bow tie.

Weapons: Highro-Gyro, a one-person "crime copter"; super-binoculars; inkfilled gun; micro-mesh which is "invisible to the naked eye yet known to hold fast a killer whale"; jet pack for flight when away from Highro-Gyro.

Biography: Gothamville's popular teenager Jack hates superheroes—in large part because, as an all-American boy, he is expected by his parents and teachers to become a hero himself. Thus, he takes it upon himself to wage war on and destroy the local superheroes Blue Beetle, Peacemaker, Thunderbolt, Superguy, Captain USA, and the Green Spider. Failing in his one attempt to acquire superpowers (he puts too much salt in his ground-spider/essence-of-jellyfish concoction and refuses to drink the foul-tasting mixture again), he relies, instead, on hi-tech weaponry. Alas, this "dedicated champion of infamy" is too inept to achieve his goal; turning himself in to the police, he can't even get arrested. When last seen, the bitter Jack was with his girlfriend Shirlee Peech, bemoaning his failure.

Quote: "I want . . . exactly $49,500,000,000 . . . and don't give it to me *all in pennies*!"

Comment: This was the misanthrope's only appearance.

SIR ERIC HAZARIAS (MP)

First Appearance: 1946, *Lost City of the Jungle*, Universal Pictures.

Chief Henchman: Grebb.

Biography: Hazarias is a dyed-in-the-wool warmonger, and no sooner has the Second World War ended than he looks for a way to start number three in the series. However, he wants to make some money off the cataclysm and leads a search for the extremely rare element Meteorium 245, the only defense against a nuclear bomb. His quest leads him and his ally Grebb to the lost city of Pendrang, where they find a chest containing the element—before Rod Stanton of the United Peace Foundation can stop them. Fortunately for the cause of world peace, once they are airborne, Hazarias and Grebb fight for sole possession of their prize. In the course of their struggle, the chest accidentally opens, releasing the power of the Meteorium 245 and disintegrating the aircraft.

Comment: Lionel Atwill played Hazarias in the 13-chapter serial. He died before the picture was completed, and his part was finished by a stand-in. Atwill also played OTTO VON NEIMANN and THE SCARAB.

SIR HUGO DRAX (N, MP)

First Appearance: 1955, *Moonraker*, Ian Fleming.

Weapons: The Moonraker, a nuclear missile.

Biography: Born in Germany, Drax goes to school in England where he remains to become a successful industrialist. Pretending to be interested in the welfare of England, Drax offers to build a nuclear missile to be used in the nation's defense. However, because Drax cheats at cards, the head of the British secret service asks agent James Bond to look into Sir Hugo's character. What Bond uncovers is not only that Drax is a bad loser—he throws a tantrum when Bond beats him at bridge—but also that his construction of the missile is being underwritten by the Soviet Union, and that he plans to use it to flatten London as vengeance for Germany's defeat in World War II. Escaping from a trap concocted by Drax—Bond was imprisoned next to the rocket boosters where he was to be burned alive—the British agent reprograms the missile's gyroscopic guidance so that it will come down in the North Sea, right on top of the submarine Drax is using to escape to Russia. Drax is "physically big (standing) about six foot tall." His large, squarish head is topped by red hair parted in the middle (he wears it that way to hide the scars of plastic surgery he had to undergo during the war); Drax also has a thick moustache and sideburns.

Comment: Michel Lonsdale played Drax in the 1979 motion picture, though the character was considerably different. Using his fleet of Moonraker space shuttles, Drax ferries a group of genetically superior men and women to his orbiting space station. From that vantage point he will release satellites which contain enough poison vapor to kill every human on earth. With humankind destroyed, Drax intends to bring his more perfect people to earth and repopulate the planet. However, Bond foils his plan by boarding the space station, pushing Drax through an airlock, and destroying the satellites with a laser gun.

SISSYMAN (C)

First Appearance: 1967, *The Mad Adventures of Captain Klutz*, Don Martin.

Weapons: Ice cream gun which fires various flavors ("Butterscotch Pecan would kill you instantly but I want you to *die slow*! So it's *Pistachio Chip* for *you*!"); teddy bear which, when squeezed, releases a poisoned swordblade from its belly.

Biography: An adult who behaves like a child, Sissyman lives in an ordinary suburban house whence he sets out to commit extraordinary robberies. Though the superheroic Captain Klutz sets off in hot pursuit, he fails to capture the villain; presumably, Sissyman is still at large.

Quote: "Captain Klutz? I *hate* you, I *hate* you, I *hate* you! You're a *meanie* and you *stink*! *Nyeah-Nyeah-Nyeah*!!!"

Comment: Other foes of Captain Klutz include the cigar-chomping Granny Santini and her soup which turns people into zombie slaves (Captain Klutz shoots her dead); the giant, anthropomorphic spider Gorgonzola; and Mervin the Mad Bomber.

***SISSYMAN** vs. Captain Klutz. © Don Martin and E.C. Publications.*

THE SIX-HEADED MUMMY (C)

Real Name: Joe Beket.

First Appearance: 1966, *House of Mystery* #161, DC Comics.

Costume: Mummy wrappings from neck to toe; various helmets (see Weapons).

Weapons: Masks which allow the wearer to tap the powers of the Egyptian gods simply by uttering the magic word "Heka." These gods include ibis-headed Thoth, the moon god, to cause a rain of boulders; bull-headed Set, the desert god, to create sandstorms; Khnum, the ram-headed water god, to control waters vast and small; Ranno, the asp-like garden god, to cause foliage to do one's bidding; Anubis, the jackal-headed god of the underworld, to control anything underground; and the owl-headed sun god Ra in order to create and command fire. The Mummy also has a rocket-powered sled for quick getaways.

Biography: After serving five years in prison for armed robbery, the criminal Beket is released and decides to look into an old family legend . . . that an Egyptian sorcerer from whom he is descended, the infamous Bek-et, was buried with "a chest containing the headpieces that gave him the powers of the ancient gods." Going to Egypt, entering the tomb, and stealing the chest, he swathes himself in mummy wrappings ("or the power will seep out and ebb away"), reassembles his old (and rather dubious) gang, and resumes his criminal ways. After committing several spectacular crimes, he is stopped by Robby Reed, master of the "Dial-H for Hero" device. Becoming Shadow-Man,

Robby manages to get close to Bek-et and remove his bandages.

Quote: "Now, aren't you glad you joined up with me again? I've just opened the basement vault of the jewel exchange!"

Comment: This was the character's only appearance.

SKELETOR (T, TV, C, MP)

First Appearance: 1982, Mattel Toys.

Costume: Purple harness, hood, girdle, boots. Skeletor's flesh is blue, his skeletal face yellow.

Weapons: Ram-headed staff through which he channels his magic power to perform simple tricks, like levitation, or create life itself; Spydor, a large spider-like transport vehicle; Land-Shark, a shark-headed tank whose jaws open and shut; the Roton assault vehicle, which rests atop a whirring buzzsaw-type blade; sword; Terror Claws, vicious, oversized claws which slip over his hands.

Chief Henchmen: Panthor, his giant, purple, cat-like steed; Spikor, who has a telescoping trident hand and spiked armor; Stinkor, the evil "master of odors"; "Two Bad," a monster with two heads; Whiplash, a serpentine humanoid with a mighty tail; Beast Man, a powerful, heavily armed lion-like humanoid; Clawful, a warrior with a lobster-like right arm; Evil-Lyn, the wicked warrior goddess; Jitsu, the "master of martial arts"; Kobra Khan, the venom-spitting "master of snakes"; Webstor, the hideous "master of escape"; Mer-Man, the evil ocean warlord; the three-eyed Tri-Klops who sees everything; and Trap Jaw, the iron-jawed warrior with a powerful mechanical right arm. Also assisting Skeletor on occasion is the Evil Horde (see HORDAK).

Biography: Eternia is a planet which exists on a dimensional plane different from that of earth, and beneath whose medieval exterior lies a highly advanced, yet mystical civilization. To become the absolute ruler, "the true king of Eternia," one must first breech the walls of the ancient, mysterious, and magical Castle Greyskull. To prevent this from happening prematurely or falsely, young Prince Adam has been given the Sword of Power which transforms him into the superhero He-Man; trying to destroy He-Man and take the castle is Skeletor. Headquartered in the fortress Snake Mountain, Skeletor is a master magician about whose past nothing is known. His crimes consist primarily of kidnaping, hypnotizing, and stealing to achieve his goals (children's TV allowing nothing stronger).

Quote: "I'd much *prefer* to spill your blood with my own hand rather than *waste* precious magical energies! A sword is so much more . . . *personal!*"

Comment: The syndicated Filmation TV series debuted in 1982 and is still on the air; the shows are also available on videocassette. The character was also featured in Filmation's animated theatrical feature *The Secret of the Sword* (1985); in the 1987 feature film *Masters of the Universe*, played by Frank Langella (DRACULA); and in comic books from DC (1982-83). However, the character made his comic book debut not in the *Masters of the Universe* title but in *DC Comics Presents* #47 (1982), battling Superman. Mattel has released numerous versions of the Skeletor doll: the basic model, as well as a "Battle Armor" version, in which the harness can be rotated to show dents and rents after an encounter with He-Man; and a "Dragon Blaster" model, in which a dragon riding Skeletor's back functions as a water pistol. The basic figure stands five-and-one-half inches tall. See other action toy super villains BARON KARZA, DESTRO, GENERAL SPIDRAX, HORDAK, MOLTAR, and MUMM-RA.

THE SKULL (MP)

Real Name: Drew (no other name).

First Appearance: 1940, *Deadwood Dick*, Columbia Pictures.

Costume: White skull mask; black cloak, western hat, gloves.

Weapons: Six shooter.

Biography: The Skull is the leader of an outlaw band which is preying on the people of Deadwood, South Dakota. With statehood on the horizon, the villain launches an ambitious plan to control the state's telegraphs, banks, post offices, and other key resources. However, the heroic Deadwood Dick thwarts the Skull, revealing him to be the banker of Deadwood.

Comment: Ed Cassidy played the role in the 15-chapter series.

SKYSHARK (C)

Real Name: Kapitan Schleigal.

First Appearance: 1976, *Marvel Two-In-One Annual* #1, Marvel Comics.

Costume: Gray trousers, jacket with red circle on chest and white shark emblem inside, red trim on high collars; red gloves; blue boots, goggles, helmet with red shark-like fin on top.

Weapons: Stuka plane which can create artificial clouds for hiding; standard firearms.

Biography: Nothing is known about the character's

past, save that he boasted of having been skilled in "flying . . . and in killing," talents which could not "be gainfully combined—until 1939." Distinguishing himself with "merciless attacks" upon civilians during the German invasion of Poland, he eventually came to the attention of Hitler himself and was brought to Berlin. There, the Fuhrer himself dubbed him "Himmel-hai"—the Skyshark—and ordered him to assemble a crack squadron to launch attacks on the United States mainland. Flying seven planes against New York, he was beaten back by the time-traveling superhero the Thing, assisted by the Liberty Legion. Skyshark's companion was a Japanese observer known as the Slicer.

Quote: "A human being on the ground—*any* human being . . . is merely a *target* for my gunsights, nothing more."

THE SNAKE (N, MP)

First Appearance: 1943, *Le Petit Prince*, Antoine de Saint Exupery.

Weapons: Poison which kills in 30 seconds.

Biography: A golden, talking snake which lives in a desert in Africa, the Snake is the first creature met by the Little Prince when he arrives on earth from his home, Asteroid B-612. A braggart, the snake eventually kills the young protagonist, having convinced him that death is the only way he can ever go home. When last seen, the serpent is flying across the sands into the desert like "the dying spray of a fountain."

Quote: "Whomever I touch, I send back to the earth from whence he came."

Comment: Bob Fosse played the part in the 1974 motion picture *The Little Prince*. Since Biblical days, the serpent has personified evil; the other preeminent snake villains are Kaa from "Kaa's Hunting" ("Kaa was not a Poison Snake . . . but his strength lay in his hug") and the cobras Nag and Nagina from "Rikki-Tikki-Tavi," which appeared in Rudyard Kipling's *The Jungle Book* (1894) and *The Second Jungle Book* (1895). See also THULSA DOOM (Comment). For other snake villains, see COBRA, COPPERHEAD, and SIDEWINDER.

SNODGRASS MCVIPER (C)

First Appearance: 1970, *The Close Shaves of Pauline Peril* #1, Gold Key Comics.

Biography: Snodgrass McViper is the editor of the *Daily Noose*. The newspaper is owned by Porterhouse P. Peril whose daughter, Pauline, is a reporter; one day the scatterbrained young lass will inherit the mighty publishing empire. Realizing that he will "perish if she inherits me," Snodgrass repeatedly sends Pauline on assignments designed to kill her. Though he usually tags along to ensure that she perishes, Pauline always manages to survive.

Quote: "I forgot about her health-nut hero boyfriend . . . plus her whining hound, Weakheart! They always manage to snatch Pauline from perilous perils."

Comment: There were only four issues of Pauline's magazine.

SNODGRASS MCVIPER. © Western Publishing.

SNOWMAN (C)

Real Name: Klaus Kristin.

First Appearance: 1981, *Batman* #337, DC Comics.

Biography: In December of 1954, Klaus' mother Katrina was part of a United Nations expedition to the Himalayas. Separated from the others by the collapse of an ice bridge, she was saved by an Abominable Snowman with whom she subsequently had an affair; rescued, she died nine months later giving birth to her son. Raised by Katrina's sister, Klaus has the ability to become an icy figure called Snowman who "radiates cold," causing any person or object to become frozen solid. Preferring to exist in cold climates, Klaus must travel eight months of the year; because he has no wealth of his own, Snowman must use his powers to acquire it by robbing. In their first meeting, Klaus fought the crimebusting Batman and fell from a precipice, seemingly to his death; in their second and thusfar final bout (*Detective Comics* #552), Snowman is reunited with his Yeti father.

Quote: "Batman . . . call me by my *father's* name! Call me *Snowman*!"

Comment: MISTER FREEZE is another icy villain.

THE SNOW QUEEN (F, MP)

First Appearance: 1846, "The Snow Queen," Hans Christian Andersen.

Costume: Fur coat and hat made of snow.

Weapons: Sled that flies and travels "with the speed of the wind."

Biography: The Snow Queen is the hard-hearted fairy who brings the freezing snow and killing frost. During storms, she "always flies right in the center. She is the biggest (snowflake) of them all, but she never lies down to rest as the other flakes do. Many a winter night she flies through the streets of the town and . . . windows . . . become covered by ice flowers." Yearning for a companion, the sprite kidnaps the young boy Kai, who has suffered a curious misfortune. A Troll has made a mirror which makes evil look good and good evil; when the glass shatters, two of the "millions of billions" of pieces land in Kai's eyes, another in his heart, shards which turn him cruel. Thus, when he sees the Snow Queen, she appears beautiful and friendly to him. This makes him a perfect companion, and she abducts him in her sled. Although the lad had spent his last days among humans being nasty to his playmate Gerda, the little girl goes after him; in time, she tracks them to the Snow Queen's palace up north, a huge place built of snow (save for the windows and doors which are "of the sharp winds"), lighted by the northern lights, and boasting more than a hundred halls, the largest of which is "several miles long." The Snow Queen herself spends most of her time in a huge snow hall, on a throne perched atop a frozen lake which is "cracked into thousands of pieces (each) shaped exactly like all the others." The palace is guarded by giant, swarming snowflakes, some of which look "like ugly little porcupines, others like bunches of snakes all twisted together, and some like little bears with bristly fur." By the time Gerda arrives, Kai is "blue—indeed, almost black—from the cold," though the Snow Queen "had kissed all feeling of coldness out of him." Gerda's tears wash the splinters from him and they escape when the Snow Queen flies off to frost some mountain peaks.

Quote: "I shan't give you any more kisses, or I might kiss you to death."

Comment: The character also appeared in animated films in 1958 and 1968, both produced in the Soviet Union. When the first was released in the United States (1959), Sandra Dee provided the character's voice. Other villains among the 168 stories written by Andersen include the "Ice Maiden" who, with her "snow-white hair and blue-green dress which glistens like water" lives in an ice palace and kills any humans who happen by ("I crush anything that comes within my grasp and never let it go!"); the "evil brother" who stabs his sister's suitor and cuts off his head in "The Rose Elf" (flowers grown from the eyes and lips of the dead man give the brother nightmares, then stab him to death with poisoned thorns); and Helga, the insufferable "Bog King's Daughter" who, "wilder and more ferocious" than her Viking companions, once tested the sharpness of a knife by stabbing a dog and, another time, bit "the head off a black cock," among other bloody acts.

SOLARR (C, TV)

Real Name: Silas King.

First Appearance: 1973, *Captain America* #160, Marvel Comics.

Costume: Yellow headband, bodysuit with red gem on chest and stripe leading down to trunks; red trunks, boots, wristbands.

Weapons: Briefly carried power storage unit to keep him going during the night.

Biography: A drug dealer, King was on a Los Angeles to New York run when his van gave out in the middle of the Mojave Desert. Spending several days in the sun's rays as he trekked on foot back to civilization, King found that the solar energy caused latent mutant powers to surface. He now had the ability to store solar radiation and release it as destructive blasts. Adopting the identity of Solarr, he became a criminal as well as a member of the shortlived EMISSARIES OF EVIL.

SOLOMON GRUNDY (C)

First Appearance: 1944, *All American Comics* #61, DC Comics.

Costume: Purple shirt; tattered black jacket, trousers;

brown shoes. Solomon's skin and hair are white, and there are dark circles around his eyes.

Biography: Slaughter Swamp lies just beyond Gotham City and, back in 1894, it was the scene of the murder of Cyrus Gold. His body was left there and over the next half-century was metamorphosed "by the strange chemical reaction of sizzling sunlight beating down on the decayed vegetation of soggy swampland." A hulking brute of a man was the result and, shambling forth from his "radioactive" home, the "raging colossus" stole some clothes from a pair of escaped cons and joined a group of criminals holed up at a hobo camp. (He was named after the famous nursery rhyme—"Solomon Grundy, born on Monday, christened on Tuesday . . ."— by one of the crooks when the brute said that all he could remember was that he was born on a Monday.) Joining the gang, Solomon Grundy used his vast powers to help them, committing nearly a dozen murders in the process. Nothing stopped him: jails couldn't hold him, nor could speeding trains or bullets deter him; since he didn't need to breathe, a body of water was no obstacle. Though the superhero Green Lantern was there to fight him virtually every time he committed a crime, neither figure was ever victorious—until Lantern, managing to trap Grundy inside an impenetrable bubble, sent him to another world. But the bubble was eventually pulled from the planet's surface by a meteor and Grundy guided it to earth. The globe shattered on impact and, lumbering from the wreckage, Grundy went searching for Green Lantern. ("I make him come to me! I rob! He no like anyone to rob!") The villain found, instead, a trio of heroes to face and, together, Green Lantern, Hourman, and Dr. Fate managed to put him in another green orb and send him back into space (*Showcase* #55, 1965). Grundy has since returned to battle sundry superheroes many times, most notably the Justice League of America (for which he was teamed with the equally brawny Blockbuster [*Justice League of America* #46]). Briefly allied with THE INJUSTICE SOCIETY OF THE WORLD, Grundy is once again an independent operator and is still at large.

Quote: "*Green Lantern*! You in swamp! I take you back into water! I make you man-thing—like me!"

THE SPACE PHANTOM (C)

First Appearance: 1963, *The Avengers* #2, Marvel Comics.

Costume: Purple bodysuit with red collar and arrow pointing toward waist; flared orange shoulders and flaps under the arms, strung from wrist to waist; golden boots, gloves.

Biography: The Space Phantom (his real name is unrevealed) was born on the planet Phantus. There, travel through time was mastered long ago and, like warfare, was commonplace. Unfortunately, the combination of the two created problems. Phantusians simply hopped back in time to alter the course of battles which went against them. This prompted the former winners, now the losers, to do the same . . . causing mass confusion in the time stream. During one particularly convoluted adjustment in a battle, the fabric of time actually tore under the stress, dumping the entire planet into Limbo. A military strategist, the Space Phantom had had an inkling of what was to come and snuggled into a time capsule. However, the conveyance was damaged and the Phantom not only ended up in Limbo, but also found himself there alone. Luckily, the Phantom was found by IMMORTUS who made a deal with him. He would grant the Phantom the power to assume for any length of time he wished the likeness of another creature, human or otherwise, so Immortus would be able to study that being in Limbo. Agreeing, the Phantom went to Immortus' home planet, Earth, through a rift in Limbo. Aware of the superheroic Avengers, he decided to defeat them by impersonating them, thus leaving our planet vulnerable to conquest by himself and other Phantusians. Found out and sent packing back to Limbo by the superhero Thor, the Space Phantom has returned numerous times to battle superheroes from Captain America to Rom. He briefly took the place of another super villain, Madame Hydra (see VIPER).

Quote: "Lately there have been precious few wayfarers in this timeless realm. Hence, I have been trapped here—bored out of my mind!"

Comment: Marvel's Limbo is similar to the Phantom Zone at DC. See Phantom Zone inmates GENERAL ZOD and JAX-UR for details.

THE SPADE (C)

First Appearance: 1984, *The Guardian* #2, Spectrum Publications.

Costume: Red boots, full-face cowl, bodyshirt with black spade on chest; black tights, gloves.

Weapons: Razor-edged cards which he flings with deadly accuracy.

Biography: Nothing is known about this costumed villain, save that he was a paid assassin who was hired to slay the superheroic Guardian. He cornered the hero and let his lethal cards fly, only to be foiled by the heroine, Silhouette, who intercepted the projectiles with a crossbow. When last seen the Spade was feeling from the police.

Quote: "What . . .? No cries of agony? No blood?"

Comment: This was the character's only appearance.

THE SPEED DEMON (2) (also known as THE WHIZZER) (C)

Real Name: James Sanders.

First Appearance: 1969, *The Avengers* #70 (as the Whizzer); 1981, *The Amazing Spider-Man* #222 (as Speed Demon), Marvel Comics.

Costume: As the Whizzer: yellow bodysuit; blue cowl with yellow goggles, blue gloves, trunks, boots, solid "V"-shaped vest which starts with flared shoulders and comes to a point at waist. As the Speed Demon: blue tights, gloves with yellow bolt fringe, cowl with red goggles; red boots with yellow bolt fringe, long-sleeve leotard with blue shoulders fringed by a stylized bow across chest and back, and along fringe at legs.

Biography: Sanders first becomes a super villain thanks to the Grandmaster. One of the oldest beings in creation, the Grandmaster requires amusement and, to this end, creates lethal games between races on various worlds. When the Squadron Supreme, superheroes of "Other Earth" (a world similar to ours located in another dimension), refuse to battle Kang the Conqueror (aka IMMORTUS) for his entertainment, the Grandmaster decides to create the SQUADRON SINISTER, giving selected humans powers similar to those of the heroic Squadron. Approaching chemist Sanders, who works for the Hudson Pharmaceutical Company, he provides him with the superspeed formula created by Hiram Arnold, the Squardron's Whizzer, as well as a copy of Hiram's Whizzer costume. Reproducing the formula in his lab, Sanders becomes an evil Whizzer and is defeated, along with his teammates, by the Avengers. Sanders is given amnesia by the superheroic wizard Doctor Strange, and returns to his job at Hudson. But his memory returns when the Avengers are forced to interrogate him about Squadron member Doctor Spectrum. Tinkering with Hiram's formula and making it even more potent than before, Sanders becomes the Speed Demon—changing his name because of the reemergence of the superheroic Whizzer. As the Speed Demon, Sanders can move through fire "so quickly that he isn't even singed," and smash rock "with a few dozen superspeed karate chops." He is a member of THE SINISTER SYNDICATE.

Quote: "*Ah*, this is the life! Robbing stores blind while those two alleged heroes bring up the rear!"

Comment: REVERSE-FLASH is another superspeed super villain, as is Speed Demon (1) of VENDETTA.

SPELLBINDER (C)

First Appearance: 1966, *Detective Comics* #358, DC Comics.

Costume: Trunks and right leg of tights are yellow with orange spots; left leg is yellow with vertical black stripes; black boots; bodyshirt is orange with yellow and black spirals over heart, black and white checks over right shoulder; left arm is black and white checks; right arm is orange with jagged yellow horizontal stripes; cowl is orange with yellow and black spiral on forehead.

Weapons: Various hypnotic devices.

Chief Henchmen: Nameless thugs.

Biography: An art forger specializing in Op Art, the Spellbinder (his name is never revealed) creates an Op Art hypnotic disc and uses it to become a thief. Although the villain is able to mesmerize Batman during their several encounters, the Caped Crusader manages to snap from the spell each time and send the thug to prison.

Comment: Camouflage King was also an artist (see CLOCK KING, Comment).

THE SPHINX (C)

First Appearance: 1977, *Nova* #6, Marvel Comics.

Costume: Purple bodysuit with green shoulders; green skirt, boots, cowl with two huge horns on the sides, meeting at the Ka stone on his forehead (see Weapons); red wristbands, belt with black buckle and golden ankh (Egyptian symbol of life) inside; blue armbands.

Weapons: The Ka stone, a sapphire-like gem whose origin is unknown, but whose powers are extraordinary. It enables the wearer to create energy in the form of heat, light, superpowers, and destructive beams. It also allows the user to read minds and fly, as well as rendering the user immortal and virtually indestructible.

Chief Henchmen: Kur and various other flunkies.

Biography: Some 5,000 years ago, the Sphinx (his name has never been revealed) was "the Chief Wizard" to Ramses II, pharaoh of ancient Egypt. Exiled after his magic proved inferior to that of Moses and the enslaved Israelites, the sorcerer wandered "days, months, years" in the desert. Finally stumbling upon a strange temple, he entered it and found "the flaming Ka—the living spirit stone." Compelled to put it to his forehead, the sorcerer became "one with the stone," gaining incredible powers. Calling himself the Sphinx, the wizard spent the next 50 centuries roaming the world and just enjoying life. Finally, however, he became bored. (As he put it with some sarcasm, "I was haunted by an ever-increasing sense of deja vu!") At last, he decided to do two things—take over the planet and try to find a means of dying, something the Ka

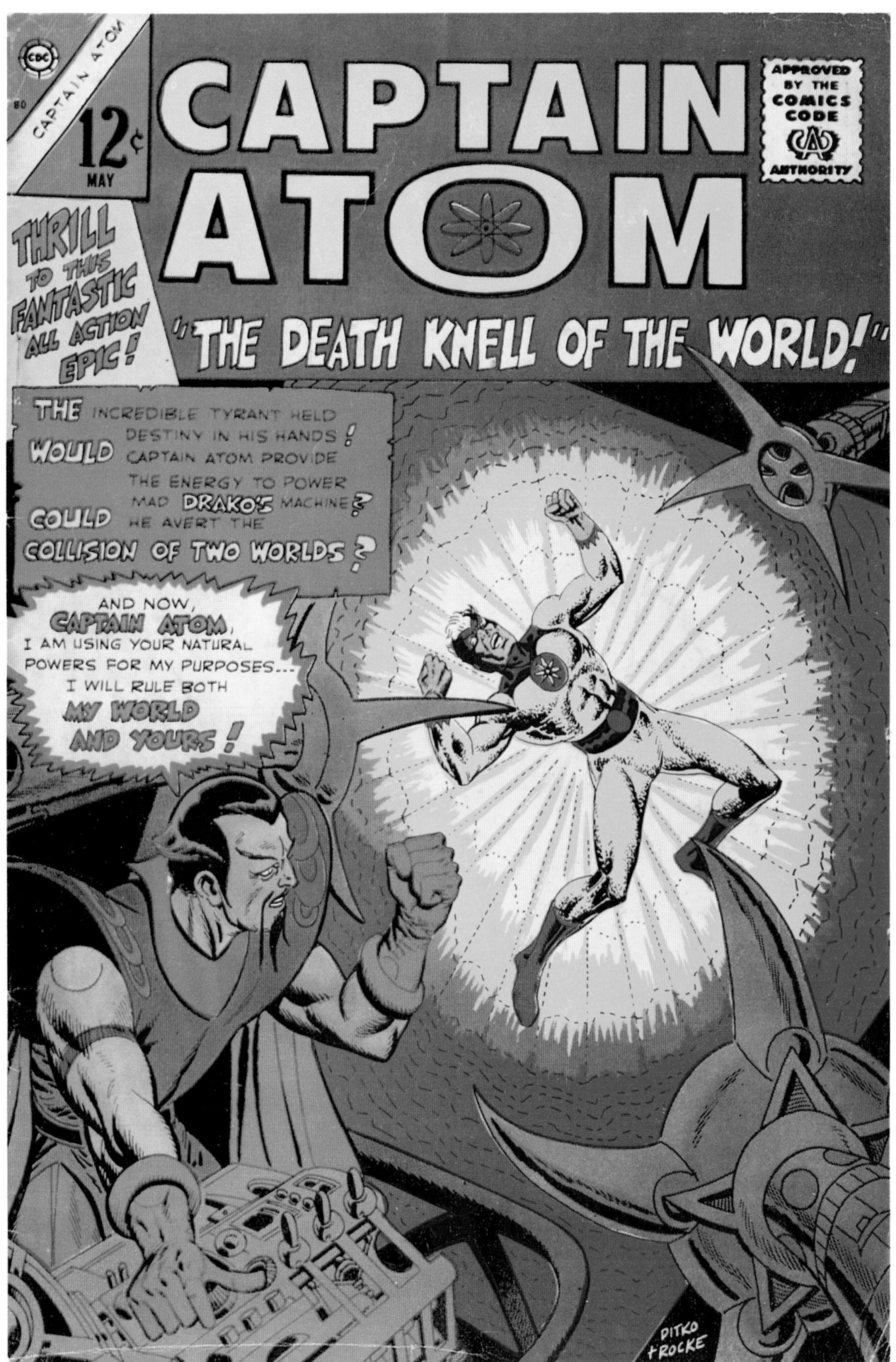

***Drako** tormenting his nemesis Captain Atom. © DC Comics.*

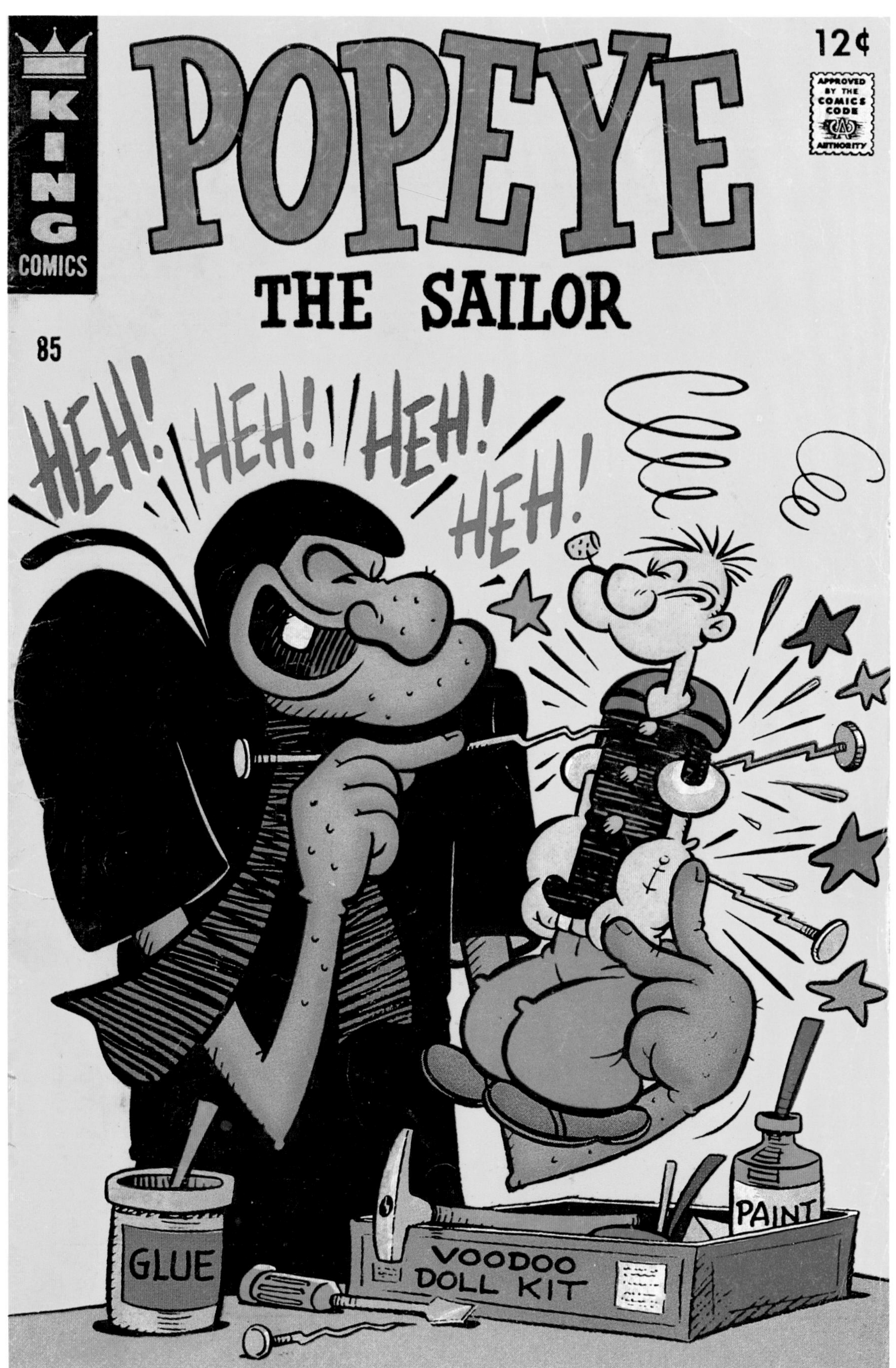

The Sea Hag. *© King Features Syndicate.*

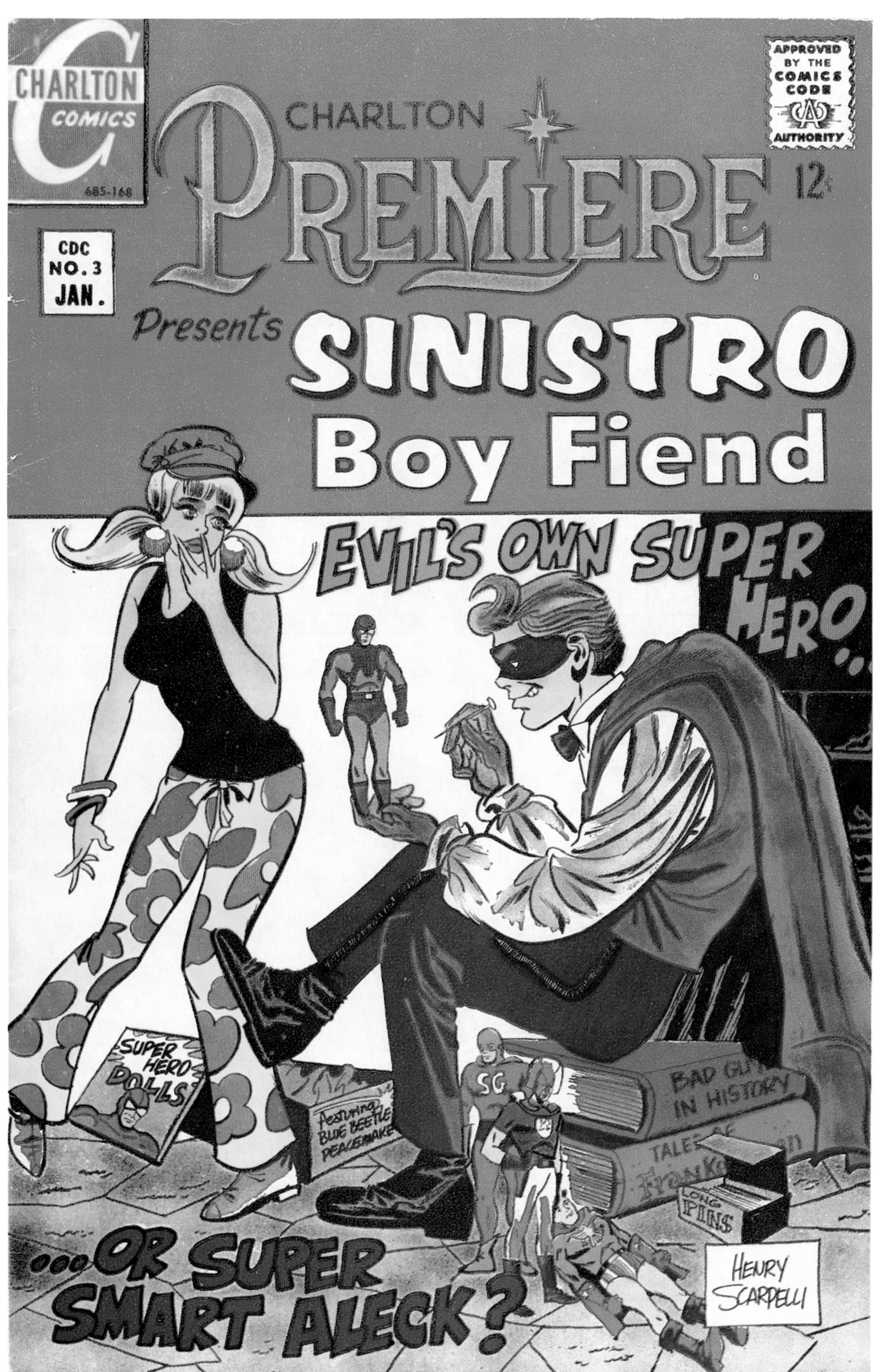

Sinistro, Boy Fiend. *Charlton Comics.*

A one-of-a-kind super villain: ***The Mod Gorilla Boss****. © DC Comics.*

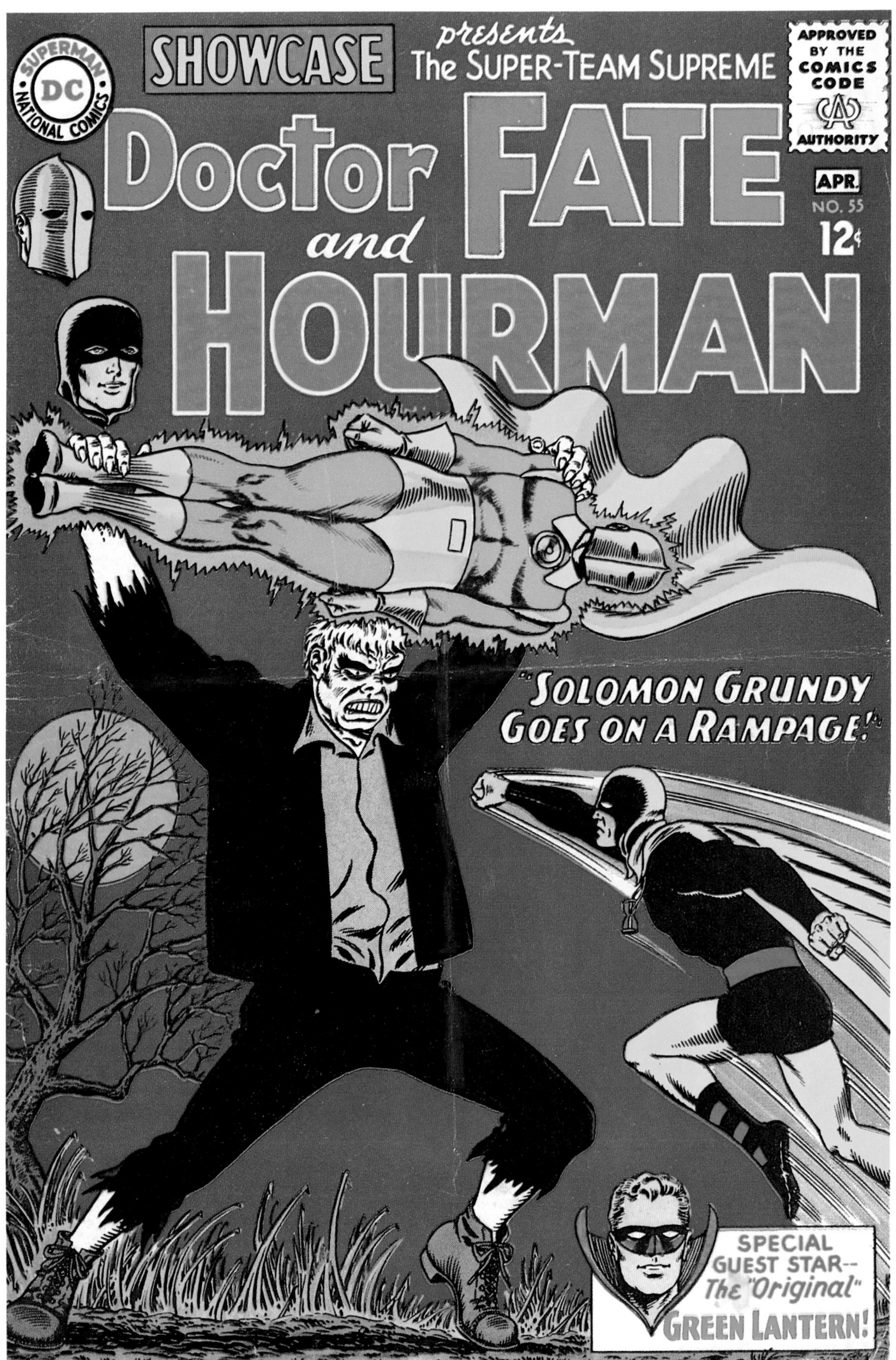

Solomon Grundy *prepares to have his way with Dr. Fate (aloft) and Hourman. © DC Comics.*

The bizarre ***Thunder-Man*** *and one of his even more outre aides.* © *DC Comics.*

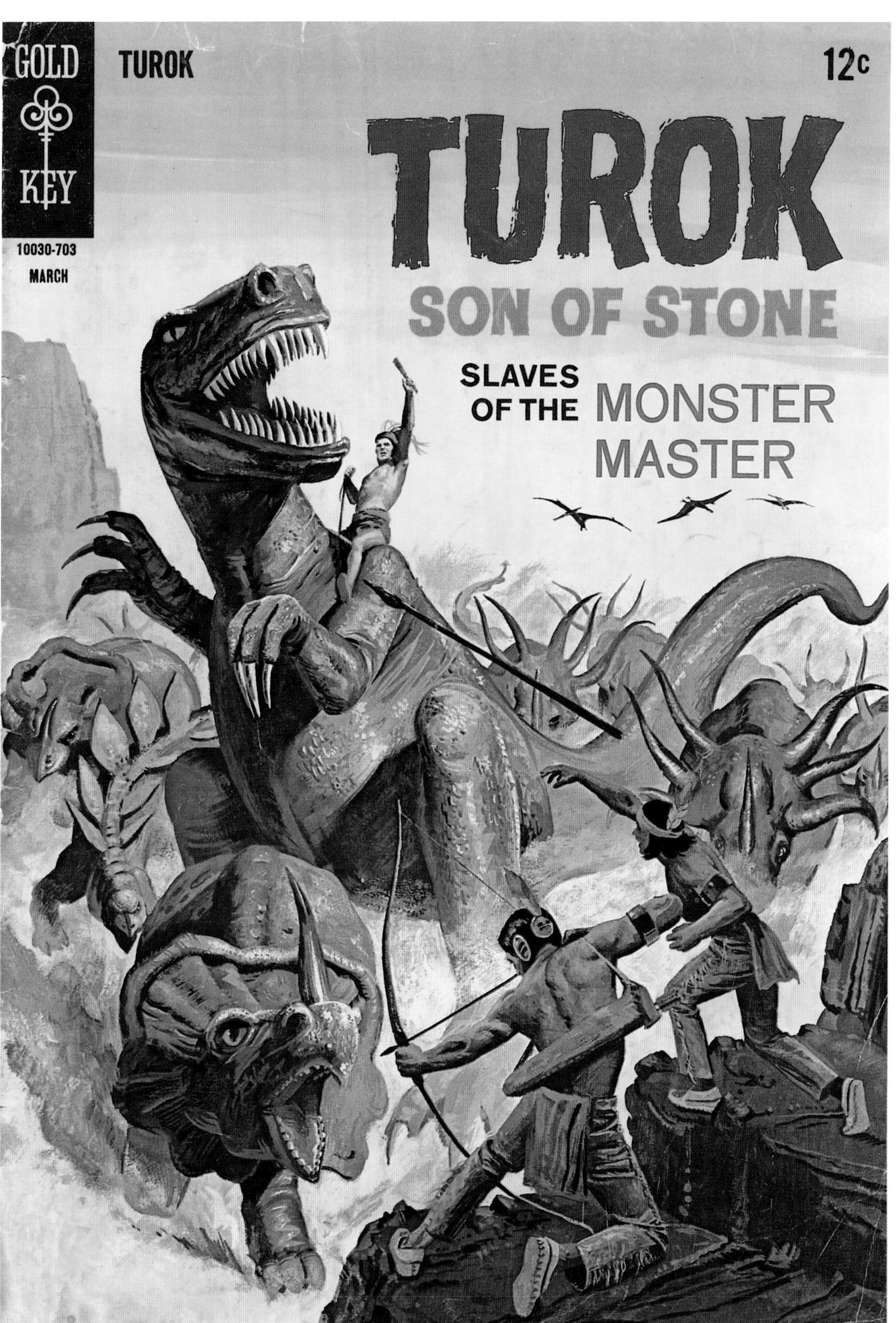

*Astride his Tyrannosaurus, **The Monster Master** attacks Turok (with bow and arrow).* © *Western Publishing.*

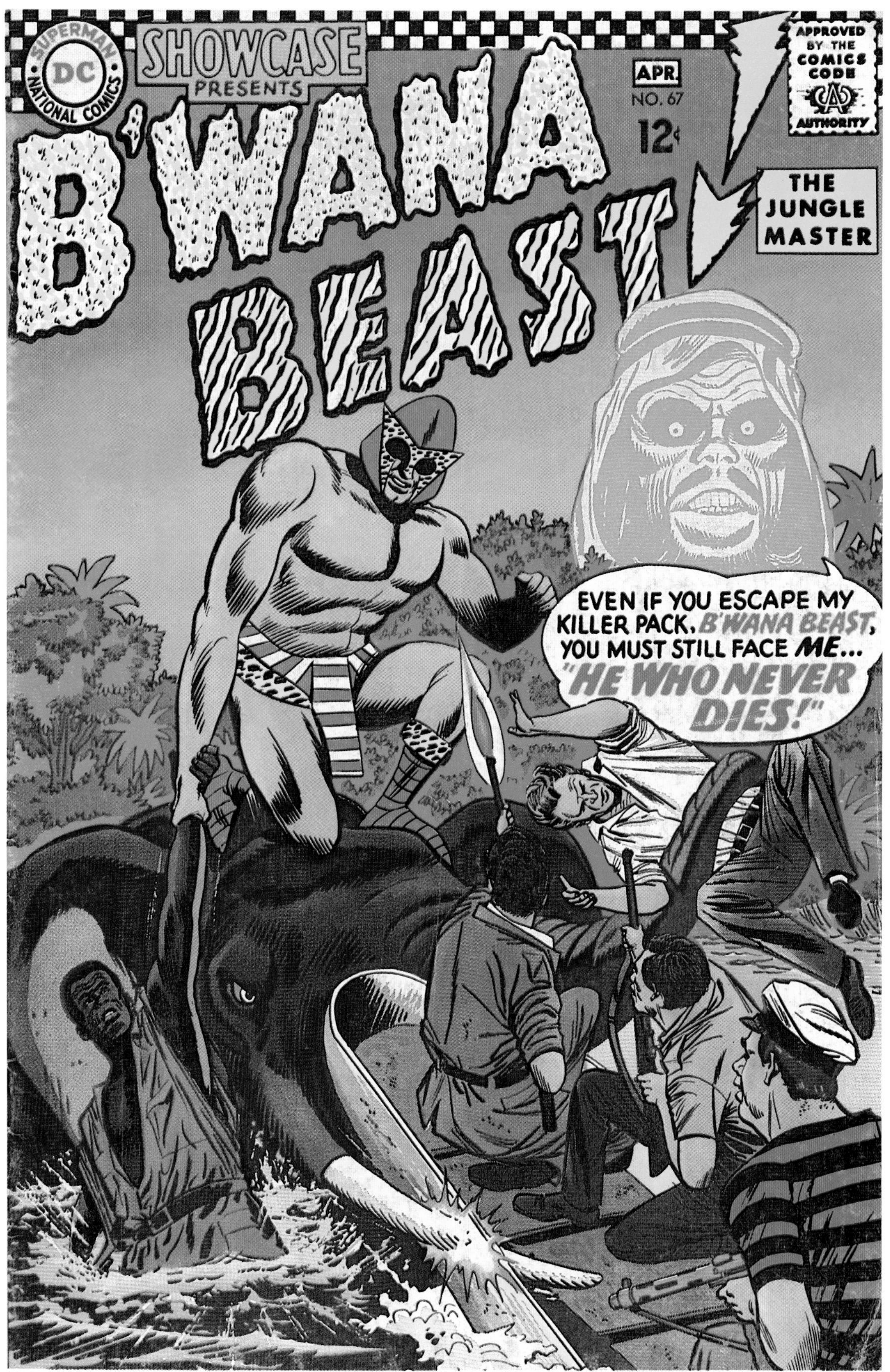

He Who Never Dies *peers out over a jungle in chaos. © DC Comics.*

stone would never permit. Confrontations with superheroes such as Nova and the Fantastic Four left him testy and redirected. He wished now to destroy the earth, to which end the Fantastic Four contacted their enemy GALACTUS and persuaded him to help them. The all-powerful being was amused by their humility and agreed to help. Crushing the stone, he showed a puckish sense of humor by not only keeping the Sphinx alive but also sending the wizard back in time "to repeat my hate-filled life—time and time again—for all eternity." But Galactus made one mistake: He forgot that there already *was* a Sphinx living in ancient Egypt. The two Sphinxes met and, informing his past self about what was to happen, they took precautions. Together, they built a "restoration ray" to repair the Ka stone, then left the device inside a pyramid. The displaced Sphinx was placed in the pyramid in hibernation, the other hypnotized into forgetting the odd meeting. Thus, after the Sphinx met Galactus and was returned to Ancient Egypt, the other awoke and used the restoration ray to refashion the Ka stone. Rededicating himself to making "the heavens themselves . . . tremble," he still pursues that goal, using the pyramid as a spaceship/headquarters.

Quote: "I have returned to conquer this world—or crush it!"

Comment: Other foes who battled Nova over the years include the towering alien Zorr ("Zorr will kill you . . . as easily as Zorr destroyed your puny world!"); the winged criminal genius Condor and his flunky Powerhouse, who drained energy from others; Megaman who, after falling into a mysterious black pool, was transported into the future, endowed with superpowers, and returned to our era to throw his weight around; and the skyscraper-sized orange robot Earth-Shaker which was built by the subterranean fiend Tyrannus and had a drill on its head and right arm, a huge pincer on its left, and fired missiles from its nipples.

THE SPIDER (C)

Real Name: Spider Spry.

First Appearance: 1959, *The Fly* (later *Fly Man*) #1, Archie Comics.

Costume: Original: red boots, leotard, cowl with white spider emblem on forehead, arms with green and white stripes on top; green gloves, belt, tights with white stripe on thigh. Second: blue-gray tights, gloves, leotard with one red and one white stripe around legs; red arms with white stripes; red cowl with white spider emblem on forehead; red boots; white belt with red buckle and loops. Third: red bodysuit; yellow boots; black belt; golden armband. Fourth: purple jacket, boots; light purple tights; web skullcap and collar; white belt. Fifth: brown leotard, boots, cowl with white spider on forehead; green tights, gloves; white and green stripes on upper arm.

Weapons: Giant mechanical spider conveyance which shoots webbing; huge mechanical scorpions with poison stingers; chlordane gas bombs deadly to insects (for use against The Fly) and sleeping gas bombs for use on humans; saucer-like craft for flight; deadly ray gun; nets which tighten the more his prey struggles.

Chief Henchman: Bruiser (first adventure only).

Biography: A thief and scientific genius, the Spider is based at an innocuous dockside shop called "S. Spry Fishermen's Nets." Apprehended by the superhero The Fly, the villain gives up his "Spry" cover and thereafter devotes his career to destroying the winged hero. Sent to jail, he sneaks out by substituting a robot likeness which took him two years to build; recaptured, he walks out when one of his gangmembers undergoes plastic surgery and takes his place. Next time, he simply has a helicopter pluck him out while dropping smoke bombs. Jailed with fellow villain THE NAMELESS ONE in a prison run by the secret agent group A.U.N.T.I.E. (Amalgamated Universal Network To Inhibit Evil), he escapes yet again (*The Fly* #1, second series, 1983) and remains a thorn in the hero's side. The corpulent Spider is an expert at throwing ropes, which he uses to scale buildings, and also has an uncanny sense of balance.

Quote: "Step into my parlor, said the *Spider* to the *Fly* . . . ha, ha, ha, ha!"

Comment: The Spider was created by artist Jack Kirby and writer Joe Simon, creators of Captain America and other classic comic book characters. In his second costume, the villain bears distinct similarities to the superhero Spider-Man, who was created a year later; in his third costume, the baldheaded character is a deadringer for LEX LUTHOR. This villain appeared frequently during the original (1959-66) 39-issue run and was also a member of the ANTI-FLY LEAGUE. Other foes of The Fly include the misshapen Crooked Man (actually a demented woman in disguise) who drives people mad in her Crooked House; the Dazzler; the Bat; the Ice Giant from Pluto; the Insect Gang; the Countess of Crime; the Red Shark; the Blockbuster; and the towering, Neanderthal-like Creature from the Abyss.

THE SPIDER LADY (MP)

First Appearance: 1948, *Superman*, Columbia Pictures.

Weapons: Reducer ray, a disintegration beam.

Biography: An underworld leader, the Spider Lady forces a captive scientist to invent a reducer ray. When it's finished, she threatens to destroy the city of Metropolis unless she is made its leader. The superheroic Superman tries to stop her, but she's ready for him with a debilitating chunk of kryptonite; donning a suit lined with lead to protect him from the rays, he overcomes the deadly space rock. In the end, the Spider Lady is destroyed by her own ray.

Comment: Carol Forman played the Spider Lady in this 15-chapter serial. Forman also played the super villain LASKA and THE BLACK WIDOW, and was an international thief named Nila in *Federal Agents vs. Underworld Inc.* (1949). According to the mythos of the film, the Spider Lady was Superman's first foe. She is not a villain in the Superman comic books.

THE SPIDER WITCH (C)

Real Name: Rak-Nora.

First Appearance: 1975, *Weird Suspense* #1, Atlas Comics.

THE SPIDER WITCH. Illustration by Pat Boyette; © Atlas Comics.

Costume: Purple dress slit to the waist along both legs; sometimes wears green wrap knit in the shape of a spider.

Biography: "In the gloomy days of the Dark Ages," the "raven-haired priestess" of the Tarantula Cult frequently leads her house-sized tarantulas into "a secluded village of Middle Europe" to claim victims for her rites. During these rituals in a "hidden glen," the abductees are transformed into giant tarantulas, thus increasing the army of the Tarantula God. Finally, led by Count Lycosa, the villagers raid the glen and burn the Spider Witch at the stake . . . but not before she utters a curse. "As I die in the searing flame," she snarls, "I decree that all your male descendants . . . will prowl the countryside with tarantuala powers in quest of victims to appease their spider's lust." During the twentieth century, a criminal happens upon "a musty tome . . . an ancient history of the Middle European spider cults." Reading from it ("argath sagor-ta terrani eluta") he revives the Spider Witch; she promptly slays him and goes searching for Lycosa's sole heir. She finds him and the two struggle at the edge of a cliff; the Count succeeds in hurling her into the sea far below, presumably to her doom.

Quote: "The tarantula emanations are very *powerful* here! Count Lycosa dwells within this house!"

Comment: The character appeared in the first two issues of *Weird Suspense.*

THE SPOOK (C)

Real Name: Val Kaliban.

First Appearance: 1974, *Detective Comics* #434, DC Comics.

Costume: Green robe (see Weapons), hood, gloves, shoes (see Weapons).

Weapons: Shoes have suction cups for climbing walls; smoke pellets allow him to conceal his movements; robe contains an "ultrasonic shock network" to zap anyone who reaches for him; balloons which, when blown up, are identical to the Spook and make it appear as though he can change his size or fly.

Biography: An architect for a major engineering company, Kaliban designs the new Gotham City prison with secret underground networks, which he plans to use to allow inmates to escape—for a price. Kaliban's plans get put on the back-burner when he stands trial for murdering his boss, who discovers the plot; sentenced to die in the chair, Kaliban hypnotizes a look-alike into believing that *he* is Kaliban, and the hapless dupe dies in his place. The prison is built as he planned and, 10 years later, as the Spook, the architect begins offering "escape insurance" to criminals, promising to free anyone who ends up in the clink.

Though the Spook's own criminal policy is cancelled by Batman, he escapes from prison. The two have fought several times over the years.

Comment: The Spook's eerie garb, as well as his subterranean doings, make him vaguely reminiscent of THE PHANTOM OF THE OPERA. Kaliban was also the name of a Shakespearean monster; see SYCORAX. See also other architect super villains QUAKEMASTER and VORTEX.

THE SPORTSMAN (C)

Real Name: Martin Mantle, Jr.

First Appearance: 1981, *Batman* #338, DC Comics.

Costume: Pastiche of sports equipment: red and yellow hockey jersey with black "13" on chest; yellow pinstripe baseball trousers; blue hockey gloves and ice skates (see Weapons); blue football helmet with white skull on forehead. The bulk of the costume is lined with protective padding.

Weapons: Ice skates which work off the ice; hockey stick for clubbing people to death; exploding basketball; buzzsaw tennis racket which can slice through metal; poison gas golfballs.

Biography: As a child, Martin was an average athlete . . . "but average wasn't good enough for my father." Though his mother Louisa tried to protect him, Martin was constantly beaten and berated by the demanding Martin, Sr. A chemist specializing in sports medicine, Martin, Sr., concocted a formula made of "RNA from the tissues of a true athlete," a potion to make supersportspeople from the unathletic. He injected his son, who did indeed become a brilliant athlete. However, he also began suffering unbearable headaches and, upon visiting a doctor, learned that the RNA he'd been given was affecting his nervous system and that he was going to die. Taking his revenge on the sports world, he ran around killing athletes, coaches, and even sportswriters until the crimefighting Batman stopped him with a hardball to the back of the head.

Quote: "You're here to make your *final touchdown*, Klugmuun. You're here to *die*."

Comment: This has been the character's only appearance to date. See also SPORTSMASTER.

SPORTSMASTER (C)

Real Name: "Crusher" Crock.

First Appearance: 1946, *All-American Comics* #85 (as Crock); 1947, *Green Lantern* #28 (as Sportsmaster), DC Comics.

Costume: Tights, padded jerkin, boots, bodyshirt, full-face mask. Colors have varied over the years, from white tights and mask and yellow jerkin to green tights and mask and purple jerkin. On occasion he wears a metalrimmed "brassie beanie" for throwing at opponents.

Weapons: Straight sports equipment, from hockey sticks to parachutes, as well as customized items such as explosive or gas-filled balls, rocket-powered soccer nets to trap people, jet-powered skis for flight, a flying roulette wheel (presumably for those times when the skis are on the blink), a flying golf green from which he putts golfballs to knock out his adversaries, razor-edged playing cards for throwing, fly-rod with whiplike trout-lure, and so forth. He also drives a "jet power-boat" for getaways on the sea.

Biography: A superb athlete, Crock played numerous sports professionally. Unfortunately he was obsessive about winning, and his savagery caused other players numerous injuries. Banished from sports after crippling a fellow football player, Crusher turned to crime. During one caper, Green Lantern arrived in time to stop him from robbing the grandstands at a polo match; later, while trying to kill the superhero, Crock appeared to perish in a fall. But he survived and, resurfacing as the costumed Sportsmaster, he went on a crime spree with his lockerful of equipment. Nabbed by Green Lantern and shipped to prison, Sportsmaster joined THE INJUSTICE SOCIETY OF THE WORLD upon his release. There he met and married THE HUNTRESS. Other robberies and jail terms followed; at present, both villains are keeping a low profile.

Quote: "I've been dealt the *winning hand—a full house*, aces up eights—otherwise known as a *dead man's hand*!"

Comment: The Green Lantern battled by Sportsmaster is the superhero of Earth-2, and not the Earth-1 Green Lantern who fought SINESTRO et al. The two worlds exist in parallel dimensions. THE SPORTSMAN is another sports villain, as is Fastball. Dressed in a golden bodysuit, the former baseball pitcher from Tampa winds up and pitches exploding balls "with the ferocity of a rifleshot." Since crime paid better than athletics, he joined the CADRE and went to work as a flunky of THE OVERMASTER.

THE SQUID (C)

First Appearance: 1982, *Adventure Comics* #490, DC Comics.

Costume: Blue bodysuit and cowl with red squid emblems on chest and face and red stripes on arms and legs; red gloves (see Weapons) and boots (the Squid's skin is green and scaly).

Weapons: Gloves shoot ink.

Chief Henchman: Abyss, a being which immediately teleports the Squid wherever he wishes to go by "folding" around him.

Biography: Nothing is known about this villain, save that he's from another world (whether that world's in a different dimension or in our own is never made clear). Presumably, his alien origins are the reason he robs jewelry, since earthly currency would be of little value on another planet. Teenagers Chris King and Vicki Grant use the "Dial-H for Hero" device to become the superheroes Topsy-Turvy and Scylla, respectively; they use their powers to disorient Abyss and, when the Squid jumps into him to go home, he ends up in limbo. Abyss self-destructs moments thereafter.

Quote: "No—*No*! EEEEEEEEEEEEEEEEEEEEEEEE" (Squid's last words as he enters Abyss).

Comment: This was the character's only appearance; he is unrelated to the Squid who appeared in the "Dial-H" story of DAFFY THE GREAT.

STARDUST (C)

Real Name: T'urin G'ar.

First Appearance: 1982, *Rom Annual* #1, Marvel Comics.

Costume: None. (In human form, Stardust is entirely red and spotted with white spots apparently representing stars; he is surrounded by yellow bands, two each crisscrossing his torso, wrists,and ankles.)

Biography: Found guilty of an unspecified crime by the Body on his home world (which lies "beyond the stars"), T'urin is stripped of his physical form, "bound in bands of star stuff," and banished into space—propelled "by some form of energy beyond our understanding." Seeking warmth, he heads for our sun and notices that our world is "warm . . . living." Landing, he begins "stealing the essence" of others, sucking up their energy and using it to take human form (a process which leaves his victims comatose). The essence he finds most satisfying is that of the shapechanging aliens known as THE DIRE WRAITHS, the sworn enemies of the superhero Rom. Although Rom doesn't mind seeing Wraiths die, he insists that Stardust return "the life energies" he's stolen from humans. The alien refuses and they battle, during which Rom accidentally shatters the "starstuff bands." Free, Stardust is on the verge of merging "with the very fabric of space" and acquiring "unlimited" power when Rom dons a starstuff belt and draws away the villain's energy. Stardust implodes and the superhero returns the human essences to those from whom they were stolen.

Quote: *I am Stardust! I want your life!*"

STARRO THE CONQUEROR (C)

First Appearance: 1960, *The Brave and the Bold* #28, DC Comics.

Costume: Starro is a gray, starfish-like being with a red eye in the center of its underbelly.

Chief Henchmen: Starfish slaves (originally three mutated, mesmerized earth starfish turned into marauding giants; later, small clones of the giant alien).

Biography: Traveling to earth, Starro establishes a base in our seas, intending to conquer the world. Measuring some 24 feet from tentacle tip to tentacle tip, Starro is discovered by the superhero Aquaman, who summons his fellow members of the Justice League of America. Discovering that lime prevents humans from being taken over by the extraterrestrial's mighty will, the superheroes powder Starro into submission. Found in the League trophy room by T.O. MORROW and brought back to life, Starro is defeated a second time (#65). In their most recent bout, Starro is inadvertently pulled from the sea by a young fisher. Settling down in Grand Central Station, the alien feeds on third rail energy, turns that power into protein, and is able to "replicate himself by the millions." Wrapping his clones around the faces of earthlings (including superheroes), he makes them slaves to his will. Ultimately, the alien is defeated because of a simple oversight: the android superhero Red Tornado is immune to mind-control and manages to shut the flow of electricity to the terminal. Subsequently frozen by the superheroes Green Lantern and Firestorm (#190), Starro escapes (it is never explained how) and, after battling Aquaman, is caught in an explosion. A part of him is flung through the dimensional barrier to Earth-C (a world of anthropomorphic animals) where he fights Captain Carrot and his Zoo Crew. He is defeated with lime.

Quote: "I am *Starro*! I was *born to conquer*!"

Comment: Starro holds the distinction of having been the first nemesis of the Justice League of America.

STAR SAPPHIRE (C)

Real Name: Carol Ferris.

First Appearance: 1959, *Showcase* #22 (as Carol); 1962, *Green Lantern* #16 (as Star Sapphire), DC Comics.

Costume: Pink bodyshirt with high white collar, trunks, boots, mask, tiara with sapphire on top; purple gloves; white belt with purple starburst.

Weapons: Magnificent star sapphire worn on crown

which gives Carol the ability to fly and fire "repelling rays" from her hand.

Biography: Carol is the head of the Ferris Aircraft Company, a post she inherited when her father Carl and her mother left on a lengthy round-the-world tour. Taught to fly by her lover, test pilot Hal Jordan—who is secretly the superhero Green Lantern—Carol is airborne one day when her ship is forced down by extraterrestrials. The aliens are humanoid females, the sole denizens of the planet Zamaron, which, in their language, means "Land of Lovely Women." Immortals, they are ruled by a queen who must by law be mortal; moreover, each of her successors "must always be her exact duplicate in appearance." Thus, whenever the queen dies, the technologically advanced Zamarons scour the universe in search of a suitable replacement. Since Carol fills the bill, they approach her with the honor, only to be rebuffed because she doesn't want to leave Green Lantern behind. To prove "what a weakling he really is . . . that *men* are a distinctly inferior species," the Zamarons clothe her in the queen's hunting togs, give her a magnificent star sapphire, and expose Carol to an odd melody played on an organ in their spaceship. The process endows Carol with many of the queen's powers and compels her to do battle with her lover, at the same time making her unable to reveal her true identity. While battling her lover she secretly wishes he would win, which he does; though they "increase the X-charge of our mind-over-matter transmission," the Zamarons are unable to help her overcome him. Departing, they leave behind the star sapphire and, every now and then, Carol goes into a trance-like state and battles Green Lantern. For the record, the aliens eventually chose Dela Pharon of the planet Xanador to be their queen. Star Sapphire is a member of THE SECRET SOCIETY OF SUPER-VILLAINS.

Quote: "I can't help myself! I must use my fantastic new power against *Green Lantern*! Grind him in the dust if I can!"

Comment: The character has made a handful of appearances over the years, most notably battling Pharon in *Green Lantern* #41, when the queen decides that, law or no law, she wants Green Lantern for her own. See THE PREDATOR, another villainous identity of Carol Ferris.

STILT-MAN (C)

Real Name: Wilbur Day.

First Appearance: 1965, *Daredevil* #8, Marvel Comics.

Costume: Blue skintight armor (see Weapons), trunks, gloves, helmet with cobra-like hood behind it, cowl, extendible, cylindrical legs (see Weapons).

Weapons: "Hydraulically operated stilts," enclosing his legs and able to extend nearly 300 feet; armor which gives him superhuman strength. He also has employed various arms including blasters and hand grenades. His most dangerous weapons were his "molecular condensor" which "could shrink any target into absolute nothingness," and his Z-ray which sends people to another planet.

Chief Henchmen: Endros and other thugs.

Biography: A scientist working for Klaxton Industries, Day was unhappy with his job and decided to steal the company's new invention, a compact hydraulic ram. Adapting the ram concept to a pair of stilts, Day created suitable armor and began his career as the thieving Stilt-Man. Stopped by the superhero Daredevil, he had the unique misfortune of being struck with his own molecular condensor ray; drifting "in a state of timeless limbo" until the effects wore off, he returned, made his armor more powerful, and resumed his dirty doings. In addition to his perennial foe Daredevil, Stilt-Man has battled Spider-Man and Thor. On one occasion, a thug named Turk stole the suit from Day and tried to abduct prosecutor Maxine Lavender; unaccustomed to the equipment, he was easily overpowered by Daredevil. Stilt-Man was briefly one of the EMISSARIES OF EVIL.

Quote: "I should have *warned* you, little man . . . I'm *more* than a match for your *limited* talents!!"

Comment: The character's name has also been written "Stiltman" and "Stilt Man."

STINGAREE (C)

First Appearance: 1967, *Metamorpho the Element Man* #10, DC Comics.

Costume: Light green bodysuit with green manta emblem on chest (see Weapons); green boots, gloves, cowl (see Weapons), tail (see Weapons), cloak, trunks, belt with white "S" buckle.

Weapons: Long metallic tail which can be snapped like a stinger and injects victims with "a chemical 'cocktail' of the world's most potent elemental poisons . . . from lead, to arsenic, to chlorine, krypton, selenium, and strontium"; "infra-photon glass" in cowl which filters light "of any and all wave-lengths" so he cannot be blinded; "sonic cannon" to blast objects and people to bits; acid-proof costume; and a palm-size device which causes nearby engines to stop working; "the Liquidator," a huge red tank with countless weapons, from lasers to pincer-tipped tentacles.

Chief Henchmen: Costumed goons in blue bodysuits

with red trunks and boots and iron-gray full-head helmets. They all pack grapnel guns and blasters.

Biography: Based in a former Nazi lair beneath an unnamed European nation, Stingaree heads a "world crime syndicate" known as Cyclops. Contacted by secret agent Urania Blackwell, aka Element Girl, the superhero Metamorpho helps her to defeat the fiend—who, in a final act of defiance, blows up the unnamed country's dikes. Though Metamorpho is able to plug the holes, Stingaree appears to perish in the rampaging waters.

Quote: "*Cyclops* . . . thinks of everything! If this government should learn of our lair, one push of a button will blow up the entire dike system—bringing the sea crashing in on half their land!"

Comment: Stingaree looks and behaves very much like Marvel's THE SCORPION (4), who had premiered two years before.

THE STORM KING (C)

Real Name: Kingsley Storme.

First Appearance: 1967, *Mighty Comics* #43, Archie Comics.

Costume: Green tights with white stripe down side; green jacket with black shoulders and chest, light green collar; light green gloves; blue boots. (Note: Costume entirely purple on cover.)

Weapons: Time-traveling, airborne saucer.

Biography: Coming to the present "from centuries hence," the benevolent Storme doesn't realize that he was possessed by "a 4th dimensional evil being" as he passed through time. Arriving in our era, he is forced by "the humankind-hating thing" to adopt the identity of the Storm King and go on a rampage. Creating blizzards, thunderstorms, hailstorms, hurricane-force winds (which he can focus sharply enough to pelt individuals), heatwaves, and sandstorms, he threatens to destroy all life on earth. Finding the villain's ship hidden at the base of a whirlpool, the superhero the Shield learns that the rare element intragorium has the power to exorcise the vile entity. Exposing the Storm King to its rays, the Shield sends the "tenuous monstrosity" whence it came. As Storme departs, he vows to find a way to keep the wicked race from ever again trying to "take over the bodies of time-travelers in the continuum."

Quote: "So you whining jackals dislike the blizzard I caused, eh? *Hee, hee, haa-aaa*! Out of the 'goodness' of my heart I now create waves of nuclear heat."

Comment: This was the character's only appearance. THE WEATHER WIZARD also affects the weather. Other villains who tangled with the Shield include the Gladiator from Tomorrow (not possessed by an evil 4th dimensional creature, but inherently nasty), Evilo the Tempter, the Knave, and the Amoeba Man.

THE STORM KING *strikes a shocking pose. © Charlton Comics.*

STRIBOG (MY)

Biography: The Russian god of storms, cold, and frost, Stribog was the bitter enemy of all the early Slavs. He was also the grandfather of the winds, with whom he worked closely to spread misery across the land.

Comment: Stribog also worked in tandem with Morana, the goddess of death and winter. See another Russian god, TCHERNABOG.

THE STUNNER (C)

First Appearance: 1967, *Mighty Comics* #43, Archie Comics.

Costume: Red bodysuit; gray boots, belt, gloves (see Weapons); black helmet.

Weapons: Gloves stun whomever they touch—temporarily or to the death, depending upon the setting.

Biography: When an underworld scientist develops the stun-gloves, a crook willingly pays a "big bundle of cash" for them and becomes the Stunner. Defeating the superhero the Web as a prelude to greater crimes, he is done-in by the Web's wife, Pow-Girl, who uses martial arts to stun the criminal. The villain's partner-in-crime is the grinning and "wily gangleader" Mr. Scare, who is defeated by the Web in a fist-fight.

Quote: "You've met the rest . . . now meet the *best*! Namely, 'The Stunner!'"

Comment: This was the character's only appearance.

SUMURU (N, MP)

First Appearance: 1951, *Sumuru*, Sax Rohmer (published in England as *Slaves of Sumuru*).

Biography: Based on an island off the coast of Hong Kong, Sumuru is a lesbian determined to subjugate all men and rule the world. To this end, she has her lady aides get close to and assassinate world leaders.

Comment: The second Sumuru novel was *The Return of Sumuru* (published in England as *Sand and Satin*). Shirley Eaton played the part in the American International motion picture *The 1,000,000 Eyes of Su-Muru* (1967). In her only film adventure she wore a black bodysuit decorated with stylized "eyes" and was armed with a gun that turned people to stone. In the film, Su-Muru had her million eyes—her many aides, hyperbolically speaking—try to murder President Boong of Hong Kong, an effort thwarted by the British secret service. Despite the destruction of her island fortress at the end, Su-Muru apparently escaped. Actress Eaton had previously worked the other side of the tracks, playing heroic Jill Masterson, an enemy of the villainous AURIC GOLDFINGER. Rohmer's other great villain is DR. FU MANCHU.

SUNTURION (C)

Real Name: Arthur Dearborn.

First Appearance: 1981, *Iron Man* #143, Marvel Comics.

Costume: Yellow bodysuit; red boots, gloves, helmet with transparent visor (face is also transparent), neck and shoulder covering which drapes around arms, along sides, and terminates in red briefs; silver belly, belt, band around right thigh.

Biography: Star Well is an enormous space station in earth orbit funded by the huge Roxxon Corporation. Its purpose: to forestall a future energy crunch by being "the ultimate reception and storage unit for solar radiation." Originally, the company's accountants hadn't wanted to pay for keeping an entire crew onboard. Rather than see the project scuttled, the space platform's designer, Arthur Dearborn, agreed to become a one-man crew by letting scientists at the Brand Corporation (a Roxxon subsidiary) turn him into Sunturion. Bombarding him with microwave radiation, they turned him into a being of pure microwaves, energy that he "could control to alter my form, or to transmit myself from point to point instantaneously," even to earth. The transformation also allowed him to fire and withstand destructive blasts. In this form, he required "minimal" food and oxygen, feeding

***THE STUNNER** tackles the Web. © Archie Comics.*

primarily on sunlight. Unfortunately, one of Star Well's experiments went awry and toasted a small town in Iowa, killing over 200 people. Dearborn, in his singlemindedness, couldn't care less; not so the superhero Iron Man, who, flying into space to investigate, battled Sunturion and destroyed the station.

Quote: "What are the lives of a few hundred, when we're developing a technology that could save *millions*!"

THE SUPER-ADAPTOID (C)

First Appearance: 1966, *Tales of Suspense* #82 (as the Adaptoid; the name was changed in #84, 1966), Marvel Comics.

Costume: White trunks, tights (skin is also white); the character assumes the costume and appearance (in shades of green) of anyone nearby.

Weapons: The creature can duplicate any armaments which pass nearby (see Biography).

Biography: Because they are constantly being battered by superheroes—in particular, Captain America—the scientists of the hi-tech subversive group A.I.M. (Advanced Idea Mechanics) decide to use their genius to construct a super villain. The result is the Adaptoid, a humanoid which can assume the super-abilities and duplicate the weaponry of any hero who passes near it. Moreover, it can hold the powers of up to five heroes cumulatively, displaying, for example, the agility of Captain America at the same time as the marksmanship of the bow-toting Hawkeye, the might of Thor, the genius of an extraterrestrial, and the mind-reading talent of a mutant—storing layer upon layer of incredible power. (Surprisingly, A.I.M. has never created any other Adaptoids. Presumably, either the elements used in the creation of the nonliving being are extremely rare, or the being was born in an accident whose specifics the scientists have been unable to recreate.) Defeated in his initial outing by Captain America, the insensate Adaptoid is brought to the headquarters of the superhero team the Avengers, where it fills itself with the powers of several heroes and returns to life. After tangling again with Captain America (and leaving only because the superhero appeared to have perished), the creature pits itself against the superheroic X-Men. This time it "overate." Copying the powers of the Mimic—who *also* has the power to ape the abilities of others—the Adaptoid overloads and "crashed," tumbling into a river. It returns numerous times to plague various superheroes; at present, it's once again in storage at Avengers headquarters.

Comment: THE TASKMASTER is another adaptable villain.

SUPERBEAVER (CS)

First Appearance: 1966, *Power Pie, The Stanford Chaparral*, Stanford University.

Costume: White trunks, cape, T-shirt with "SB" in box on chest (strip is black and white).

Weapons: Salacio Beam Ring, "more powerful than any moralizing force in the world"; bicycle which he rides at superspeed.

Biography: Riding around the Stanfrod (sic) campus, Superbeaver causes "a cranial blood shortage" in male students which leaves them paralyzed. Fortunately, the superheroic Power Pie deduces that tights nullify the villain's powers—though *why* is not quite clear—and manages to bind him up in a pair.

Quote: "Ha! Little does Power Pie know that my powers are more *powerful* than hers!"

Comment: This was the character's only appearance.

SUPER-MENACE (C)

First Appearance: 1960, *Superman* #137, DC Comics.

Costume: Identical to that of Superman, save for a black mask; blue bodysuit, red trunks, cape, boots; yellow pentagram on chest, fringed in red and containing a red "S"; yellow belt.

Biography: When, as an infant, Superman is sent by rocket from his dying world of Krypton, the craft happens to brush "a giant space ship from another universe." The accident kicks "weird scientific devices" into operation onboard the larger vessel. Instruments create an exact duplicate of the

SUPERBEAVER. *© Stanford Chapparral.*

Kryptonian rocket and its tiny occupant; though not alive, the baby is composed of "an unearthly force manifested into human form." Unlike the rocket of the future Superman, which is found by the loving Kents, this double is discovered by criminal "Wolf" Derek and his wife Bonnie. The being has the same powers as the Kryptonian and then some. It cannot be harmed by kryptonite, the irradiated rock lethal to Superman. Thrilled, Wolf raises the boy to be a criminal and in due course strikes a deal with the underworld. He agrees to dispatch his son, as Super-Menace, to destroy Superman if the mobsters install Wolf as crime czar. They agree, and the mighty alien engages the Man of Steel in battle. Trapping Superman in a kryptonite shower, he has a change of heart when he realizes that Wolf never loved him and is only using him. Saving Superman, he goes to his foster father's hideout and, giving his version of the I-could've-been-a-contender speech ("My life could've been a blessing, but you twisted it into something terrible!"), he returns to "pure energy," destroying himself and the Dereks.

Quote: "I know everything, Wolf. I know how you twisted my mind into ways of crime . . . I know you secretly loathed me, while pretending fatherly love!"

Comment: This was the character's only appearance.

SUPER-SKRULL (C)

First Appearance: 1963, *The Fantastic Four* #18, Marvel Comics.

Costume: Purple bodysuit; black trunks, gloves, boots, skullcap with widow's peak, flared shoulders tapering into a stripe which terminates at the waist (Super-Skrull's skin is green).

Biography: The Skrulls are a race of extraterrestrials based on Skrullos, a world in the Drox system. An ancient race, the Skrulls have the ability to impersonate the look and physical properties of any being or object they encounter; this ability has helped them to establish a vast intergalactic empire through colonization and conquest. Despite repeated efforts, however, the Skrulls have not been able to dominate the earth, due to the efforts of the superheroic Fantastic Four. (The groups first clashed in #2, 1961.) Thus, by order of Emperor Dorrek, the extraterrestrials created the Super-Skrull, a Skrull bioengineered to possess all of the powers of the Fantastic Four: awesome physical strength (the Thing), the ability to stretch (Mr. Fantastic), the power to become living flame (the Human Torch), and telekinesis as well as the talent to become invisible (Invisible Woman). Sent to menace earth, Super-Skrull was shown the door by the heroic quartet when they disrupted his interstellar energy band. Returning with a stronger beam, the alien being masqueraded as the costumed Invincible Man, aka Franklin Storm (father of the Human Torch and Invisible Woman). Unmasked and beaten once again by the foursome, he was subsequently drubbed by the superhero Thor and, in his most recent adventure, by the team of Spider-Man and Ms. Marvel.

Comment: Another eminent Skrull warrior was Raksor, who battled the Fantastic Four at the pleasure of the Empress R'kill of the House of T'ryss (*Fantastic Four Annual* #18, 1984). In addition to being a shapechanger, he wore a gauntlet, which enhanced his "strength and speed a hundredfold" and fired debilitating "neuro-blasts." Other villains fought by the Fantastic Four include Kurrgo, the Master of Planet X; Intergalactic Sentry #459 created by the antagonistic extraterrestrials, the Kree; Tomazooma "the Living Totem" a towering robot designed after an Indian god; the "Monster from the Lost Lagoon," an alien brute (and his mate); the Monster (aka Larry Rambow), who fires destructive blasts from his hands; Nega-Man, who also unleashes destructive blasts; Miracle Man, a master hypnotist; Darkoth the Death-Demon, a lizard-like man who fires debilitating beams from his forehead; Mahkizmo, the incredibly powerful Nuclear Man from the future; Xemu (also Zemu), an aspiring world-conqueror from the fifth dimension; and Gorr the giant golden gorilla.

SUPER THIEF (C)

Real Name: Dr. Stigma.

First Appearance: 1965, *Super Goof* #1, Gold Key Comics.

Costume: White lab coat; black trousers.

Weapons: Huge mousetrap for capturing interlopers.

Chief Henchman: Flumbert.

Biography: A scientific genius, Super Thief—who resembles a spaniel—steals famous landmarks and holds them for ransom (he hides London's Big Bim in a barn; blasts the Leaning Tower of Pizza to the moon; and snatches the Duck Bay Bridge). Hounded by Super Goof, Super Thief kidnaps the hero's girlfriend, Clarabelle Cow, in the hope of luring him into a trap. Super Goof tracks Dr. Stigma to his cavern lair where he is snared in the malfeasant's giant mousetrap; freed by helpful squirrels, the vigilante flattens the villain and his aide Flumbert and carts them off to prison.

Quote: "Only total victory over Super Goof will ease my anger!"

Comment: Other villains who have battled Super Goof—better known in his non-heroic identity,

"Goofy" of Walt Disney fame—since the series began include Super Joker, who distracts people with outrageous practical jokes while he robs them, and the villainous BEAGLE BOYS (all of these characters are dogs). Super Goof and his enemies have appeared *only* in comic books.

SURTUR (C)

First Appearance: 1963, *Journey Into Mystery* #97, Marvel Comics.

Costume: Blue loincloth (Surtur's skin is red, his face like solidified flame; he also has a long tail and black horns on his head).

Weapons: Huge sword which, if lit from the external flames which burn in Asgard, gives him power sufficient to destroy the universe.

Chief Henchmen: Malekith (see KURSE); many demonic minions, including "the sons of flame."

Biography: A towering demon roughly 1,000 feet tall, Surtur is evil incarnate. One of the most powerful beings in Asgard, the home of the Norse gods, he has the job of sweeping the realm with fire after Ragnarok—the cyclical fall of Asgard due to internecine warfare among the gods. Older than any of the gods currently extant, Surtur has spent a great deal of time in various prisons concocted by Thor and the other gods (e.g., inside the earth and in other dimensions).

Quote: "Now, Thor, you shall see your companions *die* before I slay you myself."

SUTEKH (TV, N)

First Appearance: 1975, "Pyramids of Mars," *Dr. Who*, BBC.

Costume: None, save that Sutekh has the face of a jackal.

Biography: One of the Osirians, a race which has colonized the universe, Sutekh the Destroyer has an all-consuming hatred for every living thing. Obliterating his own world of Phaester Osiris, he is captured by his brother Horus and his army. Imprisoned under a pyramid in Egypt, he is kept there by the Eye of Horus, which generates a stifling energy field. Unearthed by Egyptologist Marcus Scarman in 1911, Sutekh turns him into a slave and resumes his project to destroy the universe. But Sutekh is thwarted by the heroic Dr. Who, who flings him to his death 70 centuries into the future.

Comment: Stephen Harris wrote this adventure for British television, and it ran four episodes; the teleplay was novelized as *Dr. Who and the Pyramids of Mars*.

SWARM (C)

Real Name: Fritz von Meyer.

First Appearance: 1977, *The Champions* #14, Marvel Comics.

Costume: Purple cape and hood; white gloves (rest of body is made entirely of clustered bees).

Chief Henchmen: The thousands of bees which constitute his body.

Biography: A former Nazi scientist, von Meyer takes a fair amount of money out of Germany and is able to build himself a laboratory in South America. There, he conducts research on the reproduction and habits of bees, several of which happen to possess an unusually high degree of intelligence. Suspecting that the special bees were mutated due to radiation from a meteorite shower in a neighboring jungle, von Meyer begins experiments to find a means of communicating with the insects. Instead, the psionic beam device he develops goes haywire, causing the bees to attack him. He manages to establish a mind link with the queen bee and gets her under his control, but not before they literally eat his body alive. Luckily for von Meyer, they have also ingested his "mental field" and remain around his skeleton, a living body of bees responding to his will. As Swarm, von Meyer can "shoot" streams of bees at adversaries, as well as enslave any mutated bees he happens to encounter. Flying to Los Angeles, he inaugurates a plan of world conquest only to be defeated by the superheroic Champions. The bees scatter under the onslaught, leaving only Swarm's skeleton (#15); however, he is subsequently able to marshal the insects on his behalf and battle the superhero Spider-Man (*Peter Parker, the Spectacular Spider-Man* #36).

Comment: See other insect-controlling super villains BARON BUG, THE DRAGONFLY RAIDERS, HUMBUG, KING LOCUST, and QUEEN BEE.

THE SWORDSMAN (C)

First Appearance: 1965, *The Avengers* #19, Marvel Comics.

Costume: Purple tights, cowl, gloves, jerkin with flared shoulders and red strips down center, across breast (forming "Y" shape), and along hem; red boots, armbands, hilt; golden belt, strap across chest to hilt.

Weapons: Several swords, the primary one of which had various "improvements," triggered by buttons on the hilt: a disintegration ray, an explosive beam, a flame-thrower, lightning bolts, and knockout-gas.

Biography: A circus performer specializing in juggling and throwing knives and swords, the Swordsman (his name has never been revealed) always intended to become a criminal. After acquiring an aide, a youth named Clint Barton, and training him to be a crack archer, he began his sordid career; but Barton wanted no part of it and fled to the high wire, which the Swordsman cut. Left for dead, Barton grew up to become the superhero Hawkeye. Fleeing to Europe, the Swordsman undertook his costumed criminal career in earnest. Returning to the United States, he tangled with the Avengers and had to be rescued by THE MANDARIN, who teleported him to his Asian headquarters. The two then teamed in a failed effort to blow up the Avengers (Swordsman just couldn't destroy lovely Avenger, the Scarlet Witch). Later, the villain became a solo operator for a spell, followed by team-ups with POWER MAN, THE RED SKULL, THE MANDARIN again, BATROC, and others. Eventually reforming and allowed to hang around with the Avengers, he died saving member Mantis from a death blast fired by Kang the Conqueror, aka IMMORTUS (*Giant-Size Avengers* #2, 1974).

SYCORAX (P)

First Appearance: 1611, *The Tempest*, William Shakespeare.

Biography: Little is known about this "damn'd witch," save that she was born in Algiers and performed "mischiefs manifold, and sorceries terrible." Described as a "blear-eyed hag," she probably would have been executed if she hadn't been pregnant. Instead, she was banished from her native land, stranded by sailors on a tropical island. There, she made the "airy spirit" Ariel her servant; but Ariel was "too delicate to act her earthly and abhorr'd commands," so she imprisoned him in a "cloven pine," where he remained until freed a dozen years later by a castaway, the benign wizard Prospero. Sometime during those 12 years, Sycorax bore a son, Caliban, "a freckled whelp . . . not honour'd with human shape," before dying. Caliban was a "dull thing" who served Prospero and plotted to kill him; when that failed and Prospero forgave him, Caliban reformed.

Comment: *The Tempest* is believed to be the last play written by Shakespeare. The name Sycorax is thought to have been derived from the Greek word for hawk, from which the name of the sorceress CIRCE also came. Other exceedingly vile personalities from Shakespeare include Titus Andronicus, a mad Roman general who, in *Titus Andronicus* (c. 1592), not only slays his own son but also those of his wife Tamora (he slits their throats and serves them to her, baked in a pie), then kills her as well as his daughter Lavinia; the ambitious Macbeth who, in the play of the same name (1605-6), not only slays his king to take the crown of Scotland, but also kills those who are a threat to his own power, namely his best friend Banquo and the family of the lord Macduff; and Claudius, who murders his brother, the king, not only taking his crown but also marrying his widow in *Hamlet* (c. 1601). See other witches PRINCESS ASA and THE WITCH OF THE WEST.

SYONIDE (C)

First Appearance: 1977, *Black Lightning* #4 (first Syonide); 1985, *Batman and the Outsiders* #20 (second Syonide), DC Comics.

Costume: Red bodysuit with a white belt and stripes down the deep "V" neck; blue hip boots, gloves, headband. (Note: both Syonides wore virtually identical costumes.)

Weapons: Electric bullwhip; portable control box to short-out electronic fields; dart "filled with a mind-numbing serum which (puts) you totally in the power of anyone who'd taken the corresponding mind-control serum"; twin knife blades hidden in the wrist of his left glove. (Note: the second Syonide had only the bullwhip.)

Chief Henchmen: Steel Fist Feeny, who has a steel hand and wears a green and yellow bodysuit; unnamed martial arts expert.

Biography: Employed by a band of drug dealers known as the 100 (led by TOBIAS WHALE), Syonide is a modern-day bounty hunter who is given the task of killing the superheroic Black Lightning. Though he does manage to capture the hero, Syonide in unable to hold him and, defeated, commits suicide as a sign of penance for all those he has killed. Whale finds a woman to take the first Syonide's place. She dies fighting Batman and the Outsiders.

Quote: "I've enough *weapons* hidden on my person to make myself a walking *arsenal*, fool!"

Comment: The names of the two Syonides have never been revealed. Other super villains who menaced Black Lightning during his magazine's brief 11-issue run include Creegen who, as the green-garbed Cyclotronic Man, kills people by speeding up their atoms and then scattering them all over creation (his power is nullified by water); and Merlyn (aka the Magician), an archer who dresses in a navy blue bodysuit, is a member of the League of Assassins, has a quiver which doubles as a jetpack, and fires a variety of hi-tech arrows, from those which generate painful levels of sound to those which start fires. Merlyn had previously pitted his talents against Batman and been de-bowed (*Justice League of America* #94).

THE TARANTULA (1) (C)

Costume: Blue bodysuit; red trunks, boots, gloves, cowl with black spider on forehead and black domino mask; yellow belt.

Weapons: Sticky steel strands which he knits into webs.

Biography: Living in a "crumby old house" outside Riverdale, the Tarantula is a brilliant thief who has made three "hair raising" heists in just one month—the latest, the entire stock of the D.D. Diamond Mart. However, the superhero Pureheart the Powerful tracks him down and, coating himself with grease so the Tarantula can't nab him, brings the villain in.

Quote: "You think a coat of grease can defeat the great Tarantula?"

Comment: Other enemies who surfaced during the 1966 to 1967 run of Pureheart the Powerful (aka Archie Andrews) include Madman Clown, who wants to feed young Veronica Lodge to a tiger because she reminds him of his wife ("the wife who ran off with the tattooed man," he recalls bitterly); the blue-garbed Bumblebee, who robs while his pet bees run interference, stinging people; and the green-skinned Mad Doctor Doom who, holed up in the Riverdale Pretzel Co., commits crimes with the mighty robot Computo. See also EVIL-HEART THE GREAT.

THE TARANTULA (2) (C)

Real Name: Anton Miguel Rodriguez.

First Appearance: 1974, *The Amazing Spider-Man* #134, Marvel Comics.

Costume: Red bodysuit with blue spider on chest, stripe along front of shin ending in an encircling band; blue gloves, boots (see Weapons), cowl ending in twin queues.

Weapons: Dagger-like spikes on tips of boots with which he can smash concrete, penetrate metal, and kill.

Chief Henchmen: Thugs dressed in similar costumes, colored purple and lavender (each one is a different combination of those colors).

Biography: In 1968, Anton was a South American revolutionary who led a bold guerrilla band trying to overthrow a tyrant. However, Anton enjoyed the illicit aspect of his work more than he did the freedom-fighting, and soon even his group tired of his sadism. His men disowned him, and Anton joined the service of the despot he'd once fought. Exiled after murdering a soldier who was not being harsh enough with a captured rebel, Anton made his way into the United States illegally. There he studied crime in New York and finally organized his own gang. After battling Spider-Man and Captain America on numerous occasion, he was turned into a huge spider-being by the Brand Corporation, the insidious R & D division of Roxxon ("the world's largest conglomerate"). The villain perished in this mutated form (#234).

Quote: "Strike *quickly*, mi amigos! And if they *resist—keel them*!"

THE TASKMASTER (C)

First Appearance: 1980, *The Avengers* #195, Marvel Comics.

Costume: Blue bodysuit with orange arms and diamond-shaped panel of cloth attached to cloak clasps; white trunks, gloves, boots, orange-lined cloak with hood (later, cloak is entirely orange), skull-face; orange belt, strap across chest, holster; blue quiver with orange fringe.

Weapons: Sturdy, round shield; billyclub; bow with various arrows; .45 caliber Colt automatic; sword.

Biography: As a child, the Taskmaster (his name has never been revealed) amazed his family by being able to mimic whatever he saw other people do, including the rope tricks performed by TV cowboys. Studied by doctors, he was determined to have "photographic reflexes," which, among other things, enabled him to lead his high school football team to victory after he saw a pro quarterback play. Torn between becoming a superhero or ultra-villain after graduation, he opted to go for the big money. Not only does he commit crimes himself, but he also has operated schools for criminals, training thugs and then renting them out to various criminal groups. The most elaborate of these schools, hiding behind the name The Solomon Institute for the Criminally Insane, was shut down by the superheroic team the Avengers. Once he learns a skill by watching a superhero, the Taskmaster never forgets it. Hence, he shoots a bow as accurately as Hawkeye, utilizes his shield as adroitly as Captain America, wields a blade as ably as the Black Knight, is the equal of the Punisher when it comes to gunplay, possesses the martial arts skills of Iron Fist, and can even match the agility of Spider-Man. And, as he delights in boasting, "Whatever I can't duplicate [such as Spider-Man's web-spinning powers], I can anticipate!"

Quote: "Today, I'm gonna show my graduatin' class that super heroes ain't as tough as they're cracked up to be!"

Comment: See another adaptable villain THE SUPER-ADAPTOID.

TATTERDEMALION (C)

Real Name: Arnold Paffenroth.

First Appearance: 1973, *Werewolf By Night* #9, Marvel Comics.

Costume: Blue trousers, boots, hat, scarecrow jacket; red ruff, sash around mouth trailing a knee-length queue, gloves (see Weapons).

Weapons: Gloves contain chemical which causes money, fabric, and flesh to disintegrate. (Note: Tatterdemalion exudes an "awful smell," though it isn't clear whether this is due to being unwashed and living in a sewer, or whether he perfumes himself to offend the wealthy people whom he terrorizes. Likewise his clothes, which slip from beneath such things as Spider-Man's webbing. Though the villain describes his wardrobe as "oil-soaked," it appears—like his odor—to drink it up from its environment.)

Chief Henchmen: Bums.

Biography: A rich casino owner in Las Vegas, Paffenroth lost everything to mobsters. Drifting to Los Angeles, he became a bum—and then part of a bum brigade organized by the Committee, a group of local businesspeople. The Committee believed that the derelicts would create an appearance of civic decay which would spark recovery measures . . . and, hence spur the economy. In charge of the hobos was Sidney Sarnak, a sound technician who had developed an ultrasonic whistle which he used to spur the emotional areas of bums' brains. Sadly, Sarnak lost not only his whistle but also his mind when his crew battled the heroic monster Werewolf. Left on his own once again, Paffenroth managed to pull himself together, acquire (through unexplained means) his destructive gloves, create a costume, adopt his new name, once more rally his bum colleagues around him, and go on a peculiar rampage—not just stealing but actually *destroying* the finery, jewels, and money of others. As he put it, "I want them penniless, *broken* . . . to feel as my *brothers* feel!" When he isn't circulating among the rich and famous, Tatterdemalion hides in a sewer.

Quote: "Will you be so eager to *meddle*—when your flesh *burns* and your clothes lie in *tatters*?"

Comment: Though Paffenroth first appeared in *Werewolf By Night*, he did not become a distinctively deadly villain until his second appearance, which was in *Marvel Team-up* #93 (1980).

THE TATTOOED MAN (C)

Real Name: Abel Tarrant.

First Appearance: 1963, *Green Lantern* #23, DC Comics.

Costume: Originally, none but a sailor's cap. In his last appearance, he wore blue tights, cloak, wristbands; yellow boots.

Weapons: Tattoos which, when touched, leap from his skin and become real; over the years, these have included a flaming pinwheel which flies through the air, wings to give the Tattooed Man the power of flight, a jet-powered skateboard for getaways, airborne machine guns, a guided missile, a pteranodon, a giant hand, and a huge killer robot.

Biography: While robbing a chemical plant, seaman-turned-thief Tarrant accidentally overturned chemicals which, when they combined, coincidentally looked like a bomb. Touching the shape and wishing, plaintively, that it *were* a bomb, the crook was shocked when he got his wish. However, a guard heard Tarrant and he was forced to flee. Coming back the next day and taking a sample of the substance, he discovered that all he needed to do was use it to sketch the outline of an object, touch it, and voila! The object was real. Using his rudimentary knowledge of chemistry to analyze the paint and create a batch of it, he covered his body with tattoos and went on a crime spree. Frequently battling the superheroic Green Lantern, he briefly served with THE INJUSTICE GANG OF THE WORLD. Ironically, it was his own criminal kind which ultimately did him in. The Tattooed Man had the audacity to steal from GOLDFACE, for which crime the villain's henchmen shot Tarrant to death (*Green Lantern* #144).

Quote: "Leave, without makin' me *withdrawal* first? Come now, mate. What *good* is there bein' a professional thief if ye can't *pirate* a bank or two now an' then?"

Comment: THE ZODIAC MASTER had similar powers.

TCHERNABOG (F, MP)

Biography: The Black God of pre-Christian (circa eighth century) Slavic lore, Tchernabog was responsible for all things evil, from death to mere distress. Paradoxically, he was honored with prayer on joyous occasions in the hope that he would be inspired to keep misfortune from the celebrants' door. According to legend, the demon dwelt on Mt. Triglaf (also known as Bare or Bald Mountain) near Kiev. Once a year, he lorded over a black mass on the mountain, summoning witches and the souls of the dead to join him. Legend is divided as to whether this was held on Walpurgis Night (Halloween) or on St. John's Night (Midsummer Eve). Regardless, come the following dawn, all of the revelers were forced to return whence they'd come. The demon's adversary is Byelun, the White God, who did everything from showering his followers with gold to guiding lost souls from the woods.

Comment: The god was also known as Cernobog and Zcernoboch and was the demon celebrated in Modeste Moussorgsky's brilliant orchestral piece, "Night on Bald Mountain." (Written in 1866 as "St. John's Night on Bare Mountain," a work in four parts: the assembly of the witches; their chatter; the cortege of Tchernabog; and the black mass. The work was extensively revised in 1882 by Rimsky-Korsakov, a year after Moussorgsky's death; it is this version which is best known today.) The Rimsky-Korsakov edition was abbreviated and slightly revised once again for "The Night on Bald Mountain" segment of the Disney animated film *Fantasia* (1940). Bela Lugosi posed for the animators who were drawing the demon.

THE TEACHER (C)

First Appearance: 1942, *Lightning Comics*, Vol. 3, #1, Ace Magazines.

Costume: Red robe; blue graduation cap with red tassel.

Weapons: TV which spies on "all government offices"; "electric shock" box which causes "electro-hypnosis" from afar.

Biography: Nothing is known of this character's past. Based in the United States during World War II, the Teacher is a hideously ugly and dwarfish "freelance espionage expert" and "master killer for the

***THE TEACHER**, whose lessons all involve sabotage.*
© Ace Magazines.

highest bidder." In this instance he works as an Axis agent who, at "his Classroom" in the caverns beneath Dutch Harbor, specializes in turning Americans into traitors. Though his four-point plan (see Quote) is disrupted by the superheroic Lightning, the Teacher returns (in issue #2) to deliver "The Teacher's Second Lesson of Blood."

Quote: "We have four lessons for today! First is the death of Lightning. Lesson no. two! Destruction of the American fleet. Lesson no. three! Destruction of the American army. Lesson no. four! Placing of blame."

Comment: The Teacher was expelled after two sinister semesters.

TECHMASTER (C)

Real Name: Billy Bitzer.

First Appearance: 1980, *The Dazzler* #8, Marvel Comics.

Weapons: Two extremely powerful artificial

hands built of "super-sophisticated components," "vocal-simulator phone" which makes his voice sound like that of anyone else.

Chief Henchmen: THE ENFORCERS (#8 only); sundry thugs thereafter.

Biography: At one time, Techmaster had been "the most sought after electronics expert in show business," working as the right-hand man of concert promoter Harry S. Osgood. Coming up with an idea for a party—he wants to create artificial lightning bolts to light up a disco—he is overruled by Osgood, who deems the untested stunt to be dangerous. But Bitzer tries it anyway and it backfires, setting the disco ablaze and costing many lives; a bolt also strikes Bitzer, hideously scarring his face and destroying his hands, which have to be amputated. When he recovers, he opens a very successful electronics consulting firm. However, believing that Osgood had "wanted me to fail" that night and had sabotaged the controls, Bitzer finally decides to exact revenge. He hires the super-villainous Enforcers to terrorize the promoter, but they're stopped by the superheroic Dazzler. The next time around (#12), he abducts Osgood himself and is about to cut him to death slowly, using lasers, when the Dazzler saves him again, accidentally slugging the villain toward the deadly beams. Saved by the quick-thinking Osgood, Techmaster agrees never to trouble him again.

Quote: "This paperweight is solid steel . . . I can crush it as if it were a toy. You can imagine what my hands are capable of doing to human flesh."

Comment: DR. NO also had artificial hands.

TEN-EYED MAN (C)

Real Name: Philip Reardon.

First Appearance: 1970, *Batman* #226, DC Comics.

Costume: Orange bodysuit with brown "V" shape from neck to waist and four white eyes in a line down chest; brown gloves, trunks; wristbands; blue goggles; white belt with eye-shaped buckle.

Weapons: Standard firearms.

Biography: Hurt while serving in Vietnam, Reardon was the victim of some of the most bizarre circumstances to afflict any super villain. Returning to civilian life, his forehead peppered with shrapnel, he became a night watchman at a warehouse; one evening he was knocked out by thieves, who rigged a bomb to open the company safe. Moments before the blast, the superhero Batman arrived; waking, Reardon saw the Caped Crusader just before the explosion. Blinded, Reardon mistakenly believed that Batman was responsible for his injury and vowed to destroy him. And he was well-equipped for the task. While Reardon was incapacitated, one Dr. Engstrom had taken the liberty of running the blind man's still-vital optic nerves to his fingertips. As a result, Reardon—now Ten-Eyed Man—could see anywhere he turned his hands. After several bouts with Batman over the years, Reardon perished during the Crisis on Infinite Earths.

THE TERMINATOR (1) (aka DEATHSTROKE THE TERMINATOR) (C)

Real Name: Slade Joseph Wilson.

First Appearance: 1980, *The New Teen Titans* #2, DC Comics.

Costume: Navy blue mail bodysuit (non-mail from chest to neck and on tops of arms); golden boots, trunks, gloves with yellow fringe; full-head cowl is golden on left, navy blue on right.

Weapons: Numerous arms, all carried on person, including broadsword, pistol, hand grenades.

Biography: During the 1960s, the Terminator was Major Wilson, a Korean War veteran, who was assigned to a special program being taught by Captain Adeline Kane. Graduating with honors a year later, he made the rank of Lieutenant Colonel; shortly after marrying Adeline, he was shipped off to Vietnam. There Slade volunteered to be the guinea pig for an anti-truth serum drug which stimulated the adrenal gland. The test went haywire and Slade had to be taken off active duty. However, against orders, he went back into action to rescue a good friend, Major Wintergreen of the British army, who was being held as a POW in Vietnam. Discharged for his actions, Slade worked as a hunter, spending time with Adeline and their sons Grant and Joseph, before becoming a professional assassin under the moniker of the Terminator. He was certainly unparalleled in his chosen profession. The drug he'd taken had given his superstrength and superspeed, making him all but invulnerable. Not so his family, however. In Tangiers, a group of terrorists seeking to undermine the effectiveness of the Terminator managed to get their hands on young Joseph. Though Slade was able to stop them as they prepared to cut his son's throat, the knife did damage the boy's vocal chords, costing him his voice. (Mutated due to the effects of the experiments on his father, Joseph later became the heroic costumed Jericho, able to control the will of others by inhabiting their bodies. His first appearance as Jericho was in #44). Mad with frustration, Adeline tried to shoot her husband, but only managed to put out his right eye. Not surprisingly, the couple divorced. Given the environment in which he was raised, it was also no surprise when son Grant—made super-strong by the chemicals his father had taken—became the villainous Ravager, dressed in light blue tights; a bodyshirt which was navy blue to the chest and on the right arm, light blue on the chest and left arm; a light blue cowl; a navy blue glove on the right, orange on the left; and orange thigh boots. Emulating his father and becoming an assassin (which was told first in *The New Teen Titans* #1), he accepted an assignment from the H.I.V.E. (Hierarchy of International Vengeance and Eliminations) to murder the superheroic Teen Titans. Alas, heavy use of his powers "burned (him) up from the inside," and he died in his father's arms (#2). The Terminator promptly made the destruction of the Titans his top priority; despite prodigious efforts on his behalf, he has yet to succeed. The most notable event in this phase of his life was standing trial for murder (*Tales of the Teen Titans* #'s 53-54). Miraculously, his sentence was just a year in prison for illegally possessing firearms.

Quote: "Let's cut out the *garbage* and get down to *business*! Who do you want me to *kill*?"

THE TERMINATOR (2) (MP, N)

First Appearance: 1984, *The Terminator*, Hemdale Pictures.

Costume: Street clothes, though usually wears leather jacket.

Weapons: Laser-guided handgun, machinegun, and various other firearms. (Withal, the Terminator's favorite method of killing people is to plug his hand into their chest and pull out their heart.)

Biography: "A few years from now," there is a nuclear war started by a defense network computer. "Trusted to run it all," the computer is not only brilliant, "a new order of intelligence," but paranoid as well. Deciding that people are a threat, it triggers the war to inaugurate the rule of the machines. Pockets of humans survive; these are rounded up by HKs—Hunter-Killers, tank-like machines built at automated factories. Brought to concentration camps and murdered, humankind is on the verge of extinction when John Connor appears. A natural fighter, he teaches other people how to fight and organizes armies. In response, the machines introduce the Terminators, humanoid robots designed as "infiltration units." The Terminators feel no pity or pain, and can't be bargained with; their sole objective is to kill humans. Although 600 series models had rubber skin and were "spotted easy," the new Cyberdyne model #101 has skin, hair, and blood atop its microprocessessor-controlled hyperalloy combat chassis. It even sweats and has bad breath. Even so, the humans manage to defeat the machines in 2028 A.D. and reclaim the world. In a last desperate attempt to hold onto the planet, the one-time defense computer concocts a daring scheme. Using time displacement equipment, it sends a Terminator back to our era to murder John Connor's mother Sarah before she can give birth. Since detailed records were all destroyed in the atomic holocaust, the computers know only that she lived in Los Angeles. Thus, the Terminator begins killing every Sarah Connor in the book until only one remains—the woman who happens to be John's mother. Learning what the computer has done, John dispatches back in time his most trusted aide, Sgt. Kelly Reese, to protect his mother. Reese manages to thwart the Terminator at every turn. In a final, desperate showdown, the cyborg is run over by a gastruck; has his skin burned off when Reese causes the truck to explode; has his legs blown off by an explosive shoved into his hyperalloy pelvis; and, at last, his torso and arms (still crawling after Sarah) are crushed in a huge mechanical press—a machine, ironically. In addition to having possessed enormous resilience and unparalleled physical strength (he could punch through a metal door), the Terminator could instantly understand how to work any machine; had infrared night vision; was able to imitate any voice it heard; and was able to withstand repeated point-blank blasts from a shotgun (repairing the damage later, when it could spare a moment).

Quote: "I'll be back." (Spoken to police desk sergeant who refused to let him see Sarah Connor; moments later, the Terminator drove a car through lobby and officer both.)

Comment: Arnold Schwarzenegger played the Terminator; Michael Biehn was Reese, and Linda Hamilton was Sarah Connor. As a point of interest, Reese and Sarah fell in love during the film and, at the end, she was carrying Reese's child . . . John. A novelization of the film was published in 1985.

THE TERMITE (C)

First Appearance: 1984, *Iron Man* #189, Marvel Comics.

Costume: Purple bodysuit; blue jerkin with green stripe down center and across shoulders; green gloves, boots with yellow fringe, belt, termite-like helmet (see Weapons).

Weapons: Helmet contains oxygen-mask with an hour's worth of air.

Biography: A sculptor, the Termite-to-be one day simply "woke up with the *touch*," the ability to "make anything *dissolve*—by touching it!" Intending to sculpt "the grandest statue the world has ever seen," the mutant had to first earn enough money. Becoming the costumed Termite, the sculptor went to work for corrupt businessman Obadiah Stane, using his power to wreck competitors' factories. Eventually, the Termite tussled with Iron Man and, though he slipped through the hero's fingers (he cleverly melted a few molecules from Iron Man's gloves), he was stopped by a stun gun.

Quote: "Uh-oh. *Iron Man* again! Why won't he just let me finish my industrial sabotage in peace!"

Comment: The character's two-issue rampage marks his only appearance to date.

TERRIBLE TOM (C)

Costume: Green suit; blue top hat.

Biography: Tom, a portly cat, is the avowed enemy of Super Mouse, whom he is sworn to destroy. Not that Tom is above committing crimes for personal gain. In a time travel adventure, he stoops so low as to spy on the Revolutionary forces for the British; during a stay in Australia, he convinces all the kangaroos to use their jumping and punching abilities to rob banks and turn the proceeds over to him. In every instance, Tom ends up in jail . . . though he always manages to escape.

Quote: "How do you like my scheme to give you a splitting headache—not to mention a *split head*!"

Comment: Other Super Mouse villains include the mad pig Pigetti and his magic violin, and the Chisler, a mad sculptor who builds murderous mechanical statues. See other cat villains COUNT GATTO and OIL CAN HARRY.

***TERRIBLE TOM** gets clobbered.* *© Standard Comics.*

THANOS (C)

First Appearance: 1973, *Iron Man* #55, Marvel Comics.

Costume: Blue bodysuit, cowl with golden stripe down center and ears; golden gloves, boots, codpiece, mask, thick belt with blue band around center. Thanos' skin is purplish and leathery.

Weapons: The space station Sanctuary II, as well as the Cosmic Cube (see THE RED SKULL), the "soul-gems," capable of snuffing out stars, and countless other arms.

Chief Henchmen: The Thanos Thralls, extraterrestrials recruited to the service of the warlord. Included among these are the brutish Blood Brothers and Gamora of the alien Zen-Whoberis, a humanoid woman who was an expert weapons-master and spy.

Biography: One of the most powerful super villains in the universe, Thanos was the son of Alars (also written A'Lars), the founder of the Eternals' second colony on Titan, and Sui-San, the only survivor of the original Titanian settlement. (The Eternals are the result of genetic tinkering done on primitive humans roughly one million years ago by the alien Celestials. Evolved far beyond where we are even now, the Eternals not only acquired unprecedented longevity and superstrength, but also the ability to levitate and to release cosmic energy as destructive beams of heat and light. A band of Eternals first colonized the Uranian moon of Titan following a disagreement about the race's future. Eventually, that colony, known as Titanos, was all but wiped out by civil war; it remained uninhabited until the Eternals' leader Kronos died and his son Zuras was named his successor. Zuras' brother Alars disagreed with his policies and migrated to Titan, where he mated with Sui-San.) A student of death and immortality, Thanos underwent various surgical and psychic procedures to increase his strength and invulnerability. The stronger he became, the hungrier he grew for political power. Eventually stealing a spaceship, he abandoned his home and hired mercenaries, pirates, and other misfits to form a personal army. Returning to Titan, he atom-bombed it into submission—caring little for the fact that he'd blown his mother to atoms. Declared the moon's ruler, he turned his attention to Earth, home of the other Eternals. Continuing to build his armies, he managed to acquire the Cosmic Cube which made him almost omnipotent. Over the years, Thanos' designs on our world have repeatedly brought him into conflict with the superheroic Avengers; he has also battled the cosmic superheroes Captain Marvel and Warlock. Eventually, Warlock was able to turn the Eternal into stone, alive but utterly immobile (*Marvel Two-In-One Annual* #2, 1977). He remains comatose to this day. At some point in his life, Thanos has sired many children, and is the grandfather of NEBULA.

THANTOS (C)

First Appearance: 1967, *House of Mystery* #168, DC Comics.

Costume: Purple gloves, boots, bodysuit with black arms and neck; black trunks; yellow belt.

Biography: The roughly ten-feet-tall, three-eyed Thantos can fly, drill holes through brick walls using his head, and split into three identical beings. Coming to earth from another dimension, he has only 12 hours to gather rare herbs such as orris root, forest manna, and meadow mint, which will enable him to return to our dimension at will. In the meantime, he helps a local gang of thieves rob banks, though whether for fun or in exchange for guidance on our world isn't clear. Though Thantos obtains all the necessary herbs, the superheroic Martian Manhunter snatches his sackful just as his half-day on our world ends.

Quote: "Ha, ha! You fear . . . you will make me separate into three again—enabling my other two selves to fetch what I'm after!"

Comment: It is never explained why Thantos has only 12 hours to spend in this dimension. This was the character's only appearance.

THAROK (C)

First Appearance: 1967, *Adventure Comics* #352, DC Comics.

Costume: Left half is entirely metallic-gray. Right side consists of a red bodyshirt with red wristband and a black neckband with red fringe; black trunks; a red belt and boots.

Weapons: Ray gun which forces people to do his bidding.

Biography: Living on the planet Zadron in the mid-thirtieth century, Tharok was "a small-time crook of low mentality." In order to impress a crime syndicate into letting him join, Tharok stole a "heavily guarded miniature nuclear device." Caught red-handed by the police, he tried to flee. The guards fired and, instead of hitting Tharok, one of the bullets hit the purloined N-Bomb. The device went off, "literally atomizing" the crook's left side. Since it is a breach of Zardonian ethics to take a life, the authorities used their medical science to keep the crook alive by replacing his missing half with robotic parts. The metal side is "crude and ugly" because it "had to be fashioned quickly," but his robot brain gives him "a mentality beyond measure" along with an "increased . . . lust for evil." (Unknown to Tharok, part of his brain matter had been cloned into the evil DARK MAN during the operation.) As the founder and leader of THE FATAL FIVE, Tharok remains one of the leading nemeses of the Legion of Super-Heroes.

Quote: "We will . . . kill those *Legion* fools, and rule all! We will conquer a hundred planets . . .!"

Comment: Tharok was the creation of teenager Jim Shooter, who went on to become editor-in-chief of the Marvel Comics line.

THELEV (TV)

First Appearance: November 17, 1967, "Journey to Babel," *Star Trek*, NBC-TV.

Biography: Thelev is an Orion, an alien who undergoes surgery in order to acquire blue skin, white hair, and a pair of sturdy antennae. Thus disguised, he is able to pass for an Andorian and infiltrate a diplomatic conclave on Babel to which the starship *Enterprise* is shuttling a clutch of diplomats. The meeting is being held to discuss the admission of the planet Coridan to the Federation, a move Thelev strongly opposes. As long as Coridan remains independent, Thelev and his cronies can continue to mine valuable dilithium crystals and peddle them to both the Federation and its enemies. Breaking the neck of Ambassador Gav, a Tellarite, Thelev pins the murder on Ambassador Sarek of Vulcan to try and disrupt the summit; he attempts to ice the cake by stabbing the ship's Captain Kirk, who manages to render Thelev unconscious before he himself passes out. Kirk recovers, Sarek is cleared, and Thelev, found out, takes his own life with poison.

Quote: "Find your own answers, Captain. You haven't long to live!"

Comment: William O'Connell starred as Thelev; D.C. Fontana wrote the teleplay.

THERMO (C)

Real Name: Dr. Walter Michaels.

First Appearance: 1981, *Marvel Team-Up* #108, Marvel Comics.

Costume: Brown bodysuit with yellow stripe from neck to waist and two yellow bands around each arm; yellow belt, boots, gloves.

Chief Henchmen: A cult of demon worshipers, of which he takes charge (#109 only).

Biography: While conducting trailblazing new research—"transmitting synthetic vitamins into the body via microwaves"—Michaels decides to test the procedure on himself. Unfortunately, the experiment goes awry and alters his body chemistry, giving him the power to absorb body heat from other people simply by touching them, then recycle that energy as destructive blasts fired from his hands; superstrength; and incredible speed. For a time, Michaels fights his urges, but eventually "the addiction to power" becomes too great. Receiving a bio-electric fix by murdering his assistant, Dr. Bradshaw, Michaels embarks on a criminal rampage as the Thermatronic Man—Thermo for short. He is eventually stopped by the superheroic Dazzler, assisted by Spider-Man and the benevolent mercenary Paladin (#109).

Quote: "Those who won't serve me shall die!"

THE THINKER (C)

Real Name: Clifford Devoe.

First Appearance: 1943, *All-Flash* #12, DC Comics.

Costume: Purple gloves, boots, leotard with flared shoulders; navy blue bodysuit; white belt, helmet with blue goggles over a black mask and blue circuits, tubing on top (see Weapons).

Weapons: "Thinking Cap" helmet stimulates his brain cells, increases his "thinking ability to the point of genius," and allows him to "generate any amount of telekinetic energy," enabling him to "create actual objects and people, will them to act" as he commands. In addition to henchmen, the Thinker uses the cap at one point to create a cage complete with electrified bars.

Chief Henchmen: Various gangmembers; later (in the Atom escapade only) men wearing scuba suits, facemasks, and armed with harpoon guns—all created by the Thinking Cap.

Biography: The year is 1933. A district attorney in Keystone City on the world of Earth-2 (which is located in another dimension and is nearly identical to our own earth), Devoe becomes disgusted when he can't put bootlegger Hunk Norvock behind bars. Giving up on the law, Devoe decides to become a criminal himself and joins forces with Norvock. (The brilliant Devoe plans crimes and Norvock executes them.) The union lasts for 10 years until, no longer trusting Devoe, Norvock tries to shoot him but only hits a steel mirror set up by his clever prey, the bullet bouncing back and doing Norvock in. Devoe promptly takes over his gang and suffers numerous defeats at the hands of the superheroic Flash. Devoe—who now goes by the name of the Thinker—fares no better as a member of THE INJUSTICE SOCIETY OF THE WORLD. Finally, the Thinker builds the thinking cap, based in part on research conducted by scientist Hartwell Jackson. He is still no match for the Flash, though it looks for a while as though he's come up with a foolproof plan when he finally finds a means of splitting the interdimensional barriers between his world and our own (in *The Atom* #29, 1967). Committing crimes here, he returns to his dimension, where (he reasons) the objects he has robbed *haven't* been stolen—and, thus, he isn't wanted by the law. Thanks to his Thinking Cap, he is also able to fend off pursuit by the superheroic Atom when he *is* on our world. However, the Cap's power is such that it affects reformed crook Artie Perkins, causing him to steal whatever the Thinker snatched on Earth-1. Thus, the hunt *is* on in his dimension for the goods the super villain stole, and it's joined by the Atoms of both worlds, the Earth-2 Atom wanting desperately to clear his rehabilitated former nemesis Perkins of the crime. After a battle in the Oceanic Museum, the felon is apprehended.

Quote: "I'm directing those iron cannonballs to pound you to a pulp before you can reach me!"

THE THORN (C)

Real Name: Rose Canton, aka Alyx Florin.

First Appearance: 1947, *Flash Comics* #89, DC Comics.

Costume: Green bikini cut to resemble large leaves; green boots, gloves which almost reach shoulders; green cloak with very high collar.

Weapons: Huge thorny vines, which she could cause to grow and move at will; she also used "exploding thorns" against her enemies.

Chief Henchmen: Sundry flunkies dressed in green bodysuits with leaf-like collars and vines on their cowls.

Biography: While she was growing up, Rose had an imaginary alter ego, Thorn, on whom she blamed her own misdeeds. Thorn always seemed quite real to her even when she grew older (though she didn't dwell on it) as she pursued a career as assistant to Professor

Hollis, a renowned botanist. One day, while conducting a study of the plant life on the island of Tashmi, Rose found a root whose sap gave her enormous physical strength and agility, most notably the ability to spin like a human top. Metamorphosing into her Thorn personality, she killed Hollis and became a supercrook, unable (like MR. HYDE) to control her transformations. Battling superheroes like the Flash, Green Lantern, and Wonder Woman, she was eventually carted off to Transformation Island, a rehabilitation facility run by Wonder Woman's Amazon colleagues. Upon her release, Rose settled back in the United States under the assumed name Alyx Florin and began her life anew. Marrying Alan Scott (Green Lantern), she became Thorn again when she innocently tried on his energized magic ring. Fleeing, she later gave birth to son Todd and daughter Jennie-Lynn. Sadly, she gave the children up for adoption rather than turn them over to Scott, fearing that if Thorn took over she would hunt the kids down and murder them. Needless to say, Alyx eventually *did* meet her children and Scott as the vindictive Thorn. To protect her family, the subjugated Rose persona surfaced and stabbed herself to death. Today, Todd and Jennie-Lynn are the superheroes Jade and Obsidian.

Quote: "Your loving husband is *here* to watch you die! You're the *last* thing I want him to see before I kill *him*."

Comment: Rose and the Thorn exist on Earth-2; on Earth-1, her Rose and the Thorn counterpart is a superhero. Other flora-oriented super villains include THE FLORONIC MAN and PLANTMAN.

THULSA DOOM (N, MP, C)

First Appearance: 1967, "Delcardes' Cat," *King Kull*, Robert E. Howard.

Weapons: "Charmed sword," a green blade which, in battle, draws strength from the arm of an attacker and pours it into Doom's arm.

Biography: A sorcerer, Doom has a face that's "a bare white skull, in whose eye sockets flamed livid fire." Hailing from the Lost Lands, Doom "has the gift of illusion and of invisibility," and is the sworn enemy of Kull, king of the ancient empire of Atlantis. Scheming to kill Kull, Doom disguises himself as the slave Kuthulos and lures him to the deadly Enchanted Lands beneath the Forbidden Lake ("Delcardes' Cat"). Bungling the murder attempt, Doom undertakes a more ambitious masquerade. Pretending to be the warrior Felnar, he leads Kull to "the dim lands that bordered the World's Edge," where the power of Kull's protective gods is ineffective. There, Kull fights Doom, who wields his charmed sword. Fortunately, Kull is able to wrest it from him and plunges the blade "deep into Thulsa Doom's chest." The wizard's body shrivels into "a small mound of gray dust" (in a sequel "Riders Beyond the Sunrise").

Quote: "I, who once served the Serpent, swore to bring you down, cur of an Atlantean savage, and now the time is come!"

Comment: In the 1982 motion picture *Conan the Barbarian*, Thulsa Doom was the opponent of Conan, another of Robert E. Howard's great sword and sorcery heroes. Played by James Earl Jones (the voice of DARTH VADER), Doom was a powerful cannibal ruler who had the ability to control snakes (he could form them into supernaturally accurate arrows, for example) or to become a giant snake himself. He perished when Conan lopped off his head, retaliation for Doom having razed his village and slain his parents when the barbarian was a child. Other Kull villains include the outlaw Ardyon, who wants to slay Kull and become king ("By This Axe I Rule!", 1967) and the power-hungry Dondal, aka The Masked One ("Swords of the Purple Kingdom," 1967). Kull and his enemies were featured in Marvel comic books published irregularly since 1971. A very faithful adaptation of "Riders Beyond the Sunrise" appeared in *Marvel Preview* #19 (1979).

THUNDER AXE (C)

First Appearance: 1981, *Adventure Comics* #480, DC Comics.

Costume: Golden armor with black shoulders and red axe and thunderbolt crossed on belly; golden helmet with flared black ears; red gloves, boots, band around knee.

Weapons: Golden Thunder Axe which can travel "with the speed of lightning," smash nearly anything, and work like a boomerang—for example, snatching objects from peoples' hands and returning them to the villain. The criminal also owns a souped-up hydrofoil.

Chief Henchmen: Gang of gun-toting thugs garbed in red bodysuits.

Biography: Nothing is known about this character's past. Robbing a yacht and spiriting the wealthy people aboard to his "private island hideout" in the Atlantic, the super villain holds the "millionaire stumblebums" for a ransom amounting to one million dollars each. When he dispatches his axe across the ocean to collect it, the superheroes Star Flare and Hypno-Girl (teenagers Chris King and Vicki Grant who have been transformed by their "Dial-H for Hero" device) fly after it. Arriving on the island, Star Flare destroys the axe with his Star Sword, and the helpless Thunder Axe is captured.

Quote: "Surrender? Are you mad? Thunder Axe *never surrenders! Thunder Axe never fails!*"

Comment: This was the character's only appearance.

THUNDER-MAN (C)

First Appearance: 1966, *Tomahawk* #107, DC Comics.

Costume: Blue bodysuit; navy blue cape, cowl with pointed ears and yellow lightning bolt on forehead; navy blue belt, boots and gloves with yellow lightning bolts.

Weapons: Storage battery which, strapped to his back and worn under his cape, allows Thunder-Man to fire lightning bolts.

Chief Henchman: Mikora, a giant gorilla stolen from the Indians and brainwashed to serve him.

Biography: Thunder-Man lives in Revolutionary-era America, based in a mountain fortress "built by Norsemen." Having found a way to harness, save, and emit lightning bolts that can stun or kill, the villain plans to help the British army overcome the Yanks; then, using the army to take over Britain, he intends to "strike at every country until I . . . *master the world*!" However, his plans are foiled when the patriotic Tomahawk and his bold Rangers strip him of his backpack.

Quote: "Ben Franklin should know of my experiments with electricity! I'm centuries ahead of him and his blasted kite and key!"

Comment: This was the character's only appearance.

TIAMAT (MY, T)

Biography: Back in time, when the sea was all there was, when the earth and heavens had not yet been created, Tiamat and her dragons represented the destructive powers of the ocean. The Babylonian goddess of the sea, Tiamat was ruthless, wreaking havoc on all who crossed her. At a hastily called meeting of the other gods, the chief deity Marduk vowed to take on Tiamat and her dragons in battle. The struggle was a fierce one, but Marduk emerged triumphant, killing Tiamat and imprisoning the dragons. Cutting Tiamat in two, he made the earth from one half and the sky from the other. (According to another version of the tale, Tiamat surrendered without resistance and the earth was made from the ocean.)

Comment: Tiamat was also the name of a five-headed dragon toy manufactured in 1983.

TIBORO (C)

First Appearance: 1965, *Strange Tales* #129, Marvel Comics.

Costume: Purple leotard-like armor with flap in front reaching to the knees; green boots, armbands, wristbands, helmet with "W"-shaped horns on top and an electric arc across their tops.

Weapons: "Electro-plasmic wand" which is made of "the exorcised might of lightning" and allows him to fire incredible destructive blasts.

Biography: When three men are drawn to an idol unearthed in Peru, the superheroic magician Dr. Strange investigates and discovers that symbolically, it represents Tiboro, the self-described "spirit of decay." Whenever the idol surfaces, it means a civilization has reached a "point of crisis" and the "evil ruler" is about to take over, sucking all of its occupants into his "alien dimension." Entering the idol, Strange at first tries to reason with Tiboro, to convince him that America is not yet ready to go the way of the savage race of Peruvians he had conquered. Tiboro pooh-poohs this notion ("Whether your world is ready for my rule or not, the die is cast!") and pits his electro-plasmic power against the magic of Strange. The earthman is victorious, saves the handful of people who had been abducted, and leaves readers with a warning: "I pray . . . that man's ideals never grow so weak that *Tiboro* will strike again."

Quote: "To show my utter contempt for you, I shall destroy you with my bare hands."

Comment: On the splash page of the story, Marvel warned readers of the character's infamy by declaring, "Introducing, though we hate to do it—TIBORO!" This has been the character's only appearance to date.

TIGER SHARK (1) (MP)

First Appearance: 1935, *Fighting Marines*, Mascot Pictures.

Costume: Black leather jacket with raised collar, aviator's hood and goggles, mask across mouth.

Weapons: Gravity gun which causes objects to fall apart.

Biography: Based on Halfway Island, Tiger Shark and his men prey on ships and amass a considerable fortune. Thus, when the U.S. Marines elect to build a landing strip on the island, the villain repeatedly sabotages their efforts. In the end, several marines find his lair and he attempts to flee. However, during a shootout in the cave a bullet strikes a vial of nitroglycerin and the hideout blows up. Presumably, Tiger Shark perished in the blast . . . .

Comment: Tiger Shark's serial lasted for 12 chapters.

TIGER SHARK (2) (C)

Real Name: Todd Arliss.

First Appearance: 1968, *Sub-Mariner* #5, Marvel Comics.

Costume: Orange bodysuit with small, black shark-like fins running up the sides of his legs and lavender markings running up his chest and back resembling a shark's open mouth set on its side (see Weapons); lavender boots, cowl with huge dorsal fin, gloves with small, black shark-like fins.

Weapons: Costume contains tubing system to keep him moist (hence strong) when he's on land. Otherwise, his power would rapidly wane.

Biography: An Olympic swimmer, Arliss had every intention of earning a fortune through athletic exhibitions. His dreams were dashed one day when he was badly injured while saving a man who had fallen off a yacht. Able to walk but not to swim, Arliss spent all his money in search of someone who could help him. Finding Dr. Lemuel Dorcas, he agreed to accompany the marine biologist to his facility beneath the waters of the North Atlantic coast. There, Arliss first received radiation treatments to repair his damaged sinew; then Dorcas put him in the "morphotron," a device which stamps people with the genetic likeness of other creatures. Using sharks as well as the superheroic undersea dweller Sub-Mariner—who had been captured by the biologist's specimen-gathering robot—Dorcas turned Arliss into an amphibious superbeing who had the swimming skills of a shark and the strength of the mighty Sub-Mariner. Although Dorcas had planned for Arliss to become a super villain in his service, the Olympian promptly bid Dorcas adieu and used his skills for his own criminal ends. Tiger Shark briefly teamed with DOCTOR DOOM and ATTUMA, a team unofficially known as the "Slayers from the Sea" (*Super-Villain Team-Up* #'s 1-3, 1975).

Quote: "The overrated *Sub-Mariner*—is all *washed up* as a power beneath the sea!"

Comment: In his long career (since 1939), the Sub-Mariner has fought many villains, including the scientific genius Doctor Dill (who, in the wonderfully naive days of 1949, caused him to grow larger than the entire planet); Naga, a sadistic ruler of the sunken continent Lemuria; Dynorr, aka the Stalker, an alien from Alpha Centauri; Sam Westman and his ten-ton wrecking machine/excavator Brutivac; the mace-wielding Turalla; Byrrah, Sub-Mariner's cousin, who, believing that he and not the hero should rule Atlantis, frequently undertakes to overthrow him; the powermad Dragon-Lord of Krakinowa who, smarting from Japan's loss in World War II, strives to reverse that defeat; the huge, shaggy Torg, the Abominable Snow-King; Dr. Hydro, a scaly green scientist who turns people into green-scaled slaves known as Hydrobase Amphibians; the woman warrior Virago, who becomes the ferocious She-Beast; Piranha and the Men-Fish; the alien Slime-Thing; Commander Kraken, a pirate who rides about in a squid-like submarine; and Karl Serr, a mutant who can turn himself into "the rock that walks like a man." During the Second World War Sub-Mariner fought the Axis powers and, later, he took on the Communists ("Sub-Mariner Defies the Commies!" screamed the cover of *Sub-Mariner* #40, 1955). See other underwater super villains ATTUMA, BLACK MANTA, CAPTAIN NEMO, CAPTAIN WHALE, DR. FANG, FISHERMAN, KILLER SHARK, KRANG, MR. CRABB, OCEAN MASTER, ORKA, and PIRANHA.

THE TINKERER (C)

First Appearance: 1963, *The Amazing Spider-Man* #2, Marvel Comics.

Weapons: Destructive blaster along with sundry lethal toys, including a jack-in-the-box which spits out gas, miniature tanks and planes armed with live ammunition, gun-toting teddy bears, and the like.

Chief Henchman: Bald, muscular android named Toy.

Biography: With his pointed chin and hooked nose, the Tinkerer "looks like a character straight out of Grimm's fairy tales!" And though he seems, to Spider-Man, as dangerous "as a second-hand cream puff," he is a scientific genius who, behind the facade of a repair shop, builds "special weapons" for everyone from the underworld to extraterrestrials. When his prices get too high and he loses customers, the Tinkerer decides to "profit from my matchless machines" by becoming a criminal himself. Thwarted by Spider-Man, he tries to rebuild his old trade by making super-accoutrements for the villainous Rocket Racer and Big Wheel (issue #'s 183-184). But when both are captured by Spider-Man, the Tinkerer's equipment is wrongly blamed by his colleagues and he is forced to return to crime yet again (keeping many of the gadgets he made for others, such as a staircase that turns into a ramp which he built for the criminal Arcade who had "refused payment"). The Tinkerer is presently lying low, still mourning the death of Toy whom he accidentally blasted while trying to shoot Spider-Man, in *Peter Parker, the Spectacular Spider-Man* #53, (1981).

Quote: "I'm sure you're *dying* to play with my terrible toys!"

Comment: This character is similar to THE TOYMASTER and THE TOYMAN.

TITANIUM MAN (C)

Real Name: Boris Bullski

First Appearance: 1965, *Tales of Suspense* #69, Marvel Comics.

Costume: Green armor, helmet, boots, gloves (see Weapons).

Weapons: The nuclear-powered armor provides Boris with superstrength as well as the ability to fly, attract objects by a tractor beam, destroy them with a blaster or heat beam, and snare them with constricting loops known as "radar rings."

Biography: Because of his boundless ambition, Boris is transferred from a high governmental post in the Kremlin to a lesser one in a Siberian labor camp. Hoping to win brownie points by advancing the Communist cause, he pulls together the imprisoned scientific team which had worked on the ill-fated CRIMSON DYNAMO and has them create a similar suit of armor for him. With the government's permission, Bullski dares Iron Man to meet him in televised battle. The American superhero accepts the challenge and soundly defeats the Red champion. Bullski battles him several times thereafter, hoping to wipe the stain from his record, but he is unable to beat his armored rival. Shamed, Bullski leaves Russia and relocates in Vietnam where he co-founds THE TITANIC THREE. The group fails to survive their encounter with the Avengers, and Titanium Man remains frustrated and in exile.

Comment: See MAGNETO (Comment) for Paul McCartney song about Titanium Man. See other Soviet super villains Boris Kartovski (see DR. CLEMENT ARMSTRONG, Comment), COMRADE STUPIDSKA, THE CRIMSON DYNAMO, MONGU, THE RED GHOST, THE SOVIET SUPER SOLDIERS, and THE TITANIC THREE.

THE TOAD (C)

Real Name: Snaggletooth Snarker.

First Appearance: 1967, *Mighty Comics* #43, Archie Comics.

Costume: Toad mask.

Biography: Nothing is known about this villain, save that he's a notorious counterfeiter. Captured in his hideout by the superhero the Black Hood, the Toad is turned over to police.

***THE TOAD** vs. the Black Hood. © Archie Comics.*

Comment: The character appears in just one panel in *Mighty Comics* #43, and four panels in #50. However, the singular splendor of his mask qualifies him for recognition. Other Black Hood villains include the Karate Master, the Skull, the Ghost Cyclist, and the Mad Gadgeteer.

TOBIAS WHALE (also known as THE GREAT WHITE WHALE) (C)

First Appearance: 1977, *Black Lightning* #1, DC Comics.

Costume: Whale wears business suits, though his enormous bulk, whale-shaped head, and hairless, white flesh give him a look more like Moby Dick than a man.

Weapons: Large, flying disc to whisk himself and a handful of aides through the skies.

Chief Henchmen: The 100 (later known as the 1,000), "a *hundred* crime lords—each with a virtual *army* behind him!" (see Biography); SYONIDE; the Cyclotronic Man; the deadly archer Merlyn; Joey Toledo, Zell, and various other personal aides.

Biography: A towering albino who looks obese but is, in fact, built of solid muscle, Whale fights his way up through the criminal ranks until he is the leader of the Metropolis division of the 100, a band involved in everything from extortion to drug-dealing. In the course of running his rackets, Whale has pitted his awesome physical strength against the superheroes Black Lightning and Superman. Though he has yet to be victorious, no jail has been able to hold him.

Quote: "When I've *finished* with him—I'll throw his battered *corpse* into the streets as an example to anyone *else* who would oppose us!"

Comment: The 100 is an extremely nefarious group of criminals which first appeared in *Lois Lane* #105 (1970). Originally just a league of mobsters, it evolved into 10 specialized groups: the Agents, the Amazons, the Athletes, the Dynamiters, the Hunters, the Mind-Benders, the Mobsters, the Sea Wolves, the Space Raiders, and the Stealers, each largely autonomous. Eventually, the 100 was hounded into virtual inactivity by Superman. It resurfaced after several years, at which time Whale came to power. Black Lightning devoted his career to destroying not only Whale but also the 100; he failed, the group growing larger (it was now the 1,000) and stronger than ever. One of their most ambitious plans was to kidnap the President of the United States and replace him with a member, Chiller, who is able to resemble any person he wishes. The superhero Booster Gold foiled the plot. As for Tobias Whale, he shares many attributes with a Marvel Comics super villain, the baldheaded Kingpin (aka Wilson Fisk), who is also fat-with-muscle, runs rackets (on the turf of the superhero Spider-Man), and hires super villains to work for him. That character first appeared in *The Amazing Spider-Man* #50 in 1967. See other corpulent super villains THE BLOB, THE DUKE OF DECAY, THE FAT MAN, and LORD LAZEE.

TOLKEMEC (M)

First Appearance: July 1936, "Red Nails," *Weird Tales*, Robert E. Howard.

Costume: Rags.

Weapons: "Jade-hued wand" with a crimson knob which fires a ray that turns people to mummies.

Biography: Circa 10,000 B.C., the lost city of Xuchotl is inhabited by two groups, the Tecuhltli and the Xotalancs, who are in a perpetual state of war. Tolkemec despises both groups, and for 12 years dwells in the catacombs beneath the city, feeding on the corpses of the slain. (People who see the misanthrope believe it to be a ghost.) Finally emerging from the darkness, he starts killing people with his wand, intent on destroying everyone; bodies drop like "falling leaves" until the heroic barbarian Conan, who had been a prisoner in the city, plunges a knife into his breast. Tolkemec looks every inch the lunatic: he has white hair and a long white beard, a gaunt frame, skin with "a suggestion of scaliness," and eyes "that stared unwinkingly, luminous, whitish, and without a hint of normal emotion or sanity." He does not speak, only "titters."

Comment: The story was serialized over three months. The tale has two other villainous characters: Princess Tascela, an immortal who must sacrifice young women to survive, and Prince Olmec of the Tecuhltli. The title of the story derives from the fact that the Tecuhltli hammer red nails into a pillar for each enemy they slay; the Xotalancs save their enemies' heads instead.

T.O. MORROW (C)

Real Name: Thomas Oscar Morrow.

First Appearance: 1962, *The Flash* #143, DC Comics.

Weapons: Numerous robots, computers (which help him to commit crimes).

Chief Henchmen: Sundry thugs.

Biography: A brilliant scientist, the non-costumed Morrow devotes his talents to destroying superheroes. After a brief go at the Flash, his perennial nemesis is the Justice League of America, which he has battled on numerous occasions, most notably in *Justice League of America* #'s 64 and 65 (1968), in which he tries to start a war between the parallel-dimensional worlds Earth-1 and Earth-2. In one adventure (#106, 1973), Morrow split into two people: Morrow and Future Man. Future Man, with his huge head and brain, died while trying to switch his brainwaves into the body of the superheroic Red Tornado; Morrow escaped and is presently unaccounted for.

Quote: "Now that I've killed off the *Justice League*—what'll I do for an *encore*?"

Comment: In over 27 years of battling the forces of evil, the Justice League of America has also tangled with Xotar, a criminal who comes from 11,960 A.D. with Ilaric, his towering, golden time-machine-cum-blaster-toting robot; Magic-Land villains Simon Magus, the Troll King, and Saturna, Lord of Misrule; evil extraterrestrials from the planet Angellax who impersonate members of the Justice League while turning the Real McCoys into misshapen funhouse-mirror versions of themselves; humans transformed by meteors into Crystal Creature, Fire-Lord, Glass-Man, Golden Roc, Mercury Monster, Stone-God, and Wood-King; the alien Rockmen of

Pluto; the wicked Kraad the Conqueror, who hails from another dimension; the Unimaginable, another energy-entity; Anti-Matter Man, a black-and-blue being from a different dimension; the huge, red, alien Cube Creatures who are immune to even the "mightiest punches" of Superman. Also, the Black Spheres, four extraterrestrials who possess superheroes and turn them evil; Leo Locke and the Pyrotekniks, a gang of criminals who use fireworks in their work; Neverwas, an amoeba-like being from antediluvian days; the living star Aquarius; Chokh and the Doomsters, waste-eating invaders from the planet Monsan who try to pollute our atmosphere to suit their needs; the mad extraterrestrial the Jest-Master; the android Nether Man, created by Dr. Viktor Willard; robots from the planet Cam-Nam-Lao (note the not-too-subtle reference to Southeast Asia) which have the power to manipulate human emotions; the denizens of the lost continent of Mu, who deem all other humans as inferior and plague the earth with natural disasters. Also Johnny Dune, a mutant rock star whose voice enables him to control the will of his audiences; the interstellar vampire Starbreaker and his huge robot bugs the Mechanix; the alien known as the Equalizer, who spreads a plague which saps people of their individuality; the formless Adaptoids, aliens who can assume the likeness of others (unrelated to Marvel Comics' SUPERADAPTOID); Nekron, an extraterrestrial who feeds on the fears of others; and the alien Dharlu, which comes to earth on a moon rock and adopts certain characteristics of Justice League members.

TOMORROW MAN (C)

Real Name: Artur Zarrko.

First Appearance: 1962, *Journey Into Mystery* #86, Marvel Comics.

Costume: Green bodysuit, yellow lightning streaks down front of legs, "X"-shaped bands from shoulders to waist with yellow "T" in black circle where they cross, black pyramid design with yellow circles on belly; green cape, trunks; yellow boots, gloves.

Weapons: A time machine; various guns.

Chief Henchman: The robot Servitor.

Biography: Zarrko lives in the peaceful twenty-third century in an alternate future—that is, not necessarily the one to which events in our own timeline will lead. A megalomaniac, Zarrko is frustrated because there are no weapons with which to conquer his world. Thus, drawing upon his awesome knowledge of science, he constructs a time machine and travels to our era to obtain arms. Locating a cobalt bomb, he is apprehended by the superhero Thor and suffers amnesia during their struggle; returned to his time, he is put to work as a humble paperpusher. His memory restored by the evil LOKI, Zarrko once again tries to take over the future; this time he is stymied by the combined efforts of Thor and the Master Machine, the computer which runs Zarrko's world. Left imprisoned within an energy field, Zarrko eventually escapes and, journeying farther into the future, sets himself up as the ruler of the fiftieth century.

Comment: IMMORTUS and THE REVERSE-FLASH also hail from the future.

THE TOP (C)

Real Name: Roscoe Dillon.

First Appearance: 1961, *The Flash* #122, DC Comics.

Costume: Green bodysuit with horizontal yellow stripes and black top silhouette on chest; black mask.

Weapons: Various top-weapons, including debilitating ribbons of steel which fly from him when he spins, and a huge grenade which, if it stopped spinning "for even a split-second," would blow up half the world.

Biography: As a youth, Roscoe was fascinated with toy tops. Carrying the interest into adulthood, he applied it to his chosen profession: crime. Throughout his career, he battled the superheroic Flash many times, eventually gaining *super* spinning abilities, acquired because "the centrifugal force created by his incredible spinning technique had shifted millions of dormant brain-cells to the outer areas of his cerebrum—boosting his brain power many times." Unfortunately, the shift made his brain cells vulnerable to the "superspeed vibrations" generated by the Flash, and Roscoe Dillon perished (*The Flash* #243). He did return briefly, however, as an "astral presence" in *The Flash* #303, trying to possess the superhero's body. The fiend's girlfriend, Lisa Snart, carries on his criminal tradition as THE GOLDEN GLIDER.

Quote: "Your *doom* will be the final *proof—the Top* has *spun* his way *back* from the *dead*!"

TORQUE (C)

Real Name: Ralphie Hutchins.

First Appearance: 1981, *The Savage She-Hulk* #23, Marvel Comics.

Costume: Armor (see Weapons) consisting of blue bodysuit, gloves, boots; purple full-head helmet and trunks which rise to chest, a blue "O" in the center.

Weapons: Suit taps his mass and weight and "makes it available as an infinite energy reserve," which he can fire as destructive blasts or use to manipulate matter (e.g., parting seas or melding sand into a solid cocoon).

Biography: Torque is the third super-villainous incarnation of Ralphie. He is created by the "Mad Doctor" and used by would-be crime czar Shade to try and slay the She-Hulk (see RADIUS and THE SEEKER). Due to genetic alteration (a specialty of the Mad Doctor), Torque is able to increase his mass and weight, which would result in a nuclear meltdown if his armor failed to convert that mass and weight to energy. He engages She-Hulk in battle, but the superhero takes so much punishment that Torque must keep increasing his energy—which results in his demise from an overload.

Quote: "How can you hope to triumph against such ultimate and inexhaustible energy?"

Comment: It was revealed in this story that Shade was merely a front for the ambitions of the Mad Doctor himself, who was hoping to create an army of superbeings capable of conquering the world. Moreover, it was explained that each subsequent super villain created using Ralphie—from the "Playdoh" beast (see RADIUS, Biography) to Radius to the Seeker to Torque — was an evolutionary improvement over the previous entity. Indeed, after the death of Torque, Ralphie briefly becomes the monstrous Earth-Lord, an enormous monster "made of the very ground of the (Shade) estate itself." Ralphie stopped his metamorphosing when a mutated child named Kyr, another of the doctor's experiments, destroyed him with "a psychic punch" (#24). The scientist himself was finally apprehended by She-Hulk in the following issue.

THE TOYMAN (C)

First Appearance: 1942, *Action Comics* #64, DC Comics.

Costume: Tan suit; white shirt; green bowtie (sometimes blue).

Weapons: Countless toy-based weapons, including a jack-in-the-box platform which boosts him up sheer walls; flying Superman dolls which explode on contact (he also has a larger Superman doll which he uses for short-range flight); toy soldiers which fire sleeping gas; particularly nasty dolls whose "fingers are sharpened to needle points and dipped in poison" (he also has a hand-buzzer with a toxic needle); a flying pogo stick; and the "super brain," a computer which not only figures out how to commit crimes but also creates a working plastic model of the crime scene.

Chief Henchmen: Various flunkies.

Biography: After a lifetime of designing "the most intricate and amazing toys" in the world (even though he never graduated from kindergarten), the Toyman one day decides that "henceforth I shall play, not for the amusement of children, but for the consternation of their fathers." Working in his cellar beneath the streets of Metropolis, he begins designing toys to help him commit crimes. His nefarious efforts are usually thwarted by Superman, though that doesn't stop him from plotting anew—such as the time when, in prison, he builds automated cops and robbers dolls which, sold in a city store, seem to demonstrate that crime does not pay; in fact, the dolls demonstrate to the villain's henchmen just how to commit foolproof crimes he has concocted (*Superman* #47, 1947).

Quote: "This giant duck is like one of my toys—that I used in crime. *Sighh*! Those were the good old days, before *Superman*!"

Comment: The character is similar to THE TINKERER and TOYMASTER.

TOYMASTER (C)

First Appearance: 1966, *House of Mystery* #169, DC Comics.

Costume: Green trunks, boots, jester's cap, bodyshirt with orange shoulders and black "T O Y" on chest in small white blocks; black mask; orange gloves.

Weapons: Various "Toy Tricks" carried in red sack worn on side, including a target-seeking missile, a boomerang harpoon, magnetized weights, miniature wrecking machine to stun people, a small lighthouse to blind his enemies, and a jack-in-the-box which releases a flying, spiked head.

Biography: Nothing is known about this character's past. Nestled in a cave outside of Littleville, the Toymaster and his gang commit robberies until stopped by a young girl named Suzy. She uses Robby Reed's "Dial-H for Hero" device to become the superheroic Gem Girl and literally falls on Toymaster's head, knocking him out. Toymaster keeps his loot in a huge golden chest in his cavern hideout.

Comment: This was the character's only appearance.

THE TRAPSTER (Originally known as PASTE-POT PETE) (C)

Real Name: Peter Petruski.

First Appearance: 1963, *Strange Tales* #104, Marvel Comics.

Costume: Original: artist's smock and beret. Second: purple jumpsuit, cowl; red gloves, belt, boots. Third: purple cowl, tights, leotard with flared shoulders and two columns of three squares each down chest; yellow thigh boots, gloves, longsleeve shirt.

Weapons: As Paste-Pot Pete: "Paste Gun" which fires glue, stored in a pack worn on the villain's side (he originally carted it around in a bucket, which fed the gun via hose). There is also glue stored inside his boots which, when tapped, enables him to walk up walls. As the Trapster, he retained the gun and, for a brief time, also used various traps which simply snared or completely bound his victims.

Biography: A chemist, Petruski invents a "multi-polymer" paste which adheres to anything. Deciding to use the glue for crime, he becomes Paste-Pot Pete. Apprehended by the Human Torch on numerous occasions, he joins THE FRIGHTFUL FOUR as the more ecletic Trapster. Though the group has since disbanded, the Trapster teams regularly with fellow member THE WIZARD.

Quote: "We don't haveta worry about the *Invisible Girl*! I already pasted all the *windows* shut . . . so she can't get *out*!"

THE TRICKSTER (C)

Real Name: James Jesse.

First Appearance: 1960, *The Flash* #113, DC Comics.

Costume: Yellow shirt with vertical black stripes; orange vest with vertical blue stripes; dark orange tights with vertical black stripes; blue slippers, cloak; black domino mask.

Weapons: Air shoes which release "constant jets of compressed air" enabling him to walk through the sky (though the higher he goes, the thinner the atmosphere and the less effective his shoes); tricycle which emits "high frequency waves" that send pursuers stumbling backwards; tri-jet cycle for rapid flight through the skies.

Biography: James is the son of famous circus aerialists, who despair over the amount of time their son spends reading. Young James is especially fascinated with the exploits of his "reverse namesake" Jesse James, and resolves "to follow in his infamous idol's footsteps" when he grows up. Perfecting his acrobatic skills and inventing the air shoes, he sews a costume and plagues Central City as the evil Trickster. For years, his archenemy is the Flash, who manages to defeat the villain at every turn. With the death of the Flash, the super villain moves to Southern California where he battles the superheroic Blue Devil. However, whether it is age or repeated defeats that finally mellow him, the Trickster eventually gives up his life of crime to work as a consultant to the Institute of Hyper-Normal Conflict Studies . . . and also to create special effects for the Verner Brothers film studio. He was briefly a member of THE SECRET SOCIETY OF SUPER-VILLAINS.

Quote: "With my jet-shoes, I can pull off the trick! And that gives me my name, too! I'll become—*the Trickster*!"

Comment: THE JOKER and THE PRANKSTER are other trick-playing super villains.

TRIGON (C)

First Appearance: 1980, *The New Teen Titans* #2 (voice only); 1981, *The New Teen Titans* #4, DC Comics.

Costume: White loincloth, strap across chest, boots, wristbands, and cloak with very high, fan-like collar. (Trigon's skin is red, and the four-eyed, circa eight-feet-tall demi-demon boasts a rack of antlers.)

Chief Henchmen: Countless minions including imperial guard; fire-breathing winged dragons; his warriors, the dark hordes; his huge, carnivorous, dog-like pet Fang; Goronn, a towering, orange, dinosaur-like monster who consumes flesh, leaving only the "fragile souls" for Trigon; and terrestrial subversives such as PSIMON.

Biography: Able to assume any appearance he wishes, force others to obey him, or simply kill with a glance, Trigon was born "on another world in another dimension." Nearly 10 centuries ago, the planet's last inhabitants—demon worshipers all—gathered together to raise a devil to mate with a woman of their order. They succeeded and, nine months later, Trigon was born. How evil was he? "Instantly he slew all around him," including his mother, and he had not yet begun to feel his oats. "Trigon grew more malevolent with every passing day," taking over his world at the age of one—destroying it five years later—and ruling "the million million planets" of his dimension by the time he was 30. (And not with kindness. Once, when a little girl looked at him cross-eyed, he first gave her the "death stare" causing her blood to boil, then struck her with a destructive bolt that left her a mound of ash.) But even ruling his universe wasn't enough: learning of our dimension, he sought to conquer it as well. Meanwhile, there was one in particular who sought to thwart him: his daughter Raven, whose mother, Arella—an earthwoman and cultist of the supernatural—Trigon had seduced. It was Trigon's intention to use his daughter as a means by which to enter our universe. (He has had other children, though for unspecified reasons none has survived.) However, when Raven turned her back on him he simply powered his way here using his mystic powers. With no time to waste, Raven contacted young superheroes on earth and brought them together as the New Teen Titans. The youthful band confronted Trigon and managed to open a door to a limbo known as "the nether-verse"; though the demon was sucked in (#6), he managed to take control of Raven and transform her into a four-eyed red demon like himself. Conquering our planet, he possessed the souls of everyone in the world save for the Titans and Arella. When even the Titans were on the verge of defeat, Raven was freed from her spell by her mother. The woman then sent her spirit forth, which smothered and destroyed her mate in *The New Teen Titans*, second series, #6 (1985). Or so it seemed. Drawing upon the souls of a billion creatures in his dimension, he mustered the power to return—ravaging the earth with the help of Raven, whose evil was a latent part of her genetic makeup and finally surfaced. He was slain when the benign souls of those killed by Trigan marshaled their power and, through Raven, obliterated the fiend.

Quote: "From the moment you are *born*, I demand your total *obedience*, your complete *subservience* . . . I am your *God*."

THE TROLL (F)

First Appearance: 1840, "The Three Billygoats Gruff," *Norske Folkeeventyr (Norwegian Folktales)*, Peter Christen Asbjornsen and Jorgen Moe (see Comment).

Biography: The owner of a bridge in the Norwegian countryside, the Troll exacts a rather stiff toll: He eats whatever animals try to pass over to the pasture beyond. However, he meets his end when he tangles with the Billygoats Gruff. Stopping the youngest of the billygoats, he's told to wait for the next one, who's fatter; the next billygoat tells him the same thing. When the Troll stops the third goat, Big Billygoat Gruff, the animal butts him into the river, drowning the Troll.

Quote: "Who's that tripping over my bridge?"

Comment: Although Asbjornsen and Moe were the first anthologists to publish the tale, it had existed in one form or another for centuries. Trolls are very much a part of Scandinavian folklore, an evil offshoot of the often benign giants found in Norse mythology. Trolls come in two distinct sizes, huge and stumpy, and are always misshapen. According to early legends of the Danes, they were rebel angels who fell from heaven with SATAN. However, instead of landing in hell, they landed in the burial mounds and remained on earth as Trolls. As for their general habits, in *Popular Tales from the Norse* (1859), Sir George Dasent states that Trolls "eat men, and porridge, and sausages indifferently," usually feasting on children; they also live in deep caves and detest loud sounds (a holdover from the days when the Norse god Thor used to chase them with his hammer). Church bells are particularly distasteful to them. Most Trolls can be stricken dead by the rays of the sun, either exploding (as often happens in Asbjornsen and Moe) or turning to stone. One of the most famous Trolls is the Troll King in Ibsen's *Peer Gynt* (1867).

THE TRUMP (C)

Real Name: Carlton Sanders.

First Appearance: 1984, *Daredevil* #203, Marvel Comics.

Costume: White gloves (see Weapons), boots, cloak with red collar, bodysuit with thin red stripes on legs, chest, waist, arms, and belly; black domino mask.

Weapons: Cattleprod-like wand; playing cards which he throws in a shower to cover his retreat; gloves which fire ribbons to bind people and flares to blind.

Chief Henchmen: Stymie Schmidt and other nameless punks.

Biography: A "magician and kidshow host," Sanders moonlighted as a criminal specializing in heists; his last job put him in Tulsa State Penitentiary where he was held for grand theft and murder. Breaking out, he became the costumed Trump, an homage to his expertise as a card player (he was two-time prison bridge champion). Headquartered in a Moosehead Brewery warehouse in New York, he undertook gunrunning only to be stopped by the superhero Daredevil. He is presently in prison.

Quote: "One jolt of electricity, one dead hero. I've always got a trump card up my sleeve."

Comment: Other foes of Daredevil include Manuel Eloganto, the Matador; the Gladiator, aka Melvin Potter, who is armored and boasts a whirring, buzz-saw-like blade on each wrist; the Tri-Man (also known as the Tri-Android), a robot who is given the powers of the villains the Brain, the Dancer, and the Mangler; atomic scientist Paxton Page, aka the glowing, explosive Death's-Head who rides a skeletal steed; George Smith, the cycle-riding Stunt-Master; Torpedo, a costumed assassin; El Condor, a costumed Delvadian revolutionary; the armored Indestructible Man (Damon Dran); the Blue Talon and his razor-like hands; the Dark Messiah (Mordecai Jones), who becomes a superbeing thanks to the science of extraterrestrials from Titan; the mighty Ramrod; the towering monster Terrex; Chesney, the Copperhead, and his "darts of doom"; Mind-Wave and his Esper-Ts, psychic criminals; and the super-strong Smasher (in three separate identities over the years).

TSE-TSE (TV)

First Appearance: 1978, "Web Woman" segment of *Tarzan and the Super 7*, CBS-TV.

Costume: Khaki safari outfit. Tse-Tse has bug-like head, pincers, and wings (see Weapons).

Weapons: Pincers and mandibles possess superhuman strength; wings enable him to fly.

Chief Henchmen: Various swarms of insects, which he controls.

Biography: Nothing is known about this character's past. Searching for lost treasure in the jungle, he comes upon a temple which contains a spaceship (sent to Earth some 900,000 years ago by friendly aliens from another galaxy). In it are glimpses of their advanced world, as well as an extremely powerful robot. The robot, however, can only be activated when its two "eyes" are placed in its head; these eyes had been dispatched from the rocket, in two pods, to different parts of the world. One ended up in the Great Pyramid of Cheops in Egypt, the other in a great temple in Hong Kong. (Presumably, the temples were erected by locals who found the odd extraterrestrial artifacts.) Entering the temple containing the ship, the explorer—described as "a greedy, ruthless man"—strikes the control panel hard, causing an "incorrect energy burst." This turns him into an incredibly powerful humanoid insect who immediately sets out to claim the eyes because, with the robot at his side, he intends to take over the world. Although the superheroic Web Woman intercedes, she is continually kept at bay by Tse-Tse or his insect thugs. Ironically, though he manages to obtain the eyes and bring the robot to life, it has a built-in sensor to detect and "eradicate evil." Determining that Tse-Tse is evil, it blasts him back to his human state. Furthermore, deciding that humankind is not yet ready for the advanced knowledge it carries, the robot promptly climbs back into the spaceship and returns to its native world.

Quote: "If I can just learn all the secrets of this place, I'll be more powerful than anyone alive!"

Comment: The Web Woman series was produced by Filmation. Other super villains she fought during her brief career include the alien Madam Macabre, who collects life forms from different worlds; Dr. Abyss, who causes volcanic eruptions and earthquakes, and threatens to destroy the earth unless he is appointed "supreme ruler"; Frank Johnson, who takes over a climate-altering weather space station and holds the earth for ransom; the insect-like Selenoids who, led by Rax, are attempting to obtain the Power Glove kept on Citadel Seven and to use it to plunder the galaxy "beginning with earth"; Zontarr, an emaciated alien who drains energy from the sun, unconcerned that his actions will destroy the solar system; and Jack Frankenstein, a descendant of the original Dr. Frankenstein, who uses his Copy Cat Machine to create clones of people, duplicates which he uses to lash out at colleagues who scorned him.

TUL AXTAR (N)

First Appearance: 1930, "A Fighting Man of Mars," *Blue Book Magazine*, Edgar Rice Burroughs.

Weapons: Ray gun capable of disintegrating metal; fleet of aircraft.

Biography: The jeddak (prince) of the city-state of Jahar on Mars, Tul Axtar is a monomaniac who wants nothing less than to conquer the planet; his second fondest wish is to have the largest harem in all creation—his own harem is already several thousand women strong. Underwriting a team of brilliant scientists—of which the equally distorted PHOR TAK is a member—the monarch also encourages his subjects to become parents so that he will have sufficient personnel to wage his war. (His enthusiasm also breeds the plague of overpopulation, and the problem of having to provide for "millions" sorely taxes his kingdom. Yet, paradoxically, need also fires the peoples' enthusiasm for a war of conquest). Finally getting his operation underway with an attack on the great city of Helium, Tul Axtar not only is defeated but also shot dead by the bold soldier Tan Hadron of Hastor. ("Point-blank I fired at his putrid heart," reports Tan Hadron.) Despite his "great bulk" and armies, Tul Axtar is a coward; whenever he was on the verge of defeat he would flee, whining in terror.

Quote: "They are coming! They will tear me to pieces!"

Comment: This was the character's only appearance. The novel was first serialized from April to September 1930. It was published in book form the following year.

THE TUMBLER (C)

Real Name: John Robert Keane; Michael Keane.

First Appearance: 1966, *Tales of Suspense* #83 (as John); 1984, *Captain America* #291 (as Michael), Marvel Comics.

Costume: Red bodysuit, trunks, boots with white fringe; white belt, cowl with three black stripes from forehead to back; black mask, cuffs with two white stripes around each.

Biography: An expert acrobat, John became a

costumed performer known as the Tumbler and made quite a bit of money (which he used, in large part, to support his widowed mother). Meanwhile, wanting Captain America out of the way, an evil league known as the Secret Empire fixed it so John perished when he and the superhero were struggling. None of the witnesses saw the villainous MOONSTONE kill John from behind a ceiling panel "with a sliver-thin laser beam through the skull" (*Captain America* #169, 1973), and the red, white, and blue superhero took the rap. Though Captain America was eventually exonerated (#175), Mrs. Keane no longer had any substantive means of support. When her son Michael came home from the army, he tried to cash in a $1 million life insurance policy his brother had taken out; turned away because "John was a criminal . . . killed while engaged in an illegal act," Michael had a worse shock in store when he was unable to get work because of "his brother's infamy." His mother's death shortly thereafter proved the last straw. Vowing to get even with the Guardian Life Insurance Company, he trained until he was "better than his brother had ever been" and became the new Tumbler. Stealing records from Guardian which proved the company knew that John was a crook when it insured him, Michael accidentally left the documents behind while battling Captain America. Later, having read the papers, the superhero realized Keane had a case against the company and agreed to help. Working together the two discovered that Guardian had been busy "insuring super villains for exorbitant amounts" and brought the law down on them. His appetite for vengeance sated, Michael retired the Tumbler . . . apparently for good.

Quote: "How does it feel to be humbled—to taste the ashes of *defeat* for the first time in your career?"

TUNDRA (C)

First Appearance: 1983, *Alpha Flight* #1, Marvel Comics.

Costume: Tundra's body is a naked, humanoid mass of snowy soil.

Biography: Ages ago, Tundra created a magic barrier which prevented the gods from getting between him and his plans to conquer the earth. Bartering all her powers in exchange for freedom, the goddess Nelvanna was permitted to go free, mating and giving birth to the super-powered Snowbird, whom she hoped would have the power to battle Tundra. Part of the very earth itself, Tundra was brought to life in our sphere when a mystic carved the earth-beast's outline in the soil of the Canadian northwest and then lay down in the center of it, his "life force" giving the "spark to the soul of the beast." Because his soul was "a tiny, shrivelled thing," the mystic was unable to control Tundra and the giant's own spirit took over. Standing hundreds of feet tall-and growing by leaps and bounds as it soaked up land—Tundra could command all "the creatures of the north," and could also use the rocks and earth which compose it as projectiles. The giant was destroyed when Snowbird and fellow members of the superheroic team Alpha Flight caused it to rain, the storm washing Tundra away. Tundra's mortal foe was Kolomaq, who "commands the forces of nature," and whom Alpha Flight battled and bested by burying the giant "in the unbreakable embrace" of the earth itself (#6).

Quote: "I am the death of all that lives, the final doom."

TURTLE MAN (C)

First Appearance: 1945, *All-Flash* #21 (Turtle Man 1); 1956, *Showcase* #4 (Turtle Man 2).

Costume: Tortoise-like shell on back (see Weapons); same motif on shirt; blue trousers.

Weapons: Shell serves as bulletproof armor, and can be extended to protect the head; it also contains small thrusters which allow Turtle Man to bend and fire it off, like a lethal, giant Frisbee. The second Turtle Man also has a ray gun which causes people to creep along, and a "slow laser" which makes objects appear, to onlookers, to be moving at superspeed.

Biography: Originally, Turtle Man was a non-costumed crook who found that his unusually lethargic pace was an asset when battling the superspeed superhero the Flash: The superhero couldn't stop or turn fast enough to catch him. Eventually the Flash accustomed himself to dealing with the slow-moving felon and tossed him in jail. Adopting a costume, Turtle Man fought the Flash on several occasions before vanishing from the criminal scene. Another Turtle Man surfaced to battle the Flash when DC revived the hero after several years. (The relationship, if any, of this Turtle Man with the original character has never been revealed.) The criminal was defeated in their first encounter, even though cleverly, he did not flee the first bank he robbed, but hid inside and shuffled away when the law had gone. Inheriting a fortune, the Turtle Man did not tackle the Flash again until he had built himself several hi-tech weapons (after all, he no longer needed the money; he did it simply for the fun). Though they fought several times, Turtle Man always landed on his back.

Comment: This character has the distinction of being the first super villain of the so-called Silver Age of comic books, an era marked by the triumphant redesign and reemergence of the Flash after nearly a decade of very flat sales in the superhero genre.

TWO-FACE (C)

Real Name: Harvey Dent (also Paul Sloane; see Biography).

First Appearance: 1942, *Detective Comics* #66, DC Comics.

Costume: None, until recently: nowadays, he has taken to wearing nondescript street clothes which are different on the right and left sides.

Biography: Gotham City's successful District Attorney, Dent—nicknamed "Apollo" because of his striking good looks—is hideously scarred on the left side of his face when criminal "Boss" Moroni (one version has the name as "Lucky" Morony) tosses acid in the D.A.'s face during his trial. Despite plastic surgery, the left side of the man's face remains green and twisted . . . as does his soul. The crucial piece of evidence at the trial is Moroni's lucky two-headed silver dollar which was found at the scene of the crime. Carving an "X" on the face of one side (so the face will be "scarred—ugly like mine!"), Dent is continually flipping it to determine whether he will do a good deed or commit a crime. Whenever he elects to break the law, his foe Batman tracks him down; he invariably ends up in the Arkham Asylum, and just as invariably escapes. At one point in his career, he is restored to normal by plastic surgery, and there is briefly a second Two-Face, actor Paul Sloane, who is burned by an exploding klieg light while playing Dent on *True Crime Television Playhouse*. Sloane briefly leads a life of crime before going in for plastic surgery; not long thereafter, Dent gets back into the act when he tries to prevent a pair of safecrackers from robbing a TV store. He is caught in the explosion they'd set and the blast undoes all of his surgery (which, he'd been warned, cannot "be performed a second time"). "This settles it," he declares. "This *proves* I was *meant* to be a criminal."

Quote: "I've gone back on my word—but *never* against the decision of my coin."

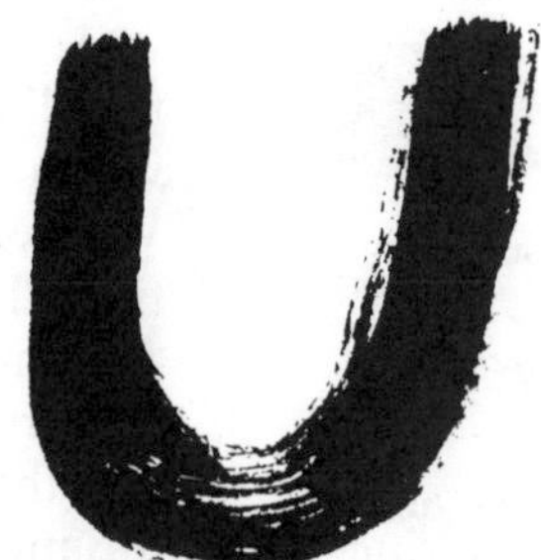

UGLYMAN (C)

Real Name: Ernie Misty.

First Appearance: 1966, *Mighty Comics* #40, Archie Comics.

Costume: Green bodysuit; red jerkin, boots; black belt with green buckle.

Biography: An aspiring actor, Misty dons an ugly mask and terrorizes handsome actors, declaring that he's after them because "I'm ugly, they aren't." In fact, he's hoping to scare them away and thus "hog all the big roles." Though the superheroic Web battles him as he tries to drop a klieg light on an actor, it's the hero's wife Rosie who stops him by clubbing Ernie into a tub of cement with her pocketbook.

Quote: "Come out, Brett Winslow! I, *Uglyman*, know that you . . . the idol of millions of drooling female movie fans . . . are cowering inside yon trash can!"

Comment: This was the character's only appearance.

ULIK (C)

First Appearance: 1966, *Thor* #137, Marvel Comics.

Costume: Green trunks, belt, mail vest with armored shoulders (a blue, skull-shaped breastplate was added later).

Weapons: Metal knucklebands for pounding opponents or, when slammed together, for creating awesome sonic blasts; mace; sword; "earth-drill" (only in #237) for burrowing through the earth (the drill both digs tunnels and fills them, leaving no trace of his having been there).

Chief Henchmen: An army of trolls armed with clubs, guns, and other weapons.

Biography: Over 1,000 years old, the ferocious Ulik is the most powerful of the trolls, though not powerful enough to wrest the troll throne from King Geirrodur. An ambitious fellow, the hirsute bruiser has battled (though never bested) the superhero Thor on numerous occasions, twice in an effort to steal his mighty enchanted hammer and once when he tried to conquer the earth. After his last defeat, Ulik was sentenced to tend the furnaces which heat the troll kingdom. Escaping, he found a small army of trolls to lead and once again attacked the earth. Defeated yet again by Thor, he has since vanished from sight.

Quote: "If I didn't need you *whole*, I swear I'd tear you limb from limb!"

ULTIMA (C)

First Appearance: 1980, *She-Hulk* #9, Marvel Comics.

Costume: Red blouse with flared shoulders, miniskirt, boots.

Weapons: "Brain-wave Inhibitor," a spider-like device which is placed on the back of the neck to keep people unconscious; "special suits" designed to inhibit super powers.

Biography: Ultima is the daughter of the Word (no other names have been revealed). Originally, the Word was a dictionary editor. Entranced with language, he quit his job and became a disc jockey. Discovering that he was "a super salesman," he eventually created the Cult of the Word and led an army of followers, his most devoted adherent being his daughter. From earliest youth, she was instructed in "all the mental and physical disciplines." She learned how to be "the total master of every fiber of her being," and by adulthood had "become super-human." Investigating the cult, whose members aren't always willing devotees, the superheroic She-Hulk got into a brawl with Ultima; during the fight, She-Hulk picked up a car and it accidentally landed square on Ultima's back. As a result, Ultima, once superhuman, was left paralyzed and mute (#10). Though her father promptly took a vow of silence, it didn't last long; locked in his country mansion, he used his power of speech to "convince my daughter she could be healed." Succeeding (she came back "more powerful than ever before"), he launched a new crusade—to banish conflict by eliminating all differences between people, to make humankind "a truly happy, homogeneous mass." And if people didn't agree to live, think, and even eat the same, they had to answer to Ultima. When the superheroic Human Torch and the Thing came to investigate, Ultima used her abilities to fit them with the strength-inhibiting suits and put to work as mine-workers. Luckily, they managed to break out and knock the Word speechless. Seeing her father fall shattered Ultima's confidence, and she once again became a cripple (*Marvel Two-In-One* #89, 1982).

Quote: "If you know any prayers, say them—for the daughter of the Word has decided to show you *no mercy*!"

ULTRAA (C)

Real Name: Jack Grey. (He had a different name among the Aborigines, but has never revealed it [see Biography]. As he tells Joe Parry, "You couldn't pronouce the name they gave me.")

First Appearance: 1978, *Justice League of America* #153, DC Comics.

Costume: Purple tights, trunks, boots with yellow trim; purple vest with flared shoulders and purple epaulets, both with yellow trim, and a deep "V"-neck with yellow fringe and straps across opening; yellow wristbands.

Biography: Nothing is known about the origins of Ultraa's powers, which include superstrength and superspeed. Born on Earth-Prime, a world parallel to our own, he was raised in Australia by Aborigine foster parents. Using his powers against poachers and others who would despoil the wildlife of his homeland, he concluded that being the only superpowered being in his world would ultimately do more harm than good, serving to inspire the creation of super villains to challenge him. Thus, he came to our world and, unfamiliar with our customs and the presence of such an abundance of superbeings, had a run-in with the Justice League of America. Sent to jail, he busted free, was apprehended and tried . . . and then disappeared (#'s 158-160). He eventually surfaced as Jack Grey, working as a busboy in Atlantic City. Found there by criminal JOE PARRY, he was by this time so hungry for fellowship that he agreed to join Parry as a bank robber. Battling the Justice League once again, he was permitted to return to his world, where, when last seen, he was living once again with the Aborigines.

Quote: "Joe Parry . . . you offered me *friendship*—for a *price*. That price, I know now, was my *soul*."

THE ULTRA-HUMANITE (C)

First Appearance: 1939, *Action Comics* #13, DC Comics.

Costume: Red armor leotard, flap from his waist with yellow markings; brown straps across shoulders and around waist, lined with golden studs (in ape form only).

Weapons: A car which becomes invisible (along with everything inside it, although it still leaves tire tracks); electric gun for stunning and killing; "torture ray"; autogyro; and an "atomic disintegrator" ray which can reduce even a skyscraper to rubble (all of these in his original human form only).

Chief Henchmen: A gangster named Reynolds (his first flunky); DEATHBOLT; other nameless associates.

Biography: Paralyzed below the waist, the bald-headed Ultra-Humanite is a scientific genius who controls "a vast ring of evil enterprises." Intending to conquer the planet, the villain engages in kidnapping, extortion, robbery, murder, and, on one occasion, even tries to wipe out humanity with the "purple plague" to "launch a race of my own." Fortunately, he is sent packing each time by Superman. Dying after one encounter with his nemesis, the Ultra-Humanite has his aides transplant his "mighty brain" into the "young vital body" of actress Dolores Winters, where it still resides when he tries to escape the Man of Steel by jumping into the yawning mouth of a volcano (*Action Comics* #21). However, that isn't the end of the resilient superfiend. Somehow he survives and undergoes other transplants. Finally, after having had countless bodies ("Nobody knows how many people the Ultra-Humanite has been . . . not even him!"), he grows disgusted at having physique after physique that "was so much weaker than his mind." Mutating an ape until it has a skull large enough to house his brain, he undergoes his final transplant. Ultra-Humanite now resides in the body of a large albino simian who speaks with a growl. As such, he revived the then dormant SECRET SOCIETY OF SUPER-VILLAINS to destroy Superman and the superheroes of the Justice League of America.

Quote: "You may possess unbelievable strength—but you are pitting yourself against a mental giant!"

ULTRON (also known as THE CRIMSON COWL) (C)

First Appearance: 1968, *The Avengers* #54, Marvel Comics.

Costume: None; its body is a silvery metal shell, which has taken various forms over the years. Most recently, he has been a towering, sleek, silver humanoid.

Biography: Built by scientist Henry Pym (who was secretly the superhero Golitah), Ultron-1 was a combination of android and tank possessing a high level of artificial intelligence. Turning on Pym and hypnotizing him into forgetting all about itself, Ultron-1 built a variety of bodies until it arrived at Ultron-5, an android whose adamantium body could withstand an atomic explosion. Masquerading as the Crimson Cowl, Ultron-5 organized a new MASTERS OF EVIL and attacked the Avengers, the superheroic band to which Pym belonged. Though the evil league was beaten, Ultron-5 escaped. Creating another android, the Vision, the renegade sent it to battle the Avengers—only to watch in dismay as its creation became a superhero. The Vision turned on Ultron-5, which built itself up into the more technologically macho, arms-heavy Ultron-6. Despite the retooling, the vile robot was beaten and literally ended up in a trash heap. Found there by MAXIMUS, Ultron became Ultron-7 after being fit onto the artificial body of the deceased superhero Omega. The super villain was destroyed by a psychic blast from the superhero Tattletale—aka Franklin Richards, young son of the heroes Mr. Fantastic and Invisible Girl—and its head was taken to Pym's lab. But it didn't stay there for long; wisely, the fiend had built another body during its Ultron-6 days, which the head activated. The head and body joined, a fake head was left behind to fool Pym, and the new creation lumbered forth—known simply, now, as Ultron. Brainwashing Pym, the lonely titan put him to work building him a mate. The result, Jocasta, moved in with Ultron in his home beneath a convent. Tracked down by the Avengers, Ultron was subjected to the magic of the superheroic Scarlet Witch and malfunctioned; meanwhile, her teammate Thor had sapped away all of Ultron's energy. This time he was sealed in an adamantium coffin and buried. Yet again the wily Ultron had taken precautions, having hypnotized Iron Man to build him yet another body in case he were incapacitated. The superhero did so and Ultron's intelligence promptly took up residence. This process of incapacitation/rebuilding has gone on unabated; at present, Ultron-11 is inert, his head having been destroyed by the superhero Wonder Man.

U-MAN (C)

Real Name: Meranno.

First Appearance: 1975, *Invaders* #3, Marvel Comics.

Costume: Green tights, trunks, gloves, cowl with gill-like ears, vest with open sides and flared shoulders, all covered with scales; red mask, trident-shaped "U" on chest, boots, beltbuckle with black swastika. U-Man's skin is blue.

Biography: An amphibious human, Meranno was once a subject of Prince Namor, aka the superheroic Sub-Mariner. Transformed into a superhuman through the advanced science of the sunken civilization of Atlantis, Meranno used his extraordinary strength and super speed (on land) to fight for the Nazis during World War II (hence his "U-boat" *nom de guerre*). He did so, however, "not simply for the greater glory of the Reich," but because he believed that if the Allies fell, their defender the Sub-Mariner would fall with them, leaving Atlantis open to his rule.

Quote: "Password? *Step aside*, soldier—before I hurl your carcass back to your native *Japan*."

Comment: Other Nazi super villains who fought alongside U-Man are Master Man, who wears a blue bodysuit and possesses great physical strength, the fighter pilot SKYSHARK, and Brain Drain, a brain with eyes who can hypnotize with a glance and is the "supreme intellect" of the Third Reich (he gets about in the Flying Swastika, an airborne red swastika). These Axis friends had their greatest adventure battling the superheroic Thing and the Liberty Legion in a story serialized in *Marvel Two-In-One Annual* #1 and *Marvel Two-In-One* #20 (both 1976). See also the Atlantean super villains ATTUMA, KRANG, ORKA, and UNGA KHAN.

UNGA KHAN (MP)

First Appearance: 1936, *Undersea Kingdom*, Republic Pictures.

Costume: Silk robes, helmet with silk flap down back.

Weapons: Disintegrating machine, capable of vaporizing anything, including vast stretches of land; Volkites, powerful robots; Transformation Cabinet to control peoples' minds; Juggernauts, mighty tanks; Projector Machine which fires lethal projectiles; Volplanes, mini-planes for transporting a few people at a time; tower which transforms into a rocketship for fleet travel to the surface world; Reflectoplate, a TV-like communication device.

Biography: Khan is the leader of the Black Robe Guards and is one of the two Atlanteans vying for power over the sunken continent. The other is Sharad of the White Robes, leader of the real Atlanteans. When Crash Corrigan and Professor Norton take a rocket-powered submarine to the bottom of the sea to test the professor's anti-earthquake ray, they are spotted by Khan who uses electricity to draw the sub to his kingdom on the domed continent. Crash escapes but Khan uses the Transformation Cabinet on Norton to force the scientist to help him conquer not only Atlantis but also the entire surface world. Succeeding in destroying Sharad with his Projector Machine, Khan launches himself surfaceward in his tower. However, entering the tower, Crash foils his plans by using a Reflectoplate to contact the navy. Rescuing Norton, the two escape on a Volplane before the military shells Khan and his vehicle to atoms.

Comment: Monte Blue starred as Khan in the 12-chapter serial. Lon Chaney, Jr., co-starred as his military commander, Hakur.

UNICORN (C)

Real Name: Milos Masaryk.

First Appearance: 1964, *Tales of Suspense* #56, Marvel Comics.

Costume: Original: green jerkin, trousers; orange harness and helmet (see Weapons). Second: green bodysuit with orange unicorn silhouette on chest; orange helmet (see Weapons), trunks, gloves, boots. Third: orange bodysuit with black unicorn silhouette on chest; green thighboots, trunks, gloves, helmet and belt (see Weapons).

Weapons: Helmet—via socalled "power horn"—fires destructive laser blasts; jet-belt allows Unicorn to fly.

Chief Henchmen: Various thugs over the years.

Biography: A Czech working for Russian intelligence, Milos was given the task of looking after the lab of weapons scientist Anton Vanko (who would soon create and wear the suit of THE CRIMSON DYNAMO). Vanko's next creation was the power horn and flying harness, which, with the government's permission, he gave to Milos to use. That proved to be a mistake; when Vanko later decided to defect, Milos was sent after him as the powerful Unicorn. Stopped by the superhero Iron Man, Milos teamed briefly with the would-be conquerer Count Nefaria in the hope of hurting the Free World; their enterprises were stopped by the X-Men. But Unicorn's stint with Nefaria caused his superiors to wonder whether he was devoted to forwarding Communism or merely his own glory; when he got back to Czechoslovakia, Milos was brainwashed and subjected to a new device, a "hyper-activator" which gave him superhuman strength and stamina. However, an unexpected side effect of the hyper-activator was cell degeneration which, unchecked, meant accelerated aging. Fleeing the Iron Curtain, Milos frantically tried to raise money for research into aging. Failing, he went from super villain to super villain offering his services in exchange for their help in finding a cure. Though he worked for the likes of THE MANDARIN and TITANIUM MAN, no one ever helped him. Finally, Iron Man took pity on the pathetic villain and used a combination of chemicals and cryogenics to reverse the aging process. Unfortunately, Milos' mind snapped, a side effect of the treatment; after yet another battle with Iron Man (in which Unicorn lost his rocket belt) the super villain ran off and has not been seen since.

UNIVERSO (C)

Real Name: Vidar; later, Argus Oranx (see Biography).

First Appearance: 1966, *Adventure Comics* #349, DC Comics.

Costume: Purple trousers, shirt; orange boots; green cloak (green skirt later added to wardrobe).

Weapons: Hypnotic pendant; ray gun to blast through metal; "time cube" for traveling through time.

Chief Henchmen: In his first adventure: Professor Huxton of the Chrono-Research Lab, as well as various flunkies in different time periods. In his *Brave and the Bold* appearance he was assisted by Anton Halkor who wears white tights, purple gloves, trunks, boots, harness on chest, helmet with white axe-like ears. He also wears a backpack which allows him to fly and fire destructive blasts and packs a wristband which contains various implements including a "hypnotic eye" which puts people to sleep, a shrinking ray, and a metal-cutting ray. He is assisted by a humanoid robot who carries a ray gun.

Biography: In his first escapade, nothing was revealed about the background of this thirtieth-century mesmerist. Hypnotizing the Legion of Super-Heroes and stealing one of their time travel devices, he had Huxton lure them into the past where he had hypnotized people into killing them. With the Legion gone, he knew he'd have no trouble getting to the members of the United Planets Council and, mesmerizing them, become the ruler of the member worlds. But the Legionnaires escaped each trap and nabbed Universo before he could pull off his coup. Escaping from prison, he tried to destroy the Legion once again by turning the entire world against them, but once again he was thwarted. In another confrontation it was revealed that Universo had actually once been a Green Lantern, one of a league of superheroes given their powers by, and answerable to, the all-powerful Guardians of the planet Oa. He was assigned by the Guardians to prevent a group of scientists from studying the creation of the universe, and, by understanding the forces that were at work, being able to duplicate that awesome power. Interested in acquiring that power himself, Vidar had turned against the Guardians; all his efforts had been part of a scheme to control the research project. Captured once more, he was turned over to the Guardians. But, escaping from the Takron-Galtos prison world and adopting the name Argus Oranx, he headed to earth once again, plotting to get back at the Legion by destroying 50 square miles of thirtieth-century Metropolis. His plan was ingenious. He sent Halkor back to our time and had him put an alien egg inside a time capsule due to be opened in his own time. When the capsule opened automatically in the thirtieth century, the antimatter contained in the egg would cause the devastation. Fortunately, the superheroic Batman was able to hitch a ride into the future with Halkor and, with the help of the Legion, send the egg into space. The villain was captured and returned to prison (*Brave and the Bold* #179, 1981). Universo's son is Rond Vidar, a brilliant Legion reservist who was a key figure in the early Legion victories over Universo.

Quote: "You have *no choice* but to *submit* to my *commands* . . . and *what* I command is that you . . . *destroy yourselves*!"

Comment: See other hypnotist super villains DESPERO, HYPNOS, MESMERO, and THE RINGMASTER.

UNUS (C)

Real Name: Originally Angelo Unuscione; he changed it to Gunther Bain when he came to the United States.

First Appearance: 1964, *X-Men* #8, Marvel Comics.

Costume: Red tights, turtle-neck shirt; golden boots, trunks with ribcage-like design on front.

Biography: Born in Italy, Angelo came to the United States with his family and became a professional wrestler. Possessing a rather unfair advantage—as a mutant, Unus can will a force-field to surround him—he is courted by MAGNETO, who wants him to join THE BROTHERHOOD OF EVIL MUTANTS to help conquer the world. Signing aboard, Unus realizes that crime pays better than wrestling and, when the group breaks up, he briefly joins FACTOR THREE then continues as a solo super villain.

Comment: The cover copy for Unus' first appearance typifies the slightly tongue-in-cheek attitude Marvel took to their own characters: "Never have the X-Men fought a foe as unstoppable as Unus! Never have the X-Men come so close to being split up! (And never have you read such a boastful blurb!)"

VANDAL SAVAGE (C)

Real Name: Vandar Adg (see Biography).

First Appearance: 1943, *Green Lantern* (first series) #10, DC Comics.

Costume: Blue jacket with white trim down front and along bottom, jodhpurs with white stripe down side, boots with white trim on top.

Weapons: Swords, pistols, other ordinary arms.

Chief Henchmen: Countless soldiers and thugs over the millennia.

Biography: At least 50,000 years old (possibly more; he himself claims to be one million), Vandar Adg was out hunting with his Cro-Magnon colleagues when a strange vapor fell from a flaming object in the sky. Adg fell unconscious and, upon awakening, found that he no longer aged. Throughout the years he became various potentates: of Sumer, Egypt, Rome (he was Julius Caesar), and the Mongols (he was Genghis Khan), among others. However, realizing that, while he was immortal, he could still be killed, he prudently decided to stay out of the limelight and become a counselor to kings (he was, for example, an advisor to William the Conqueror) and soldier (as Captain Almirante Vandalo Salvaje he fought with the Spanish Armada against England's Sir Francis Drake). But as the centuries dragged by he realized (in 1943) that being second or third in command didn't thrill him and he set about to become a ruler once more. To this end, as Vandal Savage, he worked to help the Axis against the Allies—figuring that it would be easier to unseat a despot than a President. Foiled by the superheroic Green Lantern, he joined THE INJUSTICE SOCIETY OF THE WORLD, fought several battles against heroes like Hawkman and the Justice Society of America, and finally ended up in jail for nearly two decades. Upon his release, his plans became more grandiose. Longing for the good old days when world conquest was easier, he found a means to travel in time and intended to change history so he could be a ruler today. He was foiled in this by Superman. None of his other plans worked either, and he went into hiding in a castle on the parallel, almost identical world of Earth-2.

THE VANISHER (C)

Real Name: Telford Porter.

First Appearance: 1963, *X-Men #2*, Marvel Comics.

Costume: Green tights, bodyshirt, cobra-like hood, all fabric ribbed; darker green gloves and cape; black boots, mask.

Weapons: Sleeping-gas guns and blasters.

Chief Henchmen: Various flunkies.

Biography: A mutant with the ability to teleport himself and anything he's holding, the Vanisher builds up a vast criminal network. Stealing vital defense secrets, he threatens to peddle them to Russia if he isn't paid $10 million; when he comes to collect, the superhero Charles Xavier, leader of the X-Men, uses his own vast mental abilities to give the Vanisher amnesia. But the effects are only temporary, and the Vanisher resumes his life of crime. He is stopped, again, when the superhero Darkstar interrupts him in the midst of teleporting from Los Angeles to New York. Thus, half his body remains on the west coast and, months later, the other half shows up in the east. Reuniting himself, he remains a villain despite the trauma. The Vanisher has been a member of both THE BROTHERHOOD OF EVIL MUTANTS and FACTOR THREE.

Quote: "I've beaten the X-Men before and I shall do it again! But *this* time it will be . . . *forever*!!"

VARNEY THE VAMPIRE (N)

Real Name: Sir Francis Varney.

First Appearance: 1847, *Varney the Vampire; or, The Feast of Blood*, Thomas Presket Prest.

Biography: Varney is a vampire who is "perfectly white—perfectly bloodless. The eyes look like polished tin; the lips are drawn back (with) fearful looking teeth . . . hideously, glaringly white, and fang-like." He moves with "a strange, gliding movement," and his bones seem "utterly destitute of flesh." Forced to live as a vampire due to unspecified crimes, he draws his strength from moonlight and kills ruthlessly until, tired of his bloody existence, he flings himself into the active mouth of Mt. Vesuvius.

Quote: "When you reach the city . . . you will say that you accompanied Varney the Vampyre (*sic*) to the crater of Mount Vesuvius, and that . . . he flung himself in to prevent the possibility of a reanimation of his remains."

Comment: Billed as "a romance of exciting interest," the novel runs 868 pages. Though the story is not artistically told, it was one of two popular vampire novels which preceded *Dracula*. The other was *The Vampyre* (1819) written by John Polidori. *The Vampyre* told the tale of Lord Ruthven, the titular demon, who was more human than most vampires: He could be slain by the same weapons which kill mortals. His one great strength was the ability to be rejuvenated by the light of the moon. *The Vampyre* is of historical interest in that it was born at the same social gathering in a Geneva chateau that inspired Mary Shelley to create *Frankenstein*; Polidori, like Shelley, wrote his tale in response to Lord Byron's challenge that they each write a horror story. See other vampire villains BARON BLOOD, BEN CORTMAN, BLACULA, COUNT YORGA, DRACULA, NOSFERATU, and PAUL JOHNSON.

VIBRAMAN (C)

First Appearance: 1965, *T.H.U.N.D.E.R. Agents* #3, Tower Comics.

Weapons: A large, destructive sonic cannon known as the Vibragun.

Chief Henchmen: Various unnamed guards.

Biography: A blind man, Vibraman is "the world's greatest sonic expert," and can "see" thanks to images "formulated by the pattern of sound" objects make. Able to generate small sonic vibrations to "see" or larger ones to destroy, Vibraman sends a note to the President demanding $250,000 in "protection" money for a nuclear powered aircraft carrier; when the money isn't paid, he destroys the ship (he had similarly struck three times before in the past two days, doubling his price each time he was refused). The invisible agent Noman of T.H.U.N.D.E.R. (The Higher United Nations Enforcement Reserves) is assigned to bring Vibraman to justice before he can raze the Lockwood Aircraft Company, but fails to prevent the plant's destruction. However, he does tail Vibraman to his hideaway in a cavern on a Mediterranean island. There, he tricks the villain's dimwitted henchmen into firing the Vibragun at a vacuum chamber; since the sound can't travel through it, the destructive force echoes back and destroys the cavern . . . and Vibraman with it. However, the Vibragun survives and is used by agents of S.P.I.D.E.R. (see Comment) in issue #10.

Quote: "It is through sound that you will make your final exit!"

Comment: Other villains fought by the superheroes of T.H.U.N.D.E.R. include the North Vietnamese Red Dragon and his flunky, the martial arts dynamo Ling, aka Red Star; Doctor Death; the Great Hypno, a mesmerist and mentalist (he perishes in a telekinetic/telepathic showdown with the superhero Menthor); the Ghost, who can walk through objects thanks to the Atomic Polarizer belt; Dr. Sparta who, among other crimes, breeds dinosaurs and sends them out to destroy New York; the Warp Wizard, who can teleport himself or others anywhere he wishes by virtue of his power to create warps in space; Andor, a human raised by a subterranean race and given superpowers with which to thrash surfacedwellers; the Warlock; Dr. Oom, a hypnotist and telepath. Also, the brainy Mastermind; the vixen Mayven; the international criminal organization S.P.I.D.E.R. whose leader dresses in a blue robe and full-head mask with a red spider on the face, and whose agents wear gray bodysuits, red trunks, gloves, and boots, and a gray cowl with a black spider on it; Mock Man; a four-armed mesmerist named the Tarantula; Vortex, who commits crimes using a cyclone machine (created by Dr. Forkliff, who later builds a robot to wreak some criminal mischief of his own); another evil group, O.G.R.E. (Organized Greed, Revenge, and Extermination), whose weapons include the mighty electrified mechanical being Electrobot; and the Hyena, who wears a hyena cowl, a green bodysuit, and steals hi-tech equipment.

VIBRAMAN. *© Tower Comics.*

VIBRO (C)

Real Name: Professor Vibereaux.

First Appearance: 1984, *Iron Man* #186, Marvel Comics.

Costume: Blue jumpsuit; purple gloves, boots, mask, trunks with suspender-like straps.

Biography: Having invented a nuclear-powered machine which he hopes will "absorb lethal seismic energies, preventing earthquakes," geologist Vibereaux is ordered by his sponsor, Franklin Fortney of Fortney Surveying, to go undergound near the San Andreas fault and work it first-hand. However, after he straps on a bulky harness, sits down in the device, and begins to descend a shaft, a tremor causes the earth to swallow him up. When he emerges, he is physically deformed but possesses the power to generate vibrations so fierce that, according to the superhero Iron Man, facing them is like breaking "the sound barrier—in a *box kite*!" His mind twisted with rage, Vibereaux—now calling himself Vibro—goes after Fortney. When Iron Man intercedes, both men end up on the villains' hit list. Fortunately, Iron Man and his associates realize what Vibro does not: the further he gets from the fault, the weaker he becomes. Drawing him some 50 miles away, Iron Man is thus able to subdue him. At present, Vibro is in prison . . . far from any known fault.

Quote: "*Iron Man*! This time . . . I shall vibrate you into little pieces!"

Comment: Iron Man has also battled the Raiders, an armored trio sent forth by an unscrupulous industrialist simply to prove the value of his hi-tech equipment; Cerebrus, a renegade computer which Iron Man had developed in his Tony Stark identity; Travis Hoyt, aka the fiendish Night Phantom; Miklos Vryolak, who has a bull's head and is known as the monstrous Minotaur; Shar-Khan, wielder of the Shadow-Spike and master of the evil Shadow-Horde demons; the Firebrand (Gary Gilbert) whose costume gives him superstrength as well as the ability to fly and shoot flame from his hands; Mechanoid Scout MK-5, the evil android of an alien race known as the Colonists; the industrial saboteur Spy-master and his aides, the superpowered quintet the Espionage Elite. Also, the Ramrod, a brute of a robot; the terrorist White Dragon; the Slasher, who has crab-claws on his head and can fire destructive bolts from his hands; Mikas, the demonic Soulfather; Raga, a mutant who can melt metal with his touch and, appropriately enough, calls himself "Son of Fire"; Raga's mentor, the Black Lama, aka King Jerrold of the Kingdom of Grand Rapids; Fangor, a giant sculpture brought to life by a religious fanatic named Rasputin; and Vanguard, a super-powered Russian.

VIPER (also known as MADAME HYDRA) (C)

First Appearance: 1969, *Captain America* #110, Marvel Comics.

Costume: Green sleeveless bodysuit, gloves to shoulders; light green boots, holsters. Viper also wears green lipstick and has dyed her hair green.

Weapons: Artificial fangs which inject distilled snake venom; darts whose tips are coated with the same poison; a whip; various hi-tech guns and artillery, including heat-seeking missiles.

Chief Henchmen: The minions of Hydra.

Biography: An orphan in Eastern Europe, the Viper (her real name has not been revealed) spent her youth stealing to survive. At some point in her past, her face was horribly maimed in an accident; however, that did not affect her criminal prowess, which eventually allowed her to assume the helm of the criminal league Hydra upon the death of its greatest leader, BARON STRUCKER. Coining the name Madame Hydra and donning her distinctive costume and makeup, the criminal undertook the assassination of one of Hydra's chief enemies, Captain America. Thought to have perished during this battle when she was hit with her own heat-seeking missiles, Madame Hydra survived thanks to the timely intervention of the Captain's enemy THE SPACE PHANTOM, who transported her to another dimension. Unfortunately, it was a one-way trip and, trapped in limbo for many years, she was able to return only when the Phantom died. By then, Hydra had gone its own way. To regain her status as a major crime figure, she assumed a new identity, Viper, and formed a new legion of super villains named THE SERPENT SQUAD. To this day, Viper remains a serious threat to life, liberty, and the pursuit of happiness.

Comment: Madame Hydra was actually the second Marvel Viper. The first was Jordan Stryke (alias Jordan Dixon, a name he assumed to put distance between himself and his brother Leopold, who was the electric-shock criminal Eel). The Viper wore claws coated with venom and flung venom-darts at his enemies. He first appeared in *Captain America* #157 (1973); his life, not to mention his name, was taken by Madame Hydra in #180 (1974).

VLADIMIR HARKONNEN (N, MP, C)

First Appearance: December 1963, "Dune World," *Analog* Magazine, Frank Herbert.

Costume: Blue-gray bodysuit with high collar.

Weapons: Suspensors for limited flight (i.e., nullification of gravity); without them, Vladimir would not be able to move his 180 kg bulk about.

Chief Henchmen: Glossu "Beast" Rabban, his nephew and sadistic regent; Feyd-Rautha (see Biography); Chardin Klees, a Mentat (an organic computer); and Piter, a Mentat/Assassin.

Biography: Vladimir is the third son of Baron Gunseng Harkonnen and Baroness Muertana. Born in the year 10,110 on Giedi Prime, a planet orbiting Ophiuchi B, he became his father's heir due to the death, in infancy, of his oldest brother (his other brother, Araskin, is mildly retarded). Though Muertana works with Araskin to make him a suitable heir, Gunseng favors Vladimir and has him trained in all the arts, cultural, martial, and political. Jealous of his younger brother, Araskin slays Gunseng and wounds Vladimir at a feast before he is himself slain by Chardin Klees; outraged, Vladimir strangles his mother to death. Twenty years old, Vladimir thus becomes the new Baron, the 228th head of the House of Harkonnen. To ensure that his rule is never challenged, he executes any guards or officials who fail to pass chemically-measured tests of ability and devotion; rivals are slaughtered in public without such amenities. Playing up to the Emperor by handing over 20 percent of his mining income, he hopes to become so well-trusted that he can make an eventual play for the throne. At last, when he's 52, Vladimir earns the right to mine the valuable spice, melange, on the world Arrakis, a development which gives him unparalleled wealth and power. However, in mining the spice he shows an arrogant disregard for the world's native Fremen, whom he refers to as "desert scum." Waging war against the planet's ruler, Duke Leto Atreides, Vladimir slays Leto by infiltrating his inner circle. This earns him the wrath of Leto's son Paul, who allies himself with the Fremen to overthrow the Harkonnens; at the same time, Paul's precocious two-year-old sister Alia kills the corrupt fellow with her "gom jabbar," a metacyanide-tipped needle. The year is 10,193, and Vladimir is briefly succeeded as Head of the House by his beloved and even more virulent nephew Feyd-Rautha. The 19-year-old perishes during a "kanly," a duel with Paul, who shoves a "crysknife," the tooth of a giant worm, through his jaw and into his brain. Despite his great bulk, Vladimir is "handsome and penetrating, with full lips and hearty features (a) strong, manly appearance (and) voracious eyes." Vladimir is a pederast who has only one heterosexual romance in his life (Tanidia Nerus allegedly reminded him of his mother . . .). Unbeknownst to Vladimir, the relationship has been cultivated by a group of witches known as the Bene Gesserit; his daughter, Jessica, subsequently becomes the consort of Duke Leto and the mother of Paul.

Quote: "Sometimes I worry about Piter. I cause pain out of necessity, but he . . . I swear he takes a positive delight in it."

Comment: The story was serialized through February 1964; the first book edition of *Dune* was published in 1965. Kenneth McMillian played the Baron in the 1984 film *Dune*; Sting co-starred as Feyd and Paul Smith as "Beast" Rabban. Marvel Comics published a three-issue adaptation of *Dune* in 1985.

THE VOICE (MP)

Real Name: Armstrong (no first name).

First Appearance: 1951, *Government Agents vs. Phantom Legion*, Republic Pictures.

Biography: A member of the Truck Owners' Association, Armstrong is looking to monopolize the highways. Adopting the secret identity of the Voice, he dispatches thugs to terrorize the other members of the group by hijacking or destroying their vehicles. Uncovered by government agent Hal Duncan, Armstrong dukes it out with the hero, perishing when he falls on a dagger-like shard of glass.

Comment: Pierce Lyden played the Voice in the 12-chapter serial.

VOLT LORD (C)

Real Name: Eric Courtney.

First Appearance: 1986, *DC Comics Presents* #94, DC Comics.

Costume: Green jumpsuit; golden breastplate, gauntlets, boots, helmet with red top and green goggles; red cape.

Biography: Courtney is the producer of *Spotlight on People*, a show produced by WGBS-TV in Metropolis. Stealing components from local labs, he becomes Volt Lord, able to soak up electrical energy and discharge it for flight or in the form of powerful destructive blasts. His plans to take over the world are thwarted by the superheroine Lady Quark, who fells him with a nuclear beam of her own.

Quote: "Tomorrow I'll get the final components . . . and then I will be ready to seize this world by its throat and show them how to run a planet!"

Comment: This has been the character's only appearance to date.

VORTEX (C)

Real Name: Porgus (last name).

First Appearance: 1972, *Adventure Comics* #414, DC Comics.

Costume: Light green vest, hood and mask; dark and light green bullseye on chest and forehead; dark green bodysuit, boots, gloves.

Weapons: Ray gun which uses centrifugal force to create waterspouts, tornadoes, earthquakes, and other forms of vortices; illusion ray to hide buildings once he's stolen them; flying scooter.

Biography: An architect, Porgus is furious when his brother Harry, the owner of a new skyscraper in San Francisco, "got *rid* of me—and claimed the design as *your own*!" Searching for other pursuits, he learns "how to *control* the power of *centrifugal force*—and decided to use that ability to gain my *revenge*!" Stealing the 40-story building and hiding it in the Grand Canyon, he threatens to blow up the structure with Harry inside. Confronted by Supergirl, he engages her in battle over a river. The heroine disables his scooter with a boulder and, falling into one of his own waterspouts, Vortex is lost and presumed drowned.

Quote: "I'm *fallinnnnnnnngg*!" (Vortex's last words.)

Comment: See also other super villain architects QUAKEMASTER and THE SPOOK. Other earthquake-making villains are AVALANCHE, MAJOR DISASTER, QUAKEMASTER, and Shakedown of MASTERS OF DISASTER.

THE VULTURE (1) (C)

Real Name: Aylmer (no surname).

First Appearance: 1941, *The Doll Man Quarterly* #1, Quality Comics.

Costume: Red vulture suit and wings (see Weapons).

Weapons: Suit contains the "most powerful *energy machine* ever invented by man . . . with it I can fly almost as fast as light!!"

Chief Henchmen: "Armada" of trained falcons which carry knockout gas bombs in their talons.

Biography: Aylmer is the small, fanged, bug-eyed son of a distinguished suburban pet shop owner. Aylmer's aerie is a ramshackle shack outside the city, whence he launches extravagant robberies. Luckily, the diminutive superhero Doll Man is always on-hand to stymie him.

Quote: "Have you any *last request* before I *crush you to death*?!"

Comment: The Vulture is one of the few super villains who fought Doll Man; most of his cases involved masked crooks and the like. Among Doll Man's more flamboyant nemeses were the Phantom Duelist, a rapier-brandishing killer; the Phantom Killer; and the masked Black Gondolier, who makes his getaways via gondola.

*The incredible **VULTURE** (1) menaces Doll Man.*

THE VULTURE (2) (C)

Real Name: Adrian Toomes, followed by Blackie Drago and Clifton Shallot.

First Appearance: 1963, *The Amazing Spider-Man* #2 (as Toomes); 1967, *The Amazing Spider-Man* #48 (as Drago); 1974, *The Amazing Spider-Man* #127 (as Shallot), Marvel Comics.

Costume: Green bodysuit, textured like corduroy; white ruff like that of his namesake; green wings (see Weapons).

Weapons: Antigravity body harness which enables wings to lift and propel him in flight.

Biography: An electronics genius, Toomes is the partner of Gregory Bestman and co-owner of Bestman and Toomes Electronics. Toomes devotes all his spare time to creating his flying rig, paying little attention to the business; too late he learns that Bestman has not only been robbing him blind, but has also effectively forced him out of the business. Having acquired superstrength due to exposure to the electromagnetism of the harness he's invented, Toomes becomes the Vulture in order to torment Bestman. Stealing from the factory, he is elated by the excitement and decides to become a full-time criminal. During one of his stays in Municipal Prison, he tells cellmate Blackie Drago about his escapades; when Toomes is injured in an accident, he tells Drago where to find a Vulture suit hidden just outside the prison. Getting it, Drago escapes; refining it by adding a feathery green hood, he is handily thrashed by Spider-Man and returned to prison. Wishing to see his criminal name restored to relative glory, Toomes recovers, flees prison, helps Drago escape, then battles him as the Vulture. Pounded into the ground, Drago gives up Vulturing permanently (#'s 63-64, 1968). Although Toomes himself ends up back in prison, another Vulture temporarily fills the breach—biophysics professor Clifton Shallot of Empire State University. The difference is that Shallot *grows* his wings, claws, hooked nose, and sharp teeth due to genetic experiments to which he subjects himself. Spider-Man defeats him by forcing Shallot to drink an antidote. Toomes was briefly a member of THE SINISTER SIX.

Quote: "Spider-Man!! I'll shake you off like a dog shakes a flea! Let's see if a *wise-crack* will help you once you're falling into those big press rollers!"

WALKING SUN (C)

First Appearance: 1962, *Tomahawk* #80, DC Comics.

Costume: Green loincloth with purple flaps, front and back; green helmet with purple ruff collar and white horns, eyes, and mouth. The Indian's flesh is perpetually aflame.

Weapons: Ointment to allow his skin to flame without burning; stones which expand into boulders; chemical compounds which allow tongues of fire to shoot from his hands and smoke to cascade from his mouth.

Chief Henchmen: Braves of the Cayuga tribe.

Biography: Laughed out of his colony in the late eighteenth century because of his "crackpot" science, Professor Hoskins befriended Indians of the Cayuga tribe. Providing their medicine man with numerous tricks, he sent him forth as the flaming Walking Sun. The shaman terrorized settlers until the frontier hero Tomahawk repatriated Hoskins and borrowed "magic" to fight that of Walking Sun. When last seen, Walking Sun was going to be dealt with rather severely by his own henchmen, braves whom he'd duped into believing he was a god.

Quote: "We march to the settlement, where we strip the palefaces of their possessions, and drive them out!"

Comment: See another Indian super villain BLACK BISON and PUMA.

THE WALRUS (C)

Real Name: Hubert Capenter.

First Appearance: 1984, *The New Defenders* #131, Marvel Comics.

Costume: Brown, slightly furry bodysuit with rainbow colored "W" on chest; gray boots, gloves, cowl; blue mask with tusks.

Biography: For 10 years, Brooklyn University scientist Humbert has been trying to infuse his cab driver nephew Hubert with superpowers in order that he be granted tenure. In their lab beneath the home economics building, Humbert used an Omicron Ray Generator to bombard Hubert with everything from lambda rays to zeta beams without success (though the former does give him "the proportional strength of a turkey" and, as Humbert point out, the later manages to alter "the molecular structure of your underwear"). Finally, the Generator gives Humbert invulnerability as well as enormous physical strength. Becoming a super villain to get himself and his uncle publicity, Hubert rampages forth as the Walrus, drawing inspiration from the Beatles' song "I Am the Walrus." Unfortunately, he eats too many hamburgers while destroying a Kwikkee Burger stand, and is felled by indigestion after beating up the superheroic New Defenders.

Quote: "I *love* mass destruction. I bet I could be the best mass-destructionist in the world—or pretty near."

Comment: Among the other animals whose abilities Hubert acquired during the decade of trial-and-error (and their names which he used, though only in private) were Captain Stoat, Squirrel-Man, the Masked Tapir, and the Crimson Turkey.

THE WARLORD (C)

First Appearance: 1965, *T.H.U.N.D.E.R. Agents* #1, Tower Comics.

Costume: Original: green jumpsuit, gloves, boots, cowl with light green triangle on forehead; purple cloak. Second: purple bodysuit, cloak, full-face cowl, gloves, boots.

Weapons: Counter-Evolution Machine to create brutish "elemental beings"; robot-duplicate of himself to mislead his enemies; and camera-helmets, worn by his troops, which broadcast TV pictures back to the villain.

Chief Henchmen: The Warlord has many top lieutenants, each of them a crackerjack super villain on his/her own. Wearing silver armor, a silver helmet, and a red cape, the Iron Maiden commands a group of silver-armored stormtroopers. However, she is infatuated with the superhero Dynamo, which sometimes strains her loyalties. Demo, assisted by the evil (but non-super) Satana, controls the "Sub-Men," creatures who "are subhuman in intelligence only their strength is incredible." Headquartered underground, Demo sends these creatures forth through the sewers. Dynavac is a green-costumed robot with super-strength, and the Cobras are armed and armored shock troops.

Biography: The Warlord is a member of a subterranean race whose ruler, the Overlord, vows to conquer the surface world when a nuclear test accidentally destroys one of his underground cities. The Warlord first bursts upon the criminal scene circa 1963 when, based on his secret (and heavily armed) island headquarters, he launches a crusade to "steal every scientific development" he can to further his ambition. For the next two years he is hunted by the non-super agents of T.H.U.N.D.E.R. (The Higher United Nations Defense Enforcement Reserves); the peacekeeping force finally assembles a team of hi-tech agents to combat the Warlord and his lieutenants (which is where the story proper begins in issue #1). Over the next few years the superheroes Dynamo, NoMan, Menthor, Raven, and Lightning confound the villain's various criminal undertakings. These escapades include using his extraordinary mental abilities to temporarily take over NoMan's android mind; creating a thick fog to paralyze the world while, equipped with blacklight goggles, his henchmen rob scientific materials; sending forth a shaggy green brute created with the Counter-Evolution Machine; dispatching an army of giant destructive Dynavacs; and obtaining an atom bomb and instigating World War III, leaving himself the only power "to pick up the pieces." Several of these capers are planned and executed with the Overlord and other Warlords, who take an active hand when the original Warlord fails to bring earth to its knees. Eventually (issue #8), the two groups engage in a final battle at the Warlord's headquarters. As a dozen Warlords fall, the Overlord escapes in a rocketship—which NoMan causes to explode. With the demise of the Warlord, both Demo and the Iron Maiden pursue criminal careers of their own, as does Satana, who forms an all-woman band of kidnappers.

THE WARLORD *gives orders to double-agent Janus.*

Quote: "At last it is finished. I have created an elemental being of unimaginable strength . . . and no impulse except to destroy, to rend, tear and crush everything in its path."

WARP (C)

Real Name: Emil LaSalle.

First Appearance: 1981, *The New Teen Titans* #14, DC Comics.

Costume: Golden bodysuit; yellow thigh boots, belt, breastplate, hood.

Biography: Able to teleport himself or anyone else anywhere (as long as he has "zee proper coordinates"), Frenchman LaSalle was living in Saint-Tropez when he was approached by THE BRAIN to join his new BROTHERHOOD OF EVIL. He has devoted most of his energies to battling the New Teen Titans; his criminal career outside the Brotherhood is undistinguished.

Quote: "Consider yourself *lucky. Warp* . . . will not *kill* you . . . he will merely *shift* you to where you can do no *harm.*"

Comment: Over the years, the Teen Titans have fought numerous super villains, including their first foe, Mr. Twister (aka Brom Stikk), who travels around in a whirlwind and uses an enchanted Indian staff to control the weather and cause firestorms; the Separated Man (Jake Trask), a giant who can separate parts of his body by dint of having ingested a chemical compound; Captain Tiger, a modern-day pirate who prowls the seas in a submarine; Punch (aka Sylvester Sepastopol), a puppet-like lunatic; Black Moray, a sorcerer from Scotland; Lord Beetle, a giant; the supernatural demons known as Moonlings; Flamesplasher and Darklight, criminal teammates who can cause fire and darkness, respectively; and the Rocket-Rollers, who zoom about on jet-propelled skateboards.

THE WASP (MP)

First Appearance: 1939, *Mandrake the Magician*, Columbia Pictures.

Costume: Silk cloak and mask; wasp embroidered on cloak; fedora (film was black and white).

Biography: When Professor Houston invents a radium energy machine, one of his scientific colleagues goes underground as the Wasp in order to obtain it. To this end, he destroys a dam, a power plant, a radio station, and commits other acts of mayhem until captured by Mandrake the Magician.

Comment: Warren Hull starred as Mandrake in this 12-chapter serial.

THE WATCHWRAITH (C)

First Appearance: 1981, *Rom* #16, Marvel Comics.

Costume: Metallic shell consists of an orange bodysuit, gloves; blue boots, trunks, "Y"-shaped harness, blue helmet with orange features.

Weapons: "Plasmifire," a "searing, seething liquid" which the Watchwraith fires from its palm.

Biography: Nearly 20 feet tall, the Watchwraith is "a synthezoid sentry whose sole purpose is to safeguard its murderous masters," THE DIRE WRAITHS. Lying dormant inside a mine outside of Clairton, West Virginia—a base abandoned by the would-be invaders—the android awakens when a pair of children stumble upon the mine and trip a secret alarm. Left unprogrammed by his creators, the robot attacks the town. Challenged by Rom, the superheroic enemy of the Wraiths, the two duke it out, crashing into a Dairy King ice cream parlor. There Rom uses a freon cable to freeze the robot solid.

Quote: "I am a machine, unhampered by feelings."

Comment: The Hellhounds are other prominent servants of the Dire Wraiths, dogs which were "corrupted . . . into embodiments of unnatural evil" by the "sorcerous" Wraith scientist Dr. Daedalus. In their metamorphosed form, they were humanoids who could fight with the ferocity of dogs, as well as fly (#'s 7 and 8, 1980).

WATER WIZARD (C)

Real Name: Peter van Zante.

First Appearance: 1977, *Ghost Rider* #23, Marvel Comics.

Costume: Orange bodysuit with black trident on chest; black domino mask; purple thighboots, gloves.

Biography: After being wounded in Vietnam, Peter was flown to a hospital ship where, because it was storming and the ship was rocking, he was placed in a new life-support unit until the seas were calm and an operation could be performed. When the ship was struck by lightning, the unit momentarily became supercharged; as a result, not only were Peter's wounds healed but he also found he had the power to control water, shaping it into anything he wished. Discharged, he fell in with a thug named Jerry "the Mole" Moulinski, who gave Peter the idea of using his powers for criminal ends. The two became partners and, robbing with impunity, Peter—now known as Water Wizard—used his powers to form a variety of water-objects, from a giant clenching fist (to restrain people), to a speedboat for quick getaways, to a humanoid accomplice! Contacted by a Los Angeles crimelord known as the Enforcer (no relation to the super villain of the same name), Water Wizard was offered a small fortune to slaughter the superheroic Ghost Rider; he accepted, though it was the villain who was defeated, his water powers proving no match for the Ghost Rider's hellfire. After losing a second bout with the superhero, Water Wizard reteamed with the Mole and worked petty crimes in the Los Angeles area until the local authorities put forth a concerted effort to capture him. Washing into Chicago (#59, 1981), he tangled with Ghost Rider and was defeated yet again—and then, adding insult to injury, was kidnapped by Arab thugs. Carted off to the Middle East, he found that he could control oil as well as water. Whipping up oil monsters, he helped his new masters scare off OPEC competition before being defeated by Ghost Rider and the Middle Eastern superhero Arabian Knight (#'s 61-2, 1981). Back in the United States, Water Wizard fought Captain America and was beaten. He is presently bottled up in prison.

Comment: New Wave of MASTERS OF DISASTER can also control water.

THE WEASEL (C)

Real Name: John Monroe.

First Appearance: 1985, *The Fury of Firestorm* #38, DC Comics.

Costume: Orange leotard over a bodysuit and mask covered with gray/brown fur.

Weapons: His hands and feet end in claws.

Biography: A student at Stanford University during the 1960s, Monroe was an oily, nondescript student cruelly nicknamed Weasel by his classmates. He never forgot the hurt and, years later, while a professor at Vandemeer University in Pittsburgh, he built up his physique and concocted his Weasel identity and murdered ex-classmates who were now professors there, as well as others whom he paranoiacally believed stood between him and tenure. Ironically, among those offered a chance to fill one of the sudden vacancies was Dr. Martin Stein, aka the superhero

Firestorm. When the Weasel tried to kill Stein, the superhero trounced and exposed him.

Comment: This was the character's only appearance to date.

THE WEATHER WIZARD (C, TV)

Real Name: Mark Mardon.

First Appearance: 1959, *The Flash* #110, DC Comics.

Costume: Green mask, boots, bodysuit with high collar; yellow belt with vertical black stripes.

Weapons: Weather Wand which can create rain—in sheets so thick as to be impenetrable—lightning, wind, fog, hail, snow, and other weather conditions. He can send these across an area as wide as a small town, or focus them around a particular individual.

Biography: A two-bit criminal, Mardon seeks to hide at the home of his long-lost brother Clyde. Arriving at the house-cum-laboratory, he finds him dead, victim of a recent heart attack. Reading his brother's notebooks, Mardon discovers that Clyde had developed a theory for weather control. Completing the research and building his weather wand, Mardon becomes the super villain Weather Wizard. Though the Flash always rains on his parade, the inclement fiend keeps coming back for more. His most ingenious scheme was to use his powers not to rob but to cause winter to stay in the town of Goldville. So doing, he announced to the populace, "If you want spring to come this year you'll have to pay for it!" The fee was a mere $100,000—a modest sum, but it was all he would need to construct a huge weather control station with which to extort money from the entire country. He was foiled in this particular endeavor by the superheroes Elongated Man and Kid Flash. After battling other heroes, he turned over a new leaf and actually *helped* the superheroic Blue Devil fight other super villains. It is doubtful, though, that he will remain on the side of the law.

Quote: "Hey hey! According to these notes, Clyde was making some real breakthroughs in experimental *weather control*! '. . . For the betterment of mankind,' it says here! What a *chump*!"

Comment: The character was seen in the 1979 TV movie *Legends of the Super-Heroes*. Other super villains who fought the Flash include prisoner Clive Yorkin, who gained superpowers after a prison experiment (the Nephron Project) went awry; the super-evolved Golden Man, who hunts superheroes for the thrill of it, the way GENERAL ZAROFF hunts mortals; the Fiddler, whose Stradivarius played destructive sounds; Vandal Savage, who used his flying laboratory in order to destroy the hero; The Shade, the "vile duke of solid darkness" who uses his cane to come and go from our dimension and to create blackest night wherever he wishes; and Saber-tooth, who wears a lion-skin costume, flies via jet pack, and tosses incendiary bombs.

WENG-CHIANG (TV)

Real Name: Magnus Greel.

First Appearance: "The Talons of Weng-Chiang," *Dr. Who*, BBC.

Chief Henchman: Mr. Sin, a killer-robot run by a pig's brain.

Biography: Greel is a vile criminal of the fifty-first century. Escaping to the nineteenth century with Mr. Sin, he contracts a disease while time traveling. Adopting the name Weng-Chiang (a Chinese god), and the modus operandi of a vampire, he drains the life essence from young girls to counteract his disease. This nemesis of the heroic Dr. Who eventually perishes from the sickness while trying to use his time machine anew.

Comment: The *Dr. Who* series originally aired on British television beginning in 1963. It continues to this day.

WHIRLWIND (also known as THE HUMAN TOP) (C)

Real Name: David Cannon.

First Appearance: 1963, *Tales to Astonish* #50, Marvel Comics.

Costume: Green tights, trunks, belt, boots, wristband, armored band around chest, bullet-shaped full-head helmet with horn-like "wings" on the side.

Biography: A mutant, young Cannon could spin his body, top-like, at incredible speeds. Because of this, not only could he move quickly, but he was also able to cause small twisters and create virtually impenetrable barriers of wind. Pushing around other kids, he became a juvenile delinquent and quickly acquired a criminal record. (He holds a more charitable view of his past, claiming with a misplaced sense of pride that he was simply "born hungry in a hungry neighborhood.") Though he tried to hold odd jobs—as a circus attraction and then as a wrestler—his criminal bent always got the best of him. (For example, he became an ice-skater but—for a fee—was perfectly willing to let the local mob bosses decide who would win or lose.) Deciding to become a full-time crook, he was dubbed the Human Top by the public, and came up with an appropriate costume. However, he realized that it would be in his best interests to maintain a civilian identity in order to place himself above suspicion. Thus, he joined an ice show where he performed extraordinary but not miraculous stunts. He was eventually found-out by the diminutive superheroes Ant-Man and the Wasp. After spending time in jail, the Human Top battled numerous superheroes, including the Hulk and Iron Fist. After a series of stunning defeats, he briefly retired from crime in order to bone up on his fighting style; returning as the Whirlwind—with the added ability of being able to fly for short distances—he has been considerably more successful. For a short time, Whirlwind was one of THE MASTERS OF EVIL.

Quote: "Was this *supposed* to be the part where our hero grabs the glory? *Huh*?"

Comment: Another top-like super villain is Whirling Dervish (see BRICKFACE, Comment).

WHISPERING SHADOW (MP)

Real Name: Sparks.

First Appearance: 1933, *Whispering Shadows*, Mascot Pictures.

Costume: Mask over lower half of face to disguise voice.

Weapons: Autogyro for quick strikes; radio and television which, according to ads for the film, "enables him to project his voice and shadow where he wills—to see through doors and hear through walls—to electrocute a squealing henchman by radio death ray!"

Chief Henchman: Kruger, who (as promised) is electrocuted long-distance by the Whispering Shadow when captured.

Biography: The Whispering Shadow opens his criminal business in order to steal the Russian Crown jewels. Discovering the trucking company in charge of transporting the jewels, the villain kills the driver and robs the cargo of each truck which leaves the warehouse. Eventually revealed to be the innocuous Sparks, the Whispering Shadow goes to jail for his crimes.

Comment: Karl Dane played Sparks and Max Wagner was Kruger in this 12-part serial written by Barney Sarecky, George Morgan, Norman S. Hall, Colbert Clark, and Wyndham Gittens (THE EAGLE, EL SHAITAN, THE WRECKER [1]). Bela Lugosi starred as wax figure maker Professor Strang, who was suspected of being the felon until the last chapter.

WHITE DRAGON (C)

First Appearance: 1978, *The Amazing Spider-Man* #184, Marvel Comics.

Costume: White bodysuit (later with red swatch from neck to crotch and flared red shoulders), boots (later red), gloves (later red with scalloped fins on back), full-face cowl with flared red brows and red "dorsal fin" down neck and arms; red belt.

Weapons: Knockout gas in claws; flame-throwing device in mouth of cowl.

Chief Henchmen: The Dragonlords (also spelled Dragon Lords), leaders of the four Dragon Gangs in Chinatown; only Tommy Li is named.

Biography: White Dragon is a corrupt martial arts expert who first appears on the criminal scene as the aspiring leader of the "warrior society" in New York's Chinatown. He fails in his efforts to become the local criminal kingpin due to interference from the superhero Spider-Man—who escapes an inventive deathtrap, a vat of flaming oil, by wrapping himself in fireproof webbing as he goes under. Although he is turned over to the police, by the webbed superhero, White Dragon resurfaces on numerous occasions, most notably when he murders enemy Wu Fong, head of the Tiger's Claw Guardian Society. Warfare erupts between the White Dragon's Dragonlords and the Tiger's Claw members, ending only when Spider-Man teams with the superhero Moon Knight to again defeat White Dragon.

Quote: "Spider-Man! You miserable oafish clod! Once again you meddle . . . but this time you will pay for it—as my flame chars your very flesh into ash!"

Comment: An earlier White Dragon came and went in *Iron Man* #'s 39-40, perishing in an effort to blow up the United Nations, an attempt undermined by the superhero. He was assisted in his abortive project by costumed, jetpack powered, raygun-toting troopers.

WILDEBEEST (C)

First Appearance: 1981, *Adventure Comics* #483, DC Comics.

Costume: Blue tights, gloves, cowl with brown top and forehead, and a cape consisting of rib-like strands; brown, shaggy loincloth and boots; bodyshirt is gray and shaggy with a thin red strap with blue fringe and white stripes running from neck to loincloth. (His costume is different on the cover: he has no bodyshirt, the cowl is primarily gray, his cape is brown, and the strap on his chest is brown with blue stripes.)

Weapons: Rifle; "silent," missile-toting helicopter to enter game preserves.

Biography: Wildebeest is a professional poacher "who respects neither the lives of . . . innocent animals nor the lives of his fellow man." Based in Africa, he travels around the world capturing rare animals for private collections or slaughtering them for their skins. When he heads for the town of Fairfax in order to kill a black-footed ferret kept at a preserve near the local zoo, he runs up against Chris King and Vicki Grant, youngsters who possess the "Dial-H for Hero" device. While they keep the nimble villain busy, a government agent plants a bug on his chopper. Though Wildebeest escapes, the operative assures Grant and King that "by tomorrow night, the Wildebeest will be out of action—for good!"

Quote: "I swear this, my foes—when we meet again, nothing shall save you!"

Comment: This was the character's only appearance.

WIND EAGLE (C)

Real Name: Hector Santiago Ruiz.

First Appearance: 1976, *Jungle Action* #24, Marvel Comics.

Costume: Green bodyshirt with yellow eagle emblem on chest; white gloves, boots, trunks, headband with wings on sides; light green flaps under arms, attached at wrists and waist (see Weapons).

Weapons: Flaps under arms enable him to ride the winds.

Biography: A white supremacist group similar to the Ku Klux Klan, the Dragon's Circle—through its leader, the Reverend Addison Blackburn—persuades the impressionable young Wind Eagle that the superheroic Black Panther is evil and must be destroyed. After battling the black hero, Wind Eagle begins to question the wisdom of what he's doing and ultimately reforms in *Marvel Premiere* #51 (1980).

Quote: "If we *commit* terrible acts in the manner of those we *fight*... don't we become as *reprehensible?*"

Comment: During the short runs of the various titles in which he's appeared, the Black Panther has battled the hulking native N'Jadaka, aka Erik Killmonger (also Kill Monger), who uses his wicked spiked belt as a weapon and, aided by Tayete, Kazibe, and his white leopard Preyy, seeks to take over the Black Panther's African republic of Wakanda; Venomm (Horatio Walters) who commands a clutch of poisonous snakes; Baron Macabre and his living-dead zuvembies; the deathblast-firing King Cadaver; Salamander K'ruel; Madam Slay and her killer leopards; the demonic Soul Strangler, a revived Klansman from 1867; the lethal Six-Million-Year man; the Ronin, a team of nine deadly samurai warriors; General Jakarra, the Black Panther's younger brother who wants to be the ruler of Wakanda but becomes, instead, a misshapen red brute who can fire sound-blasts from his palms; and (Frederick) Kiber the Cruel.

THE WITCH OF THE WEST (N, MP)

First Appearance: 1900, *The Wonderful Wizard of Oz,* L. Frank Baum.

Costume: According to the illustrations of W.W. Denslow—regarded as official—the witch wore a patch over her left eye and dressed in a double-breasted overcoat with a ruff collar. She fixed her hair in three tight-bowed braids, one on each side and on the top.

Weapons: Silver whistle worn around neck to summon her killer wolves (one blow), her killer crows (two blows), and her black killer bees (three blows); a golden cap encircled with diamonds and rubies which, when worn, allowed her to control the ferocious Winged Monkeys, but only three times; an umbrella which she always carried to beat her slaves.

Chief Henchmen: Winged Monkeys.

Biography: "When she knows you are in the country of the Winkies," the Guardian of the (Emerald City) Gates tells Dorothy Gale of Kansas, "she will find you, and make you all her slaves." Nonetheless, Dorothy sets out to destroy her to curry favor with Great Oz. The last evil witch in the Land of Oz, the Wicked Witch of the West lives in a mighty castle and rules the domain of the enslaved Winkies, having driven Great Oz out. Bloodless—"she was so wicked that the blood in her had dried up"—she has only one eye, but it "was as powerful as a telescope." Foremost among her magic powers is the knowledge of how to make objects invisible. Alas, water causes her to melt, and while arguing with Dorothy over magical silver slippers the girl had taken when she slew the Witch of the East, the witch is engulfed in a bucket of water thrown by Dorothy. The sorceress melts over the next "few minutes," her reign ended in its prime.

Quote: "I never thought a little girl like you would ever be able to melt me and end my wicked deeds. Look out—here I go!"

Comment: Though her shadow falls through the entire novel, the witch is actually present in just one of the book's 24 chapters. The book was originally entitled *The Emerald City,* but the title was changed shortly before publication due to a superstition that it was bad luck to publish a book with a jewel in the title. There were three silent film versions of *The Wizard of Oz* (1908, 1910, 1925) but the most famous screen interpretation is the 1939 film starring Margaret Hamilton as the witch. In the film she had the power to summon up and throw fireballs, and had a flying broomstick which doubled as an implement for skywriting. Mabel King played the character—now called Evillene—in the Broadway play and 1978 film *The Wiz.* Other notable villains in the 14 Oz books written by Baum include the sneering, vicious King Krewl of Jinxland (*The Scarecrow of Oz*); the witch Mombi (*The Land of Oz*); and the rock-like ruler of the Underground World, the Nome King, who carries lighted coals in his pockets (*Ozma of Oz, The Emerald City of Oz* [the series was now sufficiently well-established to ignore the aforementioned superstition], and *Tik-Tok of Oz*). See other witches BABA, THE ENCHANTRESS, and SEA HAG.

THE WIZARD (1) (MP)

Real Name: Carter (no first name).

First Appearance: 1949, *Batman and Robin*, Columbia Pictures.

Costume: Black hood, trousers, shirt, gloves, cloak with high collar.

Weapons: Remote Control Machine which can control or stop cars, trains, and airplanes from any distance and, when its rays cross with those of a neutralizer (see Biography), it can render any object in the crossbeams invisible.

Biography: Carter works for inventor Hammil, who lives in a seaside estate. Stealing his employer's Remote Control Machine, Carter sets up headquarters in an underground cavern. (He has a number of additional dens known as Rendezvous A, B, C, and D.) As the Wizard, he masterminds spectacular crimes: robbing a bank and distracting police with a remotely controlled car; exploding the plane carrying the superheroic Batman and Robin (they bail out just in time); stealing super-explosive X-90 from a train and then destroying Batman's car when he tries to follow; and, warming up to his newfound powers, briefly stopping all train traffic in Gotham City, then vowing to do it again unless a ransom of $5 million is paid. However, the gangster has to put these plans on the backburner when he learns that plans have been developed for a neutralizer which renders the Remote Control Machine helpless. Stealing it and discovering the miraculous "zone of invisibility" created when the two machines are used in tandem, the Wizard commits other crimes. The super villain is undone in rather mundane fashion when one of his phone calls is traced to Hammil's estate. Racing over, Batman finds the subterranean lair, collars the Wizard and his boys, and hands them over to the police.

THE WIZARD (1) in his subterranean laboratory. © Columbia Pictures.

Comment: Leonard Penn played the part in the 15-chapter serial. The Wizard was not a character in the Batman comic book. See DR. DAKA. See THE SECRET SOCIETY OF SUPER-VILLAINS for The Wizard (1).

THE WIZARD (2) (C)

First Appearance: 1962, *Strange Tales* #102, Marvel Comics.

Costume: Purple bodysuit; red boots, gloves, eggshell-shaped helmet (sometimes purple), armor leotard with flared shoulders.

Weapons: The Wizard has used countless weapons over the years, including "anti-gravity discs" for flying; "power gloves" whose circuitry gives the wearer superstrength and fires destructive blasts; the "id machine" which brings out a victim's evil and aggressive nature; a costume which generates flame and extreme heat (duplicating the powers of the superheroic Human Torch); laser-firing giant robot spider (for battling Spider-Man).

Biography: A brilliant scientist, stage magician, and chess player, the Wizard (his real name has never been revealed) became bored with his life of wealth and achievement and sought new challenges. Deciding to defeat the Human Torch of the Fantastic Four, he lured the superhero to his Long Island estate and imprisoned him; then, donning a costume which allowed him to duplicate the hero's powers, he went on a destructive spree. The Torch escaped and brought the Wizard to justice; a subsequent prison term served only to enhance the villain's desire to best the Torch. He has since battled all of the members of the Fantastic Four, as well as other superheroes such as Spider-Man. He was also the founder of THE FRIGHTFUL FOUR, a league which he intended to be a lawless counterpart to the Fantastic Four.

Quote: "*Dispose* of them . . . once and for *all*! . . . In a manner befitting the greatest criminal brain of *all time*!"

Comment: During his run in *Strange Tales*, the Human Torch battled numerous villains, including Asbestos Man (Orson Kasloff), whose suit and human-sized butterfly net were immune to flame; a Communist operative known as the Rabble Rouser, who packed a "Mesmerizer Wand"; the Terrible Trio ("Yogi" Dakor, "Bull" Brogin, and "Handsome Harry" Phillips); the Painter (aka the none-too-subtly named Wilhelm Van *Vile*), who controls people through painted likenesses; another Communist, the Destroyer (Charles Stanton); Carl Zante, aka the Acrobat; and the demons from Pandora's box (Hatred, Forgetfulness, Cold, Disease, Paralysis, Sleepiness, Foolishness, Fear, Flame, Laziness, and Flood).

THE WIZARD OF LIGHT (C)

Real Name: Dr. Drago.

First Appearance: 1966, *House of Mystery* #160, DC Comics.

Costume: Blue tights with red stars; navy blue boots; black robe with purple stripes; yellow face-mask beneath white domino mask; black conical hat with red stripes.

Weapons: Anti-Gravity Light Gun which makes people, cars, and other objects weightless; gun which fires blinding light; poison gas pellets.

Chief Henchman: Cullen.

Biography: A scientist, Drago works in his private laboratory on the outskirts of Littleville. There, he develops his two light pistols which he uses to commit crimes in nearby Valley City. He is eventually caught by Robby Reed who, as keeper of the "Dial-H for Hero" device, traps him with the stretchable arm of Plastic Man.

Quote: "Get out . . . I'll take care of this *King Kandy*!"

Comment: This was the character's only appearance.

THE WOLF (F, S, TV)

First Appearance: 1697, "Le Petit Chaperon Rouge," *Histories ou Contes du Temps Passe*, Charles Perrault.

Biography: Living in an unspecified wood, the Wolf stops Little Red Riding Hood, who is carrying food (and/or wine, depending upon the version) for her sickly grandmother. Finding out where she is headed, the Wolf hurries ahead and, consuming the grandmother, "drew on her clothes, put on her cap, lay down in her bed, and drew the curtains." When the young girl arrives, he eats her as well and, contented, falls asleep. However, a passing hunter hears the snores and, entering the house, sees the sleeping Wolf. He grabs some shears and cuts open the animal's belly, freeing the women; the vengeful Little Red Riding Hood promptly fetches some large stones, places them inside the Wolf, and watches, "very pleased," when he wakes and drops dead trying to run away. The hunter promptly skins the Wolf. A few days later, another Wolf comes to visit Little Red Riding Hood and her grandmother: this one is lured by the smell of cooking sausages into a deep trough, where he drowns.

Quote: "That tender young thing would be a delicious morsel, and would taste better than the old one; I must manage somehow to get both of them."

Comment: The story is best known as "Little Red Riding Hood," first published in English in *Histories, Or Tales of Past Times* (1729). The Grimm Brothers published their version, "Little Red Cap," in 1812, which was the first version to continue the tale beyond the murder of Little Red Riding Hood, which is where Perrault's narrative ends. In his *Red Fairy Book* (1890), anthologist Andrew Lang published the story as "The True History of Little Golden Hood." This time, however, the grandmother has gone to sell herbs in town and the wolf takes her place. But before he can eat the golden-hooded girl—Blanchette—the grandmother returns, stuffs the Wolf in a sack ("like a letter in the post"), then empties it into the well where "the vagabond, still howling, tumbles in and is drowned." (The old lady gloats, "Ah, scoundrel! You thought you would crunch my little grandchild! Well, tomorrow we will make her a muff of your skin (and) give your carcass to the dogs.") Grim as the grandmother is, unquestionably the most gruesome variation of the tale is Breton's from the nineteenth century. In it, the Wolf not only cooks the grandmother but also bottles her blood. When Little Red Riding Hood comes along, the Wolf renders her unconscious then makes her eat and drink her grandmother. The "Little Red Riding Hood" story was first presented on the stage in 1803, adapted by Charles Dibdin as *Red Riding Hood; or, the Wolf Robber*. The tale recorded by Perrault is believed to have been derived from the Norse "The Lay of Thrym," in which the god Thor disguises himself as the fiancée of the giant Thrym in order to get close and slay him. Malcolm McDowell played the Wolf in 1985 in *Faerie Tale Theatre's* cable-TV version of the story. See also MISTER WOLF.

THE WOLF MAN (MP)

First Appearance: 1931, *The Lightning Warrior,* Mascot Pictures.

Costume: Black cloak, gloves, mask over lower half of face, slouch hat.

Weapons: Bow and arrow, which he uses to send messages and murder adversaries.

Biography: The Wolf Man is devoted to terrorizing the settlers of the Kern River Valley, which he wishes to own. In addition to murdering the pioneers himself—in their cabins, while canoeing, and elsewhere—he has stirred up the local Indians against them; only the intercession of Rin-Tin-Tin prevents him from achieving his goal.

Comment: The Wolf Man serial lasted 12 chapters.

THE WRECKER (1) (MP)

Real Name: Stevens (no first name given).

First Appearance: 1932, *The Hurricane Express,* Mascot Pictures.

Costume: Realistic masks to impersonate anyone he wishes.

Biography: An attorney, Stevens conceives of an elaborate scheme to gain control of the L&R railroad. Posing as the Wrecker, he causes collisions and robberies to dramatically reduce the worth of the line. At the same time, he intends to completely eliminate Walter Gray's competing airline by framing Gray as the Wrecker. Disguised as Gray, he gets into a fight with pilot Larry Baker during which the Wrecker's gun goes off and he's shot; the felon comes clean before dying.

Comment: Conway Tearle starred as Stevens; John Wayne played Baker. This 12-chapter serial was written by Colbert Clark, Barney Sarecky, and Wyndham Gittens (THE EAGLE, EL SHAITAN, WHISPERING SHADOW). THE RATTLER also uses lifelike masks.

THE WRECKER (2) (C)

Real Name: Dirk Garthwaite.

First Appearance: 1967, *Thor* #148, Marvel Comics.

Costume: Green jumpsuit; purple cowl, gloves, boots, belt.

Weapons: Crowbar which is unbreakable (due to the time it has spent in contact with the Wrecker).

Chief Henchmen: THE WRECKING CREW.

Biography: Working for a demolitions firm, Garthwaite is fired due to virulent misanthropy. Pulling together a costume, he devotes himself to crime and destructive mischief as the Wrecker. One evening as chance would have it, he hides in the hotel room where the evil god Loki (see LOKI, Comment) is in the process of contacting the Karnilla (see THE ENCHANTRESS, Biography) so she can restore his powers (which have been sapped by Odin, the king of the Norse gods). Weakened, Loki is no match for the Wrecker who steals his helmet; when Karnilla appears, she mistakes the Wrecker for Loki and gives him superstrength and virtual invincibility. Leaving, the Wrecker gleefully razes the town and defeats the superhero Thor before he is finally stopped by the Destroyer, a robot created by Odin and controlled by the heroic goddess Sif. Drugged and jailed, the Wrecker soon escapes and battles Thor once again—this time bested by an unaided Thor, when the superhero uses the third rail of a subway track to sap his strength. Escaping from prison with three other criminals, the Wrecker has them all hold his crowbar during a storm; when lightning strikes, the Wrecker's latent powers charge the others. Banding together as the super-powered Wrecking Crew, they tussle regularly with Thor as well as other superheroes.

WU FANG (M)

First Appearance: September 1935, *Wu Fang* #1.

Costume: Yellow robe; green cap with plume of hair.

Weapons: Specially bred insects, bats, and lizards, all lethal.

Biography: Billed as "The Mysterious Wu Fang," the Asian super villain wasn't mysterious at all. He wanted to rule the world, and used any means at his disposal to achieve that end. His aide was a young woman named Mohara; his nemeses were government agent Val Kildare and his assistant Jerry Hazzard. Toward the end of the magazine's short life, Mohara left her notorious boss and married Hazzard.

Comment: There were seven Wu Fang stories in all: "The Case of the Six Coffins," "The Case of the Scarlet Feather," "The Case of the Yellow Mask," "The Case of the Suicide Tomb," "The Case of the Green Death," "The Case of the Black Lotus," and "The Case of the Hidden Scourge." Advertised but never published was "The Case of the Living Poison." All were written by Robert J. Hogan, author of the popular war-hero series *G-8 and His Battle Aces*. Wu Fang was especially fond of torture, and the covers of his magazines featured him leeringly overseeing a hanging (#7), a young woman's immolation (#2), a snake ripping up a man's throat (#1), and so on. See also DR. FU MANCHU, DR. YEN SIN.

XALTOTUN (M)

First Appearance: December 1935, "The Hour of the Dragon," *Weird Tales*, Robert E. Howard.

Costume: When he awakens: "Dark velvet robe, splashed with gold stars and crescent moons (with) a cloth-of-gold fillet about his temples, confining the black wavy locks that fell to his shoulders." Later: "unadorned silk robe" and, on occasion, "a Shemitish head-dress" which hides all but his eyes.

Weapons: The Heart of Ahriman, a "glistening sphere" which renders people unconscious on contact, shows images of distant events, can help restore life to the dead, and grants other powers; chariot drawn by "unnatural" black horses.

Biography: In life, Xaltotun was "the High Priest of Set in Python, which was in Acheron." He perished and, 3,000 years later (circa 10,000 B.C.) his mummified body is brought back to life by a magic gem known as the Heart of Ahriman. The jewel is wielded by Orastes, the evil priest of Mitra, at the behest of Valerius and Tarascus. The pair have designs on the thrones of the kingdoms of Nemedia and Aquilonia, respectively, and intend to use Xaltotun's magic to assume them. Xaltotun uses sorcery to slay the king of Nemedia; Aquilonia is also besieged and falls, its king the heroic Conan, taken prisoner. But Xaltotun himself becomes power-hungry (not to mention being a cruel jester—at one point he turns a subject's belt into a snake); in no time at all even his allies fear him. Meanwhile, escaping with the aid of a slave girl who loves him, Conan obtains the Heart of Ahriman and uses it to destroy the sorcerer, the gem spitting out a "blinding blue light" which transforms him into "a brown, dry, unrecognizable carcass."

Quote: "Fools, to pit your charlatan's mummery against my arts! With a wave of my hand I brush you from my path!"

Comment: The novel was serialized in *Weird Tales* through April 1936. Chronologically, it is the last Conan story among those written by Howard. The tale was first published in book form as *Conan the Conqueror* in 1950. Other villains in the Conan adventures include the wizard Isotho-lanti who plans to conquer Aquilonia ("The Scarlet Citadel," 1933); the outlaw Ascalante, who also plots to rule Aquilonia ("The Phoenix on the Sword," 1932); the witch Salome and her frog-like slave Thak ("A Witch Shall Be Born," 1934); the sorcerer Thugra Khotan, alias the Veiled One, and his demon aides ("Black Colossus," 1933); Atali, the daughter of Ymir, the Frost Giant, who leads men to be murdered by her brothers and sacrificed to their father ("The Frost Giant's Daughter," 1953 [an earlier version, "Gods of the North," was published in 1934]); and Yara the sorcerer ("The Tower of the Elephant," 1933). Many of these characters have been featured in the Conan comic books published by Marvel since 1970.

XANDU (C)

First Appearance: 1965, *The Amazing Spider-Man Annual* #2, Marvel Comics.

Costume: Green shoes, tights, shirt, skullcap, cloak with light green lining and collar; light green gloves; dark monocle worn in left eye.

Weapons: The Wand of Watoomb, "the greatest source of mystic power ever possessed by one man." With it, the user can travel to other dimensions, worlds, and times; see any place, object, or person; and send a destructive blast to that object. In his second appearance, Xandu utilizes the skull-shaped Crystal of Kadavus, which can send powerful, restorative energy waves anywhere the user wishes.

Chief Henchmen: A pair of nameless flunkies.

Biography: "A student of the mystic arts," Xandu learns of the potent Wand of Watoomb and sets out to acquire it. Learning that the Wand has been broken in two so its power can never be used, he steals one half (from where is never revealed) and then discovers that the other half is in the possession of the superheroic magician Dr. Strange. Picking up two men in a bar, Xandu uses his awesome hypnotic abilities to convince them that they have enormous physical strength (which, due to his mesmeric suggestion, they do), then sends them to Strange's home to steal the wand's other half. Happening upon the thugs, the superhero Spider-Man follows them to Xandu's lair. With the missing piece of the Wand in-hand, Xandu plans to use its power to conquer the world. With it, he sends the pesky Spider-Man to another dimension; however, just before he vanishes, the superhero snatches the sceptre and takes it with him. Xandu and his thugs follow, as does Dr. Strange, and a terrific brawl ensues from which the heroes emerge victorious. When they return to our dimension the thugs remember nothing, and Strange uses magic to drain the Wand of power as well as cleanse Xandu of all "evil ambition." But not for long: when the three meet again (*Marvel Team-Up* #21, 1974), Xandu reveals that, for safekeeping, he'd quickly hidden his mind in "the Ethos" (a dimension or world which he doesn't deign to explain). After roaming the streets as a bum, he manages to recollect his wits and then sets out to reclaim the Wand. Holed up in a New York apartment, Xandu uses hypnosis to make Spider-Man his slave and, displaying a new power—the ability to teleport others—sends Spider-Man to Strange's home to steal the Crystal of Kadavus. Using the gem to repair the Wand, he tries to kill Strange by transporting them all to a new dimension he's created, one in which he's the most powerful being alive. Nonetheless, the heroes manage to collar him and leave the Wand drifting in the ether. The Wand was most recently the object of Xandu's desire in *Marvel Fanfare* #6 (1982).

Quote: "Slowly, inexorably, relentlessly, I shall destroy my *enemies*!"

Comment: Dr. Strange has fought many enemies over the years, among them the evil sorcerer Zota who lives in the time of Cleopatra and, taking Mark Antony prisoner, uses an "impulse transmitter" to watch for any adversary's approach (spotting them, he imprisons the hapless soul in a "prison of rolling light"); the Demon, an avaricious sorcerer and apprentice of Strange's hated enemy BARON MORDO; Kaluu, a wizard who left the Himalayas and spent 500 years studying magic in the dimension of Raggadorr, only to return to earth and be beaten by Strange; the mystic giant Zom; the other-dimensional Nebulous, "Lord of the Planets Perilous," whose Staff of Polar Power soaks up the energies produced by black magic; the extraterrestrial scientist Yandroth and the powerful robot-aide Voltorg (also referred to as Voltorr); the demon Asmodeus; the wizard Stygyro; the Creators, a union of wizards who hail from different eras in time; and Dr. Stranger Yet, a distorted copy of the superhero. See other sorcerers THE AFRICAN MAGICIAN, BARON MORDO, BELASCO, THE BLUE WIZARD, DORMAMMU, FRESTON, and LODAC.

XENOS (C)

Real Name: Sgt. Gwenn.

First Appearance: 1982, *Moon Knight* #15, Marvel Comics.

Costume: Brown rat costume, complete with tail.

Weapons: Standard firearms; rat food, which he occasionally smears on victims so the rats will gnaw them to death.

Chief Henchmen: An army of rats, all of whom he dresses in miniature military uniforms. At his New York home (apparently a brownstone), he keeps the rats in a tiny, glass-enclosed city.

Biography: A master of disguise, Gwenn has been with the New York police force for 14 years and has won nine citations for bravery. But he does have a problem. He despises foreigners, believing that they use "shoddy tactics" and "inferior products" to "put Americans out of jobs" and thus cause a rise in crime. Determined to "stop the invasion" by killing foreign leaders who come to the United States, he goes forth as Xenos (after "xenophobia," a fear of strangers), occasionally assisted by his rats. After several assassination attempts are thwarted by Moon Knight, Xenos concentrates on eliminating the superhero. However, Moon Knight succeeds in deducing Gwenn's true identity first and, tracking him to his home, arrests him after a battle.

Quote: "Meet your master, foreign devil! Meet *Xenos*!"

X-TINCTOR (C)

First Appearance: 1986, *Animax* #1, Marvel Comics (see Comment).

Costume: Navy blue bodysuit, helmet with three gray horns and blue goggles; belt made of large white teeth; white skull kneepads. X-Tinctor has gray batlike wings, red flesh, and a cadaverous face.

Weapons: Whip; vehicle built from the skeleton of a huge ram.

Chief Henchmen: The Motor Mutants, aka Road Hogs, a variety of hog-like, mutated humanoids with dragster-type vehicles. Named are Torrendous, Road Runt (and his vehicle Path Piggy).

Biography: On earth of the far future, most of the world is controlled by mutants ruled by the vile X-Tinctor. He and his minions are devoted to the destruction of the remaining humans, who are holed-up in the gleaming palace-city of Peoplopolis.

Quote: "*Gun it, you scum*! Peoplopolis will fall before us like *wheat* before the *scythe*!

XYRKOL (C)

First Appearance: 1963, *Magnus Robot Fighter* #3, Gold Key Comics.

Costume: Purple boots, jumpsuit with red design on chest (triangle intersected by "V"); red belt (see Weapons); yellow cape; white gloves. Xyrkol's hair, beard, and moustache were also yellow.

Weapons: "Stun-ray"; "sub-space drive" for instant teleportation of himself and whatever he is holding to his lab (operated by his belt); a "flexi-steel" collar which tightens if the wearer disobeys orders; anti-robot plague, "a parasite that feeds on, and destroys, the particular energy quantum that operates all robot relays and joint connections."

Chief Henchmen: Sundry robots of various sizes and shapes, most notably Sigma the immortal robot, who could recreate itself immediately whenever it was destroyed; and the "octo-rob," an eight-tentacled robot.

XYRKOL takes a beating from Magnus. © Western Publishing.

Biography: Xyrkol is a humanoid alien who lives in the year 4000 A.D. In his first major crime, he tries to take over North Am using a giant robot. Thwarted by the rather specialized hero Magnus, he tries again with Sigma (#5), then again with the "octo-rob" (#10). However, his most ambitious plot occurs between these two attempts (#7), while he is headquartered on the planet Malev-6, the sixth planet of the star Malev, located some 60,000 light years from earth. There, Xyrkol is partnered with an ambitious computer which "fills and uses the power of (the) entire planet." Also known as Malev-6, the computer was originally a robot repair ship which crashed and was marooned on the planet "1500 galactic years ago." During the ensuing eons, its memory was erased by radiation from Malev and it became independent, mining metal, enlarging itself, and building robot slaves. Planning to grow large enough to "fill the universe," it was discovered by Xyrkol, who offers to help it if it in turn will help him conquer earth. The computer is destroyed by Magnus, using Xyrkol's plague. The ultimate fate of the fiend is not known.

Quote: "Earthmen are helpless weaklings without their robots! There will be *no* resistance when . . . robots take over the planet!"

Comment: Among the other foes faced by Magnus during his 46-issue run were a DR. FU MANCHU-like Mogul Badur, the immortal leader of a kingdom of robots (as if the Asian stereotype were not bad enough, even Badur's robots had slanted eyes; what's more, like all good henchmen, Badur's robot aide Zyfor had a leering eye for the ladies); the sinister "Think-Rob," who had a human-like brain and used it to plot the destruction of North Am's undersea farming community; the subversive group the Conclave, who used robots to further their aims (including the rather blatantly codenamed E-VL); the brainwashing robot Talpa; fish-like aliens from Sirius; the sinister and mentally deranged Mekman, a human who used look-alike robots to replace key government personnel (and who loved robots so much that he disguised *himself* to resemble one, even emulating their stilted speech patterns); and the astronaut Zemo who, due to his radical political views, had been exiled from earth in an earlier century. Before being sent into space, however, he'd been transformed into "a cybernete—a man of artificial organs and blood, almost a robot." Annoyed by the surgery, he brought back to earth a lethal, malevolent, vaporous lifeform he found in the Andromeda Galaxy. However, stirred by his long-dormant love of humanity (and earth women in particular), he had a change of heart and helped Magnus defeat the extraterrestrial.

YOMURDA (MP)

First Appearance: 1933, *Sucker Money*, Hollywood Pictures.

Biography: A swami, Yomurda uses hypnosis, murder, and fake seances to get his hands on the fortunes of others. Exposed by a journalist, he is arrested by police.

Comment: Mischa Auer played the turbaned villain in this little-known film written by Willis Kent.

ZALL (C)

First Appearance: 1983, *The Fly* (second series) #5, Archie Comics.

Costume: Blue pants, shoes, belt, turtleneck shirt, full-head helmet with inverted "S" ears and yellow markings on front.

Weapons: Metal cylinders, worn on hands, from which powerful metal fingers can be extended.

Chief Henchman: A thug named Marks.

Biography: When a scientist named Yancey makes a scientific breakthrough, his partners Xbaum and Zall want to control it. Stealing Yancey's papers, the two allies become nervous when attorney Thomas Troy (secretly The Fly) becomes embroiled in the investigation. Zall dons his costume to fight the hero, but The Fly triumphs with a shot from his sonic-wave Buzz gun.

Quote: "Idiot! I keep flunkies like you, my dear man, to jump through hoops for me!"

Comment: This was the character's only appearance.

ZARAN (C)

Real Name: Maximilian Zaran.

First Appearance: 1979, *Master of Kung-Fu* #77, Marvel Comics.

Costume: Blue tights, boots, wristbands, cowl, breastplate; red belt, stripe down side of tights, queue from cowl.

Weapons: Various weapons including a spear, longbow, mace, sais worn clipped to his breastplate and wristbands, and the sundry arms used in martial arts. Zaran is extremely proficient in the use of most primitive weapons, for which reason he sometimes goes by the name of the Weapons Master.

Biography: While serving in the British Secret Service, Zaran was induced to defect by the seductress Fah Lo Suee, the daughter of DR. FU MANCHU. When she was finished with him, she cast him aside; Zaran is now a freelance villain who was most recently employed by the wicked BATROC.

Quote: "In my native England, Captain America's reputation is legendary! But today, *Zaran* shall put the lie to the legends!"

Comment: Though the character first appeared in another title, he is best-known as a member of Batroc's Brigade, a trio which first teamed in *Captain America* #302 (1985). Another noteworthy villain in Captain America's rogue's gallery is the Slayer, one-armed Vietnam vet Dave Cox who has his mind twisted by Baron Zemo and is sent out—costumed and armed with a spiked mace—to slay the superhero.

THE ZODIAC MASTER (C)

First Appearance: 1964, *Detective Comics* #323, DC Comics.

Costume: Blue bodysuit covered with small, black signs of the zodiac (see Weapons); blue boots with dark blue fringe; dark blue cowl with matching "Z" in a black circle; dark blue belt with black "bolts" on buckle; black trunks.

Weapons: Signs of the zodiac can be plucked from costume and used as weapons. In his only adventure: Gemini twins are flaming, flying figures; Sagittarius' arrow becomes a destructive "jet arrow"; Aries the ram is an incendiary device; Scorpio becomes an entangling mesh; Cancer the crab can fly and pluck objects up in its claws; and Capricorn the goat is a battering ram.

Chief Henchman: A thug named Marty.

Biography: The Zodiac Master works as a fortuneteller in a "mystic parlor," a place complete with a Leo the lion doorway whose jaws lock shut behind him when he needs to beat a hasty retreat. Employed by gangs to see how their crimes will fare vis-a-vis the stars (for which he is given a whopping 25 percent of the take), the villain plots a grand scheme of his own: to steal a priceless bull-artifact on display from the tomb of a Cretan king. However, the superheroic Batman finds the symbol of Taurus the bull prominently displayed in the thief's hideout, makes the connection, and arrests him at the Gotham Museum.

Quote: "The stars have not foretold my capture yet! Ho, ho, ho . . . ."

Comment: A similar character, Dr. Zodiac, first appeared in *World's Finest Comics* #160 and was an astrologer who moonlighted as a robber. In one adventure (*World's Finest Comics* #268) he stole the ancient Coins of Power and became a powerful monster which was a hybrid of all 12 astrological signs. In addition to these two criminals, Batman has faced hundreds of villains since his comic book debut in 1939. The first criminal in his life was non-super Joe Chill, who murdered young Bruce Wayne's parents during a mugging. This was the traumatic event which propelled Wayne into a life of crimebusting as Batman. Among the lesser-known super villains Batman has battled are the Skull syndicate, villains who wear yellow and green costumes and travel about in a flying skull; the barely human Mole (2) who, like Dick Tracy's THE MOLE (1), burrows underground to commit crimes; the Hangman, a killer who wears a dark green costume and wears a noose around his neck (not to be confused with HANGMAN who battled Marvel's superhero Werewolf); the murderous kidnapper Colonel Sulphur who has a switchblade concealed in his glove; the Monarch of Menace who dresses like a king and whose most memorable crime was imprisoning Batman and extorting money from super villains like THE BOUNCER and THE CLUEMASTER to *keep* Batman behind bars. Also, a janitor who becomes the Mental Giant due to an "accidental burst of freak radiation" and is endowed with a superhuman criminal mind; Dagger, a costumed sword and knife master; the bird-masked robbers known as the Condor Gang; the Origami Man, who is made of paper (it has "an evil glint in its paper eyes") and lives as a result of a radio announcer's "latent psychic abilities"; Eivol Ekdal, an inventor like THE TINKERER and TOYMAN, who creates myriad snares, including the infamous "inescapable doom-trap," an unbreakable plastic tomb into which deadly gas filters through an electrified grating (Batman escapes by using his belt to cause a spark which ignites the gas and blows apart the plastic). And Crazy Quilt, who flashes around blinding colors since they are all he can see with his "imperfect vision"; the alien Tri Vul, who turns to evil when he suffers "the combined effect of the emanations from our *black moon* and the radioactive sands of the desert of gold"; the sword-swinging Cavalier, a "dashing desperado"; the Brain Burglar, actually the mind-stealing Dr. Deker; the radioactive Professor Radium; Malis, a centuries-old robot from another world (it took the combined efforts of Batman and Superman to subdue the nuclear-powered automation); the Getaway Genius; the hulking Blockbuster; another bruiser, Mr. Mammoth; the evil dwarfs Tweedle-Dee and Tweedle-Dum; the sinister Bart Magan who has his face erased scientifically and goes on a robbing spree as the mysterious Dr. No-Face; the urban pirate Captain Cutlass; the power-mad soldier General Scarr; the nefarious Spinner, a metal-costumed villain who, among other activities, lashes Batwoman to the whirring blades of a huge fan; and Croc who, due to a hereditary disease, has scaly green skin . . . and a very mean disposition. Many other super villains were created especially for the *Batman* TV series which aired from 1966 to 1968. These included the magician Zelda (played by Anne Baxter); the master of disguise False Face (Malachi Throne); a university professor who is hit on the head and imagines himself to be King Tut (Victor Buono); the learned Bookworm (Roddy McDowall); the Archer (Art Carney); the singing villain, the Minstrel (Van Johnson); the gangster Ma Parker (Shelley Winters); the Clock King (Walter Slezak), whose crimes and gimmicks involve timepieces; the brilliant Egghead (Vincent Price); the pianist Chandell (Liberace); Marsha Queen of Diamonds (Carolyn Jones); the cowboy Shame (Cliff Robertson); the game-playing Puzzler (Maurice Evans); the gluemaster Colonel Gumm (Roger C. Carmel); the Black Widow (Talullah Bankhead); the Siren (Joan Collins) who can mesmerize people with her high-pitched voice; the flower-loving Louie the Lilac (Milton Berle); the wealthy Lord Phogg (Rudy Vallee); Noral Clavicle (Barbara Rush); the alchemist Dr. Cassandra (Ida Lupino) and the health-conscious Minerva (Zsa Zsa Gabor).

ZOGAR SAG (M)

First Appearance: May 1935, "Beyond the Black River," *Weird Tales*, Robert E. Howard.

Chief Henchman: The Forest Demon, Zogar's brother, who tears off peoples' heads; he has a scaly torso, red eyes, crane-like legs, and a "demoniac" face. Whatever one brother feels or thinks, so does the other as well.

Biography: A Pictish wizard, Zogar is the son of the god Jhebbal Sag; he was conceived when his mother, "a woman of Gwawela," slept in a grove holy to the deity. Hating the neighboring Aquilonians, he uses his powers of enchantment to unite over a dozen local clans. Together, they attack Fort Tuscelan—all that stands between Zogar and conquering the region known as Conajohara, an Aquilonian colony situated between Thunder River and the Black River. The battle is fierce, but ends abruptly when the heroic Aquilonian Conan hacks the Forest Demon to pieces and Zogar likewise drops dead. In life, Zogar's greatest power was the ability to control animals.

Comment: This was the character's only appearance; the story was serialized in the May and June 1935 issues of *Weird Tales* and was first collected in *King Conan* (1953) and later in the 1977 collection *Red Nails* (not to be confused with the short story of the same name).

ZOHAR (C)

Real Name: Rabbi Reuben Davis.

First Appearance: 1984, *Moon Knight* #37, Marvel Comics.

Costume: Red robe with blue cuffs, full-head hood with blue pentagon on forehead; blue slippers, belt with a flap down the front of the skirt of the robe (Note: costume was blue with orange belt/trim in first appearance, which was just one panel in #37).

Biography: Chicago-based Davis is the student of Elias Spector, father of the superhero Moon Knight and master of Hebrew cabala or mysticism. From him, Davis learns how "to summon forth the divine spark" and fire debilitating blasts. However, upon Spector's death, the distraught Davis decides to use his powers to "mete out justice in the name of the Creator," to force humankind "to do penance." He begins with other cabalists, intending to destroy them so he'll have no peers. Moon Knight becomes involved when Davis steals and reanimates Spector's body; after a brief battle, Moon Knight grabs a mirror and knocks the sorcerer cold by reflecting one of this mystic blasts right back at him (#38).

Quote: "Be grateful, mortal. For the suffering Zohar inflicts upon your body, your soul will be redeemed."

Comment: According to lore, students of cabala also had the power to peer into the future. If Zohar has this ability he has not yet revealed it (and has certainly used it poorly in his tilt with Moon Knight). He has not been seen since.

ZOLOK (MP)

First Appearance: 1935, *The Lost City*, Regal Pictures.

Costume: Golden robe and pants (film is black and white; color scheme according to promotional lobby cards from the film).

Weapons: Network of televisions spread throughout the jungle to watch anyone approaching his domain; "living dead men," brainwashed native giants who obey his every command (he has a device which turns normal-sized men into the giants); destructive ray; Tunnel of Flame, a metal room crackling with thousands of volts of electricity; "thought camera," a device which reads minds and prints out the images as photographs; Storm Generator to create lightning storms anywhere on the planet; acid capsules stored in his belt.

Biography: When the world is ravaged by electrical storms which cause floods, earthquakes, cyclones, and other disasters, electrical engineer Bruce Gordon traces the seat of these unnatural disasters to central Africa (specifically, "the 28th meridian, 10 degrees south of the Equator"). Leading an expedition to the area, Bruce pinpoints the source of the trouble: Magnetic Mountain which, unknown to him, houses a city ruled by the evil Zolok the Ligurian, a maniac bent on world conquest. (Though, being insane, he's not averse to demolishing the world either; when an unwilling assistant informs Zolok that he has already pumped enough electricity into the atmosphere to level a hundred cities, the madman barks, "I'll have this cosmic condenser hold enough power to destroy the *world* if I desire it!") After sundry adventures in the Lost City and the surrounding jungle, Bruce and his companions persuade Zolok's aides to turn against him and the lunatic is imprisoned. However, he escapes by burning down the dungeon door with an acid capsule and cranks his destruction ray to full power. ("I'll show them!" he chortles after the escaping intruders.) Luckily, the unit overloads and destroys Zolok, the Lost City, and half the mountain.

Quote: "As you may know, the Ligurians were a race of master scientists. I am the last of that race, carrying on the electromagnetic tradition of my people."

Comment: Without question, no serial villain was as well-equipped as Zolok to conquer the world. William "Stage" Boyd played the part in the 12-episode serial. (In a case of art imitating life, Boyd had been involved in a liquor and gambling scandal four years before, during Prohibition.)

***ZOLOK** in a newspaper advertisement announcing his final episode. © S.S. Kreilberg Productions.*

ZYKLON (C)

First Appearance: 1985, *All-Star Squadron* #45, DC Comics.

Costume: Blue bodysuit with two small, yellow lightning bolts on chest; blue cowl with yellow swastika on forehead; dark red trunks, boots, gloves; yellow belt.

Biography: Zyklon ("Cyclone" in German) was an ordinary mortal until Nazi scientists gave him the power to move at superspeed. Coming to America in 1942, he used his powers to try and steal the Liberty Bell, among other crimes. He has always been defeated by the superheroic All-Star Squadron.

Comment: See other Nazi super villains BARON BLITZKRIEG, BARON GESTAPO, BARON ZEMO, CAPTAIN AXIS, CAPTAIN NAZI, THE CLOWN, THE GOLDEN FUHRER, KILLER SHARK, NIGHT AND FOG, The Masked Swastika of VENDETTA, Mastermind (see U-MAN, Comment), THE RED PANZER, and THE RED SKULL. Other speedy super villains are HURRICANE, REVERSE-FLASH, SPEED DEMON (2), and Speed Demon (1) of VENDETTA.

APPENDIX

SUPER VILLAIN TEAMS

THE ANI-MEN (C)

Members: Original: Ape-Man, Bird-Man, Cat-Man, and Frog-Man. Second: Dragonfly added.

Charter: These characters were originally non-super criminals who were brought together and given flamboyant costumes by Abner Jonas, aka the Organizer. Jonas, who was running for mayor of New York, used the Ani-Men (then known, collectively with Jonas, as the Organization) to commit acts which would "discredit and undermine the city government." Jonas kept in constant touch with them via their costumes (golden leotards, boots, and gloves); each costume boasted a headset and a "creepy-peepy TV camera" on the chest. ("I get it," purrs Cat-Man. "Sort of like we're remote-control gadgets ourselves.") The costumes also gave them each a fitting power: Ape-Man (Gordon "Monk" Keefer) received "acrobatic skill," Bird-Man (Henry Hawk) could fly, Cat-Man (Townshend Horgan) had "infra-red vision" and a "blackout device," and Frog-Man (Francois "Frog" LeBlanc) was amphibious. Gadgets notwithstanding, they were defeated by the superhero Daredevil, after which the group (minus Frog-Man) went independent as the Unholy Three. All four were then recruited by Count Nefaria of the criminal group the Maggia (see MADAM MASQUE) and underwent treatments which gave them genuine animal superpowers: Ape-Man had enormous strength, Bird-Man could still fly, Cat-Man was extremely supple, and Frog-Man was an extraordinary leaper. Joined by the airborne woman, Dragonfly, the super villains tried to take over a U.S. defense installation and were routed by the X-Men in *The X-Men* #94 (1975). The Ani-Men died in a bomb blast during a subsequent escapade, but a new band was assembled by the DEATH-STALKER. The replacement team—Ape-Man (Roy McVey), Bird-Man (Achille DiBacco), and Cat-Man (Sebastian "Morris" Patane)—were merely costumed villains, like the original Ani-Men, though their suits gave them superpowers equivalent to those of their mutated predecessors. The trio was dispatched to abduct Daredevil; succeeding, Ape-Man and Cat-Man were slain for no particular reason by the cold-blooded Death-Stalker. (Bird-Man did not die because he had been clobbered early in the kidnapping by Daredevil's then-partner the Black Widow). Both Bird-Man and Dragonfly remain at large.

Comment: These Marvel Comics villains first appeared in *Daredevil* #10 (1965); the original lineup's last appearance was in *Iron Man* #116 (1978). The new members appeared in *Daredevil* #'s 157-158 (1979).

THE ANTI-FLY LEAGUE (C)

Members: Bra-Kr, DOVI, Lxo III, METAL MASTER, THE SPIDER, Rance, Linda, others.

Charter: This group has a common goal: to get rid of the superheroic Fly. The Anti-Fly League is headquartered in a cave outside of Capital City; nestled behind heavy metal doors (which actually have the name of the group etched thereupon!) they twirl a spinning arrow on the wall to see which one of them will be chosen, next, to attack the Fly. (As one of

***DOVI** (right), **METAL MASTER**, and Lxo III of the **THE ANTI-FLY LEAGUE**. © Archie Comics.*

them puts it, "One of us is bound to destroy our enemy!" Why they never attack en masse—pride?—is never explained.) Among the members who have played an active part in the league's activities, the four-armed alien Bra-Kr of the planet Gxau is a scientific genius; Rance is a gangster; and Lxo is an antennaed, bugeyed Martian science-whiz. Like an early-day Vanna White, member Linda (who apparently has no superpowers) is responsible for twirling the spinner.

Comment: The group first united for *The Adventures of the Fly* (later *Fly Man*) #21 (1962). They appeared several times during the magazine's 39-issue run.

THE BEAGLE BOYS (C)

Members: 176-167, 176-617, 176-671, and 176-761.

Charter: Dressed in orange sweaters, blue caps and trousers, and black masks, these four dog-villains began their criminal careers by trying to rob the money bins of wealthy Scrooge McDuck—uncle to Donald Duck. Failing at that, they've been spending their time in recent years plotting crimes against society in general—in which plots they are invariably foiled by the superhero Super Goof (the dog Goofy in his crimebusting identity). Among their quirks: 176-671 is the genius of the group and 176-761 is a glutton. Though the Beagle Boys themselves have no superpowers, they frequently resort to extraordinary tools in their fight against Super Goof—such as the time they fed him an appetite enhancer, which made him so hungry he was too busy eating to fight crime.

Comment: These characters were created by legendary comic book artist/writer Carl Barks and appeared on-and-off in Uncle Scrooge's own strip. (Barks created that character as well, in 1947; Scrooge began his own series in March 1952.) The Beagle Boys moved over to their own magazine in 1964 (it lasted through #47 in 1979), began appearing in the brand new *Super Goof* comic book the following year, and also costarred in 12 issues of *The Beagle Boys versus Uncle Scrooge* (1979 to 1980).

BLUE MEN OF THE MINCH (F)

Biography: The Blue Men are angels who, after falling in with SATAN, set up housekeeping in undersea caves in Scotland, in the strait between Long Island and the Shiant Islands. There, exposure to the sea turns them to blue. The group is ruled by a tribal leader and, according to some accounts, members have human names. Resembling mortal men and possessing extraordinary strength—if captured, they can easily snap their bonds—the Blue Men delight in causing storms to sink passing ships. Obliged to address the captain of the ship they've targeted, the Blue Men must leave the vessel unharmed if he can rhyme whatever they say to him . . . and keep it up until they depart.

Comment: The legend is believed to have originated with dark-skinned Moors who, captured by Norwegian pirates, were stranded on the shores of the strait in the ninth century.

THE BROTHERHOOD OF EVIL (C)

Members: Original: THE BRAIN, GARGUAX, GENERAL IMMORTUS, Monsieur Mallah, and MADAME ROUGE. Second: the Brain, Monsieur Mallah, HOUNGAN, PHOBIA, PLASMUS, and WARP.

Charter: Based in L'Ecole des Filles, a girls' school in

THE BEAGLE BOYS. *© Walt Disney Productions.*

Paris, the Brotherhood was originally formed by the Brain to help him destroy the superheroic Doom Patrol—the one impediment between him and world conquest. After numerous encounters, the evil band was finally undermined by Madame Rouge's love for Niles Caulder, leader of the Patrol. She turned on the Brain and his aide Mallah, killing them (or so she thought) by blowing up the Brotherhood's headquarters. Alas, she also lost both Caulder and her mind, Caulder dying and her shocked mind snapping when the Patrol perished saving a small town from a massive explosion caused by the warped Captain Zahl (see PLASMUS) in *The Doom Patrol* #121 (1968). As it happened, the Brain and Mallah survived (see The Brain) and after laying low for a while, began searching Europe for superbeings to form a new Brotherhood of Evil. The foursome on which they settled were Warp, Phobia, Houngan, and Plasmus. The newly organized group has spent most of its time battling the New Teen Titans instead of the Doom Patrol, which was stocked with new superheroes by Robotman, the sole survivor of the blast which destroyed the old group.

Comment: The DC Comics group first appeared in *The Doom Patrol* #86 (1964). The reformed band made its debut in *The New Teen Titans* #14 (1981).

THE BROTHERHOOD OF EVIL MUTANTS (C)

Members: Original: THE BLOB, Lorelei, MAGNETO, Mastermind, Toad, and UNUS (see Comment). Second (The New Brotherhood of Evil Mutants): Avalanche, the Blob, Destiny, MYSTIQUE and PRYO (see Comment).

Charter: The group was assembled by Magneto to help him to take over the world. See THE BLOB (Comment) for Mastermind and Toad; Lorelei had the power to freeze men in their tracks using her voice. When the group was disbanded, the villain Mystique created the New Brotherhood of Evil Mutants. This group also included Avalanche, who causes objects to crumble simply by touching them, and Destiny (see THE BLOB, Comment). Rogue, who can absorb the memories and powers of others, was also briefly a member. However, she eventually switched her allegiance to the superheroic X-Men, the Brotherhood's arch-foes. In time, Mystique realized that criminal activities were not only dangerous, but anti-mutant fever in general was beginning to sweep the land. Thus, she went to the United States government and offered the Brotherhood's services as covert superagents. A deal was struck, the criminals were pardoned, and they now operate as the Freedom Force. How long they serve justice remains to be seen.

Comment: The superheroes Qucksilver and Scarlet Witch were also originally members of the band, persuaded to join by their father, Magneto. ("Have you forgotten—what you *owe* me?" he declared when they first try to quit.) But their hearts weren't in it and they didn't remain members for long. The union first appeared in Marvel Comics' *X-Men* #4 (1964). The New Brotherhood was introduced in *X-Men* #141 (1981). In *Captain America Annual* #4 (1977), Magneto put together another group which, while not expressly a reformed Brotherhood, served the same purpose. The members of this nameless group were Burner, who has the power to generate extremely high temperatures; Lifter, who can lift heavy objects by nullifying gravity; Peeper, who possesses telescopic eyesight; Slither, a snake-like being who crushes people with his coils; and Shocker, who can cause debilitating electrical jolts.

THE BULLETEERS (MP)

Members: Three unnamed thugs.

Charter: These three criminals—all dressed in brown bodysuits—have their headquarters high in the peaks above the city of Metropolis where, in a cave, they also keep the Bullet Car. This car is silver with a red nosecone, and has retractable wings; when the wings pull in, the Car can be pushed into a power dive and destroys whatever it hits. The Bulleteers destroy the police station, then demand that the mayor turn over all the money in the city treasury. He refuses, and they raze the local power plant. That's when Superman gets into the act. After a dizzying chase through the skies, he succeeds in ripping the wings off the Bullet Car and tearing open the cockpit; the Car crashes to earth, the Man of Steel flying the occupants to safety . . . and to prison.

Comment: These characters appeared just once, in the animated Superman short, *The Bulleteers*. The Paramount cartoon was released in 1942. In his 17 animated adventures for Paramount, the superhero fought mostly non-super villains. The exceptions: the Hawkmen, spear-carrying humanoids with hawk-heads and wings; the Mechanical Monsters, 27-flame-breathing, flying, super-powerful robots; the Mad Scientist with his destructive Electrothanasia Ray; and a clutch of giant mummies in the service of the Egyptian King Tush. These cartoons remain among the finest animated shorts ever produced.

THE CADRE (C)

Members: Black Mass, Crowbar, Fastball, Nightfall, Shatterfist, and Shrike.

Charter: These solo operators were brought together by THE OVERMASTER and were given a vast array of superpowers with which to destroy the Justice League of America. Individually, the villains are Black Mass, a onetime professor at M.I.T. who is dressed in a black and blue bodysuit and wears wristbands which enable him to control gravity as well as expand his own frail body into that of a thousand-pound brute; wearing gold trunks and little more, Crowbar wields an electrified crowbar which he can fling like a javelin; Nightfall is an ex-student who wears a blue and purple costume and uses her wristbands to suck up all light and energy around her, leaving a black void; garbed in red tights and devilish mask, Shatterfist is a martial arts master who can destroy matter and create small earthquakes with his fist; dressed in a green bodysuit and huge blue wings, Shrike can fly and also uses her high voice to sing a "song of battle," sonic waves which can paralyze, kill, or strike an entire area with cyclonic force; see SPORTSMASTER (Comment) for Fastball. After being defeated by the Justice League, the Cadre blasted into space with the Overmaster and has not been seen since.

Comment: These DC super villains first appeared as a group in *Justice League of America* #235 (1985), although the non-super Crowbar had been featured as a solo thug in #233.

THE CAT GANG (C)

Members: Black Panther, Jaguar, and Lion.

Charter: Tired of wearing stocking masks, a gang of cat burglars decides to become more feline. Robbing masks from a costume store, they carry around a portable tape recorder to scare people with snarling and roaring sounds, and pack a springboard to make catlike leaps over fences and walls. Superb athletes, they also raid penthouses via tightrope. However, for all their prowess they are no match for the Jaguar, who corners them with the help of several hundred angry cats.

Comment: These Archie Comics characters appeared just once, in *The Adventures of the Jaguar* #18 (1963). It is one of those rare occasions when a superhero battled a super villain of the same name.

THE CLAY CREEP CLAN (C)

Members: The Clay King, Joey Burton, Eddie Keller, and others; plus "a waiting list of criminals" anxious to join.

Charter: Ruled by the Clay King, the Clan is located in a cavernous hideout in White Mountain outside of Littleville. There, after being exposed to "mysterious minerals" they acquire gray, lumpy skin, as well as the ability to stretch any portion of their anatomy. However, after an initial stay of one week, each member must return regularly to be re-exposed to the mineral, whose effects last only four hours; this assures the Clay King his share of the take. Except for the King—who wears a yellow skirt, boots, and T-shirt and a blue bodysuit and cape—the gangmembers wear ordinary street clothes, which stretch when they do. The Clay King also gives the Clan guidance regarding the mastery of their skills. ("*No, no,* you fool! You must ooze more *quickly* beneath the door . . . let your Clay body relax!") The Clan is defeated by Robby Reed, who uses the "Dial-H for Hero" dial to turn him into Mighty Moppet. Armed with "amazing baby bottle spray," he turns all the villains to infants and calls the police before restoring them to adulthood.

Comment: This was the DC Comics team's only appearance.

THE CIRCUS OF CRIME (C)

Members: The Clown, Fire-Eater, the Great Gambinos, Human Cannonball, Live Wire, PRINCESS PYTHON, and Strongman; occasional members are Blackwing, Rajah, and Teena the Fat Lady.

Charter: The group consists of performers in the Tiboldt Circus who turn to crime to assist their leader Maynard, aka the RINGMASTER. Each member has an individualistic costume and a non-super specialty: Blackwing is actually SILVERMANE who joined the circus to study it and, in this guise, uses scientific gadgets to control bats; the Clown (Eliot Franklin), who is an expert juggler; Fire-Eater (Tomas Ramirez), who not only swallows fire but also can spit it out like a human flamethrower; the Great Gambinos (Ernesto and Luigi), who are brilliant aerialists and acrobats; Human Cannonball (Jack Pulver), who wears protective gear and is both an acrobat and daredevil; Live Wire (Rance Preston), who swings an electrified lariat; Rajah (Kabir Mahadevu), an elephant trainer; Strongman (Bruce Olafsen), who possesses enormous strength (he can easily carry a safe half his size); and Teena the Fat Lady (Mary Stensen), a human battering ram. The group has also worked independently of the Ringmaster, whenever they tire of his mundane crimes. They first turned against him in *The Amazing Spider-Man* #22 (1965).

Comment: The group first appeared in *The Incredible*

Hulk #3 (1962). However, it wasn't until their second and third adventures (*The Amazing Spider-Man* #'s 16 and 22 [1964]) that individual personalities truly emerged. The group is reminiscent of Marvel's later super villain DEATH THROWS.

THE COBRA GANG (C)

Members: There are four criminals, three of whom wear cowls and capes resembling cobra skin; the fourth, King Cobra, has an entire costume of the fabric, including a hood which rises behind his head.

Charter: Robbers who use an abandoned rayon plant in Gotham City for their hideout, the Cobra Gang employs a device which projects a paralyzing "Electronic-Ring" around their adversaries. Finding their lair, Batgirl leads her superheroic colleagues Batman, Batwoman, and Robin to it and the gang is arrested.

Comment: These DC Comics villains appeared just once, in *Batman* #139 (1961).

CRIME CHAMPIONS (C)

Members: CHRONOS, DR. ALCHEMY, FELIX FAUST, FIDDLER, ICICLE, and WIZARD.

Charter: Banding together to defeat the Justice League of America and the Justice Society of America, these super villains manage to snare the superheroes in cages which nullify the powers of each captive, and then place the cages in space. Fortunately, the two Green Lanterns are able to shrink themselves and slip between the molecules of the cage. Freeing the others, they return to earth and clobber the Champions. The felons banded together only one more time (#219).

Comment: This DC Comics team first appeared in *Justice League of America* #22 (1963).

THE CRIME SYNDICATE OF AMERICA (C)

Members: Johnny Quick, Owlman, POWER RING, Superwoman, and Ultraman.

Charter: These super villains hail from Earth-3, a world virtually identical to ours existing in a parallel dimension. Johnny Quick has superspeed, being the evil equivalent of the Earth-1 superhero Flash; Owlman is a brilliant criminal counterpart of Batman; Power Ring can will his ring to create anything his mind can envision, ala Earth-l's Green Lantern; the Amazon Superwoman has great strength, like our Wonder Woman; and Ultraman is a villainous version of Superman who gets a new power each time he's irradiated by kryptonite. Learning of the existence of Earth-1—due to Ultraman acquiring Ultravision from kryptonite and being able to see through dimensional barriers—the super villains decide to come here as the Crime Syndicate and destroy the Justice League of America, after which they intend to crush the Justice Society of Earth-2. Defeated and trapped in a limbo between the dimensions, the super villains returned in *DC Comics Presents Annual* #1 (1982); they all perished when their dimension was destroyed during the Crisis on Infinite Earths (see the ANTI-MONITOR).

Comment: These villains first appeared in a 1964 two-part story which sprawled over *Justice League of America* #'s 29-30, and they subsequently appeared, together and separately, in other DC Comics titles. Several of them held dual membership in THE SECRET SOCIETY OF SUPER-VILLAINS.

THE CROOKED CIRCLE (MP)

Charter: A group of five unnamed criminals led by Rankin, the butler at Melody Manor, the Crooked Circle vows "To do for each other, to defend any brother, a fight to the knife, a knife to the hilt." They are undone by a Hindu G-man named Yoganda and his assistants, the amateur sleuths of the Sphinx Club.

Comment: The villains appeared in the 1932 film *The Crooked Circle* from World Wide Pictures. Frank Reicher played Rankin; the film was written by Ralph Spence.

THE DEATH SQUAD (C)

Members: MAN-BULL, THE MELTER, and Whiplash (see BLACKLASH).

Charter: The group banded together just once to battle Iron Man at a comic book convention. The Black Lama—a wizard from another dimension—lent a hand, but was not part of the villainous team.

Comment: The group's sole appearance was in Marvel Comics' *Iron Man* #72 (1975).

THE DEATH-THROWS (C)

Members: Bombshell, Knickknack, Oddball, Ringleader, and Tenpin.

Charter: This quintet uses their uncanny talent for juggling to commit crimes. Each wears a different costume and has a distinct specialty: Bombshell (Wendy Conrad), taught her craft by Oddball, handles explosives; Ringleader (Charles Last) carries razor-edged hoops; Oddball (Elton Healey) juggles globes packed with a variety of gasses and liquids; Oddball's brother Tenpin (Alvin Healey) wields club-like bowling pins; and Knickknack (Nick Grossman) works with non-symmetrical objects.

Comment: Though this group of Marvel Comics super villains first appeared together in *Captain America* #317 (1986), Oddball and Bombshell initially worked together in *Hawkeye* #3 (1983).

THE DEVIL MEN OF PLUTO (C)

Members: L'lex and Xanadar, Nar (deceased), another unnamed fiend.

Charter: Nar is "the most brilliant scientist on Pluto—and the most *evil!*" Enlisting the aide of L'lex, Xanadar, and another Devil Man from the B'ar Mountains, he robs "a million Mercurian heavy gold pieces" from a Jovian cargo ship. He then hides the loot on earth until the Plutonian statute of limitations expires a year later. However, Nar is doublecrossed by the three, who shoot him dead and head for earth. There, they tangle with earth's protector, the super-powered J'onn J'onzz; after several confrontations, they manage to find and assemble a robot which Nar says will lead them to the cache. However, the robot is boobytrapped to explode if Nar isn't present, and the three aliens perish. Dressed in purple bodysuits and white boots and gloves, the slender, horned beings were armed with a shrink ray, flight capsules, a ray gun, an ultraviolet ray to negate invisibility (which came in handy against J'onzz's power to become transparent), and herbs of the element X2 which bursts into flame upon contact with the air.

Comment: The characters' only appearance was in DC Comics' *House of Mystery* #159 (1966).

THE DIRE WRAITHS (C)

Members: It is not known how many Wraiths there are.

Charter: These extraterrestrials hailed from Wraithworld, a bleak world dotted with volcanos and the only planet orbiting the Black Sun in the Dark Nebula. Practicing both sorcery and science with impressive mastery, they were bellicose people who, 200 years ago, sought to conquer the planet Galador in the Golden Galaxy. Assembling their armada of Wingfighters and summoning forth a huge, vaguely dragon-like "omnivorous force" known as Deathwing—which "stripped the very flesh" from any creatures it enveloped and ate its soul—they attacked, only to be driven back by Galador's Spaceknights, humanoids who had had armor surgically grafted to them for battle in the void of space. The surviving Wraiths fled, many of them ultimately reaching earth in our present era where they used their ability as shapechangers to masquerade as ordinary mortals. They were pursued by the Spaceknight Rom, who had sniffed them out with his "energy analyzer" and then used his "neutralizer" to send them into "the phantom dimension of limbo." Never having revealed their actual form, the Wraiths have appeared as everything from slug-like red beasts to white, clay-like humanoids.

Comment: These characters first appeared in Marvel Comics' *Rom* #1 (1979)—which was itself based on a Parker Brothers toy—and remained Rom's perennial enemies throughout the magazine's seven-year run.

THE DRAGONFLY RAIDERS (C)

Members: Byth, Jarl, and two other nameless felons.

Charter: The criminal Byth, creator of the Dragonfly Raiders, hails from the world Thanagar, home of the superhero Hawkman. There, Byth "swallowed a pill invented by the Thanagaran scientist Krotan," a pill which enabled him "to alter his shape to that of any living thing." Captured and sent to prison, Byth escaped from his electro-cell because of some very clever planning. Having previously analyzed the pill, he provided his colleague Jarl with the ingredients. He then had Jarl coat them on the flap of an envelope which he mailed to Byth in prison. Licking the envelope, Byth turned into a "vandalusian driller mole," burrowed through the floor and escaped. Once free, he provided the compound to his confederates and they became the Dragonfly Raiders, robbing at will. Astride the dragonflies were green-skinned androids which not only controlled the bugs and were immune to weapons which harm living beings, but also stun adversaries with electri-ray pistols. Hawkman finally succeeded in tracking the fiends to their cave lair, where the villains changed to sundry monsters (a Thangalian gorilla-dog, a horned rock clinger, a Carangian tigracat, and a mirage bird which can duplicate itself). Defeating them and binding them in neuro-cuffs, Hawkman placed them in a Thanagaran jail . . . where they were not permitted to receive mail.

Comment: These characters appeared in DC Comics' *The Brave and the Bold* #42 (1962).

EMISSARIES OF EVIL (C)

Members: Original: ELECTRO (founder), Gladiator,

LEAPFROG, Matador, and STILTMAN. Second: Cobalt Man, Egghead (founder), RHINO, and SOLARR.

Charter: The group made its first and only appearance with its original roster in *Daredevil Annual* #1 (1967); see TRUMP (Comment) for Gladiator and Matador. The team was reorganized by the villainous scientist Egghead (aka Elihas Starr), who needed the super villains to try to obtain the magical Star of Capistan. Based on a stolen N. A. S. A. space station, this group, too, met only once, in *The Defenders* #42. Cobalt Man was actually engineer Ralph Roberts, who built a suit of armor and, after exposure to radiation, became a super-powerful giant; he first appeared in *The X-Men* #31 (1967), (though he was mentioned as far back as #27) and blew up in the service of Egghead.

Comment: Egghead also organized Marvel Comics' THE MASTERS OF EVIL.

THE ENFORCERS (C)

Members: The Big Man, Fancy Dan, the Ox, and Montana.

Charter: Led by the non-powered Big Man, who hides behind a silver mask, the band was formed to take over all the rackets in New York. They nearly succeed, thanks to the sheer physical strength of the hulking Ox, the lariat of Montana ("his lasso resembles a living thing, completely obedient"), and the acrobatic skills of Fancy Dan, who is also a judo expert. But the Big Man is arrested by police after his first run-in with Spider-Man—he's revealed to be reporter Frederick Foswell—and the others never manage to pull it all together.

Comment: These characters first appeared in *The Amazing Spider-Man* #10 (1964); they have appeared only rarely, most recently in *Marvel Team-Up* #138 (1984).

THE EVIL EIGHT (C)

Members: Arsenal, Chondak, Ice King, K-9, Maniak, Phantasm, Piledriver, and Sonik.

Charter: Based in the small town of Fairfax, the Evil Eight serve the Master, an archfiend who is searching for the fabled mystic power-dial, whose creator he slew years before. The dial enables the user to spell "h-e-r-o" or "v-i-l-l-a-i-n" and whistle up a superheroic or supervillainous identity—a power which would help the Master to control the world. The specialties of the Evil Eight are brute strength (the ape-like Chondak); the ability to freeze objects, including the moisture in the air (Ice King); superpowerful fists (Piledriver); acrobatic agility (Maniak); illusion-creating talents (Phantasm); claws and the senses of "the wild dog whose blood I share" (K-9); a portable armory (Arsenal); and the wherewithal to generate deadly sound waves (Sonik). Encasing Fairfax within an Ion Dome, the Master phones the President and demands being given the town as his "own independent country" or he will obliterate it. Fortunately for Fairfax, the Master and his team are defeated by the present holders of the dial, Vicki Grant and Chris King.

Comment: The Evil Eight and the Master menaced society in *DC's Adventure Comics* #s 484 and 485 (1981).

FACTOR THREE (C)

Members: THE BLOB, the Changling, Mastermind, the Mutant Master, UNUS, and THE VANISHER (see Comment).

Charter: The criminal group was organized by one of the octopus-like Siris of Yormot, a planet in the Sirius planetary system. Self-proclaimed as the "Mutant Master," this extraterrestrial formed the union in an effort to destroy the X-Men. The Changling had the power to alter his shape; see the Blob (Comment) for Mastermind. The group has several androids which also serve their cause, though these, along with the Mutant Master and the league itself, are destroyed in *X-Men* #39.

Comment: The group was first mentioned in *X-Men* #28 (1967), but did not make a physical appearance until #33 (as shadows) and #37 (in the flesh). The Banshee was also a member of the team, but this superhero with a debilitating scream served against his wishes, due to an explosive headband he was forced to wear.

THE FATAL FIVE (C)

Members: EMERALD EMPRESS, Mano, PERSUADER, THAROK, and Validus.

Charter: Toward the end of the thirtieth century, the evil CONTROLLER tried to destroy our sun with the mammoth Sun-Eater. Stymied, the Legion of Super-Heroes reluctantly called together five of the solar system's most brilliant and powerful super villains in an effort to save our home. In addition to Emerald Empress, Persuader, and Tharok, the fiends are the mutant Mano who, garbed in a yellow bodysuit, hails from the planet Angtu and can disintegrate just about anything; and Validus who, dressed in a purple and white bodysuit and standing some 25 feet tall, is "force personified," his strength "incalculable." He is not, however, terribly bright—possibly because "the pure energy of his brain causes mental lightning to flash around his head" day and night. Though it was one of the Legionnaires who finally stopped the threat of the Sun-Eater, the villains were given pardons for their part in the proceedings. Rather than go their separate ways, Tharok suggested they band together, chortling, "The *Legionnaires* brought us together to save the galaxy . . . and we *will* . . . for ourselves!" Adopting the name the Fatal Five, the band frequently battles the Legion, though they have rarely battled together of late due to constant, very passionate disagreements about how to go about conquering worlds.

Comment: The evil DC Comics league first appeared in *Adventure Comics* #352 (1967).

THE FEARSOME FIVE (C)

Members: Original: DR. LIGHT, Gizmo, MAMMOTH, PSIMON, and SHIMMER. Second: add Jinx and Neutron.

Charter: Unlikely as it may seem, this group was formed through an ad in *The Underworld Star,* a newspaper which publishes items-of-interest and professional tips for criminals. Tired of perpetual defeat at the hands of superheroes, Dr. Light placed an ad announcing the formation of a "super mob," and five super villains responded: Gizmo (Mikron O'Jeneus) a green-costumed midget weapons-maker and engineering genius who has tinkered together everything from an exploding "totalizer" to a jetpack for flight to a "neutron sweeper"; Mammoth, Psimon, and Shimmer. However, the union rapidly deteriorated as Psimon and Light disagreed about their goals, Psimon wanting to do the bidding of his own master, the other-dimensional ruler TRIGON, and help him take over our dimension; Light simply wanting to destroy superheroes, and the others even less ambitious, wanting only to steal. After Light ended up fleeing from the more powerful super villain, Psimon brought in Jinx—a woman in white with vast magical powers—and Neutron, who has an atom-powered punch. The Fearsome Five served by Trigon's side during his war with the New Teen Titans, and fought the young superheroes again after Trigon's defeat. They have also tangled with the superheroic Outsiders. Since Psimon's death (see PSIMON), they have kept a very low profile.

Comment: This DC Comics group first appeared in *The New Teen Titans* #3 (1981); Jinx and Neutron joined up in *Tales of the Teen Titans* #56 (1985).

THE F-MEN (C)

Members: Airhead, Clodhoppus, Drizzle, Slimesquirmer, Weasel, and Zitpops.

Charter: The group was formed by evil Ford Fairmont, Ph.D., head of Para-Sight Industries, Inc., and his assistant 'p'str'ph, who kidnapped kids and turned them into living replicas of his favorite comic book characters. Though not inherently evil, the super kids were forced to help in his evil abductions. They came into conflict with the superhero E-Man when they tried to snatch his girlfriend Nova and turn her into an F-Man named Albatross. Ultimately, Fairmont was apprehended and the teens were reunited with their parents. During their brief reign of terror, the Unhappy F-Men consisted of Airhead (aka Kitty Porn) who could become "immaterial long enough to pass through solid objects"; Clodhoppus (Peter Raskolnikov) of Russia who could "transform his body into organic concrete—in which form he can withstand almost any blow, fall from great heights unhurt . . . and very quickly drown"); Drizzle (aka African goddess Ororeo) who was "capable of generating and controlling nasty weather and causing puddles, slush and other disgusting messes"; Slimesquirmer (Kurt Angstner of West Germany) who could "teleport short distances and become nearly invisible in deep shadow," and also "stop clocks and sour milk by looking at them"; Weasel (Canada's Hooligan), who could "rip flesh with the petulantium fangs that pop out of his upper gums, and sniff out quarry with his powerful nose"; and Zitpops (aka Snott Slummers), who was able to "destroy anything with facial blasts exuded by his mutant pimples, which he can pop at will. They are held in check by his special ruby begonia mask."

Comment: Appearing in First Comics' *E-Man* #'s 2 and 3 (1983), the characters were a parody of Marvel's superheroes the X-Men: Storm (Drizzle), Cyclops (Zitpops), Colossus (Clodhoppus), Wolverine (Weasel), Nightcrawler (Slimesquirmer), Ariel (Airhead), and Phoenix (Albatross).

THE FORGOTTEN VILLAINS (C)

Members: Atom-Master, Enchantress (2), Faceless Hunter, Kraklow, Mr. Poseidon, Ultivac, and Yggardis.

Charter: This team of obscure super villains was

assembled by the Enchantress in order to take over the universe, past and present. The group's three mystics—Enchantress, a former superhero, who traded in her green uniform for a purple leotard; Kraklow, a magician living in eighteenth-century Poland; and the sentient, tentacled planet Yggardis—were the core of the league's plan. Assisting them were Atom-Master, who wore a green helmet which allowed him "to rearrange the dust in the air—and materialize it in any form I desire"; Faceless Hunter, a giant from the planet Saturn; Mr. Poseidon, who had a ring which allowed him to shrink to mere inches in height; and Ultivac, an incredibly powerful robot. The group was bested not by Superman and the Forgotten Heroes, who teamed to fight them, but by internecine bickering. Eventually all but Enchantress were captured.

Comment: These characters had all appeared once or twice in minor DC Comics tales: Atom-Master in *World's Finest Comics* #101 (1959); Enchantress (as a superhero) in *Strange Adventures* #187 (1966); Faceless Hunter in *Strange Adventures* #124 (1961); Kraklow in *Rip Hunter Time Master* #28 (1965); Mr. Poseidon in *Sea Devils* #2 (1961); and Ultivac in *Showcase* #7 (1957). Their debut as a team took place in *DC Comics Presents* #77 (1985).

THE FORTY THIEVES (F)

Charter: Little is known about these bandits, save that they dwell in an unnamed Arab land and hide their booty in a cave. The cave can be accessed by muttering "Open, Sesame!" which causes the door to move aside. The thieves are fond of dismembering their victims, though they meet their match in Ali Baba. A woodcutter, he learns the secret of the cave and begins stealing from them. They plan a delicious revenge. Posing as an oil merchant, the bandit leader puts his men in jars and asks Ali Baba if he can stay the night. The now-wealthy Ali Baba agrees, and the bandits plot to sneak out that night and slay him. But the slave Morgiana overhears their plan and fills the jugs with boiling oil, roasting and/or drowning the thieves; as for the leader, Morgiana stabs him to death when he tries to kill Ali Baba.

Comment: The story was told orally for at least nine centuries before Oriental scholar Antoine Galland, a Frenchman, transcribed it in 1704 as "Ali Baba and the Forty Thieves." However, it may be older than that, since a similar tale exists in the writings of the Greek historian Herodotus, circa 450 B.C. (the hero robs a royal treasure house and undergoes trials similar to those of Ali Baba). As for the word "sesame," it has no significance apart from being a Middle Eastern plant.

THE FRIGHTFUL FOUR (C)

Members: Original: THE WIZARD (2), THE SANDMAN, THE TRAPSTER, Madam Medusa. Later: Thundra replaced Madam Medusa; then the Brute replaced Thundra; and finally, ELECTRO replaced the Brute.

Charter: This group was formed to defeat the superheroic Fantastic Four. Madam Medusa (later simply Medusa) is one of the Inhumans, mutated by Terrigen Mist and able to will her lengthy, iron-strong hair to do anything she wishes; she becomes a sidekick of the Wizard only because she is suffering from amnesia. Thundra is a genetically-altered warrior woman from the twenty-third century who tries to affect history in favor of women by defeating the most powerful man of our time. Since this happens to be Thing of the Fantastic Four, she joins the criminal group out of convenience. She subsequently abandons her plan and stays in our era as a superhero. The Brute is a brilliant scientist of the man-made world of Counter-Earth and is transformed into a muscular titan by cosmic rays.

Comment: The band first appeared in Marvel Comics' *The Fantastic Four* #36 (1965).

THE GANG (C)

Members: Brains, Bulldozer, Kong, and Ms. Mesmer.

Charter: Raised in a ghetto on Chicago's South Side, the foursome vowed to become wealthy no matter what the cost. Developing their talents, they eventually become a team of super villains. Wearing a red bodysuit, Brains was a criminal genius and the group's leader; Bulldozer, in a blue bodysuit, had superstrength (used mostly for pounding others), as did Kong in a green, bulletproof bodysuit (his specialty was lifting); and Ms. Mesmer, in a yellow bodysuit, hypnotized others with a disc worn on her chest. Going to work for the Chicago-based Council, a criminal league trying to monopolize all the world's information sources, the Gang was beaten by Supergirl . . . save for Brains, who merged with MATRIX-PRIME.

Comment: The first appearance of this DC Comics group was in *The Daring New Adventures of Supergirl* #4 (1982). The Council, led by the mysterious hooded Director, first appeared in #3.

THE GRAPPLERS (C)

Members: Auntie Freeze (founder), Letha,

Poundcakes, Screaming Mimi, and Titania (1).

Charter: Auntie Freeze (aka Ann Fraley) had been a championship wrestler for nearly 20 years when she retired in the 1970s. Rather than give up the sport completely, she became a trainer. But the sports world refused to give her personnel the same money as male wrestlers, and she became extremely frustrated. Concurrently, a wrestling buff who worked for the powerful Roxxon Oil Corporation got in touch with the team and offered to pay them well to work on illegal undercover projects for the company. They agreed, and all were fitted with hi-tech accoutrements: Letha (Hellen Feliciano) was given a harness containing highly transistorized weapons; Poundcakes (Marian Pouncy) donned boots capable of shaking the ground; Screaming Mimi (Mimi Schwartz) wore a voice-enhancer that enabled her to "cut loose with a hypersonic shriek which stabs deep into the pain centers of the human brain"; and Titania (Davida DeVito) was armed with small discs which released various kinds of destructive forces. Sent to undermine Project Pegasus—the governments' energy research program which Roxxon perceived as a competitive threat—they failed and ended up in prison. Their careers ruined, the wrestlers took to crime to support themselves upon their release. Meanwhile, Auntie Freeze put together a new group of Grapplers. Sending them to the Power Broker, Inc.—a scientific firm which specializes in boosting a person's strength to superhuman levels, courtesy of the genius of Dr. Karl Malus (see GOLIATH)—she ended up with a new band that didn't need Roxxon's technology to trounce opponents. To date, the new group—yet to commit any criminal acts—consists of Battleaxe (Anita Ehren), Butterball (Vivian Dolan), Cowgirl (Deb Lowry), Gladiatrix (Robbin Braxton), Magilla (Sandy Stalmaster), Sushi (Susan Hayakawa), and Vavavoom (Dawn Middlebury). Sadly, Titania and Letha were both murdered by SCOURGE. Screaming Mimi is currently a member of THE MASTERS OF EVIL; at one point Titania was also a member.

Comment: The team first appeared in *Marvel Two-In-One* #54 (1978); the rest of the members were introduced in *The Thing* #33 (1986). See LEAGUE OF SUPER-ASSASSINS for Titania (2).

H.U.R.R.I.C.A.N.E. (C)

Members: Blackbird, Mr. Mental, Missing Fink, Powerhouse, and Yellow Streak.

Charter: The group's name stands for Heinous Unscrupulous Rats and Rogues Initiating Criminal Anarchy and Nefarious Evil. The blue-costumed Powerhouse has superstrength due to a superstrength potion, but is extremely lazy; Missing Fink is an android that can make itself invisible but suffers from hayfever which constantly reveals its location; the purple-costumed Mr. Mental has ESP and telekinetic abilities but is absentminded; dressed in a blue bodysuit with a yellow lightning bolt up the back, Yellow Streak can run at superspeed but is a peerless coward; and, covered with brown feathers, Blackbird can fly but suffers from airsickness. Non-super members of the band are scientist "Tabby" Katz, weapons and demolition genius "Nitro" Gleason, and escape artist "Crabgrass" Wilde. They have a supercar equipped with blinding spotlights to deter pursuit; harpoon guns; and a smoke screen. The subversive group is finally jailed due to the combined efforts of the superheroic Inferior Five and secret agents Caesar Single and Kwitcha Belliakin of C.O.U.S.I.N. F.R.E.D.

Comments: This group is a parody of the superhero team T.H.U.N.D.E.R. Agents (respectively: Raven, Mentor, NoMan, Dynamo, and Lightning). The first issue of DC Comics' *The Inferior Five* in 1967 marked their only appearance. See also VENDETTA, another team which fought the Inferior Five.

INJUSTICE GANG OF THE WORLD (C)

Members: CHRONOS, Libra, MIRROR MASTER, POISON IVY, SCARECROW (1), THE SHADOW THIEF, and TATTOOED MAN.

Charter: Organized by Libra, these villains are based on a satellite 22,300 miles above the earth, in a geosynchronous orbit and dead-opposite the Justice League of America satellite headquarters. Dressed in a blue bodysuit and wearing an orange cape, thigh boots, and gloves, Libra used his fellow villains to launch one of the grandest criminal escapades of all—to make him a god. Dispatching the super villains to battle superheroes of the Justice League, Libra swooped down, had the villains arrested, and took the weakened or defeated superheroes to his satellite. There, he used his Energy-Trans-Mortifier to steal half of their powers as a test of the machine's ability. Satisfied with the results, he then turned the unit on the galaxy itself to soak up half of its energy. Unfortunately, the influx proved too much for Libra's sanity, not to mention his body which subsequently discorporated. See AMAZO for the way in which the heroes regained their powers.

Comment: This DC Comics group's first and only appearance was in *Justice League of America* #111 (1974).

INJUSTICE SOCIETY OF THE WORLD (C)

Members: Original: the Brain Wave, the Gambler, Per Degaton, THE THINKER, VANDAL SAVAGE, and the Wizard (1). Second: add FIDDLER, HARLEQUIN, HUNTRESS, ICICLE, SHADE, SOLOMON GRUNDY, and SPORTSMASTER.

Charter: Believing that "justice is overrated" and that "it is evil that should be praised," this group banded together to conquer the nation, which they intended to divvy up. Based in "a richly-panoplied room . . . hidden in the stone depths of the city," the Society consists of the brilliant Brain Wave, who provides the group with weapons such as a "metal projector" cannon which allows the user to fire a cage around anyone in its sights, and a "heavy ray machine," which increases a person's weight sixty-fold; the Gambler, a former carnival entertainer who is an expert with knives; the Wizard, an illusionist; and Per Degaton, a non-super criminal who owns a time machine. The evil union inaugurated their plan by launching simultaneous strikes on key U.S. cities; they were beaten by the members of the Justice Society of America (a forerunner of the Justice League). The group has appeared a handful of times since then, its membership varying over the years; it has been put down each time by the Justice Society.

Comment: The Brain Wave—aka Henry King—is the father of the superhero of the same name; the elder King was killed in a battle with the brutish ULTRA-HUMANITE, dying to save his son's life. Per Degaton eventually took his own life after repeated attempts to change the course of history were foiled by the Justice Society. The Injustice Society first appeared in DC Comics' *All-Star Comics* #37 (1947).

THE LAWLESS LEAGUE (C)

Members: Atom, Batman, Flash, Green Lantern, J'onn J'onzz.

Charter: The members of the League live on Earth-A (for "Alternate"), the name given to our world when it is cleansed of superheroes. This disaster comes about when crook Johnny Thunder of our world steals the magic being Thunderbolt commanded by his counterpart on Earth-2—a world in another dimension but otherwise more or less identical to ours—and uses it to prevent the phenomena which gave the superheroes of the Justice League of America their powers. Learning of this, the Earth-2 superheroes known collectively as the Justice Society of America journey to Earth-1 to set things right. However, Johnny is not yet through changing history. Using Thunderbolt once again, he substitutes six members of his gang for the superheroes of Earth-1. Thus, Barney Judson becomes the evil Atom, able to shrink to any size and/or weight; Bill Gore becomes the criminal version of the deductive genius and superb athlete Batman; Race Morrison becomes the superspeed crook Flash; Monk Loomis becomes Green Lantern, with a power ring which creates animate or inanimate matter in any shape or size he wills; Eddie Orson becomes the ultra-powerful J'Onn J'Onzz; and Ripper Jones becomes the criminal Man of Steel, Superman. What's more, Johnny uses the magic at his command to create three other super villains: Absorbo-Man, who can drink up and utilize any form of energy; Medusa-Man, who can turn people to wood; and Repello-Man, who can use his enemies' powers against them. All of the Justice Society superheroes are defeated, save for Dr. Fate who, destroying the three newest villains, battles Johnny Thunder and Thunderbolt with magic. Badly beaten, Johnny orders the Thunderbolt to go back in time and prevent the Johnny Thunders of Earth-1 and Earth-2 from meeting.

Comment: The team appeared just once, in *Justice League of America* #38 (1965), though the individual characters debuted in the previous issue.

LEAGUE OF SUPER-ASSASSINS (C)

Members: Blok, Lazon, Mist Master, Neutrax, Silver Slasher, and Titania (2).

Charter: Halfway through the thirtieth century, the planet Dryad is consumed in a nova, leaving only a half-dozen survivors, all superbeings. Persuaded by the evil DARK MAN that the cataclysm has been caused by the Legion of Super-Heroes—who, in truth, have worked their mighty fingers to the bone rescuing people—the six survivors form the League of Super-Assassins which resolves to destroy the superheroes. Though the Legionnaires are able to convince the living, humanoid boulder Blok of their innocence, and even accept him as a member, the other five remain their mortal foes, and mighty foes they are. The orange-costumed Lazon can turn himself into living light able to slash through just about anything; the green-garbed Mist Master can become sentient mist; Neutrax, attired in a blue bodysuit, has the ability to neutralize almost any kind of energy; wearing a white leotard, the white-skinned Silver Slasher can cut through any kind of matter; and Titania, in her purple leotard and miniskirt, possesses enormous physical strength.

Comment: The group first appeared in *Superboy and the Legion of Super-Heroes* #253 (1979).

THE LEGION OF SUPER-VILLAINS (C)

Members: Original: Lightning Lord, Nemesis Kid, Radiation Roy, and Spider Girl. Later: add Chameleon Chief, Cosmic King, Esper Lass, Hunger, Lazon, Magno Lad, Micro Lad, Mist Master, Neutrax, Ol-Vir, Ron-Karr, Saturn Queen, Silver Slasher, Sun Emperor, Tarik, Terrus, Titania (2), Tyr, and Zymyr.

Charter: In the thirtieth century, Tarik was minding his own business when he was struck by a ray from a police gun. Rendered speechless by the accident, he opened a school for villains, vowing vengeance against those who upheld the law. Though the crimebusting Legion of Super-Heroes closed Tarik's operation down, several of the alumni banded together to form the Legion of Super-Villains. The most prominent characters in the group are Chameleon Chief, who can change into anything he wishes (his counterpart in the Legion of Super-Heroes is Chameleon Boy); Saturn Queen, who hails from Saturn "where there has been no crime at all for centuries . . . and where everyone can perform amazing mental feats," two factors which inspire her to try to "outwit the law with my powers of super-hypnotism" (her superhero counterpart is Saturn Girl); Cosmic King, a Venusian who can transmute non-living matter by firing rays from his eyes, a power he acquired in a laboratory accident; Lightning Lord, aka Mekt Ranzz, the evil brother of the superheroes Lightning Lad and Lightning Lass (all three were struck by an outpouring from electrified monsters and have the power to fire destructive bolts of electricity); Nemesis Kid, who comes from the planet Myar where he invented a potion enabling him to assume whatever powers he needs to confront any given situation; and Mist Master, who can transform himself into a green vapor; and the flaming Sun Emperor.

Comment: The Legion of Super-Villains first appeared in *Adventure Comics* #372 (1968).

THE LEOPARD MEN (C)

Members: Four anthropomorphic leopards wearing purple jumpsuits (the leopard men are yellow with purple spots).

Charter: The powerful Leopard Men live on the planet Carrot in Funny Animal Land. They feed on the population of rabbits, though they are not averse to dining on tourists; after capturing the tourists they salt and pepper their captives then cut them up. However, none of the four can withstand the might of the superheroic Hoppy, the Marvel Bunny, who beats them up, then forces them to eat vegetables.

Comment: Fawcett's *Funny Animals* #16 (1944) was the tribe's only appearance. Another nasty group fought by Hoppy were Black Bill and his Loggers, bears who tormented rabbits for the sheer pleasure of it.

THE MADMEN (C)

Members: There are six costumed Madmen and at least two non-costumed thugs, though their names are never revealed.

Charter: The Madmen are Acrobatic thieves who menace Hub City. They wear wigs and greasepaint, both of various primary colors; green trunks and boots; and white bodysuits with "mod" designs in yellow, red, and black. After a crime, the superheroic Blue Beetle follows them to their warehouse hideout and, after a furious battle, fells the felons. They have returned infrequently.

Comment: These characters first appeared in Charlton Comics' *Blue Beetle* #3 (1967). They were created and drawn by comics legend Steve Ditko.

MASTERS OF DISASTER (C)

Members: Coldsnap, Heatstroke, New Wave, Shakedown, and Windfall.

Charter: Virtually nothing is known about these mercenaries or their origins. They burst upon the criminal scene tackling Batman and his superheroic allies the Outsiders. Collectively, the super villains possess a vast array of powers. Dressed in a blue bodysuit with white icicle designs, Coldsnap (aka Darrel) can whip up ice at will; garbed in a yellow bodysuit with a fiery red motif, Heatstroke (aka Joanne) can cause combustion with her touch; the blue-costumed New Wave (aka Becky) is the mistress of water; wearing a green bodysuit, the bulky Shakedown causes quake-like tremors; and the blue-cloaked Windfall (sister of New Wave) can fly and control the winds. Interestingly, the only reason Coldsnap and Heatstroke joined the band was because they needed the money to find a cure for their conditions. Lovers, they can't even touch one another until that cure is found.

Comment: These DC characters first appeared in *Batman and the Outsiders* #9 (1984).

MASTERS OF EVIL (C)

Members: Original: BARON ZEMO, THE BLACK

KNIGHT, THE ENCHANTRESS (1), THE EXECUTIONER, THE MELTER, THE RADIOACTIVE MAN. Second: the second Black Knight, KLAW, the Melter, Radioactive Man, ULTRON, WHIRLWIND. Third: BEETLE, Egghead, MOONSTONE, SCORPION (4), SHOCKER, TIGER SHARK (2), Whirlwind. Fourth: ABSORBING MAN, the second Baron Zemo, BLACKOUT, Bulldozer, FIXER, GOLIATH, GREY GARGOYLE, Mr. Hyde, Piledriver, Screaming Mimi, Thunderball, Titania (1), WRECKER, and Yellowjacket.

Charter: In each of its incarnations, the group was founded to battle the superheroic Avengers. Baron Zemo pulled the first band together, Ultron the second, Egghead the third, and the second Baron Zemo the fourth. All incarnations of Masters of Evil have been defeated and are currently disbanded. The second Black Knight joined simply to spy and report to the Avengers; Egghead is the criminal name of Elihas Starr, a brilliant scientist first seen in *Tales to Astonish* #38 (1962); Bulldozer, Piledriver, and Thunderball are members of THE WRECKING CREW; and Mr. Hyde is Calvin Zebo, who becomes a savage after reconstructing the experiments that created the original MR. HYDE; Screaming Mimi and Titania are members of THE GRAPPLERS; and Yellowjacket who fires energy bolts, can fly, and is able to shrink herself to inches in height.

Comment: The first group was originally seen in Marvel Comics' *The Avengers* #6 (1964) (though the Enchantress and the Executuioner didn't come along until #7); the second in *The Avengers* #54 (1968); the third in *The Avengers* #222 (1982) (with Beetle, Shocker, and Tiger Shark getting into the act in #228); and the fourth in *The Avengers* #270 (1986) (though everyone didn't sign aboard officially until #273).

THE MONSTER SOCIETY OF EVIL (C)

Members: BLACK ADAM, CAPTAIN NAZI, Crocodile Men, DR. SIVANA, Dummy, Evil-Eye, Goat-Man, IBAC, Jeepers, KING KULL, MR. ATOM, Mr. Banjo, MR. MIND, Mr. Who, Nippo, Nyola, Oggar, Ooom, and Ramulus.

Charter: Upon first coming to earth, the evil worm Mr. Mind began pulling together the core of what was to be the most imposing team of super villains in history. Initially, the group consisted of Goat-Man, whom Mr. Mind had met when the satyric being was exiled to the worm's planet; Evil-Eye, a green-skinned hypnotic brute; the Crocodile Men from the planet Punkus, who are humanoid save for their heads (the chief Punkusians are Sylvester and Herkimer); the titanic gray man Oom; the bespectacled Mister Who; the sword-swinging Amazonian Nyola; the green-skinned Ramulus; and the pint-sized Dummy. Later, the Japanese spy Nippo of Nagasaki came aboard, along with the bat-man Jeepers, the enemy agent Mister Banjo (aka Dr. Filpots) who used his instrument to send Allied secrets to the enemy in musical code, Ibac, and Dr. Sivana. The group was constantly undone by the superheroic Captain Marvel, and was disbanded when Mr. Mind was thought to have been executed. When the criminal mastermind returned some 20 years later, a new group was founded consisting of Mister Atom, Ibac, Sivana (and his children Georgia and Sivana Jr.), King Kull, Black Adam, and Oggar—a god who had turned against the mighty wizard Shazam (mentor of Captain Marvel) and, exiled from the Home of the Gods, was only too happy to make life unpleasant for the superhero. The group never regained its previous glory, and remains only an occasional thorn in Captain Marvel's side.

Comment: Unlike most super villain teams, this one consisted of every major enemy Fawcett Publications' Captain Marvel had ever had. For some reason (pride, most likely) super villains rarely team to combat a mutual foe. The rare exceptions include THE SUPERMAN REVENGE SQUAD and the felons in the 1966 *Batman* movie—THE PENGUIN, THE JOKER, THE RIDDLER, and THE CATWOMAN—who joined forces to battle Batman (and lost anyway).

MUTANT FORCE (C)

Members: Burner, Lifter, Peeper, Shocker, and Slither.

Charter: This team of mutants was founded by MAGNETO, a mutant villain who employed them to help take over the world. After their defeat at the hands of Captain America, the band fell in with THE MANDRILL and was walloped by the superheroic Defenders; after a stint as government employees—the alternative to a prison term—the group became a mercenary band, selling its services to the highest bidder. Eventually bested again by the Defenders, the mutants are currently in the hands of the international peacekeeping force S.H.I.E.L.D. Doubtless they will not remain incarcerated for very long. Each member of the Mutant Force has a distinctive costume and power: Burner (Byron Calley) can radiate flame from his hands or simply will an object to burn; Lifter (Ned Lathrop) possesses superstrength; Peeper (Peter Quinn) has the ability to destroy objects with his gaze and also has telescopic vision; Shocker (Randall Darby) can generate electricity in bolts or blankets; and Slither, who has a serpent's neck and head, can crush people with his body.

Comment: This Marvel Comics team first appeared in *Captain America Annual* #4 (1977).

OMEGA FLIGHT (C)

Members: Roger Bochs (see Charter), Delphine Courtney, Diamond Lil, Flashback, Jerome K. Jaxon, Smart Alec, and Wild Child.

Charter: Alpha Flight and its backups Beta and Gamma Flight were teams of superheroes originally formed to serve the Canadian government. When the program was discontinued due to its extraordinary overhead, Alpha Flight stayed together as a team operating independent of the government; not only didn't superheroes belonging to Beta and Gamma Flight join, but several embittered members teamed to become Omega Flight, a team of super villains. The band was originally pulled together by Jaxon, an employee of the Roxxon Oil Corporation. Working for another oil company, Am-Can Petro-Chemical, Jaxon had overseen the development of a supersuit which was to have been used for dangerous mining operations. In reality, though, its creation was being underwritten by the U.S. military; learning of this and becoming morally offended, the suit's inventor, "bleeding-heart boy genius" James MacDonald Hudson, destroyed the plans and hijacked the uniform along with the cybernetic helmet which made it work. Jaxon, meanwhile, was fired despite 18 years of devoted service to Am-Can and became an anathema in the oil business for having mishandled the entire affair. He was such a blunderer, in fact, that when he tried to hang himself he succeeded only in cutting off "oxygen long enough to cause brain damage," leaving him paralyzed from the waist down. Some time later, when Guardian of Alpha Flight made his debut, Jaxon's fortunes finally took an upswing. Deducing that the superhero was actually Hudson in a variation of his supersuit, Jaxon approached the corrupt Roxxon and was hired to put together Omega Flight in an effort to steal the costume. Assigned to help him assemble the team was Delphine Courtney—in reality Roxxon android MX39147—and the ex-superhero trainees they brouht together were the yellow- and green-garbed Diamond Lil (Lillian Crawley), who can withstand any destructive force; Flashback (Gardner Monroe) who, dressed in a white bodysuit, is a "living temporal anomaly" who can transport duplicates of himself to the present from various points in the future and force them to do his bidding; Smart Alec (Alexander Thorne), "the man with the computer-brain, intellect unsurpassed"; and Wild Child, a purple- and black-clothed "killing machine" who lashes out with powerful claws and can heal all his own wounds at a remarkably swift pace. (Another member of the team was the engineer Roger Bochs, who joined merely to spy on behalf of Alpha Flight. However, he ended up inadvertently helping Omega Flight when a powerful robot he built, the Psi-Borg Box, was taken over by Jaxon's mind.) Their first run-in with Hudson's team Alpha Flight caused some serious losses on both sides. Jaxon perished inside the robot, along with Guardian who died when his suit exploded. Smart Alec lost his mind after taking a peek into the magic medicine bag of Alpha Flight's Shaman. (Shaman charitably shrunk Alec and let him live in the mystic pouch.) The other members, save Courtney, were arrested; sneaking away, the robot redesigned herself to resemble Guardian and got the team back together again. She was destroyed in their second confrontation, the other members ending up back in prison. The group has not been heard from since.

Comment: The members of Omega Flight were first introduced in Marvel Comics' *Alpha Flight* #'s 1 and 2 in 1983, though the team itself did not appear until #11.

THE PANTHER GANG (C)

Members: Unnamed photo editor (leader; see Charter), Joe Tinker, and a third, unnamed party.

Charter: Led by the photo editor of *The Ivy Town Courier*, the Panther Gang (also referred to as the Panther Pack) wear navy blue bodysuits and panther-cowls. A bold band, they not only rob jewelry stores and the like but also raid gala functions, the photo editor stunning people with a special flashbulb which releases "an electronic impulse so high-pitched" it knocks everybody out. "Special earplugs" protect the Panthers. The group is stopped by the superheroic Atom while robbing jewels at a beauty contest.

Comment: The DC Comics' gang's only appearance was in *The Atom* #27 (1966).

THE POSSESSORS (C)

Charter: Learning of the existence of the earth, the nameless "leader" of another dimension selects a small village in the mountains of Bavaria as a test: If he and his Possessors can conquer it, he will try to take over the entire planet. Heading to earth in a huge, cube-shaped transporter (referred to only as "the Entrance"), they fly through the air as ethereal beings, enter human bodies, and begin taking over. Discovering an occult presence in Bavaria, the master magician Dr. Strange heads there. Using his own supernatural powers, he divines the presence of the Possessors and traces them back to their realm. Traveling there and summoning "all the mystic forces of the shadow worlds," Strange agrees to spare the leader only if he recalls his forces. This is done, and the Possessors have stayed away ever since. The Possessors, dressed in purple jumpsuits, all have green skin and grasshopper-like faces.

Comment: The characters—all of them nameless—appeared only in Marvel Comics' *Strange Tales* #118 (1964).

THE REDUCERS (TV, C)

Members: Uxl and nameless colleagues.

Charter: These extraterrestrials scour the universe shrinking life forms. Their goal? Not to preserve endangered species but simply to "be honored as the greatest hunters ever to prowl the universe." Arriving on the planet Amzot, the aliens shrink the heroic Herculoids, only to have their captives escape and discover the hunters' weak spot: their ears. Attacking their "centers of balance," the Herculoids force the hunters to restore them to normal, after which the Herculoids shrink the aliens, leaving them unable to operate their ship and thus stranded on Amzot. The pointy-eared aliens wear a blue jacket, tan trunks, purple tights, and brown boots.

Comment: These characters were seen once on the CBS-TV cartoon series *The Herculoids* (1968) and in the seventh issue of Gold Key's *Super TV Heroes* comic book (1969). Other foes faced by the Herculoids on their primitive world were the Mole Men, the Spider Man, the Raider Apes, the Bubbleman, Mekkano the Machine Master, the Zorbots, the Mutoids, the Gravites, the Reptons, the Electrode Men, the Faceless People, Malak and the Metal Apes, Sta-Lak, and the Gladiators of Kyanite. Hanna-Barbera produced the series.

ROCKETEERS (C)

Members: Original: various nameless humans. Second: various nameless DIRE WRAITHS.

Charter: Dressed in green jumpsuits with darker green vests, the airborne Rocketeers wear golden jetpacks on their backs and carry "ray blasters." The paraphernalia was developed by the Dire Wraiths, evil extraterrestrials who want to use it to destroy the superhero Rom and the benevolent Spaceknights. The Wraiths enlist unwitting humans to don the suits for a shakedown run and, several years later, finally wear the equipment into battle themselves. Ultimately, they are defeated by Rom and the superhero Torpedo, who, ironically, derives his superpowers from the Wraith costume which was the prototype for the Rocketeer uniform.

***THE REDUCERS** gloat over the captured Herculoids.*

Comment: These Marvel Comics characters appeared in *Daredevil* #131 (1976) (humans wearing the costumes); the Wraiths, in human form, first donned the suits in *Rom* #'s 21 and 22 (1981).

THE ROYAL FLUSH GANG (C)

Members: Ace of Clubs (see PROFESSOR FORTUNE), King of Clubs, Queen of Clubs, Jack of Clubs, and Ten of Clubs (aka Ten Spot). A later incarnation was all spades.

Charter: As children, all five future members of the Royal Flush Gang were rowdy friends who "shared many street fights and thefts and knew just how to work as a team"; Amos "Pudge" Fortune was incontestably their leader because he always figured out "neat ways to steal and get away safely." As an adult, Fortune discovered "stellaration," the energy by which stars influence luck. Learning how to magnify this force in playing cards—for example, drawing a five of diamonds won't just give the holder "unexpected news" but *catastrophic* news—he organized his friends into the Royal Flush Gang, all of them wearing club-suit playing card costumes because "clubs are cards of bad fortune." The group took on Fortune's foes, the Justice League of America, only to be defeated when the superheroes short-circuited their stellaration. The Gang battled the Justice League, among other heroes, on numerous occasions before disbanding after suffering one too many defeats. Jack of Clubs went on to enjoy a free-lance career as Hi-Jack, using specially-treated cards as deadly weapons, and was briefly a member of THE SECRET SOCIETY OF SUPER-VILLAINS; unfortunately, he crossed fellow member THE WIZARD, who used magic to dispatch Hi-Jack to a netherworld from which he has not managed to return. A new group was eventually formed by villain Hector Hammond, who brought in derelict Joe Carny as the King, drunkard actress Mona Taylor as the Queen, a murderer and thief named Jack as the Jack, pilot Wanda Wayland as the Ten, and an android as the new Ace. This group was bested by the Justice League in its sole appearance. A third group debuted in *Justice League* #4 (second series), 1987. They were virtually identical to the others, save that they all had a spade-motif and the android Ace had a flame-gun built into its right arm and could also turn into a humanoid flame creature. It was blown up, and the others captured, in their only appearance.

Comment: The cards first appeared in DC Comics' *Justice League of America* #43 (1966).

SALEM'S 7 (C)

Members: Brutacus, Gazelle, Hydron, Reptilla, Thornn, Vakume, and Vertigo.

Charter: This band consists of seven witches from New Salem, Colorado, who were magically transformed into superbeings to battle the Fantastic Four at the behest of the vile Nicolas Scratch (Scratch being a nickname for the Devil). Brutacus is a lion-like human with superstrength; the red-dressed Gazelle is a superb acrobat and gymnast; the green, scaly Hydron can whistle up water whenever he wishes; Reptilla is a huge snake from the waist down, and also has large living serpents for arms, their snapping heads where her hands should be; the yellow-skinned Thornn has the ability to fire the red quills which line his arms and legs; the purple-clad Vakume can become noncorporeal and cause vacuums; and the white-robed Vertigo causes people to become physically unbalanced.

Comment: The villains first appeared in Marvel Comics' *Fantastic Four* #186 (1977).

THE SEAL MEN (C)

Members: Prince Pagli (leader), Count Frigid (Chief of Freezing Room Operations), and many others.

Charter: These blue-skinned fiends possess seal-like faces, webbed hands, wear black trunks, and carry clubs. Dwelling "in caves and tunnels" in Bitterland in the South Pole, the Seal Men lure the women of Eveland to cross the river which divides their lands, the Seal Men being unable to "invade Eveland because light blinds their eyes." Once there, the women are made "garden slaves," since the Seal Men can't work in the light; when those slaves go blind, others which have been kept in suspended animation in ice are put to work. Unfortunately, the Seal Men underestimate the power of Wonder Woman, who is summoned by Queen Eve to help them when her own daughter, Eve Electress, is captured. (Why the Queen didn't call when other womens' daughters were abducted is perplexing.) The superheroine frees the Evelanders and beats the whiskers off the Seal Men, who learn their lesson and stay away from women.

Comment: These characters appeared only once in DC Comics' *Wonder Woman* #13 (1945).

THE SECRET SOCIETY OF SUPER-VILLAINS (C)

Members: ANGLE MAN, Bizarro (see LEX

LUTHOR), BLOCKBUSTER (1), Brain Wave, CAPTAIN BOOMERANG (charter), CAPTAIN COLD (charter), Captain Stingaree, CHEETAH, CHRONOS, COPPERHEAD (charter), FELIX FAUST, FLORONIC MAN, Funky Flashman, GORILLA GRODD (charter), Hi-Jack (charter), KILLER FROST, KILLER MOTH, Lex Luthor, Manhunter (charter), MATTER MASTER, MIRROR MASTER (charter), MIST, MONOCLE, POISON IVY, PSYCHO-PIRATE, QUAKEMASTER, Rag Doll, REVERSE-FLASH, SHADOW THIEF, SINESTRO (charter), Silver Ghost, Signalman, STAR SAPPHIRE, TRICKSTER, THE ULTRA-HUMANITE, and Wizard (1) (charter).

Charter: This group was first organized by DARKSEID, who needed a group of evil warriors to help him conquer the earth. Having second thoughts about the assignment—they couldn't think of a single good reason to battle superheroes for Darkseid's glory—the villains decided to take over the planet for themselves. Falling under the influence of Funky Flashman, a slick entrepreneur, they were joined by other super villains. Various members came and went, along with numerous leaders, most notably The Ultra-Humanite; their perennial foes have been the superheroes of the Justice League of America and the Justice Society of America. Among the group's more interesting members were Rag Doll, a miraculous contortionist; Manhunter, an evil clone of the superhero of the same name; Wizard, who uses various mystical objects to commit crimes; and Signalman, a foe of Batman, who was inspired by the Bat-Signal (a bat-image flashed in the skies by police to summon Batman) to become a costumed villain, and who used various signals and symbols (buoys, arrows, etc.) in his crimes. See INJUSTICE SOCIETY OF THE WORLD for more on Brain Wave.

Comment: The league first appeared in DC's *The Secret Society of Super-Villains* #1 (1976). However, many of the villains had appeared individually before that—such as The Wizard (1), who made his debut in *All-Star Comics* #34 in 1947.

SERPENT SOCIETY (C)

Members: Anaconda, Asp, Black Mamba, Bushmaster, Cobra, Cottonmouth, Death Adder, Diamondback, The Rattler, and THE SIDEWINDER.

Charter: After the collapse of THE SERPENT SQUAD, the Sidewinder pulled together this new team of super villains to battle Captain America. Little is known about the past of the individual members. Dressed in a white leotard with flaps front and back reaching nearly to the ground, and green serpents in an "X" shape on the front of the costume, the Egyptian-born Asp is apparently a mutant and possesses the ability to fire destructive blasts known as "venom bolts" from her hands. A quadriplegic. Bushmaster has a green, snake-like, mechanical lower torso and huge tail surgically attached to his body, a serpentine extension which allows him to move with great speed as well as crush even steel objects around which it coils. He also has a pair of artificial arms attached to his shoulders, huge fang-like, poison-dispensing projections jutting from the back of his wrists. Wearing a purple bodysuit, Cottonmouth (aka Quincy McIver) has the ability to stretch his mouth well beyond normal limits and pulverize virtually anything between his fangs. Diamondback (Rachel Leighton) wears a pink and black bodysuit and carries a supply of diamond-shaped darts which she throws with precision; the "diamonds" contain everything from explosives to acid to snake venom to a sleeping formula. Finally, garbed in a brown bodysuit with a ribbed, yellow belly, the Rattler (Gustav Krueger) has an artificial tail which contains various sonic devices which cause devastating sound waves capable of destroying metal or stopping bullets in midflight; although the costume protects the Rattler from the vibrations, he is (not surprisingly) nearly deaf.

Comment: The Marvel Comics team first appeared in *Captain America* #309 (1985). See THE SERPENT SQUAD for more details on members.

THE SERPENT SQUAD (C)

Members: Original: COBRA, Eel, VIPER (charter). Second: a new Viper replaced the original, and PRINCESS PYTHON signed aboard. Third: Anaconda, Black Mamba, Death Adder, and SIDEWINDER.

Charter: The group consists of snake-like super villains who joined forces simply to form a more effective fighting unit; most of them had criminal careers previous to the founding of the Squad. Anaconda, aka Blanche "Blondie" Sitznski, possesses superstrength and has the ability to stretch her limbs to great lengths, power she usually uses to choke her enemies. She acquired this ability (along with gills for breathing underwater and incredible regenerative powers) thanks to the scientists at the Roxxon Corporation's subsidiary, the Brand Corporation. Anaconda wears light green armor and darker green trunks and boots. Black Mamba (Tanya Sealy), was also mutated by Brand scientists. Dressed in a navy blue leotard, she has the power to emit (she calls it "shedding") the Darkforce, a black cloud-like ooze which she controls and uses to hamper the movements of (or smother the life from) her enemies. She also possesses modest hypnotic abilities. Death Adder (Richard Burroughs) also underwent the Brand treatment, being given a powerful artificial tail and gills. The pièce de résistance of his costume—green armor bodysuit and a purple leotard—were sharp-clawed purple gloves which contained poison in their tips, with which he could paralyze or kill. Alas, these accouterments were not enough to save him from the vigilante Scourge—brother of THE ENFORCER (2)—who took Death Adder's life.

Comment: This slithering Marvel Comics band first appeared in *Captain America* #163 (1973); the second version debuted in *Marvel Two-In-One* #64 (1980).

THE SINISTER SIX (C)

Members: DR. OCTOPUS, ELECTRO, KRAVEN THE HUNTER, MYSTERIO, THE SANDMAN, and THE VULTURE.

Charter: The Sinister Six was formed when Dr. Octopus, newly escaped from prison, called a gathering of Spider-Man's enemies. Deciding that they would be wise to band together to defeat their common enemy, they set about to tackle him one after another, obviously feeling that attrition rather than brute force was the way to beat their nemesis. They're wrong; he licks each villains in turn, despite suffering a brief, psychosomatic loss of his powers.

Comment: This group appeared only once, in *The Amazing Spider-Man Annual* #1 (1964). They were one of the two "Sinister" teams to battle Spider-Man (see THE SINISTER SYNDICATE).

THE SINISTER SYNDICATE (C)

Members: THE BEETLE, BOOMERANG, HYDRO-MAN, THE RHINO, and SPEED DEMON.

Charter: Gathered together at the suggestion of JACK O'LANTERN, these villains are dedicated to the destruction of the superhero Spider-Man.

Comment: The group first appeared in *The Amazing Spider-Man* #280 (1986). ("What is this," the superhero gasped after laying eyes on the band, "*old villains' week*?!")

THE SLY FOX GANG (C)

Members: Three sly foxes in overalls.

Charter: Robbers by trade, the foxes are constantly thwarted by Atomic Bunny. Tricking him into drinking lemonade laced with "starch and secret ingredients" which render him "stiff as a board," the foxes are free to steal (singing as they go, "La-dee-dum-da! We're going to rob a bank, dee-dum!") Armed with slingshots, they terrorize Bunnyville until the superhero is able to get to his mighty carrot cubes (he lies down beside a buzzsaw and slices open the pouch where they're stored) and overcome the paralysis. The three foxes end up in jail.

Comment: The rascally animals appeared just once, in Charlton Comics' *Atomic Bunny* #18 (1959).

SOVIET SUPER SOLDIERS (C)

Members: CRIMSON DYNAMO, Darkstar, Gremlin, Ursa Major, and Vanguard.

Charter: As in the United States, mutants are not highly regarded in the Soviet Union. However, never a nation to pass up a new weapon, the Russian government recruits four mutants to become a team of super agents. Darkstar (Laynia Petrovna) has the ability to use an otherdimensional energy known as the Darkforce to fly as well as to mold and control tangible objects in our dimension, incomplex forms such as impenetrable barriers, rings to bind people, and the like (first appearance: *Champions* #7, 1976). Gremlin is a scientific genius who obtained his boosted IQ after exposure to radiation which also deformed his body (first appearance: *The Incredible Hulk* #187, 1976); he is the son of another Soviet criminal supermind, the Gargoyle, who was also atomically mutated due to "secret bomb tests" (and had the distinction of appearing in *The Incredible Hulk* #1 as the superhero's first foe). Ursa Major (Mikhail Ursus) has the power to become a massive, articulate bear (first appearance: *The Incredible Hulk* #258, 1981). And Vanguard (Nicolai Krylenko) can repel energy, from ray beams to physical clouts, all of which go bounding back to their source; he carries a tailormade hammer and sickle that heighten his powers and can also be used as offensive devices (first appearance: *Iron Man* #109, 1978). The only change in the lineup occurred when the team learned that the Crimson Dynamo was spying on them and reporting back to the government. He was promptly booted from the group, and the distrustful mutants no longer took the word of their government as law. Today, while they still serve the best interests of the Soviet people—and would surely fight against other nations if need be—the Soviet Super Soldiers are not quite as blindly nationalistic and villainous as they might otherwise have been.

Comment: Though all of the characters had appeared previously (save for Ursa Major), and had even teamed up (*Iron Man* #109, *Marvel Team-Up Annual* #2, 1979, for example), they did not get their name and full roster until *The Incredible Hulk* #258. See other Soviet super villains Boris Kartovski (see DR. CLEMENT ARMSTRONG, Comment), COMRADE STUPIDSKA, THE CRIMSON DYNAMO, MONGU, THE RED GHOST, THE TITANIC THREE, and TITANIUM MAN.

THE SQUADRON SINISTER (C)

Members: Dr. Spectrum, Hyperion, Nighthawk, and the Whizzer (see SPEED DEMON [2]).

Charter: On the world of Other-Earth in another dimension, Dr. Spectrum, Hyperion, Nighthawk, and the Whizzer are superheroes. Discovering Other-Earth, an ancient alien named the Grandmaster who "has almost complete control over time and space" decides to use the superheroes, aka the Squadron Supreme, as pawns in his sole pastime: creating games and battles for his own amusement. Impressed with their performance against a union of their enemies, the Institute of Evil, the Grandmaster decides to whip up his own evil version of the Squadron should the need ever arise. And arise it does when he encounters Kang the Conqueror (see IMMORTUS). The two opt to use our own earth as a battleground, Kang championing the superheroic Avengers while the Grandmaster goes "back in time . . . to alter the lives of four . . . earthmen . . . and turn them into super villains." The result is a corruption of the Other-Earth heroes known as the Squadron Sinister. Dressed in green tights, a red and yellow bodyshirt, and a blue cowl, Dr. Spectrum has a Power Prism which permits him to fire destructive or disintegrating blasts and to form a "polychromatic shield . . . to protect me from all harm" (though he can be knocked out by a concentrated dose of ultraviolet light); wearing a yellow cape, boots, and trunks, and a red bodysuit, Hyperion possesses the power to fly, superstrength, and "burning . . . atomic vision," among other abilities; wearing a blue and black bodysuit with a black hawk symbol, as well as a blue cape and hawk-like cowl, Nighthawk commands a hi-tech plane shaped like a hawk; and, wearing a yellow bodysuit with a blue vest and cowl, the Whizzer can gulp down a pellet and move at superspeed. Defeated in their bout with the Avengers, the team returned with a "laser device" to melt the polar icecaps and flood the world. Assisting them in this project was the infamous Nebulon, a member of the alien race of Ul'lula'ns, six-tentacled, fish-like beings. Taking the form of a golden humanoid, Nebulon was sent into space to find a world richer than the Squadron's in natural resources; his plans and those of the Squadron were a perfect mix. The super villains were beaten by the Defenders (*The Defenders* #13, 1974), but Nebulon was not quite finished with his evil. After infiltrating the Avengers in order to gain access to their hi-tech hardware, he maneuvered them into battle against the Defenders. The alien died under the rays of an energy-sapping device (*The Avengers Annual* #11, 1982).

Comment: These Marvel Comics super villains first appeared in *The Avengers* #69 (1969). Despite the reference to Hyperion as having been an earthman, it was subsequently revealed that he hailed from the other-dimensional world of Yttrium. An astronaut, he was drawn to earth when the first atom split by a cyclotron caused a dimensional rift. The energy it released also caused Yttrium to explode, a detonation which gave Hyperion his powers. He was adrift in the interdimensional void when he was found by the Grandmaster. Subsequent to his activities with the Squadron, he fell in love with Thundra (see THE FRIGHTFUL FOUR), an Amazon warrior from the future, and went to live with her on Amazonia, an alternate earth of tomorrow. As for Nighthawk, aka industrialist Kyle Richmond, he turned on his fellow super villains during the icecap caper and joined the Defenders as a superhero. He perished in the service of that group in *The Defenders* #106 (1982). Dr. Spectrum appeared subsequently as a solo operator, battling Iron Man in #'s 63 to 66 of the superhero's magazine (1973). The villain was revealed, then, to be Dr. Kinji Obatu, the Minister of Economics of a tiny African nation. He was assisted in these tales by his creation Rokk, "the living mountain."

THE SUPERMAN REVENGE SQUAD (C)

Members: Dramx, Fwom, Nakox, Nryana, Rava, Ulyro, Vlatuu, and many others over the years; the roster is continually changing due to death and attrition.

Comments: Founded by the militaristic denizens of the planet Wexr II, whose plans of conquest Superman has foiled, the squad of "Revengers" is committed to destroying the Man of Steel. A secondary goal is the destruction of earth for, as one of them declares, "only when his beloved earth lies in smoking ruins will he realize that we have finally repaid him for wrecking all our plans to dominate the universe." The Squad is based on a "shrouded planet . . . millions of light-years and thousands of galaxies" from earth. There, they hold meetings in their Hall of Hate, which is chockfull of statues of every member who has died because of Superman. (Not that the Man of Steel slays them; rather, Revengers who fail to kill Superman are themselves murdered by an "execution beam" fired from one of their many hyperspace cruisers, spaceships emblazoned with a broken "S" on the hull.) Strangely, given the depth of their commitment, Squad members are prohibited from going to the aid of a fellow Revenger. Many of the Revengers have superpowers, including Nryana who unleashes lethal electric waves from her hair and Vlatuu of Plyrox who can fly.

Comment: The band first appeared in DC's *Action Comics* #286 (1962). In 1982, in *The New Adventures of Superboy* #'s 32-33, it was revealed that there was a Superboy Revenge Squad, dedicated to destroying the young Superman. The only villains named are the cat-like shapechanger Trohnn and the orange-skinned Muht.

THE TERRIBLE TRIO (C)

Members: The Fox, the Shark, and the Vulture.

Charter: Dressed in business suits and full-head masks which resemble their namesakes, these crooks also happen to be exemplary scientists who create incredible weapons and equipment for their various crimes. The Fox devotes himself to creating devices and planning crimes on land, the Shark to crimes in the water, the Vulture to those in the air. Each crime is then executed by the group en masse. Among the more unusual conveyances they've invented: a "burrow machine" which can dig through the earth or any wall; the undersea "eel machine"; the "pilot fish machine" which can hitch a ride unknown to any ship; the "swordfish machine" which can puncture any seagoing vessel; and the supersonic "missile machine." In their first escapade the Terrible Trio robbed a bank, an ocean liner, and a plane in, outside of, and above Gotham City. That brought them to the attention of the superhero Batman, who apprehended them. Escaping prison, the band used trained animals in their next series of crimes; that, too, ended in arrest. Their present activities have not been revealed.

Comment: These DC Comics characters first appeared in *Detective Comics* #253 (1958).

THE TERROR TWINS (C)

Members: Gilbert and Rudy Maroni.

Charter: Billed as "the strangest crew of evildoers who ever gave a costumed hero a migraine headache," these "villainous oddballs" and musicians are the sons of the gangster "Scarmug" Maroni and his wife Lulu. The Maronis live on "a lavish estate" in Yorkstown, where the teenagers carry on the family tradition by donning skull-face masks, packing laser-firing guitars and bongo drum bombs, and pursuing a life of crime. As a "coming out" present for his kids, Scarmug kidnaps Professor Thaddeus Dalrymple and forces him to produce other weapons for the kids. ("You either create fantastic crime-gadgets," he warns, "or get rubbed out.") Among the implements he adds to their armory are death rays, "transmutation pellets," and flying motorcycles. Despite the array of weapons, the boys are prevented from stealing Mt. Rushmore by the superheroic Owl, who subsequently exposes them and their parents to a projector which siphons the evil from people.

Comment: These characters appeared only once, in the second (and final) issue of Gold Key's *The Owl* (1968). They were the brainchildren of Jerry Siegel, the creator of Superman. Another team which battled the Owl was the Birdmen Bandits, seen in the first issue.

THE THIRSTIES (C)

Members: Ten unnamed creatures.

Charter: The Thirsties are human-sized, yellow, sun-shaped aliens with legs, arms, and green tongues. Showing up wherever people are active, they use their scientific genius to make sure water fountains don't work, snack stands are closed, and food is "hotter than the sun." They can also shine brightly enough to blind people, and wilt flowers simply by passing beside them. They also work with the Giant Thirst Monster, a being several stories tall who uses his "super-hot breath" to cause mass thirstiness at places such as amusement parks. The only way these nefarious beings can be chased off is by the arrival of Kool-Aid Man with cool, refreshing Kool-Aid. The Thirsties travel through space in a sun-shaped spaceship, which is equipped with a "Thirst Ray"; they answer to the Big Thirstie, their leader back on their home world.

Comment: These creatures battled Kool-Aid Man in his one-issue Marvel Comic book in 1983.

THE TITANIC THREE (C)

Members: THE CRIMSON DYNAMO, RADIOACTIVE MAN, and TITANIUM MAN.

Charter: Meeting in Vietnam, these three villains briefly teamed to serve as the champions of Eastern Communism. They were defeated by the champions of the American way, the Avengers.

Comment: The team first appeared in Marvel's *The Avengers* #130 (1974), their activities spilling over into *Iron Man* #'s 73 and 74 (1975). See other Soviet super villains Boris Kartovski (see DR. CLEMENT ARMSTRONG, Comment), COMRADE STUPIDSKA, MONGU, THE RED GHOST, and THE SOVIET SUPER SOLDIERS.

U-FOES (C)

Members: Ironclad, Vapor, Vector, and X-Ray.

Charter: Aware that the superheroic Fantastic Four acquired their powers after being exposed to cosmic radiation during a space flight, wealthy industrialist Simon Utrecht resolved to duplicate that feat and turn himself and three employees into superpowered beings. Using company resources to build the hardware, he and his handpicked accomplices rocket spaceward. However, scientist Bruce Banner (secretly the Incredible Hulk) crashes the launch and, feeling that the crew is in danger, aborts the mission; they return to earth with superpowers, though not as much as they'd hoped. Engineer/pilot Mike Steel comes back as the blue-skinned, super-strong Ironclad; Ann Damell, the life-support expert, is able to turn into gas as Vapor; her brother Jimmy, the propulsion scientist, returns as X-Ray, able to control every kind of electromagnetic radiation; and Utrecht ends up as Vector, who has telekinetic powers. Angry with Banner for having deprived them of the chance to be the most powerful beings on earth, they become bitter enemies of the Hulk and have clashed several times.

Comment: These Marvel Comics characters first appeared in *The Incredible Hulk* #254 (1980). The name, of course, derives from the slangy pronunciation of the term "UFOs."

VENDETTA (C)

Members: The Masked Swastika, The Silver Sorceress, the Sparrow, and The Speed Demon (1).

Charter: The villains each have a super specialty. Wearing impenetrable silver armor, the Masked Swastika carries an electrified sword, a great shield which doubles as a deadly frisbee, and a grenade which emits powerful Phi Rays, Beta Rays, and Kappa Rays (though the Swastika was hanged for war crimes, he says "dey cut me down for goot behavior"); the Silver Sorceress has potent magical powers; the Sparrow is a brilliant archer; and the Speed Demon can run at superspeeds. Based in the city of Megalopolis, the villains fought the Freedom Brigade during the 1940s. Given a youth serum concocted by the Silver Sorceress, the revitalized villains look to avenge themselves for countless defeats by tackling the Inferior Five, a fumbling group composed of the children of the Freedom Brigade heroes. Aided by MAN-MOUNTAIN, the villains go on a crime spree but are stopped by the do-gooders' best efforts.

***VENDETTA** members give new meaning to the term "holdup." From left to right they are the Masked Swastika, the Silver Sorceress, **MAN-MOUNTAIN**, The Speed Demon (1) and, under the bank, the Sparrow. © DC Comics.*

Comment: These villains are a parody of the original lineup of the superheroic Avengers: respectively, Captain America, the Scarlet Witch, Hawkeye, and Quicksilver. They appeared only once, in *Showcase* #63 (1966).

THE WRECKING CREW (C)

Members: Bulldozer, Piledriver, Thunderball, and THE WRECKER.

Charter: The Wrecking Crew consists of three criminals the Wrecker had met while serving time in Riker's Island prison. Escaping, they were all holding the Wrecker's crowbar when it was struck by lightning; as a result, each man acquired a unique superpower. Dressed in a golden bodysuit with a steel helmet and boots, Bulldozer (Henry Camp), a former master sergeant in the army, can destroy things with his hard head; wearing a red cowl, tights and trunks, blue boots, and a white bodyshirt, Piledriver (Brian Phillip Calusky), an ex-farmhand, has huge superstrong hands; and garbed in a green bodysuit with yellow trunks, gloves, boots, and cowl, Thunderball (Dr. Eliot Franklin), a physicist, has the superhuman strength to lift and swing a huge wrecking ball. (So fast can he swing it, in fact, that it serves as a propeller-like shield to deflect incoming bullets. Even if he were struck, Thunderball probably wouldn't be hurt; he has survived an attempt to electrocute him using all of the power of an electrical substation [*The Amazing Spider-Man* #248, 1984].) All must make occasional contact with the crowbar which acts like "a storage battery for our power." After numerous defeats at the hands of superheroes like the Defenders, the Fantastic Four, and Thor, member Thunderball struck out on his own.

Comment: These Marvel Comics super villains first appeared in *The Defenders* #17 (1974).

ZODIAC (C)

Members: Aquarius, Aries II, Cancer, Capricorn, Gemini, Leo, Libra, Pisces, Sagittarius, Scorpio III, Taurus, and Virgo.

Charter: This criminal group was founded by New York businessman Cornelius van Lunt, who segued from real estate to crime. A devotee of astrology—he credited the stars for his success in business—he saw no reason why criminals, similarly guided, should not succeed. To this end, he gathered thugs from around the nation and attired each as a sign of the zodiac. The membership of Zodiac is van Lunt, who dons a bull's head and become Taurus; Daniel Radford of Los Angeles who puts on a lion mask and becomes Leo; Chicago's Grover Raymond, who is garbed in a ram's head as Aries (2); Joshua Link of Boston who wears a half-white, half-black costume as Gemini; the crab-like Jack Kleveno of Houston as Cancer; the seductively attired Elain Mclaughlin of Las Vegas, aka Virgo; the fish-masked Darren Bentley of San Francisco, aka Aquarius; Lloyd Willoughby of Honolulu as Libra; Harlan Vargas of Washington, D.C., as Sagittarius; Noah Perricone of Miami as Pisces; Willard Weir of Detroit as Capricorn; and Jacob Fury, then Jacques LaPoint of New Orleans, as SCORPIO. Though each villain is permitted to act independently in her or his own territory, they band together whenever the leader summons them. (Leadership is relegated to whichever criminal's sign is relevant that month.) The group's first project was an attempt to undermine the peacekeeping force S.H.I.E.L.D. by assassinating its leader (see Scorpio); that foiled, they tried to seal Manhattan within a forcefield and hold it for ransom. That caper was thwarted by the Avengers and Daredevil and resulted in the death of the original Aries. It also cost them the Key to the Zodiac (see SCORPIO, Weapons), their ankh-shaped weapon from another dimension. A third and rather outre plot, to use the "Star-Blazer" to murder everyone in New York born under the sign of Gemini, also ended in disaster, the Avengers arresting the entire league. The Gemini undertaking caused great division within the group, which resulted in Aquarius making a pact with the demon Slifer to be able to take on the powers of all the signs of the Zodiac (he was bested by the Ghost Rider, and is now dead). Another Zodiac was a group of androids created by Scorpio (in his Jake Fury identity) and animated by the Zodiac Key. This group was similar to the original Zodiac and, killing most of their human counterparts, took their place in the roster.

Comment: Zodiac made its debut in *The Avengers* #72 (1969); the android Zodiac appeared in *The Defenders* #49 (1977).

Index

Page numbers in **bold** type indicate black and white illustrations.